THE HEALING GODS OF
ANCIENT CIVILIZATIONS

AMS PRESS
NEW YORK

ASKLEPIOS OF MELOS

See page 302.

From a cast in the School of Fine Arts,
Yale University.

THE HEALING GODS OF
ANCIENT CIVILIZATIONS

BY

WALTER ADDISON JAYNE, M.D.

EMERITUS PROFESSOR OF
GYNECOLOGY AND ABDOMINAL SURGERY
UNIVERSITY OF COLORADO

Non est vivere, sed valere, vita.
Martial.

NEW HAVEN · YALE UNIVERSITY PRESS · MCMXXV
LONDON · HUMPHREY MILFORD · OXFORD UNIVERSITY PRESS

HOUSTON PUBLIC LIBRARY

Library of Congress Cataloging in Publication Data

Jayne, Walter Addison, 1853-1929.
   The healing gods of ancient civilizations.

   Reprint of the ed. published by Yale University
Press, New Haven.
   Bibliography: p.
   Includes index.
   1. Healing gods. 2. Mythology. 3. Medicine,
Ancient. I. Title.
[BL325.H4J3   1979]   291.2'11   75-23728
ISBN 0-404-13286-3

First AMS edition published in 1979.

Reprinted from the edition of 1925, New Haven. [Trim size
of the original has been slightly altered in this edition.
Original trim size: 15.4 × 23.3 cm. Text area of the original
has been maintained.]

MANUFACTURED
IN THE UNITED STATES OF AMERICA

THE PHILIP HAMILTON McMILLAN
MEMORIAL PUBLICATION FUND

THE present volume is the second work published by the Yale University Press on the Philip Hamilton McMillan Memorial Publication Fund. This Foundation was established December 12, 1922, by a gift to Yale University in pursuance of a pledge announced on Alumni University Day in February, 1922, of a fund of $100,000 bequeathed to James Thayer McMillan and Alexis Caswell Angell, as Trustees, by Mrs. Elizabeth Anderson McMillan, of Detroit, to be devoted by them to the establishment of a memorial in honor of her husband.

He was born in Detroit, Michigan, December 28, 1872, prepared for college at Phillips Academy, Andover, and was graduated from Yale in the Class of 1894. As an undergraduate he was a leader in many of the college activities of his day, and within a brief period of his graduation was called upon to assume heavy responsibilities in the management and direction of numerous business enterprises in Detroit, where he was also a Trustee of the Young Men's Christian Association and of Grace Hospital. His untimely death, from heart disease, on October 4, 1919, deprived his city of one of its leading citizens and his University of one of its most loyal sons.

PREFACE

ALL studies of civilizations preceding the Christian era must be considered as tentative only, and as subject to repeated revisions in the future. Many original documents giving first-hand information regarding the political, religious, and social life of the early Orient have come into our possession quite recently, and a large number of them have not been critically examined or even translated; while the terms and the language used in some are not understood, nor has any key to their interpretation yet been found. Excavations yielding rich archeological returns are still in progress, others of equal promise are projected, and further important information concerning these peoples will undoubtedly be obtained in the near future. These remarks apply equally to the medicine of the ancients. Although sufficient is known from classical literature and from studies of newly discovered archeological documents to justify general conclusions regarding the therapeutic theories and practices of the ancient East, many extant medical treatises, especially of Mesopotamia and Egypt, have not been translated or adequately studied, and may easily contain statements which will materially alter our present views.

The following volume on the ancient methods of religious healing and the pagan healing gods is, therefore, presented as an introductory historical study. This particular phase of the religious and social life of the ancients is seldom considered independently, but rather in connection with an introduction to the general history of medicine, as those of Neuberger and Pagel, of Garrison, and the essay of Osler, or in papers on special aspects of the subject. Careful reviews of the origins of ancient medicine, as referred to by classical authors, are given in the older medical histories, as those of LeClerc and Sprengel, but, since these were written, much direct information has been obtained through archeological researches which has greatly broadened our knowledge of the healing practices in the cults of the pagan deities. Some part of this new material has been considered in the several brief monographs that have been published in Germany during the past forty-five years. These have not been translated; the subject has received little attention from writers of English, and as yet it has not been adequately presented to the English-speaking peoples for general study. In preparing this work from materials culled from many sources, an endeavor has been made to give a more detailed and extended exposition of the subject in a form for general survey and comparison, without attempting to cover the broader aspects of the early history of the healing art.

The author has selected for study several of those great civilizations that preceded and overlapped the Christian era, from the birth of history to the time when paganism was suppressed by the edict of Emperor Theodosius. In these nationalities, religion and healing had passed beyond the elementary stages of development and were more or less systematized under priesthoods. These civilizations had their development in an Oriental nursery, and their earliest traces are found among the Indo-Iranians and the peoples of Mesopotamia and Egypt, remarkable for their general learning and culture, their occult sciences, and the supposedly ineffable mysteries of their religions. Coming from various parts of the old world, these several nationalities were commingled by wars and conquests; and finally outgrowing their native environments, they overflowed westward. Filtering through channels that are now often obscure, the learning of the mysterious peoples of the East and their wondrous arts came to Greece, where they were undergoing examination when conquering Rome drew all civilizing influences to herself. The knowledge and arts of the great Orient came to the Occident as a mystic but lasting heritage; there to be appraised side by side with the native faiths and practices of Greece and Rome; to be refined and molded under new surroundings and other influences, into loftier conceptions of a new and higher civilization. The healing customs of these nations, and the beliefs that prompted them, were representative of their age and illustrate the ancient relations existing between religion and the healing art, which were continued under the Christian fathers in a more or less modified form.

The subject is approached strictly from a historical standpoint, all theories and controversial matters being avoided so far as possible. Facts, traditions, and myths have been gathered from archeological studies, the works of classical authors, and the treatises of authoritative commentators, and the subject-matter of each nationality is considered independently and under two sections: the first giving a general review of the salient features of their respective religions and healing customs; and the second dealing with the personalities of their deities most intimately concerned in the cure of the sick.

Owing, chiefly, to the imperfect and fragmentary character of the ancient records, no pretense can be made to completeness, especially in the lists of the healing gods. Doubtless innumerable deities who were conceived as efficient healers served their peoples and faded, leaving no tangible record behind. The names of others were probably lost in the destruction following the fall of

nations and of paganism, and still others now buried may
be disclosed on monuments and in documents yet to be
unearthed. In many instances, the healing function of a
god is vaguely referred to, or the divinity appears to be
of such minor importance that the name has purposely
been omitted. A short biographical sketch is given of
those deities whose curative acts are definitely noted, and
it is believed that the work of their cults as herein given
is fairly characteristic of the official healing practices of
their respective nationalities. The period during which
these deities were active is indicated when possible, but
this is often so indefinite that no chronological order is
feasible; and the gods are listed alphabetically.

Other kindred fields of inquiry of equal attractiveness
have not been invaded. The healing deities of the post-
Vedic religions of India, particularly the Buddhist, with
its extensions into Tibet, China, and Japan; or of the
great Slavic and Teutonic races, and those of ancient
America—the Incas, the Mayas, and the Aztecs—all present interesting racial types that would well repay a more
detailed study than has yet been given them.

The present work has been prepared in the odd mo-
ments of leisure from the active practice of medicine;
and, with a full appreciation of many shortcomings, the
general fruitage of these studies is offered with the hope
that it may have an interest for its readers, and perhaps
stimulate further and more satisfactory researches in
this by-path of early civilizations.

The author desires to acknowledge, with sincere appreciation, the courtesies and generous assistance received
from many friends during the progress of these studies,
without which they could not so nearly have approximated completeness. Especial thanks are due to Mrs.
Martha L. Crook for her active interest and coöperation,
and for her researches and translations from the Ger-

man; to the late Professor Morris Jastrow, Jr., for reviewing the manuscript of the chapter on Babylonia and Assyria; to Professors Henry F. Lutz, of the University of California, and T. George Allen, of the University of Chicago, for their comments on the Egyptian chapter; to Lieutenant-Colonel Fielding H. Garrison, U.S.A., for his interest, encouragement, and advice after reading the early draft of the manuscript; and, finally, to Professor Louis H. Gray, of the University of Nebraska, for his constant advice and many valuable suggestions.

CONTENTS

The civilization of Egypt. The Pyramid Texts. Egyptian reticence. Character of the early religion. Egyptian deities. Deities incarnate in animals. Local deities. Cosmic and tribal gods. The rise of Rē. No uniformity of belief. Osiris and Isis. The Osirian myth. Trial of the dead. The 'Negative Confession.' The 'Book of the Dead,' and 'Coffin Texts.' The life in the tomb. The soul and the body. The Sacred Eastern Sky. Spirits and demons. The priesthood. Religious festivals. Egyptian magic. Divine magic. The magic rites. Examples of magic. Divination. Dreams and oracles. Early Egyptian healing. Local healing deities. Temples of healing. Medical libraries. Preparation of the papyri. The medical papyri. The Kahun Papyrus. The Edwin Smith Papyrus. The Hearst Medical Papyrus. The Westcar Papyrus. The Ebers Papyrus. The Greater Berlin, or Brugsch Papyrus. The London Medical Papyrus. Other papyri. Papyri not canonical. Descriptions of disease in the papyri. Causes of disease. Prophylaxis. Gods suffered from disease. Physicians. Healing methods. Remedies. Medical incantations. Tests for sterility. General remarks. Profane Egyptian medicine. The old priest-physician.

'Anuqet. Apis. Bes, or Bēsa. Êpet, or Uêret. Ḥat-ḥôr. Horus, Ḥor, or Ḥoru. I-m-ḥotep. Isis, or Êset. Khonsu, or Khons. Neith. Nekhbet. Nephthys, or Nebt-ḥôt. Ptaḥ. Sekhmet. Serapis, or Osor-ḥap. Thoth, Thout, or Tahuti. Ubastet, or Bastet. Uzoit, Uazit, or Buto (Uto).

CONTENTS xvii

Demigods, Heroes, and Heroines Associated with Healing

ILLUSTRATIONS

INTRODUCTION

IT is a matter of common knowledge that from the
dawn of history the healing art has been more or
less intimately connected with religion. During antiquity the bonds uniting them were inseparable, and for
many centuries medicine was an integral part of religion.
On the free soil of Hellas, however, restrained by no
binding religious traditions and by no hierarchy, experience with the remedies of folklore and critical observations of disease permitted by an unfettered personal
judgment, backed by liberal, speculative, constructive
thought, developed, under Hippokratic influence, a scientific spirit, ethical ideals, and a definite line of cleavage.
The healing art, free for the first time from sacerdotal
surveillance directed by an organized priesthood, began
to be studied on its merits, both within and without the
temples. The scientific method, the germ of all future
progress, was then introduced, and theories were put to
the test. The breach with religion, once created, widened
slowly as medicine was independently studied by an ever-
increasing number of enthusiastic disciples' with honest
purpose and open, analytical minds. Thereafter medicine
never ceased to assert its right to its own development,
but religion, always concerned with human destiny, physical and spiritual, though relaxing its hold, continued to
retain a powerful influence over the healing art and too
often restricted efforts looking to advancement. Notwithstanding persistent struggles for intellectual freedom,
it was not until the nineteenth century that medicine, with

other sciences, gained sufficient headway to break loose
from ancient authority and traditions and to find opportunities for unprejudiced investigation, experiment, and
adoption of new principles. During the succeeding years
medicine has intrenched itself behind numerous demon-
strations of newly discovered facts, and it has finally
been accorded a high place among the sciences, although
retaining many of its time-honored characteristics as an
art.

Throughout all history of human progress, from the
primitive state to the higher intellectual levels, the race
has shown a strong conservatism of opinion, an ever-
constant tendency to cling to old beliefs and customs
while tentatively accepting newer conceptions prompted
by a broader, better knowledge of the workings of nature's laws, upon which advances in civilization have
been based. Mankind instinctively is dependent upon the
Supreme Power for life and all benefits, and it is not a
matter for surprise that many in our communities, reject-
ing modern professional ideas of disease, its causes, and
its treatment, prefer to rely, as did the people of old,
upon divinity for the preservation of health and for relief
from all physical ills. The prevalence of this faith, side
by side with 'new thought' and the many variant forms
of mental healing resulting from modern psychological
studies, excites a very special interest in the types of
belief of those ancient peoples who exercised the religious
healing function, and suggests a historical study of
these beliefs and the methods employed in such healing
by the representatives of the pagan religions of the pre-
Christian era, without, however, any attempt to appraise
the relative values of divine, mental, and material healing
practices.

In the following studies, the early types of ancient and
primitive healing are considered only as they pertain to

the spiritual beliefs of the people. Views and opinions of
compilers have been avoided unless based upon original
or sound collateral evidence, and an endeavor has been
made to cite original authors and documents as authority
whenever possible.

At the outset it should be noted that one of the most
important features of the early history of medicine is the
essential uniformity in principle of beliefs prompted by
the human religious instinct as they relate to the healing
customs of peoples widely separated by space and time,
differing only in details of racial and national coloring.
All comparative studies support the assumption that prehistoric man did not differ materially from the savage as
observed in the modern world; and in this fact is found
the explanation of the identity of all forms of ancient and
primitive medicine, and the unity of folklore. Garrison,
in his recent work,[1] forcibly summarizes these conclusions in the following words:

One of the best accredited doctrines of recent times is that of
the unity or solidarity of folklore. The collective investigations
of historians, ethnologists, archeologists, philologists, and sociolo-
gists reveal the singular fact that all phases of social anthropology which have to do with instinctive actions inevitably converge
to a common point of similarity or identity. This is true of all
myths, superstitions, laws, and social customs of primitive peoples (as also of the cruder ethnic aspects of religions) which are
concerned with the fundamental instincts of self-preservation and
reproduction. It is possible, as we shall see, that many strange
cultural practices, such as mummification, circumcision, or the
couvade, may have been deliberately transported by migrations
from one continent or island and imposed upon another (Elliot
Smith). But the fact remains that, for those human actions which
have been defined as instinctive, as based upon the innate neces-
sity which is the mother of invention, "folklore is an essential

[1] *An Introduction to the History of Medicine,* 3d ed., 1921, p. 17.

unity.'' The mind of savage man, in its pathetic efforts to form religious and ethical systems for moral and spiritual guidance, or to beautify the commoner aspects of life with romance and poetry, has unconsciously taken the same line of least resistance, followed the same planes of cleavage. The civilized mind differs from the savage mind only in respect of a higher evolutionary development. Human races and racial customs have changed as they became more highly specialized. The heart of man remains the same.

It follows that, under different aspects of space and time, all phases of folk-medicine and ancient medicine have been essentially alike in tendency, differing only in unimportant details. In the light of anthropology, this proposition may be taken as proved. Cuneiform, hieroglyphic, runic, birch-bark, and palm-leaf inscriptions all indicate that the folk-ways of early medicine, whether Accadian or Scandinavian, Slavic or Celtic, Roman or Polynesian, have been the same—in each case an affair of charms and spells, plant-lore and psychotherapy, to stave off the effects of supernatural agencies.

The people of the ancient, pagan world regarded all natural phenomena, the causes of which were not apparent, as due to unseen superhuman agencies. They believed that they were surrounded by innumerable, invisible spiritual beings of great variety, differing widely in character, who possessed supernatural powers by which they energized all nature, controlling its forces and directing its processes in their infinite detail. Each had the attribute of life, and many were believed to be immortal. A few, more highly developed in the imagination of the people, were personified and received names. They were conceived as in the likeness of man; they had human traits, were endowed with sex, and had families; and their characters were a mixture of good and bad. In general, those who represented constructive agencies helpful to man were the good spirits, while those who were destructive and harmful were, for the most part, evil spirits. Then there were hosts of others, including the ghosts of the dead, who still had power over the living, whose ethical character was not clearly defined, and who might be either good or bad. The evil spirits greatly outnumbered the good and were ever active in attempts to accomplish malevolent designs upon mankind. The spiritual beings, having both general powers and specific functions in nature, determined the collective and individual destinies of man; but the powers of the good spirits and deities were, as a rule, superior to those of evil, although they were unable wholly to conquer and control them. Because of their ethical character and superior powers the benevolent divinities were regarded as the natural protectors of mankind, and the people learned to look to them for benefits in all the exigencies of life, for defense against the attacks of those of evil intent, and especially for rescue when misfortunes befell.

The deities composing the several national pantheons were conceived in all ranks of dignity and power, and for each and every function. There were the great divinities of the heavens who were associated with the cosmogony; the deities of earth, of vegetation, and of the underworld; the tutelary gods of tribes and villages, of the household, the family; and the guardian spirits of the individual. Many gods, conceived as anthropomorphic, were grouped in families, or in triads of father, mother, and son, in enneads, or even in double and triple enneads. Some of the divinities, growing in power and importance, absorbed the attributes of lesser gods who were subordinated, or who faded and became obsolescent. Others were syncretized and had many aspects, differing with time and place. All were subject to the political, social, and religious vicissitudes of their peoples; and as nations were conquered or passed away, they were lost to memory, except a few of the more important who survived in traditions or who, adopted by victors, secured a place in the records of their respective civilizations. For the most part the gods were identified with political or social organizations, and only a few held a place in the true affections of the people.

All the activities of nature were emanations of the will and power of supernatural beings, usually referred to as gods. Divinity was, therefore, believed to be omnipresent, and in its beneficence, as the protector of mankind, gave indications of its intent for the future course of events by omens and portents, whence prognostications were of the utmost importance for guidance in all the affairs of life, both public or national and personal. Correct interpretations were earnestly sought, since the success of rulers, the destiny of nations, and the fate of individuals depended upon the forecasts and decisions of diviners. Divination and prophecy, standing midway between magic and religion, became important arts in both national and social life, in the practice of which priests acquired great skill.

Such, in brief, were the early fundamental beliefs that dominated the outward conduct of ancient peoples and prompted their flattering appeals to their many divinities for protection and help in need; but though the official religion, as interpreted by their political and religious leaders, directed the attention of the populace to the beneficence of their deities, the great mass of the general folk were often so imbued with fear and dread of the power of the malevolent gods and demons that they were more inclined to propitiate them than to rely on the worship of their benevolent deities.

Medicine-men and magicians appear as the first intermediaries with the spirit world among primitive peoples. The kings and priests rose above the common people as a higher order, and kings were occasionally regarded as divinity itself, so that many were deified after death. The priests, representing the highest learning and culture, and the instructors and intellectual leaders of their peoples, were skilled in magic and occult practices, and, according to approved formulas, served the people in their appeals to the divinities for health, happiness, prosperity, and relief from misfortunes.

In the pagan religions appeal was made to the gods by prescribed ceremonies and rituals for the welfare both of the community and of the individual. The beneficent deities were implored to exercise their superhuman, divine powers, alike in their general and in their special spheres of activity, not only to grant favors, but to restrain the powers of evil from carrying out their designs to the detriment of man; while the invocations to the malevolent divinities were intended to cause them to depart, to exorcise them, or to appease, propitiate, or coerce them to cease their malignant activities, and sometimes to induce them to accept a substitute victim. All recourse to the spiritual forces of nature was dealing with the occult, based upon the belief that man, by proper approach, could sway or control the gods according to his will; and the more primitive practices, ceremonies, and rituals representing this faith partook of the character of magic rather than of worship in its present accepted sense, which became manifest only as religion developed to higher levels. As the ceremonials of these worships are analyzed and the elements which we recognize as magic are differentiated—the manual and many of the oral rites, as the gestures with the wand, the formulas for exorcism, the incantations, the 'words of power,' and the commands—they appear as the more direct, mechanical methods of approach to the spirit-world; but they were regarded as powerful and essential for the effective coercion and control of inanimate objects and deities, even of high rank, and were believed to be potent to compel them to obey the will and commands of the magician or of the magician-priest.

Whether magic preceded religion as its rudimentary form in the evolutionary scale of human history or whether it was identified with its lowest, primitive forms has not been determined by any consensus of opinion.[2] Magic and religion had a fundamental unity in the fact that both dealt with the occult, superhuman powers of nature in an effort to control them for the benefit of man. They were, therefore, very nearly akin; and in all the great pagan religions they were interfused and insepar- able, so that in the earliest magico-religious formulas there appears no appreciation of any distinction between magic and religion, whence it is deemed improbable that any such differences between the two as are now recog- nized existed for the ancients. It is asserted, however, that a differentiation came to be made in the Semitic religions, and that "it was the community, and not the individual, that was sure of the permanent and unfailing help of its deity. It was a national not a personal provi- dence that was taught by ancient religion. So much was this the case that in purely personal concerns the ancients were very apt to turn, not to the recognized religion of the family or of the State, but to magical superstitions."[3] The individual was bound to act with the community, not for himself alone. In Greece and Rome, cults that were foreign, strange, and had no official recognition were magic, heterodox, inferior, and suspect, and were fre- quently regarded as illicit and forbidden by law. Cults

[2] For a summary of the principal theories of magic, see R. R. Marett, "Magic (Introductory)," in *ERE* viii, 245-252; and magic in pagan thought, see Thorndike, *History of Magic and Experimental Science during the First Thirteen Centuries of Our Era*, pp. 4 ff.

[3] Smith, *The Religion of the Semites*, 2d ed., pp. 263 f.

of great variety, however, both native and foreign, received recognition; and in making the distinction between magic and religion the consideration does not appear to have been one of kind, but to have been dependent, rather, upon the popularity, influence, and assumed usefulness of the cult to the people.

With the advance of ethical conceptions, magic was believed to be a bad, religion a good, method of approaching the occult. It was conceived that while the malevolent powers might be propitiated and inanimate objects endowed with activity by the magicians, so that both might be compelled by his will, the good spirits and deities occupied a sphere beyond man's control, whence their favors could be obtained only by humiliation and conciliation. Although confidence in magic declined, and it became more and more definitely allied with black art, its superstitions have shown a remarkable permanence and uniformity, continuing in the background of the consciousness of the people, occasionally leading them astray, and only partially restrained by a veneer of the more practical conceptions of advancing knowledge or even by Christianity.

In ignorance of the operation of natural laws, disease was ascribed to spiritual beings of superhuman powers; the malevolence of demons; magic influences, enchantments, and spells of the black art exercised by a sorcerer, wizard, or witch; the evil eye or the act of an enemy; or, possibly, the malady was believed to be superinduced by the gods; and, as religious conceptions reached a higher level, it was regarded as a visitation of the wrath of a deity in revenge for some act of omission or commission, neglect, or impiety, until, finally, it was held to be a punishment for sin. The individual fell prey to disease in consequence of these supernatural onslaughts, while the community, in similar fashion, was visited by epidemics.

The demons of disease gained entrance to the body through one of its natural openings in an unguarded moment, taking possession and carrying on their destructive work by so eating or gnawing away the entrails and other tissues of the body that, unless driven out, they might even cause death. Comparing such ancient beliefs with our present knowledge of pathogenesis, they are found strangely similar by simple changes in terms, substituting those of bacteriology and parasitology for the hosts of unknown and unnamed active, living forces— the invisible beings of demonology.

Diagnosis was of small importance in religious healing, since the causes of all diseases were believed to be practically the same in kind and were covered in the prescribed magico-religious formulas. Therapeutic methods differed widely in detail, but each was based upon rituals of worship, sacrifice, and purification to conciliate and gain the favor of the gods, and to entreat divine intervention for cure; or to exorcise the malignant authors of disease; to appease, frighten, or coax them, or to offer a substitute victim, and thus to be rid of them. Such appeals were supported by mystic rites, often accompanied by the administration of remedies, the exact method of treatment not infrequently being communicated in dreams and visions or by oracles; while in the cure of the sick, magic was ever an efficient handmaiden of religion. Healing was, therefore, a mystic process, which, under the ancient régime, often appeared as the successful result of a contest between invisible beings of good and evil, or was taken as proof that offended deities had been conciliated and had conferred their favor. Prevention of disease was believed to be obtained by the wearing of amulets and talismans, the power of prophylaxis being derived from some spiritual source, usually because of some inscribed divine 'words of power.'

In theory, and in large measure in practice, the deities generally were efficacious for healing, and any god might exercise his control over the demons of disease to effect a cure, or might extend his beneficent power directly for the aid of the suffering. Some divinities, however, appeared to the people to be more graciously inclined than others to aid the sick and even to be more efficient as healers, whence they became favorites and were renowned for their therapeutic benefactions in addition to other functions which they might have. A few developed as specialists; but the majority exercised their healing power sporadically and in special instances or they were merely patrons of the healing art and had little or no active function.

Such, in general terms, were the beliefs and customs of the ancient pagan civilizations in the matter of religious therapeutics. In this connection it should be remembered, however, that in most countries herein referred to there were physicians who practiced independently, side by side with temple-healing. Some were governed by custom, others by law. It is assumed that, for the most part, they gathered their medical knowledge from folklore and experience or from the priestly class; and it is known that they frequently coöperated with the priests, to whom they looked for guidance. Such independent work undoubtedly had a very definite influence on the development of the various ancient theories of disease and on the more material, practical therapeutics, fostering scientific methods and a gradual relaxation of the hold of religion on the healing art; but for these coincident phases in the history of medicine the reader is referred to the many general treatises on the subject.

LIST OF ABBREVIATIONS

ABAW	Abhandlungen der königlichen Akademie der Wissenschaften zu Berlin. Philosophisch-historische Classe.
AF	Altorientalische Forschungen.
AJA	American Journal of Archeology.
AJP	American Journal of Philology.
AJSL	American Journal of Semitic Languages and Literatures.
AKAW	Anzeiger der kaiserlichen Akademie der Wissenschaften. Philosophisch-historische Classe.
AMH	Annals of Medical History.
AMWL	Allgemeine Monatschrift für Wissenschaft und Literatur.
AP	Anthropological Papers.
APAW	Abhandlungen der königlich preussischen Akademie der Wissenschaften.
BAM	Bulletin de l'Académie de Médecine.
BCH	Bulletin de Correspondance hellénique.
BIA	Bulletino dell' instituto di correspondenza archeologica.
BKSGW	Berichte über die Verhandlungen der königlichen sächsischen Gesellschaft der Wissenschaften. Philosophisch-historische Classe.
BMJ	British Medical Journal.
BOR	Babylonian and Oriental Record.
CIA	Corpus Inscriptionum Atticarum.
CIG	Corpus Inscriptionum Græcarum.
CIGGS	Corpus Inscriptionum Græcarum Græcia Septentrionalis.
CIL	Corpus Inscriptionum Latinarum.
CIR	Corpus Inscriptionum Rhenanarum.
CIS	Corpus Inscriptionum Semiticarum.
CLC	Cincinnati Lancet-Clinic.
CMV	The K. R. Cama Memorial Volume.
CSHD	Classical Studies in Honour of Henry Drisler.
EB	Encyclopædia Britannica.
EMJ	Edinburgh Medical Journal.
ER	Egyptological Researches.
ERE	Encyclopædia of Religion and Ethics.
ESE	Ephemeris für semitische Epigraphik.
GIPA	Grundriss der indo-arischen Philologie und Altertumskunde.
IF	Indogermanische Forschungen.

IG	Inscriptiones Græcæ.
IGA	Inscriptiones Græcæ Antiquissimæ.
JA	Journal asiatique.
JAMA	Journal of the American Medical Association.
JAOS	Journal of the American Oriental Society.
JBASR	Journal of the British-American Archeological Society of Rome.
JCP	Jahrbücher für classische Philologie.
JEA	Journal of Egyptian Archeology.
JHS	Journal of Hellenic Studies.
KS	Kleine Schriften.
MAIA	Mittheilungen des kaiserlich deutschen archäologischen Instituts in Athen.
MAIBL	Mémoires de l'Institut national de France. Académie des Inscriptions et Belles-Lettres.
MAR	Mythology of All Races.
ME	Mélanges égyptologiques.
MVG	Mittheilungen der vorderasiatischen Gesellschaft.
NMBIF	Notices et extraits des manuscrits de la Bibliothèque impériale et autres bibliothèques. L'Institut impérial de France.
NYHSQB	New York Historical Society. Quarterly Bulletin.
PCC	Proceedings of the Charaka Club.
PRSM	Proceedings of the Royal Society of Medicine. Section of the History of Medicine.
PSBA	Proceedings of the Society of Biblical Archeology.
RA	Revue archéologique.
RC	Revue celtique.
RE	Revue égyptologique.
REMC	Recueil d'Études égyptologiques dédiées à la mémoire de Jean François Champollion.
RHR	Revue de l'histoire des religions.
RN	Revue numismatique.
RP	Records of the Past.
RTPA	Recueil de travaux relatifs à la Philologie et à l'Archéologie égyptienne et assyrienne.
RVV	Religionsgeschichtliche Versuche und Vorarbeiten.
SBE	Sacred Books of the East.
SGAS	Studien auf dem Gebiete der griechischen und der arischen Sprachen.
SIG	Sylloge Inscriptionum Græcarum.
UGAÄ	Untersuchungen zur Geschichte und Altertumskunde Ägyptens.

ZÄ   Zeitschrift für ägyptische Sprache und Altertumskunde.
ZDMG   Zeitschrift der deutschen morgenländischen Gesellschaft.

The following author's names stand for their works as given.

Pauly-Wissowa   Real-Encyklopädie der classischen Altertumswissen-
                schaft.

Roscher   Ausführliches Lexikon der griechischen und römi-
                schen Mythologie.

CHAPTER ONE

EGYPTIAN GODS

CHAPTER ONE

THE HEALING GODS OF ANCIENT EGYPT

PART I: GENERAL SURVEY

The civilization of Egypt.

THE ancient Egyptians were a people of superior attainments. The conditions in the Nile valley being favorable to life and conducive to prosperity, the people utilized their advantages, developed their resources, and were at least on a par with their contemporaries as pioneers and leaders in the arts of civilization.

Egyptologists assert that the more they learn of ancient Egypt the more complete and far-reaching its civilization is found to have been.[1] The attainments of their learned men were recognized and admired by their contemporaries, and the repute of their sages for wisdom was proverbial, while they were equally renowned for their skill in healing disease (Herodotos, iii, 1, 132). Many of the earlier kings, as well as those of the Thinites, in the fourth millennium B.C., and of the Third Memphite Dynasty, are reputed to have been versed in medical lore and as chief priests to have practiced healing among their peoples.[2] Specialists were attached to the courts of kings, and several physicians and superintendents of physicians were so renowned and respected that their names were recorded on stone and are known to us. The foundations of Egyptian medicine were laid in prehistoric times. The methods

[1] Budge, *The Gods of the Egyptians*, i, 118.
[2] G. Foucart, "Disease and Medicine (Egyptian)," in *ERE* iv, 751.

of healing disease, devised by the gods and communicated to their representatives, the priests, were not subject to improvement by man, hence they were jealously guarded, preserved, and became traditional. Although the practice in the different parts of the Valley may have varied, influenced by the special religious beliefs of the various healing centers, the information now available does not permit of making distinctions either for place or for possible changes in the course of the widely separated periods of ancient Egyptian history. It is believed, however, that the methods of healing developed in the early centuries were as conservatively followed, without material change in principle, as were the religious beliefs and customs with which they were associated, and of which they were an integral part.

The Pyramid Texts.

The first glimpses of the early civilization of Egypt, furnished by the Pyramid Texts from her oldest monuments, indicate that, in the fourth and third millenniums B.C., she was already far advanced in her intellectual and spiritual development.[3] At that early date Egypt had developed the peculiar beliefs and had adopted the customs and practices which influenced her whole religious career. Although characterized by a strong conservatism for previous concepts, political and tribal rivalries, as well as moral and philosophical developments, played active parts in Egypt's long history, resulting in an unfolding and a fashioning of conceptions of divinity and its powers; and many changes occurred in the religions of the several districts, or nomes, often politically detached, into which the long valley of the Nile was divided. Gods and cults were blended by peaceful combinations or were fused by conquest, with a compounding of names, a disguising of

---

[3] Breasted, *A History of the Ancient Egyptians*, pp. 30 ff.

myths, and a mass of surprising inconsistencies that have
bewildered all late observers.[4]

Egyptian reticence

The priests were extremely reticent respecting their
religion, and such explanations as they made in response
to inquiries were in enigmatical terms, hints of half-
truths, mystical suggestions, and intimations of symbolism which confused their hearers and served further to
obscure the meaning of their religious rites, rather than
reveal their sentiments. The Egyptians believed that
"words are a great mystery." The 'Divine Books' and the
books of the 'double house of life' were sacred, and none
but the initiated were permitted to see them; "it is not to
be looked at" (*Papyrus Leyden*, 348, recto 2, 7) by any
except him for whom it was intended. "The eye of no man
whatsoever must see it; it is a thing of abomination for
[every man] to know it. Hide it therefore; the Book of the
Lady of the Hidden Temple is its name.'"[5] The Egyptians,
however, illustrated and liberally portrayed the practical
application of their religious beliefs and customs on their
monuments; but they were silent concerning their philosophy and theology, while it is doubted whether they ever
attempted to formulate theories or to establish principles.

Character of the early religion.

The religion of the Egyptians appears to have had its
origin in animism, out of which its polytheistic pantheon
is assumed to have developed.[6] From prehistoric times it
had grown out of their crude beliefs and, without control
or guidance, had evolved the innumerable traditional

[4] Breasted, *Development of Religion and Thought in Ancient Egypt*,
p. 369.

[5] Budge, *Egyptian Magic*, p. 116; also Baillet, *Idées morales dans
l'Égypte antique*, pp. 72-75.

[6] Müller, *Mythology, Egyptian*, pp. 15, 214.

myths of the many independent deities of the Nile valley. It presented itself to a late observer [Herodotos] as "a religion of innumerable external observances and mechanical usages carried out with such elaborate and insistent punctiliousness that the Egyptians gained the reputation of being the most religious of all peoples.'"[7] The earliest glimpses of the life of the people, the evidences of the Pyramid Age, show that they were pious and devout (Herodotos, ii, 64), tenacious and sincere in their beliefs, and with a high moral discernment for truth, righteousness, and justice.[8] These sentiments influenced their daily lives, and by such standards they were judged after death. Moral purity and justice in this life gained for them a life after death, in many respects like unto that upon earth.

Egyptian deities.

The recognized religion of the Egyptians was based upon polytheism. Although some Egyptologists find suggestions that a belief which may practically be characterized as monotheistic was ancient when the pyramids were built, more particularly in the cult of Osiris and as early as 3300 B.C.,[9] it never gained definite recognition or influence, not even in the ephemeral religious revolution of Aten.[10] In their primitive days, the Egyptians had conceived the forces of nature and other influences affecting their lives as living, breathing, thinking beings, revealed and manifested in various forms, as fetishes in wood or stone, or as abiding in animals, birds, and reptiles, so that earth, air, and sky teemed with spirits of all sorts carrying on the works of nature and aiding or obstructing mankind. The Egyptian deities were developed from among

[7] Breasted, *op. cit.*, p. 367.
[8] *Ib.*, pp. 165 ff.
[9] A. H. Gardiner, "Egypt, Ancient Religion," in *EB* ix, 52.
[10] Budge, *Gods*, i, 119, 147; also Breasted, *op. cit.*, p. 6.

these spirits. Mythical tales were conceived concerning them, and they acquired personal traits, qualities, functions, powers, and attributes. Gods for all functions were evolved according to the expanding intellectual, spiritual, and imaginary needs of the people and their leaders; and these divinities had natures like unto those of man, although, with greater powers of concentrating their energies, they were superior to humanity. They had need of food and drink; they had passions and emotions of grief and joy; they were subject to disease and death; they grew old and had the infirmities of age, became enfeebled, tottered, druled, and were helpless; and finally, like man, they went forth to the tomb and were there subjected to the same moral inquisition.[11] Their bodies were mummified and preserved in appropriate tombs; but the spirit of the divinity was transferred to the mummy, or to an image of the god, and dwelt therein, the god or goddess receiving the same homage and worship as before.

Deities incarnate in animals.

Apparently as an outgrowth of prehistoric animistic beliefs,[12] the spirits of the divinities were incarnate in the forms of certain animals, birds, and reptiles. As representatives of their respective deities, such sacred animals received homage and developed cultic worship (Herodotos, ii, 65, 66).[13] Very early certain other gods and goddesses were conceived as having human bodies with the head of the animal or bird that was identified with them; and the name became a distinctive part of the title of the divinity, as the ibis-headed Thoth (or Thout), the hawk-headed Horus, and the lion-headed Sekhmet.[14] A

[11] Maspero, *The History of Egypt, Chaldea, Syria, Babylon and Assyria,* i, 151, 162, 225 ff.; also Müller, *op. cit.,* p. 80.

[12] Müller, *op. cit.,* p. 159.

[13] Budge, *op. cit.,* ii, 345 ff.

[14] Gardiner, *op. cit.,* p. 50.

few deities, particularly Osiris and Ptaḥ, were represented with human heads and faces; and it has been suggested that this may be attributable to a possible Semitic origin, or as being examples of the deification of ancient rulers.[15] Emblems, often suggestive of their functions, were acquired; and these, together with the animal forms, served to identify the gods in pictorial representations in the tombs and on the monuments. Such characterizations were constant from very ancient times and became distinctive of the divinity, except that in subsequent syncretisms, deities borrowed the heads and emblems of other gods as indicative of additional functions and aspects which they had assumed, although the worship of Osiris, Neith, and Ḥat-ḥôr, as known in late periods, retained many of the characteristic aspects shown by pre-Dynastic and archaic monuments.

Local deities.

Each political district (or nome), city, and tribe throughout the Nile valley had its own local divinity who bestowed life, health, and prosperity upon his or her people, who was its patron, protector, and ruler, whose divine, sovereign power was recognized, and whose supremacy was upheld against all rivals.[16] The real names of the gods were known only to the priests, if at all; they were too sacred to be mentioned, whence the deities received substitute names, some being best known by their home seats, as 'He of Edfu' (Tbôt) or 'She of Dendera' (Enet).[17] Such deities might be either male or female; and there was usually a consort, possibly a neighboring god or goddess, and a child, making a triad or family of divinities. At the seats of the greater deities, the number asso-

[15] K. Sethe, "Heroes and Hero-Gods (Egyptian)," in *ERE* vi, 648.
[16] Budge, *op. cit.*, i, 95 f.
[17] G. Foucart, "Names (Egyptian)," in *ERE* ix, 153.

ciated in the sanctuary was frequently larger—an ennead, as at Heliopolis (An or On), or a 'circle of associated gods,' as that surrounding Thoth at Hermopolis (Khmu-nu) ; and there was sometimes a double or triple ennead.[18] Each nome and city had its temple sacred to its official deity, and lesser divinities associated with the chief god were assigned shrines in the sanctuary relative to their importance, receiving appropriate shares in the worship and sacrifices. Each family, almost each individual, pos-sessed a god or fetish who had a niche or shrine in the household and who was loved, respected, worshipped, con-sulted, and obeyed as the family or personal guide in the various contingencies of life.[19] As nomes and cities in-creased in importance, their respective deities, develop-ing independently of each other, advanced in prestige and formed relations, friendly or otherwise, with neighboring gods. Myths and tales were repeated, and the local divin-ities often became famed beyond their borders for certain functions and attributes.[20] Local priests were quick to take advantage of any opportunity to enhance the posi-tion of their god, frequently accomplishing it by a blend-ing with a more important deity.[21] Thus at Heliopolis the nome-god Atum was united with the great sun-god Rē and became the more dignified Atum-Rē, rising in rank by re-flected glory and appropriating his attributes and his powers. In such cases the local divinity did not lose his identity, but gained in prestige by the additional aspect of a composite character.[22] Thus Horus was syncretized and presided over three nomes in Upper and two in Lower Egypt, while Ḥat-ḥôr had five seats in Upper and one in

[18] Budge, *op. cit.*, i, 85 ff.; also Müller, *op. cit.*, p. 216.
[19] Maspero, *op. cit.*, i, 172 f.
[20] Müller, *op. cit.*, pp. 202, 204.
[21] Budge, *op. cit.*, i, 175.
[22] *Ib.*, i, 102.

Lower Egypt.[23] Such syncretism became a common practice.[24] Local deities assumed correlation with the great
gods, used their attributes, and exercised their powers,
with resulting conflicts of personality, indistinctness of
character, fanciful variations, and a mystic confusion that
is bewildering to the stranger, though it apparently enhanced the beauty of the mythological conception for the
Egyptian imagination.[25] Thereafter the great gods could
best be identified by their original residences, as 'Rē of
Heliopolis' or 'Ḥat-ḥôr of Dendera.'

Cosmic and tribal gods.

Two phenomena appear to have been prominent in the
development of the religious thought of ancient Egypt:
first, the sun, "the most insistent fact in the Nile valley,"
or the solar system; and, second, the life-giving Nile.[26]
Very early the gods were conceived as being of two
groups: those representing the cosmic forces of nature,
the sun, moon, and stars, the atmosphere and earth, which
are referred to as the solar group; and the tribal or official divinities of the nomes and cities. In the solar pantheon, the sun was viewed differently in various places,
and had several names. At Edfu he appeared as a falcon,
as a winged-disk (Ḥor or Ḥoru), or as Ḥar-akhti, 'Horus
of the Horizon,' and there were four Horuses in the Eastern Sky. The sun-disk with falcon's wings was one of the
most common symbols of Egyptian religion. In many
places the sun was a winged beetle, Khepri,[27] rising in the
eastern sky; the material sun of noon-day was Rē; and
the evening sun, Atum, appeared at Heliopolis as an old

[23] Moore, *The History of Religions*, p. 146.
[24] Menzies, *The History of Religions*, p. 145.
[25] Müller, *op. cit.*, p. 92.
[26] Breasted, *op. cit.*, pp. 9 f.
[27] Budge, *op. cit.*, i, 294.

man tottering to his grave in the west.[28] Originally distinct, these sun-gods were correlated. Horus became the 'son of Rē,' and they coalesced as Rē-Atum (*Pyramid Texts,* §§1694, 1695). The moon, Thoth, an eye of the sun-god, was called the 'Horus-eye,' and this was the holiest symbol of Egypt.[29] Horus was supposed to prepare the way for Rē; when he opened his eyelids, dawn appeared; when he closed them, the dusk of night fell. Rē, the Horus-eye, traversed his kingdom across the sky by day in his 'Boat of Millions of Years,' returning to the east by another boat by a passage through Duat (the Underworld) or by way of the dark north.[30] Ibis-headed Thoth was the moon-god; Qêb was the earth-god; and Nut, his consort, was the sky-goddess, supported by Shu, god of the atmosphere. Numberless deities were developed for minor functions.

The rise of Rē.

In the earliest temples the sun-god was the source of life and increase. The priests of Rē at Heliopolis fostered the solar theology, and during the Fifth Dynasty (*circa* 2750 b.c.) it was established as the state religion, Rē thus becoming the universal divinity of Egypt,[31] though he was not the nome-god, but a deity of priests. Atum, the nome-god of Heliopolis, gained prestige by his assimilation with Rē; and it then became popular for other local deities to identify themselves with Rē, so that, in the end, Rē was combined with nearly every deity of Egypt, Ptaḥ being a notable exception.[32] The process of assimilation continued until after 1600 b.c., when it ended with a radical syncre-

[28] Müller, *op. cit.,* p. 83.

[29] Breasted, *op. cit.,* p. 10; also Budge, *op. cit.,* i, 352.

[30] Budge, *op. cit.,* i, 206 ff.; also Breasted, *op. cit.,* p. 144; W. M. Flinders Petrie, "Egyptian Religion," in *ERE* v, 244.

[31] Moore, *op. cit.,* p. 153.

[32] Budge, *op. cit.,* i, 330, 333, 349.

tism in the pantheistic approach to monotheism set forth by Aten.[33] The sun-god was believed to be an ally and protector of the kings of Egypt, who, about the Fifth Dynasty, assumed the title 'Son of Rē,'[34] every Pharaoh thenceforth claiming to be a divine incarnation, a living representation of the sun-god,[35] a bodily son of Rē by his queen-mother,[36] and often acting as the first priest in official ceremonies as an intercessor for the people.

No uniformity of belief.

The gods and the beliefs associated with them never had any general acceptance throughout the Nile valley; views differed in each district and in each age; and it has been said that there was no such thing as "the Egyptian religion," but that, rather, "during thousands of years there were ever-varying mixtures of theologies and eschatologies in the land," though the funerary side of the religion became better known than any other.[37]

Osiris and Isis.

According to the myths of the Pyramid Texts, Osiris of Mendes (Dêdu) in the Delta was the Nile-god, the fertilizer of the soil and the beneficent deity of vegetation;[38] while his sister and consort, Isis of Buto (Per-uazit or Per-uzoit), also in the Delta, represented the rich black soil of the Valley and was the divinity of love and fecundity. Osiris also symbolized the doctrine of the after-life, the future life in the grave, an early feature of Egyptian religious thought; and the tomb was the kingdom of

[33] Müller, op. cit., pp. 28, 218, 224 ff.

[34] Breasted, op. cit., p. 15; Budge, op. cit., i, 329.

[35] Müller, op. cit., p. 170.

[36] Note, an early example, if not the origin, of the idea of 'virgin birth.'

[37] Petrie, in ERE v, 236.

[38] Breasted, op. cit., p. 143.

Osiris. Between the sun-god Rē and Osiris, as the deity of the Underworld, there existed from the beginning a serious rivalry for the highest place in religion; and this continued throughout the many centuries of Egypt's history until after the Christian era.

The Osirian myth.

According to the myth, which has many variations, Osiris had incurred the enmity of his brother, Sêth,[39] who murdered him and threw his body into the Nile, where it was found by Isis and, by the aid of Thoth, was temporarily restored to life. His posthumous son, the child Horus, seeking justice for his father, introduced him into the Great Hall at Heliopolis for justification from the charges brought by Sêth before the tribunal of the gods; and at the trial the accuser was defeated by Horus, with the moon-god Thoth as the ally and advocate of Osiris, or as "Judge of the Rivals who reconciled the gods,"[40] while Osiris was vindicated ('justified') by the gods and was made Lord of the Underworld and Judge of the Dead, superseding Anubis (Anupu), the old Lord of the Sepulchre. According to another form of the myth, the body of Osiris, dismembered and scattered by Sêth, was diligently sought and gathered up by the faithful Isis, put together by Thoth, embalmed by Anubis, and placed in the tomb at Abydos (Abotu), of which he became lord, whence that necropolis was, thereafter, the center of his cult, this concept of him overshadowing his aspect as the Nile-god.[41] In his person Osiris had suffered indignity and death at the hands of his enemies, had risen from the dead, and had made his moral justification before his judges, being

---

[39] Müller, op. cit., pp. 72-73.

[40] Müller, ib., pp. 117-118; also Boylan, Thoth, the Hermes of Egypt, p. 42.

[41] Ha'pi, represented as a fat man, was also a Nile-god.

awarded everlasting life in the 'Land of the West,' and,
later, a more glorified existence in the Eastern Sky. The
Osirian doctrine was a popular one, but while it was
accepted by the more cultured and refined among the
people, it did not satisfy their aspirations, though it gave
to every Egyptian the hope of securing moral purification
after death, of attaining everlasting life, and of becoming
an Osiris.

Trial of the dead.

The Judgment scene in Amenti, of which there are three
accounts, a part of the *Book of the Dead* and the most
common in the papyri, is depicted on the walls in many
tombs. The deceased is conducted to the trial chamber,
the Hall of Ma'at, by Thoth; and his heart is weighed in
the Great Balance against an ostrich feather representing
Ma'at, the goddess of right and truth, by Anubis supervised by Thoth, who records the result and reports it to
Osiris (*Book of the Dead,* chap. cxxv).[42] The deceased is
then led before his judges, Osiris and the forty-two counsellors, by Horus and there makes his profession of a
moral, just, and pure life on earth, denying all wrong. In
this 'Negative Confession,' of which there are several
versions, the deceased addresses Osiris as follows:[43]

Homage to thee, O Great god, thou Lord of Ma'at! I have
come to thee, O my lord, and I have brought myself hither that I
may behold thy beauties. I know thee, and I know thy name and
I know the names of the two and forty gods who exist with thee
in the Hall of Ma'at, who live on evil doers and devour their
blood. . . . Hail to thee, great lord, lord of truth! . . . Behold I
come to thee; I bring to thee righteousness and I expel for thee
sin. I have committed no sin against the people, . . . I have not

----

[42] Boylan, *op. cit.,* p. 142.
[43] Breasted, *op. cit.,* pp. 299-306; also J. Baikie, "Confession (Egyptian)," in *ERE* iii, 827-829; Budge, *Magic,* p. 163; Budge, *Gods,* ii, 159-
160.

done evil in the place of truth. I knew no wrong. I did no evil thing. . . . I did not do that which the god abominates. I did not report evil of a servant to his master. I allowed no one to hunger. I caused no one to weep. I did no murder. I did not command to murder. I caused no man misery. I did not diminish food in the temples. I did not decrease the offerings of the gods. I did not take away the food offerings of the dead. I did not diminish the grain measure. . . . I did not load the weight of the balances. . . . I did not withhold the herds of the temple endowments. I did not interfere with the god in his payments. I am purified four times. I am pure as that great Phœnix is pure which is at Hierakonpolis [Henen-nesut]. For I am that nose of the Lord of Breath who keeps alive all the people. . . . There arises no evil thing against me in this land, in the Hall of Ma'at, because I know the names of these gods who are therein, the followers of the Great God.

If the deceased is found 'true of speech,' the gods say, "Pass onwards," and he is guided by Horus. After traversing the Seven Halls of Osiris and answering correctly the names of the many pylons and other questions, the god of the pylons says, "Pass on, thou art pure,"[44] and he becomes one of the 'People of the West,' in the land of Sekhet-Earu, or 'Field of Rushes.' By the side of the Great Balance sits a monster, Sobk, the 'Devouress,' with the body of a hippopotamus and the jaws of a crocodile,[45] to whom Anubis tosses the hearts which do not weigh against the feather, of the unfortunates who fail to justify themselves, or of those who are condemned to torments or to punishments that mean annihilation or long agony.

The Book of the Dead and 'Coffin Texts.'

In order to pass the ordeal successfully and to become one of the blessed, enjoying everlasting life in the 'Land of the West,' the deceased must not only know the names of

[44] Budge, *Magic*, p. 167.
[45] Müller, *op. cit.*, pp. 148, 179-180.

his judges, the counsellors, and other persons and things he meets on his journey, but he must be prepared to avoid the pitfalls and dangers of the passage to his final resting place. "I know you, and I know your names, therefore know ye me, even as I know your names."[46] Accordingly all the necessary information was prepared and buried with the dead—lists of names, prayers, texts, hymns of praise, and especially magic words of power—to enable him to answer all questions correctly and to arrive at his final home in the 'Field of Rushes,' the celestial realm of the early kings. "The dead are glorious by reason [means] of their equipped mouths."[47] King Unas at his burial (3300 B.C.) was provided with a book of words of power in which it was stated that "the bone and flesh which possess no writing are wretched, but behold, the writing of Unas is under the great seal, and behold, it is not under the little seal."[48] The devouring crocodile was held back by these means: "Get thee back, return, get thee back, thou crocodile fiend, Sobk! Thou shalt not advance to me, for I live by reason of the words of power I have with me"; or, "I am clothed and wholly provided with thy magical words, O Rē, the which are in heaven above me, and in the earth beneath me."[49] These matters are contained in the Pyramid Texts, originally the mortuary customs for kings engraved on the walls of the royal tombs; but after the Old Kingdom, the belief in the effectiveness of the uttered word developed to such an extent that they were appropriated by the middle and official classes, thus coming to represent a similar funerary literature of the populace of the Feudal Age.

The texts were written on rolls of papyrus which have

[46] Budge, *op. cit.*, p. 165.
[47] Breasted, *op. cit.*, p. 94.
[48] Budge, *op. cit.*, p. 124.
[49] *Ib.*, pp. 126-127.

commonly come to be called the 'Book of the Dead,' the
official version, which was built up gradually and which
became standardized in some measure, even canonical in
the Saïte period, finally containing 165 chapters. Copies
of extracts from these documents, about equally divided
between the popular mortuary literature and the Pyramid Texts, were supplied by the priests to the coffin-
makers of the Feudal Age; and scribes copied them in
pen and ink on the inner surface of the cedar coffins, in-
serting the name of the deceased, whence they came to
be known as 'Coffin Texts.'[50] In some of these copies the
successful issue of the trial, as anticipated by the deceased
and his friends, was depicted, and the word 'justified'
was appended to his name on the tomb.[51]

The life in the tomb.

In the cult of the dead, the after-life in the tomb, in
Amenti, was an active one, similar in many respects to
that on earth; and a text in the *Book of the Dead,* chap. cx,
gives a man power of "doing everything even as a man
doeth on earth.'"[52] While the present life was in every way
preferable, that of the dead was not gloomy, but was joyous and happy if their wants were supplied; though neglect rendered their existence correspondingly wretched.
Those in the tomb required food, drink, clothing, utensils,
and servants (*ushebtiu*) as when on earth; but for these
they were entirely dependent on the good will and sacrifices of their family, their friends, and those who followed
them. Since, therefore, there was constant dread that their
stores in the tomb should fail, endowments were established to guard against such a contingency, and other

---

[50] Breasted, *op. cit.*, pp. 272 ff., 293, 296 f.

[51] Gardiner, in *EB* ix, 56.

[52] Budge, *Gods*, i, 168; see further, A. H. Gardiner, "Life and Death
(Egyptian)," in *ERE* viii, 19-25.

measures were taken that the supply should be continuous and permanent.[53] Providing for the deceased became a heavy financial burden upon the people until it was finally lifted by the ingenuity of the priests with the aid of the magic of daily life, which was brought more and more to bear on the hereafter and which was increasingly placed at the service of the dead.[54] All things pictured on the walls of the tomb mystically became real and alive, ready for the service of the occupant by the mere magic of word-formulas. Hence, all the necessaries of life, including arable fields,[55] and servants and animals to work them, were imitated in figures or were portrayed on the walls; and when given a name, they supplied all wants, thus permanently securing the future comfort of the departed by "those things which chanted declamation makes real."[56] Appeals to passers-by were engraved on the tombs, requesting them to utter a prayer, *i.e.*, to recite the magic formulas that procured these essentials for the happy life of the dead, saying, "It will cost but a breath of the mouth."[57] It may be noted that wild and dangerous animals, such as lions and elephants, were often pictured as incomplete and as lacking an essential part if it was thought that they might be dangerous to the occupant when they became alive.[58]

The soul and the body.

The Egyptians believed that both gods and men were composed of at least two elements, a body and a soul. The body had a double, a *ka,* an incorporeal reflection which

[53] Breasted, *op. cit.*, pp. 267 ff.

[54] *Ib.*, pp. 294 ff.

[55] Müller, *op. cit.*, pp. 177 ff.

[56] Foucart, in *ERE* ix, 152.

[57] Gardiner, in *EB* ix, 56; also Breasted, *op. cit.*, pp. 272 ff.

[58] P. Lacau, "Suppressions et modifications de signes dans les textes funéraires," in *ZÄ*, 1914, li, 1-64.

was born with him and which awaited him at the tomb as a kind of superior genius to act as his monitor and guide. When a man or god died, it was said that he had gone to live with his *ka,* which dwelt in the sky when it was a god or a king.[59] In the tomb of King Pepi, who died about 3200 B.C., it was recorded that "Pepi goeth forth with his flesh; Pepi is happy with his name; and he liveth with his *ka;* he [the *ka*] expels the evil that is before Pepi, he removes the evil that is behind Pepi" (*Pyramid Texts,* 908).[60] The soul, or *ba,* associated with the breath, was depicted as a bird with a human head, hovering over the mouth of the deceased, giving him breath with its wings, and awakening him to the after-life.[61] The body remained on earth, and the soul dwelt above; nor did the soul or shadow of a divinity differ from those of a man, except that they were stronger and more ethereal. The amuletic *sa,* circulating among the gods, gave greater vigor, which they could transmit to man; and when they became exhausted, they renewed their strength at the 'Pond of Sa' in the Northern Sky.[62]

The Sacred Eastern Sky.

The Osirian heaven was in the gloomy west, the 'Field of Rushes,' or 'Earu,' and Osiris was 'Lord of the People of the West.' From earliest times the kings of Egypt, and later (2950-2475 B.C.), the nobles and great men had been accorded a happier celestial realm,[63] where they blended with Horus, the sky-god, and where they were given a seat in the Sacred Eastern Sky. Even from the beginning the bitter rivalry for the highest place in Egyptian religion

[59] Breasted, *op. cit.,* pp. 52 ff.
[60] Budge, *Magic,* p. 158; also Breasted, *op. cit.,* p. 53.
[61] Breasted, *op. cit.,* pp. 56 ff.
[62] Maspero, *op. cit.,* i, 151.
[63] Breasted, *op. cit.,* p. 139.

had continued. The solar theologians of Heliopolis had actively supported the claims of Rē and had succeeded in advancing him to supremacy; but the ethical teachings of the Osirian faith made a powerful appeal to the common people and had a rapid growth after the Pyramid Age,[64] gaining strong adherents and attaining such influence that the cult became a dangerous rival to the adoration of Rē. During the Middle Kingdom the worship of Osiris made irresistible progress, gained moral supremacy, and confusions developed between Osiris and Rē. Osirian theology was combined with that of Heliopolis and the Osirian hereafter was celestialized and received an honored place in the happier celestial realm in the Sacred Eastern Sky, which was reached by a ladder,[65] or by a boat, the 'Boat of Millions of Years' of which Rē was the ferryman, or which was guided by the strange ferryman "whose face is backward."[66]

Spirits and demons.

Reflecting the ideas of prehistoric animism, the Egyptians imagined that every living being or thing had its spirit or demon, and that spirits existed in vast numbers in the heavens, earth, and nether-world. They were never specifically good or bad in origin or disposition; but in their development, according as they were controlled or directed by a master spirit or by a personal whim, some proved friendly to man, while others were hostile. Spirits became detached from their objects; and as they emerged and were recognized, they received names and might become deities.[67] The classes of spirits were not clearly de-

[64] Breasted, op. cit., p. 285.
[65] Ib., pp. 148, 153, 158; also Budge, Gods, i, 167; ii, 241.
[66] Müller, op. cit., pp. 58, 176; also Breasted, op. cit., pp. 157 ff.
[67] For a general survey of this subject see G. Foucart, "Demons and Spirits (Egyptian)," in ERE iv, 584-589; also Budge, op. cit., i, 3 ff.

fined, though they ranked between gods and the king and queen;[68] but there were the *baiu* and the *khuu*, the latter being also the name for the ghosts of the dead. These terms were interchangeable for a time; but later the *baiu* appeared more beneficent, and the *khuu* more maleficent, although the essential natures of demons and gods were the same. Then there were the *rekhtiu* ('the knowing ones, the wise'),[69] who, though full of wisdom, were mischievous and were the personifications of the powers opposed to the divinities. There was also the great and powerful master-spirit of evil, the serpent 'Apop, the arch-fiend, who represented darkness, who was spiritually opposed to Rē,[70] and who, with his fiends, as the 'children of rebellion,' was equally hostile to man.[71] Each morning he fought with Rē to prevent the rising of the sun,[72] and though he was always defeated, he renewed the struggle daily to continue the darkness. The god of Upper Egypt, Sêth, the brother of Osiris and Isis, in early times beneficent, a friend of Horus (*Pyramid Texts*, 141, 370, 473), and a helper of the dead, became the deadly enemy of Osiris and of Horus the child, thus developing into a persistent doer of wickedness, to whom were attributed most of the misfortunes and calamities befalling mankind. In late times he was known to the Greeks as Typhon. Malignant spirits, like gods, were syncretized and blended, and Sêth-'Apop became a composite agent of evil.

In the *Book of the Dead* the innumerable evil spirits receive much attention.[73] These beings, like the ghosts of the dead, were recognized in religion and were made

[68] Sethe, in *ERE* vi, 647.

[69] Müller, *op. cit.*, pp. 379-380, notes 18, 31.

[70] *Ib.*, p. 104.

[71] Budge, *op. cit.*, i, 159, 324.

[72] *Ib.*, i, 324; ii. 245.

[73] Foucart, in *ERE* iv, 585.

prominent by many magic practices, yet it appears that they were more important in the imagination of the people than in the minds of the priests, for they were not officially listed, they did not form a fixed caste or develop into a demoniacal hierarchy, and there were no such monsters, hideous and bloodthirsty, as those of Assyria and Babylonia. The contest to overcome the malign influence of maleficent spirits was constant and it received the earnest attention of the people, but they were not oppressed by such fear as were many of their contemporaries. Sêth and his partisans were definite and active spirits creating evil, spreading disease, madness, and all forms of malignity; their eyes shed tears that, dropping upon the ground, made plants poisonous; their sweat, saliva, and blood were deadly and, falling upon the earth, germinated into scorpions, venomous reptiles, and strange, deadly plants.[74] There were spirits for each mischief, of every rank, chiefs and attendants; but all were subject to the higher will of their leaders and of the gods and their ministers who possessed the secret names and words of power.

The priesthood.

Egypt had numerous temples in the nomes and cities of the Nile valley, and a retinue of priests, priestesses, and lay attendants, varying in number according to the importance of the sanctuary, was attached to each.[75] All were governed by strict rules and traditions, and purity in everything connected with the shrine was invariably an essential. The priests were divided into classes, differing in rank and each having special duties which were exacting and onerous; and lay priests served for one fourth of each year. The temple duties commenced early

[74] Maspero, *op. cit.*, i, 225.

[75] A. M. Blackman, "Priest, Priesthood (Egyptian)," in *ERE* x, 293-302; also Breasted, *History*, p. 64.

in the morning with the breaking of the clay seals which
protected the sacred rooms and with the routine ritual
of personal attentions to the deities,[76] these consisting of
the toilet of the god (washing, anointing, and perfuming
the idol, and burning incense before it), chanting hymns,
bowing in adoration, and making sacrifices and libations.[77]
Then followed numerous rites and ceremonies which continued during the day and often into the night, and there
were also the special ceremonies of the several festivals.
The priests cared for the sacred books, upheld the supremacy of their local divinities, and, when possible, enhanced their reputation and position by relation with
other deities. Sacerdotal schools, each known as 'the house
of life' (per-'onkh), were conducted in connection with
the temples of the greater gods, as at Heliopolis, Hermopolis, Abydos, and Thebes (Wēset or Newt). During
the New Empire the priesthood and the sacerdotal colleges, growing in wealth, acquired great influence and
power in matters political, so that the Pharaohs consulted
the priests in state affairs, bowing to their dictates, while
the chief priest of Amon of Thebes was made primate of
Egypt.[78]

Religious festivals.

Egypt was extremely rich in festivals and fasts, upward of fifteen hundred for all periods and places being
listed; and these formed an important element in the daily
and religious life of the people.[79] A large number were in
honor of the gods, while others were to celebrate important events, such as the seasons, the 'arrival of the river,'
or the opening of the canals. Festivals were held to ex-

[76] A. M. Blackman, "Worship (Egyptian)," in ERE xii, 776-782.
[77] Moore, op. cit., p. 156.
[78] Breasted, Development, p. 363.
[79] Foucart, "Festivals and Fasts (Egyptian)," in ERE v, 853-857;
also Petrie, in ERE v, 238 ff.

change visits between the divinities of different cities, as between Horus of Edfu and Ḥat-ḥôr of Dendera, long retinues of priests and attendants accompanying the deities; and during the ceremonies sacred dramas were performed, based upon some legendary incident in the lives of the gods, as at the festival of Horus at Edfu and in celebration of the mysteries of Osiris at Abydos.[80] The festivals of the divinities of the dead were of a funerary character, and those of Osiris were fused with those of the cycle of the cult of Ptaḥ-Sokar-Osiris. Festivals lasted for days, weeks, and even a month, and were occasions for general rejoicings, with music, dancing, and often noisy, licentious gaiety.

Egyptian magic.

Like peoples of other races, the Egyptians sought to better their condition and destiny by enlisting the aid of supernatural forces to modify the natural order; and acting upon their belief that the gods and various spirits had the requisite power, they entered into dealings with them by methods known as hīke', the best English equivalent for which is 'magical power.' An essential element in all such dealings was mystery, and they had the clear implication of demand upon the unseen for the exercise of supernatural, miraculous powers for the benefit of the living, actions which, when analyzed, are found to be magical, leaving little that may be described as religion. Hence it is claimed that from the Egyptian point of view, there was only hīke', but no such thing as religion, which should be considered in the tripartite division of its active aspect into the worship of the gods, cult of the dead, and magic.[81] In the estimation of the people, hīke' was effica-

[80] Moret, Mystères égyptiens, pp. 15 ff.; also id., "Mysteries (Egyptian)," in ERE ix, 74-77.

[81] A. H. Gardiner, "Magic (Egyptian)," in ERE viii, 262-269; also Erman, Die Ägyptische Religion, 2d ed., chapters i-vi.

cious and was, consequently, held in high esteem; magic was sacrosanct and unchangeable, the oldest and most characteristic element of the so-called religion;[82] it was applied religion, and all rites and ceremonies were full of it. There was even a deified concept of *hīke'*, a special divinity (who may have been a form of Thoth), the 'god of the Magic Formulas,' who, in the Pyramid Texts, was represented as a sphinx, bearing a scourge, a shepherd's staff, and the scepter of venerability or life;[83] physicians of the Old Kingdom were 'priests of Ḥīke' ';[84] and several well-known divinities, Thoth, Isis, Rē, and Sêth, were called 'great of the magic formulas.'

Divine magic.

The magic of the gods differed from that of man only in its superior power.[85] Possession of the secret names of deities gave dominance over demons and over all evil spirits, enabling the magician to compel divinities of inferior rank to that of the deity whom he invoked, and whose true name he knew, to do his will.[86] Hence both gods and men sought diligently to obtain the secret names of the mightiest divinities. The mere possession was sufficient, the name was seldom pronounced, and the few secret names that are mentioned in the texts appear simply as cabbalistic gibberish. It is related that Isis rose from a lowly rank in the house of Rē and became the great enchantress of Egypt by her guile, tricking the sun-god into yielding up his true name to her.[87] The mechanism of or-

[82] Budge, *op. cit.*, i, 13.

[83] Wiedemann, *Magie und Zauberei im alten Ägypten*, p. 23.

[84] Mariette, *Les Mastabas de l'ancien empire*, p. 96.

[85] Gardiner, in *EB* ix, 56.

[86] Müller, *op. cit.*, pp. 200-201; also Wiedemann, *op. cit.*, pp. 143-145.

[87] Budge, *op. cit.*, i, 360 f.; and for the myth related in verse, see Müller, *op. cit.*, pp. 80-83.

dinary magic was essentially the same as that which is observed in the worship of the gods and in the cult of the dead. The most common use of magic was to cure the sick; but black magic and sorcery were used for corrupt and degraded purposes, and could be purchased for the injury and misfortune of others.

The magic rites.

In order to approach the supernatural agencies by successful magic, it was necessary to break down the mystic barriers through the medium of the ritual—specified word-formulas and acts, homage and sacrifice—and purity in all things was a prerequisite for receiving benefits. The priests, versed in secret lore and adepts in all these practices, had exclusive charge of the divine books, including those of the 'double house of life'; and magic in the hands of the proper person, the theologian, became religion.[88] The ibis-headed moon-god, Thoth, was the chief magician, and Isis was his counterpart. He knew the mystic names, the mighty hidden words of power, the secrets of the gods; and hence he was master of them all, having authority over heaven, earth, and the Underworld. He knew the prayers, the ceremonies, and the formulas for all occasions, using them in the 'correct voice' and with the proper gestures; while magicians educated at his school at Hermopolis had powers which approximated his own.[89]

Examples of magic.

The power of Egyptian magic was boundless, and the oldest Pyramid Texts describe the wonders performed by magicians, usually the 'lector-priests' (kher-ḥab). Devils were cast out, the sick were healed, life was restored, the

---

[88] Müller, op. cit., p. 198.
[89] Budge, op. cit., i, 408; also Maspero, op. cit., i, 246.

corruptible body was transformed into the incorruptible, human beings assumed other shapes at will, and inanimate objects, becoming animate, obeyed commands and then returned to their normal state. The powers of nature were under the control of the magician. Wind, rain, rivers, and seas obeyed; waters were separated and piled up on one side; the earth was rent; the sun was made to stop in its course; and all the mysteries of life, death, and the future belonged to him who possessed the lore of the book of 'the double house of life.' The Westcar Papyrus, of about 1500 B.C., tells of many feats performed by the 'chief-lectors' in the reign of King Cheops (Khufu) of the Fourth Dynasty.[90] Teta, a magician, demonstrated before the Pharaoh his power of revivification by cutting off the head of a goose, a snake, and a bull, after which, at his command, each head moved forward, and joined its respective body, thus restoring life.[91] Again when one of the royal rowers lost her jewel in the lake, a magician was commanded to secure it, which he did by separating the waters, piling them on either side, walking between on dry ground, picking up the jewel, and restoring it to its owner; and the same papyrus contains an account of another magician who fashioned a wax crocodile which, placed in the river, devoured an adulterer when he came to bathe.[91] At a much later date, Moses, who "was learned in all the wisdom of the Egyptians" and, like her magicians, was "mighty in words and deeds," performed things which they also did, as well as others which exceeded their powers.[92]

[90] Paraphrase of the Westcar Papyrus, see Flinders Petrie, *Egyptian Tales*, i, 97-142; also Erman, *Die Märchen des Papyrus Westcar*, i, 21 ff.; Wiedemann, *Altägyptische Sagen und Märchen*, pp. 1-24.

[91] Erman, *op. cit.*, i, 8 ff.; also Budge, *Magic*, pp. 18-19, 9-10, 67-69; Maspero, *Popular Stories of Ancient Egypt*, pp. 33-34, 28-30, 24-27.

[92] Exodus, vii, 10-11, 20-22; viii, 5-7, 16-18; Acts vii, 22.

Divination.

In common with other peoples of the ancient Orient, the Egyptians resorted to divination to learn the future and the disposition of the gods toward them. The earlier mantic processes, depending upon the interpretation of dreams, upon the readings of the stars, and upon estimates of their position and influence (little used in healing practices), as well as upon the direct manifestation of the divine will by the deities themselves, appear to have been simpler than those of their contemporaries, which, however, were introduced in the late period under Asiatic and Hellenic influences.[93]

The most characteristic Egyptian means of learning the divine will and of securing benefits was by direct appeal to the image of the deity, the response being made by 'seizing' the person chosen, as in the selection of a king; or by acquiescing in the prayer by gestures, this being accompanied in some instances by the spoken word, 'as a father to a son.' Such consultations were made according to an established etiquette at certain times and places, when the priest, approaching the statue, began the invocation (*âsh*) in court language, asking if it were convenient for it to listen to such and such an affair. According to the records, the "chief of the temple has a consultation of the god," and this was made orally by prayer or by reducing questions to writing after carefully arranged formulas, and depositing them under seal before the image of the deity, the petition usually beginning as follows: "O God of Goodness, my Lord," or "Lord, may we lay before thee a serious affair?" and then stating the case. The reply often came in sealed writing, but in certain instances the response proceeded directly from the statue of the divinity; if it remained motionless, the request was refused;

---

[93] G. Foucart, "Divination (Egyptian)," in *ERE* iv, 792-796.

but if the deity consented to listen and to acquiesce, it performed *hanu* (making some movement of the head or arms) "twice with decision," or spoke words, the decree (*utu*) being recorded, sometimes on the walls of the temples, as the "words of the god himself." Numerous examples of such responses may be found in the cults of Amon-Rē of Karnak, of Khonsu of Thebes, of Isis of Koptos (Kebtōyew), and of the Ethiopian Amon of Napata.[94] Divination, like exorcism, healing, and the possession of the amuletic *sa,* was the exclusive privilege of the 'essential' statue, although it had the ability of transmitting its magic power to one of its images, as when the statue of Khonsu "made four passes of its magic fluid."

Dreams and oracles.

The origin and extent of the use of dreams and of the dream-oracle in Egypt are obscure; but the power to dream or to cause others to dream was prized and encouraged, and sleeping in the temples to obtain a mantic response and a remedy (incubation) was a current practice among princes and private individuals. Diodoros says (i, 28) that "in Egypt dreams are regarded with religious reverence," and that the prayers of the devout are often rewarded by the gods with an indication of the remedy which their sufferings require; but this and magic (*Wisdom of Solomon,* xvii, 7-8) were only the last resource when the skill of the physician had been exhausted and when all hope of recovery was gone. A similar feeling toward the gods induced them to offer ex-votos in the temples for the same purpose (Clemens, *apud* Origenes, viii, 41).[95]

[94] Foucart, in *ERE* iv, 793-794.

[95] *Id.,* "Dreams and Sleep (Egyptian)," in *ERE* v, 34-37; also Wilkinson, *Manners and Customs of the Ancient Egyptians,* ii, 356, 462 ff.

Appeals were made to the divinities to 'hear the prayer' and to reveal themselves—"Turn thy face towards me"; " 'Tis thou who dost accomplish miracles and art benevolent in all thy doings; 'tis thou who givest children to him that hath none," or " 'Tis thou who canst grant me the means of saving all." The invocation having been made in the temple, the response was awaited in sleep. In the vision "the god N.[96] [or some one in his name] spake to him saying . . ." The divinity begins by identifying the person addressed: "Art thou not *such an one,* son [father, wife, etc.] of *so and so?*" The god then tells the suppliant at what place, 'when morning comes,' a sealed *naos,* or box, will be found containing a certain book which must be copied and replaced. The directions, to be followed by a certain result, were in direct language requiring no interpretation, and it is believed that in the Pharaonic period there were no groups of official interpreters.[97] In the later epoch, the interpretation of visions, especially those of a symbolic character, was assigned to the 'Masters of the Secret Things,' or to 'the Learned Men of the Magic Library,' who, early in the Christian era, formed a guild at the Serapeum in Memphis.[98] In the sanctuary of Ptaḥ-Sotmu at Memphis oracles were given during the Pharaonic period to sufferers who consulted it; and the demotic inscriptions of Nubia mention other deities who, during long centuries, had been sending dreams to reveal remedies to persons sleeping in their temples, as well as the oracles of Isis at Philæ (Pi-lak) and Thoth at Pnubs, all these being purely Egyptian in character without for-

[96] N. and NN. are conventional indications that a proper name is to be supplied according to circumstances, and are often expressed by the phrase *such an one.*

[97] Foucart, in *ERE* v, 36.

[98] Letronne, "Notices et textes des papyrus grecs du Musée du Louvre et de la Bibliothèque impériale," in *NMBIF,* pp. 81, 321.

eign elements.[99] Deities who manifested themselves as
hearers of petitions[100] were represented as having a large
number of ears. One deity was alleged to have 77 eyes and
as many ears (*Harris Magic Papyrus,* vii, 6),[101] and a
king, who was regarded as equal to the god, was endowed
with innumerable ears (*Anastasi Papyrus,* II, vi, 3 ff.; IV,
v, 6 ff.).

Early Egyptian healing.

The art of healing in Egypt emerges from the mists of
prehistoric times as the gift of the gods to men. The
earliest definite knowledge of Egyptian therapeutic customs is obtained from the several medical papyri that
have been discovered, the oldest coming from the Twelfth
Dynasty, about 2000 B.C. Later texts have parts common
to the older documents, evidently being compilations from
more ancient writings; and this fact, together with the
grammar and the language, tends to confirm the most
ancient traditions, which attribute a large share of the
essential contents of these papyri to the early kings. It
was the duty of the Pharaohs to maintain the health of
their subjects. From Manetho (*apud* Africanus, *Fragmenta historicorum Græcorum,* ed. Müller, ii, 511 ff.) we
learn that King Athotis, of the First Dynasty of the
Thinites, practiced healing and wrote anatomical works.
The kings of the Third Memphite Dynasty were sons and
representatives of the gods, and in their capacity of chief
priests would naturally be acquainted with the methods
of healing of their time and would apply them among their
people, King Tosorthros (Zoser) in particular fostering

---

[99] E. Révillout, "Un page de l'histoire de la Nubie," in *RE,* 1888,
v. 72-77; and ["Letter upon Nubian Oracles,"] in *PSBA,* 1888, x,
55-59.

[100] W. Spiegelberg, "Ερμῆς ὁ Θηβαῖος" in *ZÄ,* 1908-1909, xlv, 89-90.

[101] Budge, *Facsimiles of Egyptian Hieratic Papyri,* pl. 26.

the healing art in the person of one of his wisest advisers, I-m-ḥotep, who was deified in Ptolemaic times.[102] The invention of medical science was constantly ascribed to Thoth, the ibis-headed moon-god, the originator of all learning; and a legend for the use of the dead, engraved on lapis lazuli, supposedly in the fifth millennium B.C., runs as follows: "I am Thoth, the inventor and founder of medicines and letters; come to me, those that are under the earth, rise up to me, thou great spirit."[103] Ptaḥ and the demigod I-m-ḥotep performed miracles of cure, and in later times were extolled as the inventors of healing; but Thoth, who in the Græco-Roman period was confused with Hermes Trismegistos,[104] always held the first place in the minds of the Egyptians.

Local healing deities.

The deities of Egypt, especially the local divinities, were beneficent and watchful over the welfare of their peoples. They were the sole defense against the machinations of their enemies and by reason of superior knowledge had devised means by which evil spirits were exorcised and the sick were healed, these methods having been taught by (or stolen from) the gods for the service of mankind, and their application having been entrusted to the priesthood.[105] As permanent and precious gifts, these sacred revelations must be jealously guarded and transmitted; and having implicit faith in their divinities, the efficacy of such therapeutic methods was never doubted by the people, so that they became an integral part of the common religion. Very many of the minor deities of the Nile valley practiced healing, and some gained repute as

[102] Foucart, in *ERE* iv, 751.
[103] Budge, *Magic*, p. 43.
[104] Griffith, *Stories of the High Priests of Memphis*, p. 58.
[105] Foucart, in *ERE* iv, 750.

I-M-ḤOTEP

THE EGYPTIAN ASKLEPIOS

Courtesy of the Metropolitan Museum of Art.

healers, while occasionally one of them was associated with the greater gods at their celebrated sanctuaries.

Temples of healing.

There were many healing temples in the Valley, but eventually all the great medical centers were located at the chief capitals along the Nile; and large numbers of people, many travelling long distances, and others making annual pilgrimages, sought the curative beneficence of their favorite divinities. The remains of the temple at Philæ and of Khonsu at Karnak afford ample testimony of the beauty and extent of such shrines, and are evidences of the honor and respect paid to the deities presiding over them. The great sanctuary of Thoth at Hermopolis, where a clinic for the gods was held during the long battle between Horus and Sêth for the succession,[106] was renowned; and others of prominence were those of Neith, of Nekhbet, of Ptaḥ, of I-m-ḥotep, and of Min at Panopolis (Epu), while, although Isis had little part in the politics of Egypt, her temple at Koptos was, perhaps, the most popular of all.

Medical libraries.

These healing shrines were reputed to be the depositories of medical lore, and the ancient traditions are confirmed by lists of diseases and their cures, and by recently discovered evidence from the library ('hall of rolls') at Heliopolis, prescriptions found in the temple of Ptaḥ,[107] and inscriptions of the library of the temple at Edfu mentioning books which it contained "for the turning aside of the cause of disease" (Clemens Alexandrinus, *Stromata*, vi, 4). Clement (*ibid.*), fully in accord with ancient traditional belief, also refers to forty-two her-

[106] Budge, *Gods*, i, 489; also Wiedemann, *Magie und Zauberei*, p. 19.
[107] Wilkinson, *op. cit.*, ii, 355, 358; also Foucart, in *ERE* iv, 751.

metic books in the temple at Hermopolis, six of which (xxxvii-xlii) were medical, representing Thoth as the inventor of formulas for giving remedies. On the walls of sanctuaries were inscriptions and votive tablets in commemoration of miraculous cures, and round about, within the sacred precincts, were steles and statues erected by former patients in grateful recognition of cures effected by the divinity. Here, in 'the house of life' (*per-'onkh*), priests and lay brethren who were to practice healing pursued their studies and took their oath (*Harris Magic Papyrus*, vi, 10), while a physician was enabled to restore the *per-'onkh* at Saïs ''because his majesty knew the value of this [medical] art.''[108]

Preparation of the papyri.

It was the duty of rulers to continue the work of the good gods who had founded Egypt (Manetho, *apud* Eusebios) ;[109] and since healing had been devised by the divinities, it was not subject to improvement by man. The medical papyri, the 'divine books,' were, therefore, prepared with meticulous care, and old manuscripts were copied by the 'Scribes of the Double House of life,' or by 'the Learned Men of the Magic Library,' for preservation of their lore and for use at other sanctuaries; but no changes from the original were allowed, only notations, or glosses in rubrics, were made, generally on the margins or backs, relating cases of some god or distinguished person, such as a prince or a king, who had been cured by certain remedies or prescriptions (*Ebers Papyrus*, lxiv, 4; lxvi, 15).[110]

The medical papyri.

The chief papyri which are known as medical and that are now available for study and reference are as follows:

[108] Gardiner, in *ERE* viii, 268.
[109] Foucart, in *ERE* iv, 751.
[110] *Ib.*, p. 750; also Erman, *Life in Ancient Egypt*, p. 359.

1. The Kahun Papyrus,[111] the oldest, probably dating from about 2000 B.C., is a short text consisting of only three columns which treat of the symptoms, diagnosis, and therapeutics of gynecology and veterinary medicine. It contains no magic or incantations, and this fact has led a few writers to assume that the practice of its period was empirical and free from magic elements; but since it is incomplete, too much reliance should not be placed upon such an omission, which may pertain only to this part of the document. It is interesting to note that the text gives directions for determining the sex of the unborn babe: "Prescription No. XXXI. Another time: if thou seest her face green, but in the green (?) thou findest things upon her like . . . [she will bring forth a m]ale (?) (child), but if thou seest things upon her eyes, she will not bear ever."

2. The Edwin Smith Papyrus, recently announced, is superior in scientific value to the Ebers Papyrus, which it probably exceeds somewhat in age, since it dates from about 1600 B.C. and possibly from the seventeenth century B.C. So far as known, it is the "oldest nucleus of really scientific knowledge in the world," and "contains incomparably the most important body of medical knowledge which has survived to us from ancient Egypt, or, for that matter, from the ancient Orient anywhere.'"[112] It is a roll 184½ inches long by 13 inches wide, with twenty-two columns of writing, or five hundred lines. On the face of this papyrus, which deals with surgery and internal medicine, are seventeen columns describing forty-eight cases of injury of the upper half of the body (head, neck, thorax, and spine), with a discussion of the examination of patients, diagnosis, prognosis, and treatment, with explana-

111 *The Petrie Papyri; Hieratic papyri from Kahun and Gorob* . . . , ed. F. Ll. Griffith, p. 10.

112 J. H. Breasted, "The Edwin Smith Papyrus," in *NYHSQB*, April, 1922.

tory glosses, after which it ends abruptly. On the back are five pages of magic incantations. It appears that all was written by the same hand, but that the sources from which the recto and verso were taken were different.[113] Only a preliminary examination of the papyrus has as yet been made, and the contents have not thus far been critically studied and interpreted.

3. The Hearst Medical Papyrus,[114] which is ascribed to a period between the Twelfth and Eighteenth Dynasties and which is somewhat earlier than the Ebers, consists of eighteen pages, at least part of which came from the same source as the Ebers, since about one half is similar to that text, though not duplicating it. This papyrus contains references to illnesses of Rē and prescriptions for him, and formulas and enchantments to be repeated over the sick when taking remedies.

4. The Berlin Papyrus 3033,[115] the Westcar, or, as sometimes called, the Lesser Berlin Papyrus, and presumed to be of about 1600 B.C., consists of twelve pages, containing wonder-stories of the performances of magicians and sorcerers.

5. The Ebers Papyrus,[116] the most important, except possibly the new Edwin Smith Papyrus, was probably written about 1552 B.C. and consists of 110 pages inscribed in different dialects. Coming from Thebes, it shows more skill, a riper knowledge, and a more systematic arrangement than others; and it gives evidence of having been copied from a collection of documents, combining several small writings in one. It deals both with medicine and sur-

[113] J. H. Breasted, "The Edwin Smith Papyrus," in *REMC*, Paris, 1922, pp. 393-394.

[114] Reisner, *The Hearst Medical Papyrus*, Leipzig, 1905.

[115] Erman, *Die Märchen des Papyrus Westcar*, Berlin, 1890.

[116] Ebers, *Papyrus Ebers. Der Maasse und das Kapitel über die Augenkrankheiten*. Leipzig, 1889; also Joachim, *Papyrus Ebers*, Berlin, 1890.

gery, and contains prescriptions for various diseases with incantations and enchantments.

6. The Berlin Papyrus 3038,[117] the Greater Berlin, or the Brugsch Papyrus, which is of later date and is believed to have been inscribed about 1350 B.C., consists of twenty-three pages, treating of twenty-five different medical subjects in much the same manner as the Ebers Papyrus. Very curiously, the same, or a practically similar, test for female sterility contained in this papyrus is found in the article on this subject ($\pi\epsilon\rho\iota$ $\dot{a}\phi\delta\rho\omega\nu$) in the *Corpus Hippocraticum*.

7. The London Medical Papyrus (British Museum No. 10059),[118] is of the most recent date and is supposed to have been written about 1000 B.C. It consists of nineteen columns, largely medical, but with a generous commingling of magic, suggestive of an increased tendency to a reliance on the magical arts which is said to have characterized that period. This papyrus is in a poor state of preservation.

Other papyri.

Other texts, known as the Leyden Papyrus,[119] Turin Papyrus,[120] Harris Magic Papyrus,[121] Louvre Papyrus,[122] Boulaq Papyrus,[123] Vatican Magical Papyrus,[124] and

[117] Wreszinski, *Der grosse medizinische Papyrus des Berliner Museums*, Leipzig, 1909.

[118] Wreszinski, *Der Londoner medizinische Papyrus und der Papyrus Hearst*, Leipzig, 1912; also Griffith and Thompson, *The Demotic Medical Papyrus of London and Leiden*, London, 1904.

[119] Pleyte, *Étude sur un rouleau magique du Musée de Leyde*, Leyden, 1866.

[120] Pleyte and Rossi, *Papyrus de Turin*, 2 vols., Leyden, 1869-1876.

[121] Akmar, *Le Papyrus magique Harris*, Upsala, 1916.

[122] Maspero, *Mémoire sur quelques papyrus du Louvre*, Paris, 1875.

[123] Mariette, *Les Papyrus égyptiens du Musée Boulaq*, Paris, 1871.

[124] A. Erman, "Der Zauberpapyrus des Vatikan," in *ZÄ*, 1893, xxxi, 119-124.

Mother and Child Papyrus (Berlin Papyrus 3027),[125] contain occasional references to medico-magic subjects.[126]

Papyri not canonical.

While no definite statement is possible, it appears improbable that any of these documents formed part of the hermetic books mentioned by Clement, although the latter are believed to have been written at a much later date. It is known that Egyptian practitioners obtained from priests transcripts of the approved healing methods and prescriptions to be used in the authorized manner, and these may be such examples; but the exact status of these texts under the old régime cannot now be clearly established.

Descriptions of disease in the papyri.

It is of interest to note that, however crude and erroneous their healing practices may appear to modern minds, the ancient Egyptians made such careful observations and gave such clear descriptions that about 250 different diseases may be distinguished, and many can be identified, as, for example, stomach, bowel, and bladder complaints, asthma, angina pectoris, anemia, hematuria, skin diseases, smallpox, pyorrhea alveolaris, cancerous

[125] A. Erman, "Zaubersprüche für Mutter und Kind," in *APAW*, Berlin, 1901.

[126] In addition to these technical works of reference, the following studies published in medical journals are enumerated, the more important medical papyri being ably considered from the physician's point of view. C. H. von Klein, "The Medical Features of the Ebers Papyrus," in *JAMA*, 1905, xlv, 1928-1935; J. D. Comrie, "Medicine among the Assyrians and Egyptians in 1500 B.C.," in *EMJ*, 1909, ii, 101-129; J. Offord, "A New Egyptian Medical Papyrus," in *PRSM*, 1912-1913, vi, 97-102; J. Finlayson, "Ancient Egyptian Medicine," in *BMJ*, 1893, i, 748-752, 1014-1016, 1061-1064; B. Holmes and P. G. Ritterman, "Medicine in Ancient Egypt," in *CLC*, 1913, cix, 566-570, 590-603, 624-629.

tumors, menorrhagia, dysmenorrhea, metritis, conjunctivitis, ectropion, styes, and purulent ophthalmia.[127]

Causes of disease.

The Egyptians did not deal in theories, and their literature affords little information concerning their view of disease; but they never resigned themselves to the idea that death was natural and inevitable.[128] Life, once begun, should continue indefinitely. The people had the same belief in the malignant activity of spirits toward mankind as their contemporaries. Demons prowled around at all times; and when disease and death overtook a person, it was the result of curses or attack from an enemy, visible or invisible, a man with an evil eye, an animal or reptile, a maleficent spirit or ghost of the dead, or even an inanimate object; and death was practically regarded as an assassination or murder. The malevolent being gained entrance to the body by supernatural means in an unguarded moment through the eyes, ears, mouth, or nose and then made a vicious attack, breaking bones, sucking the marrow, drinking the blood, gnawing the intestines, heart, or lungs, and devouring the vital substance,[129] death ensuing unless the intruder was driven out before irreparable damage had been done. There were unlucky days, and certain seasons of the year were particularly dangerous, the intercalary, or epagomenal, days being fraught with exceptional risks,[130] since on them evil spirits had greater power. "Numerous harmful germs penetrate the clothing," and especial care must be taken lest "infection steps in and causes death."[128] Persons born on such days were particularly liable to die of certain maladies, and the

[127] Foucart, in *ERE* iv, 749.

[128] Maspero, *History*, i, 152 ff., 308.

[129] Foucart, in *ERE* iv, 750-752.

[130] Frazer, *Adonis, Attis, Osiris*, 3d ed., ii, 28, note 3; also Budge, *op. cit.*, ii, 109.

injunction was given, "go not forth from thy house; from
any side of it; whosoever is born on this day shall die of
the disease *aat*."[131] Diseases of animals were caused by
similar attacks of evil spirits, and were cured by the same
methods as were used for men.[128] The Egyptians, in common with other primitive peoples, believed that the great
scourges, or epidemics (*iatu*), were sent by the gods; but
it seems to have been foreign to their views that deities
inflicted disease upon individuals in punishment of sin,
though it was recognized that such visitations were made
in resentment for a personal offense or as penalty for an
indignity toward a divinity.[129]

Prophylaxis.

Although Egypt was considered a salubrious country,
the people took studious precautions to preserve their
health,[132] selecting their diet with care and for three successive days each month taking purges, emetics, and clys-
ters to guard against bowel troubles (Herodotos, ii, 77).
They were cleanly, bathed frequently, and wore white
linen garments, admirably adapted to the climate. Osiris
set an example; it was a source of great joy that he had
the power to lave himself; and both he and his *ka* washed
before sitting down to break bread together[133] (cf. *Pyramid Texts*, 564, 1537). Familiarity with the names of the
epagomenal days was a safe method of protecting oneself
against their perils (*Leyden Papyrus*, 346, 2, 6). All the
people wore about the neck amulets, charms, and talismans of stone or knots of cloth on which magic words of
power had been inscribed, or over which priests had recited magic texts,[134] the 'eye of Horus,' 'the intact eye'

[131] Budge, *Magic*, p. 227.
[132] Maspero, *Life in Ancient Egypt and Assyria*, p. 118.
[133] Budge, *Gods*, ii, 118.
[134] E. Naville, "Charms and Amulets (Egyptian)," in *ERE* iii, 430-
433.

(*uzait*), which gave health and soundness of sight, being the most popular protection against illness.[135] If the books in the library of Edfu "for turning aside the causes of disease" referred to prophylaxis, these customs may easily have been a part of the religious instructions.

Gods suffered from disease.

Gods suffered from maladies in the same manner as men, and when ill they applied to their fellow-divinities for help, as Horus and Sêth at Heliopolis (*Ebers Papyrus,* ii, 3-6; *Hearst Medical Papyrus,* 70, V, 9, 12, 15). Rē had sudden diseases of the eye (assumed to have been symbolic of eclipses), together with other ailments, and came near death when a scorpion stung his heel;[136] Isis was afflicted with an abscess of the breast following the birth of Horus; and Horus suffered from headache and internal pains,[137] and not only had dysentery and an anal weakness, but would have lost his life from a scorpion's sting had it not been for the prompt help of Isis and Thoth.[138] The liability of gods to disease was officially recognized, and in many temples were prescriptions both for divinities and for men, one of which had been composed by the invalid Rē (*Ebers Papyrus,* xlvi). The deities defended themselves more effectively than man because of their superior ability to concentrate their energies against their enemies, but the methods of cure were identical.[136]

Physicians.

The chief physicians (*sunu-oiru*) of the Pharaohs, from

135 Müller, *op. cit.,* p. 91.
136 Budge, *op. cit.,* i, 372 ff.; ii, 214.
137 *Leyden Papyrus,* ed. Pleyte; also Naville, *Études dédiées à Leemans,* pp. 75 ff.
138 Budge, *op. cit.,* ii, 208 ff.; also H. Brugsch, "Eine geographische Studie," in *ZÄ,* 1879, xvii, 1 ff.

the Memphite Dynasties to the Ptolemies, were high ecclesiastics.[139] The physician (*sunu*), who might be a layman attached to the temple, was not the same as the magician, who was a priest; the former healed "mechanically and by book," the priest on the other hand was "acting through his own religious feeling."[140] Herodotos (ii, 84) described the physicians as specialists, each one taking care of a certain class of diseases, and some were concerned with only one malady; but having been instructed in the divine methods, they had no personal choice in treatment and were obliged under risk of severe penalties, even of death, to follow the prescribed rules, which finally became canonical (Diodoros, i, 82), although Aristotle says (*Politica*, iii, 5) that if no improvement was noted after four days of treatment, the physicians were allowed to change their method. However, the practice of healing, at least under the native Egyptian régime, was essentially the monopoly of those who possessed a higher, deeper knowledge of the secret nature of things and had the power to control mysterious forces and to ward off invisible perils:[141] the magician-priests, especially the 'lector-priests' (*kher-hab*) (*Brugsch Papyrus*, vii, 10), since they had discovered incantations (*shinet*) and were endowed with the gift of prophecy (*London Medical Papyrus*, viii, 12).[140]

Healing methods.

The sacerdotal methods of healing consisted in magico-religious rites (*hīke'*), ceremonies and formulas which brought forth the mysterious, miraculous powers of deities and other supernatural beings, and which centered about the idea of exorcism, of expelling the unseen, mali-

[139] Foucart, in *ERE* iv, 752.
[140] Gardiner, in *ERE* viii, 268; also Wilkinson, *op. cit.*, ii, 354-358.
[141] Boylan, *op. cit.*, p. 124.

cious spirits which caused disease. Appeals to the gods
for the cure of disease were made orally or in writing.
The magician-priest approached the patient in a formal
manner, made his examination of the indications of disease, and followed with the ceremonial form for diagnosis,
"so shalt thou say" "a sufferer with ———" (naming the
disease), after which he classified the case according to
his prognosis: "an ailment I will treat," "an ailment I
will contend with," or, "an ailment I will not treat."[142]
Then came the treatment, which consisted of incantations,
prayers, and sacrifice, and possibly the giving of some
remedy, with the aid of all the devices and accessories of
magic, oral and manual,—commands, conjurations, threat-
enings, coaxings, aspersions, spells, and fumigations,—
the incantations and gestures being repeated four times.[143]
All these formulas and acts of the magician were supposed to have some mystic or symbolic meaning, which,
however well understood by the priests, served to impress
the people. It was deemed advisable, if not essential, for
the magician to know the name of the demon concerned in
each case. When known, it was called by name and, upon
the authority of a deity or (generally) deities of superior
powers whose names the magician claimed to know, it was
commanded or persuaded to come forth and depart, and
to be exorcised. The specialization in vogue among the
Egyptians assumed that the body was divided into thirty-
six parts, each of which was in charge of a certain god
("There is no limb of his without a god," *Leyden Papyrus*, 348, verso 6, 2), "and so invoking these, they heal the
diseases of the limbs" (Origenes, *contra* Celsum, viii, 58),
this responsibility of the god continuing in the after-

[142] Breasted, in *NYHSQB*, p. 15; also Gardiner, in *ERE* viii, 267;
Erman, *Life in Ancient Egypt*, p. 358.
[143] Müller, *op. cit.*, p. 199.

life.[144] On occasion the magician would put on a disguise and would appear as the god himself, imitating him in voice and gesture, and employing his relics and charms to deceive the demon and to cause him to depart. Such deception, like the use of the secret names of the deities, whether obtained properly or by stealth, was not considered an impiety or an offense against the divinity.[145]

Remedies.

Remedies (*pakhret*) were commonly employed to assist the magic formulas for exorcism and for the cure of disease; and in many cults they were revealed by the gods in dreams, such visions being regarded with religious reverence.[146] The gods had devised some of these remedies for themselves or for other deities (*Hearst Medical Papyrus*, pp. 9-10, V, 7, 9, 10, 12, 15). Drugs of many kinds were used, vegetable, mineral, and animal; and while some were loathsome, as the urine of animals,[147] the greater number were wholesome, time having proved the value of a goodly number of those then employed, such as castor oil, aloes, mint, myrrh, copper, lead, salt, goose oil and fats, opium, coriander, turpentine, cedar, hyoscyamus, and others that are still used in pharmacy.[148] The magic with which they were given did not hide their intrinsic healing properties from physicians, who were also acquainted with panaceas (*Ebers Papyrus*, xlvi, x-xlvii), "a true remedy on many occasions" (*Leyden Papyrus*, 347, xiii, 2, 3). Drugs were given internally or were applied externally, usually in combinations, numbers being

[144] Wiedemann, *op. cit.*, p. 24; also, Gardiner, in *ERE* viii, 265; Foucart, in *ERE* iv, 750.

[145] Foucart, *loc. cit.*

[146] Wilkinson, *op. cit.*, ii, 356.

[147] Griffith, *Petrie Papyrus*, pl. 5, 1, 18.

[148] Budge, *The Syriac Book of Medicines*, i, cxxxiv.

believed to increase their potency; and there were many long prescriptions. All these were prepared in conformity with traditional formulas to the accompaniment of prayers and incantations, "words to be said in the preparing of medicines for all parts of the body of the patient" (*Ebers Papyrus*, p. 1)[149]—and there were also "incantations of the measure when taking it to measure a prescription" (*Hearst Medical Papyrus*, p. 12, XIII, 12-17), as well as for oil (*ib.*, XIV, 4), besides "chapters for drinking remedies" (*Brugsch Papyrus*, p. 20, line 9)[150] and for applying them externally (*Ebers Papyrus*, I, 1-11). Remedies without magic were valueless or failed of their full effect, and the incantations were frequently written down, washed off, and drunk.[151] Healing had developed with magic, it was inseparably connected with it, and all evidence indicates that it was never emancipated from it.[152]

Medical incantations.

The function of the medical papyri is stated in the opening paragraph of the Ebers Papyrus: "This is a book for healing all disease''; and the two incantations following are examples found in that document:

Formula for drinking a remedy: Welcome, remedy, welcome, which destroyest the trouble in this my heart and in these my limbs. The magic (*hīke'*) of Horus is victorious in the remedy'' (recto, page 2, lines 1-2).

Another [*remedy*] *for driving away the cataract in the eyes:* Come verdigris ointment! Come verdigris ointment! Come thou verdant one. Come afflux from the eyes of Horus. Come thou effu-

---

[149] Joachim, *op. cit.*, p. 1.

[150] F. J. Chabas, "La Médecine des anciens Égyptiens," in *ME*, 1 sér., 1862, p. 67.

[151] Müller, *op. cit.*, pp. 83, 199.

[152] Foucart, in *ERE* iv, 750.

sion from the eyes of the god Turu! Come ye stuffs, ye who proceed from Osiris! Come to him [the patient] and take from him the water, the pus, the blood, the pain in the eye, the chemosis, the blindness, the flow of matter, which are worked there by the god of inflammations, of each kind of death, of each kind of pain and of all the evil things which are found in the eyes . . . so many of them there are too. So it is to be recited over the verdigris ointment, dissolved in beetle honey, with which we should mix Cyperus, which should then be laid upon the eyes in the specified fashion.[153]

The next incantations are found in the Brugsch Papyrus:[154]

Incantation for the quaffing of a remedy: —Thou awakenest beautiful, enduring unto eternity, in that every pain that is before thee is dispelled. Thy mouth is opened by Ptaḥ, thy mouth is unclosed by Sokaris with this iron hook of his.

. . . . .

O thou remedy, that dost loose the . . . , that dost dispel weakness, the ḥrj-ẖ-t is loosed by that which the divine Isis hath done; the ꜥꜣꜥ of the dead, which is in the limbs of [NN], born of [NN], is dispelled by the incantations of Nephthys. They are serviceable to him like that which is in the sparrow-hawk, as when the ꜥẖj-bird is struck, as when the sea hears the voice of Set.

. . . . .

I am Horus, who spendeth the night . . . , who spendeth the day in Abydos; my staff doth afford protection. —Praise be unto thee, thou proper staff that dost protect the limbs, thou wand of the sacred acacia. The 7 Ḥat-ḥôrs, who . . . the limbs, so that my limbs are healthy, just as Rēꜥ appears unto the earth. [My] protection is in my hand [i.e. the magic wand]; it is the great Isis who doth complete the works of Rēꜥ, [by means of] the physician Nṯr-ḥtp.

---

[153] Ebers, op. cit., p. 60.
[154] Wreszinski, Der grosse medizinische Papyrus des Berliner Museums, text pp. 43-44; tr. pp. 102-103; text p. 44, tr. pp. 103-105.

The following incantations for the protection and cure of a child are found in another papyrus:[155]

Protective charm for the protection of the body, to be recited over a child when the sun rises.

Thou dost rise, Rē,
Thou dost rise.

.   .   .   .   .

She [the dead one] will not take her son upon her lap.
'Thou dost save me, my lord Rē,'
Says [NN] (fem.), born of [NN].
I do not surrender thee,
I do not give [my] burden to the robber and the female robber of
    the realm of the dead.
My hand lies upon thee,
My seal is thy protection.
Rē doth rise,
Extend, O thou protection.

[Extract] My hands lie upon this child, and the hands of Isis lie upon him, as she lays her hands upon her son Horus.

[Extract] To drive away the *nsw* from all the limbs of a child. —Thou art Horus, and thou shalt awake as Horus. Thou art the living Horus; I drive away the malady that is in thy body, and the malady (?) that is in thy limbs. [etc.]

The Hearst Medical Papyrus contains incantations for broken bones, "A prescription for uniting a broken bone, the first day,"[156] and the following incantation from the London Medical Papyrus is believed to have been designed for wounds:[157]

O Horus, O Rē, O Shu, O Qêb, O Osiris, O Hekaw, O Nut, praise be unto you, ye great gods, who have brought the heavenly one (?)

[155] Erman, in *APAW*, pp. 43-44, verso 3, line 8, to page 4, line 2; p. 15, recto 2, lines 6-10; p. 19, recto 2, line 10, to page 5, line 7.

[156] Reisner, *Hearst Medical Papyrus*, p. 12, XIV, 13, 14, 15.

[157] Wreszinski, *Der Londoner medizinische Papyrus und der Papyrus Hearst*, pp. 148, 187, recto 8, lines 1-7.

to the underworld, ye who grant that he wander to this region,
ye who conduct Rē when he ascends out of the horizon, ye who
ride along in the evening bark and pass along in the morning
bark. Come ye unto me, arise unto me, unite yourselves with me,
for all sorts of evil hath befallen me, all sorts of evil ⳑ|-maladies,
all sorts of evil ḥȝj-t-maladies, which are in this body [of mine]
and in all these limbs of mine.

Tests for sterility.

The Brugsch, or Berlin Papyrus 3038, contains two formulas for determining whether or not a woman is sterile,
the first (verso, p. 1, lines 3-4, section 193) is as follows :[158]

To distinguish a woman who will bear a child from a woman
who will not bear a child. —Watermelons, pounded, to be saturated thoroughly with the milk of a mother of a boy, and to be
made into a śᶜm-dish. To be eaten by the woman. If she vomits,
she will bear a child; if she has flatus, she will never bear a child.

This same prescription, in slightly different form, is
found in the treatise "On Sterility" in the *Corpus Hippocraticum,* of nearly a thousand years later, and Diogenes
Lærtios (viii, 87) offers the explanation that Eudoxos,
a Knidian physician and mathematician, spent fifteen
months with the Egyptian priests at Heliopolis during
the reign of Nektanebos (384-362 B.C.).[159] The Greek text
(ed. Kühn) mentions two ingredients which should be
used with the milk, one, σικύα, a cucumber or gourd-like
plant, the other, βούτυρον. Hesychios explains the latter
component as a plant (βοτάνης εἶδος), and in view of a

---

[158] Wreszinski, *Der grosse medizinische Papyrus des Berliner Museums,* text, p. 45, tr. p. 106.

[159] Strabo states (XVII, i, 29 = p. 805 C) that Eudoxos was reputed
to have come to Egypt with Plato and to have lived at Heliopolis for
thirteen years; and Plutarch (*de Iside et Osiride,* 6, 10) refers to books
that he wrote.

passage of Athenaios (ix, 395 A), it is inferred that it was odoriferous.[160]

The second formula (verso, p. 2, lines 2-5, section 199) runs thus:[161]

Another test whether a woman will bear a child [or] will not bear a child. —Wheat and spelt which a woman daily wets with her urine, like dates and like the baked food š͑-t, in two sacks. If both of them grow, she will bear a child; if the wheat grows, it will be a boy; if the spelt grows, it will be a girl; if they do not grow, she will not bear a child.

General remarks.

During the last millennium B.c., following the decline of the New Empire, and during the Saïte régime, when attempts were being made to stem the course of the rapid disintegration of ancient Egyptian civilization by a revival of primitive traditions and customs in their original purity,[162] the native healing practices present no new features, except a corresponding decline in confidence in

[160] The nature of this plant is not clearly set forth: Chabas, in *ME*, 1 sér., 1862, pp. 69 ff., gives it as *batatu*, or Bull *batatu;* Brugsch (*Notice raisonnée d'un traité médicale datant du XIVme siècle avant notre ère* . . . , Leipzig, 1863, p. 17) writes "Herb. *Boudodou-kå*," etc. (see note), and referred to it in *AMWL*, 1853, pp. 44-45; Renouf ("Note on the medical papyrus of Berlin," in *ZÄ*, 1873, xi, 123 ff.) claims that the characters can equally well be read *buteru*, and tries to connect this with βούτορον of Hippokrates; while Wreszinski translates it as "Wassermelonen" (watermelons), and for an ancient Egyptian picture of the vegetable, see Wiedemann, *Das alte Ägypten*, p. 278. Littré (*Œuvres complètes d'Hippocrate*, viii, 415) construes βούτορον as butter, which Renouf regards as an error. *Note.*—In commenting on this subject, Dr. William F. Egerton (in a personal communication) says: "It would seem that the last part, k ꜣ ('kå' according to Brugsch's system) meaning 'of bulls,' 'bull-', was not an essential part of the noun. May one not suppose the 'bull-melon' meant 'big-melon'?"

[161] Wreszinski, *op. cit.*, text, p. 47, tr. p. 110.

[162] Breasted, *op. cit.*, p. 365.

old methods and a like tendency to decadence. Traditionally the Egyptians avoided the use of the customs of other
peoples (Herodotos, ii, 91), but the invasions from Asia
and Greece, with incidental foreign rule, forced many
changes, and these are doubtless reflected in the writings
of classical authors who were unable to gain a clear in-
sight into their more ancient, native methods of religious
therapeutics. Ptolemy Soter, in sympathy with Hellenic
influences, reorganized religion and introduced the adoration of Serapis in the place of that of Osiris-Apis (Osor-
ḥap). Although coldly received, his worship, through its
association with that of Isis and under official pressure,
made rapid headway in the North; and his healing cult
gained popularity, especially among foreigners, through
the prominence given his dream-oracle with interpretations of visions by priests, in which appeared intimations of what are now known as hypnotism and suggestive
therapeutics.[163] In these Ptolemaic times foreign influences were dominant, and the old Egyptian art of divine
healing, which had been declining for several centuries,
now passed into oblivion, leaving no definite information
for contemporaries, and for modern investigators only
vague and imperfect records which have recently been
discovered.

Profane Egyptian medicine.

Turning aside for a moment to the more practical, profane side of the native medical practice, which is beyond
the scope of this study, it is of interest to consider that
"Egyptian medicine was at its best in diagnosis and in
its physiological speculations; the *materia medica*, on the
other hand, remained permanently under the influence of
magical conceptions."[164] The Egyptians practiced sur-

[163] Hamilton, *Incubation*, p. 105.
[164] Joachim, *op. cit.*, pp. 99, 100, 103; also Gardiner, in *ERE* viii,
268.

gery, performing operations with flint knives, as vene-
section, circumcision,[165] castration, and lithotomy.[166] Like
all primitive peoples, their civilization was permeated
with gross and childish beliefs side by side with their
noblest, highest conceptions of ethics and religion. They
studied nature's laws, but they did not theorize or attempt to deduce general principles from observed facts,
and were content with a traditional, conservative em-
piricism.[167] Their facts, intermingled with the mysteries
of their faith, were not divulged to their contemporaries;
and the writings of classical authors of the Græco-Roman
period bear testimony of failure fully to comprehend
what they observed and were told. The Egyptians did,
however, succeed in laying broad foundations for future
medicine from observed facts; and while their visitors
gained only a superficial understanding of their attainments, they proved, in reality, a mine from which the
ancients borrowed freely, copying and adapting, too often
without credit to the originators and teachers. Plato is
said by Clemens Alexandrinus (*Stromata,* i, 15) to have
remarked, concerning the Greeks, that ''Whatever we receive from the barbarians we improve and perfect''; and
it is believed that they were indeed indebted to Egyptian
physicians for many valuable medical suggestions.

The old priest-physician.

The priest-physicians of ancient Egypt were persons
of education and of social standing, famed throughout the
Orient from earliest historic times. Homer bears testimony for his own day in saying (*Odyssey,* iv, 231-232), of
Egypt, ''There each physician is skilled above all other

[165] G. Foucart, "Circumcision (Egyptian)," in *ERE* iii, 670-677;
Budge, *Gods,* i, 119; Wilkinson, *op. cit.,* iii, 385-386.

[166] Budge, *The Syriac Book,* i, cxxxiv; also Müller, "Surgery in
Egypt," in *ER,* Washington, 1906-1910.

[167] Schneider, *Kultur und Denken der alten Aegypter,* pp. 317 ff.

men; for truly he is of the race of Paian.'' The repute of
the skill of the priest-physicians was spread along the
caravan routes farther east (Herodotos, iii, 1), and Egyptian prescriptions have been found in the archives of
Nineveh. The general testimony of writers of the last
centuries B.C. is rather specific that the physicians of
the Nile valley, of whom a fine portrait is drawn for us
by Chairemon (*Fragmenta historicorum Græcorum,* ed.
Müller, iii, 497; Strabo, XVII, i, 29 = 805 C), still stood
forth as noble and beneficent figures of Egyptian civilization.

PART II: THE HEALING DEITIES

Few of the many gods of ancient Egypt were prominent
as healers. Doubtless a large number of deities practiced
the curative art as a part of their general protective
beneficence, of which little or nothing is recorded; but
much of the information which has come down to us is
only vague and suggestive. It is impossible to make a
list of the healing divinities which may be regarded as
even approximately complete; and the deities who are
here discussed, some of them the chief gods of the pantheon and with other, perhaps more important, functions,
are set forth on the hypothesis that the practices in their
cults represent the religious healing customs of ancient
Egypt.

'Anuqet.	Neith
Apis.	Nekhbet.
Bes, or Bēsa.	Nephthys, or Nebt-ḥôt.
Êpet, or Uêret.	Ptaḥ.
Ḥat-ḥôr.	Sekhmet.
Horus, Ḥor, or Ḥoru.	Serapis, or Osor-ḥap.
I-m-ḥotep.	Thoth, Thout, or Tahuti.
Isis, or Êset.	Ubastet or Bastet.
Khonsu or Khons.	Uzoit, Uazit, or Buto (Uto).

Minor divinities of Child-birth and Nursing.

Ḥeqet.   Renenutet, or Rannu.
Meskhenet.

'ANUQET

'ANUQET, a goddess of the South, of the region of the
cataracts, and apparently of Nubian origin, was the third
of the triad of Elephantine (Abu), Khnûmu and Satet
being the other members. She was a deity of fertility, and
like Ḥeqet (the later consort of Khnûmu) was a goddess
of child-birth; while at Dakkeh (Per-Selket), the Greek
Pselchis, she was represented as the nurse of a king[168]
and was a "giver of life, and of all health, and of all joy
of the heart."[169] She was one of the goddesses of an island
near the First Cataract, on which was her temple, the
center of her worship, whence she was called 'Anuqet, the
'lady of Satet' (*i.e.*, 'the Island of Seheil').[168] She had the
same attributes as her sister-goddess, Satet, who was worshipped with her; and she wore a feather crown of unusual form, arranged in a circle, suggestive of her foreign
origin. 'Anuqet was equated with Nephthys (Nebt-ḥôt),
and the Greeks identified her with Hestia.[170]

APIS

APIS (pronounced Ḥap), the great god of Memphis and
one of the deities of Egypt from early dynastic times,
was worshipped in the form of a bull,[171] this being the
incarnation of Osiris, the "beautiful image of the soul
of Osiris" (Plutarch, *op. cit.*, 30), the 'son of Ptaḥ,'
and later the 'living replica of Ptaḥ.' The animal repre-

[168] Wilkinson, *op. cit.*, iii, 181.
[169] Budge, *Gods*, ii, 57-58.
[170] Müller, *op. cit.*, p. 131.
[171] *Ib.*, p. 162.

senting the god was carefully chosen, being recognized by characteristic black and white spots, a triangle or square on the forehead, an eagle on the back or a crescent on the flank (Pliny, *Historia Naturalis*, viii, 71), and double hair on the tail (Ailianos, *Historia Animalium*, xi, 10; Herodotos, iii, 28). When he had been found, he was escorted to Memphis, where, with much pomp, he was installed in his temple, the Apiæum, as "the holy god, the living Apis";[172] and when he died, his mummified body was buried with elaborate ceremonies in the Serapeum or in a rock tomb near the pyramid of Saḳḳâra.[173] Osiris was blended with the hawk Sokari, a deity of the dead related to Apis, and later with Ptaḥ as Osiris-Apis (Osor-Ḥap), who became Serapis in the Greek period.[174] The bull Apis was consulted for divination and Pliny (*loc. cit.*) and Ammianus Marcellinus (xx, 14) relate that the omen was good or bad according as Apis accepted or refused the food offered by worshippers.[175] Apis was a healing divinity, one to whom the origin of medicine was ascribed (Eusebios, *Præparatio Evangelica*, X, vi). Pausanias (VII, xxii, 3, 4) says that the manner of consulting the god was the same in Egypt as in Greece; the lamps were filled with oil, money was placed on the altar,[176] and, with his mouth to the bull's ear, the suppliant whispered his request, drawing his answer from the first words of the first person whom he met.

Although Apis was usually depicted as a bull, he was also represented with a human body and the head of a

[172] Müller, *loc. cit.*

[173] Budge, *op. cit.*, ii, 350; also Strabo, XVII, i, 33 = p. 807 C.

[174] Müller, *op. cit.*, p. 98.

[175] Foucart, in *ERE* iv, 793.

[176] See *infra*, page 332. These auguries refer especially to the classical period. Egypt had no coinage until after she had been conquered by Persia (525 B.C.).

bull, wearing a globe, symbolizing the moon, between the horns.[177]

BES, OR BĒSA

BES, though originally a foreign deity, either from Arabia or, more probably, from Central Africa, and deriving his myths from Nubia,[178] had been adopted into the pantheon from early dynastic times, the first mention of him being in the Pyramid Texts (no. 1786). Recent studies tend to the view that he was a purely human god, of negro or negroid character, and that he was in origin a person of magic power, personified as a divinity and introduced into the pantheon to execute special dances designed for protection and to remove bad influences, evil genii, and monsters of all sorts.[179] Thus he appears as a deity of pleasure, mirth, laughter, music, and dancing; amusing, while protecting, children and their nurses. He strangled or devoured serpents, and caught dangerous animals, while his image was placed above the doors of sleeping-rooms to keep away noxious beasts and evil spirits. The most ancient images of the divinity, which date from the Middle Empire, often represent him as holding a serpent in each hand, in the rôle of protecting infants. He became a companion of Êpet (Uêret) as a protector of child-birth and children and is frequently portrayed with her in the birth-chamber of princesses, as in a painting, dating from about 1500 B.C., found at Deir-el-Baḥri.[179]

During the Saïte epoch, the images of the deity multiplied and they became more varied, receiving a number of accessories, many of which were symbolic of other divinities and which were assumed to augment his mysterious power.[180a] At Thebes he was represented as wear-

[177] Budge, op. cit., ii, 346-351; also Wilkinson, op. cit., iii, 86-89.

[178] Budge, op. cit., ii, 284-288; also Wilkinson, op. cit., iii, 148-150.

[179] Budge, op. cit., ii, 285.

[180a] G. Jéquier, "Nature et origine du dieu Bes," in RTPA, 1915, xxxvii, 114-118.

ing emblems of war, but although this has been construed as indicating that he was a god of slaughter, it is probable that these arms were for protection or for attack on animals rather than for aggression. Armed with sword and shield, and wearing a panther's skin, he performed dances which were like the warrior dances of equatorial Africa. Represented with full face as an ugly dwarf with goggle eyes, flat nose, thick lips, protruding tongue, beard, shaggy brows, short, bent legs, and the grotesque figure of a mountebank, Bes, like other dwarfs of Egypt, has been regarded by writers on medical iconography as an example of achondroplasia. The Metternich stele gives proof that the head of Bes was a mask.

Although widely worshipped among the lower classes, Bes is not mentioned in inscriptions of the Græco-Roman epoch.[180b] He was associated with magic, and with its recrudescence in the late period he became so prominent that he appears to have ousted Serapis from the temple at Abydos, where an oracle flourished until it was suppressed by Constantine II, while in Roman times he was worshipped at the Serapeum at Memphis, where divination by incubation for healing was practiced. Bes was placed among the stars, corresponding with the serpent-strangling constellation Ophiouchos (Serpentarius) of the classical world.[181]

ÊPET, OR UÊRET

ÊPET, a strange goddess of foreign importation, probably from Central Africa, appears in a picture, from the temple of King Sethos I, of a constellation near Ursa Major, the old name being 'Ox-Leg,' or 'Club' or 'Striker.' She is portrayed as a composite being, standing upright, sometimes crowned with plumes or wearing the disk be-

[180b] J. G. Milne, "Græco-Egyptian Religion," in *ERE* vi, 383.
[181] Müller, *op. cit.*, pp. 61 ff.

tween two horns, and as having elements which belong to
the crocodile, the lion, and to man, as much as to the hippopotamus, with a strong, pointed head, a straight mouth
and a double row of small, sharp teeth, human breasts,
the enormous body of a hippopotamus (perhaps pregnant), and the paws of a lion. She was a creation of a
magic order with a terrifying aspect to frighten away
hostile and malevolent spirits; and she, like Bes, had the
duty of protecting children from the moment of birth
through their early, defenseless years.[182] Monuments
show that there were a dozen Êpets, each presiding over
a month.[183] It is believed that at one time she was widely
worshipped, since the month Epiphi was named for her,
whence her name Uêret, which appears in Greek as
Thouéris ('the Great One');[184] and she is assimilated with
many divinities. She was a benevolent deity, the 'mistress
of talismans,' helpful in parturition, and a protectress
from illness; and she appears each morning at the birth
of the sun, as also in the evening at his death, while in a
Pyramid Text she is represented as a divine nurse. Bes,
who became her companion, was sometimes regarded as
her husband; and in a picture from the temple of Deir-
el-Baḥri she is shown standing with him beside the couch
at the supposed birth of the daughter to the queen of
Thutmose I.[185]

ḤAT-ḤÔR

Ḥat-ḥôr ('House of Horus,' *i.e.*, where the sun lives in the
sky), one of the most ancient divinities of the Egyptian
pantheon, was first a goddess of the Eastern Sky and then

---

[182] G. Jéquier, "Thouéris," in *RTPA*, 1915, xxxvii, 118-120.
[183] G. Daressy, "Thouéris et Meskhenit," in *ib.*, 1912, xxxiv, 189-
193.
[184] Often spelled Toëris.
[185] Müller, *op. cit.*, pp. 59-62; also Budge, *op. cit.*, ii, 235, 359.

of the whole heaven, finally being numbered among the cosmic deities. She was the 'Mistress of Heaven,' the counterpart of Rē, and more frequently the consort of Horus the Elder. As the 'Mistress of Heaven' she sat beside the Persea tree, the celestial tree sacred to her;[186] and as a goddess of the Underworld she received the dead, bestowed new life upon them, and from the fruit of the tree gave them drink and heavenly food. She was the deity of love, the patroness of women, joy, and music, and was not only equated with 'Astart and Aphrodite, but was identified with all other female divinities, especially with Nekhbet, Uzoit, Ubastet, and Neith, who were sometimes referred to as goddesses of child-birth. Thus she was a protectress of the parturient and of mothers, and represented all that was best in women as daughter, wife, and mother; while she was even multiplied into seven Hat-hôrs who foretold the future of every child at birth.

Hat-hôr was accorded the most extravagant titles, such as 'mother of the world' and 'creator of the heavens,' of the earth, and of everything in them. The most laudatory salutations were used in paying homage to her in worship, and, given every attribute, she was worshipped throughout Egypt under many titles or names of other divinities, as Isis at Panopolis, and Neith at Saïs, although her home and the center of her worship were at Dendera in Upper Egypt. The cow was sacred to her, and she was represented as a cow or as having a human body and the head of a cow, with a globe (the solar disk) between her horns.[187]

HORUS, HOR, OR HORU

HORUS was a generic term for very many deities of the Egyptian pantheon, all of whom were variants of essen-

---

[186] Müller, *op. cit.*, pp. 37, 39-42.
[187] Budge, *op. cit.*, i, 428-438, 467.

tially two personalities, 'Horus the Elder' (Ḥar-uêr, the Aroueris of the Greeks), and 'Horus the Younger,' or 'Horus the Child' (Ḥar-pe-khrad, the Harpokrates of the Greeks).

Horus the Elder was the son of Rē and Ḥat-ḥôr, or of Qêb and Nut, and was the brother of Osiris, Isis, Sêth, and Nephthys, born on the second of the five intercalary days,[188] an old hymn, copied on a papyrus about 310 B.C., containing the following lines:[189]

Qêb and Nut begat Osiris, Horus (the one before the eyeless) (?), Sêth, Isis, and Nephthys from one womb, One of them after the other.

He was a solarized divinity, connected with the theology of Heliopolis, 'Horus of the Horizon' (Ḥar-akhti), who prepared the way for the sun-god Rē, the falcon, whose symbol, the winged disk, was seen in the sky. Horus, the face of the heavens by day, as contrasted with Sêth, the face of the heavens by night,[190] was one of the very oldest deities of the pantheon;[191] and his ancient and principal seat of worship in Lower Egypt was at Edfu, though it is quite probable that the earlier, and perhaps original, center of his cult was at Hierakonpolis (Nekken), 'the City of Hawks,' in the South.[191] At Ombos (Ombite) he was the chief of a triad.[192]

Horus the Younger, or Horus the Child, was the posthumous son of Osiris by Isis, the reincarnation of Osiris, the third member of the Osirian triad, and one of the principal divinities of the Osirian circle of the Underworld, superseding Anubis as the conductor of souls, although by a confusion he was also referred to as a solar deity, the

[188] Frazer, *The Scapegoat*, pp. 340 ff.
[189] Müller, *op. cit.*, p. 69.
[190] Breasted, *History*, p. 36; Budge, *op. cit.*, i, 467.
[191] Müller, *op. cit.*, pp. 27, 101-102.
[192] Petrie, in *ERE* v, 245.

'Rising Sun,' to whom were given the two eyes of Rē.[193] In the late dynastic period, when the worship of Osiris and Isis had become dominant, Horus absorbed the attributes of all Horuses, and in him was finally blended every variant personality, from Horus the Elder to the least significant. Beginning with the New Empire, Horus became more and more important; and though mentioned by different names, he was identified and worshipped with all the deities of the pantheon,[194] while the Greeks equated him with Apollo.

Harpokrates, the Greek name of a variant of 'Horus the Child,' was a late development who, with Serapis and Isis, was the third member of the divine triad at Alexandria, Philæ, and Fayum, and was worshipped with Isis at Panopolis.[195] He had the functions of Horus, and in Ptolemaic times assumed the attributes of the local deities with whom Amon-Rē had been identified, and even those of this deity at the center of his worship, at Thebes. Without temples, he was worshipped as a deity of the lower classes and of the home, and was often represented as a young boy standing between Isis and Nephthys, or as a child seated on a lotus flower with a lock of hair on the right side of his head and holding his finger to his lips. This figure has been misconstrued as commanding the faithful to be silent concerning the mysteries of their religion[196] and was so interpreted by the Greeks, who sometimes called the deity Sigalos, equating him with Akesis, Telesphoros, and Euamerion of the retinue of Asklepios (Plutarch, op. cit., 19, 68).[197]

The mother of Horus taught him the arts of magic, the

[193] Müller, op. cit., p. 83.
[194] Budge, op. cit., i, 486.
[195] Milne, in ERE vi, 379.
[196] Müller, op. cit., p. 243.
[197] Wilkinson, op. cit., iii, 129-132.

maladies of mankind, and their cures, and he rendered signal service in healing by his oracles (Diodoros, i, 25). Horus of Letopolis (Khem) was the 'chief physician in the house of Rē' (*Turin Papyrus*, 124, 5), and one of his most important sanctuaries of healing was situated there, other well-known temples being at Edfu, Tanis (Zanet), Philæ, and Abydos, while he was especially venerated at Heliopolis.

Horus the Child was the subject of some of the most venerated and popular myths of Egypt. As the son of Osiris and Isis, his life was sought by Sêth, his father's bitter enemy and murderer; and Isis saved him only by hiding in the papyrus swamps near Buto, where he was born. While in the rushes, he was bitten by a scorpion and was *in extremis* when found by Isis, who called upon Rē in the heavens to save him, whereupon, leaving his 'Boat of Millions of Years' in mid-sky, he sent Thoth, who, with his magic words of power, restored the child to life.[198] When Horus had grown to manhood, undertaking to be avenged on the murderer of his father and to establish his own legitimacy, he engaged in a three days' battle with Sêth, who was defeated and lost his virility, while Horus himself was deprived of an eye, which, however, was restored when Thoth spat upon the wound and healed it.[199] Sêth was in danger of forfeiting his life, but was saved by the interference of Isis, upon whom Horus turned in anger and cut off her head, which Thoth replaced with the head of a cow,[200] or, according to Plutarch (*op. cit.*, 19), removed from it the symbols of her authority. Later, when Osiris was vindicated of the charges made by Sêth before the great tribunal of the gods at Heliopolis, Horus

---

[198] Budge, *Magic*, pp. 133-136; also, for text in parallel, *id.*, *Gods*, ii, 233 ff.

[199] Breasted, *Development*, pp. 29-31.

[200] Müller, *op. cit.*, p. 126; also Budge, *op. cit.*, i, 489; ii, 212.

succeeded to the inheritance and the throne of his father, receiving sovereignty over the whole world.[201]

Horus was one of the most universally recognized, beloved, and worshipped deities of the pantheon. The hawk was sacred to him, and he was usually represented with a human body and the head of a falcon, being called the 'hawk-headed Horus'; or he was pictured as a child in the arms of Isis or some other goddess, and occasionally as a boy (Harpokrates) standing by her side.[202]

I-M-ḤOTEP

I-M-ḤOTEP, the architect of King Tosorthros (Zoser) of the Third Dynasty (*circa* 2900 B.C.), the builder of the Sakḳâra Pyramid, an astrologer of the priests of Rē, and a distinguished leech, was renowned for his wise sayings and became a patron of learning, of scholars, and especially of physicians. After the New Kingdom (1580 B.C.), writers made libations to him; and gradually losing his humanity, he was deified after the Persian period (525 B.C.) and elevated to the rank of a healing divinity.[203] In his divine character he was the 'Son of Ptaḥ' and of Sekhmet, and having displaced their son Nefer-têm, he was made the third member of the great Memphite triad. Related to Thoth in function, I-m-ḥotep occasionally absorbed his funerary duties, and as 'scribe of the gods' he was the author of words of power which protected the dead.[204] He was also closely related to the deified sages Amon-ḥotep and Teos,[205] who were associated with healing.

I-m-ḥotep, 'He who cometh in peace,' owed his fame and

---

[201] Breasted, *op. cit.*, pp. 33-37; also Budge, *op. cit.*, i, 489.
[202] Budge, *op. cit.*, i, 466-499.
[203] Sethe, in *ERE* vi, 650-651.
[204] Budge, *op. cit.*, i, 522.
[205] Boylan, *op. cit.*, pp. 166-168.

power to his skill in the healing art. He was the good physician both of deities and of men, "the god who sent sleep to those who were suffering and in pain, and those who were afflicted with any kind of disease formed his especial care."[206] He was the divinity of physicians and of "all those who were occupied with the mingled science of medicine and magic." His suppliants usually received information of the curative remedy in dreams by incubation, as shown by epigraphs and related in tales (Diodoros, i, 25); and in the vision the deity usually began by identifying the suppliant, and then revealed the directions for treatment.[207] Satni relates that his wife Mahituaskhit appealed to the god for relief from sterility, prayed and slept in his temple, and dreamed that he told her to pull a living colocasia plant, leaves and all, and making a potion, to give it to her husband. This she did and she conceived at once.[208] Another case of sterility, cured by a remedy similarly revealed in a dream during temple-sleep, is recorded on the Memphite Stele of Psherenptah of the Augustan period.[209]

The cult of I-m-hotep was originally attached to his tomb near the Pyramid of Sakkâra, and his earliest important sanctuary was erected near the Serapeum close to Memphis. After the New Empire was established, his worship grew rapidly in popularity and importance; and during the Saïte period and the later Ptolemaic age he was greatly honored. He was revered and adored in his own city, as well as at Thebes, Edfu, and elsewhere; he was prominent in the temple of Kasr-el-'Agûz, erected to Teos, a sage or god similar to Thoth; while the Ptolemies built a small but beautiful temple to him on the island of

---

[206] Budge, op. cit., i, 523.
[207] Foucart, in ERE v, 35-36.
[208] Maspero, Popular Stories of Ancient Egypt, pp. 146-147.
[209] Foucart, in ERE v, 35.

Philæ, upon which was placed the following inscription:
"Great one, Son of Ptaḥ, the creative god, . . . the god
of divine forms in temples, who giveth life unto all men,
the mighty one of wonders, the maker of times, who
cometh unto him that calleth upon him wheresoever he
may be, who giveth sons to the childless, the chief 'lector-
priest' (*kher-ḥab; i.e.,* 'wisest and most learned one'), the
image and likeness of Thoth the wise one.'"[210]
The bronze figures of this hero-god in the museums are
all of the Twenty-second Dynasty, and represent him as
a bald man, sometimes wearing a cap, seated, with a book
or roll of papyrus on his knees,[211] and without any of the
customary ornamentations of Egyptian deities. I-m-ḥotep
was called Imuthes by the Greeks, who identified him with
their Asklepios (Stobaios, *Ecloga,* I, xli, 44); and his
temples were termed Asklepieia.[212]

ISIS, OR ÊSET

Isis, one of the very ancient goddesses of Egypt, the most
beloved and generally worshipped as a 'protective deity,'
held a place in the affections of the people above that of
all other female deities. Born on the fourth epagomenal
day, she was the daughter of Qêb and Nut, the sister of
Osiris, Horus the Elder, Sêth, and Nephthys, the wife of
Osiris, and the mother of the Child Horus. Becoming the
consort and mother of the sun-god, with the solarization
of Osiris she was identified with all other celestial goddesses and was most intimately assimilated with Hat-
ḥôr;[213] while she was also one of the chief divinities of the

[210] Budge, *op. cit.,* i, 523.

[211] Erman, *Ägyptische Religion,* p. 174.

[212] Müller, *op. cit.,* p. 171; and for further details consult G. Foucart,
"Imhotep," in *RHR,* 1903, xlviii, 362-371; K. Sethe, "Imhotep der
Asklepios der Aegypter," in *UGAÄ,* 1902, ii, 98 ff.

[213] Müller, *op. cit.,* p. 99.

ISIS
WITH HORUS THE CHILD
IN THE PAPYRUS SWAMPS

ATTENDED BY UZOIT, THOTH, AND NEKHBET

*Reproduced from "The Gods of the Egyptians," by the courtesy of
Sir E. A. Wallis Budge.*

Underworld, the Kingdom of the Dead, and, as the consort
of Osiris, appears with him in the judgment scenes represented by Ma'at, and receives the title 'Goddess of the
West' as a result of her identification with Ḥat-ḥôr. In
her original character she was the rich, black soil of
Egypt, fertilized by the Nile;[214] but later she was conceived as the goddess of fertility and love, the close friend
and protectress of women in all the vicissitudes of their
lives, and was equated with 'Astart, Aphrodite, Demeter,
and Persephone. Originally independent, political changes
united her with Osiris, but she was always the more popular of the two, and more a divinity of the home and person
than of the temple and priest. Until the Twenty-sixth
Dynasty she was seldom shown as a nursing mother, but
thereafter the worship of the mother and child became increasingly general and during the Roman period was
widely spread.[215]

In the *Book of the Dead* and in the Pyramid Texts, Isis
is associated with many of the most important myths of
the Egyptian religion. As the faithful wife of Osiris she
sought and found the body of her husband, which had been
dismembered and scattered by Sêth, his murderer; breathing into his mouth, she restored him, and receiving his
seed, she secreted him in the papyrus swamps against the
further enmity of Sêth; and there, aided by Thoth and
attended by her sister Nephthys and by other goddesses
of child-birth, she brought forth Horus, nurturing him
among the rushes.[216]

Isis gained her unusual powers as a magician by means
of a stratagem through which she learned the secret name
of the supreme god Rē, when he was old and feeble. Originally a humble member of his household, she mixed his

[214] Maspero, *History*, i, 132.
[215] Petrie, in *ERE* v, 246.
[216] Budge, *op. cit.*, ii, 233 ff.; also Müller, *op. cit.*, p. 116.

spittle with earth and created a scorpion, which was placed in the path until Rē should walk forth, when it stung him on the heel. Not knowing what the trouble was, and feeling himself dying, he called loudly for help, where-upon, Isis, among others, came with profuse protestations of sympathy. During his extreme suffering she begged Rē to disclose to her his secret name that she might use it for his cure, but he long demurred, saying that his father had locked the name in his breast in order that no god should have power over him, and declaring that it could be obtained only by a surgical operation. Rē finally yielded, however, and Isis performed the operation, se-cured the name, cured the god,[217] and thus became the supreme enchantress of Egypt, a sorceress often referred to as Wēret-ḥīke', 'she who is great of magic' (*Turin Papyrus*, 131-133).[218]

Isis, a healing divinity of the first rank (Diodoros, i, 25), cared for the health of her people and was especially skilled in the treatment of children, having gained her knowledge by devising charms and remedies for her infant son (*Turin Papyrus*, xxxi, lxxvii, 6; *Ebers Papyrus*, i, xii). To the suffering she came "bringing with her words of magical power, and her mouth was full of the breath of life; for her talismans vanquish the pains of sickness, and her words make to live again the throats of those who are dead."[219] In the preparation of remedies she was appealed to by incantations, as in the following from the Ebers Papyrus:

May Isis heal me as she healed her son Horus of all the pains which his brother Sêth brought on him when he slew his father

---

[217] Budge, *op. cit.*, i, 372-387, gives the story in parallel texts.

[218] K. Sethe, "Zur altägyptischen Sage vom Sonnenauge das in der Fremde war," in *UGAÄ*, 1912, v, 128; also Budge, *Magic*, pp. 137-141; Gardiner, in *ERE* viii, 268.

[219] Budge, *op. cit.*, p. 139.

Osiris. O Isis! Thou great enchantress, heal me, save me from all evil things of darkness, from the epidemic and deadly diseases and infections of all sorts that spring upon me, as thou hast saved and freed thy son Horus, for I have passed through fire and am come out of the water. May I not light upon that day when I shall say "I am of no account and pitiable." O Rē, who hast spoken for thy body. O Osiris, who prayest for thy manifestation. Rē speaks for the body, Osiris prays for the manifestation. Free me from all possible evil, hurtful things of darkness, from epidemic and deadly fevers of every kind.

To those who sought her aid in illness she disclosed her remedies through dreams by incubation, more especially in the later period, when she was associated with Serapis at Alexandria and at Philæ;[220] and her temples, notably those at Koptos and at Panopolis, were depositories of ancient medical lore. She was also a child-birth goddess, and in this function she was associated with other divinities, as Nephthys, Ḥeqet, and Meskhenet.[221]

Isis of 'ten thousand names' was venerated and worshipped throughout the whole of the known Nile valley. From the period of the New Kingdom she was assimilated with practically every goddess in Egypt, absorbing their attributes, overshadowing them, and being worshipped in very many aspects in the shrines of other goddesses, either under their names and attributes or under compound names, such as Isis-Ḥat-ḥôr or Isis-Neith. The original seat of her cult appears to have been at Per-ehbet, near the city of Buto;[222] and she had other temples in different parts of the country, one of the most beautiful being that erected under the Ptolemies on the sacred

[220] Révillout, in *PSBA*, 1887, x, 58.

[221] Erman, *Die Märchen des Papyrus Westcar*, pp. 60 ff.; also Maspero, *Popular Stories*, pp. 36 ff.; Wiedemann, *Altägyptische Sagen und Märchen*, pp. 1-24.

[222] Müller, *op. cit.*, p. 99.

island of Philæ, the remains of which are still of great architectural interest.

In the reorganization of religion under Ptolemy Soter, Isis was associated with the new god Serapis at Alexandria, where she was the second member of the triad; and this new cult, gaining in popularity, especially among foreigners, soon spread to Greece, Rome, and its provinces, although in Rome it was long discredited because of cultic abuses. After it had been suppressed elsewhere in the general movement against paganism, the worship of Isis continued in Egypt even to the middle of the fifth century A.D., owing to the faithful support given it by the Nubians.[223]

KHONSU, OR KHONS

DURING the Early Empire, Khonsu, the son of Amon and Mut, and the third member of the Theban triad, appears to have been a travelling deity, a messenger of the gods in the form of the moon;[224] and with the rise of the Theban Empire and the advancement of Amon to supremacy as a national divinity, he was recognized as an ancient form of the moon-god, and the son of Amon-Rē. The earliest certain mention of Khonsu is of his close association with Thoth as a moon-god, and before the Middle Kingdom he seems to have been little known, especially outside of Upper Egypt. In his development he was associated with Horus as Khonsu-Horus, and at a late date with Rē as Khonsu-Rē. During the period between the Twelfth and Eighteenth Dynasties he came into notice more and more frequently and thereafter he became an important deity, his healing cult developed rapidly, and he was widely renowned for his miraculous cures, but there are no legends

[223] Budge, *Gods*, ii, 202-240; also Müller, *op. cit.*, pp. 98-101; Petrie, in *ERE* v, 246; Milne, in *ib.*, vi, 378; G. Showerman, "Isis," in *ib.*, vii, 434-437.

[224] Müller, *op. cit.*, p. 140; Wilkinson, *op. cit.*, iii, 484, 513.

of him before the Ptolemaic period.[225] He was greatly
honored at Thebes, and Rameses III (1200-1100 B.C.)
erected a large and beautiful temple for him at Karnak,
on the east bank of the Nile, within the precincts of the
great temple of Amon. There were three shrines: the
'House of Khonsu,' 'the beautiful resting one'; the 'House
of Khonsu in Thebes, Nefer-ḥotep'; and the sanctuary of
Khonsu as 'the god who carries out his plans in Thebes,'
i.e., the divinity energized to permit his power to act
outside the temple.[226] The deity was also worshipped elsewhere, as at Edfu and Hermopolis, where he was assimilated with Thoth as Khonsu-Tahuti, but the chief interest
attaches to his form as Khonsu-Nefer-ḥotep, who ruled
over the month, "the great god who driveth away devils"
of sea, earth, and sky which are hostile to man and which
attack him, causing pains, sickness, madness, decay, and
death. Khonsu made women and cattle to become fertile.

As the 'god in activity,' the divinity cured Ptolemy
Philadelphus of a dangerous disease; and in gratitude
the monarch erected, in honor of the deity, a statue adjoining his sanctuary, the base of which is still preserved.[226]

The image of Khonsu contained the soul of the god, and
it announced his will by *hanu,* movements of the head.
Khonsu-Nefer-ḥotep was credited with the ability to
effect cures by substitution, loaning the healing forces
from his own 'soul energy' (*i.e.*, his *sa*) to an image or
double, "bestowing upon it [by the nape of the neck] its
protective fluid at four intervals." The 'true name' thus
conveyed gave the statue power to cast out demons and
to cure disease, but the 'best of the divine substance' was
always kept at Thebes. An instance of the efficacy of this

[225] A. M. Blackman, "The Pharaoh's Placenta and the Moon-God
Khons," in *JEA*, 1916, iii, 235-249.

[226] Wiedemann, *Magie und Zauberei,* pp. 19-21.

transmitted power is related on the so-called Bakhtan stele, now in Paris.[227] The father-in-law of Rameses II, a powerful prince of Mesopotamia, requested him to send one of Egypt's sages to heal his daughter, who was afflicted with a disease which had resisted all efforts at cure; and Rameses accordingly deputed "a man wise of heart and cunning of finger";[228] but, when he reached his destination, he found himself helpless to aid the princess, since she was possessed of a demon (or a ghost, or spirit of the dead) of superior rank. A second appeal was made to Rameses, who then consulted Khonsu, whereupon the god "nodded firmly twice," thus consenting that one of his doubles, to whom he transmitted his healing forces in fourfold measure, should be sent to Bakhtan. Upon the arrival of the deity, the evil spirit at once recognized his master, made submission, and offered to return to his own place; but begged that first a feast should be held at court at which he might be present. This request was granted, and when the god, the prince, and the demon had spent a pleasant day together, the evil spirit went to his home, and the princess was cured; while Khonsu was thereafter highly honored at Bakhtan, where he remained for more than three years. Recent critics declare that the stele is of late Greek origin, and that the story was probably invented to enhance the waning influence of the deity.

Khonsu was variously represented with the figure of a man and the head of a hawk, or a human head, surmounted by a lunar or solar disk and with the crescent or uræus; he is also depicted as a child, bearing a relation to the god similar to that of Harpokrates to Horus;[229]

[227] Budge, *Magic*, pp. 206-213; also *Gods*, ii, 38-41; Maspero, *op. cit.*, pp. 175-179.

[228] *I.e.*, *rakhikhet*, "a knower of things" (*Ebers Papyrus*, I, ix).

[229] Müller, *op. cit.*, p. 140; Budge, *op. cit.*, ii, 33-41; Wilkinson, *op. cit.*, iii, 174-176.

but the most characteristic form is that of a young prince
with a side lock of hair, clothed in antiquated royal ap-
parel with the insignia of royalty, the whip and crook.[230]

NEITH

NEITH, one of the most ancient deities of the pantheon and
probably of Libyan origin, adopted during the First
Dynasty,[231] had as symbols the shuttle, and a bow and
arrows; whence it would appear that she was a divinity
of weaving (perhaps of handicrafts) and of the chase,
though in her later aspect she was regarded as a form of
Ḥat-ḥôr and as a sky-goddess. Presiding over the city of
Saïs, in the Delta, she was frequently referred to under
that name; and being associated with the theology of
Atum-Rē at Heliopolis, the father-god, she was called the
'mother-goddess,' 'Neith, the mighty mother who gave
birth to Rē,' the 'great lady,' the 'lady of heaven,' and
the 'queen of the gods'; while the term 'self-born' or 'self-
produced' was applied to her, and she was said to have
brought forth Rē without the aid of a husband.[232]

Although a prominent and highly respected member of
the pantheon, she was always surrounded with an air of
mystery; the many texts concerning her have not been
harmonized; and her composite, complex character has
not been clearly interpreted. She was assimilated with
many of the principal goddesses of Egypt in their varied
aspects, being allied with Isis as a protector of Horus and
as a form of the magic powers of these deities, and with
Sekhmet, Mut, Ubastet, and Uzoit, divinities having child-
birth functions, her symbol being the vulture, indicative
of maternity and of an obstetric function. She was also
a healing deity, her temple at Saïs being celebrated as a

[230] Blackman, in *JEA*, 1916, iii, p. 247.
[231] Budge, *op. cit.*, i, 475.
[232] *Ib.*, i, 459.

healing sanctuary, and having attached to it a medical school which was restored (by direction of Darius) during the Persian occupation.[233]

The Greeks, who equated the goddess with Athena, attributed to her remarkable powers;[234] and a statue of Neith, which is supposed to have symbolized Truth and of which much has been written, bore an inscription given by Plutarch (*op. cit.*, ix) which he assumed to refer to Isis and which read: "I am all that hath been, and that is, and that shall be; and my veil none hath uncovered (or revealed)."[235]

The worship of Neith was widely extended throughout Egypt, the chief seats in the South being at Elephantine, where she was the consort of Khnûmu, and at Letopolis (Te-snēt);[236] and her annual 'Festival of Lamps' at Saïs was famous (Herodotos, ii, 59, 62).[237]

NEKHBET

NEKHBET, the tutelary goddess of the cities of Eileithyiaspolis (Nekhab), the modern El-Kab, and Hierakonpolis, 'the White City' of hawks, was the best-known divinity of child-birth in the pantheon;[238] while in the early period she was one of the 'two mistresses' of the prehistoric kingdoms into which the country was then divided; Nekhbet ruling the South, while her sister, Uzoit of Buto, reigned over the North.

Although she is described on monuments as a deity of child-birth, she is more commonly referred to as a nurse who protected kings, as in the instance of Pepi, whom she

[233] Gardiner, in *ERE* viii, 268.
[234] Wilkinson, *op. cit.*, ii, 42.
[235] Budge, *op. cit.*, i, 458.
[236] *Ib.*, i, 450-465; also Wilkinson, *op. cit.*, iii, 39-44.
[237] Wilkinson, *op. cit.*, iii, 380.
[238] Müller, *op. cit.*, pp. 101, 142-143.

suckled.[239] The vulture, whose hieroglyph was used for
'mother' (Ailianos, *op. cit.*, x, 22), was her emblem and
was very commonly shown with outspread wings; while
Nekhbet herself was represented with a human figure and
the head of a vulture, or sometimes of an asp;[240] with the
head of a woman wearing the white crown of Upper
Egypt; with a cap and the two ostrich feathers of Osiris;
and occasionally with the globe of Ḥat-ḥôr as a sky-
goddess.

Nekhbet is named in the myths as one of those in attendance upon Isis at the birth of Horus, and she was
intimately associated with the other divinities of parturition, especially with Uzoit, Ubastet, and Ḥat-ḥôr, as
well as with Meskhenet (or Rannu), who was more definitely a nurse, particularly of kings and princes; while
other deities of Egypt are occasionally mentioned in connection with gestation and child-bearing, such as Nut,
Mut, and Typho.[240] Nekhbet further appeared together
with a goddess of the North, Uat or Uati, modern variants
of one name, ordinarily called Buto (more accurately
Uto), who was also a 'protectress of Monarchs' and who
was likewise represented in the form of a vulture and
worshipped with the same honors at Thebes, but who was
placed in opposition as having a contrary character.[240]
The Greeks equated Nekhbet with Eileithyia, and the
Romans with Lucina; and the city of Nekhbeyet was called
'Civitas Lucinæ.'[241]

NEPHTHYS, OR NEBT-ḤÔT

NEPHTHYS, the 'Mistress of the temple' and an ancient
deity of the Osirian cycle, was, in general character, the
goddess of death, whence she was called 'Mistress of the

[239] Breasted, *op. cit.*, p. 130.
[240] Wilkinson, *op. cit.*, iii, 194-200.
[241] Budge, *op. cit.*, i, 438-441.

West'; yet her personality was essentially passive, and she appears as complementary to Isis. Born on the fifth epagomenal day, she was the daughter of Qêb and Nut, and the sister of Osiris, Sêth, Horus the Elder, and Isis; but though she was the wife of Sêth, she was an attendant upon Osiris in the judgment scenes and a faithful friend to Isis. She aided her sister in searching for and collecting the remains of Osiris, and in carrying them to Abydos for interment; and she watched over Isis in the swamps while awaiting the birth of Horus, afterward being one of the child's nursing mothers. She was intimately associated with Nekhbet and Uzoit, Ḥeqet, and Meskhenet, and co-operated with them as deities connected with child-birth (*Westcar Papyrus*, pl. 9, i, 21 ff.).

Like Isis, Nephthys was skilled in magic, 'mighty in words of power,' and a healing divinity, while with Osiris and Isis she was one of the 'great sovereigns' of Mendes in the Delta. She had numerous titles, of which the most common were 'lady of heaven,' 'mistress of the gods,' and 'great goddess, lady of life'; and she was worshipped in many places, especially with Isis at her great temple at Per-ehbet (Plutarch, *op. cit.*, xxxviii, lxiii).[242]

PTAḤ

PTAḤ, one of the primeval deities, called 'the very great god,' represented wisdom[243] and was a cosmic divinity, 'the creator of the gods and of the world,' a fellow worker with Khnûmu in the creation of the universe, molding the solar and lunar eggs on the potter's wheel,[244] and executing the commands of Thoth and of the Seven Wise Ones of the goddess Meḥ-urt who planned the world.[245] As a

[242] Müller, *op. cit.*, p. 110; Budge, *op. cit.*, ii, 254-260; Petrie, in *ERE* v, 246.

[243] Budge, *op. cit.*, i, 501.

[244] Müller, *op. cit.*, pp. 144-145.

[245] Budge, *op. cit.*, i, 516.

creator he was Ptaḥ-Tetenen and an architect,[246] a divine
artist in stone and metal 'who formed works of art,'
his high priest being the 'chief artificer.'[247] Ptaḥ partook of the nature of Thoth and was called 'lord of Ma'at'
at Memphis, which was named Ḥat-ka-Ptaḥ, 'Place of the
Soul of Ptaḥ,' and in which he had been adored from
archaic times as the greatest of all divinities.[247]

Ptaḥ, "the god of the 'propitious' face," was the chief
of the Memphite triad, his wife Sekhmet and his son
Nefer-têm (or, later, I-m-ḥotep, who displaced Nefer-têm)
completing the group.[248] He was identified with many
other deities whose powers he was supposed to possess,
but more closely with Apis and Osiris than with others.
Apis was regarded as the incarnation of the soul of Ptaḥ,
and in dying became Sokari,[249] who was a divinity of a
place near Memphis and who was transformed into a god
of the earth and of the dead when this became a necropolis.
Ptaḥ was then blended with Sokari, and later, when absorbed by Osiris as Osiris-Apis, they became Osor-ḥap,
the Serapis of Ptolemaic times.[250]

Ptaḥ was a therapeutic divinity of great renown, and
his temple at Memphis was celebrated for the marvellous
cures which he effected. It appears that from early times
the remedies for the healing of diseases were revealed to
suppliants at his shrine in dreams during sleep in his
sanctuary. As an incubation deity he received the epithet
Sotmu,[251] and it was chiefly in his aspect as Ptaḥ-Sotmu
that he was adjured to 'hear the prayer,' and when morning came the response, when made, was interpreted by

[246] Breasted, op. cit., pp. 45-46.
[247] Müller, op. cit., pp. 144-145, 220-222.
[248] Budge, op. cit., i, 520.
[249] Maspero, History, i, 163.
[250] Müller, op. cit., pp. 98, 149, 162.
[251] Sotmu meaning ears or hearing, Ptaḥ-Sotmu is construed as 'Ptaḥ
who hears,' Foucart, in ERE v, 36.

the 'Learned Men of the Magic Library,' or was found in
a sealed box containing a book with direct instructions to
be copied and followed.

The scarabeus was the sacred emblem of the deity, although he was occasionally represented by the frog. He
was commonly depicted as a bearded man with close-
fitting garments and a cap without ornament, seated and
holding in his hands the emblems of life and stability; but
occasionally he wore the ostrich feathers of Osiris and
held his staff. The Greeks equated him with their Hephaistos.

SEKHMET

SEKHMET was the second member of the Memphite triad,
the consort and female counterpart of Ptaḥ; and her
name, assumed to have been derived from *sekhem*
('strong'), corresponded to her personality, which was
strong, mighty, and violent. She represented fire and the
intense, destroying heat of the sun, and was at times an
avenging deity, the 'Lady of pestilence.'[252] Rē employed
her to destroy the wicked, but she became so fond of the
blood of man and carried her destruction so far that he
was alarmed for the human race, and seeking to restrain
her, caused to be made a mixture of blood and mandrake
which the goddess drank with such avidity that, becoming
intoxicated, she forgot to slay.[253]

Sekhmet was a therapeutic divinity and was associated
with Ptaḥ at his healing shrines, her priests being celebrated in the curative art and reputed to have unusual
skill as bone-setters.[254] She overplayed the part of protecting the good and annihilating the wicked, and bore
many titles, as 'greatly beloved of Ptaḥ' or 'lady of

[252] Budge, *op. cit.*, i, 515; Gardiner, in *ERE* viii, 264.
[253] Müller, *op. cit.*, pp. 73-75; Maspero, *op. cit.*, i, 234 ff.
[254] Maspero, *op. cit.*, i, 308.

heaven, mistress of two lands,' although her most common epithet was the 'Lady of Flame.' She was assimilated with Mut and Neith, and both she and her sister Ubastet were identified with forms of Ḥat-ḥôr, while in dynastic times she was blended with Rē and Ubastet, being called Sekhmet-Ubastet-Rē. She was ordinarily confused with Ubastet and Uzoit. Her close relations in religion with Amon and Mut at Thebes have been shown in modern excavations at Karnak by the finding of more than one hundred and eighty statues of her in heroic size bordering the avenue leading to the temple of Amon.[255] The goddess was represented with the head of a lioness, usually surmounted by a solar disk with the uræus.[256]

SERAPIS, OR OSOR-ḤAP

SERAPIS was introduced into the Egyptian pantheon by Ptolemy I with the intention of establishing a god in whose worship the Greeks could join at a common shrine and who would be distinctive of his reign.[257] Finally, in a dream, he saw the great statue of a deity which he was told to bring to Alexandria[258] (Plutarch, op. cit., xxviii, xxix), and, after a search, the image, found at Sinope in Pontus, was obtained with some difficulty and taken to the capital, where it was set up with great pomp and ceremony, the temple of Osiris-Apis being rebuilt, and the large, celebrated Serapeum of Alexandria becoming the center of the divinity's cultic worship. The Egyptians were told that the god was a fusion of Osiris and of Apis of Memphis, and they discerned in him

---

[255] Many of these statues have been removed to museums of the Western world.

[256] Budge, op. cit., i, 514-520.

[257] Ib., ii, 195.

[258] Bouché-Leclercq, Histoire de la divination dans l'antiquité, i, 78; also Budge, op. cit., ii, 199.

Osiris-Apis (their own *wesjr ḥapi, i.e.,* the dead Apis, the blended Osor-ḥap);[259] but the deity was received with coolness and never become popular, although, as a result of official pressure, his cult was widespread, especially throughout Lower Egypt. Serapis assumed the titles of Osiris, as the Nile-god, the god of the Underworld, and the judge of the dead, and absorbed all his functions, although the ceremonial rites were changed,[260] and Isis was associated with him in cultic worship. The Egyptian origin of the name is preferred by good authority, but many opinions have been expressed concerning the antecedents of the divinity; that he was the Ba'al, or Belzipur, of Babylon who was equated with Zeus; or, more probably that he was the great Babylonian healing deity, Ea of Eridu, under his common title Sar-apsi, 'King of the Watery Deep,' with his dream oracle;[261] while Bouché-Leclercq remarks that "under his [Serapis's] name were collected the debris of numerous divine personalities worn out by time."[262]

Serapis was a complex character, but he was a healing divinity *par excellence,* an iatromantic deity working with the dream oracle and other forms of divination with incubation, magic, and like mystic practices. The old Egyptian ritual was superseded, and the compulsory interpretation of dreams by priests, who thus controlled the oracle, gave rise to many abuses. A Louvre papyrus of late date contains a journal of a Greek attendant at the Serapeum at Memphis, of about A.D. 164, which suggests that the writer belonged to a guild of professional me-

[259] E. Thrämer, "Health and Gods of Healing (Greek and Roman)," in *ERE* vi, 542, 549.

[260] Wilkinson, *op. cit.,* iii, 95-98.

[261] F. F. K. Lehmann-Haupt, in Roscher, 1910, iv, 340; Müller, *op. cit.,* pp. 98, 389.

[262] Bouché-Leclercq, *op. cit.,* i, 78.

diums who incubated for suppliants and who were called
by the Greek name *katochoi*,[263] such priests being supposed to be inspired by a divinity and to act as the mouth-
piece of the oracle of the god.

The great Serapeum at Alexandria was always the chief
seat of the worship of Serapis and Isis in the Ptolemaic
age; and it was adorned by a statue of the deity, a colossal
work of art by the famous sculptor Bryaxis (Tacitus,
Historia, iv, 83), a contemporary of Skopas.[264] The two
other centers of his worship were at Memphis, where he
displaced Apis, and at Abydos, where he took over the
temple of Osiris. Another Serapeum which was renowned
and held in great veneration was situated at Canopus,
where suppliants incubated for themselves, or others did
for them; and marvellous cures were reported (Strabo,
XVII, i, 17=p. 800 C). The cult, acquiring renown, spread
to Greece, where it proved a powerful rival to that of
Asklepios, and it also found its way to Rome and its
provinces until it was forbidden, and the Serapeum at
Alexandria, with all its accumulations of Oriental literature, was destroyed shortly after the edict of Theodosius
which finally suppressed paganism.[265]

THOTH, THOUT, OR TAHUTI

THOTH, the Egyptian moon-god installed by Rē,[266] personified the intellect of the lunar deity, as well as his
creative and directing power; and he was the orderer of
the cosmos, speaking the words which resulted in the
creation. He was the divinity of wisdom through whom
all mental gifts were imparted to man, and was the possessor of every kind of knowledge and of everything that

[263] Hamilton, *op. cit.*, p. 105.
[264] Cumont, *The Oriental Religions in Roman Paganism*, p. 76.
[265] Budge, *op. cit.*, ii, 195-201; also Milne, in *ERE* vi, 376-378.
[266] Müller, *op. cit.*, pp. 84-85.

contributed to civilization and refinement, whence he was the inventor of letters, language, and numbers, and of the arts and sciences, including astronomy, architecture, medicine, and botany. He was the founder of the social order, the author of the institutions of temple worship, and the builder of shrines,[267] besides being the 'Lord of the Divine words' who devised the sacred ritual for proper approach to deity with prayers and sacrifices. He was, moreover, the 'Lord of Laws,' the master of law in its physical and moral conceptions, the 'knowing one' who "looketh through bodies, and testeth hearts"; and, accordingly, he became the divine arbiter to whom appeal was made for assistance in important matters under dispute. He was also 'great in magic,' the mightiest of all magicians; and the god Ḥike' of the Old Kingdom was possibly a form of Thoth,[268] while he was regarded as the personification of the intelligence of Ptaḥ. Thoth thus appears as above the ordinary Egyptian divinities, "a god whose mind is all-penetrating, and all-comprehending," 'the Mysterious,' 'the Unknown.'[269] "The character of Thoth is a lofty and beautiful conception, and is, perhaps, the highest idea of deity ever fashioned in the Egyptian mind.''[270]

Thoth was intimately associated with the myths of the Osirian cycle. In the Underworld he was a divinity of Ma'at ('Justice'), who, in the judgment scene, stood by the Great Balance and determined the weight of the human hearts against the ostrich feather; and he was the recording deity, the 'scribe of the gods,' who reported the results to Osiris and his assessors, who replied, saying: "That which cometh from thy mouth is true, and the de-

[267] Boylan, op. cit., pp. 88-89, 93, 101-103.
[268] Ib., p. 125.
[269] Ib., p. 102.
[270] Budge, op. cit., i, 415.

ceased is holy and righteous.''[271] He outwitted Rē by creating the intercalary days, thus enabling Nut to give birth to Osiris, Horus the Elder, Sêth, Isis, and Nephthys,[272] and the chapters of the *Book of the Dead* are declared to have been composed by him. He put together the scattered members of the murdered Osiris (*Pyramid Texts,* 639, 747, 830); he provided the magic words by which Isis revived Osiris that she might receive his seed and conceive Horus; and Rē chose him to go with mighty words of power which cured the dying Horus of the scorpion's sting.

Thoth was a protector against evil, and especially against illness, delivering man from the perils that threatened him, as well as from the evil demons that beset him. "My god Thoth is a shield round about me" (*Anastasi Papyrus,* I, viii, 3). The essentials of medicine consisted in the rites and formulas by which unseen malicious beings which caused disease were exorcised and expelled from the bodies of victims, and hence were magical, so that, as a magician, he was a powerful patron of physicians, who besought him to give skill to 'those who know things,' to 'physicians who are in his train' (*Hearst Medical Papyrus,* vi, 10). An enormous number of amulets in the form of figurines of the god have been found in all parts of Egypt, and are supposed to refer to his functions as magician and healer;[273] while according to the old texts, he played the part of the 'physician of the eye of Horus' (*Hearst Medical Papyrus,* xiv, 9), healing the 'eye of the sun''[274] when he restored the eye of Horus after his fight with Sêth; and he was especially efficacious against the attacks of scorpions. With his spittle he healed the wound

[271] Budge, *op. cit.,* i, 408.
[272] Frazer, *op. cit.,* p. 341.
[273] Boylan, *op. cit.,* p. 131.
[274] Müller, *op. cit.,* p. 32.

of his own arm, received while endeavoring to compose the Horus-Sêth struggle (*Pyramid Texts*, 535, 2055), and in invocations he was reminded of his own physical troubles, possibly of this incident: "O Thoth, heal me as thou didst heal thyself" (*Book of the Dead*, 71, 6).

A period of exceptionally intense veneration for the divinity began with the Eighteenth Dynasty, and in the Græco-Roman epoch his popularity had a rapid growth, his shrines existed everywhere, and he appeared definitely at Philæ and in the Nubian temple at Dendûr as the Egyptian Asklepios, holding the serpent-encircled staff; while his epithet '*Iśtn* connects him with I-m-ḥotep at Philæ as "He who comes to him that calls him." In the late period the name of Thoth-*Śtm* became familiar, *Śtm* being regarded as an appellation of the oracle, as well as of the healing god Thoth;[275] and at the shrine at Medinet Habu (Djeme) he was sometimes confused with Teos (*Ḏḥr*), a divinity of healing who, it is conjectured, was a deified priest of Memphis.[276] In the text of the dedication of this sanctuary it is said that Thoth (and possibly Teos) was accustomed to descend on the temple each evening in the form of an ibis, going forth every morning; and it is, therefore, assumed that the fane was regarded as the focus for oracles received through incubation.[277]

Thoth had a primitive shrine at Hierakonpolis, where standards show the sacred ibis, but the first trace of a cultic center was at his sanctuary in Hermopolis, which became probably the greatest healing temple of ancient Egypt. A medical school and library were connected with it, and Clemens Alexandrinus (*Stromata*, vi, 4) describes forty-two hermetic books, 'books of Thoth,' which were discovered there, six of which, numbered from thirty-

---

[275] Boylan, *op. cit.*, pp. 89, 91, 131-132, 159, 166-168.
[276] Sethe, in *ERE* vi, 651.
[277] Boylan, *op. cit.*, p. 168; also Mallet, *Kasr-el-Agouz*, pp. 99-101.

seven to forty-two, were medical.[278] Presumably, as an assistant, Safekht (or Sekhauit) was attached to the library, being the 'lady of letters, mistress of the house of books.'[279] At the temple of Philæ, Thoth was especially venerated and received the titles of 'Lord of Philæ,' 'Lord of Eshmunein,' 'Thoth of the Abaton,' and 'Thoth of Pnubs.'[280] His cult was fostered in Nubia, his chief sanctuary there being at Dakkeh, and another was at Dendûr; but in both he appeared in the form of Shu. The use of the dream-oracle by incubation in the temple at Hermopolis is confirmed by numerous texts, and there are many suggestions that it was in use at his other shrines.[281]

At his own city of Hermopolis, Thoth was the chief of a company (paut) consisting of an ogdoad of four pairs of male and female deities, his own feminine counterpart and consort being the goddess Ma'at. In the most ancient texts, an ibis on a perch is the symbol of the god, and he was usually represented with a human body and an ibis-head, occasionally surmounted by a feather crown, though he is also depicted as an ape or dog-headed baboon.[282] The Greeks equated him with Hermes, as Psychopompos.[283]

UBASTET, OR BASTET

UBASTET, the 'Lady of the West' of the Delta and one of the most prominent of the ancient deities of the pantheon,[284] was primarily, like her sister Sekhmet, a god-

[278] Wilkinson, op. cit., iii, 171.

[279] Müller, op. cit., pp. 52-53, 200; also Petrie, in ERE v, 249; Budge, op. cit., i, 424.

[280] The name p-nbs or pr-nbs is construed 'House of the Sycamore' (Boylan, op. cit., p. 169).

[281] Foucart, in ERE v, 35.

[282] Hopfner, Der Tierkult der alten Ägypter, pp. 26-32.

[283] Boylan, op. cit., pp. 136 ff.; also Budge, op. cit., i, 400-415.

[284] Müller, op. cit., p. 150.

dess of fire, but expressed the idea of the milder heat of the sun, the warmth which germinates the seed and encourages vegetation.[285] She was sometimes represented as a huntress and was also a healing divinity to whom the origin of the medical art was ascribed, a goddess of the birth-chamber, and a protectress of children. The center of her worship was at Bubastet (Per-Baste), and her temple and festivals were among the most interesting in Egypt (Herodotos, ii, 59, 60, 137, 138; Diodoros, xvi, 51; Pliny, op. cit., v, 9; Strabo, XVII, i, 27, 28 = pp. 805, 806 C). Identified with most of the well-known feminine deities of the Nile valley and worshipped under their names, she was known at Thebes as Mut-Ubastet and was depicted as Isis, while at Memphis she had a temple where she was identified with her sister Sekhmet and where they both represented the devouring, destructive heat of the sun (Herodotos, ii, 156). Her association with Khonsu at Thebes has led to the surmise that she was a moon-goddess. The cat was sacred to her, and being depicted with the head of that animal, she was called 'the cat-headed goddess'; but in the later period she was regarded as a variant of Sekhmet, and then had the head of a lioness, surmounted by the uræus. The Greeks equated her with Artemis (Herodotos, loc. cit.).

UZOIT, UAZIT, OR BUTO (UTO)

Uzoit was one of the old divinities of the pantheon, the 'goddess of the North,' who with her sister Nekhbet at their respective ancient capitals of Lower and Upper Egypt, Buto in the Delta and El-Kâb in the South, ruled over these prehistoric kingdoms;[286] and they were called

---

[285] Budge, op. cit., i, 444-450.
[286] Breasted, op. cit., p. 130.

serpent goddesses, since they often symbolized the two
Egypts in this form.[287]

Like her sister Nekhbet, Uzoit was a deity of child-
birth and was also a celebrated magician, frequently
identified with Isis. She assisted Nephthys in hiding Isis
and in caring for her in the papyrus swamps, and with
Nekhbet and other goddesses she superintended the birth
of Horus, subsequently acting as one of his nursing
mothers.[288] Her own city, the chief seat of her worship,
was at Buto, and here, in her great temple, Pe-Dep, she
conducted a renowned healing oracle (Herodotos, ii, 83-
84). During Ptolemaic times, the *pr-mst*, 'birth-house,'
also called the *ht-'bw*, 'house of purification,' in which
women are supposed to have remained fourteen days
after delivery, was attached to the temples of goddesses.
Uzoit was called 'mistress of all the gods,' or 'Uzoit, Lady
of heaven,' and was assimilated with Hat-ḥôr, Nekhbet,
and Isis. Her symbol was the uræus, and she wore the
asp on her headdress, being called the 'Uræus Goddess.'
The Greeks identified her with Leto.[289]

Minor deities of Child-birth and Nursing.

IN addition to the two principal divinities of child-birth,
Nekhbet and Uzoit, there were several minor goddesses,
connected with the lying-in chamber, who gave easy births
and cared for the child, but whose personalities were not
clearly developed and defined. Among the more notable
of these were Ḥeqet, the later consort of Khnûmu, a birth-
deity and 'goddess of the cradle';[290] Meskhenet ('birth-
place'), who though associated with the dead, is more
frequently mentioned in connection with the birth-

[287] Müller, *op. cit.*, pp. 132, 361.
[288] Budge, *op. cit.*, i, 441.
[289] *Ib.*, i, 438; ii, 285, 441-444.
[290] Müller, *op. cit.*, p. 52.

chamber and with the care of children, and who was sometimes regarded as a feminine deity of fate;[291] and Renenutet, a divinity of nursing,[292] who was identical with the asp-headed Rannu, and who was called a divine nurse of princes.[293] Meskhenet, the name of the brick or couple of bricks on which women crouched in giving birth, was a symbolic goddess, personified under a sign on the head interpreted as a bicornate uterus (?). In the texts she is coupled with Khnûmu or with Renenutet.[294]

[291] Müller, op. cit., pp. 52, 95, 137; also Budge, op. cit., ii, 144, 359; Maspero, Popular Stories, p. 36; id., Études égyptiennes, i, 27.

[292] Müller, op. cit., pp. 66, 116.

[293] Wilkinson, op. cit., iii, 213-214. Note.—Others are mentioned in ancient Egyptian literature but they do not appear sufficiently definite to be included here. See A. M. Blackman, "Some Remarks on an Emblem upon the head of an Ancient Egyptian Birth-Goddess," in JEA, 1916, iii, 199-206.

[294] Spiegelberg, Aegyptologische Randglossen zum Alten Testament, pp. 19-25.

CHAPTER TWO

BABYLONIAN AND ASSYRIAN GODS

THE HEALING GODS OF BABYLONIA
AND ASSYRIA

PART I: GENERAL SURVEY

THE people of Babylonia and Assyria believed that disease was supernatural in origin and that it was due to the activities of unseen enemies, particularly to the presence of some spirit, such as a ghost or a demon, in the body of the sufferer. Often it was superinduced by a deity or by a human sorcerer, and cure was dependent upon the dislodgment and expulsion of the evil being by some higher, divine power. The treatment of disease was, therefore, a matter which pertained to religion and which was under the direction of the priests.

General views of the people.

The ancient civilizations of Mesopotamia, which flourished in pomp, magnificence, and power in the valleys of the Tigris and of the Euphrates, and which included the surrounding countries, extending their control to the Mediterranean and into Egypt, referred every phenomenon of nature to supernatural causes, believing that all nature was controlled by superhuman or divine beings, or spirits, who might be either good or evil in intent. Man sought to obtain the blessings which nature provided and to escape the misfortunes of life which malicious beings of the spirit-world brought upon him; and to this end he invoked the gods, who were his natural friends and protectors, and who were generally more powerful than the beings of evil. Supplications were made to them to thwart the evil designs of the enemy spirits, and, expelling those who already possessed the sick and suffering, to grant the blessings of health and of prosperity. These appeals were supported by religious ceremonies which included prayers, incantations for exorcism, sacrifice, symbolic magic, occult practices, and mysterious pseudo-sciences, in all of which the priests were adepts. Such beliefs and usages were an integral part of the accepted religion; and instructions derived from magic practices and from occult learning, transmitted through the priests, were the voices of their honored deities by which their daily lives were guided, both in personal and in national affairs.

Ancient records.

The Old Testament and the ancient historians, including the Babylonian Berossos, fragments of whose works have been preserved to us, furnish scant information concerning these great nations, and the interest which they have always aroused has been only partially satisfied by further details of their history and civilization disclosed by ancient records found in modern excavations. These tablets of clay, engraved in cuneiform characters, many of them from the great library of Assurbanipal at Nineveh, generally date from about the seventh century B.C., although it has been determined that many are copies of much older documents. While the cuneiform sources do not begin until about 3000 B.C., there are evidences that the people of Sumer occupied the southern Euphrates valley as early as 5000 B.C., and even 8000 B.C. is mentioned.[1] The most ancient records of the valley yet discovered (legends, ritual texts, hymns, contracts, and word-lists) are in the Sumerian tongue, which was for many centuries the classic, scientific language of the

---

[1] H. Zimmern, "Babylonians and Assyrians," in *ERE* ii, 309.

invaders from the north; and they suggest that the Sumerians had attained a higher type of civilization than that which was possessed by their Semitic conquerors.[2] The Semites of Akkad, who are supposed to have made their appearance in the land not later than about 4000 B.C., grew in strength until about 2300 B.C., when the Sumerian states were transformed into a collection of Sumero-Akkadian states; and Semitic speech, serving with Sumerian as the official language during the third millennium, became predominant both for popular and for official use after about 2000 B.C., when the Semites gained full control of the valley.[3] Many of these records are broken and imperfect, very many others are as yet undeciphered; but, although our information is still fragmentary, sufficient is known to construct a fairly accurate picture of many of their customs, as well as of their religious beliefs and practices.

The respective civilizations.

The closely related civilizations of Babylonia and Assyria were very much the same, but Babylonia cultivated literature and the arts, and gave thought to religion to a larger extent, while Assyria, dominated rather by the spirit of conquest, manifested greater materialism with a stronger undercurrent of animism in her religious cults. Whatever individuality was shown in Assyrian beliefs and customs, they were ever influenced and tinctured by the higher and more vigorous culture of the Babylonians, from whom they borrowed much.

The religion.

The religion of the Babylonians and Assyrians never

[2] T. G. Pinches, "Sumero-Akkadians," in *ERE* xii, 43; cf. also Winckler, *Die Völker Vorderasiens*, p. 5.

[3] Jastrow, *The Civilization of Babylonia and Assyria*, pp. 120 ff., 148.

rose far above a relatively primitive stage of development, its dominating feature being polydæmonism, in which were a multitude of divinities.[4] This seems to have superseded earlier animistic beliefs which were still a powerful underlying element in the imagination of the people; and its survivals appeared in all the popular forms of religious observances, so that a subjective religion apparently existed side by side with, yet apart from, the official creed, which was diligently followed by those whose thought never attained the higher levels of speculation.[5]

The pantheon.

The many deities of Babylonia and Assyria were, for the most part, ancient gods of local origin, identified with the several states and cities, though others had been brought in from neighboring states after invasion and domination, and had been accepted as members of the pantheon. The old Sumerian and Semitic divinities with their consorts had been acknowledged and assimilated, but the Sumerian names greatly exceeded those of Semitic origin, and everything goes to show that the Sumerian elements in the population had the same preponderating influence in religious matters that they enjoyed in literature and in art.[6] There were cosmic and national deities; each city had its chief divinity; around each great god were grouped lesser deities, demigods, and those of a still lower order; and these were subdivided, some being good and some being evil spirits, hostile to man and possessed of power to do him injury. The good spirits were guardians of mankind, and one was supposed to be assigned to each person for guidance and for protection; while the

[4] L. B. Paton, "Baal, Beel, Bel," in *ERE* ii, 295.
[5] Jastrow, *The Religion of Babylonia and Assyria,* pp. 116 ff., 180 ff.
[6] Pinches, in *ERE* xii, 42.

gods were patrons and defenders of their respective cities and peoples. A few of the older deities were credited with cosmic functions, and their deeds in bringing order out of chaos, and in developing the heavens, the atmosphere, and the earth are related in the religious traditions and myths. The more important divinities were grouped in triads, the first of which consisted of Anu, the great god of the heavens, supreme over all, whose chief seat was Uruk; Enlil, the deity of the atmosphere and of the earth, whose abode was at Nippur; and Ea, the divinity of the waters, whose city was Eridu. A second triad was composed of Shamash, the sun-god; Sin, the moon-god; and Ishtar, the goddess of love and fertility; and there were many other divinities having various functions, such as Nusku and Gibil, or Giru, deities of fire, and Ninib, a divinity of war.[7]

The rank of deities.

The fortunes of all deities varied with the changing circumstances of their devotees, with the favor and power of rulers, and particularly with the activity and influence of the several priesthoods in the development of their favorite divinities. Local gods gained popularity and prestige, and were accepted and worshipped in other cities as their authority extended with the increasing power of their peoples.[8] Some were thus raised to a high rank and prestige, and some received national recognition and power, while others were displaced, their attributes and rites were absorbed, and they receded to subordinate rank, though frequently retaining the love and respect of their local worshippers and still enjoying a limited influence. Marduk, the national god of Babylonia, is the most striking example of rise in fortunes; from an

---

[7] Jastrow, op. cit., pp. 188 ff.; Zimmern, in ERE ii, 309-313.

[8] Jastrow, op. cit., pp. 107-108.

insignificant local divinity of the city of Babylon he became more and more prominent as the city increased in power until finally he attained supremacy over all other divine beings of Babylonia and secured recognition of his might in several neighboring states. He absorbed the attributes, functions, and honors of other deities, reduced them to a secondary place, and finally contested, though unsuccessfully, the independence of Assur, the national god of Assyria. Even the traditional myths were altered to glorify him, and he received credit for the cosmic deeds of other divinities.[9]

Temples.

The deities were worshipped with much formality and pomp. Elaborate rituals and complicated symbolic ceremonies were handed down by tradition for these functions, and great festivals, lasting for days, were held in honor of certain divinities at stated times of the year.[10] Numerous temples were erected for the patron deities of cities, and some of these acquired high renown, as E-Apsu, the temple of Ea of Eridu, and E-Sagila, the great sanctuary of Marduk at Babylon; while gods of lesser rank were honored with fanes of their own or were received in the great temples, where they were assigned private shrines according to their importance.[11]

The priesthood.

Priests, and occasionally priestesses, were attached to the sanctuaries, and were trained in the special duties pertaining to their class. One group supervised sacrifices and offerings; another attended to hymns, prayers, and lamentations; another, which included physicians, con-

[9] Jastrow, *op. cit.*, pp. 106 ff., 116 ff.
[10] *Ib.*, pp. 462 ff., 675 ff.
[11] *Ib.*, pp. 612 ff.

ducted the rites of incantation which dispelled evil spirits, exorcised demons of disease, purified the unclean, and thwarted wizards and practitioners of black magic; while still another group directed oracles, divination, interpretation of dreams, and omens from the movements of the heavenly bodies, arts in which the priests, particularly the Chaldæans, were adept. The priesthood had great prestige and influence, both in religious and in political affairs, and guided the destinies of their patron deities, besides holding practical control of all learning, culture, and the arts, and conducting schools in the temples where scribes, physicians, and priests were educated.[12]

Religious literature.

An examination of the religious compositions of Babylonia and Assyria discloses the fact that their religion was based upon fear of demons and upon belief in the power of the gods over them, rather than upon ethical considerations, which came only as a much later development. As used in the great majority of the texts, the terms sin, sickness, and possession by evil spirits were synonymous, and indicated merely the physical condition of an evil state of the body, from which relief was sought. Misery, sorrow, and contrition were frequently expressed, often with great feeling; but in the penitence there was seldom even a suggestion of moral wrong. The appeals to the deities, and the religious practices by which it was hoped to obtain release from misfortune, after overcoming or exorcising the demons, must be termed, for the most part, according to modern views, magic in character, being formulated on the theory that

[12] Jastrow, op. cit., pp. 655 ff.; also id., Aspects of Religious Belief and Practice in Babylonia and Assyria, pp. 273 ff.; T. G. Pinches, "Priest, Priesthood (Babylonian)," in ERE x, 285-288.

the priests were thus enabled to exercise control over unseen, supernatural powers, whether of good or of evil. Magic and magic practices, accordingly, permeated all the religious thought of Mesopotamia and dominated its ceremonies.[13]

The after-life.

The hereafter engaged the attention of the people, but their ideas of immortality remained vague. Death was an unmitigated evil—the end; and its occurrence was a time of sorrow without mercy, for though the future did not involve extinction of conscious vitality, yet it was gloomy, since Assyro-Babylonian belief pictured the departed as huddled together deep in the bowels of the earth in a place called Aralû, over which presided the goddess Allatu and her consort, Nergal, whose subjects were doomed to perpetual inactivity in a realm of neglect and decay. There was an absence of all ethical considerations in the allotment of the abode of the dead, and no theories of rewards and punishments were associated with their fate. In a fashion they were associated with the gods, and some of them were regarded as heroes; but all interest centered in the present life, and the deities were not concerned for those who had departed from this earth, but who, nevertheless, had an undefined influence over the affairs of mankind and at times exercised a malign power upon them. They were the source of occasional oracles which were believed to have divine sanction,[14] and which are well illustrated by the Old Testament example of Saul calling upon the dead Samuel, through the medium of a sorceress, to declare what the outcome of a battle was to be.[15]

[13] Zimmern, in *ERE* ii, 316-317; also L. W. King, "Magic (Babylonian)," in *ERE* viii, 253-255.

[14] Jastrow, *Religion,* pp. 559-560.

[15] I Samuel, xviii, 8-19.

Belief in demonology.

Belief in the activities of evil spirits and demons was personal and vital with the people of Mesopotamia, embittering and oppressing their daily lives with fear. All evils, misfortunes, and mishaps that befell mankind were due to them, except such as were inflicted by offended divinities; and even then, the demons were used by the gods as instruments of punishment. Malicious spirits and demons inimical to man existed on every side, ever ready to assail him and to do him all possible injury, often making their attacks in groups of seven or of twice seven, and many having special functions or bringing certain diseases and misfortunes. In the later period, the deities were credited with greater control over the spirits of evil, so that it then came to be believed that the demons were able to effect their malevolent designs upon man only as they were given license by the gods.[16]

The demons.

The invisible evil spirits, devils, and demons were divided into three general classes: (a) disembodied spirits of the dead, ghosts or *edimmu;* (b) unhuman, supernatural beings differing from the gods by being of a lower order, and named in groups as the *utukku,* the *rabisu,* and the *gallû,* or the triad *labartu, labasu,* and *ahhazu,* and others; and (c) half-human, half-supernatural beings, born of human and ghostly parentage, awful monsters, and also named in groups, as *lilû, lilîtu,* and *ardat lilî.* There were, besides, many others, especially the *labbu,* a fabulous, lion-like, raging monster, allied to the mythical sea-serpent and a bitter enemy of man.[17]

[16] Jastrow, *op. cit.,* pp. 260 ff.

[17] R. Campbell Thompson, "Demons and Spirits (Assyro-Babylonian)," in *ERE* iv, 568-571; also Zimmern, in *ERE* ii, 315.

Attitude of the deities.

The gods were regarded as the champions, protectors, and defenders of man, and since, except by virtue of their intervention, he had no adequate defense against the attacks of his enemies, the deities were invoked for help through the medium of the priests as representing divinity. The religious ritual forms and ceremonies by which the gods were approached for release from all malign influences were systematized by the priesthood, who alone knew the methods which propitiated and appeased the divinities, gained their favor, averted misfortune, exorcised demons of disease, and secured protection and guidance for the future. Soothsayers and exorcists were, therefore, held in high esteem by the people.

Rituals.

All rituals and ceremonies were essentially twofold; (1) appeals to the deities for assistance, particularly for the exorcising of demons; and (2) divination to learn the disposition and the will of the gods. Entreaties to the divinities took the shape of hymns of praise and of prayers introductory to incantations, or *shiptu,* all of which partook of the nature of a curative remedy for present misfortunes, sickness, and suffering.[18] The forms of these hymns, prayers, and incantations were built up by the priests from age to age until they became rigid, traditional formulas of approved ritual invocation, arranged for all occasions and to be followed without variation. In the library of Assurbanipal have been found elaborate series of incantation-texts which were to be uttered in connection with certain sympathetic and symbolic magic rites, the sole object of all these prescribed magic texts and of the ceremonies accompanying their

[18] Jastrow, *Aspects,* pp. 299 ff.

recitation being to combat the demons, to exorcise and drive them away, or to transfer them to substitute victims. If recognized, the particular malevolent being concerned was addressed by name; but if he was unknown, a long list of ghosts and evil spirits, any one of whom might be the active agent, was enumerated with a command to depart.[19]

Purification.

Purification was regarded as of essential importance, and water and fire, both having a sacred significance, were the chief elements used for the purpose in connection with sympathetic and symbolic magic rites, particularly in the cults of the healing divinities for purifying the sick. The god Ea of Eridu supervised the ritual use of water, usually by sprinkling or pouring; and appeal was made to the deities Gibil (or Giru) or Nusku in the fire-rituals. Sickness was an uncleanness, and purification of the person and of the house in which he had lain was necessary, especially after recovery; while in the case of kings the use of torches and of censers is mentioned.[20] In the performance of these rites the exorcist was known as the *ašipu*-priest, and the purifier was termed the *mashmashu*.

Divination.

Every effort was put forth to penetrate the veil of the future for divine help and guidance.[21] Special priests (the *bârû*, or diviner) were assigned to the study and the interpretation of signs and omens; and the omen-texts show that Shamash, the sun-god, and Adad, the storm-god, were addressed as the gods of divination. The liver

---

[19] Jastrow, *Religion,* pp. 252 ff.; also Zimmern, in *ERE* ii, 317-318.

[20] Jastrow, *Aspects,* pp. 312 ff., 318.

[21] L. W. King, "Divination (Assyro-Babylonian)," in *ERE* iv, 783-786.

was regarded as the chief organ of life, as the seat of life in fact, and its conformation and markings were assumed to be true indications of the disposition of the divinities toward the affairs of man, so that examination of the livers of sacrificial animals (hepatoscopy), particularly of the sheep, was resorted to for guidance in matters of public welfare, and especially for official decisions.[22] The signs of the heavens (astrology),[23] the movements of the sun, moon, and planets, and of the many signs of nature, the condition of the atmosphere, the abnormalities of infants at birth,[24] omens from animals[25] and from oil and water,[26] and dreams[27] all gave more or less important indications of the divine will for the future, chiefly for the use of rulers in national affairs. The application of astrology for personal interests had scant development in Mesopotamia, since the reading of the heavens for the individual horoscope came only later, being engrafted upon astrology with Greek astronomy and applied in Greece and Rome.[28]

Dreams and oracles.

Oneiromancy, the art of divination by dreams, was recognized as a means of involuntary divination and had an important place in the beliefs and practices of the people of Mesopotamia.[29] The gods, it was held, revealed themselves and their will to favored ones in dreams, which were a regular medium of communication between

[22] Jastrow, op. cit., pp. 148 ff.; and id., Die Religion Babyloniens und Assyriens, ii, 23-215.

[23] Id., Religion, pp. 356 ff.; and Die Religion, ii, 415-748.

[24] Jastrow, op. cit., ii, 836-946.

[25] Ib., ii, 775-836.

[26] Ib., ii, 749-775.

[27] Ib., ii, 946 ff.

[28] Id., Aspects, pp. 243-244.

[29] Id., Religion, pp. 402 ff., and Aspects, pp. 204 ff.

deities and men, and which were supposed to be sent by some divinity, usually when the soul was untrammelled by the burden of material sense. Thus the deity Ningirsu appeared to Gudea of Lagash in a vision and declared the divine pleasure that a great temple should be erected in his honor according to specified plans, all this being interpreted to him by his goddess mother, Nina.[30] Supplications were made to the divinities for helpful dreams, of which the following is an example:

O god of the new-moon, unrivalled in might, whose counsel no one can grasp,
I have poured for thee a pure libation of the night, I have offered thee a pure drink,
I bow down to thee, I stand before thee, I seek thee!
Direct thoughts of favor and justice towards me!
That my god and my goddess who since many days have been angry towards me,
May be reconciled in right and justice, that my path may be fortunate, my road straight!
And that he may send Zakar,[31] the god of dreams, in the middle of the night to release [forgive] my sins.[32]

Affairs of state were frequently directed by dreams. Ishtar, as the goddess of war, appeared to Assurbanipal in a vision and directed the march of his army to victory; and again, when he was disheartened, she promised in a dream to give him her aid and to enable him to overcome his enemies in battle.[33]

Dream deities.

The importance of dreams developed divinities who

[30] H. F. Lutz, "An Omen Text Referring to the Action of a Dreamer," in *AJSL*, 1919, xxxv, 145; also A. H. Sayce, "Dreams and Sleep (Babylonian)," in *ERE* v, 33.

[31] Zakar is here the 'envoy' of the moon-god.

[32] Jastrow, *op. cit.*, p. 335.

[33] Lutz, *loc. cit.*

presided over them, such as Makhir (Mamú), a goddess who had a small shrine at Balawat; and there were also Mamu-da-ge, Zakar, and Zakar-màš-gê. These were not independent deities, however, since Shamash, as *bêl-biri*, the 'lord of visions,' outshone them all, and they became subject to him as his court attendants. These divine beings were addressed in penitential prayers, of which the following is a specimen:

Reveal thyself unto me and let me see a favorable dream,
May the dream that I dream be favorable,
May the dream that I dream be true,
May Mamú, the goddess of dreams, stand at my head;
Let me enter E-Sagila, the temple of the gods, the house of
    life.[34]

Temple-sleep or incubation.

It was believed that answer to prayer and divine guidance could best be obtained in sacred places, and that inspired dreams were induced by the presence of deity. Suppliants therefore visited the temples, where, after offering prayer and sacrifice, they slept in the hope of having a vision from the god which would carry supernatural directions for relief of present misfortunes and suffering, and for avoidance of future ills. Such dreams were more apt to come toward morning; and all visions were interpreted by the *sha'ilu*,[35] or *bârû*-priest, the answer of such a priest or priestess being the *têrtu*, the divine decision, or oracle of the god. Temple-sleep (incubation) for inspired dreams was resorted to for all emergencies, especially for the cure of disease, and was systematized as a recognized religious procedure by the priests, who became professional dreamers for suppliants as well as interpreters of their visions, while relatives

[34] Lutz, *op. cit.*, p. 146.
[35] Jastrow, *Civilization*, pp. 272, 273, 274.

and friends of those unable to attend the temple often incubated for them. It is related (Arrianos, *de Expeditione Alexandri*, VII, xxvi) that, during the fatal illness of Alexander the Great at Babylon, his generals slept for him in E-Sagila, the temple of Marduk, in the hope of receiving a revelation by which he might be cured.[36] The use of the dream-oracle was a common practice throughout the Orient, in Western Asia, in Egypt, and in Greece. The origin of the custom has been the subject of several studies of the ancient currents of religious and civilizing influences between Oriental nations, but positive proofs are thus far lacking, and the matter is still undetermined,[37] though it would appear that temple-sleep for inspired dreams had an earlier and possibly a more authoritative development in the religions of the Euphrates and Tigris valleys, particularly in the cult of Ea of Eridu, than elsewhere.[38]

Causes of disease.

Disease was ascribed to the open attack of a demon, to the possession by some evil spirit, to the breach of a tabu, to the evil eye, to the machinations of a sorcerer, or to the attack of an enemy through the aid of a wizard or witch, a practitioner of black magic; or it might be due to such influences initiated and directed by some offended deity.[39] If the person was smitten in the neck, it was the hand of Adad; if in the neck and breast, it was the hand of

[36] Gauthier, *Recherches historiques sur l'exercice de la médecine dans les temples, chez les peuples de l'antiquité*, pp. 107-108; E. Thrämer, "Health and Gods of Healing (Greek and Roman)," in *ERE* vi, 541-542.

[37] For further details concerning the history of incubation the reader is referred to the works of Hamilton, Bouché-Leclercq, and Deubner listed in the General Bibliography.

[38] Thrämer, in *ERE* vi, 542.

[39] Jastrow, *Religion*, pp. 260 ff.; and *Aspects*, pp. 319 ff.

Ishtar; and if in the temples, a ghost had seized him. Evil spirits of all kinds—fiends, devils, and demons—had special powers and caused particular diseases. The *utukku* were extremely vicious, and with several attendant fever-demons they assailed the throat; *alu* attacked the chest; *gallû*, the hand; *rabiṣu*, the skin; *labartu*, a horrible monster, caused nightmare and ills of women; *labaṣu* brought epilepsy, and *lilû* and *lilîtu* were the source of infirmities of the night (probably excessive *pollutiones nocturnæ*); *ashakku* caused wasting sicknesses, fever, and consumption; *t'iu* brought headaches with fever; and other fiends were equally capable of causing dread maladies. Namtar, the messenger of Allatu, the queen of the Underworld, who sent sixty diseases, and Ura, a form of Nergal of the Underworld, were deities of pestilence, as was Nergal himself;[40] while witches were supposed to make men impotent and to rob women of the fruit of the womb. It was believed that the demons of disease gained entrance through some natural, but unguarded, opening of the body, as the mouth, nose, ears, or eyes; and sickness thus became a struggle between the patient and the demons, in which the aid of the gods was sought, the cure being effected when the spirit causing the malady had left the body.

Physicians and physician-priests.

Herodotos (i, 197; cf. Strabo, XVI, i, 20 = p. 745 C) declared that in Babylon the sick were brought into the public squares that they might seek counsel concerning their disease from those who had been similarly afflicted; and he attributed this custom to the lack of physicians

[40] R. C. Thompson, "Disease and Medicine (Assyro-Babylonian)," in *ERE* iv, 741-746; also Jastrow, *Civilization*, p. 456; and "The Medicine of the Babylonians and the Assyrians," in *PRSM*, 1913-1914, vii, 114.

in the city. Information derived from texts leads to the conclusion that this statement was incorrect, for the sufferers were probably desirous of alms rather than of counsel; and his error seems to have arisen from overlooking the relation between religion, the priests, and disease. For the most part, certain priests acted as physicians, and the old Sumerian name for a medical man, *A-Su*, or *asu*, "one who knows water," passed into the Semitic languages.[41] Physicians and surgeons are frequently mentioned in the medical texts, which give the rigid laws governing their practice, more particularly that of the surgeon, and which prescribe their fees and penalties according to the Code of Hammurabi (*circa* 2200 B.C.).[42] They also refer to the use of bronze knives for injuries,[43] and lists of herbs and of other remedies are recorded, in addition to letters of advice from doctors to their patients, as one from Avad-Nanâ to the king's son.[44] Physicians appear to have been a well-organized body, but it is believed that those who were not also priests were held in comparatively small esteem by the general public, since magic with religious ceremonies, in connection with the administration of drugs, as performed by the *aśipu*-priest, were very generally preferred as being more efficacious.

Medical texts and aśipu-*priests.*

The medical tablets in the *Shurpû* and *Maklû* series, which come chiefly from Assyrian sources, give numerous illustrations of the practice of the time. Of approximately 30,000 fragments of clay documents from the library of

[41] M. Jastrow, "Babylonian-Assyrian Medicine," in *AMH*, 1917, i, 233.

[42] "The Laws of Hammurabi, King of Babylon," in *RP*, 1903, ii, 84-85.

[43] Jastrow, in *AMH*, 1917, i, 239, 252 ff.

[44] *Id.*, in *PRSM*, 1913-1914, vii, 149 ff.

Assurbanipal, not less than 800 are medical; but comparatively few have yet been deciphered, and many of the texts are copies of originals from the libraries of Chaldæa, or of tablets of ancient Sumer and Akkad.[45] From these documents much information is drawn concerning magico-religious practices and drugs used for the cure of the sick, demonstrating the prevalent belief that maladies, being supernatural in origin, could be successfully combated only by the aid of powers more than human, and showing that healing without magic and occultism was practically unknown. The demons of disease must be driven out, and water and fire were the sacred elements most prominently mentioned in the texts for exorcism. The *aśipu* was the priest whose function it was to dislodge these fiends.[46] He was learned in the traditions of maladies and their causes, and was an adept in the ritual of prayers, incantations, rites of purification, and all formulas for expelling malevolent beings, with magic, sorcery, and material remedies for ridding the sick of the demons which possessed them. The mysterious arts of the *aśipu*-priests were jealously guarded, and being preserved in families, they were transmitted from father to son.[47] There were schools where medicine was taught, one of which, celebrated for its instruction, was situated at Borsippa, across the river from Babylon. There were libraries containing rituals and incantations for all occasions, and these were augmented by borrowing texts and formulas which had proved efficacious. The great deities had sufficient power over all ills, mental and spiritual as well as physical; and the *aśipu*-priest acted as the intermediary in approaching the gods and in securing the

[45] Jastrow, *op. cit.*, pp. 110-111.

[46] Weber, *Dämonen-Beschwörung bei den Babyloniern und Assyriern*, pp. 4-5.

[47] Thompson, in *ERE* iv, 743.

divine aid. It was customary for him to inquire whether or not the sick person had been guilty of some misdeed that was the cause of the malady, not for the purpose of penitence or reparation, but rather to determine, if possible, the reason for his falling under the ban and to enable him to differentiate and to select the appropriate ceremonies and formulas for each case, since success depended not only upon the power of the proper formula, but upon its correct application. Error might be fatal; exactness in word and in intonation was essential—the ritual for the fever-demon would not be efficacious for the devil of headache, nor would Nergal respond to an exorcism addressed to Namtar. The 'word of power,' recognized by all magic, was of the greatest efficacy; and usually the name of some superior spirit or high deity was used as authority for the command that the malignant being withdraw from the victim.

Formulas for exorcism.

The medical texts give many formulas for exorcism "when a ghost seizes a man," the following being some of the more common: "In the name of the great god Ea, whose servant I am," "By the name of the great gods," or "By Heaven be ye exorcised! By Earth be ye exorcised!"[48] It was considered very necessary to be acquainted with the appellation of the evil spirit concerned and to require exorcism in person, as: "Depart, Namtar, black demon! I am the beloved of Bel, depart from me!" If the name was not known, the priest would recite a long list of malevolent beings of various kinds, ending with the command, "Whatever be thy name, depart!" The art of exorcism occupied an important position in the rituals,

[48] Thompson, in ERE iv, 742.

and Ea and Marduk were the chief deities of the healing cults. In an incantation text the exorciser asks Marduk to

> Expel the disease of the sick man,
> The plague, the wasting disease . . .[49]

The tamarisk (or some similar tree) was held aloft during the act of expulsion by the priest, the following being a form of such an incantation:

The man of Ea am I, the man of Damkina am I, the messenger of Marduk am I, my spell is the spell of Ea, my incantation is the incantation of Marduk. The ban of Ea is in my hand, the tamarisk, the powerful weapon of Anu, in my hand I hold; the date-spathe (?), mighty in decision, in my hand I hold.[48]

Another, rather similar, charm reads:

The man of Ea am I, the man of Damkina am I, the messenger of Marduk am I. The great god Ea hath sent me to revive the . . . sick man; he hath added his pure spell to mine, he hath added his pure voice to mine, he hath added his pure spittle to mine, he hath added his pure prayer to mine; the destroyer(s) of the limbs, which are in the body of the sick man, hath the power to destroy the limbs—by the magic word of Ea may these evil ones be put to flight.[50]

The following is an incantation for unknown spirits in which the exorcist calls upon several deities to support his demand:

When [I] enter the house, Shamash is before me, Sin is behind [me], Nergal is at [my] right hand, Ninib is at my left hand; when I draw near unto the sick man, when I lay my hand on the head of the sick man, may a kindly spirit, may a kindly guardian angel stand at my side! Whether thou art an evil spirit or an evil demon, or an evil ghost, or an evil devil, or an evil

---

[49] Jastrow, *Religion*, p. 308.
[50] Thompson, in *ERE* iv, 743.

god, or an evil fiend, or sickness, or death, or phantom of the night, or wraith of the night, or fever, or evil pestilence, be thou removed from before me, out of the house go forth! [For] I am the sorcerer-priest of Ea, it is I who [recite] the incantation for the sick man.[51]

Marduk was the son of Ea and, acting as a mediator between the sick man and the supreme healer, he sought the advice of his father, the following being an example of such a consultation:

Marduk hath seen him [the sick man], and hath entered the house of his father Ea, and hath said, "Father, headache from the under world hath gone forth." Twice he hath said unto him, "What this man hath done he knoweth not; whereby shall he be relieved?"

Ea, preserving the dignity of Marduk and giving him credit for equal knowledge with himself, suggested the cure, replying:

O my son, what dost thou not know, what more can I give thee? O Marduk, what dost thou not know, what can I add to thy knowledge? What I know, thou knowest also. Go, my son, Marduk. To the house of purification bring him [i.e., the sick person], break the ban! Release him from the curse![52]

Purification and exorcism.

If a god was to be appeased, emphasis was given to hymns of praise, penitential prayers, confessions, lamentations, purifications, and sacrifices. Purification was effected by the symbolic use of water, oil, or fire, and these were connected with the rituals of Ea and of the fire-gods, Nusku, Gibil, and Giru, the sick person being sprinkled or bathed with sacred water, usually that from

---

[51] Thompson, *Devils and Evil Spirits of Babylonia*, i, 15.
[52] *Id.*, in *ERE* iv, 742; also Jastrow, *Aspects*, p. 93.

the Euphrates or the Tigris, or being rubbed with oil.
The following are examples of such texts:

> Glittering water, pure water,
> Holy water, resplendent water,
> The water twice seven times may he bring,
> May he make pure, may he make resplendent.
> May the evil *rabisu* depart,
> May he betake himself outside,
> May the protecting *shedu*, the protecting *lamassu*,
> Settle upon his body.
> Spirit of heaven, be thou invoked!
> Spirit of earth, be thou invoked![53]

A simpler water-ritual runs thus:

All that is evil, . . . [which exists in the body] of N. [may it
be carried off], with the water of his body, the washings from his
hands, and may the river carry it away downstream.[54]

In another incantation, while rubbing the patient with
oil, the priest recites the following formula appealing to
Ea:

Pure oil, shining oil, brilliant oil.
Oil which makes the gods shine,
Oil which mollifies the muscles of man.
The oil of Ea's incantation, with the oil of Marduk's incantation
I pour over thee; with the healing oil,
Granted by Ea for easing [pain] I rub thee;
Oil of life I give thee;
Through the incantation of Ea, the lord of Eridu,
I will drive the sickness with which thou art afflicted out of
    thee.[55]

In the use of fire, an image of the demon, wizard, or
witch was made of wax or other inflammable material,

---

[53] Jastrow, *op. cit.*, pp. 289-290.
[54] Thompson, in *ERE* iv, 742.
[55] Jastrow, *Civilization*, p. 253.

and with hymns, sacrifices, and elaborate ceremonies, the gods of fire, usually Gibil and Nusku, were invoked to consume it. When it had disappeared, the sufferer was supposed to be purified and to be relieved of the demoniacal possession. The following is an example of such a hymn addressed to the fire-god and his reply:

Nusku, great offspring of Anu,
The likeness of his father, the first-born of Bel,
The product of the deep, sprung from Ea,
I raise the torch to illumine thee, yea, thee.
[sorcerers, sorceresses, charmers, witches who had bewitched the
    sick man],
Those who have made images of me, reproducing my features,
Who have taken away my breath, torn my hairs,
Who have rent my clothes, have hindered my feet from treading
    the dust,
May the fire-god, the strong one, break their charm.

Immediately following comes an incantation directed against the demons:

I raise the torch, their images I burn,
    Of the *utukku*, the *shedu*, the *rabisu*, the *ekimmu*,
    The *labartu*, the *labasi*, the *akhkhazu*,
    Of *lilu* and *lilitu* and *ardat lili*,
    And every evil that seizes hold of men.
Tremble, melt away, and disappear!
May your smoke rise to heaven,
May Shamash destroy your limbs,
May the son of Ea [*i.e.*, may the fire-god],
The great magician, restrain your strength (?).[56]

Substitute victims.

Under certain circumstances, it was customary to offer the demons a substitute victim for the sick person, generally a kid or a sucking pig, the sacrificial animal being killed, and the carcass being laid beside the invalid while

[56] Jastrow, *Religion*, pp. 286-287.

the exorcist transferred the evil spirit to it. In the following text, Ea, the supreme healer and 'lord of incantation,' shows the method of treatment, and placing the victim before Marduk, he says:

The kid is the substitute for mankind,
He giveth the kid for his life,
He giveth the head of the kid for the head of the man,
He giveth the neck of the kid for the neck of the man,
He giveth the breast of the kid for the breast of the man.[57]

Sacrifices.

In addition, the gods received offerings of various kinds, such as a bullock, a sheep, or a goat, or usually a kid or a lamb; or, for bloodless sacrifice, oil, dates, figs, incense, bread, grain, or honey.

Drugs.

While reciting such incantations in appeals to the deities, the priest usually performed manual magic by gestures and passes, and administered various remedies, alone or in combination, with suggestions of their mystic and magic value. The ritual texts enumerate many remedies used by the ašipu-priest in connection with incantations, these including herbs, roots, and other drugs, such as onions, dates, palm-blossoms and palm-seeds, milk, butter, cream, honey, wine, oil, meat, salt, flour, and the juices and seeds of various trees and plants.[58] Many substances that were foul and ill-smelling, as dung, urine of animals, and decaying matter, were administered, apparently with the intention of disgusting the demon, and of making his stay so disagreeable that he would depart.[59]

[57] Thompson, *Devils*, ii, 21.

[58] Zimmern, *Beiträge zur Kenntniss der babylonischen Religion*, pp. 98 ff.

[59] Jastrow, in *PRSM*, 1913-1914, vii, 116-117; and in *AMH*, 1917, i, 240-248.

Prophylaxis.

Prognosis in disease and guidance in life to forestall and to avoid the misfortunes of illness and of death were sought by the interpretation of dreams and omens, by the reading of stars and planets, and by hepatoscopy and other forms of divination. Charms and amulets, talismans made of knots of cord, pierced shells, bronze or terra-cotta statuettes, and bands of cloth, inscribed with magic words, were very commonly worn as being potent in warding off the evil eye and the enchantments of the black art, as well as averting disease and other misfortunes;[60] while, for similar purposes, 'words of power' were engraved on cylinders of stone, on hematite, agate, rock-crystal, onyx, lapis lazuli, or jasper, and were worn on the head, neck, limbs, or hands and feet. The demon *labartu*, who lived on the mountains and in the cane-brakes of marshes, was greatly feared for young children, and as a protection against her they hung around their necks a stone with the following inscription: "By the great gods mayst thou be exorcised; with the bird of heaven mayst thou fly away!" Pregnant women, in like fashion, were accustomed to wear bands with inscriptions claiming the protection of some deity, such as, "I am ————, the servant of Adad, the champion of the gods, the favorite of Bel."

Appeals to the demons.

In addition to the entreaties addressed to the deities for assistance in overcoming the activities of the evil spirits, and frequently instead of making such an appeal, these malevolent ones were approached directly through the medium of a magician, and various methods were used to divert them from their purpose, or to appease and

[60] R. C. Thompson, "Charms and Amulets (Assyro-Babylonian)," in *ERE* iii, 409-411.

to propitiate them, and thus gaining their favor cause them to depart. Such practices and ceremonies were similar to those of 'medicine-men' among savage tribes and consisted in singing, wild dancing, shouting, beating of drums, and asserting that the demon or devil had been removed from the sick man and had been transferred to an animal or to the medicine-man, or had been driven away. In certain instances, the spirit of the invalid was assumed to have been carried off, and the medicine-man would be sent, often long distances, to recover it and to fetch it back to its owner.

Uniformity of belief in Mesopotamia.

The standards of religious beliefs as they pertained to disease and its treatment appear, so far as known, to have been practically the same throughout Mesopotamia and the neighboring non-Indo-Iranian tribes and nations.

A pious sufferer.

The following excerpts are from texts on tablets expressing the laments and observations, the sufferings and despair, of a man who seems to have been a ruler of Nippur who strove, and failed, to understand the mysterious ways of the gods. Having been faithful in the performance of his duties to the deities, he is not conscious of guilt, yet he is stricken with disease and cannot find help or consolation until, at the last extremity, a high divinity intervenes, and he recovers. His poem gives many details of his disease and sufferings, but the principal facts, illustrative of current beliefs as discussed above, are given in the following extracts:

(My eyeballs he obscured, bolting them as with) a lock
(My ears he bolted), like those of a deaf person.
A king—I have been changed into a slave,
As a madman (my) companions maltreat me.

I had reached and passed the allotted time of life;
Whithersoever I turned—evil upon evil.
Misery had increased, justice was gone,
I cried unto my god, but he did not show me his countenance;
I prayed to my goddess, but she did not raise her head.
The diviner-priest could not determine the future by an inspection,
The necromancer did not through an offering justify my suit,
The zakiku-priest I appealed to, but he revealed nothing,
The chief exorciser did not by (his) rites release me from the ban.
The like of this had never been seen;
Whithersoever I turned, trouble was in pursuit.

As though I had not always set aside the portion for the god,
And had not invoked the goddess at the meal,
Had not bowed my face, and brought my tribute,
As though I were one in whose mouth supplication and prayer was not constant,

I taught my country to guard the name of the god,
To honor the name of the goddess I accustomed my people.
The glorification of the king I made like unto that of a god,
And in the fear of the palace I instructed the people.
I thought that such things were pleasing to a god.

Despite his devotion, he is smitten with disease and indulges in gloomy thoughts, despairs of pleasing the gods, recounts his sufferings, and tells how the demons have laid him low:

An evil demon has come out of his (lair);
From yellowish, the sickness became white.
It struck my neck and crushed my back,
It bent my high stature like a poplar;
Like a plant of the marsh, I was uprooted, thrown on my back.
Food became bitter and putrid,
The malady dragged on its course.

I took to my bed, unable to leave the couch.
The house became my prison;
As fetters for my body, my hands were powerless,
As pinions for my person, my feet were stretched out,
My discomfiture was painful, the pain severe.

The disease of my joints baffled the chief exorciser,
And my omens were obscure to the diviner,
The exorciser could not interpret the character of my disease,
And the limit of my malady the diviner could not fix.
No god came to my aid, taking me by the hand,
No goddess had compassion for me, coming to my side.
The grave was open, my burial prepared,
Though not yet dead, the lamentation was over.
The people of my land had already said "alas" over me.
My enemy heard it and his face shone;
As the joyful tidings were announced to him his liver rejoiced,
I knew it was the day when my whole family,
Resting under the protection of their deity would be in distress.

Another tablet continues the plaint and passes on to an
account of a dream sent to the sufferer in which Ur-Bau,
as a "strong hero decked with a crown," appears, bringing a message from Marduk that the patient will be
released from his sufferings.

He sent a mighty storm to the foundation of heaven,
To the depths of the earth he drove it,
He drove back the evil demon into the abyss.
The nameless Utukku he drove into his mountain house.
He confounded Labartu, forcing him back into the mountain.
On the tide of the sea he swept away the ague.
He tore out the root of my disease like a plant.

My ears which had been closed and bolted as those of a deaf
        person,
He removed their deafness and opened their hearing.
My nose which through the force of the fever was choked up,
He healed the hurt so that I could breathe again.

My lips which had been closed through exhausted strength,
He reduced their swelling (?) and loosened their bonds.

My entire body he restored,
He wiped away the blemish, making it resplendent,
The oppressed stature regained its splendor,
On the banks of the stream where judgment is held over men
The brand of slavery was removed, the fetters taken off.

The patient then closes with the advice never to despair.

Let him who sins against E-sagila, let him learn from me,
Into the jaw of the lion, about to devour me, Marduk inserted
   a bit.
Marduk has seized the snare (?) of my pursuer, has encompassed
   his lair.[61]

PART II: THE HEALING DEITIES

DURING the many centuries of the existence of these great
Empires of Mesopotamia, many changes occurred in the
status, rank, and influence of their various divinities, and
there appears to have been a strong tendency toward
centralization and the concentration of religious control
in the hands of a few great gods, particularly in respect
to political affairs. The functions of deity as they pertained to personal relations with the people, at least so
far as they may now be determined, were of a general,
rather than of a specialized, character; the particular
traits and powers that characterize the healer are recognized in but few, and the success of such divinities in the
exercise of their curative aspects caused them to be
known as 'great physicians.' Others exercised their
therapeutic powers as a minor function, and still others
are mentioned in the incantation-texts in a manner that
suggests the lower and dependent rank of attendants and

[61] Jastrow, *Civilization,* pp. 477-483.

aids to the greater gods. For the present, the list of therapeutic divinities must remain indefinite and imperfect, and the few here named are mentioned in the texts in connection with healing, although not all of them may be classed as strictly healing gods. Those who appear most prominently are:

Allatu, or Ereshkigal	Ishtar	Nusku
Ea	Marduk	Sarpânîtum
Gibil, or Giru	Nabû, or Nebo	Shamash
Gula, Bau, or Nin-karrak	Ninib, or Ninurta	Sin

ALLATU, OR ERESHKIGAL

ALLATU ('Goddess'), or Ereshkigal ('Queen of the Lower World'), the chief goddess of the Underworld and the consort of Nergal, was also a healing deity in a limited sense, being especially mentioned in connection with the cure of fevers. In the nether-world she was reputed to have a spring ('the water of life'), the waters of which did away with pain and brought the dead to life.[62]

EA

EA ('House of Water'), the third member of the first triad of cosmic gods and one of the chief deities of the Babylonian pantheon, was associated with all the myths of the Babylonian cosmogony; and in the division of the Universe with the divinities Anu and Enlil, he became the 'King of the Watery Deep,' the god of the Persian Gulf, of the ocean, rivers, and springs, and of all waters. Ea appears as a syncretism resulting from his identification with one of the oldest and most respected Sumerian deities, Enki, 'lord of the land,' who, as a 'mountain

[62] Jastrow, op. cit., p. 280; Zimmern, in ERE ii, 316; Neuberger und Pagel, Handbuch der Geschichte der Medicin, i, 71.

EA OF ERIDU

Courtesy of the late
Professor Morris Jastrow, Jr.

deity' had been given the added distinction of 'lord of the Deep' when his people reached the Euphrates valley.[63] Ea, the old water-god was adopted by the Babylonians, becoming the patron god of the city of Eridu, south of Babylon at the mouth of the Euphrates, where his celebrated temple, E-Apsu, was located. He is represented as semi-human and semi-piscine, the lower part of his body and legs being fish-like and covered with scales.

Ea was conceived in a universal sense, and his fame had descended from very ancient times as the friend and general protector of the human race. He was the inventor of writing, the possessor of supreme wisdom, and a teacher who instructed his people in the arts of civilization, industries, literature, and all culture.[64] He was the source of general beneficence, and so of the healing art, and he was the 'lord of incantations,' knowing the potent magic which averted evil, thwarted the designs of evil spirits, demons, and witches, exorcised the demons of disease, appeased the gods, and gained their favor.[65] When he opened his mouth and gave a decision, his word was law; and his oracles were announced with the sound of the roaring surf. The learned priests of the temples conducted schools and were adepts in the rituals of incantation, in the magic arts of divination and astrology, and in the interpretation of all omens and portents, while the highest culture of Babylonia came from his temple at Eridu.

Ea, representing the healing qualities of springs and waters, was the supreme god of healing and was the last resort of the sick and suffering.[66] Appeal was made to

[63] Jastrow, "Sumerian and Akkadian Views of Beginnings," in *JAOS*, 1916, xxxvi, 287, 294-295; and in *AMH*, 1917, i, 234.

[64] Jastrow, *Aspects*, pp. 89, 93, 95.

[65] *Id., Religion*, pp. 275, 276.

[66] *Id., Civilization*, p. 211.

him by sacrifices, prayers, hymns, and incantations, and
his ritual revolved about the use of water and of oil,
especially the former.[67] The body of the sufferer was
sprinkled or bathed with the waters of the Euphrates or
of the Tigris, or with those of some sacred stream or
spring, to the accompaniment of incantations for purification and for exorcism, the image of the demon of
disease being plunged in water and symbolically drowned,
or being placed in a boat which was blown away or cap-
sized.[68] Ea was credited with the power of raising the
dead,[69] and Damkina, his consort, was sometimes appealed to by the sick, being mentioned in several incantation texts.[70] After the rise of Marduk, who was accepted
as the son of Ea, he became the intermediary through
whom invocations were made to Ea; Marduk was addressed, but he was supposed to consult with Ea and to
receive instructions concerning the methods for healing,
Ea being the source, and Marduk the manifestation, of
the creative power. The priests of Ea, dressed in robes
resembling fish-skins as representatives of the god,[71]
recited the rituals of incantation, performed the rites of
purification and of sacrifice, and directed the administration of the various remedies with oral and manual magic,
the water-expert (the *asu*, or physician) being a servitor
of Ea, and knowing how to secure the coöperation of the
deity. The cult of Ea, extending throughout Babylonian
and Assyrian territory, retained the respect of the people
and continued to exert a strong influence long after the
fall of the Mesopotamian Empires.[72]

[67] Jastrow, *Religion*, p. 289; *id.*, *Civilization*, p. 253.

[68] Jastrow, *op. cit.*, p. 247.

[69] M. Jastrow, "Babylonia and Assyria, History," in *EB* iii, 102.

[70] Zimmern, in *ERE* ii, 310.

[71] Jastrow, in *AMH*, 1917, i, 234.

[72] *Id.*, *Civilization*, pp. 210-211; also Thompson, in *ERE* iv, 742;
Zimmern, in *ERE* ii, 310.

GIBIL, OR GIRU

GIBIL, a fire-god and a healing deity of Babylonia, assimilated to Nusku and sometimes to Nabû,[73] is mentioned in the incantation-texts as directing the fires for purification and is named in the performance of the rites of symbolic magic by fire which destroyed demons of disease. He also acted as a mediator between the sick and Ea.[74]

GULA, BAU, OR NIN-KARRAK

GULA, an early goddess of the Assyrians, originally appearing as Ma-Ma,[75] was a divinity of fertility, the 'mother of mankind,' and the consort of Ninib at Nippur and at Calah, being honored with him both by the Assyrians and by the Babylonians. She was identified with Bau, the consort of Ningirsu,[76] and was a celebrated healing divinity,[77] her name frequently occurring in incantation-texts, sometimes as the 'guardian patroness' of the curative art.[78] She was a 'great physician' and a 'life-giver' who preserved health, removed disease by the touch of her hand, and "leads the dead to new life"; but at times she exercised her diametrically opposite power of inflicting evil and misfortune. In portrayals of her, the dog appears as her emblem.[79]

ISHTAR

ISHTAR, the most prominent and most popular goddess of the Assyro-Babylonian pantheon, was of Semitic

[73] Jastrow, *Religion*, p. 220.
[74] *Id., Civilization*, p. 226; also Zimmern, in *ERE* ii, 313.
[75] Jastrow, *Religion*, p. 105.
[76] *Id., Civilization*, p. 200.
[77] *Ib.*, p. 199.
[78] Zimmern, in *ERE* ii, 312; Jastrow, *Religion*, p. 175.
[79] Jastrow, *Civilization*, p. 417.

origin and was universally worshipped by that people throughout Mesopotamia; but unlike other consorts of the male divinities, who were only pale reflections of their husbands, she was an independent deity of rank and dignity, and was unsurpassed in splendor. In Assyria she was Bêlit[80] ('Mistress'), the goddess of battle, the goddess of heaven, the 'Goddess of Totality,' second only to the national divinity, Assur, as whose co-equal she at times appeared. As a deity of war she manifests herself robed in flames, armed with quivers, a bow, and a drawn sword, declaring that she marches before Assurbanipal; and again, when the king is discouraged, she promises through a dream that he shall have his heart's desire, and that his strength shall not fail in battle.[81]

In general, Ishtar was the gracious mother of creation, and the goddess of love, of fertility, of child-birth, and of healing. She was the kind, sympathetic mother of mankind who listened to the supplications of sinners,[82] and she was invoked for relief from pain, from suffering, and from demons of disease,[83] while as a goddess of child-birth she received the epithet Mylitta, 'she who causes to bear.'[84] In the Etana legend, although appeal was made to Shamash for the birth-plant which insured happy delivery, the imperfect lines of the text seem to imply that it was obtained from her.[85]

Ishtar absorbed the titles, rites, and functions of other female divinities in their own sanctuaries, and thus she appears in different aspects and in different characters

[80] Paton, in *ERE* ii, 297.
[81] Sayce, in *ERE* v, 33.
[82] Jastrow, *op. cit.*, pp. 233, 308.
[83] *Ib.*, p. 234.
[84] L. B. Paton, "Ashtart (Ashtoreth), Astarte," in *ERE* ii, 116.
[85] Jastrow, *Religion,* pp. 519-523; Ward, *The Seal Cylinders of Western Asia,* p. 142; Zimmern, in *ERE* ii, 315; T. G. Pinches, "Birth (Assyro-Babylonian)," in *ERE* ii, 644.

in various places devoted to her worship.[86] She was the tutelary deity of many of the cities of Babylonia, being known as Nanā at Uruk, as Bau at Shirpurla (Lagash), and as Anunītu at Akkad,[87] while in Assyria she appeared as three goddesses at as many seats, being a divinity of war at Nineveh and Arbela, and a deity of love at Kidmuru. Priestesses were attached to her temples, and licentious, immoral practices were officially recognized as a part of her religious rites, while in some places, especially at Uruk (Herodotos, i, 199), prostitution was associated with her worship (Strabo, XVI, i, 20 = p. 745 C).[88] Ishtar was an exacting divinity and visited her wrath upon those who disobeyed her mandates, smiting them and inflicting disease in punishment. The lion was her sacred animal, and possibly the dove belonged to her.[89] She was equated with 'Astart of the Phœnicians, with Aphrodite and Eileithyia of the Greeks, and with Venus of the Romans.

MARDUK

MARDUK, 'king of the gods,' 'glory of Thebes,' 'founder of the zodiac,' and 'lord of planets,' was a solar deity, probably Sumerian in origin, who enjoyed only a modest rank in the pantheons of Eridu and Babylon until his rapid rise to power as the chief divinity of Babylonia through the favor of Hammurabi (*circa* 2200 B.C.), who effected the union of the Babylonian city-states and caused their cults to become national.[90] He finally claimed

---

[86] Jastrow, *op. cit.*, pp. 83-88; also Zimmern, in *ERE* ii, 311.

[87] L. B. Paton, "Ishtar," in *ERE* vii, 428-434.

[88] Frazer, *Adonis, Attis, Osiris*, 3d ed., i, 38 f.; also Jastrow, *op. cit.*, pp. 475 ff.

[89] Jastrow, *Civilization*, pp. 232-236; Zimmern, in *ERE* ii, 311.

[90] Jastrow, *op. cit.*, p. 213; Paton, in *ERE* ii, 296-297; Zimmern, *loc. cit.*

to be the supreme god of the Universe and even contested the position of Assur, the national deity of Assyria, though in this he was frustrated by the prestige and power of the Assyrian priesthood. As he rose to eminence, he was held to be the son of Ea of Eridu, who conferred equal wisdom upon him; and combining in himself the functions of Enlil and of Ea, he was recognized not only as the chief of the pantheon, but also as a cosmic divinity. He then appropriated the rites, titles, attributes, functions, and powers of all Babylonian deities, overshadowing them and reducing them to subordinate rank in their own cities, except in the case of Ea, whose preeminence was such that Marduk was content to be adopted as his son and as his co-equal in wisdom and dignity. He arrogated to himself the great cosmic deeds of the older gods, and many Babylonian myths appear to have been reëdited or rewritten to glorify him in the performance of the early cosmic exploits, as when, in one of the most important texts, he displaces Enlil of Nippur as the hero who killed the demon Chaos, Tiamat, in the presence of the gods, and thus freed mankind.

Next to Ea, Marduk was the most prominent divine healer of Babylonia.[91] He was regarded as the intermediary between man and Ea and had the power of calling not only upon him, but also upon other members of the first triad of gods, Anu and Enlil, although Ea was the last resort and the supreme authority in matters therapeutic, his preëminence in this domain admitting no rival. Supplications were commonly made to Ea through Marduk, who, when implored for aid, was supposed to confer with his father and to ask what the sick man must do to be healed, but in reporting the consultations with Ea, the dignity of Marduk was preserved by the specific declaration of the former that his son knows all that he knows,

91 Zimmern, in *ERE* ii, 312.

while still giving directions for treatment.[92] In the texts he is called Marduk of Eridu, thus suggesting the city of his early residence, as well as his close association with Ea and with the temple E-Apsu, the home of the rituals of exorcism, while his own temple at Babylon, called E-Sagila ('Lofty House'), enjoyed great renown. In all the texts the methods of healing are by purification, incantation, and exorcism. His consort, Sarpânîtum, is mentioned with him in some texts; and the dog was his sacred emblem.

NABÛ, OR NEBO

NABÛ ('Proclaimer'), an old Sumerian deity presiding over wisdom and over all culture, was the inventor and the divinity of writing, revelation, and prophecy, and was "a seer who guides all gods." He was the patron deity of Borsippa, across the river from Babylon, where stood his celebrated temple, E-Zida ('True House') and a renowned school which included medicine;[93] but his supremacy in his own shrine was usurped by Marduk, and he became the son of the national god. He still retained his local influence, however, and was worshipped with Marduk, even after the Persian conquest, besides receiving adoration in Assyria, where a temple, similar to that at Borsippa, was dedicated to him at Calah. In incantation-texts he is invoked as a healer in connection with Ea and other deities; and the formulas of greeting in letters from Assyrian physicians introduce Nabû and Marduk, or invoke Nebo and his consort, Nanā.[94] Nabû was sometimes amalgamated with Nusku and identified with the planet Mercury.[95]

[92] See page 109, also Thompson, in *ERE* iv, 742; Jastrow, *op. cit.*, pp. 212-217.

[93] Neuberger und Pagel, *loc. cit.*

[94] Jastrow, in *AMH*, 1917, i, 251, note.

[95] *Id., Religion*, pp. 220-221, 459.

NINIB, OR NINURTA

NINIB, an early patron of Nippur, but overshadowed and displaced by the cosmic god Enlil, whose son he became,[96] was a divinity of agriculture, a 'lord' of the fields, and a god of the chase, as well as a solar deity, dissipating darkness, while in Assyria he was worshipped as a war-god, 'mighty in battle.' He was a beneficent divinity, a renowned healer (especially in Babylonia), and one who dispensed justice; and with his consort, Gula, he saved his subjects from the clutches of disease,[97] bringing back to life those who were near death. In Babylonian letters Ninib and Gula were the deities always invoked for relief from maladies,[98] and they were affectionately remembered by their people, great festivals being held in their honor at certain times of year, especially at Calah. Ninib had a temple, E-shu-me-du, at Nippur,[99] and another at Calah in Assyria.[100]

NUSKU

NUSKU, a conqueror of all evil and a promoter of all good, was a fire-god (originally a sun-god), a divinity of charms, and a messenger between Ea and Marduk, as well as between other deities. He was equated with Gibil, their names often appear together as Gibil-Nusku; and he was associated with Sin, the moon-god. In incantation-texts he is invoked to destroy the demons of disease by fire,[101] and in this same manner he symbolically annihilates wizards and witches, practitioners of black magic.[102]

[96] Jastrow, *Civilization*, p. 197.

[97] *Ib.*, p. 199.

[98] *Id.*, in *AMH*, 1917, i, 251.

[99] *Id.*, *Civilization*, pp. 198, 201.

[100] *Id.*, *Religion*, p. 215; Zimmern, in *ERE* ii, 312; Jastrow, *Civilization*, pp. 196-201.

[101] Jastrow, *op. cit.*, p. 247.

[102] *Ib.*, pp. 226-228, 411; *id.*, *Religion*, pp. 220-221; Zimmern, in *ERE* ii, 313.

SARPÂNÎTUM

SARPÂNÎTUM, the consort of Marduk and primarily a solar divinity, was a goddess of healing who also interceded with Ea for the sick, for methods of purification, and for the exorcism of demons of disease.[103] Her name (Sarpânîtum, 'Silvery Bright One') was transformed, by a false etymology, into Zēr-banītum, 'Seed-Creatress' or 'Offspring-Producing,' and she was accordingly amalgamated with an ancient goddess Eru'a ('Conception'), whence her special function was believed to be protection of progeny in the mother's womb, and she received other names bearing on this function, as Nin-dim, 'the lady of procreation,' Šasuru, 'the goddess of the fetus,' and Ninzizna, 'the lady of birth' (?).[104]

SHAMASH

SHAMASH, the sun-god of Babylonia, the chief of the second triad of cosmic deities, and a son of Sin, the lunar-divinity, was a champion of good and an avenger of evil, representing justice and being the supreme judge both in heaven and on earth. The kings of Assyria addressed him as the supreme oracle-deity; he was known as the 'lord of divination,' or as the 'lord of visions,'[105] and his worship was widespread, so that at Larsa in the south and at Nippur in the north temples were dedicated to him, both called E-babbar ('House of Lustre'). Shamash was likewise a prominent healing divinity, his name frequently appearing in incantations for the sick; and he was invoked to prolong life.[106]

[103] Neuberger und Pagel, loc. cit.
[104] Pinches, in ERE ii, 643; also Jastrow, op. cit., pp. 121-122.
[105] Jastrow, Civilization, p. 225.
[106] Ib., p. 246; also Zimmern, in ERE ii, 311.

SIN

SIN, the deity of wisdom, the 'lord of knowledge,' and a divinity of light adored throughout Babylonia, was the ancient Sumerian moon-god and a member of the second triad of cosmic deities. He was called the son of Bêl (Enlil of Nippur) and was the patron of Ur, at the mouth of the Euphrates, where he was worshipped as Nannar ('Furnisher of Light') at his famous temple, E-gishshir-gal ('House of Light'), although his cult was most celebrated at Harran, where he was termed Bêl-Harran.[107] He was an oracle-god, though second, in this aspect, to Shamash, and was an ancient divine physician, his name occurring in many incantation-texts, usually in a secondary capacity as supporting other divinities in their demand for exorcism and for the departure of the demons of disease.[108]

[107] Jastrow, *Religion,* pp. 75, 76, 78.
[108] Neuberger und Pagel, *loc. cit.*

GODS OF THE PAGAN SEMITES
OF THE WEST

CHAPTER THREE

THE HEALING GODS OF THE PAGAN SEMITES OF THE WEST

PART I: GENERAL SURVEY

LITTLE is known of the views of the Phœnicians and other Pagan West-Semites concerning disease; and the only survivals of their practices of healing are a few general facts which indicate that their methods were essentially theurgic in character.

The Semites of the West and their records.

Active in manufacture and commerce, and bold in seafaring, the Phœnicians, of whom we are least ignorant in the present connection, were skilled craftsmen; and their enterprise in carrying their wares, their arts, and their sciences to the farthermost parts of the world then known made them rich and powerful. Peacefully inclined, however, they became a prey to other nations, who conquered them, levied heavy tributes upon them, and held them in subjection, so that, from prehistoric times, they were dominated in turn by Egypt, Assyria, Babylonia, Persia, Greece, and Rome. All records of their national life and of their religious beliefs and customs have disappeared, except the fragments of the writings of Mochos the Sidonian and Sanchuniathon, which are regarded as apocryphal in their present form,[1] and inscriptions on monuments and tablets which have been found in the ruins of their towns and temples. These remains, supple-

---

[1] Cooke, *A Text-Book of North-Semitic Inscriptions,* p. xviii, note.

mented by comparative studies of similar neighboring peoples of the same epoch, the records of Assyro-Babylonia and Egypt, and the comments of the writers of the later period of Greece and of Rome, form the fragmentary and imperfect material upon which the existing outlines of Phœnician beliefs, practices, and general civilization have been constructed.

The Phœnicians and their deities.

The Phœnicians, like other members of the Semitic race, exhibited a strong inclination toward religion. The gods of their pantheon represented the various powers of nature; the sky, the earth, and every important object was animated by a divinity. There were celestial deities with cosmic attributes, and there were terrestrial, tribal, departmental, and adopted foreign gods, to say nothing of compound divinities, such as Eshmun-'Astart, or Melqart-Resheph, new deities who formed individual traits; Shemesh was the sun-god; Yerah, the lunar deity; Resheph, the divinity of lightning; and 'Anath, the goddess of war. Some of the deities had been brought to Phœnicia by the early immigrants, but more had been transplanted by their conquerors or had been adopted from other nations as they severally exercised a dominating influence on or intermingled with the people, among the more prominent of these being Shamash and Nergal of Assyro-Babylonia; Osiris, Isis, Ubastet, and Bes of Egypt; and Aphrodite, Dionysos, Helios, Asklepios, and Poseidon of Greece. After the conquest of Alexander the Great, the relations between Phœnicia and Greece became very close, and many elements of Hellenic religious life mingled with those of Phœnicia, especially the identification of deities with the adoption of Greek names.

The nature of their gods.

The generic West-Semitic name for 'god' was *ēl*, and

for 'goddess,' *ēlōt;* but the all-inclusive term for nature spirits was *ba'alîm,* who represented holy stones, trees, water, and mountains, the word *ba'al* meaning primarily 'owner, master, lord,' and expressing the totality of character and powers possessed by all deities. Melqart, the great national god of Tyre, who was equated with Herakles, bore this name and was known as Ba'al Melqart ('Lord City-King'); and kings often had *ba'al* as a component of their names or compounded them with those of deities to secure divine protection, as Eshmun-'asōr ('Eshmun hath helped'), their real names in many instances being unknown.[2]

'Astart.

The chief goddess of the pantheon was Ba'alath or 'Astart, the Hebrew 'Ashtoreth, who was mistress of the city of Gebal, or Byblos, and she was one of the most important deities of Phœnicia. She represented love, fertility, and the general reproductive powers of nature; and was assimilated to Ishtar of Babylonia and Assyria, Kybele of Phrygia, and Aphrodite of Greece, having numerous temples in Phœnicia and being worshipped in its colonies and wherever Phœnician influence extended. Hierodules (*qĕdhēshîm,* 'sacred men,' and *qĕdhēsôth,* 'sacred women')[3] frequented the temples of the goddess; and sacred prostitution, which was general in similar cults throughout Western Asia, was a prominent feature of her rites (Herodotos, i, 199); women, even virgins, sacrificing their chastity in honor of the goddess and to gain her favor (Lucian, *de Dea Syria,* 6). 'Astart does not appear as having a definite association with healing (unless possibly in her general divine capacity), except as suggested by the myth that she discovered the meteor

---

[2] L. B. Paton, "Phœnicians," in *ERE* ix, 889.

[3] Frazer, *Adonis, Attis, Osiris,* 3d ed., i, 17-18, 37, 70 ff.

stone, or stones with souls which breathed a prophetic spirit and cured diseases.[4]

Functions of deity.

The Phœnician deities were over-lords and rulers of the people; and each town had its own tutelary divinity, a *ba'al* who was its owner, king, lord, ruler, or protector, and the source of the fertility of its fields and of its prosperity. The gods were conceived and described as good, and as helpers who heard, knew, guarded, sheltered, judged, redeemed, and saved their people; these relations being based upon the general Semitic conception of the majesty of deity and the subjection of men; hence, the people frequently declared themselves as the slaves of such and such a divinity.

Shrines and temples.

The situation of shrines and temples was determined by the sacred character attributed to some natural object, as a tree, pillar, standing stone, spring, or stream, in which a *ba'al* dwelt; and such a spot was called a *bama,* or 'high-place,' fenced about or walled off as a sacred enclosure in which worship was performed. In early times there was neither temple nor image, merely a venerated altar; but at a later period idols came into limited use. In towns and cities permanent structures, roofed and with a pillared wall at the entrance, were erected to shelter the deity and the treasures of the sanctuary. Both priests (*kōhănîn*) and priestesses (*kōhănōth*) had charge of the religious exercises; and diviners, or *ṣôphē,* are also mentioned as being in attendance (*CIS* i, 124, 6).

---

[4] Hirschell, *Compendium der Geschichte der Medicin,* p. 27; and for further details, see L. B. Paton, "Ashtart (Ashtoreth), Astarte," in *ERE* ii, 115-118.

Religious rites.

Relatively little remains to indicate the character of the worship of the Phœnicians, but it is highly probable that their religious ceremonies were in all essentials similar to those of other West-Semitic peoples of the same period and stage of civilization. Their rites consisted of prayers, sacrifices, hymns, and votive offerings; and animals (Philon Byblios, 35 b; especially the first-born, *ib.*, 38 d) were sacrificed, a part of the flesh becoming the perquisite of the temple attendants, and the remainder being consumed by the worshippers (*CIS* i, 165, 12; 166, 3, 7, 167).[5] First-fruits (*CIS* i, 5) were also offered, usually with libations; and sacrifice of human victims, usually of first-born children, were made in times of great distress (Philon Byblios, 40 c),[6] and also others than first-born, or children (Diodoros, xx, 65).

PART II: THE HEALING DEITIES

Ba'al-marpē   Eshmun   Tanit

BA'AL-MARPĒ

A DIVINITY, Ba'al-marpē (or Ba'al-mᵊrappē), 'Lord of Healing' (or 'Healing Lord'), is mentioned in a Phœnician inscription from Cyprus (*CIS* i, 41), though *marpē* ('healing place'), or *mᵊrappē* ('healer') may have been merely the name of a medicinal spring, whence the 'lord' in question would be only a local *ba'al*.[7]

ESHMUN

ESHMUN, one of the great deities of the Phœnician pan-

---

[5] Cooke, *op. cit.*, pp. 117-121.
[6] Paton, in *ERE* ix, 896.
[7] L. B. Paton, "Baal, Beel, Bel," in *ERE* ii, 289.

theon, was the god of healing, and the chief male divinity of Sidon, possessing uranic and cosmic aspects in addition to his therapeutic powers. A female deity of Sidon, Ashima(t),[8] his consort, is mentioned in inscriptions as though she was superior to him (*CIS* I, iv, 5); but it is claimed that this goddess was none other than 'Astart.[9] It has been suggested that Eshmun was originally a nature-divinity, and possibly of spring vegetation, especially if he was identical with the Babylonian Tammuz,[10] and that, being a favorite deity of the people, he was brought with them in their migration to the Mediterranean, where, as the Phœnicians developed prosperity and influence, he was advanced in rank from a humble place until he stood next to Ba'al, Melqart, and 'Astart in the pantheon. Under this assumption, Eshmun has been considered a counterpart of Tammuz of Babylonia, and as holding the same intimate relations with 'Astart at Sidon as that deity sustained toward Ishtar in Assyria and Babylonia.[11]

By repute, Eshmun was 'the most beautiful of all gods,' and a legend runs that when the mother-goddess Astronoë fell in love with him while hunting in the forest, Eshmun, to escape her, emasculated himself. Afterward 'Astart transported him to the skies (Damaskios, *apud* Photios, *Bibliotheca*, p. 573), where he became a god of the northern heavens and the moon-deity; and another myth gives him a celestial aspect, related to the starry sphere.

The meaning of the word Eshmun is by no means cer-

[8] Cf. II Kings, xvii, 30.

[9] Eiselen, *Sidon*, p. 127.

[10] W. W. Baudissin, "Der phönizische Gott Esmun," in *ZDMG*, 1905, lix, 502; also Jastrow, *The Religion of Babylonia and Assyria*, p. 588.

[11] Eiselen, *op. cit.*, p. 126.

tain, Damaskios and Philon Byblios regarded him as 'the Eighth,' evidently through confusion with Phœnician *šymuna* ('eight'). Possibly Eshmun may be cognate with the Hebrew *shāmēn*, 'fat, robust,' and Arabic *samina*, 'to be fat,' whence the name may mean 'very stout, very strong.'[12] Following a late tradition, Damaskios (*ib.*, 352 b) makes Eshmun the eighth son of Sydyk;[13] while Philon Byblios states (36 a) that seven of Sydyk's sons were the Kabeiroi, and that one of the Titanides bore him as the eighth, Asklepios (*i.e.*, Eshmun). On the authority of Sanchuniathon, Philon further writes: "From Sydyk came the Dioskouroi, the Kabeiroi, or Korybantes, or Samothrakes, who were the first to invent a ship. From them have sprung others who discovered herbs, and the healing of venomous bites, and charms. These things did the seven sons of Sydyk, the Kabeiroi, and Asklepios, their brother, the eighth son, first of all write down in the records, as the god Tauut [*i.e.*, Thoth or Thout] had enjoined them," and to whom he disclosed the cosmogony which they passed on.[14]

The name of the divinity first appears in Assyro-Babylonian treaty between Asarhaddon and the King of Tyre (seventh century B.C.) in the form Ia-su-mu-nu,[15] and later as 'ŠMN, conventionally pronounced Eshmun. Although the god is vaguely portrayed in the myths and scanty records of Phœnicia, he emerges from antiquity through the medium of inscriptions and the writings of classical authors, with a more distinct personality and a

---

[12] Baudissin, *Adonis und Esmun*, pp. 203 ff.; also Lidzbarski, "Der Name des Gottes Esmun," in *ESE*, 1915, iii, 260-265.

[13] *I.e.*, 'just, righteous.' A Phœnician and Canaanite divinity bore this name (L. B. Paton, "Canaanites," in *ERE* iii, 183; also in *ib.*, ix, 893).

[14] E. Meyer, "Esmun," in Roscher, i, 1385-1386.

[15] Baudissin, *op. cit.*, p. 205; also Winckler, "Bruchstücke von Keilschrifttexten," in *AF*, 1898, i, 12; note p. 192, line 14.

more clearly defined character than any other Phœnician deity except Ba'al, Melqart, and 'Astart. He appears as having characteristics possessed by no other god; while his special function of healing is asserted by all classical authors who refer to him, and by comparisons made in all bilingual inscriptions in which he is mentioned. Recognizing him from early times as the counterpart of their therapeutic deities, the Egyptians equated him with Thoth (Tauut or Thout), Ptaḥ, and I-m-ḥotep; and adjoining nations made similar assimilations. The Greeks identified him with Asklepios, as is shown both by literature (Philon Byblios, v, 8; Damaskios, *apud* Photios, *Bibliotheca*, p. 573) and inscriptions,[16] this equation being further supported by abundant evidence in bilingual inscriptions; while a votive tablet on which the name 'Asklepioi' was inscribed was uncovered in excavating the temple at Sidon.[17] A Phœnician coin found at Sidon bears the image of Asklepios; a Roman coin from Berytos has the youthful figure of Eshmun, of the type adopted by Kalamis for his statue of Asklepios at Sikyon, rather than the more usual one resembling Zeus; and a coin of Septimus Severus shows the Romano-Punic assimilation of Eshmun and Asklepios, youthful and beardless, supported by two serpents and with a baton in his hand, a type derived from the Græco-Phœnician period.[18] The earliest evidence for the identification of Eshmun with Asklepios is given by two coins of Marathos and by one of Ptolemais-Akka (about the third century B.C.), if these may be regarded as Greek transformations of the native

[16] Baudissin, *op. cit.*, pp. 221-238; also Eiselen, *op. cit.*, p. 135.

[17] W. von Landau, "Vorläufige Nachrichten über die im Eshmuntempel bei Sidon gefundenen phönizischen Alterthümer," in *MVG*, 1904, ix, 289.

[18] Anonymous, "The Figure of Æsculapius in Ancient Art," in *Lancet*, 1904, ii, 1362-1363.

Eshmun.[19] A river near Sidon was named Asklepios, and a grove between Sidon and Berytos was called Asklepios's grove (Strabo, XVI, ii, 22 = p. 756 C).

The clearest and most direct evidence of the equation of the two deities in the character of healers comes from a trilingual inscription on the base of a bronze altar, dedicated to them about 180 b.c., and found near a thermal spring in Sardinia (*CIS* i, 143).[20] The text is written in Phœnician, Greek, and Latin, and mentions Eshmun, Asklepios, and Æsculapius, each being given the obscure epithet 'Merre,' the meaning of which is not clear, though it has been interpreted as 'life-giving,' 'life-prolonging,' or 'protector of wayfarers,' etc. The Latin version, which almost exactly follows the Greek, runs: "Cleon salari-[us]soc[iorum] s[ervus] Æscolapio Merre donum dedit lubens merito merente." "Partem phœniciam sic verte: Domino Eśmuno Merre: Altare æreum ponderis librarum centum c, quod vovit Cleon, [servus sociorum] qui in re salaria; audiit vocem ejus, sanavit eum. Anno suffetum Himilcati et Abdeśmuni, filii Himilci." The translation of the Punic text reads: "To the lord Eshmun Merre—the altar of bronze, in weight 100 pounds, which Cleon of ḤSGM, who is over the salt-mines (?), vowed; he heard his voice [and] healed him. In the year of the Suffetes Himilkath and 'Abd-eshmun, son of Himilk.'"[20]

To summarize, although neither Philon nor Damaskios refer to Eshmun as a healing deity and his relation to medicine is, therefore, traditional, Eshmun and Asklepios were regarded as identical at Sidon in the Phœnician motherland and, if we may believe Damaskios, at Berytos; they were possibly so equated at Marathos, Ptolemais-Akka, on the island of Ruad, and at Duma near Byblos; probably so at Oia, in Africa Proconsularis, and

[19] Baudissin, *op. cit.*, p. 221.
[20] Cooke, *op. cit.*, pp. 109-110.

in the Spanish and Sicilian settlements of the Carthaginians; and certainly so at Carthage and in Numidia, Mauretania, and Sardinia.[21]

That the worship of Eshmun was general is shown by the remains of sanctuaries dedicated to him in Phœnicia and many of its colonies. Eshmun-'azar, King of Sidon, and his mother erected a temple in honor of the divinity at Sidon, south of the river Nahr-al-Auwaly; and Bod-'Astart either completed it or built another to the god (*CIS* i, 3, 17). Excavations in 1900 at the site of the shrine revealed its ruins and an inscription running as follows: "King Bod-'Astart, King of the Sidonians, grandson of King Eshmun-'azar, King of the Sidonians, [reigning] in Sidon by the sea, Shamin Ramin, the land of Reshaphim, Sidon of Mashal, 'ŠBN, and Sidon on the plain—the whole (?) of this temple built to his god, Eshmun, Prince of Qadesh.''[22] Eshmun also had a temple at Berytos (Damaskios, *loc. cit.*); several sanctuaries dedicated to him have been discovered near springs and streams, suggesting that water was a part of the healing ritual; and the ruins of a shrine at Cherchell in Algeria, supposed to have been for Eshmun, were found to contain a rough, crude image of the god about a metre in height.[23] Of all the temples of Punic Carthage, the only one whose site appears fixed both by ancient texts and by modern discoveries is that which was situated on the summit of the citadel dedicated to Eshmun, destroyed in the siege of 146 B.C. Carthage was called the 'City of the King of Health,' and the god was termed Eshmun-

---

[21] Baudissin, *op. cit.*, p. 230.

[22] Cooke, *op. cit.*, pp. 401-403; cf. Eiselen, *op. cit.*, pp. 143 ff.; C. C. Torrey, "A Phœnician Royal Inscription," in *JAOS*, 1902, xxiii, 156 ff.

[23] A. Maury, "Sur une statuette du dieu Aschmoun ou Esmoun trouvée à Cherchell," in *RA*, 1846, iii, 763-793; also C. Texier, "Extrait d'un aperçu statistique du monuments de l'Algérie," in *ib.*, pp. 729 ff.

'Astart (*CIL* i, 245, 3-4), an association which may receive support in the collocation of Æsculapius (Eshmun) and Dea Cælestis ('Astart) in a Latin inscription from Africa Proconsularis and another from Dacia (*CIL* viii, suppl. 16417; iii, 993; cf. Tertullian, *Apologeticus,* xxiii). A sanctuary to Eshmun-Melqart stood on a low hill, called Batsalos, in the salt lagoons, near the site of Kition in Cyprus (*CIS* i, 16); and excavations in 1894 revealed the foundations of a small building, probably the shrine of this deity, a portion of these ruins being placed in the Ashmolean Museum at Oxford.

Beyond the assimilations mentioned, the evidence at hand gives no indication of the nature and character of the deity as conceived by the Phœnicians. No object referring to him as a healer was found at the temple at Sidon, and nothing is known of his worship or of the therapeutic practices of his worship, although it is assumed that they were similar to those of other Semitic healing cults of the same period.

It would seem, on the whole, that Eshmun was primarily a deity of the renewal of life in the changing seasons of the year. Accordingly, he was associated with 'Astart, the goddess of reproductive nature, and with Melqart, the revivifying divinity; and was perhaps identified with the Greek Dionysos,[24] as the god who again awakens the forces of life, and certainly with Asklepios, as granting the new life of health.[25]

TANIT

TANIT,[26] an important goddess of Carthage, but unknown outside that city and its dependencies in North Africa,

[24] Baudissin, *op. cit.,* p. 241; and in *ZDMG,* 1905, lix, 483-484.

[25] *Id., Adonis,* p. 282.

[26] Such is the conventional pronunciation of *TNT,* whose real signification is uncertain.

was probably a "native, possibly a pre-Carthaginian, deity, who in the process of religious syncretism, so characteristic of Semitic genius, was identified with various goddesses according to circumstances, with 'Ashtart, with Demeter, and with Artemis.'"[27]

Her temple stood on the Byrsa of Carthage near that of Eshmun, and a large number of inscriptions to her have been found at Carthage, many addressing her as 'the Lady of Tanit of Pne-ba'al"[28] (*CIS* i, 181) and as 'the great mother Tanit' (*ib.*, 195, 380). She may have been regarded as a daughter of 'Astart;[29] but almost nothing is really known of her, although her identification with Iuno, Diana, and Venus[30] has led to the belief that she was also a healing deity, as well as a protectress of child-birth and of children.

Note.—It is highly probable that all the great West-Semitic pagan stocks possessed healing deities as did the Phœnicians; but the only name of such a divinity which has survived is Yarḥibôl ('moon-Ba'al'), a lunar god who presided over a medicinal spring at Palmyra; Baethgen, *Beiträge zur semitischen Religionsgeschichte*, p. 87.

[27] Cooke, *op. cit.*, p. 133.

[28] For the various interpretations of this phrase (literally, 'face of Ba'al') cf. P. Berger, "Tanit Pene-Baal," in *JA*, VII, 1877, ix, 147-160; Cooke, *op. cit.*, p. 132; Paton, in *ERE* ix, 892.

[29] Baudissin, *op. cit.*, p. 267.

[30] Wissowa, *Religion und Kultus der Römer*, p. 373.

CHAPTER FOUR
INDIAN GODS

THE HEALING GODS OF ANCIENT INDIA

PART I: GENERAL SURVEY

The Aryans and disease.

AMONG the Aryans of Ancient India, disease was considered a manifestation of the will or power of some supernatural being. It might be from the gods in punishment for sin, as in the case of dropsy caused by Varuṇa; or it might be due to a mere caprice of a malevolent deity. From the earliest times, all morbid conditions of the mind and body—except such as were regarded as divine vengeance—were believed to result from attacks or possession of evil spirits which surrounded man on every side. A cure could be effected only by propitiating, appeasing, or expelling them; and the gods were appealed to for assistance through the use of Vedic hymns, prayers, and sacrifices. Often the gods were vague and uncertain, and the people, believing that magic acts and words had power to compel the gods to perform the will of man, mingled the arts of magic and sorcery with their religious ritual and practices.

The Vedas.

These beliefs were a part of the religion of the ancient Aryans of India as contained in their oldest records, the Vedas (knowledge), the ancient sacred literature of India. Of these, the Rigveda, the earliest, though often ascribed to the early date of 2000-3000 B.C., is now generally supposed to have been begun about 1500 B.C., and

parts are believed to have originated as late as 300 B.C.
The Vedas also contained the germs of many of the most
important and time-honored myths and legends of the
Indians, and these were closely interwoven with their
religious beliefs. They taught the worship of the chief
energies of nature, which are represented as superior
and supernatural beings, personified and ranked as the
greater gods. There were inferior deities, representing
the more routine phenomena of nature and other functions in a descending scale, besides a host of other spirits
and demons, greater and lesser, but below the rank of
gods, whose activities more nearly concerned the common
people and their affairs for weal or woe. These received
scant consideration in the more strictly religious literature and are treated with much more detail in the myths
and legends of the Sanskrit epics and in classical Indian
literature.[1]

The pantheon.

The great gods, whose noble and miraculous deeds had
brought all the benefits of nature to man, were celebrated
in the Vedic hymns of praise. However real and active
they were in the beginning, the results of their beneficence had long been in the possession of the people.
Although they were anthropomorphic, they were not
sympathetic. They concerned themselves less and less
with the affairs of men and finally became abstractions
increasingly distant and more vague. Thus the religion
of the Rigveda, which found expression in hymns of
praise and adoration, intermingled, in its later portions,
with naïve speculations of things divine and human and
with mythical tales, gradually faded as a vital force. It
gave place to sects characterized by lofty conceptions,
philosophical speculations, metaphysical abstractions,

---

[1] A. A. Macdonell, "Vedic Religion," in *ERE* xii, 601-618.

refinements of the 'Unknowable,' beliefs "so abstract that they escape the grasp of the most speculative intellect." From its inception, Brāhmanism inherited the myths, legends, and gods of the old Vedic literature. The great gods were theoretically the same, but as the Brāhman priests gained control of the sacrificial interests, the ancient deities lost their pristine dignity and, while still considered powerful, their share in the popular worship became less. By the same influences, the lesser deities faded and ceased to appeal strongly to the people. Their aspect changed. Some were regarded as separate from the Vedic divinities, or became demigods and godlings. Many of the older deities were forgotten or survived only in name, and their cults were absorbed by later sectarian gods; some of them were adopted from the aborigines whom the Aryans had conquered. Thus the places of the ancient divinities were taken by new ones, a host of minor deities and departmental gods of tribes and villages, who became anthropomorphic through the hands of the poets of the epics. Polytheism became sectarian and more extensive. The later Buddhists made the polytheistic Brāhman pantheon a nucleus and created new deities representing the forces of nature and abstract conceptions of religion, incorporated the pantheons outside of India, and formed the basis for the extension of a 'world-religion.'

The early Hindu period.

The higher classes of the priesthood and of the laity devoted themselves to lofty metaphysical speculation, dealing with the prospects of happiness in the future life and with abstractions of higher truths. The common people, on the other hand, were personally engaged in counteracting the machinations of the hosts of evil spirits who infested their lives and threatened them on every side with misfortune, famine, epidemics, individual disease, and death, and of whom they lived in daily dread. Such spirits, opposed to the gods, were often merely 'non-gods' (*a-suras*). Spirits once benignant became malevolent and separated themselves from the gods. The worship of ninety per cent of the masses was one of fear, and nothing being feared from the good spirits adoration was paid to a black god, or demons. The deities waged incessant warfare against the demons and were victorious because of their superiority; but it was immortality against immortality, and wherever one group of fiends was routed, another took its place, and the attack was renewed. The older Vedic gods were enfeebled, their opponents had become stronger. The enemies of the divinities—the *asuras,* the *daityas,* the *dānavas,* the *rākṣasas* and the *piśāchas*—organizing, attacked in compact bodies and fought more successfully. Some of them lived in magnificent mansions in the Underworld. They had strongholds in the depths of Pātāla, and three fortresses —one of iron, one of silver, and one of gold—in the heavens.[2]

The folk-belief.

Throughout and underlying the great religions—Vedism, Brāhmanism, Buddhism, Jainism, and Muhammadanism—and unaffected by wars and political changes, the real faith of the common people of India was the deep-seated belief in the vast number of mischievous, harmful spirits who fill the sky, clouds, earth, trees, water, and beasts, and to whom was ascribed the inception of magical practices.[3] Magic was closely allied with religion, and witchcraft was blended with the holiest rites. These convictions of the people were recognized in religious observances and penetrated to the higher religion of the Brāhman priests.

[2] Fausbøll, *Indian Mythology,* p. 3.
[3] Oldenberg, *Die Religion des Veda,* pp. 39 ff.

Mythology.

The principal myths of India, of its gods and their deeds, form an integral part of the religion and are related in the Rigveda, and especially in the *Brāhmaṇas*, the epics, and the *Purāṇas*. They are largely of Indo-Aryan origin, and the later myths are tinctured with the same poetic spirit. The mythology of India claims unique interest because of its unparalleled length of life. During 3,500 years it has had a constant and organic development. Other mythologies have perished before the onslaught of loftier faiths and survive in little else than folklore. "In India, on the contrary, though foreign invasion has often swept over the north-west of the land, though Islam has annexed souls as well as territories, though Christianity (especially in the south) has contributed elements to the faith of the people, still it remains true that the religion and the mythology of the land are genuinely their own and for this reason have in themselves the constant potency of fresh growth."[4] Underlying the mythology of the epics, the idea is clear "that the gods themselves are no longer independent eternal entities, but, however glorious and however honored, are still like man, subject to a stronger power. Indeed, in the epic the gods are chiefly conspicuous by reason of their impotence to intervene in the affairs of men; with the exception of Viṣṇu they can merely applaud the combatants and cannot aid or succor them, in strange contrast with the gods of Homer. There are real gods, however, as well as phantoms. . . . Such in essence is the attitude of the epic to the Vedic gods, who appear as feeble creatures, unable to overpower the *asuras* or to effect their purpose of winning immortality by the use of the *amṛta* (ambrosia) until aided by Śiva and Viṣṇu."[5]

[4] Keith, *Indian Mythology*, p. 5.
[5] *Ib.*, pp. 105-107.

Disease in Vedic literature.

References to disease, its origin and treatment, to the rites of sacrifice to induce the gods to protect the body and its several parts, to cure sickness, and to bestow health and long life, are found scattered through Vedic literature. Those contained in the Rigveda, the Yajurveda, and the Atharvaveda are representative, and the chief sources of information for the study of the ancient Indian views of disease and methods of healing, but passages in the *Brāhmaṇas*, the *Upaniṣads*, the *Sūtras*, and the epics, furnish many instructive examples.

Disease in the Rigveda.

In the Rigveda there is little mention of disease as such. Several diseases are named; *yakṣma* (disease in general or phthisis) in X, lxxxv, 31, 97; *hṛdyota* (heart disease) in I, xxiv, 8; *vandana* (? exanthema) in VII, i, 2; *apvā* (dysentery ?) in X, cii, 12; and *hariman* (jaundice and heart disease) in I, i, 11-12. The acts of the gods as physicians are related, and freedom from disease in response to invocations is granted, the disease sometimes being the result of sin committed (I, xxiv, 9). The healing powers of water are emphasized (I, xxiii, 16-24), and the successful use of amulets and charms to relieve the sick (X, clxi; X, lvii-lx; X, lxiii), and against poison (VII, 1) are described.

Disease in the Yajurveda.

In the *Vājasaneyi Saṁhitā* text of the Yajurveda a few other diseases are mentioned: *arśas* (hemorrhoids) in xii, 97; *arman* (disease of the eye) in xxx, 11; skin disease in xxx, 20; and *kilāsa* (leprosy) in xxx, 17. The gods hold similar relations to illness as those referred to in the Rigveda, their healing acts are noted, and collections of *mantras* for ceremonies connected with disease are given.

Disease in the Atharvaveda.

The principal source of our knowledge of ancient Indian medicine is the fourth Veda, the Atharva, as here the earliest medical book of India. Here the coarser anatomy is given. Many diseases are named, and among them: *jalodara* (dropsy), referred to in I, x; VI, xxii-xxiv, xcvi; *apachit* (sores or pustules) in VI, xxv; *akṣata* (tumors) in VI, xxv, lvii; VII, lxxiv, 1-2; *takman* (fever) in I, xxv; V, xxii; VI, xx; *vidradha* (abscess) in VI, cxxvii; *pakṣahata* (paralysis) in *Kauśika Sūtra*, xxxi, 18; *kās* or *kāsa* (cough) in I, xii, 3; V, xxii, 10-12; *balāsa* (consumption) in VI, xiv, 2; IV, ix, 8; VI, cxxvii; XIX, xxxiv, 10; and *apasmāra* (epilepsy) in *Kauś.*, xxvi, 14-21. Disease is popularly ascribed to some supernatural power, generally to one of the host of demons by which man believed he was surrounded. Methods of treatment by remedies, water and herbs especially, and magico-religious ceremonies for the control of demons are indicated.[6] More than one hundred hymns and parts of hymns intended for appeal to the gods for the cure of illness, with sacrifices, incantations, remedies, magic formulas and charms are given with much detail in the Atharvan *Saṁhitās*.[7] The practices with which these are to be accompanied are found in the *bhaiṣajya* chapters (xxv-xxxii) of the *Kauśika Sūtra*. The difference between the Rigveda and the Atharvaveda is not of time or medical progress, but rather the attitude of the priest or physician in liberality in the use of the resources of the other. The more practical and later medicine was supernaturally revealed by Brahmā and Indra (see Dhanvantari). This is found in

[6] See, for a general survey of disease and medicine in the Vedic period, Zimmer, *Altindisches Leben*, pp. 374-399; and for the whole subject, see J. Jolly, "Medicin," in *GIPA*, III, x, 1901.

[7] See, in general, M. Bloomfield, "The Atharvaveda," in *ib.*, III; B. 1899, pp. 58-83.

the *Charaka Saṁhitā,* alleged to have been written by
Charaka, the Hindu Hippokrates (first century A.D.),
under inspiration, and the Yajurvedas, as 'after-Vedas'
(*upavedas*) of the Atharvaveda, composed by Suśruta
(not later than the fourth century A.D.) from divine
dictation.[8]

Ancient Indian views on disease.

Disease was therefore, in the view of the ancient Indians, the result of an attack or of possession, direct or
indirect, by an evil spirit or demon, or a punishment for
sin. Indirectly it might come from the curse of an enemy,
the evil eye, or magic practices, or by transference from
another person or sorcerer. After the Hindus had accepted the doctrine of the transmigration of souls, disease
and infirmities were traced to sins or offenses committed
in a previous existence by a 'ripening of deeds' (*karma-
vipāka*) (*Viṣṇu Sūtra,* xlv). The demons of disease are
generally vague in outline and indefinite in number, and
are known as *rākṣas* ('injurer'), *atrin* ('eater'), *piśāchas,
kaṇva* (the latter two of unknown meaning), and the like.
Takman (fever), a demon, 'king of diseases,' was flatter-
ingly implored to leave the body and was threatened with
annihilation if he should not choose to do so. Śītalā (the
'Cool Lady,' with an euphemistic allusion to the burning
fever) was smallpox; mania, a possession by *bhūtas,* or
ghosts; and epilepsy was the result of possession by a
dog-demon. Convulsions were due to Grāhī, a she-demon,
'she who seizes' (Atharva., II, ix, 1; II, x, 6; III, xi, 1).
Jambha ('Crusher'), a godling, seized children and
caused convulsions and trismus (*Kauś.,* xxxii, 1-2). Apvā
(dysentery?) was a disease-demon (Atharva., III, ii, 5),
a goddess of impurity who was invoked to crush enemies
(*ib.,* IX, viii, 9).

[8] Jolly, *op. cit.,* pp. 11-13; also Macdonell, *The History of Sanskrit
Literature,* pp. 435-436.

Deity and disease.

In theory the deities were the benevolent patrons and natural protectors of mankind; and when misfortune befell them, the people looked to the divinities for relief. Disease was one of the calamities and throughout the term of his existence man prayed urgently and passionately that the gods should exercise their functions for protection, healing, and long life. Nevertheless, neither the Vedic nor the Hindu pantheon developed a divine healer of preëminence who devoted himself to the people. Dhanvantari was the only real divinity of this type, and he was a pale, shadowy personality, practically unknown, having no following and arising at a late period when medicine was about to emerge from its sacerdotal seclusion. The Aśvins were highly skilled, but exercised their healing functions sporadically and were not depended upon by the people.

Invocation of the gods.

The miraculous cures wrought by the gods are related in the Rigveda, the Atharvaveda, in the legends and myths of the epics and in classical literature. The hymns and prayers of the Vedas and the later liturgical texts of the *Brāhmaṇas,* in connection with the rites, formulas, and charms of the Atharvaveda indicate the methods of appeal to the gods. Each deity addressed was extolled in extravagant terms as the highest and most powerful, irrespective of all others.[9] The divinities, although anthropomorphic, were not clearly defined and individualized. Whatever their original character as portrayed in the Vedas and myths, they became indefinite in outline and their personalities became confused. Gods originally representing diverse phenomena and forces of nature,

[9] For the real meaning of this type of exaltation, see E. W. Hopkins, "Henotheism in the Rig-Veda," in *CSHD,* pp. 75-83.

upon which the welfare of mankind depended came to have common attributes. They were syncretized, grouped, and called by name, while their older, distinctive characteristics were forgotten. Many of the deities had possessed (and some still possessed) the power of assisting mankind in some manner. Their blessings had long been enjoyed by man, but now they had ceased their activity, or, if they continued to manifest their energy, they performed their functions with an aloofness that was not conducive to an intimate, sympathetic relation. They were remembered in the Vedic hymns, the myths, and the epics, but they were no longer concerned with the ordinary affairs of life and dwelt in eternal calm, indifferent to man's misfortunes. The rituals and magic employed by the priests acquired, in the belief of the people, a potency and efficacy apart from the gods; and the priests themselves were considered to have spiritual power over both gods and demons. The functions of the Vedic divinities were further blurred by the greater reliance which the people came to place on the Grāmadevātas, the tribal and village deities who were in close touch with their daily interests, and to whom they paid honor by devout household rites of sacrifice, purification by fire to drive away the evil spirits that infested the home, and other elaborate rites.

Appeals to demons.

The less intelligent classes retained their traditional, primitive animistic beliefs. The fear of spirits of evil oppressed them and overshadowed their respect and confidence in the gods, whom they regarded as indifferent to the calamities brought upon them by the 'non-gods' or demons. Instead of supplicating the deities, they sought to propitiate, appease, and gain the favor of the 'non-gods,' and especially of the *asuras, dānavas, daityas,* and *rākṣasas,* superhuman beings hostile to the gods and to all the powers of nature. This worship developed into a cult which was widely recognized and practiced, quite apart from, and independent of, the orthodox religion, though occasionally mingled with it. In this system the godlings of disease were worshipped, blood sacrifices were made, and food, honey, milk, fruits, and flowers were offered. The medium excited himself to a frenzy and, dancing wildly, proclaimed that the malignant spirits had passed out of the patient and had possessed him or an animal. It was, in great part, a shamanistic cult of typical form.

Magico-religious treatment of disease.

Disease and its treatment were, however, still matters of religion, and the gods were appealed to through the medium of the priests, who used prayers and *mantras* ('spells'), sacrifices, the healing waters, purification by fire, and remedies, intermingling charms, amulets, and the arts of magic and sorcery.[10] The priests were concerned merely with the symptoms of disease; diagnosis as now understood was unimportant, and there does not appear to have been any serious attempt to differentiate between diseases. Therefore few diseases are named in the sacred books except in connection with the demons supposed to have caused them, and wherever possible these evil spirits were named in the ceremonies for exorcism. The Atharvan treatment was always magic veneered with religion—a hymn with an oblation or prayers addressed to the gods, to the disease or demon of disease, or to the remedy. If the name of the disease was known, it was used in the order to depart; but often it was not known, and the command was given in general terms, as

[10] G. M. Bolling, "Disease and Medicine (Vedic)," in *ERE* iv, 762-772.

"whatever be thy name, go hence." Ceremonies with sacrifice to propitiate the gods and to gain their favor, or to appease, exorcise, and drive away evil spirits, together with amulets, charms, and incantations, fumigations, purifications by water and fire, and transference of the disease-demon to some other being (usually an animal), were all recognized in the Atharvaveda as effective means of dispelling the causes of disease and bringing about a cure, whether with or without remedies and magic substances, and whether given internally or applied externally.[11] The Atharvan materia medica contained many substances, some of recognized intrinsic virtue, and many more peculiar to the people and their religious beliefs, the efficacy of which did not depend entirely on the remedy but more frequently on the method of preparation and administration, and in connection with magic.

Remedies.

Waters were sacred and are frequently mentioned in the Vedic literature for their healing powers (cf. Āpaḥ). "The waters, verily, are healers, the waters are scatterers of disease, the waters cure all disease" (Atharva., III, vi, 5). They are besought to bestow their remedies, to carry away sin (Rigveda, I, xxiii, 16-24), and are frequently referred to in prayers for long life. They are panaceas (Kauś., xxv, 20) and employed to cure dropsy (ib., xxx, 11-13). Flowing waters, as from the Sindhu (Indus), are "the most skilled of all physicians" (Atharva., VI, xxiv). Waters containing the leavings of offerings are poured on, or sprinkled on, and the patient is given some to drink (Kauś., vii, 26). Plants were the offspring and essence of waters, and many were used for

[11] Bloomfield, op. cit., pp. 58-63; see also Henry, La Magie dans l'Inde antique, pp. 178-210.

their medicinal properties (Atharva., VIII, vii). Hymns
are addressed to them as panaceas that free from calamities, curses, the toils of Varuṇa (dropsy), and every sin
against the gods (*ib.*, VI, xcvi). Next to plants in holiness
were the products of the cow, the butter, the milk, and
even the hair, the cow-dung, and the urine (*jālaṣa*).[12]
Pieces of earth were used as remedies, and the earth
from a mole-hill was given for constipation (*Kauś.*, xxv,
11).

Magic and magical remedies.

In the Vedic religion man sought by hymns, prayers,
and sacrifice to gain the favor of the gods and lesser
divinities, and thereby to receive benefits according to his
desires. He also sought by magic, its 'spells' and rituals,
to constrain supernatural beings and influence, or control, the course of events according to his will. The tone
of the earliest Vedic literature is eminently religious, the
Rigveda consisting, in very large part, of hymns addressed to the gods in praise and for general welfare, for
the use of the priests, and contains only a few that are
concerned with magic. The subject-matter of the Atharvaveda, on the other hand, represents the popular side of
religion and is essentially magic, consisting of a collection of metrical 'spells' to aid the magician and to injure
his enemies. The later literature, dealing with the humbler aspects of life, shows that the domestic observances
of daily life were saturated with magic beliefs and
practices. The religious forms were propitiatory or persuasive in character. The magical were coercive, and in
practice both elements were blended.[13] Remedies were conceived as having magical powers to cure disease and were
given in connection with *mantras*—spoken charms, or

[12] M. Bloomfield, "On Jālaṣah, Jalāṣabheṣajaḥ, Jalāṣam and Jālāṣam," in *AJP*, 1891, xii, 425-429.
[13] A. A. Macdonell, "Magic (Vedic)," in *ERE* viii, 311.

'spells'in metrical form, as hymns and prayers addressed to the gods. Many of the Atharvan ceremonies were exorcistic in character (*Kauś.*, xxv, 22-36). Many substances were believed to have magical powers when brought in contact with the patient, by inhalation or fumigation, as the smoke from burning wood for expelling demons (*ib.*, xxv, 23; xxxi, 19, 22), and for worms (*ib.*, xxvii, 17, 20). Cure of disease is effected by the laying-on of hands in connection with expelling hymns (*ib.*, xxvi, 6; xxxii, 18), and a ring of magic powder is drawn around the house to prevent the return of the demon (*ib.*, xxviii, 11). A trap appears to be laid for the demon by making an offering in a fire surrounded by a ditch containing hot water (*ib.*, xxxi, 3). Poison is driven out by rubbing the patient from head to foot (*ib.*, xxxii, 23). External applications, as of ointments, must be made downward to drive the trouble where it will do the least harm, and finally out of the feet (Rigveda, X, lx, 11-12). Diseases are charmed forth (Atharva., IX, viii). Amulets were 'god-born,' and many substances were worn, as of the vegetable kingdom, metals, stones, strings, and knots, to ward off evil influences from the person.[14] "Indra placed thee [a plant] upon his arm in order to overcome the *asuras*" (*ib.*, II, xxvii, 3). Amulets are worn against disease in general (*Kauś.*, xxvi, 37); for the cure of excessive discharges (*ib.*, xxv, 6); for *kṣetriya* (chronic or hereditary disease) (*ib.*, xxvi, 43); for constipation or retention of urine (*ib.*, xxv, 10); and for diseases conceived as due to possession by demons (*ib.*, xxvii, 5). Man is released from demons by an amulet of ten kinds of holy wood (Atharva., II, ix, 1). Demons are slain by amulets (*Kauś.*, xlii, 23); sorcery is repelled (*ib.*, xxxix, 1); and triumph is gained over human enemies (*ib.*, xlviii, 3). Gold worn as an amulet confers longevity (Atharva., XIX, xxvi, 1). Charms

---

[14] G. M. Bolling, "Charms and Amulets (Vedic)," in *ERE* iii, 470.

against disease are also mentioned in the Rigveda (X, lvii-lx, clxi, clxiii), and against poisons (*ib.,* VII, 1).

Physicians.

Physicians were recognized as constituting a profession (*Vājasaneyi Saṁhitā,* xxx, 10), and the Atharvaveda recognizes physicians as well as priests as agents for the ceremonial cure of disease (e.g., V, xxix, 1; VI, xxiv, 2; VIII, vii, 26). Under the Brāhmans, a certain number of priests pledged themselves to the exclusive study of healing and formed a second brotherhood, ranking below the sages, who were occupied solely with metaphysics and theology. Later, the *kṣatriyas* ('warriors') devoted themselves to medicine, and shortly thereafter the profession of healing declined in rank to the castes of *vaiśyas* (merchants, etc.) and *śūdras* (conquered races). All these acted as, and assumed to be, physician-priests practicing theurgic medicine with ceremonies and sacrifices, magic arts and sorcery, and often descending to shamanism.[15] These classes came to be despised by the priests and warriors and they were excluded from all ceremonies sacred to the manes and to the gods. According to the *Taittirīya Saṁhitā* (VI, iv, 9³), "a Brāhman must not perform healing," this prohibition being due, at least in part, to the defilement of his caste by being brought into contact with all sorts of men (*Maitrāyaṇi·Saṁhitā,* IV, vi, 2), and for this reason the Aśvins were excluded from the sacrifice. Offerings presented to a Brāhman acting as a physician became pus and blood (*Mahābhārata,* XIII, xc, 14). So, too, a physician must be avoided at a sacrifice (Manu, iii, 152) and must not be invited to one (*Vasiṣṭha Dharma Sūtra,* lxxxii, 9); neither may his food be eaten (*Āpastamba Dharma Sūtra,* I, vi, 18²¹; xix¹⁵).

[15] Bruzon, *La Médecine et les religions,* p. 13; also Macdonell and Keith, *Vedic Index of Names and Subjects,* ii, 104-106.

Neither Buddhist nor Jain monks may be physicians (*Uttarādhyayana*, xv, 8; *Aṭṭhakavajja*, xiv, 13; *Tevijja Sutta*, ii, 7).

PART II: THE HEALING DEITIES[16]

IT has been seen that the ancient gods of the Indians were not strictly specialized. The function of healing pertained to a number of deities who are mentioned in the hymns and the epics as physicians, but (with the possible exception of Dhanvantari) as an incident to their more important duties of directing the various forces of nature. They appear as working cures in a detached and sporadic fashion rather than as a matter of devotion to the sick and suffering. The chief Indian deities who are mentioned in the Vedic hymns, the epics, and the myths, as exercising their divine powers for the healing of mankind, though not healers in the larger, specific sense, are the following:[17]

The Ādityas	Bṛhaspati	Sarasvatī
Agni	Dakṣa	Savitṛ
Āpaḥ	Dhanvantari	Soma
The Aśvins	Dhātṛ	Sūrya
Bhaiṣajyarājā, and	Indra	Tvaṣṭṛ
Bhaiṣajyaguru	The Maruts	Varuṇa
Brahmā	Rudra	Vāta, or Vāyu

[16] For additional information and Vedic references to the healing deities of ancient India, see Mukhopādhyāya, *History of Indian Medicine*.

[17] Several other deities of minor rank are mentioned in the Vedas in connection with medicine, and ancient sages, often referred to as divine, are referred to in Indian literature. Rākā, Sinīvālī, Guṅgu, and Anumati were goddesses associated with procreation and child-birth (Rigveda, II, xxxii, 6-8; X, clxxxiv, 2). Other references to Anumati will be found in Muir, *Original Sanskrit Texts*, v, 346, 398. Trita Āptya is

THE ĀDITYAS

THE ĀDITYAS were a group of deities who varied widely, not only in number (sometimes three, six, seven, eight, or twelve), but also in name (Mitra, Aryaman, Bhaga, Varuṇa, Dakṣa, and Aṁśa; or Mitra, Varuṇa, Aryaman, Aṁśa, Bhaga, Dhātṛ, Indra, and Vivasvant, etc.). Their appellation shows that they were 'children of Aditi' (the 'Boundless One'), and some of them are solar deities (e.g., Mitra) or sky-gods (e.g., Varuṇa). They are many-eyed, and sleepless; they are blameless, pure, and holy. They see what is good and evil in men's hearts and distinguish the honest from the deceitful. From Varuṇa they have received the moral duty of punishing sin and rewarding virtue. They bestow light, long life, offspring, and guidance; and are celestial deities who ward off sickness and distress (Rigveda, VIII, xviii, 10), though the reference to the latter function is only of the most general character.[18]

AGNI

AGNI ('Fire') was one of the great original deities of the Rigveda, just as fire was a principal divinity of other Indo-European peoples—Iranians, Greeks, Latins, and Balto-Slavs. In later speculation Agni symbolizes the immaterial fire of divine intelligence and is the conservator of the world. He is the divinity of sacrificial fire, Gṛhapati, the 'lord of the home,' the 'closest friend,' whom the people keep always at their hearth-side. He is the god of priests and the priest of the gods. He changes his form at will, and one of his great deeds was to burn the rākṣasas who infested the sacrifice. He inspires men

referred to as a divine healer (Keith, op. cit., p. 56) but the authority for this statement is not entirely reliable. Bharādvāja and Ātreya are examples of ancient sages reverenced as divine.

[18] A. A. Macdonell, "Vedic Mythology," in GIPA, 1897, pp. 43-45; also Bergaigne, La Religion védique, iii, 98-110.

and protects them from evil (Rigveda, I, lxxxix). In the Atharvaveda, he is the divine 'physician, a maker of remedies' (V, xxix, 1), who is invoked to restore to the sick man the flesh eaten away by the *piśāchas* (*vv.* 4-5, 12-13). He burns away the poison of snakes just as in the Vedas he burns goblins (*ib.*, VII, 1), and he is invoked to give relief in insanity (Atharva., VI, cxi). The invocation to the fire-god for snake bites and skin disease (? cancer) is suggestive of the possible use of the actual cautery. The principal Agni sacrificial rite against possession by demons was the burning of fragrant substances and fumigation. Agni is invoked in prayer chiefly to protect the body, the sight (*Vājasaneyi Saṁhitā*, iii, 17), the hearing, to quicken the mind and prolong life (Atharva., III, xi, 4), and his healing functions occupy a relatively unimportant place in the myths told concerning him.[19]

ĀPAḤ

ĀPAḤ represented the 'Waters,' divine mothers who abide on high, cleanse from moral guilt and purify. They are remedial, they grant remedies for healing, long life, and immortality (Rigveda, I, xxiii, 19-21; VI, 1, 7; X, ix, 5-7), and in the house they watch over man's health (*Hiraṇyakesi Gṛhya Sūtra*, II, iv, 5). In the Atharvaveda they are besought for procreative vigor (I, v, 3); they heal heart-burn (VI, xxiv, 1); they bring health and medicine, drive disease away, and cure all maladies (VI, xci, 3; cf. III, vii, 5); they are better healers than physicians (XIX, ii, 3). Likewise, in the White Yajurveda, they contain healing medicine (ix, 6), and are besought to flow with health and strength for their worshippers (xxxvi, 12).[20]

[19] Macdonell, *op. cit.*, pp. 88-100; Bergaigne, *op. cit.*, i, 11-148; Hopkins, *Epic Mythology*, pp. 97-107; Muir, *op. cit.*, v, 199-223.

[20] Macdonell, *op. cit.*, pp. 85-86.

THE AŚVINS

In the Vedic pantheon the Aśvins ('Horsemen') are the twin sons of the sun,[21] or of the sky, of the heavens, of the ocean, or of the universality of created things, and occupy a prominent place in the Rigveda. They are the personification of the twilight that precedes the dawn, or of the morning and evening twilight; they are celestial horsemen who ride in a shining, honey-hued car, swifter than thought, and announce the coming day or the approach of evening. They are ever young and beautiful, their skin is filled with honey, and they can change their form at will. They are the Indian counterparts of the Greek Dioskouroi (Kastor and Polydeukes) and reappear in Baltic myth. They possess profound wisdom, and as the guardians of immortality ward off death. They are invariably beneficent and merciful, succoring those in distress or in peril. They are extraordinary surgeons of great renown, and many legendary tales are told of their marvellous, even miraculous, deeds. In the *Brahmāṇas* and *Purāṇas* the Aśvins lose their cosmic character. They are still beautiful youths and physicians, but new myths are developed concerning them, so that they appear in a somewhat different light and have other names, Nāsatya ('True') and Dasra.

The Aśvins are the 'physicians of the gods' (Rigveda, VIII, xviii, 8), and they restore sight and cure the sick and maimed (*ib.*, I, cxvi, 16; X, xxxix, 3). At the prayer of the she-wolf, they restored the sight of Rijrāśva, who had been blinded by his father because he had killed one hundred and one sheep and had given them to the she-wolf (*ib.*, I, cxvi, 16; cxvii, 17-18). They restored the sight of Upamanyu after he had fallen into a well (*Mahābhārata,* I, iii, 33-77). They cured Parāvṛj of both blindness

---

[21] Or Bhāskara, considered as the fountain head of all knowledge in medicine (Mukhopādhyāya, *op. cit.,* p. 83).

and lameness (Rigveda, I, cxii, 8).[22] They provided Viś-
palā with an iron leg to replace the one she lost in battle
(*ib.*, I, cxvi, 15). They knew how to replace the head when
cut off (*ib.*, I, cxvii, 22), and they could restore life. They
could make old men young; they protected the aged Kali
so that he took a young wife (*ib.*, X, xxxix, 8). As a boon
to his beautiful wife, they restored her husband, Chyavāna, to youth with all its powers (*ib.*, I, cxvi, 10). Allusions are made to a number of other cures wrought by
them (*ib.*, cxii, cxvi-cxix).

The Aśvins were not in good repute with the other gods
and were shut out from the sacrifice, because they "have
wandered and mixed much among men, performing
cures" (*Śatapatha Brāhmaṇa*, IV, i, 5[13-14]), lowering their
caste. They insisted that the gods should receive them on
a footing of equality, and eventually they regained their
share in the sacrifice. The Aśvins thus shared in the *soma*,
but the special offering made to secure their favor was
surā (a kind of brandy) with honey (*ib.*, IV, i, 5). They
played a part in helping to transmit the Yajurveda, with
its medical knowledge, from the gods to mankind.[23]

BHAIṢAJYARĀJĀ AND BHAIṢAJYAGURU

BHAIṢAJYARĀJĀ (Bhaiṣajyaguru) ('King of Healing'),
in the later Buddhism of the Mahāyāna ('Great Vehicle')
school, is one of the many Bodhisattva Mahāsattvas (potential Buddhas of the highest class), and it is he who
has become the healing god of the Northern Buddhists.

---

[22] The ground for their cures, especially of blindness, is that dawn
brings to light that which has been lost in darkness (Macdonell, *op. cit.*,
p. 51).

[23] Jolly, *op. cit.*, p. 12; Macdonell, *op. cit.*, pp. 49-54; Bergaigne,
op. cit., ii, 431-510; Keith, *op. cit.*, pp. 30-32, 86-87, 141-142; Muir,
op. cit., v, 234-257; also Myriantheus, *Die Aśvins oder arischen Dioskuren*, Munich, 1876.

In Tibet, China and Japan he is replaced by Bhaiṣajya-guru, whose cult became very popular.[24]

BRAHMĀ

BRAHMĀ is the great Hindu god of Indian speculative thought, the chief of a Paurāṇic triad—Brahmā, Viṣṇu, and Śiva. He is the creator of all things, the self-existent, the starting point of the cosmic system which is set in motion by his will. He is the possessor of all power, and of all knowledge and science. He is a lofty, philosophic conception of supreme might and wisdom, and is the author of all; he observes all, but does not concern him-self with the machinery of the universe, nor with the affairs of man, except in a contemplative manner. His functions are vague; he has not impressed the popular imagination, and few temples and altars have been built in his honor. He transmits his infinite wisdom and science to humanity, or permits it to be transmitted, and medi-cine has thus come to man from him (see Dhanvantari). Brahmā is considered a healing deity, but not an active healer; and few personal appeals are made to him. He is a deity who has fallen into obliviscence.[25]

BRHASPATI

IN the Vedas, Bṛhaspati is the father of the gods, the priest above all others, the domestic priest, the 'Lord of Prayer,' the 'Lord of Devotion.' In the *Brāhmaṇas,* he is the 'Lord of Brahmā,' the heavenly prototype of the earthly Brahmā, the impersonation of the powers of devotion. He is golden-colored and ruddy, pure and clear-voiced. He sings chants, and his song goes to heaven. He rides in a car drawn by ruddy steeds. Without him the

[24] *Saddharmapuṇḍarīka;* tr. H. Kern, pp. 376-392; also, *SBE* XXI.
[25] Hopkins, *op. cit.,* pp. 189-198; Keith, *op. cit.,* pp. 107-109.

sacrifice does not succeed. He is Indra's ally against the
asuras, and he is closely allied to Agni, with whom he
appears at times to be identified; and it is possible that
originally he was Agni in his special function of divine
priest. He protects the pious man from dangers, curses,
and malignity. He blesses him with wealth and prosperity. He prolongs life and removes disease (Rigveda,
I, xviii, 2-3). He knows the demons; he wards off fiends;
and destroys the *asuras* (Atharva., X, vi, 22). He is
invoked to aid against sorcerers (*ib.*, I, viii, 2), and to
conquer the poison of serpents (*ib.*, VII, lvi, 5). He is
invoked to cleanse from sin; for life's vigor (*ib.*, II, xxix,
1), and long life (*ib.*, III, xi, 4).[26]

DAKṢA

THE Paurāṇic god Dakṣa is the son of Brahmā and sometimes appears as an Āditya. His name indicates intelligence, ability, competency, and he is regarded as a clever
god. He is credited with creative power and received the
Yajurveda from Brahmā, and helped to transmit it to
mankind.[27]

DHANVANTARI

DHANVANTARI was the chief Indian god of healing, the
physician of the gods, and the Asklepios of India. He
was, however, a deity of minor rank, of late development,
and of a shadowy personality. In what seems to be the
earliest reference to him (*Kauś.*, lxxiv, 6) his sacrifice is
to be made "in the waterholder to Dhanvantari, the
ocean, plants, trees, sky, and earth," which suggests that
he was primarily a deity of healing herbs; and his asso-

[26] Macdonell, *op. cit.*, pp. 101-104; Hopkins, *op. cit.*, pp. 180-181;
Muir, *op. cit.*, v, 272-283.
[27] Jolly, *op. cit.*, p. 12; Macdonell, *op. cit.*, p. 46; Muir, *op. cit.*, v,
48-53.

ciation with water, so often an element of healing, especially in connection with sacred springs, is implied by his origin from the cosmic ocean. The meaning of the name is uncertain, and it has been interpreted as "he who passes through (*tari*) the bow (*dhanvan*)," as "an island in the 'sky-ocean!' " *i.e.* 'a cloud,' and it is suggested that he may have been a cloud or celestial divinity. Dhanvantari is not mentioned in the Vedas, and it may be that he was absorbed by the rain-god Parjanya.[28]

Dhanvantari is a figure in the epics and *Purāṇas;* he is worshipped in the *Sūtras;* and is remembered in the folk-stories of the Punjab of the present day. He lives in the northeast (*Mārkaṇḍeya Purāṇa*, xxix, 17), in which direction sacrifice should be offered to him; as to the gods of the *Agnihotṛ* (Agni-Soma, Indra-Agni, Sky-Earth, the All-Gods, and others), and this oblation (being clarified butter) should be offered at evening and morning (*Mahābhārata*, XIII, xcvii, 12; Manu, iii, 85). His sacrifice is also mentioned in the *Sūtra* literature (*Aśvalayana Gṛhya Sūtra*, I, ii, 1-2; iii, 6; xii, 7; *Gautama Dharma Sūtra*, v, 10; *Mānava Gṛhya Sūtra*, I, xviii, 8; II, xii, 2-3, 19). A Brāhman priest was requisite at such rites. An annual sacrifice of a goat or a sheep must be made to Agni and Dhanvantari; and he was to receive a leaf of a plant named after him.

In the *Mahābhārata* (III, iii, 25) Dhanvantari is an epithet of the sun, who is also a god of healing; and it is likewise one of the one thousand and eight names of Śiva (*ib.*, XIII, xvii, 24). It is doubtful, however, if this identification is of real significance in view of the tendency to identify deities of divergent character, by syncretism and henotheism.

In epic myth (*Mahābhārata*, I, xviii, 39; *Rāmāyaṇa*, I, xlv, 31-33) Dhanvantari, with other desired things, arose

[28] Bergaigne, *op. cit.*, ii, 27-28.

as the result of the churning of the cosmic milk-ocean, holding in his hands a staff and a bowl of *amṛta* (ambrosia, Soma, *q.v.*), "Life-giving draught—longed for by gods and men."[29]

According to the *Purāṇas*, Dhanvantari was the twelfth and thirteenth avatar of Viṣṇu (*Bhāgavata Purāṇa*, I, iii, 1 ff.; ii, 7); and the *Viṣṇu Purāṇa* (IV, viii) makes him incarnate in King Divodāsa of Kāśi (Benares). "He was free from human infirmities and possessed universal knowledge in every incarnation. In the life just previous to his avatar as Dhanvantari, Viṣṇu had conferred upon him the boon of being born a Kṣatriya and of becoming the author of medical science, besides being entitled to a share of the oblations offered to the gods." According to medical tradition (*Suśruta Saṁhitā*, I, ii, 12, 16), "the divine physician Dhanvantari, incarnate as Divodāsa, King of Kāśi, received the Āyur-Veda from Brahmā through the successive mediation of Prajāpati (or Dakṣa), the Aśvins, and Indra, and then taught it to Suśruta and the latter's six colleagues. To Dhanvantari are likewise ascribed the *Dhanvantarinighaṇṭu*, the oldest Indian medical glossary (though not of very ancient date), and a number of minor treatises." Having acquired knowledge of the Āyur-Veda from Bharādvāja, he divided the duties of physicians into eight classes and conferred his lore upon his disciples."[30] Dhanvantari is called 'The Health Bestowing One,' but it is not known that he had any cult following.

It is related that Dhanvantari suffered demotion. An attempt was made to euhemerize him, and from an independent divinity he became an avatar and, finally, an

[29] Moor, *The Hindu Pantheon*, pp. 180-183.

[30] L. H. Gray, "The Indian God Dhanvantari," in *JAOS*, 1922, xlii, 324, 325; also Jolly, *op. cit.*, pp. 12-14.

The following genealogy is given by Mukhopādhyāya (*op. cit.*, Part

earthly king and leech who was mortal. According to a
Punjab legend Dhanvantari died of a bite of a serpent.[31]

DHĀTṚ

DHĀTṚ ('the placer') is a deity of the Hindu pantheon;
an agent-god[32] who occasionally appears as an Āditya; a
creator, a fashioner, a developer, one who puts things in
place; and he is accordingly invoked in cases of fracture
(Atharva., IV, xii, 2). He was likewise a 'departmental'

II, p. 123), based on *Suśruta Samhitā*, i, 1; *Aṣṭāṅgahṛdaya Samhitā*, i,
1; *Bhāvaprakāśa*, i, 1; and *Caraka Samhitā*, i, 1:

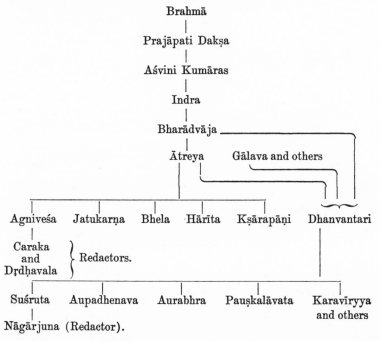

Brahmā

Prajāpati Dakṣa

Aśvini Kumāras

Indra

Bharādvāja

Ātreya   Gālava and others

Agniveśa Jatukarṇa Bhela Hārīta Kṣārapāṇi Dhanvantari

Caraka
and   } Redactors.
Dṛdhavala

Suśruta Aupadhenava Aurabhra Pauṣkalāvata Karavīryya
                                                and others
Nāgārjuna (Redactor).

[31] Temple, *The Legends of the Punjab*, i, 451, 490-492, 494, 499-505,
512; Crooke, *The Popular Religion and Folklore of Northern India*, i,
196; ii, 285.
[32] Macdonell, *op. cit.*, p. 115.

birth-god who ordained procreation, and is thus invoked, with other divinities (Rigveda, X, clxxxiv, 1): "Let Viṣṇu shape the womb; let Tvaṣṭṛ mold the forms; let Prajāpati pour in (the semen); let Dhātṛ place the embryo" (cf. Atharva., V, xxv, 4-5, 10-13).

INDRA

In the Vedas, the great divinity, second only to Agni, is Indra; but in the *Purāṇas*, he ranks after the triad, Brahmā, Viṣṇu, and Śiva. He is the favorite national deity of the Vedic Indians, is closely associated with Agni, is 'lord of a hundred powers,' and is identified with Sūrya (the Sun). He is sometimes styled an independent, a universal ruler, though this title belongs more properly to Varuṇa. He is a warrior-god *par excellence*, and in this capacity he performs his greatest feat, the conquest of the demons of drought and darkness and the killing of Vṛtra, who had impounded the waters, thereby liberating them and winning light for mankind. His weapon is *vajra* (the thunderbolt) (Atharva., VI, ii, 3), and the rainbow is called 'Indra's bow.'

Indra is the most anthropomorphic of all the Hindu deities. He has a thousand eyes and many hands; but he differs from other Vedic gods in their essentially moral character, and his body is covered with eyes (originally *pudenda muliebris*) through Gautama's curse in punishment for adultery with Ahalyā, the wife of the sage. He was addicted to soma, into which he was beguiled by the demon Namuci,[33] and drank it to the detriment of his moral standing. Chyavāna paralyzed his arm when he attempted to prevent the Aśvins from making him young, but this was subsequently relieved by the Aśvins with the assistance of Sarasvatī by the use of an amulet (*Vājasa-*

[33] M. Bloomfield, "The Story of Indra and Namuci," in *JAOS*, [1891]-1893, xv, 143-163.

neyi Samhitā, xix, 80-95). In modern India, Indra is a rain-godling of minor rank.[34]

Indra is a healing deity in a very minor capacity. He cured Apālā of skin disease, and her father of baldness (Rigveda, VIII, lxxx). Indra and Agni are called upon to cure children of worms and they succeeded in slaying those female demons (Atharva., V, xxiii, 1). His physicians have many healing remedies (*Vājasaneyi Samhitā,* xix, 12, 16; xx, 3, 56 ff.). The knowledge of medicine was supernaturally revealed by Indra, who aided in transmitting it to mankind (cf. Dhanvantari).[35]

THE MARUTS

IN the Vedas the Maruts are given a prominent place. They are the storm-gods, the storm-clouds, the storm-winds. They are brothers or sons of Rudra and are identical with the Rudras. They are of the company of 'thrice ten gods,' and are also called the 'hosts of the Maruts,' while their number is given as thrice seven and thrice sixty. "They were born from the laughter of lightning." The brothers are of equal age, have grown up together, and are of one mind; they are self-luminous and golden, of sun-like brightness. They ride in a car which gleams with lightning. They are fierce and terrible, yet playful as children. They make a noise like thunder and are the singers of heaven, while their great exploit is the making of rain. Like Rudra, they have a dual aspect; frequently they are malevolent, and at times they are truly benevolent. They are mentioned together with their father Rudra (*q.v.*), as possessing pure and beneficent remedies (Rigveda, II, xxxiii, 13; VII, xxxv, 6) which they bring from afar, from the rivers of Sindhu and Asiknī, the sea

[34] Crooke, *op. cit.,* i, 66, 73, 77.

[35] Macdonell, *op. cit.,* pp. 54-66; Bergaigne, *op. cit.,* pp. 159-196; Hopkins, *op. cit.,* pp. 122-141.

(*i.e.,* cloud-ocean), and the mountains; and these they bestow like rain (*ib.,* VIII, xx, 23-26).[36]

RUDRA

In the Vedic pantheon, Rudra is the storm-deity, the 'Howler,' the 'Roarer,' the 'terrible god of storms.' From the *Brāhmaṇas* on, he is identified with Śiva and is called Rudra-Śiva. He bears the name Tryambaka, as being born of three mothers; and is the father of the Rudras, or Maruts (*q.v.*). He shines like a brilliant sun and rides in a dazzling car; he wears a wonderful necklace and in his hands holds bows and arrows and the thunderbolt; his lightning shafts descend upon the earth and bring disease and death to men and cattle. He is fierce and strong, a terrible deity whose anger is feared; and he is implored to restrain his wrath. He has a dual aspect. He is malevolent, a cheat, a robber, and a deceiver; but he is also intelligent, wise, beneficent, and the master of purifying winds which drive away miasms and other poisons from the atmosphere. His arrows and spear were reputed to bring disease and sharp pains (? colic) and Rudra's 'dart' (*śūla*) is invoked (*Kauś.,* xxxi, 7). In his hands he holds the fairest remedies (Rigveda, I, cxiv, 5), a thousand remedies (*ib.,* VII, xlvi, 3) for illness, with which he is implored to remove (Atharva., XIX, x, 6) all disease from man and beast and to make them sound and well (*ib.,* I, xliii,6; cxiv,1). He has a potent remedy called *jālaṣa,* which was probably his urine (*i.e.,* rain) (*ib.,* VI, lvii, 2), though according to a late interpretation it was cow's urine (*ib.,* II, xxvii, 6). Vāyu or Vāta is associated with him. Rudra is a 'divine physician' (White Yajurveda, xvi, 5), the 'physician of physicians' (Rigveda, II,

[36] Macdonell, *op. cit.,* pp. 77-81; Bergaigne, *op. cit.,* ii, 369-402; Hopkins, *op. cit.,* pp. 169-170; Keith, *op. cit.,* pp. 39-40; Muir, *op. cit.,* v, 147-154.

xxxiii, 4), and his hand is restorative and healing (*ib.,* II, xxxiii, 7). He is lord of all remedies (*ib.,* V, xlii, 11) and bestows them (*ib.,* II, xxxjii, 12), so that he is besought by his worshippers to avert suffering from their children (*ib.,* VII, xlvi, 2). His healing functions are also appealed to for a wound or bruise (Atharva., VI, lvii), and his curing aid is invoked with Soma's (*ib.,* VII, xlii).[37]

SARASVATĪ

In the Rigveda, Sarasvatī is the goddess of rivers and is spoken of in connection with Agni and Savitṛ. In the *Brāhmaṇas,* she is the goddess of eloquence and wisdom. Sarasvatī assisted the Aśvins in restoring to Indra the vigor he had lost (White Yajurveda, xix, 12), she is associated with deities who assist procreation and bestow wealth, progeny, and immortality (Rigveda, II, xli, 17; X, xxx, 12; clxxxiv, 2; Atharva., V, xxv, 3).[38]

SAVITṚ

In the Rigveda, Savitṛ ('Stimulator') is a form of the sun-god, personifying the divine power of the sun. He alone is 'lord of vivifying power,' the exciter of all motion and activity. To him is attributed mighty splendor, and he goes in a golden car, seeing all creatures. The 'golden-handed Savitṛ' moves between heaven and earth; he sets the sun in motion. He is a divine physician who drives away disease (Rigveda, I, xxxv, 9) and removes it (*ib.,* X, c, 8); and he bestows long life on man (*ib.,* IV, liv, 2). In modern science he would represent heliotherapy.[39]

[37] Macdonell, *op. cit.,* pp. 74-77; Bergaigne, *op. cit.,* iii, 31-38; Keith, *op. cit.,* pp. 38, 82-83; Muir, *op. cit.,* iv, 299-320.

[38] Macdonell, *op. cit.,* pp. 86-88; also Bergaigne, *op. cit.,* i, 325-328; Muir, *op. cit.,* v, 337-343.

[39] Macdonell, *op. cit.,* pp. 32-35; Bergaigne, *op. cit.,* iii, 38-64; Muir, *op. cit.,* v, 162-170.

SOMA

Soma ('Pressed Juice'), a Vedic deity to whom the
whole of the ninth book of the Rigveda is devoted, is
identical with the Avestan Haoma (*q.v.*), and the sacrifice to him forms the main feature of the ritual of the
Rigveda. He was a drink made from a plant which cannot
be identified with any known existing species, and whose
abode was on the top of the mountains, whence it was
brought to Indra by an eagle. The juice was pressed from
the young shoots of the plant, and being filtered and
mixed with milk, sour milk, honey, or barley water,
became soma (or *amṛta*), the celestial nectar of the gods,
loved by gods and men, which gave immortality to those
who drank it. The juice, of a ruddy, brown color, flowed
with the speed of lightning and gave out a sound like
thunder. It was exhilarating and caused ecstasy of feeling, its deification probably being due to these qualities.
Most of the great and successful feats of the gods were
performed under its influence, with the strength and
courage it gave them. Soma is called the celestial child,
born of the sun and sky, bird of heaven, lord of plants,
king of the gods and mortals, king of the whole earth. He
was a healing deity. He was medicine for the sick, healed
whatever was sick (Rigveda, VIII, lxi, 17), and made the
blind to see and the lame to walk (*ib.*, VIII, lxviii, 2; X,
xxv, 11). He was the guardian of men's bodies (*ib.*, VIII,
xlviii, 9), bestowing length of life in this world (*ib.*, I, xci,
6; VIII, xlviii, 4, 7; IX, iv, 6; xci, 6). He rendered poisons
powerless (Atharva., IV, 6). He gave light, granted blessings, slew demons, dispelled sin from the heart, and promoted truth.

In post-Vedic literature (and perhaps in the late Vedic
period), Soma is connected with the moon and becomes a
lunar deity.

According to the epic and *Purāṇas,* Soma at one time

CHURNING THE OCEAN OF MILK
FOR THE *AMṚTA*

*Reproduced from "The Mythology of All Races," by
permission of Marshall Jones Company, Boston.*

was lost in the flood with many other precious things, and both gods and demons desired it. The deities consulted Viṣṇu, since without it they had been waning in power, so that the demons were gaining the advantage in their conflicts. Viṣṇu advised that the ocean of milk should be churned, and to assist he became incarnate as a tortoise (the second Great Avatar). After prolonged churning by means of the mountain Mandara, which was poised on the tortoise, and around which the cosmic serpent, Vasoky, was wrapped and pulled from either end by gods and demons, Dhanvantari (*q.v.*), the physician of the gods, appeared bearing the cup of *amṛta*. This delighted both gods and demons, but the former finally gained the *amṛta* and thereby acquired sufficient strength to drive their enemies, the demons, to their underground abode. In this myth, the celestial origin of Soma from the sky-ocean is obvious.[40]

SŪRYA

SŪRYA, one of the early Vedic divinities of the sun, whose name is etymologically connected with the Greek "Ἥλιος, is the most concrete of the Indian solar deities, and in India absorbs the function of the special sun-gods, such as Savitṛ (*q.v.*). Although he became a faded deity, according to the *Brāhmaṇas*, his worship continued under the name of Sūraj. In the Rigveda, he drives away disease and evil dreams (X, xxxvii, 4). In the Atharvaveda (I, xxii; cf. Rigveda, I, l, 11), he is invoked to cure heartburn and jaundice, and to bring back the ruddy hue of health; he is besought to heal pustules (Atharva., VI, lxxxiii, 1); indirectly he cures cough (*ib.*, VII, cvii); and he is entreated for clear vision (*ib.*, XIX, xliii, 3).[41]

[40] Macdonell, *op. cit.*, pp. 104-115; Bergaigne, *op. cit.*, i, 148-225; Keith, *op. cit.*, pp. 46-48, 90-91, 136-137; Spiegel, *Die arische Periode und ihre Zustände*, pp. 168-178; Muir, *op. cit.*, ii, 469; v, 258-271.

[41] Quackenbos, *The Sanskrit Poems of Mayūra*, no. 32.

There was in ancient India a widespread cult of the sun, and the Sauras, as his worshippers were called, formed one of the great sects of early Hinduism, especially in the north. The Iranians later exercised much influence on this sect. To this latter source is probably due the tradition associated with the Sanskrit poet Mayūra (presumably of the first half of the seventh century A.D.), who, afflicted with leprosy, was healed by Sūrya, in whose honor he then composed his *Sūryaśataka* ("Hundred Verses in praise of the Sun").[42] In like manner, Samba was cured of leprosy by Sūrya;[43] and the tradition is doubtless to be connected with the old Persian belief (Herodotos, i, 138) that leprosy and white leprosy were in punishment for sin against the sun. According to the *Sūryaśataka* (No. 101), the sun not only gives freedom from disease, but he alone makes anew and cures those who, because long rank with multitude of sins, have shriveled noses, feet, and hands, whose limbs are ulcerous, and who make gurgling, indistinct noises (No. 6).[44]

TVAṢṬṚ

TVAṢṬṚ is an obscure member of the Vedic pantheon of very feeble personality. As his name implies, he is a fashioner, a cunning artificer, a divine artifex who is concerned in the repair of man's body (*Vājasaneyi Samhitā*, xxxviii, 9). Once (Atharva., VI, liii, 3) he is entreated to "smooth down what of our body is torn apart," and he is invoked for long life (*ib.*, VI, lxxviii, 3). He formed the germ in the womb following impregnation (*ib.*, V, xxv, 5), and was, therefore, believed to preside

---

[42] Quackenbos, *op. cit.*, pp. 23-32, 34-37.

[43] *Ib.*, pp. 35-37.

[44] Cf. *ib.*, pp. 114-115; Macdonell, *op. cit.*, pp. 30-32; Hopkins, *op. cit.*, pp. 83-89; Keith, *op. cit.*, pp. 26, 86, 138-139, 183-184; Muir, *op. cit.*, v, 155-161.

over generation and to bestow offspring (Rigveda, III, iv, 9; Atharva., II, xxix, 2).[45]

VARUNA

VARUNA is one of the oldest deities of the Vedas, where he ranks only second to Indra (*q.v.*); and in many respects his position is comparable with that of Zeus in the Greek pantheon. He is closely related, at least in function, to the Iranian Ahura Mazda. He is 'lord over all,' 'lord of the all-embracing-circle of the heavens, earth and sea,' 'lord of both gods and men,' 'King of Waters,' and 'lord of the Ocean.' In the oldest strata of the Rigveda he has been regarded as lord of light, both by day and by night, but later he is, rather, lord of the sky by night. On the other hand, he is closely associated with water. In the Atharvaveda he is only a lord of waters, and it is conjectured that primarily he was a god of the celestial river— *i.e.*, of the Milky Way. He is closely associated with Mitra, a sun-god. His abode is in the sky, in a golden mansion in which he sits looking on all deeds and to which he mounts in his shining car. He is the upholder of physical and moral order; he punishes sin and rewards virtue. He is the guardian of immortality (Rigveda, VIII, xlii, 2), and he can take away life or prolong it (*ib.*, I, xxiv, 11; xxv, 12; VII, lxxxviii, 4; lxxxix, 1). He is a 'healing seer' (*ib.*, I, xxiv, 8, 11); "Thy remedies, O King!.are a hundred, a thousand" (*ib.*, I, xxiv, 9). As a moral governor and lord of the waters he sends dropsy in punishment for sin and especially for falsehood (*ib.*, VII, lxxxix), and he is repeatedly besought to loose from the fetters with which he has bound the offender (*ib.*, I, xxiv, 15; xxv, 21; V, lxxxv, 8; VI, lxxiv, 4; Atharva., I, x). In the Atharvaveda (I, xxv, 3) in punishment for sin he sends fever;

[45] Macdonell, *op. cit.*, pp. 116-118; also Bergaigne, *op. cit.*, iii, 38-64; Hillebrandt, *Vedische Mythologie*, i, 513-535.

especially dropsy (*ib.*, IV, xvi, 7); and he is invoked to relieve from dropsy, evil dreams, and misfortune (*ib.*, VII, lxxxiii); but in the White Yajurveda he is a physician (xxviii, 34) and lord of physicians (xxi, 40); while one who performs the rite in honor of his ancestors under Varuṇa's constellation Śatabhiṣaj ('Hundred-Remedies') will become a successful physician (*Mahābhārata*, XIII, lxxxix, 12).[46]

VĀTA, OR VĀYU

VĀTA, or Vāyu, is a Vedic deity of air and winds, a companion of Indra, and as a soma-drinker is second only to him. He is also associated with Rudra. He rides in a car which is drawn by ninety-nine, or sometimes one thousand, horses. He rushes through the air and never rests. His roaring is heard, but he is never seen. He is the breath of the gods, and in his flight he wafts healing and blessings upon mankind (Rigveda, X, clxxxvi), this power being doubtless representative of the purifying nature of wind (Atharva., III, xxxi, 2). He bestows vital breath (*ib.*, XIX, xliii, 2); and in the White Yajurveda (xx, 15) he is besought to free from all distress.[47]

[46] Macdonell, *op. cit.*, pp. 22-29; Hopkins, *op. cit.*, pp. 116-122; Bergaigne, *op. cit.*, iii, 110-149; Hillebrandt, *op. cit.*, iii, 3-76; Muir, *op. cit.*, v, 58-76 d.

[47] Macdonell, *op. cit.*, pp. 81-83; Keith, *op. cit.*, p. 37; Bergaigne, *op. cit.*, i, 24-28; Hillebrandt, *op. cit.*, iii, 326-331.

CHAPTER FIVE
IRANIAN GODS

CHAPTER FIVE

THE HEALING GODS OF ANCIENT IRAN

PART I: GENERAL SURVEY

IN ancient Iran, medical doctrines and practices were
determined by the sacred books and were under the
direction and control of the priests, acting as physicians.

Iranian religion. The Avesta.

The Iranian religion, which, as reformed by Zoroaster,
was conceived on a highly moral and elevated plane, prevailed in the land from an early period; but of its holy
texts, the Avesta, only about one third has survived to
form the scriptures of the Parsis of India and of their
co-religionists, the Gebers, in Persia. Originally inscribed
with golden ink on thousands of cow-hides, it was reli-
giously guarded in the 'Stronghold of Records'; but a
large part is traditionally said to have been destroyed
during the invasion of Alexander the Great, so that the
Avesta, as it exists today, is a reconstruction dating from
the reign of Shāpūr II (A.D. 310-379). The portion called
the *Gāthās* ('Songs') bears internal evidence, in phrase-
ology and dialect, of being the oldest, and is ascribed by
tradition to Zoroaster himself; but some other parts
reveal the fact that they were written, at least in their
present form, in a dead language. The Avesta is divided
into the *Yasna* (including the *Gāthās*), the *Yashts*, the
Visparad, the *Vendīdād*, etc.; and treats of Zarathustra
(Zoroaster) and his teachings, cosmology and legends,

precepts for sanctity and a religious life, the moral and civil law, and liturgy and ritual. Of all these texts, the *Vendīdād* (or *Vīdērdāt,* 'Law against Demons') is of special interest to physicians, since it makes frequent mention of disease, while chapters xx-xxii are almost wholly medical.

The religion of Zoroaster.

The salient feature of the religion of Zoroaster is an essential monotheism with an apparent dualism. The Principle of Good is Ahura Mazda (or Ormazd), and the Principle of Evil is Angra Mainyu (Ahriman), each attended and aided by lesser divine or infernal beings, partaking of their respective characters, depositories of their respective powers and attributes, and acting as agents with varied functions to carry out their leader's will and to assist in waging the incessant warfare in which their principals are engaged. High above all others, Ahura Mazda, the omniscient creator of the universe and of all good things, is supported by six Amesha Spentas (or Amshaspands), the 'Immortal Holy Ones' who form his court; while occupying an auxiliary place, the Yazatas ('Venerable Ones') are his angels. To these is opposed, in unremitting, malevolent, bitter conflict, Angra Mainyu, the 'Enemy Spirit,' who, ignorant and short-sighted, created darkness, sin, disease, suffering, and evil of every kind. With him are six Arch-Fiends, the antitheses of the Amesha Spentas, who are his commanders and who direct the activities of untold hordes of diabolical, malignant spirits, seeking to overcome and enslave Ormazd, and by every means in their power to create confusion in all his good works and to destroy them, assailing man to his detriment and destruction. Man always has a part in the struggle, aiding the one or opposing the other according to his moral attitude; and every deed is an act of warfare for the good or for the bad. This conflict between the powers of good and evil continues without cessation through eons of time until eventually the world will undergo an ordeal by which it will be purified, after which evil will be eliminated, and Ahura Mazda and goodness will reign supreme.

Mythology.

Many of the myths of Iran date from the period of Indo-Iranian unity, whence, compared with those of the Vedas, they show a marked similarity in theme and form, varying only in personalities and details. They center about the theme of the struggles between the agencies of good and evil, and, for the most part, tell of creation and of the valiant endeavors of kings and ancient heroes to secure for earth and for mankind light, rain, and other blessings of Nature against the opposing forces of evil, of dragons, and of tyrants. These cosmic and terrestrial conflicts are often in the storm-cloud, amid raging elements, on a mountain or in a cavern, with thunderbolts, wind, and fire as weapons for the confusion and destruction of the demons.

The creation of remedies.

The myth of the creation of the vegetable kingdom, later furnishing all medicinal plants, is of special interest (*Būndahishn*, ix, xviii; cf. *Vendīdād*, xx, 4; *Yasht*, i, 30).[1] Ameratatāt ('Immortality'), one of the Amesha Spentas, who had vegetation under her guardianship, pounded the dry plants very small and mixed them with water, which Tishtrya, the dog-star, who was a good genius in Iran, made to rain upon the earth, so that plants sprang up like hair on the head of man, ten thousand growing to overcome ten thousand produced by evil spirits, and these ten

[1] *SBE* v, 30-31, 65-66.

thousand becoming an hundred thousand. From the same germs arose the 'Tree of All Seeds' which stood in the middle of the deep sea Vourukasha; and near this tree was the Gaokerena ('Ox-Horn') tree, the miraculous 'All-Healer,' from which came all healing plants. This tree was necessary for the renovation of the universe, that immortality might follow; and it was that "with which they restore the dead" (*Bŭndahishn*, xxiv, 27). The Evil Spirit, Ahriman, set a lizard in the sea to injure the tree, but Ormazd, to keep the monster away, created ten kar-fish which, circling about it constantly, guard it from harm. They are both fed spiritually and will watch each other until the universe is renovated. The Gao-kerena tree is the White Haoma, a manifestation of the mystical haoma plant (*Bŭndahishn*, xxvii, 4); and a part of the Avesta now lost told of "the production of entire species of plants by Aŭharmazd for the curing of the creatures from disease; the success of the Gōkerenō plant—which is the white Hōm—in curing, as compared with other plants; and the diligence of Aīrmān in the medical treatment of the world" (*Dīnkart*, VIII, xliv, 80).[2] According to another myth (*Bŭndahishn*, x, 1),[3] the bull created by Ahura Mazda was killed by Ahriman; but its death gave birth to vegetable life on earth, while from it grew "twelve species of medicinal herbs."

Disease and dualism.

All disease, regarded as a diabolical entity, and often named after the particular demon causing it, was supposed to be governed by the quasi-dualism which ruled the cosmos; and since it was regarded as an attack or as a possession by spirits of evil, the power of good spirits must be invoked to secure relief. Sin and disease were on

[2] *SBE* xxxvii, 165.
[3] *SBE* v, 31-32.

much the same plane; sin was a spiritual, and disease a bodily, malady, being a breach of the moral or physical order resulting from pollution, visible or invisible, but substantial. This pollution must be removed by some rite or act which would effect purification; and supernatural powers were summoned by invocations, hymns, and conjurations, often in conjunction with natural remedies administered with rites and ceremonies.

'Countless' diseases.

Ahura Mazda declares that Angra Mainyu created 99,999 ('countless,' *Yasht*, xiii, 59) diseases (*Vendīdād*, xxii, 2); and in the *Vendīdād* he reveals to the human race, through Zoroaster, the means whereby man may free himself from their power. Two Amesha Spentas, Haurvatāt ('Wholeness, Health') and Ameratatāt ('Immortality'), were assigned as special guardians of man, while Ahriman directed Taurvi and Zairika to oppose them, the latter actively sowing seeds of suffering, disease, and death, and the former provided with remedies to combat these ills, both the supernatural powers of Ahura Mazda, of which they were the repository, and the natural means which Ormazd revealed to Zoroaster by many hundreds, thousands, and tens of thousands (*Būndahishn*, xxviii, 11; xxx, 29; *Vendīdād*, xx, 4).[4]

The cure.

The cure is effected by the Amesha Spenta Asha Vahishta through the medium of the physician (*Dīnkart*, VIII, xxxvii, 14);[5] and the Avesta names several divisions of the healing art: "One health by righteousness,

---

[4] *SBE* v, 107, 128; Dhalla, *Zoroastrian Theology*, pp. 168, 265; *id.*, *Zoroastrian Civilization*, p. 152.

[5] *SBE* xxxvii, 116; also A. J. Carnoy, "Magic (Iranian)," in *ERE* viii, 294-295.

one health by the law, one health by the knife, one health
by plants, one health by (holy) texts; of healing things
the most healing is he who healeth by the holy text"
(*Yasht*, iii, 6; cf. *Vendīdād*, vii, 44).

Healing texts.

Many Gāthic verses were used in effecting cures, gaining force and efficiency by frequent repetition (cf. *Vendīdād*, ix, 27; x, 4-17; xx, 12; *Yasht*, iii, 5; xviii, 8); occasionally the formulas were themselves personified and
invoked, as, "Mayest thou heal me, O Holy Text right
glorious!" (*Vendīdād*, xxii, 2); and incantations also
occur, e.g., "I conjure thee, disease, I conjure thee, death;
—I conjure thee, fever,—I conjure thee, evil eye" (*ib.*,
xx, 7). Charms and amulets were also used to ward off
disease or to avert the evil eye;[6] and fire is mentioned
(*Dīnkart*, III, clvii, 8)[7] as a therapeutic agency. Furthermore, "all remedies of waters and animals and plants"
were in the keeping of the divine Ashi (*Yasna*, lii, 2); and
the rain banished disease and death, besides revivifying
vegetation (*Vendīdād*, xxi, 3). The waters and the plants
were healing (*Yasht*, viii, 47; *Vendīdād*, xx, 4), beginning
with the Gaokerena tree, already mentioned; and such
plants were used, together with manthras, in effecting
cures (*Dīnkart*, III, clvii, 45).[8] The Amesha Spentas and
Ahura Mazda (*Yasht*, i, 2-5, 8, 12), the moon (*Yasht*, vii,
5; *Nyāish*, iii, 7), the star Vanant (? Vega; *Yasht*, xxi, 1),
and the constellation Haptōiringa (Ursa Major; *Sīrōzāh*,
i, 13; ii, 13) also received the epithet 'healing,' the two

---

[6] J. J. Modi, "Charms or Amulets for some Diseases of the Eye," in
his *AP*, 1911, pp. 43-50; Kavasji Edalji Kanga, "King Farīdūn and a
few of his Amulets and Charms," in *CMV*, 1900, pp. 144-145.

[7] L. C. Casartelli, "Traité de médecine mazdéene," in *Le Muséon*,
1886, v, 534-535.

[8] *Ib.*, pp. 546-547.

latter as opposed to Angra Mainyu and his creatures
(*Yasht,* xxi, 1; viii, 12); while the Fravashis (guardian
spirits) likewise had this term applied to them (*Yasna,*
lv, 3; *Yasht,* xiii, 30, 32, 64).

Disease of animals.

The diseases of animals were governed by the same
principles as those of men, and similar measures were
employed for their cure (*Vendīdād,* vii, 43; xiii, 35; *Dīnkart,* VIII, xix, 39; xxxvii, 29; xxxviii, 54).[9]

PART II: THE HEALING DEITIES

THE Avesta associates the origin of the healing art
with Thrita (*Vendīdād,* xx, 2) and other divine beings or
heroes, possessed of marvellous skill, who were benefactors of the human race as physicians, but they brought
cures to man only in a theoretic manner, and, with the
exception of Haoma and Mithra, they developed no cults.

Ahurāni	Cisti	Thrita
Airyaman	Drvāspa	Tishtrya
Aredvī Sūra Anā-	Haoma	Verethraghna
hita	Mithra	Yima
Ashi	Thraētaona (or	
	Farīdūn)	

AHURĀNI

AHURĀNI ('Daughter of Ahura'), an Iranian water-god-
dess (cf. *Yasna,* xxxiii, 3) to whom the sixty-eighth chapter of the *Yasna* is devoted, is invoked (*Yasna,* lxviii, 2)
"for health and healing, for prosperity and growth," as
well as for other blessings of every kind. According to

[9] *SBE* xxxvii, 48, 118, 129.

the *Great Bŭndahishn*,[10] she presided especially over rain, standing waters, and the like.

AIRYAMAN

AIRYAMAN, a deity dating from the Indo-Iranian period, is celebrated in the Avesta as a benevolent being and as a healer. After the Holy Text had failed, Ahura Mazda called upon him for coöperation in expelling disease and death, saying: "I bless thee with the fair, holy blessing, the friendly, holy blessing that maketh the empty full and the full to overflow, that maketh the unsick sick, and maketh the sick man sound," whereupon he performed the rites of purification, so effectively that he caused 99,999 diseases to cease (*Vendīdād*, xxii, 7-19). His special prayer (*Yasna*, liv, 1) is "the most healing of divine manthras" (*Yasht*, iii, 5); and in a passage of the *Great Bŭndahishn* translated by Darmesteter[11] it is he "who gives the world healing of all pains, as it is said; '[with] all the drugs that creatures take to destroy pain, if I, Aŭhrmazd, had not sent Īrmān with his power of cure, pain would indeed remain!'" (?).

Airyaman, whose middle Persian (Turfan) equivalent means 'friend' (the modern īrmān, 'guest'), finds an Indian counterpart in the obscure Āditya Aryaman (apparently also signifying 'friend, comrade').[12] His original function is uncertain, but he acted as groomsman in the marriage ceremony (Rigveda, X, lxxxv, 36-43; *Yasna*, liv, 1); and he has accordingly been interpreted as representing marriage,[13] while others regard him as an incar-

---

[10] Darmesteter, *Le Zend-Avesta*, i, 267; cf. Dhalla, *Theology*, pp. 141-142.

[11] Darmesteter, *op. cit.*, ii, 319.

[12] Hillebrandt, *Vedische Mythologie*, iii, 77-90.

[13] Dhalla, *Civilization*, p. 81.

nation of submissive piety[14] or as "a god of rain and fertility who is essentially helpful to man," whence his function of healer naturally developed among the Zoroastrians.[15]

AREDVĪ SŪRA ANĀHITA

AREDVĪ SŪRA ANĀHITA ('Lofty, Mighty, Spotless [Lady]'), a divinity of the waters, especially of the mystic river Aredvī (*Vīsparad,* i, 5; *Yasht,* i, 21; *Vendīdād,* vii, 16),[16] is the only deity, except Mithra, who is mentioned beside Ahura Mazda in the Achæmenian inscriptions (Artaxerxes Mnemon, *Susa* a, 5; *Hamadan,* 6). The fifth *Yasht* is devoted entirely to her laudation, and from it we learn that she dwells among the stars, guarding all holy creation. To her countless sacrifices are offered, among her suppliants being not only earthly heroes, including Yima, Thraētaona, and Zoroaster, but even divine beings like Haoma, and Ahura Mazda himself. The prayers of the righteous she grants, but those of the ungodly, such as Azhi Dahāka, she rejects. She rides in a chariot drawn by four white steeds created by Ahura Mazda, and they are, respectively, wind, rain, cloud, and sleet; while so detailed is the description of her that some scholars[17] hold that she was represented in glyptic form, particularly as Berossos tells us (*apud* Clemens Alexandrinus, *Protreptica,* V, lxv, 3) that Artaxerxes Mnemon introduced statues of her among the Persians.

---

[14] Darmesteter, *op. cit.,* i, 350.

[15] A. J. Carnoy, "The Iranian Gods of Healing," in *JAOS,* 1918, xxxviii, 295.

[16] Geiger, *Ostiranische Kultur im Altertum,* pp. 45-50, etc., identifies this river with the Oxus; but it is, in all probability, wholly mythical.

[17] Darmesteter, *op. cit.,* ii, 364-365; A. V. W. Jackson, "Images and Idols (Persian)," in *ERE* vii, 153, hesitates to accept this interpretation.

The Avesta states (*Yasna,* lxv, 2; *Yasht,* v, 2, 5, 87; *Vendīdād,* vii, 16) that she purifies the *semen virile* and the womb, gives easy delivery, and creates milk in the breasts, besides being, in general, healing (*Yasna,* lxv, 1) and entreated for health of the body (*Yasht,* v, 53). The cult of Anāhita, who may be Semitic or Elamite in origin,[18] spread widely in the ancient world, notably in Armenia,[19] Pontus, Cappadocia, and Lydia, and she was identified with the Great Mother of the Asianic peoples;[20] while in Greece she was commonly equated with Artemis, and occasionally with Aphrodite.[21]

ASHI

ASHI ('Reward, Destiny'), the genius of sanctity, representing "the life of piety and its concomitant reward," and standing physically for plenty, morally for righteousness, and eschatologically for the heavenly reward of earthly sanctity,[22] is celebrated in the seventeenth *Yasht.* The daughter of Ahura Mazda and Spenta Armaiti, and the sister of Daēna ('Religion') and of the Amesha Spentas, as well as of Sraosha, Rashnu, and Mithra, she was invoked by Haoma, Yima, Thraētaona, Zoroaster, Vishtaspa, and others. She brings riches, abundance, and prosperity; she increases offspring and abominates celibacy and impurity; and as a healing deity she possesses all remedies of waters and kine and plants (*Yasna,* lii, 2; cf. lx, 4; *Vīsparad,* ix, i-2; *Yasht,* xiii, 32;

[18] Moulton, *Early Zoroastrianism,* pp. 66, 238-239; *id., The Treasure of the Magi,* p. 88.
[19] H. Gelzer, "Zur armenischen Götterlehre," in *BKSGW,* 1896, xlvi, 111-117.
[20] F. Cumont, "Anāhita," in *ERE* i, 414-415; also Gruppe, *Griechische Mythologie und Religionsgeschichte,* p. 1594.
[21] Gruppe, *op. cit.,* pp. 1094, 1265, 1552.
[22] Dhalla, *Theology,* pp. 43, 122.

xvii, 1). Her name appears under the form Ardokhro on coins of the Indo-Scythian Kings Kanishka and Hu-vishka (second century A.D.), where she is represented as bearing a cornucopia.[23]

CĪSTI

CĪSTI ('[Religious] Wisdom'), a minor divine being,[24] is once (*Visparad,* ix, 1) mentioned as having healing agencies; but no details are given.

DRVĀSPA

DRVĀSPA ('Possessed of Sound Horses'), the genius of the animal world, and especially of horses,[25] is the hero-ine of the ninth *Yasht,* invoked together with Geush Tashan ('Shaper of the Ox') and Geush Urvan ('Soul of the Ox'), and the recipient of sacrifices from Haoma and many heroes. Yima made offering to her that he might avert from men death and the infirmities of age (*Yasht,* ix, 10); and it is she who keeps cattle, friends, and chil-dren sound, being healing in her activities (*Yasht,* ix, 1-2). In Mithraism she was identified with Silvanus.[26]

HAOMA

HAOMA, the Iranian counterpart of the Vedic Soma, was an Iranian deity from primeval times, appearing in terrestrial form as the yellow haoma used in the Indo-Iranian sacrifice, though later there was also a mystic White Hōm, identified with the Gaokerena or Gōkart tree (*Bundahishn,* xxvii, 4; cf. ix, 6; xviii, 1-6; xxiv, 27).[27] Ac-

[23] M. A. Stein, "Zoroastrian Deities on Indo-Scythian Coins," in *BOR,* 1887, p. 165.
[24] Dhalla, *op. cit.,* p. 101.
[25] *Ib.,* p. 125.
[26] Cumont, *The Mysteries of Mithra,* p. 112.
[27] *SBE* v, 31, 65-66, 91, 100.

cording to the Avesta (*Yasna,* x, 23, 90), the juice of this plant was first extracted by Mithra from a health-giving, invigorating herb brought from lofty Haraiti (Mount Elburz) by birds (*Yasna,* x, 10-11); and in its sacred character, it was the ceremonial drink which gave strength and life to man, prepared by the priests with elaborate, prescribed ritual prayers and ceremonies.[28] The haoma was first offered to Ahura Mazda by Vīvangh-vant; its medical properties were associated with the joys of the Amesha Spenta Vohu Manah (*Yasna,* ix, 4; x, 12); and it was invoked for health and all bodily blessings (*Yasna,* ix, 17, 19; x, 9).

The exhilarating juice of the haoma plant gave a sense of power and ability (*Yasna,* x, 13); and though it seems at one time to have been banned by the *Gāthās* as inspiring orgies (cf. *Yasna,* xxxii, 14; xlviii, 10),[29] it later reappeared, but without objectionable features.

MITHRA

MITHRA, the Mitra of the Vedas, was an Iranian deity of great antiquity, and according to the Avesta, Ahura Mazda created him "as worthy of honor, as worthy of praise as myself, Ahura Mazda" (*Yasht,* x, 1), whence he was the most important Yazata. Though regarded by the majority of scholars as primarily a solar god, he seems, in reality, to have been originally the apotheosis of the contract, the pledge, whence he was later identified with the all-seeing sun.[30] Among the Iranians, accordingly, he

---

[28] Darmesteter, *op. cit.,* i, lxxvii-lxxx; also Haug, *Essays on . . . the Parsis,* 3d ed., pp. 399-403; J. J. Modi, "Haoma," in *ERE* vi, 507-510.

[29] Moulton, *Zoroastrianism,* pp. 71-73, 357-358, 379.

[30] A. Meillet, "Le Dieu indo-iranian Mitra," in *JA,* X, 1907, x, 143-159. For the Vedic Mitra see Macdonell, "Vedic Mythology," in *GIPA,* 1897, pp. 29-30, and references there given; see also Hillebrandt, *op. cit.,* iii, 53-59. For a survey of the Iranian Mithra see Dhalla, *op. cit.,* pp. 103-111, 239-240.

was the divinity of righteousness and of the plighted
word, and the protector of justice, the defender of the
worshippers of truth and righteousness in their struggles
against Angra Mainyu, and the god of battles who gave
victory over the foes of Iran. He is invoked, *inter alia*,
for healing and for physical soundness (*Yasht,* x, 5, 94),
and is entreated to "be present at our sacrifices, be present at them hallowed; gather them for atonement; lay
them down in the House of Praise" (*Yasht,* x, 32).

Little is known of the ritual of the Iranian worship of
Mithra; but his cult in the Occident was identified with
occultism, magic, astrology, and mystic ceremonies, much
of which is believed to have been injected under the influence of the 'Chaldæans' and during its spread through
Babylonia and Asia Minor. Mithra was essentially a
moral mediator, struggling against the powers of evil
to redeem mankind, this eternal contest being symbolized
by the slaying of the bull for regeneration; while other
ceremonies included communion with bread and wine and
ointments of honey for consecration, all of which were
mystic remedies of Mithra for the healing of the body and
for the sanctification of the soul.[31]

The cult of Mithra, popular and powerful in Iran,
spread rapidly to Asia Minor, to Greece, and finally over
the Roman Empire, carrying with it the occultism of the
Chaldæans and the mysterious sciences of the Orient, so
that Romans saw Mithra's astrologers passing whole
nights on the tops of their towers, and his magicians
practiced their mysteries on the slopes of the Aventine
and on the banks of the Tiber.[32] The cult encountered
bitter hatred and the violent opposition of all Christians,
and this religious struggle continued in the more remote

[31] Cumont, *op. cit.,* pp. 157-160, 206.
[32] Bruzon, *La Médecine et les religions,* p. 137.

quarters of Europe perhaps as late as the fifth century of our era.

THRAĒTAONA (OR FARĪDŪN)

THRAĒTAONA, son of Āthwya, and the Farīdūn of Persian and Arabic authors, is apparently the Iranian counterpart of the Indian Traitana, who is mentioned only in a single passage of the Rigveda (I, clviii, 5).[33] His *fravashi* is invoked against itch, fever, and two other (unknown) diseases (*Yasht*, xiii, 131), and a Pazand charm[34] contains the words: "May N.N., by virtue of the strength and power of the virtue of Fredūn, the son of Āthwya, by virtue of the strength of the northern stars, be healthy in body." According to the Pahlavi writings, Frētūn (Thraētaona) was "full of healing" (*Dātistan -i Dīnīk*, xxxviii, 35);[35] but subsequently he became fused with his doublet, Thrita, in the national hero Farīdūn, who, in mighty struggle, overcame his father's murderer and his own inveterate foe, tyrant Azhi Dahāka, a monster created by Ahriman with three jaws, three heads, and six eyes, while on its shoulders grew two snakes from kisses imprinted by the arch-fiend. After conquering the demon, the hero fettered him with chains in a cavern on Mount Damavand for a thousand years and took possession of his palace, reigning peacefully for five centuries (*Yasna*, ix, 7-8; *Yasht*, v, 33-35; ix, 13-14; etc.; *Būndahishn*, xxix, 9; xxxiv, 6).[36] Thraētaona has been interpreted as a wind-deity.[37]

[33] Cf. Macdonell and Keith, *Vedic Index of Names and Subjects*, i, 331.

[34] Modi, in *AP*, p. 48; two other charms of similar character are given by Kanga, in *CMV*, pp. 144-145.

[35] *SBE* xviii, 90.

[36] *SBE* v, 119, 150.

[37] Carnoy, in *JAOS*, 1918, xxxviii, 297-299.

THRITA

THRITA (? 'Third'), the third to strain the haoma-juice, his reward being parentage of two heroic sons (*Yasna*, ix, 9-10), was the first who "held disease to disease, held death to death," receiving from Ahura Mazda, for this purpose, "medicine and the boons of Khshathra Vairya," *i.e.*, apparently (since this Amesha Spenta presided over metals), herbs and the surgeon's knife (*Vendīdād*, xx, 1-3). He is the Iranian counterpart of the Indian Trita Āptya,[38] but in the Avesta Āptya appears as a separate being, Āthwya (*Yasna*, ix, 6-7); and Thrita himself is superseded, at an early date, by the cognate figure Thraētaona. He has been explained as originally a water-god.[39]

TISHTRYA

TISHTRYA (Sirius), the star-genius who presides over rain, and the center of devotion in the ninth *Yasht*, white, shining, and exalted, grants fertility to the fields and happy abodes to man, and is the lord of all stars, as worthy of sacrifice, invocation, propitiation, and glorification as is Ahura Mazda himself. When due offerings are made to him, he sends rain and other blessings; and he is especially renowned for his victory over the drought-demon Apaosha. He is described as healing; as washing away, by his waters, all abomination from all creatures, and thus healing them; but as removing every remedy from the presence of the wicked (*Yasht*, viii, 2, 43, 60).

VERETHRAGHNA

VERETHRAGHNA, the genius of victory, is the Iranian counterpart of the Vedic Vṛtrahan ('Slayer of Vṛtra'),

[38] See *supra*, p. 160; and cf. Spiegel, *Die arische Periode*, pp. 257-271; C. Bartholomæ, "Arica I," in *IF*, 1892, i, 180-182.

[39] Carnoy, *loc. cit.*

a frequent epithet of Indra, though used also of Agni and Soma.[40] According to the fourteenth *Yasht*, which is devoted wholly to his laudation, he grants victory over the foe and, if proper sacrifice is offered him, he guards the Iranian lands against every enemy. When he revealed himself to Zoroaster, he appeared successively as the wind, a bull, a white horse, a rutting camel, a boar, a youth, a raven, a ram, a goat, and a warrior; and a feather from his bird, the raven, averts the enchantments of enemies, giving its possessor strength and victory (*Yasht*, xiv, 34-40).

He brings healing and power, and is the mightiest in healing; in answer to Zoroaster's prayer he gave him virility, strength of arm, bodily endurance, and keenness of vision; but, on the other hand, he can cause illness and death, taking away his agencies of healing, as he does when the evil and the unchaste dwell in the land (*Yasht*, xiv, 2, 3, 29, 47, 52).

Under the name of Vahagn, Verethraghna was worshipped as one of the three chief deities of Armenia, produced by the travail of Earth and triumphing over dragons.[41] He appears bearing sword and spear, and with a bird (probably a raven) perched on his helmet, on a coin of the Indo-Scythian King Kaṇishka (second century A.D.), where he is called Orlagno;[42] and in an inscription of Antiochos I of Kommagene (first century B.C.) he is identified, under the name Artagnes, with Herakles and Ares.[43]

[40] Spiegel, *op. cit.*, pp. 194-197; Oldenberg, *Die Religion des Veda*, p. 134; Macdonell, in *GIPA*, 1897, pp. 60, 66, 109, 114, 158. Cf., also Dhalla, *op. cit.*, pp. 112-114; Carnoy, *Iranian Mythology*, pp. 271-273.

[41] Gelzer, *op. cit.*, pp. 104-109.

[42] Stein, *op. cit.*, p. 159.

[43] Dittenberger, *Orientis græci inscriptiones selectæ*, Leipzig, 1903-1905, no. 383.

YIMA

Yima, an ancient Indo-Iranian hero, the Yama ('Twin') of the Veda and the Jamshid (Avesta Yima Khshæta, 'Brilliant Yima') of the Persian epic, appears in the Avesta as the son of Vīvahvant (*Yasna*, ix, 4) and the hero of a myth of the early expansion of the world (*Vendīdād*, ii).[44] In his golden age he reigned for centuries over a distant realm where food and drink never ceased, where man and beast never died, where water and plants never dried up, and where there was neither age nor death (*Yasht*, xix, 32-33; cf. *Yasna*, ix, 5). Nevertheless, he committed sin, either by giving man forbidden food (*Yasna*, xxxii, 8) or by yielding to falsehood (*Yasht*, xix, 34 ff.); and, in consequence, he lost both his kingly glory and his realm and was slain by the dragon Azhi Dahāka, with whose life his own seems to run parallel, and who extended his malignant sway until he, in turn, was overpowered by the hero Thraētaona (Farīdūn). According to Persian tradition, Jamshid knew

> Next leechcraft and the healing of the sick,
> The means of health, the course of maladies.[45]

Yima is interpreted by some scholars as the setting sun,[46] an explanation which has also been advanced for the Vedic Yama, though he seems rather to have been originally the first man, and thus the chief of the souls of the departed.[47]

---

[44] Cf. Carnoy, *op. cit.*, pp. 304-319.

[45] Firdausi, *Shāh-Nāmah*, tr. A. G. and E. Warner, i, 133; Mirkhond, *The History of the Early Kings of Persia*, p. 121.

[46] Carnoy, *op. cit.*, pp. 312-317.

[47] Macdonell, in *GIPA*, 1897, pp. 171-174.

CHAPTER SIX
GRECIAN GODS

CHAPTER SIX

THE HEALING GODS OF ANCIENT GREECE

PART I: GENERAL SURVEY

SCATTERED references in the *Iliad* and *Odyssey* make it clear that in the early period the Greeks believed that the deities sent disease and death upon mankind in anger and revenge, for impiety, vows unperformed, sacrifices unoffered, and unjust deeds, or because of the wickedness of the human heart. To free themselves from their evil plight, men were advised to sacrifice, to pray, to make atonement, and to propitiate the gods, who in this relation had power to avert pestilence and cure disease. "It is by no means possible to avoid disease sent from Zeus; yet do thou at least pray to thy father, even unto King Poseidon" (*Odys.*, ix, 411-412). The healing art of the early Greeks was, therefore, intimately connected with their religion and mythology.

The origin of the gods.

The Greek world of spiritual beings was evolved from the prehistoric blendings of the religious faith and practices of immigrant races coming from the north—chiefly of the Achaian, Minyan, and Dorian migrations—with those of the peoples of ancient Mediterranean stock, of which the Aigaian civilizations were composed. The imagination of the people interpreted these potencies of the pantheon as divinities and daimons. These conceptions were personified, and the fancies of the poets, the speculations of the philosophers, and the skill of the artisans, guided by an æsthetic sense, combined to transform the primitive deities into a higher order of beings, superhuman, of superior strength, similar in appearance to man, yet idealized and glorified, and to invest them "with a 'sovereign grace and a serene majesty." The gods had arisen from many independent sources with the freedom and indefiniteness of traditional tales. Some had evolved from the myths which had grown up about the 'good daimon,' or ancestor of a family or tribe, who had acquired a superhuman status, certain functions, and a recognized worship. The Pelasgians of Arkadia and Boiotia declared that their deities were born, and Greek myths recount the circumstances surrounding the birth, and sometimes the death, of many of their gods and goddesses. Hesiod (*Opera et Dies,* 107) says: "And ponder it well in thy mind, that from the same origin sprang gods and mortal men." Pindar (*Nemea,* vi, 1-7) expressed the same view:

Men and the Gods above one race compose:
  Both from the general parent Earth
  Derive their old mysterious birth:
But powers unlike their differing nature shows;—
  Man breathes his moment, and is nought
While, like their brazen heaven's eternal base,
Gods live forever: th' illumined face,
  Th' illustrious form, th' inspiring thought,
  Proclaim him kindred of the skies.

The nature of the gods.

As disclosed in the epics, Greek religion had already developed far beyond the elementary stages of evolution to the form of an advanced anthropomorphic polytheism. The gods were concrete, clearly defined personalities, of superhuman substance, living on nectar, and immortal. They were invisible, yet able to appear in various disguises; they passionately exercised human emotions and were loosely correlated in a divine family or state having one supreme ruler. They were of two classes: those of a celestial or uranic nature, who lived on the mystic heights of Olympos, and whose personalities were celebrated in verse; and those of chthonic character and functions, who belonged to the earth and Underworld, whose awe-inspiring personalities were not always pleasing to contemplate, and who were referred to vaguely in literature, usually under veiled expressions.

The gods and man.

The Greek deities prompted no spiritual aspirations and were not looked upon as beings of moral excellence or wisdom. They were unmoral, yet ethical in preserving the respect and sanctity of the oath witnessed before the gods of either the upper or lower world. They were so nearly related to human kind that they sustained injuries and suffered from diseases similar to those of man. They held friendly communion with man. They were his invisible companions and took an active part in the intimate affairs of his daily life as helpers, advisers, and friends; or, as enemies, they opposed him and brought misfortune upon him. Things without visible cause were ascribed to the supernatural powers of the gods and to spiritual beings of lesser rank. Man looked to the divinities for his welfare and enjoyment in this life and depended upon their supernatural, divine powers for help and protection in times of need. The residence and rank of deity were so accessible that some of the heroes ascended and became members of the divine family.

The pantheon.

Each settlement, village, tribe, community, and state had its own independent and favored tutelary deity and

form of worship. The rituals and ceremonies of the
several cults were conducted side by side; and the gods
were frequently blended, or one gained supremacy, as
Hera in Argolis, Athena in Athens, and Poseidon in
Corinth. The family or tribal conceptions of deity developed the larger aspect of the father and protector of
the state and of mankind. Some were regarded by local
traditions as the divine ancestor of the community, as
Hermes in Arkadia, and Apollo in Delos. The pantheon
was also invaded frequently by deities of foreign tribes
who brought to the land of their adoption their personal
gods and forms of worship, and established their cults.
Hellas was a free soil. Foreign deities were permitted
a foothold and gained favor, influence, and prominence.
Zeus, supposed to have been of Aryan origin, established
himself at Dodona and finally became ruler over all.
Dionysos and Orpheus were from Thrace, others were
from Pelasgia and Phrygia (Herodotos, ii, 53); and in
the late period, with loss of national independence,
deities were introduced from Egypt, Syria, and Persia;
while their cults definitely affected the character of the
later Greek religions. Gods of one community were
adopted by others, and the worship of many became general, but the rituals were adapted to local ideas and usage.
These deities were plastic and developed consistently
with the unfolding of the religious conceptions of the
people. They had varied functions and readily acquired
new phases and aspects, as of different personalities.
Such variants tended to develop into separate and distinct deities, as Eileithyia, who is supposed to have
emanated from Hera and to have represented her obstetric function; but others never evolved further than
to receive an adjectival name. The religions of Greece
were a composite of many cults, existing side by side yet
differing in conception and in ritual.

The divine functions.

The gods had general supernatural powers, and in addition many acquired special functions which frequently overlapped or were duplicated by others, no deity having a monopoly. Apollo was famous for prophecy, but his Delphic oracle, "the center of Greek inspiration," had many rivals, as those of Dionysos at Amphikleia, Hades at Nysa, and Trophonios at Lebadeia. Herakles, as well as many other gods and heroes besides Asklepios, practiced healing. Deities had various aspects and attributes according to place and circumstance, and received qualifying appellatives, usually surnames. Athena as guardian of the city of Athens was Athena Polias; as protector of its health she was Athena Hygieia; and as the guardian of eyesight she was Athena Ophthalmitis at Sparta. Pater remarks[1] on the indefiniteness characteristic of Greek mythology, "a theology with no central authority, no link on historic time, liable from the first to an unobservable transformation." "There were religious usages before there were distinct religious conceptions, and these antecedent religious usages shape and determine, at many points, the ultimate religious conception, as the details of the myth interpret or explain the religious custom."[2] There were priests but no theological priesthoods, no guiding authority, and each cult or center of worship was a law to itself. There were brotherhoods, as the *selloi* (or *helloi*) at Dodona and the later Orphic *thiasoi*, but they never gained social, political, or religious influence beyond their own cults. Therefore transformations were common, and the modes of worship were pliantly adaptable to changing conditions in social and political life.

[1] *Greek Studies,* p. 101.
[2] *Ib.,* p. 120.

New conceptions.

For centuries the old religions had sufficed. The gods had given to the individual the good things of this life, health, happiness, and longevity; and to the state, protection and prosperity. With the development of new conceptions came a great diversity and broadening of religious thought and purpose. The Orphic *thiasoi* spread their doctrines, the cult of Dionysos found a purpose beyond the celebration of the fruit of the vine, the Mysteries and worship of Demeter and Kore were developed at Eleusis, and other religious centers were established. The Greek mind was awakened to the needs and aspirations of the soul, to its divine nature, to the hope of a closer communion with the saving deity, and even of salvation, with a happier lot after death than that of others who descended to the prison house of Hades. Themistios, in the later period, interpreted the initiation into these great mysteries as in the nature of a rehearsal of the experiences the soul was supposed to undergo at the time of death.[3] Referring to the Eleusinian Mysteries, which were exceedingly popular with the Athenians, Sophokles, in one fragment (719), exclaims: "O thrice blessed those mortals, who having beheld these mysteries descend into Hades; to them alone it is given to live; for the rest all evils are there."[4] The nature of deity, of cults and practices, became subjects of infinite speculation by philosophers; and theories, naturalistic and agnostic, were constantly formulated. Whatever the trend, political events intervened; and the old gods, to whom people and states had appealed in their extremity, gave moral judgment for Hellas, granting victory over their enemies and preserving the country from foreign

[3] Farnell, *The Cults of the Greek States,* iii, 179 f.
[4] Cf. Homer, *Hymn to Demeter,* 480.

domination. The land was purified of the polluting presence of the Persian barbarians by fire brought from Delphoi, and the Greeks "raised an altar to Zeus the god of the free, a fair monument of freedom for Hellas" (Pausanias, IX, ii, 5).[5] The simpler faith of the tried and beloved deities revived, and the populace celebrated and honored them with great national festivals, stately processions, and decorous rituals; while the highest æsthetic sense interpreted their gods before the eyes of the multitude in terms of majesty and ideal beauty.

Absence of dogma and moral restraint in religion.

The multiplicity of gods, of cults, and of cultic practices resulted in a complexity of religious ideas that defies close analysis. The philosophers were perplexed, and Plato characterized "one who undertook to unravel the tangled web of Greek polytheism as a 'laborious, and not very fortunate man' " (*Phaidrus*, 229 D). Religion was an affair of rituals, not beliefs. There was never in Greece a systematic theological belief or doctrine. There were no religious opinions, merely traditional usages that everyone was expected to observe, and sacrifice was the recognized expression of piety from early times. There was no orthodoxy or heterodoxy in the ordinary acceptance of these terms, although it was not permitted to deny or neglect the gods. There was little or no moral restraint on the conscience, and the religion has been subjected to "the monstrous reproach of a theology altogether without moral distinctions and a religion altogether without reverence."[6] Family life and the worship of its 'good daimon' may have engendered a moral sense,

---

[5] A fragment, attributed to Terpander, expressed the majesty of the god (Zeus) as: "the primal cause of all things, the Leader of the world" (Bergk, *Poetæ lyrici Græci*, iii, frag. 1).

[6] Blackie, *Horæ Hellenicæ*, p. 78.

and the sanctity of the oath enforced by Apollo and other gods is believed to have influenced both public and private morality. In the fourth century B.C. came a tendency to eliminate the immoral stories of the deities and to create an ethical sentiment. Epicharmos expressed the idea of purity which was the basis of the cathartic ritual, "If thou art pure in mind, thou art pure in thy whole body" (Clemens Alexandrinus, *Stromata*, p. 844). From whatever source it came, there appears from the age of Perikles onward a gradually deepening sense of the influence of religion on morality. Although religion exercised so little restraint upon the individual, the impiety of defaming or denying the divinities was punished. There was a certain obligation of deference and sacrifice to the deities for bounties received, and loyalty was due to the family, the tribal, or the state god which called for the ritual forms; but beyond that, each one was free and independent to worship when and whom he pleased.

Shrines and religiosity.

The primitive custom of recognizing a natural cave, a tree trunk, a post, or a mound of stones as a 'holy pillar,' the residence of a god, and erecting there an altar for worship, and the later wayside shrines, the numerous temples, and the splendid sanctuaries, monuments, and festivals all testify to the religiosity of the people, their every-day dependence on their gods, and their constancy in observing the forms of worship. Their attitude toward the deities was not timorous, but intimate and friendly, as on a basis of quasi-equality with the supernatural world. Their religion and worship of the celestial divinities was joyous and bright, not solemn. Herakleitos may have reflected this close sympathetic relation in his remark that "men are mortal gods, and gods are immortal men."

Chthonic deities.

There was, however, a phase of their religion which was connected with the dark and hidden powers of the earth and Underworld and which was not genial or cheerful. These chthonian powers and their gloomy worship were referred to briefly by Homer and Hesiod. The poets, dramatists, and philosophers make frequent allusions to them, but treat the subject vaguely. Plutarch remarked (*de Defectu Oraculorum,* xiv) that it was from the mysteries that they had gained their best knowledge of the daimonic elements of life.[7] Something is known of the rituals of these "mysteries of which no tongue may speak," but if anything was taught by them, very little is known of it.[8] It is from later records and excavations that philological and archæological studies have disclosed the primitive features, the great antiquity, and many details of the chthonian worships. These cults, which then included that of the dead, were not prominent in the early period, but in the later days of Greek religion they became a distinctive feature. Many of the primitive rites of the cults, based on old superstitions, endured and were observed side by side with the more advanced conceptions of later religious thought.

Chthonic character.

The divinities of the earth and Underworld were numerous and varied. Some were beneficent and had functions that were essential to life and the happiness of mankind, but all were potential powers for evil and many were "fearsome and awe-inspiring."[9] They ranged from

[7] Cf. Harrison, *Prologomena to the Study of Greek Religion,* pp. 337 ff.

[8] Cf. P. Gardner, "Mysteries (Greek, Phrygian, etc.)," in *ERE* ix, 77-82.

[9] L. R. Farnell, "Greek Religion," in *ERE* vi, 398-399.

Hades, the great death-god, and his consort, the dread Persephone, rulers of the Underworld realm (Hesiod, *Theogonia*, 765), to daimons, demigods, heroes, and the vast horde of the spirits of the dead. The religion of the chthonioi has been called the "religion of fear" as contrasted with the "religion of duty" of the uranic deities.[10] The powers of the nether-world avenged the broken oath, punished sinners after death, and were able to bring all misfortunes and death upon those who incurred their enmity. Although conscious of these dread potencies, as were the people of Argolis of Poine, the evil spirit which ravaged their homes (Pausanias, I, xliii, 7), the Greeks do not appear to have been oppressed in their daily lives by the terrors of the daimonic Underworld, nor were they subject to morbid fear and anxiety concerning their destiny and the after-life. The myths of early Greece were not overburdened with goblins and specters, nor do the relics of the early cult of the dead suggest any spirit of terrorism. The temperament of the people had not been tainted with the morbidity of their neighbors of Mesopotamia. The powers of darkness had to be reckoned with, and the chthonic rituals of prayer and sacrifice were faithfully performed to appease the wrath or to placate and to gain the good will and favor of these dread powers that evil might be averted, present misfortune removed, and purification obtained from pollution and guilt. These gloomy ceremonials over, the people resumed their ordinary cheerful relations to the life about them. These rites were of the nature of 'riddance' or 'aversion' addressed to an order of beings entirely alien, as contrasted with those of 'tendance' or " 'service' addressed to Olympians.' "[11]

[10] F. H. Garrison, "The Gods of the Underworld in Ancient Medicine," in *PCC* v, 35-36.

[11] Harrison, *op. cit.*, p. 7.

Chthonic functions.

Certain of the deities of the Underworld had benign functions. They dispensed the hidden wealth of Mother Earth, advised mankind by prophecy and dreams, and aided in misfortune and suffering. For Homer and Hesiod, Demeter was a goddess of blessings, not of terror. She was the beloved divinity of fertility, of vegetation, of the happy revival of nature in springtime. Later, the Mysteries of Eleusis promised her initiates greater contentment in the present life and a happier lot than that of others after death. Her power was, however, feared. The Black Demeter of pre-Homeric times, the gruesome, threatening figure of the horse-headed goddess with snake locks in the dark cave at Phigaleia, was not forgotten (Pausanias, VIII, xlii, 4). Dionysos was the god of industry, of vine culture, and of wine, and his cult fostered gaiety and wild revelry, but he also offered worshippers the hope of a future life. Asklepios and other heroes administered by healing to sufferers. There was, therefore, much that was conducive to cheerfulness and to be thankful for in the chthonian cults, and their deities were honored, and their favorable aspects were dwelt upon in the hope of propitiating them and minimizing their disposition to work evil. They were never addressed directly and were seldom referred to by their own dread names. Hesiod speaks of Hades as Zeus of the Earth, implying beneficence. Hades was also called Plouton, 'the Rich One'; and Persephone ("the maiden whom none may name") was termed Kore, 'the Maiden.' The altar to the chthonioi at Myonia in Lokris was dedicated to 'the Gracious Gods' (Pausanias, X, xxxviii, 8). Most of the chthonioi were nameless, and many were described by adjectives, as 'Kindly Goddess,' 'Revered One,' or 'Easy-to-be-entreated.' The same idea was carried out in

art. Farnell remarks[12] that the Greeks would not brook
the full revelation of the dark features of the chthonioi,
and that ideal Greek art expressed in palpable forms of
benign beauty the half palpable personages of the lower
world, banished the uncouth and the terrible in religious
imagination, and helped to purge and tranquilize the
Greek mind by investing chthonic powers with benevo-
lence and grace. On coins Persephone is represented as a
beautiful, hopeful maiden, and the horse-headed Demeter
is transformed into graceful human form with no intimation of the original except the horse's hoof as a pendant
to her necklace.[13]

The daimons.

According to Greek belief, the shades of the departed
descended into the earth, to the prison house of Hades.
The spirits of those "who died before their time" and
of the uncremated dead, however, remained outside the
portals and had power to return to the upper world and
disturb the living. The ghost of Patroklos appeared to
Achilles in a dream and begged that his funeral rites be
performed that it might pass the gates of Hades (Il.,
xxiii, 70). The shades of the dead became earth-spirits,
daimons, heroes, and possibly wandering ghosts.[14] 'Daimons' (or demons) was a term of early Greece for the
invisible spirits of supernatural power, a primitive conception of broad meaning that did not carry with it any
moral taint. Hesiod (Op. et Dies, 122, 159, 172, 251) regarded daimons as ranking between gods and men, of a
higher grade of dignity, but otherwise indistinguishable
from heroes, who were a god-like race of men of the
Golden Age, watchers, set apart from mortals. The

[12] In ERE vi, 412.
[13] Ib., p. 404.
[14] A. C. Pearson, "Demons and Spirits (Greek)," ERE iv, 590-594.

Greeks held them to be kindly, guardian spirits, standing
by to initiate men in the mysteries of life and to guide
them after death (Plato, *Phædo,* 130). Plato said they
were interpreters and messengers between gods and men,
and other philosophers looked upon them as having
powers for both good and evil. Aristophanes says (*Equi-
tes,* 85) that the Athenians made libations of wine to the
'good daimon,' or Genius, after dinner. In Boiotia they
sacrificed to the 'good daimon' when testing new must.
Daimons sent dreams, which were signs of disease and of
good health. The ritual prescription marks an early an-
tipathy between the hero and the Olympian, but this was
compromised by an appearance of decent friendliness.[15]
In the classical age it was believed that the good
ascended, that the shades of the dead might become
heroes, that heroes became daimons and demigods, and
that a few rose to the rank of gods with a defined personality.

The worship of heroes.

From the earliest times the Greeks had paid respect
to ancestors of both family and tribe. They were regarded by the writers of Attika as the 'good daimons'
of the household, and were sometimes represented by a
serpent.[16] Libations were made to ancestors at family
meals, and such honors led to a close family tie or clan-
feeling. The memory of men who had distinguished themselves was reverenced by their family, their tribe, city,
or state. Through the mists of early Greek tradition
certain personalities stand forth as humanitarians and
as having had unusual gifts of wisdom and foresight,
favorites and 'sons of the gods.' These were the heroes
who had been inspired with the arts of civilization for
the benefit of mankind, and, possessing the mantic gift,

[15] Harrison, *op. cit.,* p. 338.
[16] Farnell, *Cults,* iii, 10.

were renowned as seers and prophets. Their mantic gifts were supposed to be hereditary and to pass to their descendants, who frequently retained the name of their ancestor as the collective by which the gifted family or race was known. Such benefactors of the people were glorified after death and honored with cultic worship, and a few were deified. They were generally worshipped as heroes, and their graves were the centers of their cults. If they gained fame and importance, shrines were built and they were accorded public honors, and possibly festivals. Such hero cults were pre-Homeric and appear to have been a survival of a primitive custom prior to the growth of the cults of the greater gods. They became prominent in post-Homeric days and were well established throughout Greece about the seventh century B.C. As chthonian earth-spirits the heroes acquired their attributes and emblems, the oracle and the serpent. The snake as an emblem, common to all chthonic characters, represented the incarnate form of the hero or god in which he was frequently worshipped, and it was thus used in statues, bas-reliefs, and other works of art. Vergil (*Æneid*, v, 84) recognized this relation when he told of the enormous serpent which appeared to Aineias as he performed the sacred rites at the tomb of his father on the anniversary of his death. Heroes were helpers in time of need and were protectors in battle; while, as the gods had favored them with skill beyond mortal man, many were healers of the sick. They avenged a slight, it was considered dangerous to meet them in the darkness or speak of them in other than pleasing terms. Hesychios (*s.v. kreittonas*) explains that heroes "seem to be a bad sort of persons; it is on this account that those who pass hero-shrines keep silence lest heroes should do them some harm."[17]

[17] Harrison, *op. cit.*, p. 339.

Ceremonials.

The Greek modes of worship and the sacred formulas used at the temples and festivals were, as a rule, decorous, wholesome, and refined. Licentious emblems and rites are rarely mentioned and were practically confined to the vegetation cults. The elements of the ritual appear to have differed materially with the various worships and with time and place.[18] They have, however, been grouped as honorific, to honor the gods as benefactors of the individual, the city, and state; as apotropaic, to acknowledge their services as averters of evil, misfortune, sickness, and death; as hilastic, to atone for offenses and to propitiate; and, as cathartic, to cast forth contamination and to purify. The gods were given the adjectival titles *lysioi, apotropaioi, alexikakoi,* and *aleximoroi,* as averters of and deliverers from evil and death; and these epithets were placed above the doors of dwellings for their magic influence. The honorific and apotropaic ceremonies consisted of pæans or hymns of praise, prayers, libations, and thanksgivings, with ritual sacrifice of animals and offerings of first-fruits, cereals, honey, wine, incense, *et cetera.* The hilastic ceremonies were similar, except that they partook of an expiatory character to appease the anger of the gods and, by placating them, to obtain a riddance of all evil spirits and their works, misfortune, sickness, or threatened death. Perfect hecatombs were offered Apollo to appease his wrath and rid the Greek camp of the scourge (*Il.,* i, 315). Odysseus was instructed to sacrifice black animals within a trench in which honey, wine, and water had been poured, and thus entreat the "illustrious nations of the dead" (*Odys.,* x, 520). Fire was used to dissipate evil spirits. Whatever the practice of human sacrifice in the dark and savage

[18] A. W. Mair, "Worship (Greek)," in *ERE* xii, 782-788.

ages, it was rare in Greek societies of the fifth and fourth centuries B.C.[19] Cathartic rites were intended to purge from stain, from the *miasma* of blood-guilt, and from spiritual pollution through contact with the impure and guilty, and consisted of the usual prayers and sacrifices, and particularly of lustrations by water or blood for ceremonial purification. Lustral water from a spring was used for bathing or it was sprinkled over the person; barley-meal was scattered with the hand on the cleansing flame, and heifers were slain. Sometimes the blood of a chthonic animal was used for lustration. The Homeric Greeks purified themselves with water and cast the ablutions into the sea (*Il.*, i, 313). Apollo, for whom the dictatorship was claimed over cleansing for blood-guilt during the eighth and seventh centuries B.C. (Aischylos, *Eumenides,* 620), had himself been sent to Crete to be purified of the blood of Python (Pausanias, II, xxx, 3); and Achilles was bidden to go to Lesbos to be cleansed by Apollo and Artemis from the stain of murder.[20] Odysseus purified his house from the pollution of murdered suitors by the burning of sulphur (*Odys.*, xxii, 481). In the ritual of sacrifice to the uranic deities the head of the victim was held up; in the chthonic offerings the head of the animal (a sheep, a ram or a lamb, black by preference) was held down, and the blood flowed into a hole in the ground (*bothros*) or altar. In honorific and apotropaic sacrifice to the uranic deities the flesh was eaten; but in oblations to the chthonic divinities the flesh was wholly burned, the remains with other offerings were thrown into a hole in the altar, and no part was eaten. During the early days, at least, the chthonic rites were held at night and frequently they were continued until the approach of dawn,

[19] Cf. A. C. Pearson, "Human Sacrifice (Greek)," in *ERE* vi, 847-849.

[20] Farnell, in *ERE* vi, 406.

as those described by Pausanias (X, xxxviii, 8). Such cultic ceremonies once established were generally conserved, little affected by modifications in the conception of the god to whom they were addressed.[21]

Oracles and divine communications.

The gods held frequent intercourse with men and by many signs, more particularly by oracles, dreams, dream-oracles, and visions, revealed the divine will, both as to the present and the future, "Telling to many a mortal wight, as he lay asleep in darkness, what has been, and yet shall be" (Euripides, *Iphigenia in Taurica*, 1261 ff.). Such communications came from gods and heroes alike and were made manifest through diviners and seers, through the medium of priests and priestesses, or directly to the individuals by dreams. These messages and their interpretation were eagerly sought by all classes, and seers, augurs, and soothsayers were held in high esteem, so that at one time large numbers of all degrees practiced their arts in Athens and throughout Greece. Only those inspired of old by Apollo uttered oracles, and the skill of soothsayers lay in the interpretations of dreams and omens (Pausanias, I, xxxiv, 4).

During the Trojan War Melampous, through his descendants, had gained fame for mantic gifts (*Odys.*, xv. 224). At the inception of the War, Kalchas, the best of augurs, who knew the present, past, and future, was besought to interpret the cause of the anger of Apollo and to indicate how it might be appeased, thus averting further destruction by pestilence in the camp (*Il.*, i, 70).

[21] For further and more detailed information concerning the chthonic deities in connection with ancient Greek medicine attention is invited to the excellent articles by Lt. Col. F. H. Garrison, in *PCC* v, 35-51; and "The Greek Cult of the Dead and the Chthonian Deities in Ancient Medicine," in *AMH*, 1917, i, 35-53.

Such powers were personal and were used in the manner of one skilled in an art, but although a cultic practice, it was not a priestly function. Achilles prayed directly to Zeus of Dodona, whose responses came from the leaves of "the many tongued oak," or the dreams of the *selloi* of unwashen feet (*ib.*, xvi, 236).

Oracles were associated with the earth and were, therefore, regarded as a function of the chthonic rather than of the uranic deities. Each oracle was inspired by the god or hero presiding over it. Special virtues attached to certain spots which were supposed to favor inspiration, as clefts in the rocks or earth from which vapors arose, often of a noxious character, as at the Ploutonia in the Maiandros valley, or at bubbling hot or cold springs, as at the Gates of Thermopylai (Frazer, *Pausanias,* iii, 297). Some of these places had more virtue than others, as Delphoi in Phokis, the seat of the Pythian, the greatest of all oracles, which was inspired by Mother-Earth through Python long before it was captured by the Olympian Apollo. Its authority had such weight, especially in political matters, that it was believed that the inspiration came from Zeus and was transmitted through his son. Oracular responses were usually given while the priestess or medium was in a state of trance, ecstasy, or madness, as Pythia sitting on a tripod over the cleft at Delphoi chewing laurel leaves, drinking water, breathing the rising vapors, and muttering disconnected, half-articulated words or sounds.[22] Plato (*Phaid.*, 244) considered this a divine madness, an ecstasy in which the human soul is possessed of a deity. At first, oracles and interpretations of dreams were delivered in plain language, but later the utterances became enigmatical, ambiguous, and incoher-

[22] Farnell, *Cults,* iv, 180 ff., 222; Moore, *The History of Religions,* p. 476.

ent, and were announced by official interpreters who translated them into hexameters.

Dreams and the dream-oracle. Incubation.

Dreams were universally regarded as divine and prophetic, whether coming to an individual or through an oracle. Aristotle acknowledged (Plutarch, *de Placitis Philosophorum,* v, 2) the mantic efficacy of 'natural' dreams, and Sokrates believed that the visions of good men were pure and prophetic, that when neither appetite nor surfeiting may trouble during slumber "that part which is best in him, but may suffer it, alone by itself, in its pure essence, to behold and aspire towards some object, and apprehend what it knows not—some event, of the past, it may be, or something that now is, or will be hereafter"; with peace within, that part "wherein reason is engendered, on the move:—you know, I think, that in sleep of this sort he lays special hold on truth" (Plato, *de Republica,* 571 C).[23] In the *Iliad* (i, 63; ii, 6) Zeus is a sender of dreams, both true and false; but they were, however, more commonly ascribed to the inspiration of the lower world, so that Euripides (*Hecuba,* 70) could speak of "O Earth, dread Queen, mother of dreams that flit on sable wings!" Dreams were of two kinds; "divine oracles given in dreams," and individual, the "oracle of the soul itself in dreaming." Artemidoros (I, i b-2) divided them, further, into "dreams to be followed literally," which at times had to be explained, and "dreams which indicate the remedy indirectly," these always requiring an interpreter. The divine and prophetic nature of such visions was a part of the Orphic and Pythagorean doctrines and was described by Pindar (*Thranoi,* ii, 4-5, ed. Mommsen): "The soul slumbers while the body is active; but, when the body slumbers,

[23] Pater, *Plato and Platonism,* p. 138.

she shows forth in many a vision the approaching issues of woe and weal." Aischylos (*op. cit.*, 104) expressed the same view: "In slumber the eye of the soul waxes bright, but by day-time man's doom goes unforeseen." Demokritos believed in daimons who revealed themselves in the form of personal emanations (Plutarch, *op. cit.*). Poseidonios declared his belief in these divine communications and held that one way in which such perceptions arose was that the air was full of immortal spirits in whom all signs of truth were stamped and visible (Cicero, *de Divinatione*, i, 30). Efforts were made to entice dreams, and when sought for divine direction for healing or any other purpose, the suppliant (or any kinsman representing him) retired to the shrine of the god or hero whose inspiration was desired, and slept in the portico of the temple, or near the image of the divinity. Only the pure were permitted to approach the god, and such temple-sleep, or incubation (*egkoimesis*), was always preceded by rites of purification and by abstinence from wine and food for varying lengths of time, and a customary ritual was for the suppliant to sleep on the skin of the victim he had sacrificed (Lykophron, 1050). These ceremonies are described by Aristeides (*Oratio Sacra,* i) and were designed, in part at least, to increase the tendency to dreaming and to enhance the clearness of the vision. Such visions were more prone to occur during the early hours of the morning, "for then the soul is free from the effects of material sustenance" (Philostratos, *Vita Apollonii,* ii, 36). This dream-oracle was assumed to be more definitely inspired by the divinity, and it was, therefore, more authoritative than the ordinary vision or dream. Deities and heroes having a dream-oracle showed a strong tendency to exercise the healing function. Temple-sleep was a characteristic practice in ancient Babylonia, but it is not altogether clear how it arose in Greece, whether independently, by importation via Lydia, from Egyptian travellers, or later with the cult of Sarapis and Isis, as is sometimes asserted.[24] Indications of an ancient dream-oracle may be noted in the practice of the *selloi* at Dodona,[25] but incubation is believed to have come into use after Homer's time, and long before 333 B.C., when the first Egyptian temple in Greece was erected at Peiraieus to Aphrodite as Isis at the instance of Ptolemy I.

Priests and incubation.

The frequent allusions to priests acting as intermediaries between the suppliant and the deity, and the fact that in the cult of Sarapis and Isis it was customary for them to incubate for their patients, have led to the belief that the practice prevailed in Greek cults, though perhaps to a lesser extent. In this incubation, and the subsequent interpretation of the visions and dreams, the priests were supposed to be inspired or possessed by the god, and often appeared to be in a state of ecstasy like that of the priestesses of Pythia. At Amphikleia the oracles of Dionysos were given out by a priest who was believed to be inspired by the god and to be acting as his mouthpiece, as a *katochos,* and it is known that the same custom was followed at the Ploutonia of Hades and Persephone, and sometimes at the shrines of Asklepios (Pausanias, X, xxxiii, 11). Whether or not this led to a more or less organized profession of priests as mediums in Greece, as at the Serapeum at Memphis, is not known.[26]

[24] Gauthier, *Recherches historiques sur l'exercice de la médecine dans les temples, chez les peuples de l'antiquité,* pp. 106 ff.; also L. H. Gray, "Incubation," in *ERE* vii, 206-207.

[25] Welcker, "Zu den Alterthümern der Heilkunde bei den Griechen," in *KS* iii, 90.

[26] Hamilton, *Incubation, or Cure of Disease in Pagan Temples and Christian Churches,* p. 105; cf. *supra,* pp. 78-79.

Decadence of cults and oracles.

With the loss of independence to Rome, the Greek institutions, including the great national cults, declined. Their individuality was invaded and confused with those from Egypt, Syria, and farther east. The oracles weakened, their suppliants were few, and the most of them became silent. Plutarch in commenting on this fact (*de Defec. Orac.,* ix) quotes Sophokles as saying: "Though the gods never die, yet their gifts do." The philosophers trimmed their views to the new influences and endeavored to adjust their speculations and theories to Oriental mystic theosophy. At the same time the Eastern type of incubation, with magic and various methods of divination, was emphasized with a freshened interest in the marvellous.

Animal incarnations.

In the early Hellenic religions there are traces of animal worship and of a belief in animal incarnation of a divinity, ancestor, or hero. Apollo Lykeios was a reminder of the time when he was still a god of the wild and associated with the wolf, his sacred animal (Pausanias, II, xix, 3-4).[27] The serpent may have been worshipped in his own right, as in the old Delphic religion, with which the snake was always connected, or as the incarnation of Zeus Meilichios, Asklepios, or some other chthonian divinity.[28] The serpent was a familiar animal in Greek religion and mythology as a sacred and mystic being having magic powers which were associated with prophecy, dreams, and healing (Apollodoros, i, 96).[29] Hellenos, Kassandra, and Melampous acquired their super-

[27] Farnell, *op. cit.,* iv, 113-116.

[28] *Id.,* in *ERE* vi, 399, 404.

[29] *Id., Cults,* iii, 10; also E. Küster, "Die Schlange in der griechischen Kunst und Religion," in *RVV,* 1913, xiii, 1-172.

natural understanding and mantic powers after their ears had been cleansed by the tongue of a serpent.[30] The serpent always had a chthonic significance. It was used as a symbol of the Underworld deities and heroes, and was frequently associated with the healing cults (Ailianos, *Historia Animalium,* viii, 12; xvi, 39; also Pausanias, IX, xxxix, 3). The oracles of Trophonios at Lebadeia were delivered by a serpent (Frazer, *op. cit.,* v, 203).

Disease ascribed to superhuman agencies.

It has been shown that disease and death, like other processes of nature, the causes of which were not visible, were ascribed to superhuman agencies of celestial or chthonic origin. Zeus sent disease, yet he declared to the immortals: "Alas! How, forsooth, do mortals reproach the gods! For they say that their evils are from us; whereas they themselves, through their own infatuation, suffer griefs beyond what is destined" (*Odys.,* i, 30). Apollo sent disease and sudden death among men (*Il.,* i, 50), and Artemis inflicted disease, especially mental and nervous disorders, and death among women.[31] The chthonioi caused disease and were feared particularly for their attacks upon the nervous system, resulting in madness, hysteria, epilepsy, and general neuroses. Heroes, daimons, spirits of the dead, and the 'hounds of Hekate' were all potential agents in bringing illness among mankind. Such popular beliefs are referred to in the Hippokratic treatise, *de Morbo Sacro:*[32]

> But terrors which happen during the night, and fevers, and delirium, and jumpings out of bed, and frightful apparitions and fleeing away—all these they hold to be the plots of Hekate, and the invasions of the Heroes.

[30] Halliday, *Greek Divination,* p. 70.

[31] Gruppe, *Griechische Mythologie und Religionsgeschichte,* pp. 1273-1274.

[32] Adams, *The Genuine Works of Hippocrates,* ii, 337.

Herakles developed madness through the chthonian
Lyssa by direction of Hera. Poseidon, Ares, and Herakles are all mentioned as causing disease; and Greek
literature contains many such allusions. Long, painful,
and wasting illness was due to being "grazed" by a hate-
ful deity (*Odys.*, v, 395-396). Vengeful fiends brought
disease (Sophokles, *Trachiniæ*, 1236). Sudden illness was
ascribed to Pan (Euripides, *Medea*, 1170 ff.). It was not
clear whether Phaidra's wasting disease was caused by
Pan, Hekate, the Korybantes, Kybele, or Diktynna (*id.*,
Hippolytus, 170 ff.). Epilepsy was supposed to be passed
from one person to another. Contagion as the cause of
the spread of disease was not recognized by the Greeks,
and such apparent diffusion of convulsive disease was
probably of the hysterical variety, similar to the chorea
and religious frenzies of more recent date.

Attitude of divinity toward disease and healing.

Such misfortunes were visited upon mankind in anger,
revenge, and punishment, but (in the time of Homer at
least) it appears that all gods had equal powers for protection and relief. The Greek traditions and myths contain numerous instances of many gods, heroes, and heroines exercising their supernatural powers for healing;
but only two deities, Paian and Asklepios, are known
exclusively as healers. The earliest traditions of Greek
healing cluster about the divinity Paian, the Centaur
Cheiron, and the hero Asklepios, with Apollo as an oracular deity in an honorary capacity.

Paian and Apollo.

Paian was the first Greek divinity who specialized in
healing, and his name frequently appears in classical
literature as a generic term for divine skill in the healing
art (*Odys.*, iv, 232), while as the physician of the Olym-

pian circle he dresses the wounds of injured deities (*Il.*, v, 401, 900). Although often confused with Apollo, Paian is distinct in all early Greek literature (Hesiod, *Fragmenta*, 144); and as mentioned by Homer (*Il.*, xvi, 514-529).[33] Apollo was not a healer, but acted merely as a friendly, divine helper when, in response to the appeal of Glaukos, he "dried the black gore from the grievous wound and instilled strength into his [Sarpedon's] soul." Solon in the sixth century B.C. still speaks (xii, 53-62; *Frag.*, 13, 45) of Paian and Apollo as separate personalities, describing the followers of the former as "physicians having the task of Paian, rich in herbs"; but in referring to Apollo and his priests, he omits any mention of a healing function. The epithet Paian as applied to Apollo is first found in the Orphic hymns (xxxiv, 1) of the late sixth century B.C. Pindar (*Pythia*, iv, 480) gives him the same title; while Aischylos (*op. cit.*, 62) ascribes to Apollo Loxias the surname *iatromantis*, and after about this time Apollo is frequently referred to as the supreme divine healer. It is significant that these titles indicative of the healing function were given Apollo after the time when the alliance with Asklepios is believed to have been effected in Phokis. Although Apollo bore the epithets he does not appear as active in healing, but rather as having honorary titles and exercising a general, vague supervision over the art. Notwithstanding the popularity of the Delphic oracle, only two cases of minor illness have been found recorded as having appealed to him there. The active duty of healing the sick was performed by his son Asklepios, the Thessalian hero-physician, to whom he, as Apollo Maleates, gave his divine approval.

[33] Le Clerc, *Histoire de la médecine*, 2d ed., pp. 18-19; also, Usener, *Götternamen*, p. 153.

The cradle of Greek medicine.

Of all the many states of Greece, Thessaly stands forth prominently in medicine as being the cradle in which the early healing customs and traditions of the Greeks were fostered. Here on the slopes of Mount Pelion, Cheiron, the mystic Centaur, lived, famed for his scientific attainments and his knowledge of the medicinal properties of plants. A tribe of Thessaly and near-by Magnesia claimed descent from him, worshipped him as a divine physician, and treasured his plant-lore as a hereditary and sacred possession. Even the witches of Thessaly, whom the people credited with making the moon descend to earth, were botanists and were acquainted with the marvellous virtues of medicinal plants.[34] In this environment Asklepios had his mythical birth and breeding. The god Herakles and many of the ancient heroes who developed healing functions were also pupils of Cheiron and learned the precepts rare that enabled them "Disease and mortal pain to 'suage" (Pindar, *op. cit.*, iii, 45-46).

Early healing customs.

The epics relate that the knowledge of the healing properties of plants which Asklepios had received from Cheiron was applied by those "excellent physicians," his sons Machaon and Podaleirios, during the Trojan War, and, according to all tradition, they transmitted their learning to their descendants, the clan of Asklepiadai, as a sacred heritage. In this heroic age, wounds were treated by those "skilled in many remedies," who adopted the rational methods of removing foreign bodies and dressing with mild, soothing, salubrious, or bitter, pain-assuaging roots and herbs (*Il.*, iv, 219; xi, 512, 830, 845; xvi, 29); the only mention of magic is when it was used

[34] Cumont, *The Oriental Religions in Roman Paganism*, p. 186.

to stay the black blood of the wounded Odysseus (*Odys.,* xix, 456). When disease came and the camp of the Greeks was decimated by pestilence, they sought a seer, a prophet, a priest, or one informed in dreams to tell them how to appease the wrath of the gods; and they offered prayers and unblemished hecatombs for sacrifice in atonement and expiation. Disease, as it affected the individual, had little interest for the writers of the epics, yet they indicate the means ordinarily taken for relief by declaring that the gods were the sources of health. The beloved father lies in a disease and wasting for a long time; "and the gods have freed him welcome from his evil plight" (*ib.,* v, 397).

The healing rituals and miracles.

The general powers of the gods and the mantic potencies of the seers and heroes were invoked for healing by the customary rituals, hymns of praise, prayers, and sacrifice; and it may be surmised that the wonder-working imagination of the people idealized the subsequent cures as the superhuman, beneficent acts of friendly deities, demigods, and heroes, irrespective of all other means employed. Recoveries from serious illnesses were beyond any understanding that the people had of the natural laws governing the body in health and disease, and being, therefore, regarded as miracles wrought by a superhuman, spiritual power, they were so recorded on steles and tablets.

Magic and healing.

Magic, that "bastard sister of science,"[35] which included rites of positive efficacy both with and without appeal to divinity,[36] had dominated religion and the heal-

[35] Frazer, *The Magic Art,* 3d ed., i, 222.
[36] Farnell, in *ERE* vi, 401.

ing art in Mesopotamia and Egypt for centuries before the traditional settlement of Hellas, warping the mind and effectually dwarfing intellectual progress. A similar relation existed in Greece, though materially tempered in quality. The affinity of magic with religion in antiquity was so close that they were not differentiated clearly, but for Greece, and especially for Rome, it may be understood that, as a general proposition, the worship of the native gods recognized by the State, and the ceremonials prescribed by officials, were the tests of orthodoxy and religion. The cults of other gods and their rites, as well as the foreign religions (Theokritos, ii, 462), especially those of the Orient, were magic and heterodox.[37] This, however, did not necessarily impair belief in the reality and power of magic. The hymns of the Orphic cult were full of magic incantations and formulas. Incantation and exorcism were a part of the hilastic rites for the cure of disease, but the æsthetic sense, serene temperament, and freedom of thought saved the Greeks from debasing and degrading their religious ideals with the darker, cramping superstitions and sorcery of their neighbors.

The methods of religious healing.

The cures reported in Greek religious practice may be grouped as effected by either one of two methods, (a) the direct; healing by direct divine intervention, very commonly by the transmission of the divine power by means of some agent or sacred object; and (b) the indirect; healing by the employment of measures directed by divine communications through oracles, dreams, visions, or omens.

The direct method.

The healing power of the gods was transmitted by the

[37] K. F. Smith, "Magic (Greek and Roman)," in *ERE* viii, 284 ff.

simple divine presence, by the laying-on of hands, through some sacred relic, or through the medium of a priest, priestess, or sacred animal. In these cases, the god repeatedly appears in person, and may apply reme- dies, but seldom or never fails to be attended by some member of his official family; he is often represented by one of them, as by a priest in the garb of the deity, and occasionally by a sacred animal, usually the serpent. The hand of the deity was believed to have both apotropaic and healing powers; and healing by coming in contact with the image of the god, or by the laying-on of the hand was a common practice in many cults, especially in those of Asklepios, Dionysos-Epaphios, Sabazios, and Eilei-thyia. The right hand was considered beneficent, but the left hand had an opposite or sinister influence, somewhat akin to the reputed power of the Gorgon's blood; that from the right side being curative, and that from the left having injurious, even fatal, effects (Apollodoros, III, x, 3). The right, or healing, hand of the god was repre-sented as being raised, with the palm outward and the thumb and first two fingers open, the other two being partly closed, very much as used in the gesture of sup-plication and blessing (Pausanias, V, xxv, 5; Frazer, *Paus.*, iii, 641).[38] The raised hand of Asklepios and Sara-pis not only healed the sick, but saved from shipwreck and other dangers. The closed right hand, or the use of the left, was of sinister import and was believed to check all progress at child-birth. In sculptures, the god is shown approaching the bedside and extending the right hand over the patient, or touching him with it. Such use of the hand for healing and protection was expressed by the epithet Hyperdexios, which was given Zeus and Apollo, and Hyperdexia, given to Athena (*IG* XII, i, 22).[39]

[38] The attitude of prayer in ancient art.
[39] Weinreich, *Antike Heilungswunder*, p. 41.

Examples.

Suidas reports that Asklepios healed Theopompos, the writer of comedies, by the laying-on of hands, as was shown in an Attic relief;[40] and another cure was effected by his healing right hand and a healing drink (*IG* iv, 952, 122 ff.). Diogenes Laertios (v, 76) says that Demetrios of Phaleron wrote pæans as a votive offering of gratitude to Sarapis, who had restored his sight by his healing touch.[41] A barren woman, sleeping in the temple, dreamed that Asklepios came and divested her of her clothing, after which he touched her body with his finger, where-upon she was healed of her disability and bore a child to her husband (*IG* iv, 952, 60 ff.). A man having but one eye slept in the *abaton,* and dreaming that Asklepios applied an ointment to the empty socket, he awoke in the morning with two sound eyes (*IG* iv, 951, 120 ff.). Herai-eus of Mitylene, who was bald, slept in the *abaton* and dreamed that the god applied an ointment to his head; when he awoke, he had a thick growth of hair. Galenos was cured as the result of a dream in which Asklepios appeared to him; he then became a physician, healed by the dream-oracle, and, directed by dreams, he performed operations and practiced optics.[42]

The divine healing power was transmitted through sacred serpents and dogs (*CIA* II, iii, 1651; Pausanias, II, xxvii, 2). A man's foot that had been badly lacerated by the bite of a wild beast was promptly cured after the wound had been licked by one of the cult reptiles. Thyson of Hermione was blind in both eyes, but recovered his sight at once after they had been licked by a sacred dog. Marinos tells of Proklos,[43] the philosopher, who, suffering

[40] Weinreich, *op. cit.,* p. 2.
[41] *Ib.,* p. 6.
[42] *Ib.,* p. 77.
[43] *Ib.,* p. 90, note 3.

probably from arthritis, had covered the part with a
cloth. A sparrow, sacred to Asklepios, plucked the cloth
away and the disease with it. The statues of Theagenes in
Thasos, and of Pulydamas at Olympia cured fevers (Frazer, *op. cit.*, iv, 39). The statue of the Corinthian general
Pelichos, which possessed healing powers, saved from
fevers; and Eukrates was so grateful for his own cure
that he plated the breast of the effigy with gold.[44] Gaining power to cure oneself by touching the image of the
god, or his altar, was recognized; and healing by kissing
some sacred object, or being touched by the foot of a holy
person, is vaguely referred to.

The indirect method.

Accounts of cures by following directions received
through dreams and visions are more common and are
often more circumstantial. An extant fragment from the
shrine at Lebena records cures due to the application of
remedies indicated by the god in visions.[45] The remedies
prescribed varied widely from mild and innocent purga-
tives, roots, herbs, diets, fasts, baths, and rubbings with
ointments, to gymnastics and general regimen. These
various measures were usually applied with some sympathetic magic, or were accompanied by the use of magic
formulas and incantations. Sometimes the remedies were
heroic, as repeated emetics, bleedings to exhaustion, and
plunging into streams in midwinter (Aristeides, *op. cit.*,
i, ii). During the third century B.C. Hierophilos remarked
that remedies were the gifts of the gods, and, when rightly
used, were "the hands of the gods,"[46] and, in parts of
Greece, an herb, called 'the hand of the mother of god,'

[44] Weinreich, *op. cit.*, p. 137.

[45] J. Zingerle, "Heilinschrift von Lebena," in *MAIA*, 1896, xxi, 67-
92.

[46] Dyer, *Studies of the Gods of Greece*, p. 219.

was scattered about before and after a birth as a protection to the parturient woman.[47] Purifications and fasting before incubation, followed by prescriptions received by visions or dreams, appear as the ordinary procedure in the cults of many deities, heroes and heroines; exemplified especially in those of Hades, Dionysos, and Amphiaraos, as well as that of Asklepios; the inspired message being received by the patient, or through the medium of a priest, relative, or friend.[48]

Sacred waters.

Many of the waters and streams of Greece, especially the rivers Acheloos and Kephisos, were spiritualized and had remarkable curative virtues (Pausanias, IV, xxxi, 4; V, v, 11; VIII, xix, 3). Mineral springs and baths, many sacred to Herakles, are first mentioned by Ibykos (*Frag.*, 46). Sophokles refers (*op. cit.*, 634) to the hot baths at Mount Œta (near Thermopylai), and the poet Krates and his friends visited a hot bath where there was a sort of hospital, called *paioneion,* at which Paian was invoked (Belluæ, *Frag.*, 2). All healing sanctuaries were abundantly supplied with water; and although some of these waters appear to have had definite medicinal properties, they were, for the most part, magical. The drinking of the water at the spring at Pergamon gave speech to a mute, while upon another it conferred the gift of prophecy (Aristeides, *Oratio in puteum Æsculapii,* i, 447). The Boiotians divined by means of a drinking well among the

[47] Weinreich, *op. cit.,* p. 12, note 3.

[48] For further details concerning the cures effected by Greek religious methods and the inscriptions relating them, consult Weinreich, *ib.;* J. Baunack, "Epigraphische Kleinigheiten aus Griechenland," in *Philologus,* 1889, xlviii, 385-427; T. Baunack, "Inschriften aus dem kretischen Asklepieion," in *ib.,* 1890, xlix, 577-606; and J. Baunack, "Inschriften aus dem Asklepieion zu Epidauros," in *SGAS,* 1886, i, 120-144.

ruins of Hysiai, at the half-finished temple of Apollo
(Pausanias, IX, ii, 1); and the water from the spring at
Kassotis ran underground and inspired women with the
spirit of prophecy in the shrine of Apollo at Delphoi (*ib.*,
X, xxiv, 7).

Votive offerings.

Fees were paid, and objects of various kinds were
presented as thank-offerings for cures, often in compliance with previous vows. Such gifts were of money,
sculptured replicas of parts cured, inscriptions on tablets, bas-reliefs depicting the god and his attendants in
healing scenes, statues of the deity, or ornaments and
relics dedicated to the divinity and his temple. Hymns
of praise composed for the deity were offered, and
several orations of Aristeides eulogizing Asklepios are
supposed to have had a similar origin. Aristarchos was
healed by the extended right hand of the god and was
required to write a votive drama based upon Asklepian
legends.[49] Side by side with tablets relating cures were
others warning of dreadful happenings if the suppliant
should fail to keep his vows or should neglect to reward
the services of the deity.[50] Instances are given of cures
that were revoked and of punishments that were inflicted
upon such recreants.

General evidences of Greek religious healing.

Such are a few of the records illustrative of traditional
religious healing that have been found on the sites of the
old healing sanctuaries of Asklepios, chiefly at Athens
and Epidauros, in inscriptions, and classical literature.
Further excavations, especially on the sites of the shrines
of other deities, would doubtless corroborate the references made by classical writers indicating that the heal-

[49] Weinreich, *op. cit.*, pp. 4-5.
[50] *Ib.*, p. 4, note 2.

ing practices of other cults, as of Herakles at Thermopylai, Dionysos at Amphikleia, Amphiaraos at Oropos,
Hades at Acharaka and Nysa, and Trophonios at Lebadeia, were of a similar general character. The religious,
magic, and rational elements of practice were probably
blended at all such sanctuaries, but the religious features
continued to predominate over the practical. The religiosity of the people and their faith in their gods would
have prevented those engaged in healing from wholly
disregarding religion or even from making a wide departure, if they had so desired. It is known that physicians
practicing among the people independently of the cults
were not permitted to neglect the healing gods. At
Athens, and probably elsewhere, they were obliged to
sacrifice to Asklepios and Hygieia twice each year for
themselves as healers and for their patients (*CIA* ii,
352 b).

Miraculous cures.

The character of the cures recorded on the tablets
found in the excavations at Epidauros and Athens led
Kavvadias to assert that the recoveries at the Asklepieia
during the Greek period were entirely of the class of
these *iamata*, or miraculous acts of the god, and that only
later, during the Roman period, when the dream-oracles
were more in evidence, was there an infusion of ration-
ality in the treatment of disease. It has been pointed out,
however, that in all religions there are tales designed for
edification and traditions of miracles illustrative of the
divinity and power of the god; and that these records on
steles and tablets should not be regarded as historical
documents, but rather as collections to influence doubters
and for the gratification of the credulous (Frazer, *op.
cit.*, ii, 239).[51] Mythical tales were current concerning all

[51] Kavvadias, *Fouilles d'Épidaure*, p. 115; also E. Thrämer, "Health
and Gods of Healing (Greek and Roman)," in *ERE* vi, 542.

Greek divinities, and there were legends of miraculous cures effected by deities who practiced healing occasionally, as well as those definitely identified with therapeutic cults. They were the stock stories of the cults and were freely used to impress the suppliants with the belief that the supernatural powers of the divinity were still available for them. At the sanctuary of Epidauros, as probably at the shrines of other healing gods and heroes, they were diligently used as exhibits to render the mind more susceptible to dreams and visions, as well as to make it more pliable for mental suggestion and for carrying out the practical measures directed by these divine revelations. The records found represent the superstitious elements always present in religious healing, and the cures recited were actual miracles, evidences of the divinity of the healer, or pious frauds, according to the point of view. These testimonials and ex-votos do not in any way negative the cultic traditions and collateral evidence that rational remedies were used in connection with theurgic practice, and in compliance with the interpretations of dreams and visions.

Origin of rational medicine in temple practice.

It has been shown that the use of remedies from plants was a customary practice among the early tribes and their descendants; and it cannot be doubted that this traditional therapeutic folklore was transmitted by the Asklepiads to their brethren of Knidos and Kos, and formed the basis for the observations from which the early endeavors for scientific methods in medicine were developed. There was a current tradition that Hippokrates learned and practiced the dietetic part of medicine from the narratives of cures suspended in the temple at Kos (Strabo, XIV, ii, 19 = p. 657 C; also Pliny, *Historia Naturalis,* xx, 100). Such legends are upheld by the testi-

mony of many ancient writers, particularly by Apollodoros (iv, 22) and Iamblichos (*de Mysteriis,* iii, 3), that
profane medicine and the use of remedies and regimen
arose in cultic practice in association with the dream-
oracle, the θεῖοι ὄνειροι, and the interpretation of dreams,
and more definitely in the healing shrines of Asklepios,
who, more than all others, represented the highest type
of religious healing in ancient Greece.

Religious and practical medicine.

The Hippokratic writings indicate that the Asklepiadai
of the early medical schools conducted within the cult of
Asklepios were exceedingly practical in their modes of
thought. That such was the fact is clearly shown by the
remark of a Knidian author that "to offer up prayers is
no doubt becoming and good, but while praying to the
gods a man ought also to use his own exertions" (Hippokrates, *de Insomniis,* Sec. IV, ch. ii (87)).[52] Although uti-
lizing the religious methods according to the universal
belief of their time, they endeavored to eliminate superstition and to place the practice of healing on a more
rational footing, based upon observations, many of which
were made a matter of record. A recent writer, referring
to ancient Greek medicine in general, very aptly remarks
that "Without any method of centralizing medical education and standardizing teaching there was a great
variety of doctrines and of practice in vogue among them,
and much of this was on a low level of folk custom. Such
lower grade material of Greek origin has come down to
us in abundance, . . . But the overwhelming mass of
earlier Greek medical literature sets forth for us a pure
scientific effort to observe and to classify disease on
rational grounds, and to apply remedies, when possible,

[52] Adams, *op. cit.,* i, 68; also *Opera Omnia,* ed. Anutius Foesius,
1662, i, 376.

on a reasoned basis.''[53] Thus lines of cleavage between theurgic and practical medicine were present as early as the fifth century B.C. The spirit of religious tolerance in antiquity permitted the application of rational measures in the treatment at the temples with the same freedom and independence of religious control that characterized the formulation of theories by philosophers. It may be that Aristotle (*Politica*, iii, 15) wished to draw a contrast and to emphasize the absence of prejudice and control when he called attention to the restrictions placed upon Egyptian physicians in being obliged to follow established and officially authorized methods of treatment. The encouragement of, and the coöperation in, the use of rational therapeutics in the cult of Asklepios is illustrated, if not fully confirmed, by an Athenian votive tablet of the fourth century B.C. found in the excavations, showing a patient lying on a couch and a physician attending him, while the larger, passive figure of Asklepios stands by, supervising, and by his presence giving his divine sanction to the treatment.[54] In a dedication found at Kibyra, in Asia Minor, the person healed gave thanks to Asklepios, to the Tyche of the city, and to Dionysios, the physician who treated him, indicating the coöperation between theurgical and practical therapeutics.[55]

Introduction of foreign healing cults.

In the later period, under Roman domination, foreign cults were introduced. Isis and Sarapis had already come from Egypt, and their worship spread rapidly, threatening serious rivalry with that of Asklepios. The cult of Mithra and other Oriental deities gained a foothold and

[53] Singer, *Greek Biology and Greek Medicine*, p. 82.

[54] Holländer, *Plastik und Medizin*, p. 122, fig. 26.

[55] W. Kubitschek and W. Reichel, "Bericht über eine im Sommer 1893 ausgeführte Reise in Karien," in *AKAW*, 1893, xxx, 104.

a certain following in Greece, but Asklepios never failed to hold the first place in the pantheon as the active, representative god of healing. About this time there appeared a growing tendency toward magic and a craving for the marvellous. Stimulated apparently by foreign influences, the evils attendant upon incubation, especially the interpretation of dreams by priests, became pronounced. Whatever of deception had been practiced by the cults in the earlier, Greek period, frauds of a grosser character frequently developed into a cause of scandal. These abuses, occurring in a period coming within the scope of early history and commented on by satirists and historians, were so emphasized that several modern writers have assumed that such practices characterized all Greek religious therapeutics, and that "the priest-physicians were only unworthy charlatans who were able to advance their own fortunes, but not the science of medicine,"[56] and the healing sanctuaries have been stigmatized "as hives of priestly chicanery and senile superstition."[57]

The descent of Greek medicine.

Greek medicine appears to have arisen from the early folklore of the people blended with their religious beliefs. The descent from this general fount was early divided into two main streams, the one flowing through cultic channels to Hippokrates and his followers; the other through physicians who practiced outside the cults. As history emerges from the mists of fable and poetry, skilled physicians appear as practicing among the people and as official doctors of the larger cities, and as independent of the beliefs in theurgic medicine as their per-

[56] Malgaigne, *Lettres sur l'histoire de la chirurgie*, pp. 59-70; also Daremberg, *État de la médecine entre Homère et Hippocrate*, pp. 57-58.

[57] Thrämer, in *ERE* vi, 542.

sonalities and the sentiment of the age permitted. Many prominent citizens of older Greece may be considered in this category, although most of them are better known as philosophers, such as Thales, Anaximandros, Phere-kydes, Empedokles, Epimenides, Pythagoras, and Anax-agoras. Self-styled physicians worked among the people from very early times, and in the later Greek period (possibly much earlier) they had their offices (*iatreia*) on the streets and conducted hospitals. Many cities had physicians under salary who were heads of public hospitals with a full equipment of consulting rooms, pharmacies, and operating rooms with instruments. Demokedes of Kroton held such an office at Athens in the sixth century B.C. and became the most distinguished physician of his day (Herodotos, iii, 125). An inscription from Karpathos praises the physician Menokritos for remaining at his post during the plague, and another from Athens tells of the award of a wreath to Pheidias, a Rhodian physician, for offering his services as a public doctor gratis.[58] Allusions in literature suggest that physicians practicing outside the temples were regarded with contempt by those within, but they carry no conviction that such statements were justified. The Greeks of all classes were faithful to their gods, and it is believed that physicians, both without and within the temples of the several States, looked up to Asklepios as a divine exemplar (*CIA* ii, 352 b). Under the fostering care of the healing temples on the one hand, and the independent physicians and philosophers on the other, medical knowledge was enriched by facts gathered from many recorded observations; and questions arising from natural phenomena of human life were examined, coördinated, and clarified until the healing art emerged from temple schools, chiefly from Knidos, Kos, Kroton, and, finally,

[58] Gardner, *New Chapters in Greek History*, p. 360.

Alexandria, and from the *iatreia* of the cities, elucidated and systematized by tentative theories for further study, application and preparation for indefinite development.

PART II: THE HEALING DEITIES, HEROES, AND HEROINES

THE deities, heroes, and heroines sketched in this section embrace those who were recognized as healers, and many others known in mythology in various other spheres of activity, but who, on occasion, exercised their curative powers for the sick and wounded.

THE HEALING DEITIES

Asklepios[59]	Hades	The Nymphs
Amphiaraos	Hekate	Orpheus
Aphrodite	Helios	Paian
Apollo	Hephaistos	Pan
Aristaios	Hera	Persephone
Artemis	Herakles	Poseidon
Athena	Hermes	Prometheus
Auxesia	Hygieia	Rhea
Damia	Isis	Sabazios
Demeter	The Kabeiroi	Sarapis
Dionysos	Kirke	Telesphoros
Eileithyia	Leto	Themis
Epaphos	Maleates	Trophonios
Genetyllis	The Muses	Zeus

ASKLEPIOS

ASKLEPIOS, first mentioned by Homer (*Il.*, iv, 194) as a "blameless physician," eventually became the chief heal-

[59] Asklepios, being the chief exemplar of all divine healing in ancient Greece, is placed at the head of the list and considered first.

ing divinity of the Greeks, the most respected exemplar of divine healing of the pagan world, and one of the most prominent deities of the pantheon. About him centered the famous and widespread cult whose devotees, the Asklepiadai, were the earliest to develop and record the clinical observations that inaugurated the evolution of medicine from a purely theurgic to a scientific basis, and whose ethical standards have been accepted throughout the Christian era.

The name.

According to an Epidaurian legend, the name Asklepios was derived from Aigle, one of his reputed mothers; but by another tradition it was traced to a combination of Askles, the name of a king whom he cured of eye-disease early in his career, with Epios ('Mild'), a term by which the god had been known.[60] The correct etymology is quite uncertain, but it is of interest to note that the legends of Phokis associate Asklepios with Apollo at Delphoi, while those of Messenia and Lakonia bring him into relation with the sun-god Helios. Hence as a deity he appears to have been an amalgamation of a chthonic hero and a solar divinity.

His origin.

History makes no reference to the origin of Asklepios except as drawn from local traditions and myths celebrated by early Greek poets and other writers, which were evidently altered and distorted from time to time in the interest of the cult and its chief divinity. The estimates of tradition assign his life to a period anterior to the Trojan War, and about the thirteenth century B.C. Homer (*Il.*, ii, 729; iv, 219; xi, 512) refers to him as a

---

[60] Gruppe, *op. cit.*, pp. 1441-1442; also Fox, *Mythology, Greek and Roman*, p. 279.

native of Thessaly, one of the Greek heroes who was instructed by Cheiron in the use of herbs and roots and the art of healing, and whose sons, Machaon and Podaleirios, led the men from Trikke, hilly Ithome, and Oichalia to the Trojan War, where they applied the healing art taught them by their father with such skill that they gained renown as men worth many others. It is related that, in his youth, Asklepios accompanied the Argonauts on their voyage to Kolchis, where he outstripped all other pupils of Cheiron in healing. The Minyai were among his early devotees, and it may be that it was on this expedition that he gained the favor of the tribe.

An earth-spirit and hero.

Asklepios was ranked as a hero of ancient Greece, and his cult at its inception was, accordingly, that of an earth-spirit, the soul of an ancestor worshipped by his descendants. The serpent was his symbol, and he acquired an oracle. These essentially chthonic characteristics served to class him from the beginning and throughout his long career as belonging to the Underworld, notwithstanding the many aspects of a solar deity and god of light which he acquired after his apotheosis, and in which he appeared at many of his later sanctuaries. The traditions of Thessaly indicate that his own tribe and their neighbors regarded him as a hero.

Development of the cult. Asklepios and Apollo.

The cult of Asklepios, developing about the memory of his deeds of healing, grew in favor, and from Trikke, his most ancient shrine (Strabo, IX, v, 17 = p. 437 C), spread to Ithome, across the borders of Aitolia to Oichalia, to Minyean Northern Boiotia, and rested for a time at Orchomenos, near the Lebadeian shrine of Trophonios, who was then dispensing similar benefactions.[61] The cult soon gained a footing at Hyettos, Thespiai, and Thisbe. It was carried into Phokis, where the traditional and implacable attitude of the Phlegyan tribe, under whose patronage the Asklepian cult was extending, toward the cult of Apollo, which had forcibly established itself at Delphoi and presided over its oracle, resulted in a clash of interests. The compromise effected proved of advantage both to Asklepios and to Apollo. Apollo retained the Delphic oracle which he had won from Python, and Asklepios was adopted as the son of the great Olympian. The natures of the two, one a hero and the other the god of light, poetry, and music, differed materially, yet their common interest in the oracle and in healing served as a lasting bond between them. Asklepios, the earth-spirit, became subordinate to Apollo, but retained full independence for himself and his cult. Henceforth he was not only the physician and benefactor of mankind, but he was the active, efficient agent who bestowed his blessings under the divine sanction and patronage of the supreme healer. Asklepios was accorded the Homeric epithet Paian; while Apollo assumed the title Maleates, the name of a god who was supposed to have come from the North with Asklepios, so that as Apollo Maleates he presided over the great healing sanctuary of Epidauros. Apollo received a share of the shrine at Trikke, which, Isyllos intimates in a pæan, retained a relic of the primitive ritual, a cave into which the suppliant descended to communicate with the earth-god or hero.[62] It may be surmised that the adjustment effected at Delphoi and the association at Trikke marked the beginning of the traditions

[61] E. Thrämer, in Pauly-Wissowa, ii, 1643.

[62] Walton, *The Cult of Asklepios*, pp. 43 f.; cf. also von Wiliamowitz-Möllendorf, *Isyllos von Epidauros*, and Baunack, *Arische Studien*, i, 147-160.

that connected Apollo with the birth-legends of Asklepios, and that the original tradition gave the honor of the
paternity of Asklepios to a certain Ischys rather than the
mythical Apollo.

The birth-legends.

The oldest definite and most generally accepted legend
of the birth of Asklepios follows the account found in
the Homeric *Hymn to Asklepios*, Hesiod's *Fragmenta*,
and Pindar's third *Pythian Ode*, which make him a member of the Phlegyan tribe, inhabiting the Magnesian coast
and Phthiotis, and possibly related to the Lapithai. The
Homeric *Hymn* is as follows:

> I begin to sing of Asklepios, son of Apollo and healer of dis-
> eases, whom fair Koronis, daughter of Phlegyas, bare in the
> Dotian plain, a great joy to men, a soother of cruel pangs. Hail
> to thee, my lord; in my song I make prayer to thee!

The story runs that Koronis, daughter of King Phlegyas, while with child by Apollo, fell in love with the Arkadian Ischys; and Hesiod (*op. cit.*, 148) says that "to him,
then, came a crow as messenger from the sacred feast to
most holy Pytho, and he told unshorn Phoibos of secret
deeds, that Ischys, son of Elatos, had wedded Koronis,
daughter of Phlegyas, of birth divine" (cf. Ovid, *Metamorphoses*, ii, 600 ff.). Pindar varies the tale, relating
that Apollo in his omniscience was aware of the unchaste
deed and sent his vengeful sister to Lakereia, where she
punished the guilty Koronis and many of her friends
with death. When Koronis lay on the funeral pyre, Apollo
relented, seized the babe from its mother's womb, and

> Away the struggling child he bare,
>   And bade the Pelian Centaur sage
> Store its young mind with precepts rare
>   Disease and mortal pain to 'suage (*Pyth.*, iii, 45-46).

And thus on the slopes of Mount Pelion, fostering
Cheiron

The hero Asklepios bred;
Who first taught pain the writhing wretch to spare,
Touch'd by whose healing hand the pale diseases fled (*ib.*, 5-7).

There were variations of these legends: that because
of its evil tidings Apollo cursed the crow, which from
white became black (Scholion on *Pyth.*, iii, 48); that
Apollo slew Ischys; and that Hermes, at the instance of
Apollo, rescued the child and carried it to Cheiron (Pausanias, II, xxvi, 6). According to another legend, Ischys,
the father of Asklepios, was a Thessalian and a son of
Elatos; but confused with another Ischys, son of Elatos
of Arkadia. The Asklepian myths are thus an integral
part of the traditions of the Thessalian tribes; and that
Trikke on the Lethaios river was the birthplace of the
god and the cradle of the cult is supported by Homer in
his *Catalogue of Ships* (*Il.*, ii, 729-732) and is emphasized by Strabo (IX, v, 17; XIV, i, 39 = pp. 437, 647 C;
cf. oracle in Eusebios, *Præparatio Evangelica,* III, xiv,
6). A Messenian tradition traces the descent through the
Lapithai tribe, from Lapithie, son of Apollo and Stilbe.
The Scholiast on Pindar (*op. cit.*, iii, 14), quoting the poet
Asklepiades, tells of another mother and a sister: "And
Arsinoë, uniting with the son of Zeus and Leto, bare a
son Asklepios, blameless and strong," while a sister was
born of the same union, "Eriopis, with lovely hair."

The Epidaurian legends.

The Epidaurian legend (Pausanias, II, xxvi, 4-5) gives
that sanctuary additional prestige by transferring the
birth of Asklepios thither. The story told is that Koronis
accompanied her father, King Phlegyas, to Argolis, and,
unknown to him, with child by Apollo, gave it secret birth
on the slope of Mount Tittheion, formerly Mount Myr-

gion. Here the babe, nursed by a goat of a near-by herd, was guarded by the watch-dog of the flock,[63] and when discovered by Aristhanas, the shepherd, it shed a radiance that declared it to be of divine parentage, thus gaining for Asklepios the later epithet Aiglær, a light-god. When he was a lad, he could cure the sick and raise the dead. Another version of the birth-legend, issued from the *hieron* of Epidauros with the authority of the Delphic oracle, was celebrated by the poet Isyllos in a pæan during the third century b.c.[64] Here all suggestions of secrecy and unfaithfulness were omitted, and Asklepios was declared to be a native of Epidauros, the son of Apollo by his marriage with Aigle, a daughter of Phlegyas, who was called Koronis because of her beauty. The babe was born within the sacred precinct, and Apollo named him Asklepios, "the reliever of disease, giver of health, a boon to mortals," after his mother. This legend of the Peloponnesos connects Asklepios with the sun-god Helios, since, according to Messenian and Arkadian traditions, Arsinoë, the parent or, as sometimes claimed, the wife of Asklepios, was the daughter of Helios; and Aigle, the wife of Helios, becomes in the legend the mother of the healing god.

Other legends.

According to another Messenian legend, the mother of Asklepios was Arsinoë, the daughter of Leukippos (Pausanias, II, xxvi, 6; III, xxvi, 4); and this was supported by the fact that in Messenia were towns called Ithome and Oichalia, with a deserted Trikke near by (*ib.*, IV, iii, 2), although it is asserted that these sites were built by Machaon after the Trojan War. From

[63] The dog thus became one of the symbols of Asklepios. Cf. *infra*, p. 308.
[64] Walton, *op. cit.*, p. 33.

southern Arkadia came another tradition of parentage
from Arsippos and Arsinoë, the daughter of Leukippos
(Apollodoros, III, x, 3; Cicero, *de Natura Deorum*, iii,
22). Aristeides, writing from Knidos, attempts to explain the different names of the mother by saying that
Arsinoë was called Koronis in her youth. There are other
legends of birth which are largely local and lack substantial support, as that Asklepios was born at Telphousa and
was left to perish, but was found by Antolaos and nursed
by a turtledove (τρυγών), or, according to Pausanias
(VIII, xxv, 11), by a woman named Trygon; and another
that the child was nursed by a dog.[65]

The family of Asklepios.

The immediate family of Asklepios varies according
to several traditions. In Epidauros his wife was named
Epione. She was the daughter of Merops, King of Kos,
and the mother of Machaon and Podaleirios, and of the
sisters Hygieia, Panakeia, Iaso, and Akeso. Hygieia is
sometimes referred to as the sister or wife of Asklepios
(Aristeides, lxxix, 5; *Hymni Orphici*, lxvii, 7); and the
children by Hygieia are given as Panakeia, Epio, and
Iaso (Herondas, iv, 4-5). Legends coming from elsewhere
than Epidauros give the name of the wife as Lampetia,
who, according to Lakonian and Messenian tradition, was
connected with Aigle and Helios, and whose children
were given the same as Epione's, except that a daughter
Aigle is mentioned and Hygieia is omitted.[66] Other traditions refer to the wife under other names, as Aiglaia,
Arsinoë, Hippone, Koronis, and Xanthe. In addition to
his family, there were in the retinue of the god certain
daimons, such as Euamerion, a 'spirit of good days,' who

[65] For a more detailed discussion of these birth-legends, see E. Thrämer, in Roscher, i, 634 f., and in Pauly-Wissowa, ii, 1643 ff.
[66] Dindorf, *Aristophanis Comœdia*, iv, 228-230.

was worshipped as a god at Titane,[67] and whom Pausanias (II, xi, 7) equates with Telesphoros of Pergamon, the daimon of convalescence, and with Akesis of Epidauros; and a hypothetical son, Ianiscos.

His descendants.

The cult once established, the family of Asklepios and his descendants devoted themselves to healing, which they considered their special prerogative, creating shrines, and serving in the temples of the hero-god. Sacrifice was offered to his wife Epione at Epidauros, while his daughters attended upon him, assisted in the ritual, and administered to the sick. Hygieia was not a healer, but simply represented Health. She aided in receiving the suppliants and cared for the sacred serpents. Legends concerning her suggest that the early development of her divinity and worship was apart from the Asklepios cult, which she joined at some place unknown. Panakeia was a definite healer, being the personification of the all-healing power of herbs and representing the omnipotence of the god in his art. Iaso and Akeso are mentioned as being in the retinue of the god at Epidauros. Homer refers (Il., ii, 731-732) to his sons, Machaon and Podaleirios, as though they came from the villages of Thessaly; but it is claimed that the traditions of the cult in the North do not mention them, and that all legends concerning them are from the Peloponnesos and the Aigaian Islands. Critics affirm, moreover, that the passages in the Iliad referring to them are interpolations of a later date than the body of the work, and hold that those relating to Podaleirios are still later than those regarding Machaon, who was the older brother and the instructor, and who as the surgeon was more prominent. They were taught by Asklepios himself, and Arktinos,

[67] Nilsson, *Griechische Feste von religiöser Bedeutung*, p. 410.

in his *Sack of Ilion* (quoted by the Scholiast and Eustathios on *Il.*, xi, 515), says that to the one, the father, the
famous Earth-Shaker (Poseidon), "gave hands more
light to draw or cut out missiles from the flesh and to heal
all kinds of wounds; but in the heart of the other he put
full and perfect knowledge to tell hidden diseases and
cure desperate sicknesses," thus making the first allusion
to specialization in medicine among the Greeks.

Machaon and his sons.

According to a legend of the Peloponnesos, Machaon
lived in Messenia after the Trojan War and established
towns named from those in Thessaly; but Pausanias (III,
xxvi, 9-10), on the authority of the *Little Iliad,* says that
he was killed during the war by Eurypylos, son of Telephos, and that his bones were brought back by Nestor and
buried at Gerenia in Messenia. A bronze statue with a
wreath had been erected to his memory there, and he was
worshipped in the local sanctuary as a healing hero. His
mother came from Kos, and it is said that the traditions
of the island claim him as the founder of the State,
though more reliable legends appear to associate him
with the Peloponnesos, where he was worshipped with
his father at many shrines, rather than with the Dorian
coast, and where his sons established shrines, receiving
the homage of the people as healers. Alexanor set up a
temple in the rocky gorge at Titane, the first to Asklepios
in the Peloponnesos, and said to be the earliest trace of a
divine cult established by a descendant (*ib.*, II, xi, 5-6);
Sphyros established a sanctuary at Argos in which was
a seated image of Asklepios in white marble (*ib.*, II,
xxiii, 4); Nikomachos (a reputed ancestor of Aristotle)
and his brother Gorgasos had a healing sanctuary at
Pharai, in Messenia, where they were still worshipped
as healers when Pausanias visited the place (*ib.*, IV, xxx,

3); and Polemokrates, yet another son, had a similar shrine at the village of Eua, in Lakonia (*ib.*, II, xxxviii, 6).

Podaleirios.

Traditions concerning Podaleirios are more vague; and while he appears to have been worshipped in the Peloponnesos, various legends associate him more intimately with the Aigaian Islands. He was shipwrecked on his return from the Trojan War; and according to one tale, he landed on the island of Skyros, whence he made his way to Karia, though Pausanias says (III, xxvi, 10) that he came ashore at Syrnos on the coast of Karia, and that the king of the country engaged him to treat his daughter, who had fallen from a roof. Podaleirios bled her from both arms; and after she had been cured, the king gave her to him in marriage. They then lived on an adjoining island, and he established two cities, one of which he named Syrne for his wife. Tradition relates that the Asklepiadai of Kos, Knidos, and Rhodes were descended from Podaleirios,[68] though there are suggestions that they claimed descent from Machaon. Herakles, driven to Kos by contrary winds (*Il.*, xv, 30), established a family of Herakleidai; and the Asklepiads there traced their lineage to him on their mother's side. According to another tale (Frazer, *op. cit.*, iii, 403), Podaleirios left Karia, and wandering to Apulia in Italy, died in Daunia, where, near Mount Garganus, he had a healing shrine at which incubation was practiced. Suppliants slept on sheep-skins laid on his tomb, and his spirit (or, as others claimed, that of Kalchas, whose shrine was on the brow of the hill above) gave oracles. Strabo says (VI, iii, 9 = p. 284 C) that from the hill where he was buried flowed a stream which was a potent cure for all diseases of cattle.

[68] Thrämer, in Pauly-Wissowa, ii, 1684.

Raising the dead and the death of Asklepios.

Asklepios not only healed the sick but brought the dead to life, as Kapaneus, Tyndareus, Hippolytos, Glaukos, and others. From Athena he had received the Gorgon's blood; that from the left side producing evil and death, while that from the right side was beneficial; and with it Asklepios wrought his wondrous cures and raised the dead (Apollodoros, iii, 120-121). Another legend is to the effect that he gained the knowledge of restoring to life by watching a serpent resuscitate its companion with an herb. Pindar (*op. cit.*, iii, 110) refers to the charge that in revivifying Hippolytos Asklepios was prompted by an improper desire for gold. Because of such avarice, because he imparted his art to mortals contrary to the will of the gods and the cosmic order was being violated,[69] or because Hades complained that the success of Asklepios in averting death threatened to depopulate his realm (Diodoros, iv, 71; Apollodoros, iii, 121), Hesiod (*op. cit.*, 109) relates that

> The mighty father both of gods and men
> Was filled with wrath, and from Olympos top
> With flaming thunderbolt cast down and slew
> Latona's well-loved son—such was his ire.[70]

The burial place.

By request of Apollo, Zeus placed Asklepios among the stars; and in anger at the death of his son, Apollo killed the Kyklopes, who forged the fatal bolt. Herakleitos (*de Incredibilibus*, 26), however, attempts to explain the death on physical grounds, saying that it was due to a violent pleurisy which left a discoloration of the side as

[69] Uffelmann, *Die Entwicklung der altgriechischen Heilkunde*, p. 412.

[70] Referring to Asklepios as the son instead of the grandson of Leto (Latona).

from a stroke of lightning. There is no substantial legend regarding the place of Asklepios's burial; and no shrine was found to indicate it. Purely local traditions name Kynosoura in Lakonia or Arkadia, Delphoi, and Epidauros, but no evidence has been discovered that supports them.[71] The legend of death tends to confirm the status of Asklepios as a hero rather than as a god, since divinities were regarded as immortal. In early Aigaian civilization, however, incineration by a thunderbolt implied celestial or Olympian immortality.[72]

The transformation of the cult.

The cult of Asklepios was transformed after its relations with Delphoi were established on a friendly basis; and father and son were honored side by side at many of the shrines in Greece. The pact with Apollo, which must date before the time of Hesiod, brought the obscure Thessalian hero and earth-spirit into prominence and gave his worship an impetus that soon led to its rapid diffusion. Spreading southward, it gained a firm foothold in the Peloponnesos and came into contact with those of other healing gods and heroes, in many of whose shrines Asklepios became an associate object of adoration. He quickly overshadowed many of these superhuman beings, and taking possession of their shrines, he assumed their names and functions, adopting them as his children and grandchildren, and so increasing his retinue of attendants by numberless genii. Asklepios thus received those complexities of character, solar and chthonic, that appeared in his later manifestations, often obscuring his original underworld nature and ritual. Meeting with Helios, probably first in Lakonia, the celestial aspects

[71] Cox, *The Mythology of the Aryan Nations*, p. 280.

[72] For the classical bibliography of Asklepian legends the reader is referred to Walton, *op. cit.*, pp. 85 ff., and Gruppe, *op. cit.*, p. 1440.

already acquired from Apollo were emphasized by the aspects of a light-deity which Asklepios gained in his relations with the sun-god, who was worshipped with himself and Hygieia at Gytheion and Epidauros.

Emigration to Epidauros. Deification.

It is believed that it was sometime during the late seventh or early sixth century B.C. that Asklepios emigrated to Epidauros, where he was worshipped with Apollo Maleates. This sanctuary then became the chief center of the cult, and his power, which was destined to affect profoundly the Greek mind and civilization, was developed there. From Epidauros the worship expanded, and all the famous sanctuaries of the god were offshoots from it. Its deputies were sent to the various parts of Greece, to the Aigaian Islands, to Asia Minor, and to the Libyan coast, where they established healing shrines. The success of the cult appears to have been due to the humanity of its hero-chief and to the substantial benefits it conferred. These elements, combined with the prestige gained by a divine paternity, not only won the gratitude of his devotees, but so spread his fame beyond that of other healers that his worship soon attracted to itself the greater part of the healing functions of other Greek deities and heroes. Like others, he received the epithets *lysios, alexikakos,* and *aleximoros* ('deliverer,' 'averter of evil,' and 'averter of fate'), used in a general rather than in a medical sense; but though he still ranked as a hero, the fame of his oracle and the devotion of the increasing number of his suppliants suggest that he was rapidly developing on broader lines. Among the Kyrenaioi at Balagrai he was termed 'physician' (Pausanias, II, xxvi, 9); and Pindar (*op. cit.,* iii, 7) still called him a hero, though he treated him as a demigod. The Athenians, faithful to their Homer and Hesiod, regarded Asklepios as a hero when they invited him to Athens, and it is doubtful whether they ever accorded him full divine rank. It is not possible to follow the steps of his progress to deification, or to determine the time and place, but it would appear that his apotheosis was the result of an increasing unanimity in favor of his glorification. All indications point to the Peloponnesos, and it is entirely probable that his majesty and godhood were due to his Epidaurian associations. Early traditions emerging from Epidauros treat Asklepios as a deity, and it is certain that at this place his divinity and his cult attained their highest development. His associates there were the higher deities of the Olympian circle, whereas elsewhere they were more frequently those of lower and chthonian rank. As the centuries passed, the renown of the healing god and the fame of his dream-oracle grew until (in the time of Alexander the Great) Asklepios was known as one of the greater divinities, while in many districts he was regarded as the head of the pantheon, inscriptions of the period referring to him as the son of Zeus or as Zeus himself.[73] His votaries were numbered by the thousands, they thronged his sanctuaries, and his cult was finally dominant in healing throughout the Greek and Roman worlds. It is interesting to note, in this connection, that the traditions of Thessaly indicate that his divine nature was not recognized there until the northern states of Greece had been invaded by the southern deities.

Shrines and sanctuaries of the cult.

In the early days of the cult its shrines were located in recesses of the earth, in a mountain grotto, or in some cave, and were undoubtedly simple structures like those of other heroes, consisting essentially of low-lying altars

[73] Gardner, op. cit., p. 357.

near the level of the ground, a mound of earth or a flat or roughly hewn stone with a hole in the center to receive the blood of the sacrificial animals, and near some spring or stream of pure water for purification. As the worship developed, temples were erected, simple or more elaborate, giving shelter and privacy to the image of the hero and to the statues of his guests, as well as to their altars. The grounds around the shrines were sacred to the hero or god, and at first no other buildings were allowed; but as the fame of the cult grew, and as the shrines attracted more suppliants and became resorts, provision for guests was necessary, and tents were used. Finally, old prejudices gave way in some places, as at Tithorea, and buildings were provided both for priests and patients. With these changes a larger number of the characteristic features of the earlier chthonic worship disappeared, and only hints of the original ritual remained, though the sites of many of the Asklepieia were associated with ancient oracles and traditions.

Location of shrines by serpents.

According to legends, the sacred serpents were responsible for the selection of several places where shrines were located and the serpent, as the incarnation of the chthonian hero or god, was transferred when a sanctuary was to be established. One of them, intended for Kos, escaped from the vessel on the shores of Lákonia while in charge of deputies and vanished in the ground at Epidauros Limera, which was then selected for a shrine (Pausanias, III, xxiii, 7). The sacred serpent that was sent, as representing Asklepios, to stop the pestilence at Rome, disappeared from the ship as it was sailing up the Tiber and was lost to sight in the rushes of the Insula Sacra, whence the Romans decided to build their great Æsculapium there. A sacred serpent representing the god was sent to the sanctuary at Sikyon in a carriage drawn by mules (*ib.*, II, x, 3).

Sites of the Asklepieia.

The sites of the Asklepieia were judiciously selected with a view to their general salubrity, pure air and water, and general attractiveness. Plutarch (*Quæstiones Romanæ*, 94) asked: "Why is the sanctuary of Asklepios outside of the city? Was it because they reckoned it a more wholesome kind of living outside of the city? For the Greeks have placed the edifices belonging to Asklepios for the most part on high places where the air is pure and clear." The Asklepieia at Kyrene, Carthage, and Mitylene were on the Akropolis; that at Kyllene was in a smiling country on a cape overlooking the sea; that at Megalopolis in a wood on the side of a mountain; that at Las in Lakonia on the side of Mount Ilion near a stream of pure water; those at Epidauros and Kleitor were in open valleys protected from the winds by surrounding mountains; and that at Kos was on a slope in a suburb of the city. Ample and good water was provided by springs and streams, but the water at several of the sanctuaries was reputed to be of definite medicinal value. The location at Pergamon was one of unusual attractiveness, and the water of the spring, at the very foundations of the temple, was so delicious that Aristeides said that he preferred it to the sweetest wine. The shrine at Aigion was near a spring of bubbling water, pure and agreeable; that at Ladon was on a stream of excellent water; that at Korone in Lakonia was by the Plataian spring, celebrated for its medicinal properties; a salt, bubbling spring from the rock bathed the temple at Kenchreiai (Pausanias, II, ii, 3); and at Epidauros there was a fountain and an aqueduct in addition to the sacred spring which was enclosed by a beautiful structure. Many of the temples were surrounded by groves of trees, that of the Asklepieion at Athens being a matter of official concern and care of the Council. The grove at Epidauros was large; at Kos and Titane it was of cypress trees; and at Epidauros Limera it was of olive trees. The sacred grounds were usually enclosed, as by a hedge at Tithorea, and no buildings were allowed near by; a wall with a formal gateway surrounded the *hieron* at Epidauros, and at Athens the limits of the *temenos* were indicated by a marked stone. In the grounds of the larger sanctuaries there were altars, small shrines, and temples of the associated deities and heroes.

The healing temples.

The Greek temples were never imposing by their size, but they were "caskets to contain the statue of the deity and the dedicated gifts of votaries."[74] They accommodated only the divinity, his altars, and his divine guests; and all ritual ceremonies, sacrifices, and gatherings were held in the open air. Constructed of wood, stucco, or stone, the temples had a portico or vestibule, a cella, and sometimes an opisthodomos, the image of the god and those of his guests, as well as his altar, being placed in the cella. Sometimes the temples were crowded with such statues, of heroes as at Athens, or of the higher deities as at Epidauros. Near the image of the god were an altar and a table for receiving offerings, and near by stood a couch where the god reclined during the sacrifices on festal occasions. The table at Pergamon was three-legged with a golden image of Asklepios, Hygieia, and Telesphoros respectively at each foot. The table at Syracuse was of gold. Before the temples were placed the high altars, or *bomoi*, oblong, round, or triangular, the stone

[74] Gardner, *op. cit.*, p. 391.

on the top having a hole in the center to receive the blood
of sacrificial animals.

The sanctity of the temples.

The sanctuaries were holy and only the pure in spirit
and the initiated were allowed to enter (Porphyrios, *de
Abstentia animalium*, ii, 17; Clemens, *op. cit.*, v, 551), the
profane and the guilty being strictly excluded. At Sikyon
the temple was double, and none but priests were permitted in the inner shrine, which was sacred to Apollo
Karneios (Pausanias, II, x, 2). The sanctuaries were
usually locked at night, and the key, which was also
sacred, was in charge of the *neokoros* (temple-sweeper,
verger) or, as at Athens of an official known as the *kleidouchos* (key-holder). Occasionally the temple was closed
by a lattice door which permitted a view of the interior.

The images and emblems of the god.

The gods were represented both by paintings and
sculpture. The sanctuary at Athens was worth seeing for
its paintings and the images of Asklepios and his children (*ib.*, I, xxi, 4). Pliny (*op. cit.*, xxxv, 40) mentions a
painting by Nikophanes in which Hygieia, Aigle, and
Panakeia were grouped about Asklepios. The images of
the gods were of wood, or wood with marble parts, terra-
cotta, stone, or marble, and occasionally of gold and
ivory, but were often rough and imperfectly hewn, Pausanias (VII, xxii, 4; IX, xxiv, 3) stating that the early
Greeks worshipped unwrought stones instead of images.
Asklepios was most commonly represented with a beard,
seldom as young, seated on a throne, or standing, and
holding a staff, usually knotted, with a serpent coiled
around it, and frequently with other emblems sacred to
him, as the dog, the cock, the vulture, the owl, the fir-cone,
and occasionally a goat's head, or the omphalos. Some-

times the serpent is represented as coiled about the body and lower limbs.[75] The statues at Epidauros and Kos were colossal in size, but they were usually smaller, and at Kos small terra-cotta images have been unearthed. In some of the older statues the god held his beard in one hand and the staff with its coiled serpent in the other. The image at Tithorea was bearded, and of stone, more than two feet high (*ib.*, X, xxxii, 12). At Sikyon the statue was beardless, and of ivory and gold, the work of Kalamis. In one hand he held a scepter and in the other the fir-cone (*ib.*, II, x, 3). At Phlious the image was of a young and beardless man, and of the archaic type (*ib.*, II, xiii, 5), and at Gortys the god was represented as a beardless youth, and in the same temple was an image of Hygieia; both being by Skopas (*ib.*, VIII, xxviii, 1). A beautiful marble statue of the god of this type, recovered from Epidauros, stands in the Vatican Museum. The sanctuaries at Ladon and Megalopolis were dedicated to the boy Asklepios, and the image at Megalopolis was erect and measured about an ell (*ib.*, VIII, xxv, 11; xxxii, 5). At Titane the image was covered by a mantle and white wool, only the face, hands, and feet being visible (*ib.*, II, xi, 6). The god was generally shown as wearing the pallium, and occasionally the head was decked with a crown of laurel. The globe and scepter were attributes of the divinity only in the later days of the cult and were seldom used, since they represented aspects which were not characteristic of him.

Auxiliary deities.

Telesphoros, typifying convalescence, and represented as a boy or dwarf, cloaked and hooded, was sometimes placed standing beside the erect statues of the god. The gods Hypnos and Oneiros, who presided over sleep and

[75] Le Clerc, *op. cit.*, p. 36 (ed. 1729).

dreams, were intimately associated with the cult, and
their statues were found at the sanctuaries, both Hypnos
and Oneiros being noted at Sikyon, Oneiros at Lebena,
and Hypnos at Epidauros and Athens.[76]

Tents instead of buildings.

Visitors to the sanctuaries and priests used tents during the earlier years of the cult, Tithorea being mentioned as one of the first places at which permanent structures were allowed. For many years buildings were forbidden at Epidauros, and tents continued in use as late
as the time of Hadrian, notwithstanding the elaborate
edifices that were constructed from time to time, the tents
being limited to thirty feet in length, while their use was
subject to very stringent rules. Long colonnaded porticoes were later provided as dormitories for the suppliants of the god, although many continued to prefer to
sleep in the porticoes of the temple, near the images of
the god, or close to the statues of those of his associates
whose particular favor they sought.

The most famous of the Asklepieia.

The most ancient shrines of Asklepios were at Trikke
(which was also the most famous, Strabo, IX, v, 17 = p.
437 C), Orchomenos, Titane, and Tithorea, where he was
called Archagetes. After the settlement at Epidauros
deputies established Asklepieia at various places, many
of which became famous healing shrines, as Knidos, Kos,
Rhodes, Kyrene, and Kroton, where medical schools were
conducted, and at Corinth, Phigaleia, Sounion, Kyllene,
Megalopolis, Athens, etc. The shrine at Pergamon was
popular with the people of Asia, and Philostratos (op.

[76] U. Köhler, "Der Südabhang der Akropolis zu Athen nach den
Ausgrabungen der archäologischen Gesellschaft," in MAIA, 1877, ii,
242, note.

cit., iv, 34) says that the Cretans flocked to that at
Lebena, and this became so famous that the Libyans
crossed over to it from Africa. Epidauros, however, was
the chief seat of the worship. Here it reached its highest
development, and the sanctuary was the largest and perhaps the most characteristic of all those of the cult. In
the city there was a precinct of Asklepios with images in
Parian marble, under the open sky, of the god himself
and Epione, who, they said, was his wife (Pausanias, II,
xxix, 1).

The sanctuary at Epidauros.

The Asklepieion at Epidauros was located six miles
inland from the city in a broad, open valley between
Mounts Kynortion and Tittheion in 'holy country,' as it
is called on medals, sacred because of the legends indicating that this was the birthplace of Asklepios. The
valley was protected from the winds by the surrounding
mountains, which were from two to three thousand feet
high, and was reputed to be particularly healthful. The
Asklepieion is believed to have been established not later
than the sixth century B.C. (possibly at the end of the
seventh), and it held its vogue for upward of eight hundred years. The reverence for the god and the gratitude
engendered by the benefits bestowed upon thousands of
suppliants provided ample means for its development on
the splendid scale described by ancient writers and confirmed by modern excavations under the direction of
Kavvadias, in 1881-1887 and 1891-1894.[77] Illustrations
based upon descriptions and the discoveries at the ruins
present an array of temples, colonnaded porticoes, buildings for sacrificial and other religious ceremonies, ac-
commodations for visitors and officials, baths, gymnasiums, and a library, all in an ample grove within the

[77] Kavvadias, *Fouilles d'Épidaure.* Athens, 1893.

sacred enclosure, and, just outside, a stadium and theater. The sacred precinct, or *hieron,* was approached through a gateway, the great *propylaia,* in the southern wall, where a ceremonial purification of suppliants was performed (Frazer, *op. cit.,* iii, 234 ff.; v, 570 ff.).

The temple.

The central shrine, the temple of Asklepios, erected on the site of an earlier sanctuary, was seventy-nine feet long, forty-two wide, and forty high; and cost about 1,000,000 drachmas (approximately $25,000). It was of porous stone, or tufa, stuccoed and tinted in tones of red and blue. It was peripteral and of the Doric order, with thirty columns, six on each end and nine on each side. It faced the east and, approached by a ramp, stood on a terrace about three feet above the level of the ground. The roof was of wood, the tiles of the floor were of marble, and the sculptures on the pediments were of the best period of Greek art, that on the west end representing a battle between Amazons and the Greeks, that on the east end a contest with Centaurs. A Winged Victory stood at the apex, and the acroteria at the angles were Nereids on horseback. It is estimated that the temple was built about 375 or 380 B.C., and an inscription found on the spot, giving details of the construction, states that it took four years, eight months and ten days to complete it (*ib.,* iii, 241). There was an elaborate and beautiful ivory door at the main entrance, above which was inscribed: ''Within the incense-filled Sanctuary one must be pure; and purity is to have righteous thoughts.''[78] Inside the cella was the celebrated chryselephantine statue of Asklepios by Thrasymedes of Paros, about half the size of the great Olympian Zeus and very nearly resembling it. The flesh was of ivory, and the rest was of

[78] Farnell, *The Evolution of Religion,* p. 138.

gold enamelled in colors. The god was seated upon a
throne in a manner more nonchalant than dignified, of
benign countenance and holding a staff in one hand, while
the other rested on the head of a golden serpent reaching
up from the floor, and a dog lay at his feet. An altar stood
before the statue, and the floor was of slabs of black
marble. A large, high altar, twenty-four feet by eighteen,
was placed in front of the shrine.

The Thymele.

Southwest of the temple stood the so-called *Tholos,* or
rotunda, more properly the *Thymele* ('place of sacrifice'), as it is called in an inscription found there and giving some details of the construction (Frazer, *op. cit.,* iii,
247). This was the *chef-d'œuvre* of the *hieron,* famous
throughout antiquity and believed to be the most beautiful circular structure erected by the Greeks. It was built
about the latter part of the fifth century B.c. by Polykleitos the Younger, and since the names of twenty-one
priests are given as superintending its construction, it is
assumed that it was that many years in building. The
Thymele was 107 feet in diameter, and its foundations
were in six concentric rings with openings; but each passage had a wall across it, compelling a person to walk all
around each before entering the next compartment, thus
making it a labyrinth. There was an outside colonnade
with twenty-six Doric columns of common, but fine-
grained, stone. The walls were of various stones covered
with stucco and were tinted red and blue; the base was of
marble, white outside and black inside; the frieze was of
Pentelic marble; the roof was of wood; and the tiles of
marble. The inner colonnade was of marble, with fourteen Corinthian columns, said to have been the most
graceful ever conceived; and the pavement was of marble,
in diamond-shaped slabs alternately white and black. No

slab has been found for the central opening, which, it is assumed, was used for sacrifices and for descent into the labyrinth. On the walls were two paintings, one representing Methe (Drunkenness) drinking from a crystal goblet of such marvellous transparency that her face was seen through it, and the other portrayed Eros in the act of laying down his bow and taking up the lyre, masterpieces by Pausias (Pausanias, II, xxvii, 3). The purpose of the building has given rise to much discussion. It has been suggested that it covered the sacred well, but no evidences of a conduit have been found; while another hypothesis is that it was the home of the sacred serpents, which were bred, sacrificed to, and kept in the labyrinth until needed in the ritual or for the establishment of other sanctuaries. The name *Thymele* and the statement that it contained a shrine may imply that the building was designed for ceremonial sacrifices of some description, possibly in connection with the mysteries of the cult, of which practically nothing is known.

Auxiliary temples.

Within the *hieron* were several smaller and less elaborate, though beautiful, temples dedicated to Artemis Hekate, Aphrodite, and Themis, and the records indicate that there were shrines and chapels to Helios, Selene, Epione, Zeus, Hera, Poseidon, Athena, Leto, Akeso, the Eleusinian goddesses Demeter and Persephone, and others. The temple of Artemis Hekate had a row of marble columns, outside which stood a statue of the goddess. Her emblem, the dog, was used for decoration, and the heads of dogs were sculptured on the cornice; while at the angles of the western end were Winged Victories as acroteria. Near the Doric temple of Aphrodite a beautiful marble statue of the goddess was found. A Roman senator named Antoninus, probably the same as the Emperor

Antoninus Pius (Pausanias, II, xxvii, 5-6; Frazer, *op. cit.*, iii, 257), erected several buildings; a bath to Asklepios; a sanctuary to the 'Bountiful gods' (auxiliaries, such as Hypnos, Oneiros, and Telesphoros); and temples to Hygieia, Asklepios, and Apollo, the last two being under the surname Egyptian (or I-m-ḥotep, the god of healing).

The dormitory.

The dormitory (*abaton* or *egkoimeterion*) was a portico, open to the south, with a double row of columns of the Ionic order, thirty-six in all. It was 246 feet long by thirty-one feet wide, and at the western end was a basement connected with the main floor by a stairway. Near the middle a wall divided the portico into two parts, one for men, the other for women. The inside walls were decorated in colors and by inscriptions, Pausanias (II, xxvii, 3) describing six tablets on which were carved accounts of cures made by Apollo and Asklepios. Fragments of two of these have been found in the excavations. The *abaton* was furnished with tables, altars, lamps, and about 120 pallets.

Other buildings within the hieron.

Near the temple of Asklepios was a large, square building with an open court; and although its use has not been determined, the discovery there of ashes and the bones of sacrificial animals has led to the view that it was for sacrifices and sacrificial banquets. Pausanias says that all sacrifices were completely burned within the *hieron,* whence this building may have been used for that purpose; or it may have been a house for priests. The building dates apparently from the fifth or sixth century B.C. and was decorated with statues and inscriptions. Within the *hieron* were several quadrangular, porticoed buildings the purpose of which is not entirely clear, although they may have been for the accommodation of visitors and for protection in inclement weather, or for the priests, while some may have been used as dormitories. One of these, the Colonnade of Kotys, was restored by the Roman senator Antoninus. There were two gymnasiums within the *hieron*, and they probably occupied such buildings. In the interior angle of one of these quadrangular structures nine rows of semicircular seats were found, this space being supposed to have been an *odeion*, or music hall, or for witnessing athletic sports. Adjacent to the large *abaton* was a building containing baths and supposed to have covered the sacred spring, especially as during the excavations to the east of the *abaton*, a well was found 144 feet in depth. The library, dedicated to Apollo Maleates and Asklepios, which has never been definitely located, is assumed to have been in this structure. Near this was a building of late construction, the Roman baths; and at right angles to it was another colonnade, or stoa, before which was an open aqueduct with basins. Lastly, situated somewhat apart from the general group, there was a large quadrangular building, 270 feet square, with four quadrangles and many rooms, which is supposed to have been a hostelry or a home for the priests.

Stadium and theater.

Outside the *hieron* to the west was the stadium, 600 feet long, with fifteen rows of marble seats on the north and south ends, seating from twelve to fourteen thousand persons; and on the slopes of Mount Kynortion, southwest of the *hieron*, was the theater of Dionysos, constructed by Polykleitos the Younger in the fifth century B.C. It was described by Pausanias (II, xxvii, 5) as the next in size to that of Megalopolis (which was the largest in Greece), and of the most beautiful proportions, these statements being confirmed by the ruins, which are still in an unusually good state of preservation. The acoustics were perfect, and it is said that today a voice from the stage, a little above a whisper, may be heard in all parts of the auditorium. This open-air theater consisted of a semicircle of seats, fifty-five rows in all, divided in two sections, an upper and a lower, with thirteen stairways in the lower, and twenty-six in the upper section. The seating capacity was about nine thousand. The chorus-space was circular, and the stage rose twelve feet above it, while the proscenium was richly decorated with sculptures. The seats were placed on the incline of the mountain, the top row being seventy-four feet above the orchestra, and gave a commanding view of the valley, the *hieron,* and the surrounding mountains. On the top of Mount Kynortion, overlooking the *hieron,* stood the temple of Apollo Maleates, from which point of vantage the supreme divine healer gave his sanction to the benevolent activities of his son Asklepios. In this temple was a fine statue of the god.

The grounds.

Aristeides and other writers testify to the general attractiveness of the *hieron* and the air of sanctity which pervaded it. The large grove was artistically arranged with walks and semicircular seats, or exedra, under the trees, and was adorned with statues of friendly deities and heroes, busts and monuments to famous physicians, and steles and tablets reciting cures effected and gifts from former patients. Special efforts were made to preserve an atmosphere of hope and cheerfulness and to remove, so far as possible, evidences of suffering and sorrow. Births and deaths desecrated the holy precinct, and those threatened with either were ejected from the *hieron*, whence, in the second century A.D., Antoninus provided a building outside the peribolos for these unfortunates (Pausanias, II, xxvii, 6).

The present ruins.

The present ruins of this great sanctuary merely outline and suggest its former greatness. In 86 B.C. Sulla robbed it of its treasures, and shortly afterward it was pillaged by Cicilian pirates; in the second century A.D. it was reconstructed and regained a large measure of its former splendor; but toward the end of the fourth century, when paganism was suppressed, the worship of Asklepios was suspended. In A.D. 396 Epidauros was sacked by the Goths under Alaric I; the library was burned and the temples were destroyed, and the materials were utilized for the construction of Christian churches. The earthquake of A.D. 552 completed its ruin.

The Asklepieion at Athens.

In the hope of checking a pestilence that was raging, the Athenians invited Asklepios to their city about 420 B.C., and he was 'affiliated' with Amynos or Alkon, an earlier healing hero of Athens, and was first worshipped at his *temenos* on the west slope of the Akropolis, while another shrine was being made ready.[79] An inscription (*CIA* ii, 1649) gives a lengthy account of bringing the god from the Peloponnesos and the establishment of the Asklepieion on the south slope of the Akropolis. Sophokles, a former priest of Amynos, was largely instrumental in bringing the god to Athens, and on his arrival entertained him at his house.[80] Hygieia is said by some to have come from Epidauros with the deity, though others

---

[79] A. Körte, "Bezirk eines Heilgottes," in *MAIA*, 1893, xviii, 237; 1896, xxi, 311.

[80] Walton, *op. cit.*, pp. 29-30; also Thrämer, in *ERE* vi, 655.

deny this, asserting that she joined the divinity some
fifty years later. The Asklepieion was known as ''the
sanctuary of Asklepios in the city'' to distinguish it from
that located at Peiraieus (Frazer, op. cit., ii, 237). The
general character of the *hieron* was essentially the same
as that at Epidauros. There was a temple to Asklepios
and Hygieia, and possibly an older one near by (*CIA* ii,
1, addenda, 489 b) ; a holy well was sunk in an excavation
of the rock and connected with the *abaton*, and there was
a fountain sacred to Asklepios and Hygieia, as well as
temples and shrines of friendly deities, Themis, Isis and
Sarapis, Demeter and Persephone, Herakles, Hypnos,
Panakeia, and others.[81]

The Asklepieion at Kos.

The Asklepieion at Kos, ''the cradle of later medical
science in Europe,'' was on an island on the Dorian coast
(Strabo, XIV, ii, 19 = p. 657 C), two miles inland and
about 320 feet above the level of the sea. The buildings
were distributed on three terraces of the northern slope
of the mountain, which afforded a commanding view of
the rich fertile valley below.[82] On the highest terrace was
a rather large, peripteral temple to the god, on three
sides of which was an extensive porticoed *abaton;* on the
next were sanctuaries and shrines of other deities, the
sacred spring, altars, and a stoa (apparently designed
for an *abaton*) ; and on the lowest were the *propylaia* and
porticoed buildings with many rooms, which, it has been
assumed, were used for consultations and treatment. According to tradition, this Asklepieion was established by
a commission of priests sent from Epidauros (Herodotos,

[81] Girard, *L'Asclépieion d'Athènes d'après de récentes découvertes,*
1881, xxiii, 6.
[82] S. Reinach, "Les fouilles de Cos," in *RA,* 4 sér., 1904, iii, 127-131.

vii, 99). The sanctuary was destroyed by an earthquake, believed to be of A.D. 554.[83]

The Asklepieion at Pergamon.

The Asklepieion at Pergamon was established in the third century B.C. by a delegation from Epidauros at an exceptionally attractive spot on the coast of Asia Minor. Tradition has it that the worship of Asklepios was introduced here by one Archias, who had been healed in Epidauria of a strained limb, injured while hunting on Pindasos (Pausanias, II, xxvi, 8), or, as it is asserted, of convulsions. During the Imperial period of Rome this sanctuary became exceedingly popular and rivalled, if it did not surpass, the Epidauros of that age.

Administration of the Asklepieia, the Hiereus.

Miss Walton[84] gives a list of upward of three hundred Asklepieia in Greece and its dependencies, not including Magna Græcia, but of the great majority of these very little is known. The larger shrines were administered by chief priests or hierophants. The Hiereus, or chief priest, had general charge of the sanctuary. He directed the order of the day, conducted the rituals and sacrifices, supervised the work of the assistant priests and minor officials, and presided over the ceremonies of the festivals. Having control of the buildings and of the entire property of the *hieron,* he was responsible for all receipts, gifts, and contributions; and at the end of his term of office, usually one year, he made a full report to the Council or governing body, with an inventory of property for his successor. If the report was satisfactory, he received a vote of praise, and the decree was recorded; and

[83] For a history of Kos, see Paton and Hicks, *The Inscriptions of Cos,* pp. ix, xlviii.

[84] *Op. cit.,* pp. 95 ff.

sometimes he was voted a crown or other gift. The administration of the Asklepieion at Athens was taken over by the State during the fourth century B.C., and the cult was placed under the control of the Council or Boule. The office of chief priest was one of such dignity that a seat was reserved for him in the theater of Dionysos (*CIA* iii, 287); and both at Athens and at Epidauros the Hiereus was selected by lot by the Boule. At Hyettos the worship was similarly administered by the Sacred Senate or Council of Elders (*CIGGS* i, 2808; Frazer, *op. cit.*, v, 133); but an inscription from Chalkedon in Bithynia indicates that the office there was open for purchase at a price of 5,000 drachmas.[85] Relying, apparently, on the customs prevailing at Athens, Epidauros, and possibly some other large sanctuaries, modern authors have been inclined to assume that physicians seldom performed priestly functions at the Asklepieia;[86] but although the specific mention of their holding such office may be rare, it would appear a strange restriction to withhold sacerdotal duties from the Asklepiadai, whose relations to the cult were hereditary and intimate, and it is doubtful whether such a rule held generally in other cities and towns. In the primitive days of the cult the office of the priest is believed to have been hereditary and a prerogative of the clan of Asklepiadai, following the general customs of family and tribal worship, in which father and son took the principal parts, or in which, if there was a king, he held the office of priest. Under these conditions a priest's tenure would be for life. Several instances of physician-priests are definitely known, as in the case of Kalliphon, the father of Demokedes, who was a hereditary Asklepiad and a physician-priest at Knidos. At Kos the selection was made by lot or by oracle for one year,

---

[85] Walton, *op. cit.*, p. 50.
[86] Thrämer, in *Pauly-Wissowa*, ii, 1685.

but the position was the prerogative of the Asklepiadai. It is stated in one inscription that Soarchos, priest at Lebena, in Crete, whose father had preceded him, had already served for forty-seven years;[87] and the office was hereditary at Mitylene, as it was at Pergamon to a late day. These priests often lived within the *hieron* and had certain perquisites.

Assistant priests.

Next to the hierophant the most important official was a priest called the *neokoros* or, as at Athens, the *zakoros*. At Athens, where the office of *zakoros* was important, he was chosen for one year and was often reëlected, while inscriptions indicate that he was occasionally a physician (*CIA* III, i, 780; addenda, 780, a, b, c). At Kos and Epidauros the *neokoros* held office for life, and at Kos, Stratonikeia in Karia, and Thera there were other priests with a similar tenure. The *zakoros* or *neokoros*, as representing the chief priest, often conducted the sacrifices and other ceremonies, besides receiving the patients, recording their names and homes, and directing their care by the attendants. He usually had immediate charge of the gifts and property of the *hieron*, though occasionally a special secular officer, the *hieromnemon*, was appointed for this duty. At Kos the *neokoros* interpreted the dreams and omens, and offered prayers for the suppliants; at Pergamon there were two, who were active in all religious exercises and interpreted dreams; but at Epidauros there was only one, and he served for all the temples within the *hieron*. At Athens, where the ritual was elaborate, there were several officials who were named for minor duties. A *propolos,* who is mentioned by Aristophanes (*Plutus,* 660), held an office close to the

[87] Walton, *op. cit.,* p. 49.

priest, extinguished the lights in the *abaton*, and told the patients to sleep. The altar fires were lighted and cared for by the *pyrophoroi*, though this duty was sometimes performed by boys who were also incense-bearers or members of the choir. There were, furthermore, the *kleidouchos*, or key-keeper, an office frequently assigned to the son of the priest; the *dadouchoi*, or torch-bearers; the *kanephoroi*, or basket-bearers; the *arrhephoroi*, or carriers of the holy relics and mysteries; and priestesses and nurses, all of whom took part in the religious ceremonies and festival processions. In addition, there were a large number of assistants, who were attendants upon the sick and had various duties in the *hieron*.

The Asklepiadai. The Hippokratic oath.

Around the cult of Asklepios gathered a large and exclusive class known as Asklepiadai, or priest-physicians, originally the family of Asklepios, their descendants, and those who had been adopted by the clan. Plato remarks (*op. cit.*, X, iii) that the disciples left by Asklepios were his own descendants. They claimed that their knowledge of healing was hereditary from the god himself, and that they had imbibed it from earliest childhood in the family circle. According to Galen (*de Anatomicis administrationibus*, bk. ii, ch. 1)[88] the origin of medicine was hereditary in the family, and Aristeides (quoted by Philostratos, *op. cit.*, iii, 44) declares that for a long time healing had been considered an attribute of the Asklepiadai. Their law was that "sacred things may be revealed only to the elect, and should be confided to the profane only when they have been initiated in the mysteries of the science."[89] All were, therefore, obliged to take a sacred oath, which was finally developed as the Oath

[88] Kühn, ed. *Medicorum Græcorum Opera*, ii, 281.
[89] Sprengel, *Histoire de la médecine*, i, 169.

of Hippokrates,[90] that they would not profane the secrets entrusted to them and would divulge them only to their children and those of their masters, or to persons who had taken the same oath. A physician says of his work: "The sacred and mysterious vow restrains me, I am

[90] "I swear by Apollo the physician, and Æsculapius, and Health, and All-Heal, and all the gods and goddesses that, according to my ability and judgment, I will keep this Oath and this stipulation—to reckon him who taught me this Art equally dear to me as my parents, to share my substance with him, and relieve his necessities if required; to look upon his offspring in the same footing as my own brothers, and to teach them this art, if they shall wish to learn it, without fee or stipulation; and that by precept, lecture, and every other mode of instruction, I will impart a knowledge of the Art to my own sons, and those of my teachers, and to disciples bound by a stipulation and oath according to the law of medicine, but to none others. I will follow that system of regimen which, according to my ability and judgment, I consider for the benefit of my patients, and abstain from whatever is deleterious and mischievous. I will give no deadly medicine to anyone if asked, nor suggest any such counsel; and in like manner I will not give to a woman a pessary to produce abortion. With purity and with holiness I will pass my life and practice my Art. I will not cut persons laboring under the stone, but will leave this to be done by men who are practitioners of this work. Into whatever houses I enter, I will go into them for the benefit of the sick, and will abstain from every voluntary act of mischief and corruption; and, further, from the seduction of females or males, of freemen and slaves. Whatever, in connection with my professional practice or not, in connection with it, I see or hear, in the life of men, which ought not to be spoken of abroad, I will not divulge, as reckoning that all such should be kept secret. While I continue to keep this Oath unviolated, may it be granted to me to enjoy life and the practice of the art, respected by all men, in all times! But should I trespass and violate this Oath, may the reverse be my lot!" (Adams, *op. cit.*, ii, 278-280.)

Note.—For a similar Hindu oath see R. Roth, "Indische Medicin. Caraka," in *ZDMG*, 1872, xxvi, 445 ff.; also G. A. Liétard, "Le médecin Charaka. Le serment des hippocratistes et le serment des médecins hindous," in *BAM*, 3 sér., 1897, xxxvii, 565 ff.; Jones, *The Doctor's Oath*, pp. 58-59.

obliged to preserve silence."[91] The Asklepiadai were leaders in the cult and probably were very influential in creating the atmosphere best adapted to keep the minds of the suppliants in a frame to trust implicitly in the mysterious powers of the god and in the divine directions received by dreams and visions. Mutilated records found in Athens indicate that there was another religious order known as the Asklepiastai, which, it is assumed, was related to the cult (*CIA* II, i, addenda, 617 b). In the early traditions of Greek medicine lay physicians having no connection with the cult appear among the people, many of whom claimed descent from the god, and, all being included under the general term Asklepiadai, they became confused in early history with the priest-physicians.[92] With the lapse of time secrecy became relaxed, the knowledge of the healing art was acquired by those who did not observe the Oath, and eventually many charlatans engaged in the practice and brought discredit upon the cult—upon both priest and lay physicians.

The cult rituals.

In the early period appeals were apparently made to Asklepios for any purpose, but as he became famous in healing beyond all other heroes, especially after his alliance with Apollo, cultic practices were restricted to effecting cures, although a few records from Athens, Sikyon, and Epidauros indicate occasional consultations on other affairs. The customs in healing are known to have differed somewhat at the many Asklepieia, yet it is believed that at all of them the religious elements outweighed the practical, although the latter became more

[91] Sprengel, *op. cit.*, i, 170.
[92] Daremberg, *op. cit.*, pp. 56 ff.; also Houdart, *Histoire de la médecine grecque depuis Esculape jusqu'à Hippocrate exclusivement*, pp. 95 ff.

prominent after the Roman conquest. Our present knowledge of temple procedure has been gathered from many sources, from traditions, allusions by classical writers, inscriptions, and bas-reliefs and ex-votos found in excavations at Athens, Epidauros, and Kos. It is asserted that at some shrines the ritual summed up the whole procedure, while at others the priests performed their religious functions and then placed the suppliant in the care of assistants, who carried out the treatment according to directions received by dreams and visions; but however effected, the god alone received all the credit for the cure. The treatment at the larger sanctuaries, such as those just mentioned, and probably also at Knidos, Rhodes, Pergamon, Smyrna, and Kyrene, belonged to the latter class. In estimating the value of the evidence furnished by the relics found at the old shrines, it must be remembered that they were offered in gratitude for favors received and as testimonials of the powers of the god rather than as records of the methods of healing, and that they should not be relied on as giving any indication of the practical therapeutics used, however effective these may have been. The general attitude is probably well expressed in the *Corpus Hippocraticum* (*de Decoro*):[93]

As regards diseases and their symptoms, medicine in the greater number of cases inclines to do honor to the gods. Physicians bow before them, for medicine has no superabundance of power.[94]

The procedures at the Asklepieia.

Tales of the marvellous cures effected at the Asklepieia had spread the fame of the deity throughout Greece, and being matters of common knowledge, the sick, in going to these sanctuaries for relief, were probably

[93] Hippocrates, *op. cit.*, i, 23.
[94] Diehl, *Excursions in Greece*, p. 347.

already imbued with a certain religious fervor, while
their imagination was excited by the hope that they also
might be the recipients of the divine grace. Only the pure
were permitted to approach the god, and on entering the
hieron all were obliged to undergo a ceremonial purification (Pausanias, V, xiii, 3), this usually consisting of a
cold bath, or sometimes a salt or sea bath, which was
occasionally repeated (Euripides, *Iph. in Taur.*, 1193),
or the burning of incense and fumigations.[95] The suppliants were then instructed to make oblations to the gods
and heroes whose favor they sought. For the poor these
offerings were mostly thin, flat, perforated cakes (*po-
pana*) sweetened with honey or dipped in oil; while for
those better able, the propitiatory sacrifice was an animal, a pig, a goat, a lamb, a sheep, or a cock, Sokrates saying that the cock was an appropriate offering to Asklepios (Plato, *Phædo*, 155). At Epidauros the sacrifice of
goats was forbidden (Pausanias, II, xxvi, 9), and at
Tithorea any animal was acceptable except the goat (*ib.*,
X, xxxii, 12); but at Athens and Kyrene there was no
such restriction. Animals were burned on the altar, and
the priests usually had a share of the sacrifice. At one
shrine the legs of the fowl were their portion; but at
Epidauros and Titane no part of the offering might be
removed, and all was consumed within the *hieron*. The
serpents, as the incarnation or embodiment of the god,
were fed and sacrificed to; at Athens, Kos, and Titane it
was considered essential to feed them before benefits
could be received; but at Titane they were feared, and
food was simply left for them (*ib.*, II, xi, 8). It was impossible to approach the god without diverting the attention
of the serpents, honey cakes being favored for this purpose. Persons remaining in the *hieron* any length of time

[95] Uffelmann, *op. cit.*, p. 414.

repeated the sacrifice at intervals and were prompted to do so in dreams. Several bas-reliefs found in the ruins of the sanctuaries illustrate cultic usage. They show the god standing or seated, with Hygieia or other members of his family and a serpent beside him while a train of suppliants approach, each bearing some offering which was to be placed on a table standing near by.[96] Sacrifices were accompanied by music and fervent prayers for a revelation; but since no offerings were made without prayers, and as the suppliants often forgot the names of the deities, the priest chanted them, while the person making the sacrifice repeated them in a loud voice (Lucian, *Demosthenis encomium*, 27).[97] These prayers were called chants, and some of them were said to have been composed by Sophokles and Isodemos of Troizen (*ib.*) ("but they sang a song resembling the pæan of Sophokles which they sing at Athens in honor of Asklepios," Philostratos, *op. cit.*, iii, 17).

The ritual of the individual.

A rigorous diet, or fasting, was very commonly ordered as a preparation for incubation and treatment, and Galen states that sometimes, under the direction of the priests, the suppliants would not take wine for fifteen days.[98] Aristeides (*Orat. sac.*, i) speaks of the depressing effect of repeated fastings and baths, saying that they kept the mind in such a state of tension as frequently to weaken the faculties, and graphically gives details of treatments directed.[99] At Pergamon wine was forbidden, as Philostratos explains (*op. cit.*, i, 8), in order that the ether of

[96] Holländer, *op. cit.*, pp. 105 ff.
[97] C. Jacobitz, ed. iii, p. 374, Leipzig, 1872.
[98] Le Clerc, *op. cit.*, p. 60; also Gauthier, *op. cit.*, p. 26.
[99] For a summary of the remarks of Aristeides on the methods pursued at the Asklepieia, see Hamilton, *op. cit.*, pp. 44-62.

the soul should not be soiled by liquor. The patients were conducted through the *hieron* by attendants who related the legends of the cult and explained the remarkable cures recorded on the steles and tablets and attested by ex-votos; the rites and ceremonies being similarly interpreted, often in mystic terms. The temple of the god and the shrines of his associates were visited, and the tablets and mystic symbols that covered the walls were examined. Then, the patient being properly prepared, it was permissible for him to approach the image of the god, offer sacrifice with prayer, and allow the diseased part to come into contact with the hand or other part of the statue. An air of sanctity pervaded the *hieron,* and the sick could not fail to be deeply impressed by the majesty of the deity and by all that they heard and saw suggestive of the supernatural powers with which he was endowed, so that, with imagination fired by the marvels of the sanctuary, they awaited the mysterious events of the night.

Incubation.

As the evening approached, preparations were made in the dormitory or *abaton.* The patient, dressed in white (which was supposed to induce dreams), brought bedding and usually some food, and was assigned a pallet in the portico; or, if he was too ill to sleep there himself, a relative or friend incubated for him. As darkness came on, the lamps were lighted, and the *neokoros* with his assistants, also in white, entered. The suppliant placed some offering upon one of the small altars and retired to his couch, the *neokoros* collected the offerings, and the priest finally offered a prayer, perhaps such a one as that composed by Aristeides:[100]

O ye children of Apollo! who in time past have stilled the

[100] Pater, *Marius the Epicurean,* i, 39.

waves of sorrow for many people, lighting up a lamp of safety before those who travel by sea and land, be pleased, in your great condescension, though ye be equal in glory with your elder brethren the Dioskouroi, and your lot in immortal youth be as theirs, to accept this prayer, which in sleep and vision ye have inspired. Order it aright, I pray you, according to your loving-kindness to men. Preserve me from sickness; and indue my body with such a measure of health as may suffice it for the obeying of the spirit, that I may pass my days unhindered and in quietness.

After the prayer, silence was enjoined, and the patients were directed to be frightened at nothing, not to whisper, and to go to sleep. The lamps were extinguished, and the priests departed, all those sleeping in the *abaton* remaining the whole night. It was customary for the priests and attendants to return to the *abaton* at some time during the night, generally toward morning, one of them being in the costume of the god, carrying his attributes, and Philostratos states (*op. cit.*, i, 7) that in the temple at Aigai the god appeared to men. They were accompanied by one or more of the retinue of the god dressed as Hygieia, Panakeia, Iaso, or Akeso, his serpents, and possibly by sacred dogs. They carried jars of ointments and other remedies, and passing among the sleepers, made applications to diseased parts or directed the attention of the serpents or dogs, which was highly prized, the serpents creeping over the sleeper and being supposed to whisper the remedy into the ear, and sometimes to pinch it.[101] Occasionally the priest, in the guise of the god, would speak with the patient, ask concerning the ailment, perhaps touch or lay a hand on the diseased part,[102] apply some remedy or give advice, and leave directions for future treatment. Aristophanes (*op. cit.*, 632 ff.),

[101] Farnell, *Cults*, iii, 10.
[102] Weinreich, *op. cit.*, pp. 1 ff.

describes such a scene in the shrine at Athens. The tales and the impressions of the preceding day had prepared the mind for the prophetic vision or dream, and it was apt to come to those who expected it.[103]

The mental impressions.

The experiences of the night, acting on an overheated imagination, the assumed appearance of the deity, possibly in the form of a serpent, and the application of the hand of the god—all in the dim light while in a state midway between sleeping and waking—were readily interpreted as a divine visitation, a celestial dream or vision. It was the realization of "divine oracles given in dreams" or of "the oracle of the soul itself in dreaming," since it was generally held that in natural dreams "the soul reveals what will benefit the body."[104] The Hippokratic writings show a qualified belief in this power of the soul, in the prophetic nature of dreams, and in the conviction that the gods should be invoked:

For dreams with good omens, pray to the Sun, to Celestial Zeus (*Di Uranios*), to enriching Zeus (*Di Ktesios*), to enriching Athena, Hermes and Apollo; for bad dreams, pray to the apotropaic gods, to Gaia, and to the Heroes, that all these ills may be averted (*de Insom.*, IV, 89).[105]

In the morning, the dreams and visions of the night were told and interpreted by the priests, who then gave

[103] For an extended consideration of ancient incubation in its relation to 'animal magnetism' (? hypnotism) and somnambulism, see Gauthier, *op. cit.*, pp. 133 ff.; and for the more modern views of these subjects and suggestive therapeutics, see the works of Bertrand, Braid, Bernheim, Moll, Bramwell, and Tuckey, listed under General Bibliography.

[104] Thrämer, in *ERE* vi, 543.

[105] Garrison, in *PCC* v, 45; also Littré, *Œuvres complètes d'Hippocrate*, vi, 652.

appropriate directions for any treatment that should be carried out. Some claimed to be healed, and the priest announced a cure to others with authority, while the fortunate were congratulated, and the cures were celebrated with shouts of joy and the singing of pæans in praise of Apollo, Asklepios, and the associated deities. Those who had not received the divine communication remained in the *hieron,* made further sacrifices, and repeated the incubation; but cases proving intractable were blamed for impiety, for lack of purity or merit, and they were often advised to go elsewhere. If an invalid died, it was through lack of confidence or because of disobedience. It appears that all were kindly treated except those who were dying or expecting child-birth, but these, as polluting the sanctuary, were cast out and obliged to shift for themselves. The god had rejected them, and no one belonging to the *hieron* would give them aid.

Practical therapeutics.

Turning to the material methods used for cures, Plato (*Protagoras,* 107) names four that were employed by physicians of his day; burning, cutting, physic, and starving; while Demosthenes (*Orationes,* iv, 80), in his speech on Aristogeiton, mentions burning and cutting. Illustrations of surgical instruments on bas-reliefs from the walls of temples or *abata* give positive proof that surgery was practiced in the sanctuaries of Asklepios. These evidences come mainly from Epidauros and Kos, and it is believed that little surgery was done at Athens. The subjects for surgery were held by attendants, and the blood found later upon the floor was believed to attest the operation. Surgeons and their assistants do not appear to have belonged to the priestly class, though they were called 'sons of the god' and were probably Asklepiads. Pindar (*op. cit.*, iii, 47-53) refers to the use of magic, internal remedies, and surgery by the god:

> Each of his several bane he cured.
> This felt the charm's enchanting sound;
> That drank th' elixir's soothing cup;
> Some with soft hand in sheltering bands he bound,
> Or plied the searching steel and bade the lame leap up.

Data recorded in literature and in many inscriptions that have been found clearly indicate that the more practical therapeutics of the temple made use of external applications of lotions and ointments, exercise, baths followed by friction and other manipulation, diet, and often a general hygienic regimen. Asklepios. has been called the father of health gymnastics. It is stated that at Pergamon the xyster, or rough brush, was invented for rubbing after the bath (Martial, xiv, 51). Religious healing practice raised two important hygienic measures, cleansing the body and moderation in eating and drinking, to divine commands.[106] In addition to the above measures, there are many suggestions in the methods associated with incubation closely simulating what are now known as hypnotism and 'suggestion,' while numerous internal remedies, presumably made from herbs and roots, were combined in administration with incantations and magic formulas.

The use of animals in the cult. Serpents.

Both serpents and dogs were used in the Asklepian cultic practice as ministers of healing, usually by the use of the tongue, but it is asserted that the disciples of Asklepios sometimes recommended that the flesh of the sacred dogs be given to patients as medicine (Frazer, *op. cit.*, iii, 65, 250-251). The serpent was the emblem of

[106] Uffelmann, *op. cit.*, p. 418.

life and healing, and was used in the cult as a ritualistic symbol, being sacred and revered as the incarnation of the god. This is illustrated on a coin from Pergamon, struck during the reign of Caracalla, on the reverse side of which the Emperor is shown in military dress saluting the reptile with his right hand, while Telesphoros stands close by.[107] Pausanias (II, xxviii, 1) says the serpents— and another sort, of a yellowish hue—are considered sacred to Asklepios and are tame, and they breed no- where but in Epidauria; but they are also described (Ailianos, *op. cit.*, viii, 12) as reddish-brown, fiery, or tawny in color, sharp-sighted, with a broad mouth, and called *pareiai*, or 'puffy-cheeked.' Their bite was not venomous, and, for this reason, they were consecrated to the best of gods, and destined to his service. It was this latter species that was kept at Athens and mentioned by Aristophanes (*op. cit.*, 728 ff.). These serpents were classed by Linnæus as the *coluber Æsculapii*. Nikandros (*Theriaca*, 438) describes still another variety found near Mount Pelion in Thessaly and used at Trikke, this being of a blackish color with a green belly, three rows of teeth, a bunch of hair over the eyes, and a yellowish beard, whose bite was not dangerous. It was classed by Linnæus as the *coluber cerastes*.

Serpent legends.

It is stated that women, resorting to the shrines of Asklepios in the hope of being relieved of sterility and of bearing children, slept in the temples, where they were visited in their dreams by a serpent as the embodiment of the deity, the children born afterward being believed to have been begotten by the snake-god.[108] At Sikyon it was said that Aristodama had slept in the temple, and

---

[107] Walton, *op. cit.*, pp. 13-14.
[108] Frazer, *Adonis, Attis, Osiris*, i, 80 ff., 90.

that Asklepios was the father of her son, Aratos (Pausanias, II, x, 3). The Messenians thought that the birth of the hero Aristomenes was out of the common; for the mother, they said, had been visited by a daimon or a god in the likeness of a serpent (*ib.*, IV, xiv, 7). Similar instances of a male parentage by a serpent are related in several traditions of ancient times (Suetonius, *Vita Augustæ*, 94; Dion Kassios, XLV, i, 2).

Dogs.

Pausanias (II, xxvi, 4; xxvii, 2) refers to dogs in association with Asklepios, and tablets found by Kavvadias at Epidauros give evidence of cures by these sacred animals.[109] Dogs were kept in the Asklepieion in Crete, as in Athens, Peiraieus, Epidauros, and Cyprus.[110] Dogs guarded the sacred treasures at Athens (*CIA* II, iii, 1651; Ailianos, *op. cit.*, vii, 13), and a dog is represented as with Machaon, Podaleirios, and Asklepios on a basrelief from that city.[110] Coins of Magnesia, in Thessaly, show the dogs by the side of Asklepios, and they are occasionally seen at the feet of the deity in statues.[111] When Asklepios went to Athens, he took certain dogs with him, and since they partook of his sanctity,[112] the Athenians offered sacrificial cakes both to the god and his dogs (*CIA* II, iii, 1651).

Tablets relating cures.

Parts of the tablets mentioned by Pausanias (II, xxvii, 3) and Strabo (VIII, vi, 15 = p. 374 C) were found by Kavvadias and have been pieced together. One of these

---

[109] *Op. cit.*, pp. 23-32.

[110] S. Reinach, "Les chiens dans le culte d'Esculape," in *RA*, 3 sér., 1884, iv, pp. 76-83.

[111] Walton, *op. cit.*, p. 32.

[112] Prott-Ziehen, *Leges Græcorum sacræ e titulis collectæ*, no. 18.

is six feet high, two and a half feet wide, and seven inches thick, and is of fine-grained lithographic stone with the face carefully smoothed. The inscription (*CIG* iv, 951 f.)[113] consists of 126 lines in the Doric dialect of Argolis, and the form of the letters, as well as the simplicity of the language, indicate that it was carved not later than the third century B.C. The tablet begins:

> God [be with us]. Good Fortune [attend].
> Cures performed by Apollo and Asklepios.

A few of these testimonials of healing by the gods are, briefly, as follows:

Kleo, who had been pregnant five years, slept in the *abaton,* where she was visited by the god in her dreams; immediately after leaving the sacred precinct, she was delivered of a boy, who of his own accord washed himself in the fountain and walked about with his mother. On her offering she inscribed the verses:

Not at the size of my tablet wonder, but more at the marvel.
Kleo for five long years was bearing the weight of her burden,
Till in the temple she slept, whence as a mother she went.

Ithmonika of Pallana, desiring offspring, slept in the temple, where she saw a vision in which she seemed to ask the god that she might conceive a daughter, the reply of Asklepios being that she would become pregnant, and that if there was any further request, it would be granted. She said there was nothing more; but since she had not asked to be delivered, after three years she returned and during her sleep had a vision in which the god inquired if she had not become pregnant. She answered that she had, but that she had not been delivered; whereupon the

---

[113] Conveniently edited, with full comment, by J. Baunack, in *SGAS,* 1886, i, 120-130. Some of the cures are taken from a similar inscription in 134 lines (*ib.,* pp. 131-144). See also Hamilton, *op. cit.,* pp. 17-27.

divinity reminded her that she had not made that request, yet that this also would be granted; and going out of the sacred precinct, she at once gave birth to a girl.

A man with paralyzed fingers came to the god as a suppliant, but was incredulous and mocked at the inscriptions. He slept and saw a vision, dreaming that as he was playing dice under the temple, the god stepped on his fingers and stretched them out. After that he could bend and straighten them, and the divinity asked him if he was still incredulous. He replied, "No"; whereupon the deity said that if he should trust in the future, he would be as other believers. At daybreak he awoke cured.

Ambrosia of Athens was a suppliant because she was one-eyed [? having anchyloblepharon], but she also ridiculed the cures as impossible. Nevertheless, she slept in the *abaton,* where she had a vision in which the god stood beside her and said he would cure her, but that she must consecrate a silver pig to the sanctuary for her ignorance. Splitting open her diseased eyelids, he poured in a lotion, and she left the temple whole.

A lad who was mute had gone through the customary rites and was standing by his father when the attendant asked if he would promise to offer the proper sacrifice to the god within a year if he gained the object of his coming. The boy suddenly exclaimed "I promise," repeating the word at the bidding of his astonished father, and he was cured from that time.

Pandaros, a Thessalian, who had marks on his brow, slept in the dormitory and had a vision in which the god seemed to tie a fillet on his brow, bidding him take it off when he was out of the *abaton.* In the morning he did this, and his face was clean; but the fillet, which he consecrated to the temple, bore the marks.

Echedoros, a friend of Pandaros, had similar marks, and wishing to try the same treatment, he went to the temple as a suppliant, taking with him an offering which Pandaros sent to the god. As he slept, he had a vision in which the god seemed to command him to deposit in the sanctuary any money which he had received from Pandaros; but he declared that none had been given him, though he promised to consecrate a picture to the temple if he was cured. The god then bound the fillet of Pandaros on his brow, but when he took it off in the morning and was about to wash, he saw by the reflection in the water that, in addition to his own, the marks of Pandaros had been transferred from the fillet to his forehead.

A slave broke the drinking-cup of his master, but saved the pieces; and since it was highly valued, the god, whose power he had doubted, made it whole. A man whose child was lost applied to the deity, who directed him where it might be found. A man had had a lance-head in his jaw for six years, but while he practiced incubation, the divinity drew it out and placed it in his hand, where he found it in the morning. A man from Thrace had swallowed some leeches. During his sleep in the *abaton* it seemed that the god appeared, and cutting open his breast, removed them, sewing up the wound. In the morning he left the sanctuary with the leeches in his hand.

While a suppliant slept on a bench outside the *abaton*, a serpent came from the temple and licked the ulcer on his toe; but when he awoke cured, he declared that he had dreamed that the deity, in the form of a beautiful boy, had applied an ointment.

Nikasiboula incubated in the temple, seeing a vision in which it seemed that the divinity carried a great serpent to her and that she had intercourse with it. Afterward she bore two boys within a year.

Erasippa, who was suffering from her stomach and burning with fever, incubated and saw a vision in which she dreamed that the god rubbed her stomach, kissed her, and then gave her a vial, bidding her to drink the contents and vomit. Her mantle was filled with the evil she vomited, and she was well.

A man having an ulcer incubated and had a vision in which the divinity seemed to order the attendants accompanying him to seize and hold him so that he might cut his belly. He dreamed that he ran away, but they seized him and tied him to the door-knocker, after which Asklepios split open his abdomen, cut out the ulcer, sewed up the wound, and released him from his bonds. He went away whole, but the ground in the *abaton* was covered with blood.

Aristagoras of Troizen had a worm in her intestines and slept in the local Asklepieion, where she had a vision in which the 'sons of the god' seemed to cut off her head during the absence of the god at Epidauros; but, unable to replace it, they sent for Asklepios, who came from Epidauros the next night, put the head back, and then cut out the worm in the proper manner.[114]

Pausanias (X, xxxviii, 13) relates the case of Phalysios, who built a temple to Asklepios at Naupaktos. He was nearly blind, and the god sent the poetess Anyte to him with a sealed tablet which he was bidden to read. It seemed impossible, but hoping for benefit, he broke the seal, and looking at the tablet, he was made whole, whereupon he gave Anyte what was written ,on the tablet, namely, two thousand gold staters (about $9,500).

The sanctuary tales, although designed only in laudation, give intimations of various practical measures used by the cult, but an inscription of some five hundred years later, probably during the reign of Antoninus Pius, is

[114] Ailianos (*op. cit.*, IX, 33) repeats this cure on the authority of Hippys of Rhegion (fifth century B.C.), except that Aristagoras is there said to have come from Methuana and to have sought relief at Epidauros (see also Frazer, *Paus.*, iii, 248).

more circumstantial and is believed to illustrate the advances toward more rational therapeutics. This text, set up by a Karian sophist, Apellas, at Epidauros in the second half of the second century A.D. (*CIG* iv, 955), runs as follows:[115]

In the priesthood of Po[phios] Ail[ios] Antiochos.

I, Markos Joulios Apellas, of Idrias Mylasa was summoned by the god, for I had fallen ill repeatedly and suffered from indigestion. In Aigina, during the voyage, he bade me not be extremely irritable; and when I was in the temple, he directed me to cover my head for two days (during which it rained), to take cheese and bread, parsley with lettuce, to wash myself with my own hands, to practice running, to take the tops of citrons soaked in water, to rub myself against the wall at the Akoai;[116] to walk about in the upper portico, to swing, to smear myself with sand, to go barefoot, to pour wine into the warm water before entering the bath, to bathe alone, and to give an Attic drachma to the bath-attendant, to offer joint sacrifice to Asklepios, Epione, and the Eleusinian goddesses, to take milk with honey. One day, when I was drinking milk alone, he said: "Put honey into the milk that it may pass through" (*i.e.*, be cathartic).

And when I besought the god to set me free more speedily, I seemed to go, all smeared with mustard and salt, from the *abaton* along the Akoai; led by a little boy with a smoking censer, while the priest said, "Thou art cured, but must pay the fees for healing." I did according to my vision, and when I rubbed myself with salt and wet mustard, I suffered; but when I washed, I had no pain. These events took place in the nine days after my coming.

He also touched my right hand and breast, and when I was sacrificing on the following day, a flame leapt forth and burnt

[115] Baunack, in *SGAS*, 1886, i, 112-118 (text, translation, and commentary).

[116] Apparently a part of the Asklepieion, so called from the 'voices' heard there.

my hand so that blisters broke out; but after a little my hand was well.

As I prolonged my stay, the god told me to use dill with olive oil for headache. Formerly I had not suffered from my head, but my studies brought on congestion. After I used olive oil, I was cured of headache. For a swollen uvula, the god told me to use a cold gargle, when I consulted him about it; and he ordered the same treatment for inflamed tonsils.

He bade me inscribe this treatment, and I left the temple full of gratitude and in good health.

Popularity of the Asklepieia.

The sick came to the Asklepieia in large numbers, and Strabo (VIII, vi, 15 = p. 374 C) says that Epidauros was constantly crowded. The hope of receiving divine favor and directions for the cure of their maladies, and the reception by experienced Asklepiads, gave comfort and mental relief; while the change of scene and rest, and a simple, regular life in the open air, amid surroundings of unusual attractiveness and interest, were conditions favoring an improvement of health and probably effected many cures without other treatment. Whatever may have been the elements upon which the healing depended, the benefits conferred by cultic practices were so real and tangible that the votaries of the god increased in numbers and influence until the worship of Asklepios had conquered the whole of the Greek world and had to be reckoned with as one of the main religious forces of later Hellenism.[117]

Recreation.

Patients and visitors found much to engage their attention at the sanctuaries. If not occupied in carrying out the directions received for treatment, the sacred precinct offered varied opportunities for recreation and religious

[117] Farnell, in *ERE* vi, 418.

devotion according to taste. There were ceremonies at the chief temple and the shrines of associated deities and heroes, which were at times elaborate and interesting; in the peristyle of the temple or in the porticoes, sophists and philosophers discoursed on matters pertaining to the cult and were ready to assist in expounding dreams, visions, and mysteries, as well as the miraculous cures of the god and his associates; and there were poets always eager to recite their works (Aristeides, *op. cit.*, i; Philostratos, *op. cit.*, i, 13). Those who were able ascended Mount Kynortion and sacrificed to Apollo Maleates; and there were the Roman baths, the gymnasium, contests in the stadium, plays at the theater, musical chants and melodies, and dancing.

Thank offerings.

When a suppliant was healed, the thank offering and payment became even more important than the preliminary, propitiatory sacrifice. These offerings were made not only to Asklepios, but to the other deities represented by shrines within the precinct who were supposed to have contributed to the cure, including the auxiliary gods Telesphoros or Akesis, representing convalescence, and Hypnos and Oneiros, presiding over sleep and dreams, or incubation; while it was also regarded as a duty and a wise precaution to make sacrifice to Hygieia. The offerings (*CIA* ii, 835, 836) consisted of money payments or of some gift dedicated to the temple; but it appears that for the most part the patients discharged their debt or expressed their gratitude as they pleased, and with a great variety of gifts. If the payment required could not be made at the time, promises were accepted; and these were fulfilled within the year; although instances are recorded of suppliants refusing to pay and having their afflictions returned to them. The most common gifts were models of the parts healed, in terra-cotta, ivory, bronze, gold, or silver, and these were sometimes inscribed with the name of the donor. There were relics of many kinds. A boy gave his *astragaloi* to the god, and Alexander the Great left his breastplate and spear in the temple at Gortys (Pausanias, VIII, xxviii, 1). Others gave temple furniture, bronze rings, or ornamental objects, such as serpents in gold and silver, one of these being a gold snake coiled round a staff; and there were many inscribed tablets and works of art, such as bas-reliefs of the god and his attendants, statues, and paintings (Frazer, *Paus.*, ii, 238-239). Pæans or hymns of praise, prayers, and dramas concerning the life of the god were dedicated to the temples. At Athens such hymns have been found inscribed on stones (*CIA* iii, 171 a); while it is said that Asklepios, appearing to Sophokles, commanded him to write a pæan in his honor; and part of one, supposed to be by him, has been discovered.[118]

Public health functions.

The public recognized in Asklepios and Hygieia powers of protection of the health of the community in addition to their ability to serve the individual, and they were regarded as public benefactors. Neglect of the gods might bring disasters upon the people in the form of pestilence or war, and the State protected itself against such calamities by exercising supervision and control over the rites of prayer and sacrifice. The Council at Athens brought Asklepios and Hygieia from Epidauros (cf. Hygieia) because of an existing plague, and in gratitude for their services gave them the epithet of 'saviors.' Thereafter, in addition to the yearly festivals held in their honor, sacrifices were made during the year at intervals fixed by law, and the Boule decreed special offer-

[118] Walton, *op. cit.*, p. 29.

ings of an ox or a bull to Asklepios, Hygieia, and other
deities of the Asklepieion for the health of the Council
and that of the citizens and their families; while public
health was considered of such importance that, early in
the fourth century B.C., the Council of the city assumed
entire control of the administration of the Asklepieion.
The Epidaurians made similar appeals. Each year, with
flowing hair, clad in white, and wearing wreaths of
laurels and orange blossoms, the noblest citizens marched
from the city to the Asklepieion chanting hymns in praise
of Apollo, Asklepios, and Hygieia, and on reaching the
hieron they offered prayers and sacrifices for the health
of the citizens and their families, and for the general
welfare of Epidauros.

Public festivals.

Great public festivals, known as Asklepieia, were held
regularly with much pomp and ceremony in honor of the
god at many of his sanctuaries. They were regarded as
great fêtes and were exceedingly popular, but the details
concerning most of them are lacking. The best known
were celebrated at Athens, Epidauros, and Kos.

Festivals at Athens.

At Athens two fêtes were held yearly for Asklepios,
called the Asklepieia and the Epidauria, and both were
under the direction of the State. The Asklepieia, which
took place in March or April, was of minor importance
as compared with other festivals of the city, as the
Panathenaia and the Eleusinia; but it was more strictly
religious than at Epidauros and Kos since it was not accompanied by athletic games. The more important celebration was the Epidauria (Pausanias, II, xxvi, 8), which
was held in August-September (possibly September
fifth), during the Eleusinia. The festival was established

to celebrate the initiation of Asklepios in the Eleusinian
Mysteries and in honor of the relations between his cult
and that of Demeter and Kore. According to an early
myth, Asklepios, who was due to attend the ceremonies,
was delayed in crossing from Epidauros, arriving only
on the second day, after all others had been initiated, but
was, nevertheless, accepted.[119] The Epidauria, therefore,
began on the evening of the second day of the Eleusinia.
The ceremonies, held in the Asklepieion, lasted all night,
and in the morning the worshippers offered sacrifices
with mysterious rites. Nothing is definitely known of
these ceremonies; but it is assumed that, as they were in
commemoration of the initiation of the god, they were
of somewhat similar character. Later in the day, processions were formed; and the sacred *kiste,* relics, and re-
liefs were exhibited by bearers. It is asserted that as
many as eighty sacred dogs figured in these festivals. In
the view of the Athenians, Asklepios never lost traces of
his original character of hero as celebrated by the early
poets; and it is assumed that this aspect of the god was
honored by a festival of which little is known, the *Heroa,*
which was held at the Asklepieion, although it may have
had a more general significance (*CIA* II, i, add. et corr.,
453, b and c). In these festivals both political and religious organizations joined, e.g., the Council of the Areiopagos, the Ephebes of Telesphoros, and the Orgeones,
who had a shrine of Asklepios in the deme Prospalta,
where they conducted a special ritual (*CIA* II, ii, 990).

Festivals at Epidauros.

The Megala Asklepieia (*IG* iv, 1473), usually called
the 'Apollonia and Asklepieia,' or the shorter form
'Asklepieia,' and sometimes 'Sebasteia [revered] Askle-

[119] Farnell, *Cults,* iii, 201.

pieia' (*CIG*, 1186),[120] held at Epidauros every five years
in the month of February and lasting nine days, was the
most elaborate of all the festivals in honor of Asklepios
and attracted throngs from all parts of Greece. At first
it was conducted by the Asklepiadai, but later, probably
after the administration of the sanctuary was taken over
by the Council of Epidauros, by the Argives. The first
day was given up to the preliminaries, and the next to the
religious exercises. All the temples and shrines of the
hieron were magnificently decorated, and the whole precinct was decked for the celebration. Sacrifices were made
to the several deities, while great choirs chanted pæans
to Apollo, Asklepios, and all other divinities of the sanctuary. By an old regulation, dating probably from the
fifth century B.C., the sacrifices were made first to Apollo,
then to Leto and Artemis. The cock, the fowl appropriate
to Asklepios, was sacrificed both to Asklepios and Apollo,
with barley meal, wheat, and wine. Asklepios received a
bull, his male associates received a second one, and his
female associates a cow.[121] The image of Asklepios, in a
triumphal car, was drawn through the precinct by Centaurs carrying lighted torches, followed by priests and
acolytes chanting hymns.[122] In these processions a hymn
by Isyllos was sung in Ionic stanzas giving the genealogy
of Asklepios.[123] These processions were, in many respects,
similar to those of the Korybantes. The priests usually
announced a few miracles, which were received with loud
acclaim. Later in the day there were feasts, and the vigils
lasted through the night. The succeeding days were given
up to athletic contests in the stadium, races, wrestling,

[120] Nilsson, *op. cit.*, p. 409.

[121] *Ib., loc. cit.*

[122] A few of these pæans have been preserved, see Walton, *op. cit.*,
p. 29.

[123] Nilsson, *op. cit.*, p. 410.

and other games, plays in the theater, competitions in
music, contests of rhapsodists, and other entertainments.
Many of the best athletes of Greece contested in the
games, and at the close of the celebration prizes were
awarded to the victors. Other festivals are said to have
been held at Epidauros, one especially, possibly every
third year in August or September, within nine days
after the Isthmian games.

Festivals at Kos.

At Kos public sacrifices were offered monthly, and
there was a yearly festival to celebrate the consecration
of the newly elected Hiereus, with games, contests of
various kinds, and plays in the theater in the city following the religious ceremonies. Every fifth year the Megala
Asklepieia, a ceremony of especial magnificence, was held
in connection with the Dionysia (*SIG*, 677, line 4). For
this, preparations were made long in advance, and the
hieron was elaborately decorated for the entertainment
of the throng of visitors. There are few references in the
inscriptions to Asklepios that relate to the ritual, but
there was a celebration, of which little is known except
from an allusion in a letter of Hippokrates (*ad Senatus
Populusque Abderitamus*, II)[124] that was called 'taking
up the staff' (οἱ τῷ θεῷ προσήκοντες).[125] This rite was held
during the annual fête, and it is presumed that it referred
to the transfer of the symbol of priestly dignity in the
yearly change of chief priests.[126]

Festivals at Pergamon.

At Pergamon the festivals were observed with great
solemnity. A bull was sacrificed to Zeus, Athena, Diony-

---

[124] Hippokrates, *op. cit.*, ii, 1274.
[125] Paton and Hicks, *op. cit.*, p. 348; also Walton, *op. cit.*, p. 72.
[126] Nilsson, *op. cit.*, p. 411, note 4.

sos, and Asklepios; and after being quartered, one share was placed before each statue, while pæans were sung to each deity in turn (*CIG*, 3538). Telesphoros was especially revered at Pergamon, and during the festivals pæans were sung in his honor.

Other festivals.

In the later period, when Asklepios had become popular, games were named for him in many places. Alexander the Great worshipped at Soloi in Cilicia, where he established a magnificent festival. Megala Asklepieia were celebrated both at Ankyra in Galatia and at Thyateira in Lydia; while at Lampsakos in Phrygia two festivals were held each year, in the Lenaion and in the Leukathion, at which the citizens wore wreaths of laurel and oleander and made sacrifices, the expenses being borne by the treasury of the god (*CIG*, 3641 b). At Tamynai in Euboia the god had a festival with sacrifices at which horsemen and children under seven years took part, the names of the latter being recorded. Festivals with games were held also at Byrkos on Karpathos, Kalymna, Ephesos, Kyzikos, Prousias (ad Hypium), Nikaia, Laodikeia, Rhodiopolis, and Termesos.[127]

Medical progress toward scientific methods.

The traditions of Greek healing tend to confirm the view that, following the Trojan War, the Asklepiads continued as the chief exponents of the healing art and that the more thoughtful observers among them became increasingly impressed with the value of material remedies such as herbs, roots, and hygienic régime. The traditional development of the art toward a more scientific understanding followed the cult of Asklepios as the chief line of descent until the dawn of Greek history, after

[127] Nilsson, *op. cit.*, p. 413.

THE *ABATON* AT KOS

From an article by Richard Caton. Courtesy of the
British Medical Journal.

which its progress may be more clearly traced. As the centuries passed the Asklepiads evidently endeavored to put their experience to better use by collating their observations for the benefit of the clan. Such efforts are first made manifest in the work of their brethren of Kos and Knidos, the medical writers whose records, the *Corpus Hippocraticum,* formed the basis for later studies, and are the earliest systematic writings on the healing art that have been preserved to modern times. Formulas that had proved successful, and wise sayings or medical aphorisms, called 'Knidian sentences,' were inscribed on the walls of the temples and dormitories for ready use (Pliny, *op. cit.,* xx, 100; Strabo, XIV, ii, 19 = p. 657 C). The responsibility of the physician was recognized by the establishment of schools at Kos, Knidos, Rhodes, Kyrene, and Alexandria for the better instruction of the Asklepiadai. Records were collected, libraries were formed, and medical theorists and writers endeavored to discard error, and to establish a more accurate differentiation of disease, a more correct prognosis, and a more effective treatment, despite the strong religious leanings toward the miraculous. At Athens and Epidauros there were no such schools, yet it cannot be doubted that the therapeutics at these sanctuaries were at least on a par of intelligence and skill with those of the Dorian coast. The marvellous acts of the god recorded in a few chosen cases must not be taken as a true index of the character of the treatment of the thousands of patients applying at the Asklepieia. No records of cures have been found at Athens, only inscribed ex-votos (*CIA* ii, 835-836), and the only account of the methods used there comes from Aristophanes (*op. cit.,* 632 ff.). Medicine, in theory and practice, became more rational with the passage of time and less dependent on faith and miracle. In the late Greek period and after the Roman conquest, during the early

centuries of the Christian era, the Asklepieia were
steadily becoming more like modern sanatoria and hospitals, and it is a notable fact that these were the only
charitable institutions established by the Greeks.[128] Here
patients underwent a more systematic medical and
hygienic treatment under the direction of physicians and
in association with the religious rites of the cult. Ais-
chines, the rhetor, underwent a three months' course of
treatment at Epidauros, and Aristeides probably remained at the healing sanctuaries a still longer time.
Many of the sick at Pergamon, the Serapeum at Alexandria, and numerous other shrines were treated by prescriptions given in dreams, and the healing art undoubtedly was cultivated in the religious dreams of the
Asklepios cult (Artemidoros, iv, 22; Iamblichos, *op. cit.*,
iii, 3);[129] while Farnell[130] makes note of the "striking
divergence between the European spirit of Hellenic
religion and the Oriental spirit of Mesopotamia; the
Babylonian god practices magic, the Hellenic Asklepios
practices and fosters science; and his cures at Epidauros
. . . show the beginnings of sane therapeutics." The
Asklepiadai are credited with an endeavor to retain the
knowledge of healing among themselves, but this monopoly was never effective; and it is known that from the
seventh century onward many of the foremost Greek
philosophers included healing among the subjects of their
speculations and practiced it side by side with physicians
independently of the cults.

The cult influence.

From his earliest shrine, the cave at Trikke in Thessaly, the fame of Asklepios spread abroad, and after the

[128] Diehl, *op. cit.,* p. 331.
[129] Thrämer, in *ERE* vi, 543.
[130] In *ERE* vi, 418.

divine alliance with Apollo the scene of his activities shifted to Argolis, where, at Epidauros, was developed the most splendid and extensive resort for health and pleasure in ancient Greece, and the Delphic oracle declared: "Thou, O Asklepios! art born to become a great joy to the world." The cult was limited to healing, and Asklepios became the chief of all spiritual agencies ministering to the sick. He was exalted to the rank of a high deity, and the spirit of divine beneficence for the relief of suffering humanity radiated from Epidauros throughout the whole of the Greek world, so that his cult became a powerful influence among the Hellenes. In the later age the individual had a greater liberty in the god he might choose and was no longer limited to the cult in which he had been born. "This freedom had already for some time been offered by the *thiasoi;* and now in the Hellenistic world, especially by the powerful and wide influence of the cult of Asklepios, the idea was developed of a deity who as Healer and Savior called all mankind to himself; and it was this significant cult-phenomena that induced Kerkidas [third century B.C.]—to include Παιαν , 'the Healer,' among the true divinities whose worship ought to supplant that of the older gods.'"[131]

Recapitulation.

Reviewing the history of the cult of Asklepios, one cannot fail to be impressed with its progressive character and with its ability to adapt itself to many changes in thought and points of view, and to lead in the art of healing during an extended period of intellectual development in Greece. Receiving its inspiration from a hero of Thessaly—becoming a cave- or earth-spirit—and with certain herb remedies and an oracle, it gained fame and

---

[131] Farnell, in *ERE* vi, 422.

reigned supreme in its sphere for many centuries. Its leader continued as the "blameless physician" dispensing health and happiness. Free from the frailties of other Greek heroes and deities, devoted only to the interests of suffering humanity, he won the confidence, reverence, and worship of an independent people and, raised from the rank of a hero to that of a demigod, was finally deified with generous and general acclaim. His descendant clan, more skilful than others, maintained the religious character of the cult, and, benefiting by its experience, established scientific methods and principles,[132] laying the foundations upon which all subsequent progress in medicine has been built. The cult withstood criticism and bitter satire and spread its methods of healing throughout Hellas and its colonies. Asklepios was adopted by the Romans, brought relief to their misery, and held sway as their chief healing divinity during a considerable part of the Republic and for several centuries of the Empire until the cults of the old religions were submerged by the wave of early Christianity. The character of Asklepios was interpreted in art by the commanding figure and majestic countenance of Zeus himself, expressive of supreme benignity and paternal sympathy.

The mystic Asklepios.

Asklepios personified the mystic powers of divinity over the healing forces of the unseen world in both its uranic and chthonic aspects. His emblem was the serpent, the symbol of life, sagacity, and healing, in which the people recognized the skill and majesty of the god. It is perhaps impossible at the present day to appreciate the mystic atmosphere in which the Greeks idealized their divinities as possessing all supernatural powers. Modern materialism does not permit of feeling that sympathetic,

[132] Singer, *op. cit.*, pp. 80, 82 ff.

beneficent touch of the divine master of the healing art which drew all Hellenes and all official Rome to his feet, so beautifully expressed by Pater.[133] However, the development of this divine personality, associated with the period of the highest intellectual expression of the ancient Greeks, is a most instructive example of the psychological attitude of the pagan world toward deity in the evolution of polytheism, which may be more readily understood by an appreciation of the various transformations of the religious aspects in which he was conceived, and which may be formulated as in several stages: (1) the mortal Thessalian physician who learned the healing art from Cheiron ánd taught it to his sons, whó applied it with distinction in the Trojan War; (2) heroized after death, his spirit, conceived as an earth-daimon —a cave-spirit with the serpent as its emblem—continued his activities, sending forth from the depths cures for disease and prophecies, and celebrated by Homer and other poets; (3) he became the son of Apollo and the great Epidaurian god of healing; he was deified by a thunderbolt of Zeus, and assumed a uranic as well as a chthonic aspect, with a cult that was recognized as dominant throughout Greece; (4) the demigod and hero of Athenian tradition (*Heros-Iatros*), honored by great festivals; (5) and finally, Æsculapius, the god of healing of later Roman tradition, represented by the serpent, who faded from view in a new era.[134]

AMPHIARAOS

AMPHIARAOS was a grandson of Melampous, from whom he inherited his faculties of seer and prophet, although, according to tradition, he first developed his mantic powers after sleeping at Phlious (Pausanias, II, xiii, 7).

---

[133] *Op. cit.*, i, 27-42.
[134] Rohde, *Psyche*, i, 141-145.

He was engaged in the Theban war, and after the disaster, when pursued by his enemies, Zeus saved him from disgrace by opening the earth, which swallowed him with his charioteer, chariot, and horses (*ib.*, IX, viii, 3). Because of his valorous deeds Zeus made him immortal, and he arose as a god from the spring at Oropos (*ib.*, I, xxxiv, 4), where the people worshipped him as a deity, while all Greece counted him as such (*ib.*, VIII, ii, 4).

Amphiaraos was skilled in divination, he became renowned as a healing deity, and his dream-oracle at Oropos was held in high esteem. According to inscriptions, the Amphiareion at Oropos was founded at the end of the fifth century B.C. (Frazer, *op. cit.*, v, 31). The temple, which stood in an ample *temenos,* was ninety-five feet long by forty-three feet wide, and had a broad portico with six columns on the east side. The cella had three aisles separated by columns with a colossal statue of Amphiaraos in white stone in the center. In front of the temple was an altar of limestone twenty-eight feet long and fourteen wide, divided into five compartments, each dedicated to several divinities. One was consecrated to Zeus, Paian, Apollo, and Herakles; another to heroes and the wives of heroes; a third to Hestia, Hermes, Amphiaraos, and the children of Amphilochos; a fourth to Athena Paionia (*Kerameikos*), Aphrodite, Hygieia, Iaso, Panakeia, and Iason; and the fifth to Pan, the Nymphs, and the rivers Acheloos and Kephisos. Near by was a spring from which the god had arisen. Northeast of the temple was an *abaton,* an open Doric colonnade with forty-nine columns, three hundred and sixty feet long by thirty-six wide. There was a central line of Ionic columns dividing the stoa into two aisles, and along the inner stuccoed wall, which was decorated with paintings and inscriptions, there was a long stone bench. Adjacent to the *abaton* was a building dating from the third century

B.C. containing ten bathrooms. Near the great altar was a low semicircle of rising seats. Behind the *abaton* on the hillside was a theater with a stage forty by twenty feet, and a chorus space forty feet wide (Pausanias, I, xxxiv). At the Amphiareion healing was effected through dreams rather than by predictions of an oracle (*ib.*). An air of sanctity pervaded the *hieron;* and if anyone misbehaved, he was subject to a fine. A *neokoros* took down the name and address, and collected not less than nine obols from each patient (*IG* vii, 235). All suppliants bathed, and after purification partook of a special diet from which beans were excluded. Before incubation each one fasted, without wine for three days and without food for one day, "in order to receive the oracle with a clear soul" (Philostratos, *op. cit.*, ii, 37), and made sacrifice to Amphiaraos and the other deities. The suppliants who could do so then killed a black ram, and wrapping themselves in the skin, passed the night in the *abaton,* the men at the eastern, the women at the western end, while a few slept on the seats before the altar (*IG* vii, 4255). Those who received the desired vision or dream and were healed were the subjects of congratulations amid general rejoicings. They threw pieces of gold and silver into the sacred spring and made the usual offerings, models of diseased parts, sometimes in gold or silver, and other gifts (*IG* vii, 303, 67 ff., 3498). The daughter of the god, Alexida, and Hestia assisted the suppliants and exercised healing functions. The medical practices at the Amphiareion were the subject of bitter satire by Aristophanes in his *Amphiaraos,* produced in 414 B.C.

Amphiaraos was held in great respect, his name apparently meaning 'doubly holy.' A festival which was largely attended was held at the sanctuary every fourth year (*CIGGS,* 4253). The god was always more particularly identified with Oropos, but had other shrines at

Rhamnous, Argos, Sparta, Thebes, and Athens. In origin he seems to have been a chthonic daimon.

APHRODITE

APHRODITE, originally a sea-divinity, was the goddess of love and the reproductive powers of nature, as well as the deity of bridal and married life in the highest sense. Her cult was generally austere and pure, and she was bidden by Zeus to confine herself to the offices of marriage (Il., vi, 429). She was equated with 'Astart and other cognate Semitic goddesses of love and reproduction, and with Venus of the Roman pantheon. Sometimes she was called Mylitta ('she who brings forth children'), the Assyrian name of the goddess Ishtar (Herodotos, i, 131, 199; Frazer, op. cit., ii, 130).

She was a cherisher of children. In the cult of Aphrodite Ctesylla in Keos and its legend there is an allusion to her as a child-birth goddess, especially as she is related closely in this worship to Artemis Hekaerge,[135] and in her worship under the title of Aphrodite Kolias, on the coast of Attika, she may have been regarded as bearing the same aspect. It is possible she was invoked under the name Genetyllis (q.v.). Her association with healing is further attested by the fact that she shared an altar at Oropos with Athena the Healer and the daughters of Asklepios (CIA vii, 136), while in the form of a dove she visited Aspasia and cured an ulcer on her chin (Ailianos, Historia Varia, XII, i).[136]

APOLLO

APOLLO, the deity of light, music, poetry, archery, prophecy, and healing (Plato, Cratylus, 47), was one of the

[135] Farnell, Cults, ii, 655-656.
[136] Hercher, ed. Leipzig, 1866 (1870), p. 117.

great divinities of the Greek pantheon, though seemingly "originally the leading god of a people who migrated into Greece from the north in prehistoric times."[137] He was the son of Zeus and Leto, was the twin brother of Artemis, and was born on the island of Delos. In Greek religion Apollo represented mental enlightenment and civilizing knowledge rather than physical light; but he also typified physical health, manly vigor, and beauty of form; and as Phoibos Apollo he stood for truth, the sanctity of the oath, and moral purity. Farnell calls him the brightest and most complex character of polytheism, and his cult was both ancient and widespread in Greece.[138]

Apollo was renowned for prophecy, and his oracle, the greatest in Greece, was located in a cleft of the rocks at Delphoi in Phokis, near Mount Parnassos (Pausanias, X, ix, 1; Strabo, IX, iii, 12 = pp. 422-423 C). It was consulted on general matters, but it was most esteemed for guidance in political affairs, and individuals and deputations came from cities and states, far and near, to present their problems for solution. The authority of the oracle was so great that it was believed the inspiration came from Zeus himself (Aischylos, *op. cit.*, 575). At Hysiai was a fountain sacred to Apollo where the *hydromanteia* was practiced, those who drank the water became ecstatic and prophesied in the name of the god; a practice and a belief that prevailed also at Klaros.[139]

Apollo was both a bringer and an averter of disease.[140] In his anger the "far-darter" sent pestilence and death among men with his arrows (*Il.*, i, 45), and in this character he was worshipped at Lindos and called Pestilential (Loimios) Apollo, and persons who were consumed by

---

[137] Fox, *op. cit.*, p. 175.
[138] Farnell, *op. cit.*, iv, 98.
[139] *Ib.*, iv, 222.
[140] Le Clerc, *op. cit.*, pp. 17-18.

disease were 'Apollo-struck,' or 'sun-struck' (Macrobius, *Saturnalia*, I, xvii, 15). In his favorable moods he averted disease (Pausanias, I, iii, 4), and as a stayer of pestilence, curing disease and dispensing health, he was worshipped as Oulios by the Milesians and Delians (Strabo, XIV, i, 6 = p. 635 C). Music, of which he was the inventor, was used to overcome disease. Grecian youths sang sacred hymns and 'songs that sweetly please' to Apollo, and stopped a noisome pestilence, and the Cretan Thaletas, by music, freed the city of the Lacedaimonians from a raging pestilence (Plutarch, *de Musica*, 14, 10). It is not clear, however, that healing was a part of his early cult. Apollo, though often regarded as identical with Paian, was not so designated by Homer or Hesiod, and it is believed that they were distinct personalities, until in the sixth century B.C. an alliance was effected with Asklepios and he received the epithet Paian, and thereafter, as Apollo Maleates, was associated at Epidauros as the supreme healer of the pantheon, although the active healing was delegated to his son, Asklepios. A temple on Mount Kynortion overlooking the *hieron* of Epidauros, was dedicated to Apollo Maleates ('Apollo of Malea') and held a fine statue of the god. It is said that the old god whose temple was on Mount Kynortion (meaning 'the dog-altar') was concealed under the Epidaurian Apollo Maleates. It is assumed that the dog was originally peculiar to this god (*IG* ii, 1651; *SIG²*, 631), and that from this circumstance the dog appears first and most frequently in Epidauros as a companion of Asklepios.[141] Apollo Maleates was also worshipped at Tegea, Sparta, and Athens. Aischylos gives Apollo the epithet Loxias (of obscure meaning) and calls him an *iatro-*

---

[141] Nilsson, *op. cit.*, p. 409, note 7; cf. Fraender, *Asklepios*, pp. 22 ff.; Thrämer, in *ERE* vi, 547.

mantis,[142] or "prophet leech and portent seer" (*op. cit.*, 62). Sophokles addressed him "thou healer from Delos" (*Œdipus Rex*, 149); Euripides refers to him as a healer (*Andromache*, 900); and Kallimachos, in his hymn (68) to Apollo, speaks of him as a teacher:

> And wise physicians, taught by him, delay
> The stroke of fate and turn disease away.

Euripides (*Alcestis*, 969) says that Apollo gave simples culled for men to Asklepios's sons, and Pindar (*op. cit.*, v, 85) declares that

> Phoibos dire diseases' cure
> To seers and sapient matrons shows.

Apollo Patroos was a divine ancestor of Ion, at Delos he was called *Genetor*, 'the Father' (Diogenes Laertios, VIII, i, 13; Macrobius, *op. cit.*, III, vi, 2), and the people believed they were descended from him. At Sparta he had the epithet Karneios (Pausanias, III, xiii, 4), while at Sikyon the temple had an inner shrine consecrated to him under the same title, which only priests were allowed to enter (*ib.*, II, x, 2). Apollo was called *alexikakos* ('averter of ill'), and this title was emphasized after the Delphic oracle had stayed the pestilence during the Peloponnesian War. He bestowed protection and healing by extending the hand, and in consequence he acquired the surname Hyperdexios. Apollo was an honored guest at the healing shrine at Oropos, and was equated with the Egyptian Horus.

No public monuments to Apollo as 'The Healer' have been discovered except one from Epidauros, of Asklepios-Apollo, now in the Athens Museum.[143] Coins of late date from Thrace show Apollo *iatros* with laurel and

---

[142] Farnell, *op. cit.*, iv, 233 ff.
[143] Holländer, *op. cit.*, p. 82, fig. 32.

bow, and the attributes of a healer, the staff and serpent; while another Thracian coin portrays him as grouped with Asklepios and Hygieia, and the hooded figure of Telesphoros.[144] According to an old tradition, Apollo was killed by Python and was buried under the tripod at Delphoi.[145]

ARISTAIOS

ARISTAIOS was one of the most beneficent heroes of ancient Greece, "a personification of the period of cooling Etesian winds which gave relief to man and beast during the burning dog-days."[146] According to the most current tradition, he was the son of Apollo and Kyrene, and in mythology he was treated as a Thessalian deity akin to Zeus and Apollo (Pausanias, VIII, ii, 4), whereas in poetry he was reduced to a hero, except that Hesiod identified him with Apollo, who bore the epithet Aristaios at Keos.[147] Pindar (*op. cit.*, ix, 64) identifies him with Agreus ('huntsman') and Nomios ('herdsman'). Aristaios was a renowned pupil of Cheiron, by whom he was trained in the arts of manhood; from the Nymphs he learned agriculture; and from the Muses prophecy and healing. He was a protector of flocks and herds, and cultivated the soil; taught people how to cultivate the olive, and he was a celebrated bee-keeper. Diodoros (iv, 81) says he received divine honors for the benefits which he conferred upon man by his useful discoveries. He was worshipped at Keos (his home), in Boiotia, and in Thessaly as Aristaios-Zeus and Apollo Nomios.

Aristaios was also celebrated for his knowledge of the healing art. He stopped the plague at Keos after raising

[144] Farnell, *op. cit.*, iv, 325.
[145] Frazer, *The Dying God,* p. 4.
[146] Fox, *op. cit.*, p. 251.
[147] Farnell, *op. cit.*, iv, 123-124, 361.

an altar and sacrificing regularly to Zeus Ikmaios (Apollonios Rhodios, ii, 522).[148]

ARTEMIS

ARTEMIS was the daughter of Zeus and Leto, a twin sister of Apollo, and "an offspring lovely beyond all heavenly beings" (Hesiod, *Theog.*, 919). She was a goddess of nymphs, of the woods and wilds, a huntress queen, and one of the great divinities of the Grecian pantheon. She was an ethical and spiritual deity, although her character, as seen in mythology, was contrary and difficult to understand. Possessed of the gifts of health and strength, she was an averter of evil and alleviated the sufferings of humanity, yet she sent plagues among men by her arrows and caused mental and nervous disorders; while sudden and untimely deaths, especially among women, were ascribed to her. Women afflicted with certain diseases were called 'moon-struck' or 'Artemis-struck' (Macrobius, *op. cit.*, I, xvii, 11).

As a healing divinity Artemis was scarcely, if at all, second to Apollo, both having received their gifts from their mother. She was able to cure the diseases which she inflicted; she restored Orestes to sanity (Pherekydes, *Frag.*, 97), and as Artemis Koria tamed the daughters of Proitos (Bakchylides, x, 98), who erected two temples to her at Lousoi in gratitude (Kallimachos, ii, 234; cf. Melampous). As a physician-goddess she had broad powers, and her methods savored so much of magic that she was regarded as allied to Hekate.[149] She knew the medicinal properties of plants and was skilled in their use; she assisted Leto in dressing the wounds of Aineias (*Il.*, v, 447-448); and as Artemis Thermia she was connected with the healing fountains at Mitylene (*CIG*,

[148] Fox, *op. cit.*, p. 252.
[149] *Ib.*, pp. 182 ff.

2172), Kyzikos (Aristeides, i, 503 D), and Rhodes (*IG* I, xxiv, 4).

In her medical aspect Artemis was, however, essentially a child-birth deity, one to whom women brought their clothes as an offering when a birth ended happily (*Anthologia Palatina*, vi, 271),[150] although Homer (*Il.*, xxi, 483 ff.) declared that she was dreaded by women in child-bed. Lucian (*Dialogi Deorum*, xvi) causes Hera, in conversation with Leto, to slur Artemis, saying that "if she were really a virgin, she could not even assist ladies in the straw." Kallimachos (iii, 20-22) refers to her preference for the wilds, saying that she will mingle with people only when women, harassed by sharp throes, call on a helper. She encouraged child-bearing, and Euripides (*Supplices*, 958) says that Artemis Lochia would not greet childless women. In Delos she was known as one of the Hypoboreans, and sacred rites were performed to her under the ancient name Oupis, supposed to mean 'watcher' or 'watcher of women in travail,'[151] half-forgotten but revived by later poetry. In the Greek states Artemis and Eileithyia were in charge of the actual processes of birth, and Eileithyia was often regarded as a form of Artemis (cf. Hera). Women in travail invoked her aid, and many of her titles, Locheia at Phthiotis (*CIG*, 1768) and in Pergamon (Gambreion, *CIG*, 3562), as well as Lochia or Lecho at Sparta (*IGA*, 52), Soodina at Chaironeia (*IGS* i, 3407; *CIG*, 1595), and Lysizonos (*Hym. Orph.*, xxxvi, 5), fully attest her obstetric function and her interest in matters pertaining to the female sex.[152] At Epidauros she was Artemis Pamphylaia and Orthia;

---

[150] L. Deubner, "Birth (Greek and Roman)," in *ERE* ii, 648.

[151] Farnell, *op. cit.*, ii, 487-488; also Gruppe, *op. cit.*, pp. 45, 156, 241.

[152] Farnell, *op. cit.*, ii, 444-445, 567-568; Thrämer, in *ERE* vi, 548.

and she frequently appears as Artemis Soteira;[153] while the gold, silver, and ivory models of limbs contained in the panelling of the Artemiseion at Ephesos testify to the gratitude of her suppliants.

Her cult was a primitive one in Attika, Lakonia, and Arkadia, but her worship extended all over Greece. Cretans worshipped her as Britomartis, 'Sweet Maid.' At Lousoi there was a celebrated healing shrine which tradition assigned to her, the Artemiseion (Pausanias, VIII, xviii, 8), and she was also associated with the healing shrine at Ephesos, besides presiding over one at Alpheios in Elis, where suppliants bathed in near-by lakes and streams and were supposed to be cured by a magical ablution.[154] Artemis had a prominent place at Epidauros, where a beautiful temple was dedicated to her. By the Romans she was identified with Diana.

ATHENA

ATHENA, whose origin is referred to the archaic period in Attika,[155] was one of the most prominent goddesses of the Olympian circle, representing mentality and wisdom, and being a patroness of every art requiring skill and dexterity. She was worshipped with zeal and devotion in all parts of Greece and was regarded as a national deity. As Pallas Athena she was the goddess of battle, personifying civilized valor and war in its defensive rather than aggressive aspects; as Athena Polias she was the guardian of Athens, and the mainstay of the body politic, honored by magnificent public festivals, the best-known of which was the Panathenaia. She was given the epithet *soteira* ('savior' or 'deliverer') and was identified by the Romans as their Minerva.

[153] Farnell, *op. cit.*, ii, 572, note 53, 577, note 78; also Gruppe, *op. cit.*, p. 1268.

[154] Fox, *op. cit.*, p. 185.

[155] Farnell, *op. cit.*, i, 259.

References to Athena as a healer are somewhat vague, but there are ample evidences of her connection with the healing art. Just within the gate of the city of Athens stood a statue to the Healing Athena near those of Zeus and Mnemosyne (Pausanias, I, ii, 5), and at the entrance to the Akropolis, close to the images of Asklepios and Hygieia, was one to Athena Hygieia (*ib.*, I, xxiii, 4), erected to her by Perikles because she had healed a workman who had fallen during the building of the *propylaia* (Frazer, *Paus.*, ii, 277 ff.; Pliny, *op. cit.*, xxii, 44). The inscription on the base shows that it was dedicated by the Athenians and it is believed that it was in some way related to the cessation of the great pestilence. The Attic Athena Hygieia image is assumed to be the same as Athena Polias, reproduced from an earlier pestilence, probably that of 500 B.C.[156] (*CIA* i, suppl., 362; *CIA* i, 475). After Asklepios had been brought to Athens this aspect of Athena as Hygieia appears to have faded, although a statue to Athena Hygieia, now in the Athens Museum, has been found at Epidauros. Effigies of Asklepios and Hygieia were grouped with that of Athena Alea in her temple at Tegea and attest her relation to health and healing (Pausanias, VIII, xlvii, 1); while as a healer she was honored at the Amphiareion at Oropos and was called Athena Paionia (Pausanias, I, xxxiv, 3), an epithet used also at Athens.[157] In Lesbos she received the epithet Hyperdexia (Stephanos Byzantinos, *s.v.* Ὑπερδέξιον). Athena and Hermes cured the madness of the daughters of Proitos (cf. Melampous).[158] She was the guardian of eyesight, especially of children, and at Sparta was called

---

[156] P. Wolters, "Zur Athena Hygieia des Pyrrhos," in *MAIA*, 1891, xvi, 153-154; Thrämer, in *ERE* vi, 545.

[157] Farnell, *op. cit.*, i, 317.

[158] *Ib.*, i, 318.

Athena Ophthalmitis, the 'keen-eyed' goddess (Pausanias, III, xviii, 2). The aigis, her sacred symbol, was used in battle and for the purification of temples, and, in an Athenian ceremony, possessed life-giving power. At certain times it was carried about the city to protect it from plague and other evil, and taken by the priestess to the houses of newly-married women, probably to procure offspring. Also it was placed in the lying-in room to favor easy births.[159] In origin she appears to have been a weather deity.[160]

AUXESIA

AUXESIA ('Increase') was, as her name implies, an earthgoddess promoting growth of crops. She was closely associated with Damia (q.v.), and both were primarily local divinities of Epidauros. Their cult received its first impetus when, in time of dearth, the Epidaurians were bidden by the Delphic oracle to make them statues of olive wood from Attika (Herodotos, v, 82-83). Thence their worship spread to Aigina, Sparta, and Troizen. At Epidauros they had the joint epithet Azosioi or Azesioi (? 'Parching'),[161] and their festival included scurrilous songs sung by two choirs of women at each other (Herodotos, v, 83). At Aigina and Troizen, they were called virgins, and their feast was the Lithobolia ('Stone-throwing'; Pausanias, II, xxxii, 2),[162] a purificatory and apotropaic rite.[163] Later the pair were merged in Demeter-Kore, of whom they became mere epithets. From her original function of goddess of increase, Auxesia became a deity of travail at Epidauros and Aigina.

[159] Farnell, op. cit., i, 100, 273, 279, 288.
[160] Gruppe, op. cit., pp. 1196 ff.
[161] Ib., pp. 192-193; Usener, op. cit., pp. 129-130.
[162] Farnell, op. cit., iii, 93-94, 113.
[163] Gruppe, op. cit., p. 901.

DAMIA

DAMIA, whose name appears at Epidauros as Mn[e]ia and at Sparta as Damoia, but which is of very uncertain meaning,[164] is almost always mentioned together with Auxesia (*q.v.*), with whose functions and rites her own were identical. They were goddesses of the cornfield, and of child-birth, being themselves represented as on their knees in the act of bringing forth.[165] The worship of Damia spread, however, somewhat farther, being found also at Tarentum and Rome (see Bona Dea), and perhaps in Campania.[166] In origin she was probably a 'departmental deity' ruling over a special province akin to that of Auxesia. In an inscription from Thera she has the epithet Lochaia, being identified with a primitive Spartan goddess of child-birth who was later merged in Artemis.[167]

DEMETER

DEMETER was a celebrated and beloved goddess of the soil, of fertility, of vegetation, and of agriculture, and was considered a form of Ge or Gaia. She was the daughter of Kronos and the mother of Persephone, who, under the name of Kore ('Maiden'), was worshipped with her, especially in Attika. The cult, which was one of the most popular and renowned of ancient Greece, included the Mysteries of Eleusis, proffering the initiates the expectation of a happy life after death, and celebrated twice yearly by great festivals, the Greater and Lesser Eleusinia, with processions from Athens to Eleusis and secret religious rites. In the Roman pantheon Demeter was identified with Ceres.

---

[164] Gruppe, *op. cit.*, pp. 193, 1164; Usener, *op. cit.*, pp. 64, 129-130.
[165] Farnell, *op. cit.*, iii, 113.
[166] Gruppe, *op. cit.*, p. 370.
[167] Gruppe, *ib.*, pp. 1133, 1272; Usener, *op. cit.*, p. 144.

The healing functions of Demeter are seldom definitely referred to (*Hym. Orph.*, xl, 20), but she was 'the cherisher of children' (*kourotrophos*) at Athens, skilled in the magic of the nursery and the treatment of ophthalmitis, and a child-birth goddess in a minor capacity.[168] She was associated with Asklepios at Epidauros, Athens, and Eleusis; and she also had a shrine (*hydromanteion*) at Patrai in Achaia, where she was appealed to for divination and prophecy in cases of illness. Tying a fine cord to a mirror, suppliants let it down into a spring which was before the temple until it just grazed the water, and then praying to the goddess and burning incense, they were able to read in the mirror the outcome of their illness (Pausanias, VII, xxi, 12). At Troizen, Aigina, and Epidauros, Auxesia and Damia (*qq.v.*), local goddesses of vegetation, were so closely allied to Demeter and Kore that they were regarded as identical, though with different appellatives.[169] At Tarentum and Syracuse she was named Eleutho, and was regarded as one of the Eileithyiai (Hesychios, *s.v.* Ἐλευθώ).

DIONYSOS

It is generally believed that Dionysos was originally a foreign deity, most probably of Thracian origin,[170] who became prominent in the Greek pantheon. His name is plausibly interpreted as meaning 'Heaven-Son';[171] primarily he was a divinity of vegetation, especially of the vine; and his cult found its way into Boiotia, where Orchomenos and especially Thebes were its ancient

[168] Farnell, *op. cit.*, iii, 81.

[169] *Ib.*, iii, 113.

[170] Fox, *op. cit.*, pp. 215-216; Kretschmer, *Einleitung in die Geschichte der griechischen Sprache*, pp. 240-242.

[171] Gruppe, *op. cit.*, p. 1409, who believes (p. 1410) the god to have been of Boiotian origin.

centers. Thence it rapidly spread throughout Greece, and his festivals, held during the winter and spring, with their mysteries, orgiastic and phallic rites, and processions at night with riotous orgies and obscene songs, became popular, especially in Attika, Corinth, and Sikyon, where they caused many scandals. Nevertheless, to these mysteries, as to those of Demeter and Kore, the Greeks turned to secure the blessings of a life beyond the grave. Through his connection with the earth, Dionysos was also the god of mining and industry; and in Orphic theology he held a high place as Zagreus, 'the Great Hunter,' the son of Zeus by Persephone or Semele.[172]

Dionysos possessed gifts of prophecy and healing, which were the inspiration of many oracles; and his priests practiced healing by touch and dream-reading (Plutarch, *Quæstiones Symposiaca,* iii, 3). The Athenians were directed by the Pythian oracle to honor Dionysos as a physician (Athenaios, *Deipnosophistæ,* I, xli); he was called *iatros* and received the epithet Paian; while as Dionysos-Epaphios he removed disease by the laying-on of hands and aided child-birth in the same manner (*Hym. Orph.,* 1, 7).[173] There was a renowned Dionyseion at Marathon, and another at Amphikleia in Phokis, where remarkable orgies were celebrated with phallic rites, reputed to have been instituted by Melampous (Herodotos, ii, 49), and where the revelations by dreams and the oracles were announced by a priest acting as a *katochos,* or mouth-piece, of the god (Pausanias, X, xxxiii, 11). Dionysos had a large share in the Delphic oracle, and it is reported that he was buried near the golden statue of Apollo in a tomb on which was the inscription, "Here lies Dionysos dead, the son of Semele."[174]

[172] Gruppe, *op. cit.,* pp. 254-255, 970.
[173] Weinreich, *op. cit.,* p. 27.
[174] Frazer, *op. cit.,* p. 3.

EILEITHYIA AND CHILD-BIRTH GODDESSES

EILEITHYIA, whose worship was ancient and widespread, was the chief of the three foremost Greek goddesses of child-birth, the others being Hera and Artemis.[175] Both Homer (*Il.*, xi, 270) and Hesiod (*op. cit.*, 920) regarded Eileithyia as the daughter of Hera. The most ancient tradition is that she developed from her, representing her obstetric function, assisting in the physical process as a divine midwife, and possibly she was a detached form of the marriage-goddess. She was, however, sometimes identified with Artemis, and the two deities were frequently worshipped together. On an inscription found at Lebadeia, a woman returns thanks to 'the gentle Eileithyiai,' whom she calls Artemides.[176] The name has an adjectival form and doubtless means 'She who hath caused to come,'[177] and primarily there was, in all probability, a multiplicity of Eileithyiai as 'momentary deities' who later were united into a single divinity.[178] At Athens, accordingly, the Eileithyiai were three in number. Homer (*loc. cit.*) refers to them in the plural and speaks of the pains of a fresh wound "as when the sharp and piercing pang seizes a woman in travail, which the Eileithyiai, daughters of Hera, who preside over difficult child-birth, send forth." Pindar (*op. cit.*, iii, 7-10) describes the goddess as in attendance upon Koronis at the birth of Asklepios:

> While Eileithyia watch'd her matron cries,
> Pierced with the thrilling dart that flies
> From stern Lucina's golden bow.

[175] Preller, *Griechische Mythologie,* i, 511 ff.

[176] Farnell, *op. cit.,* ii, 609.

[177] Baunack, *Arische Studien,* i, 69-71; cf. Schulze, *Quæstiones epicæ,* pp. 259-261.

[178] Usener, *op. cit.,* p. 299.

According to Delian tradition, Eileithyia came from the Hyperboreans to assist Leto at the birth of Apollo and Artemis (Pausanias, I, xviii, 5); while the Cretans believed that she was born on the banks of the Amnisos river in Knossian territory, and Homer (*Odys.*, xix, 188) speaks of a cavern there which was sacred to her. For the Delians the mythical Lykian poet Olen wrote hymns to Eileithyia, to whom he gave the epithet Eulinos ('With the Goodly Thread') and whom he identified with Fate; and these were sung at her altar (Pausanias, VIII, xxi, 3). Pindar (*Nemea*, vii, 1) refers to her as a dispenser of destinies:

> Daughter of powerful Hera that dost cheer,
> Throned by the deep-forboding destinies,
> The laboring birth, chaste Eileithyia, hear:

Eileithyia was closely related to Themis and the Themides; and early tradition associates her with the daughters of Themis, the Horai and Moirai, representing her as the companion of these divinities of birth and destiny, who spun the thread of fate at the beginning of life and stood in the birth-chamber.

The open right hand of Eileithyia on the abdomen favored delivery. Illustrated on Etruscan and Tyrian vases,[179] the right hand was raised with thumb and two fingers open, the last two closed, or the upraised right hand with the palm opened outward, gestures of blessing and also of natural magic.[180] Besides her benevolent aspect, Eileithyia had a malignant character as a magician, sorceress, and poisoner; and when angry, she exercised her powers to delay or stop labor by gesture, "digiti inter se pectine iuncti."[180] At the instance of the jealous Hera, she availed herself of this sinister potency

[179] Weinreich, *op. cit.*, p. 15.
[180] Farnell, *op. cit.*, ii, 613-614.

to retard the birth of Herakles, when she pressed her knees together, clasped her hands with crossed fingers and muttered charms (Frazer, *Paus.*, v, 45-46), staying all progress until Galinthis, a maid of Alkmene (or Historis, daughter of Teiresias, Pausanias, IX, xi, 3), deceived her, released her knees, and unlocked her hands, whereupon Alkmene was promptly delivered (*Il.*, xix, 112 ff.; Ovid, *op. cit.*, ix, 298 ff.). Galinthis was punished, and Eileithyia, according to tradition, was exiled to Thebes, where bas-reliefs have been found representing her with these unfavorable traits. Hera detained Eileithyia on Olympos for nine days, preventing the delivery of Leto until the Delians sent Iris on a secret mission, promising her a necklace nine cubits long, of gold set with elektron,[181] and inducing her to come to Delos to assist at the birth of Apollo and Artemis (*Hymni Homerici*, i, 97 ff.).

Eileithyia had many sanctuaries throughout Greece, at Olympia, as in Argos, Arkadia, Boiotia, Messenia, and was everywhere held in respect and reverence, especially at Delos. The goddess also had shrines in Italy, one of which was at Pyrgi (Strabo, V, ii, 8 = p. 226 C). Associated with growth, the Moirai and the fortunes of the State,[182] she was an austere goddess and was always represented as draped, with a *chiton,* or with the *chiton* and *himaton,* usually with her hands extended and one holding a torch. In her temple at Athens her image was draped to the feet; and at Aigion it was of wood, except the face, fingers, and feet, which were of Pentelic marble, and was covered to the feet with a thin veil (Pausanias, VII, xxiii, 5). At Hermione she was regarded with such sanctity that only priestesses were permitted to see her image (*ib.*, II, xxxv, 11).

---

[181] A mixture of gold and silver, in the proportion of five to one.
[182] Farnell, *op. cit.*, ii, 608, 612.

The attributes of the goddess were the cord and torch, and the torch because the pangs of travail are like fire (*ib.*, VII, xxiii, 6). These emblems were likewise used to represent the obstetric function of other goddesses, as for Hera, Artemis, and Hekate, which was also commonly indicated by adding the name of the divinity, as Artemis Eileithyia at Chaironeia (*CIG*, 1596), and elsewhere in Boiotia, and Hera Eileithyia at Argos and Athens, as was found in an inscription from Thoricos.[183]

In addition to Eileithyia and other deities of child-birth above referred to, whose worship was observed generally throughout Greece, there were many local cults of child-birth goddesses, as of Locheia or Lecho at Sparta, who is mentioned in two inscriptions,[184] of Lochia or Locheia, and of Eilion[e]ia, to whom the Argives sacrificed dogs for easy delivery (Plutarch, *Quæstiones Romanæ*, 52). Dione, Rhea, Ichnaia, Themis, and Amphitrite are mentioned as waiting upon Leto (*Hym. Hom.*, i, 93). Auge ('Radiance') seems to have been a birth-goddess who brought the child to the light of day or of life. She is mentioned but seldom, and may be an equivalent for Artemis.[185] At Tegea she was identified with Eileithyia, who was represented in the market-place by an image, kneeling in the position of a parturient woman, which was popularly called 'Auge on her knees' (Pausanias, VIII, xlviii, 7).[185] She also appears as a priestess of Athena Alea, who was associated with health and healing.[186] As the need for a 'departmental deity' of child-birth diminished, Eileithyia became identified with a variant form

[183] K. Keil, "Attische Kulte aus Inschriften," *Philologus*, 1866, xxiii, 619; W. Drexler, in Roscher, p. 2091.

[184] Usener, *op. cit.*, p. 144.

[185] Farnell, *op. cit.*, i, 275; ii, 442-443; cf. Welcker, in *KS* iii, 185.

[186] Gruppe, *op. cit.*, p. 454.

of herself, Eleutho,[187] also a child-birth goddess (Hesychios, *s.v.* Ἐλευθώ), who was identified with the child-
birth goddess Leukothea, and who later was equated with
Iuno Lucina of the Romans. Then there were also divine
nurses, as the Samian goddess Kourotrophos,[188] who was
a protectress of new-born children, and possibly a form
of Hera; the Horai, who, in a hymn of Olen mentioned
by Pausanias (II, xiii, 3), are said to be the nurses of
Hera;[189] and also of Zeus and Apollo (Plutarch, *Quæst.
Sym.*, iii, 9).

EPAPHOS, OR EPAPHIOS

EPAPHOS ('Touch') was an ancient god, the son of Zeus
and Io, who healed by touch and the laying-on of
hands,[190] but lost his independence by sharing his powers
with other deities and became merely a phase-name. He
assisted at child-birth by the laying-on of hands, and in
this function his name is associated with Sabazios. He is
recognized in the healing character of Zeus Epaphos and
of Dionysos Epaphios.[191]

GENETYLLIS

GENETYLLIS, as her name implies, was a goddess of child-
birth and a protectress of births, both as an independent
deity and as a companion of Aphrodite, who later absorbed her, thus becoming Aphrodite-Genetyllis. Sometimes, however, Genetyllis, to whom a dog was sacrificed
for easy delivery (Hesychios, *s.v.* Γενετυλ(λ)ίς), was identified with Hekate, or with Artemis.[192] The name is also

187 Farnell, *op. cit.*, iii, 81.
188 Usener, *op. cit.*, pp. 124-129.
189 Farnell, *op. cit.*, i, 196.
190 Gruppe, *op. cit.*, p. 860.
191 Weinreich, *op. cit.*, p. 27.
192 Gruppe, *op. cit.*, p. 1198; cf. Roscher, ii, 1270; Rohde, *op. cit.*,
2d ed. (1898), p. 81, 1.

used in the plural for a group of midwives (or "inferior *daimones* that watched over child-birth")[193] who were in favor among the women of Attika (Pausanias, I, i, 5), who hung an olive wreath on the outer door if the child was a boy, and a wooden fillet if it was a girl. Aristophanes (*Nubes*, 52) and Lucian (*Pseudologistes*, 11) refer contemptuously to the Genetyllides, who were characterized "as powers of doubtful origin and characters who maintain themselves on the luxury and superstition of married women, and whom the husbands regard with suspicion and dislike."[194] Lucian (*Amores*, 42) mentions them in connection with the Koliades (a name applied to a group representing Aphrodite-Kolias, the obstetric goddess of a grotto on the coast of Attika) in a tirade against these "expensive divinities of midwifery."[195]

HADES

HADES, the ruler of the Underworld, was the son of Kronos and Rhea, a brother of Zeus and Poseidon, and a member of the Olympian circle. He captured Persephone, the daughter of Demeter, and carrying her off to the Underworld made her his wife (Hesiod, *op. cit.*, 913). Believed to have control of life and death, he was invoked to prolong the former and to avert the latter; and though the healing cult of Hades and Persephone was of late development, it gained considerable renown. Their oracle was located at some cave that gave forth vapors, sometimes sulphurous and usually noxious, the shrines being

[193] Farnell, *op. cit.*, ii, 614, note b.

[194] *Ib.*, ii, 519, 655.

[195] It is surmised by some authorities that Aphrodite-Kolias and the Koliades were primarily goddesses preventing birth, and that the usual explanation of the name from the promontory is later (cf. Gruppe, *op. cit.*, p. 1357, who has a similar suggestion).

known as Ploutonia or Charoneia, and suppliants for relief appealing through the medium of priests by incubation. The most celebrated Ploutonion was within a cave in a fine grove near Acharaka in the Maiandros valley, between Tralles and Nysa in Karia, the suppliants living near the grotto among the priests, who slept in the open air and directed the treatment of the sick by their dreams. The priests also invoked the gods to heal the sick and conducted those to whom the gods had sent dreams that they wished them to enter their shrines into the cavern where they sometimes remained for several days without food (Pausanias, X, xxxii, 13); but other sufferers observed their own dreams and applied to the priests (*oneiropoloi*) to interpret them and advise treatment. To all others the place was forbidden as fatal. An annual festival was held at Acharaka, during which a bull was let loose in the cave, where it promptly died (Strabo, XIV, i, 44 = p. 650 C). Another Ploutonion was at Leimon above Nysa (*ib.*). At Hieropolis, in Phrygia, high in the valley, which was all cavernous, was still another Ploutonion at a grotto about which was a railing. From the cave arose a cloudy, dark vapor which obscured the bottom; and although the air about was innocuous, animals entering within the railing died immediately, only the Galloi, or eunuchs of the Great Mother-Goddess, appearing to be immune (*ib.*, XII, viii, 17; XIII, iv, 14 = pp. 579, 629-630 C).[196] A Charoneion was located near Thymbria on the Magnesian plain near the coast (*ib.*, XIV, i, 11 = p. 636 C); and another Ploutonion was to be found at Eana in Macedonia. The only shrine in honor of Hades was in Elis.[197]

[196] Frazer, *Adonis*, i, 205-206.
[197] Fox, *op. cit.*, p. 234.

HEKATE

HEKATE, a chthonic deity, was a goddess of the lower order of Olympian divinities, although Zeus "esteemed her above all," while she received honor from the starry heavens, and especially from the immortal gods (Hesiod, *op. cit.*, 412 ff.). She was propitious to those who sought her aid; she distinguished those whom she wished among the people, giving wealth, victory, and renown (*ib.*); and Zeus made her the "nursing mother of children" (*ib.*, 450). Hekate had power in the heavens, on earth and sea, and in the nether-world; and to this fact is attributed the triple form in which she is sometimes represented, as Selene in heaven, Artemis on earth, and Persephone in the Underworld (Vergil, *op. cit.*, iv, 510).[198] It is claimed that Hekate was originally a moon-goddess, but she appeared as such only in the fifth century B.C. As a deity of the Underworld and of the night she was greatly feared, whence, in order to placate her anger and retain her favor, people were accustomed to gather in large numbers at the cross-roads on the night of the last day of the month and offer to her sacrifices called 'Hekate's suppers.'[199] Small statues of the goddess were placed before many of the houses of Athens and at the cross-roads to secure her protection.

Hekate was the teacher of all sorcery, and she practiced healing by magic and sorcery; she was also credited with having control over life and death, and was appealed to as an oracular deity. Hekate was closely associated with Artemis as a birth-goddess (Eusebios, *op. cit.*, III, xi, 23) and carried the torch of Eileithyia.[200] She was reputed to have discovered aconite. Her symbol was the hound.

[198] Cf. Gruppe, *op. cit.*, p. 1290.

[199] K. F. Smith, "Hekate's Suppers," in *ERE* vi, 565-567.

[200] Farnell, *op. cit.*, ii, 519.

HELIOS

HELIOS ('Sun') was the deity of physical light, the sun-god whose myth goes back to an Indo-European origin. The island of Thrinakia (Sicily), where his cattle were tended, was sacred to him (*Odys.*, xii, 128). He gave light to gods and men, and seeing and hearing all things, he had natural powers of divination similar to those of Demeter and Hephaistos (Sophokles, *Œdipus Coloneus*, 868). He caused blindness as a punishment, but he also restored sight, as in the case of Orion (Apollodoros, i, 43); and his aid was invoked by the blind Polymester (Euripides, *Hecuba*, 1067). Helios represented the vivifying powers of light and the sun's rays, or heliotherapy, and his relation to the art of healing was recognized by a tablet of praise and by a statue at Epidauros; while at Gytheion he was worshipped with Asklepios and Hygieia (*CIG*, 1392); and at Megalopolis he was called *soter* (Pausanias, VIII, xxxi, 7). His daughter Kirke and his granddaughters were skilled in the use of herbs and were sorceresses. From an early period temples were dedicated to Helios in various parts of Greece; but the chief seat of his cult was on the island of Rhodes, where yearly festivals were held in his honor.

HEPHAISTOS

HEPHAISTOS, a son of Hera (Hesiod, *op. cit.*, 922) and originally the god of fire, later became the divine artificer of metals and a teacher of his art (*Odys.*, vi, 233). He delighted the deities with his artistic creations, and Olympos was decorated with them (*Il.*, xviii, 377, 394); but though he was one of the Olympian divinities, Zeus in anger threw him out of heaven with such violence that the injuries which he sustained made him lame ever afterward (*ib.*, i, 593). His favorite abode was the island of

Lemnos, where he was a chief deity and exercised his powers of healing;[201] delusions, hemorrhages, and bites of snakes being mentioned as having been cured by him.[202] He had a temple at Athens and an altar at Olympia (Pausanias, I, xiv, 6; V, xiv, 6).

HERA

HERA was the wife of Zeus and the queen of heaven, the 'noblest of goddesses,' beautiful, stately, proud, and cold. She was the only Olympian deity truly married (Hesiod, *op. cit.*, 920); but though the equal of Zeus, she was subservient to him. She was jealous and quarrelsome, and caused frequent disturbances in the royal *ménage;* and though often victorious, she was severely punished by her spouse (*Il.*, i, 522). She was identified by the Romans with their Iuno.

Hera was represented as a gracious, benevolent deity especially entrusted with the affairs of women;[203] and being a motherly protectress, she was the founder of marriage, guarding the strict observance of its vows, and punishing those who violated its duties. As a goddess of fertility and child-birth, she aided women in travail, and it was she who sent the Eileithyiai when their hour had come. She thus had the power of hastening or retarding birth, and when excited by jealousy she exerted her influence to delay birth,[204] causing Leto to be in labor for nine days at the birth of Apollo and Artemis (*Hym. Hom.*, i, 97 ff.) and postponing the confinement of Alkmene, giving the priority of birth to Eurystheus over Herakles (*Il.*, xix, 112 ff.; Ovid, *op. cit.*, ix, 285 ff.). The obstetric func-

[201] Gruppe, *op. cit.*, p. 1313.
[202] T. Panofka, "Die Heilgötter der Griechen," in *ABAW*, 1843, pp. 257 ff.
[203] Farnell, *op. cit.*, i, 190 f.
[204] *Ib.*, i, 181.

tion of Hera was represented by Eileithyia, who is often regarded as a development from or a variant form of Hera, but who was, in all probability, originally a distinct deity and whom the Cretans claimed to be her daughter (Pausanias, I, xviii, 5). Hera's power to cause insanity was notorious, and was demonstrated in the case of Herakles (Euripides, *Hercules Furens*, 830), and those of Athamas and Ino (Apollodoros, iii, 28); and she cast a spell over Dionysos (Athenaios, *op. cit.*, x, 65). Hera had no oracular function.

Both Argos and Samos laid claim as being the birth-place of Hera; and at Athens and Argos she was worshipped as Hera-Eileithyia. At Samos a splendid temple, the Heraion, was erected to her by Polykrates, and here great festivals were held in her honor. She was also worshipped at Mykena, Sparta, at Plataia in Boiotia, as well as in Elis, Corinth, Euboia, and at Aigion, where her image might be seen by no one but priestesses (Pausanias, VII, xxiii, 9).

HERAKLES

HERAKLES, the most renowned hero-god of ancient times, was ranked among the lower order of Olympian deities. He was the son of Zeus and Alkmene and was ''born to avert the curse from gods and men''; but his birth was delayed by the jealousy of Hera (*Il.*, xix, 112 ff.; Nikandros, in Antoninus Liberalis, *Transformationum congeries*, 29), and in consequence of her anger he was subject to attacks of madness,[205] besides being a sufferer from epilepsy, which came to be known as the 'disease of Herakles.' In Hellenic tradition he represents morality combined with the indomitable courage that rights wrong, and he was the real warrior who yielded to the gods in

[205] Gruppe, *op. cit.*, p. 485.

repentance and expiation. He performed seemingly impossible deeds. In the Roman pantheon he appears as Hercules.

Hesiod (*op. cit.*, 527) refers to his healing functions,[206] and Prometheus besought him to alleviate his grievous wounds; while, in the Orphic Hymn (ix, 14) to Herakles, appeal is made to him: "Come, blessed one, bringing all soothements of diseases." He was revered as a divine physician at Erythrai and Hyettos in Boiotia (Pausanias, VII, v, 5; IX, xxiv, 3), and in Messene in Sicily (Aristeides, i, 59 D), and he was recognized as a healer by an altar at the Amphiareion at Oropos with other healing deities, while the Caucasians adored him with Prometheus as a deliverer from disease and epidemics.[207] He was adored and given the title *alexikakos* ('averter of evil') in the demos of Melite in Attika when he had caused the cessation of a plague,[208] and he stopped an epidemic among the Elians by changing a river-bed to flow through and drain a low, pestilential marsh (Philostratos, *op. cit.*, viii, 7). He also received the epithet *soter* ('savior') in Thasos, and at Delos and Amorgos he was worshipped as *apallaxikakos* ('deliverer from ills').[209] Owing to the evil designs of Hera, on his return from Troy he was driven to the shores of Kos, where, according to one tradition, he settled and was associated (sometimes confused) with Asklepios in healing (*Il.*, xiv, 250; xv, 30). The Asklepiadai of Kos claimed to trace their genealogy to Herakles on their mother's side, and his own descendants, the Herakleidai, were associated with the healing art.

---

[206] Gruppe, *op. cit.*, pp. 453-454.

[207] Hirschel, *Compendium der Geschichte der Medicin*, p. 29.

[208] Sprengel, *op. cit.*, i, 138.

[209] A. Hauvette-Besnault, "Fouilles de Delos," in *BCH*, 1882, vi, 342; 1891, xvi, 671.

The Greeks had a tradition that the hot springs at Thermopylai had been created by Athena in order that Herakles might refresh himself,[210] and hot springs were frequently dedicated to him. "Who ever heard of cold baths that were sacred to Herakles" (Aristophanes, *op. cit.*, 1044)? He was especially renowned in healing as the deity of the hot sulphur springs (called *Chytroi*, or 'Hot Pots,' by the inhabitants) at Thermopylai, which was a fashionable health resort (Herodotos, vii, 176; Strabo, IX, iv, 13 = p. 428 C); and he also presided over the hot springs at Aidepsos (Strabo, IX, iv, 2 = p. 425 C) which were visited by Sulla for gout (Plutarch, *Sulla*, 26). Medicinal plants were named for him. Herakles was sufficiently prominent in healing to cause Lucian (*Dial. Deor.*, xiii) to represent him as claiming precedence over Asklepios in heaven, where they engaged in an unseemly quarrel and exchanged abusive language, Herakles terming Asklepios a mountebank, a paltry herb-doctor, skilful in palming off miserable drugs on sick people, while Asklepios recalled some unfortunate incidents in the life of Herakles until Zeus intervened and settled the matter in favor of Asklepios because he had died first.

HERMES

HERMES, the messenger of the Olympian gods, was frequently called Psychopompos, the conductor of souls to the throne of the chthonic deities (*Odys.*, xxiv, 1 ff.).[211] The divinity of trade, of thieves, of travellers, and of shepherds, and hence regarded as prudent and crafty, though tricky and a thief (*Hym. Hom.*, iii, *passim*), he evolved as a god of dreams and magic, and was called Oneiropompos, whence the Greek poets refer to his magic

[210] Frazer, *op. cit.*, i, 209-210.
[211] See further, Gruppe, *op. cit.*, p. 1321.

wand as bringing sleep, and Milton (*Paradise Lost*, xi, 133) calls it his "opiate rod."[212]

There are few references to his healing function,[213] but he was the deity of the gymnasium and athletics, and a guardian of health. He assisted Athena in curing the daughters of Proitos of madness;[214] Lucian (*op. cit.*, ix) represents him as performing the operation of Cæsarian section upon Semele, who thus gave birth to Dionysos at the seventh month; and he was honored at Tanagra for stopping the plague by carrying a ram on his shoulders around the city walls (Pausanias, IX, xxii, 1). He received the epithets *soter* ('savior') and *alexikakos* ('averter of evil'), but in a general rather than in a special medical sense; and at Pharai he was called the 'Market God,' being represented by a small, square stone statue (an Athenian usage; *ib.*, IV, xxxiii, 3), beside which was his oracle, while before the image was a stone hearth with bronze lamps. Persons wishing to consult the oracle burned incense on the altar, filled the lamps with oil and lighted them, and placing a coin on the altar, whispered the question to the god. Then, stopping the ears, they left; and when away from the place, listened for the first words spoken in their hearing, these being assumed to be the oracular response (*ib.*, VII, xxii, 2, 3).[215] Hermes was worshipped at Athens and throughout Greece, but was especially reverenced among the Arkadians, who regarded him as their ancestor.

HYGIEIA

HYGIEIA ('Health'), the Greek goddess who was the guardian of health, was generally regarded as the daugh-

[212] Gruppe, *op. cit.*, p. 932.
[213] *Ib.*, p. 1337.
[214] Farnell, *op. cit.*, i, 318.
[215] *Ib.*, iv, 221 f., and compare the oracle of the Egyptian Apis.

ter of Asklepios, though she was sometimes referred to as his sister or wife (Aristeides, lxxix, 5; *Hym. Orph.,* lxvi, 7). She was the personification of physical health ('Golden Health,' Pindar, *Pyth.,* iii, 113), but was not a healing deity. The name was used as an epithet of Athena,[216] and Farnell has suggested[217] that she may have been an emanation from or a detached and personified part of Athena, originally representing mental rather than physical health. Pausanias (I, xxiii, 4) mentions a statue to Athena Hygieia as standing near the *propylaia,* the pedestal of which, discovered on its original site in 1839, seems to date from the fifth century B.C., the legend running (Plutarch, *Vita Periclis,* xiii) that Perikles dedicated a bronze statue to Athena in commemoration of her healing a zealous workman who had been injured by falling from the *propylaia* or the Parthenon during its construction. The fragment of a vase has been found in Athens inscribed to Athena Hygieia, on which is emblazoned a serpent, evidently part of a serpent-crest belonging to Hygieia. The character of the text suggests that the inscription belongs to the sixth century B.C., and it is assumed to attest the antiquity of the worship of Athena Hygieia at Athens, and long before the advent of Asklepios to that city (Frazer, *Paus.,* ii, 277-281),[218] although this is disputed.[219]

According to common tradition, Hygieia came to Athens with Asklepios from Epidauros in 420 B.C., but it is claimed that evidence of her presence there is lacking until about fifty years later. Careful studies tend to show that she had a development independent of Asklepios,

[216] Gruppe, *op. cit.,* p. 1066.
[217] *Op. cit.,* i, 318.
[218] Harrison, *The Mythology and Monuments of Ancient Athens,* pp. 389-393; also Usener, *op. cit.,* p. 169.
[219] Thrämer, in Roscher, iii, 1486.

with whom she appears at Athens in the fourth century
B.C. (*IG* iv, 1329); and if she did not come from Epidauros, where she is supposed to have joined the cult, she
came from elsewhere in the Peloponnesos, probably from
Titane.[220] Hermes was sometimes associated with her as
her spouse (Kornoutos, *de Natura Deorum,* xvi) and
they acted as guardians of health. On vases Hygieia was
represented as Euexia ('Wellbeing'), and she was identified with the Roman goddess Salus in her capacity as a
health-divinity.

Hygieia, ever the chief of the divine retinue of Asklepios, was represented as a young maiden, fresh, lithe, and
active. Bas-reliefs show her as being in attendance upon
the god, standing by him and receiving the petitions of
the suppliants, or introducing them to the god, as at
Athens;[221] without her symbol, or as caring for and feed-
ing the sacred serpents.[222] Those who were restored to
health approached her with thank offerings before leaving the Asklepieia. Ariphron of Sikyon wrote a hymn to
Hygieia in praise of her powers of exalting the happiness
of life, and Samuel Johnson, in quoting it,[223] remarks
upon its beauty and force. Hygieia was the only one of
the retinue of Asklepios who shared his exaltation to
divine rank, and on a Greek gem they appear together as
savior deities.[224] She was the intimate companion of the
god, and her statues were usually placed near those of
Asklepios, as at Titane (Pausanias, II, xi, 6); while at

[220] Thrämer, in *ERE* vi, 551.

[221] Holländer, *op. cit.,* pp. 107 ff.

[222] For representations of the goddess in ancient art, see W. Wroth,
"Hygieia," in *JHS,* 1884, v, 82-101; also F. Koepp, "Die attische
Hygieia," in *MAIA,* 1885, x, 255-271.

[223] In *The Rambler,* No. 48.

[224] E. Le Blant, "750 inscriptions de pierres gravée," in *MAIBL,*
partie 1898, xxxvi, 80-209.

Athens she was the only partner of the deity at the Asklepieion. She was a joint-possessor of an altar in the Amphiarieon at Oropos (*ib.*, I, xxxiv, 3; *IG* vii, 372, 412). The worship of Hygieia was emphasized at Argos and Corinth.

ISIS

Isis was a well-known and greatly beloved deity of Egypt, whose cult was one of the few of foreign prophetic goddesses which flourished in Greece. She was closely identified in function with Aphrodite, and a shrine was built in honor of Aphrodite-Isis at Tentyra in Upper Egypt (Strabo, XVII, i, 44 = p. 815 C); while under her own name a temple was erected to her at Peiraieus in 333 B.C. similar to her fane in Egypt, her cult being introduced despite Hellenic prejudice. Her worship was joined with that of Sarapis, and when it had become more definitely a healing cult with divination, especially through the dream-oracle with interpretation of visions by priests (Diodoros, i, 25), it had a rapid growth; so that in the period of the Ptolemies a temple was built at the foot of the Akropolis to Isis and Sarapis.[225] Many shrines were dedicated to the goddess in Greece, although the one at Tithorea, near the temple of Asklepios, was considered the holiest of all (Pausanias, X, xxxii, 13), no man living near it, and none being permitted to approach it who had not been previously invited by a dream. Two festivals were held here in honor of Isis each year. At Boiai in Lakonia, the temple of Isis and Sarapis was near that of Asklepios (*ib.*, III, xxii, 13), and at the extremity of the harbor at Kenchreiai, the port of Corinth, were sanctuaries of Isis and Asklepios (*ib.*, II, ii, 3). The principal festival to Isis in Greece, held on March 5 of each year to celebrate the opening of navigation, is rather fully

[225] G. Showerman, "Isis," in *ERE* vii, 435.

described by Apulieus (*Metamorphoses,* xi, 7-17), and during it a ship laden with spices and richly equipped was sent to sea from Kenchreiai as an offering to the goddess.

THE KABEIROI

THE KABEIROI were a group of mysterious, minor deities of obscure and probable foreign origin, whose mysteries had long been in vogue in the fifth century B.C., and are rather definitely traced to a home in Samothrake and an institution of a non-Hellenic people. They were primarily three in number, Axieros, Axiokersos, and Axiokersa, equated respectively with Demeter, Hades, and Persephone; although others held that they were only two, corresponding to Zeus and Dionysos (*Etymologicon magnum, s.v.* Κάβειροι). Early writers connect them with the Pelasgians, Samothrake, Lemnos, or Phrygia (e.g. Herodotos, ii, 51; *Anthol. Pal.,* vi, 164, 301; Nonnos, xxvii, 121 ff.). The constant Hellenic synonym for them was *theoi megaloi,* and apparently means 'the Great Ones' (cf. Hebrew *kabbīr,* 'great'), and it may be that this was a translation by Phœnician traders of their original epithet, which has vanished; though the ancients derived it from the Kabeirian Mountains in Phrygia. Later they were identified with the Cretan Kouretes and Daktyloi (Strabo, X, iii, 7, 19-20 = pp. 466, 472 C); and still later, because of their name, they were supposed to be Phœnician, and were held to be the eight sons of Sydyk ('Righteousness'), of whom the eighth was Asklepios (Eshmun; cf. Philon Byblios, in *Fragmenta historicorum Græcorum,* iii, 569; Damaskios, quoted by Photios, *Bibliotheca,* 532b).

In origin they seem to have been chthonic divinities, and with their worship (fostered in Adania, Imbros, Paros, Miletos, and generally in the Aigaian islands, as

well as on the Greek Coast, while important Kabeiraia
have been excavated at Thebes and Samothrake) there
were certain rites, of which there is no clear evidence, but
which appear to have been analogous to those of Eleusis.
The Kabeiroi-mysteries of Samothrake seem to have had
a moralizing effect on conduct, since those who had par-
taken in them became more pious and just (Diodoros, i,
49).[226] At the Theban Kabeiraion was a grove sacred to
Demeter and Kore, in which the Kabeiroi shared, to
which only the initiated were admitted, and where cultic
mysteries and healing were practiced (Pausanias, IX,
xxv, 5; Frazer, op. cit., v, 136). Suidas (s.v. ἀκωή) regarded them as healing divinities; they were known as
inventors of medicine and music (Philon Byblios, Phœni-
cum Historia, ii, 11); while navigators worshipped them
as deities of the sea and winds (Diodoros, iv, 48 ff.).

KIRKE

KIRKE was an ocean nymph, a daughter of Helios, and a
mythical enchantress, who enticed Odysseus and his companions to her island, where she retained them for a year.
She was skilled in the knowledge of herbs, and in subtile
poisons (Odys., x, 278 ff.), and occasionally practiced
healing.[227]

LETO

LETO, according to Greek myth, the daughter of the Titan
Koios and Phoibe, was the mother of Apollo and Artemis,
who were born on the island of Delos after the jealousy
of Hera had delayed their delivery for nine days (Il., xix,

[226] For further material on this extremely difficult problem, see
Farnell, "Kabeiroi," in ERE vii, 628-632; also Gruppe, Index in op.
cit., s.v. Kab(e)iroi.
[227] Gruppe, op. cit., p. 708.

112 ff.; Ovid, *op. cit.*, ix, 297 ff.). She had a knowledge of
healing, assisted women in labor, and was a protectress
of children, whence she received the epithets of *euteknos*
and *kourotrophos* (Theokritos, xviii, 50) ;[228] while Homer
(*Il.*, v, 446) refers to her in association with Artemis in
dressing the wounds of Aineias. Her home and the center
of her worship were the island of Delos. In the Roman
pantheon she was known as Latona, and she was possibly,
in origin, the Night.[229]

MALEATES

MALEATES was the name of a healing deity who was reputed to have been brought from the north with Asklepios;[230] though the word is commonly used as an epithet
of Apollo to indicate his healing function, and Farnell[231]
would supply Apollo whenever Maleates is mentioned.
Altars and sanctuaries were dedicated to Apollo Maleates
at Tegea, Athens, and Trikke (*IG* iv, 950, 29), as well as
at Sparta (Pausanias, III, xii, 8) ; but the most celebrated
shrine was erected on the summit of Mount Kynortion
overlooking Epidauros (*ib.*, II, xxvii, 7). A sacrificial
rubric found at Peiraieus and showing the name of Maleates used side by side with Apollo (*CIA* ii, 1651) is
believed to indicate that he should be regarded as a divinity distinct from Apollo, and to suggest that the identification with him came later at Epidauros. Together with
Apollo, Hermes, Hygieia, and her sisters, he received
three cakes as an offering.[232]

[228] J. G. Milne, "Greek Inscriptions from Egypt," in *JHS*, 1901, xxi,
290; cf. also Fox, *op. cit.*, p. 175; Gruppe, *op. cit.*, p. 1249.

[229] H. Osthoff, "Griechische und lateinische Wortdeutungen," in *IF*,
1895, v, 305 ff.

[230] Walton, *op. cit.*, p. 20.

[231] *Cults*, iv, 233, 235-238.

[232] Thrämer, in *ERE* vi, 547; cf. Gruppe, *op. cit.*, p. 1442.

THE MUSES

ACCORDING to the usual version, the Muses were the daughters of Zeus and Mnemosyne and were inspired goddesses of song, poetry, the arts and sciences, and of wells and springs. Originally they appear to have been only three in number, but after Hesiod there were nine (*op. cit.*, 75-79). From Thrace and Boiotia their cult spread to other parts of Greece and became firmly established. Apollo was their leader, they received inspiration from the Delphian god, and they instructed Aristaios in the arts of prophecy and healing (Apollonios Rhodios, ii, 512).[233]

THE NYMPHS

THE NYMPHS, Dryads, Hamadryads, Nereids, and similar mythic personages were nature-spirits of the hills, forests, springs, and caves; and their worship was usually conducted in the open air. Many were regarded as the daughters of Zeus by unknown human mothers, and ruling over springs, wells, and streams which had medicinal properties, they were credited with healing functions. Some were worshipped under a collective name. Thus, in the Elian village of Herakleia, at a spring flowing into the Kytheros river, there was a sanctuary to a group of nymphs who presided over it, Kalliphaïïa, Synallaxis, Pegaia, and Iasis, collectively termed the Ionides or Ioniades; and according to Pausanias (VI, xxii, 7) "To bathe in the spring is a cure for all kinds of sicknesses and pains." In the Triphylia district of Elis was a warm sulphur spring issuing from a cave on the banks of the Anigros river, over which ruled a band of nymphs called the Anigriades. These waters had an offensive odor which, it is said, they had acquired from the purification

[233] Cf. A. C. Pearson, "Muses," in *ERE* ix, 3-5; Gruppe, *op. cit.*, pp. 1075-1078.

of the wound that Cheiron had received at the hands of
Herakles, and because Melampous had used its waters in
cleansing the daughters of Proitos of madness (Strabo,
VIII, iii, 19 = pp. 346-347 C; Pausanias, V, v, 10). These
springs were a cure for all skin diseases, while the worship consisted of prayers, vows, bathing, and the use of
rational remedies. According to Hesychios (*s.v.* ἰατροί),
certain Elian nymphs were termed 'physicians.'

ORPHEUS

ORPHEUS, a hero-god, a divinity of music, and 'the father
of poetry,' was of Thracian origin and was said to have
lived before the Trojan War. According to tradition, he
was the son of Oiagros and the Muse Kalliope; but when
he was awarded divine honors for his skill, Apollo was
credited with being his father. The strains from the
golden lyre of Orpheus and his songs fascinated all animate nature, so that mankind, the beasts of the field, the
trees, and even the rocks were moved (Pausanias, IX,
xxx, 4). He was reputed to have visited Egypt and to
have brought back and originated the religious ceremonials and mysteries of Greece, especially the Mysteries
of Eleusis; while he was said to have taught the worship
of Demeter in Lakonia (*ib.*, III, xiv, 5), and to have imparted to Hekate her mysteries in Aigina (*ib.*, II, xxx, 2).
His name became a collective term applied to his descendants, and their traditions gave rise to a religious sect
which advanced religious theories of purification, consecration, rewards and punishments, and the future state
of the soul, known as Orphism; while within the sect were
developed the *thiasoi,* a powerful brotherhood, who regarded the body as the prison of the soul and sought to
diminish the influence of matter over spirit by sobriety
and personal asceticism (Plato, *op. cit.*, 38).

The influence of music over certain diseases was recognized by the Greeks from early times, and Orpheus was its chief exponent. He was a celebrated soothsayer and exercised healing powers by appeasing the wrath of the gods through his incantations, conjurations, and magic formulas (Euripides, *Alcest.*, 966). The Thracians and Thessalians revered him as a divine physician, and he discovered remedies for disease (Pausanias, IX, xxx, 4). Orpheus had a famous oracle at Lesbos, and there was an archaic statue to him in the temple of Demeter in Lakonia at Taygetos (*ib.*, III, xx, 5).[234]

PAIAN

PAIAN was the official physician of Olympos, the divinity who dressed the wounds of the gods with anodyne cataplasms (*Il.*, v, 401, 900). To the Greeks the term appears to have meant a chant, or song of victory; and this connection with music, together with the fact that Paian never developed a cult, has led Farnell to infer that it was an old appellative of Apollo, connoting his healing function.[235] Homer and Hesiod (*Frag.*, 213), however, treat Paian and Apollo as distinct personalities; and it is only after the sixth century B.C. that the epithet Paian, as applied to Apollo, is found in literature, leading to the inference that originally he was a separate deity, later amalgamated with Apollo. Homer (*Odys.*, iv, 229) emphasizes the skill of Egyptian physicians by saying that they were of the race of Paian, and the name came to be an epithet given to divine healers, Asklepios and others. The word is derived from a base meaning 'to strike' and is construed as "He who cures maladies by his magic blow."[236]

[234] Farnell, *op. cit.*, iii, 201.
[235] *Ib.*, iv, 234 f.; cf. Gruppe, *op. cit.*, p. 1240.
[236] Boisacq, *Dictionnaire étymologique de la langue grecque*, pp. 738, 740.

PAN

PAN, a god of pastoral life and of flocks, shepherds, and vegetation, was originally an Arkadian mountain-spirit and a generative daimon of flocks and herds who later became a full-fledged deity, famed for his skill on the pipes. He had mantic powers and was even credited with having instructed Apollo in prophecy (Apollodoros, i, 22); but in certain aspects he was supposed to cause panic, nightmares, and disease.[237]

With the nymphs Acheloos and Kephisos he represented the hygiene of nature at Oropos (Pausanias, I, xxxiv, 3); he stayed the pestilence at Troizen by means of his dream-oracle (*ib.*, II, xxxii, 6); and at Sikyon the porch of the Asklepieion was flanked by the figures of Pan and Artemis (*ib.*, II, x, 2). The epithet Paian was applied to him in the Orphic Hymns (xi, 11). Pan had several oracles scattered throughout Greece, one of which at Lykaion and another at Akakesion were especially well known (Pausanias, VIII, xxxviii, 5; xxxvii, 11, 12); and at the latter he was assisted by the nymph-priestess Erato, while his oracle was powerful in accomplishing men's prayers.

PERSEPHONE

PERSEPHONE, the daughter of Zeus and Demeter and the queen of the Underworld, was the wife of Hades, who had found her gathering narcissuses in a meadow and had carried her off to his subterranean realm (Hesiod, *Theog.*, 913; Pausanias, IX, xxxi, 9); but in deference to the sorrow and complaints of Demeter, Zeus enforced a compromise by which Persephone passed the winter with Hades and the remainder of the year with her mother on earth. As the queen of the infernal mansions of Hades

---

[237] Gruppe, *op. cit.*, p. 1395.

she was the 'dread Persephone' (Hesiod, *ib.*, 768), while on earth she was the maiden Kore, and intimately associated with Demeter as a goddess of vegetation in the spring.[238] The cult of Demeter-Kore, which included the Mysteries of Eleusis and the great Eleusinian festivals, presented perhaps the most serious aspect of Greek religious life and was the most prominent and popular in Greece, those who had been initiated and had witnessed these mysteries being blessed among men. Persephone appears in the Roman pantheon as Proserpina.

As a healing deity Persephone was associated with Hades at the various Ploutonia and Charoneia in Greece and Asia Minor, the most prominent being in the Maiandros valley and the best known being at Acharaka (Strabo, XIV, i, 44 = pp. 649-650 C). Beautiful temples were dedicated to her in Lokris and at Kyzikos on the Propontis; while in Aigina, Epidauros, and Troizen she was known and worshipped with Demeter as a child-birth goddess in the cult of Damia and Auxesia, and in this aspect she was given the epithet Cheirogonia (Hesychios, *s.v.*). At Patrai and elsewhere she received the epithet *soteira* ('savior').[239]

POSEIDON

POSEIDON was one of the Olympian circle and a god of the sea and all fresh waters, whom the Romans called Neptunus. His association with the healing art is slight, and the inference concerning the healing practices of his cult may be illusory. On the island of Tenos, which was an 'Asylum,' he was called *iatros* (Philochoros, in *Frag. hist. Gr.*, i, 414), and this fact has been considered as suggesting that the priests of his cult practiced healing at

---

[238] Fox, *op. cit.*, pp. 230-231; Gruppe, *op. cit.*, p. 1182, regards her as the crescent moon.

[239] Gruppe, *op. cit.*, p. 1175.

the health resorts situated there.[240] As tending to confirm this inference, the Tenians had a tradition that Machaon and Podaleirios were the sons of Poseidon (Eustathios, on *Il.*, xi, 515). There are traces of a belief that he made the insane to whinney like horses and that he was one of the deities who caused epilepsy (Hippokrates, *de Morb. Sac.*, 2).[241]

PROMETHEUS

PROMETHEUS seems originally to have been a deity of fire, particularly in its beneficent and helpful aspects, and later to have been conceived as a creator-divinity of the 'divine-smith' group;[242] while finally he was held to typify the endeavors of man to gain enlightenment by subduing the forces of nature to his will and controlling them for his own purposes. As referring to creation, according to a legend of the Alexandrian period, probably of Babylonian origin, he mixed earth and water and making it pliable fashioned man, having summoned Athena to aid in the work (Lucian, *Prometheus*, 13; Horace, *Carmina*, I, 16; Hyginus, *Fabulæ*, 142). The most popular legend concerning him relates that he stole from Hephaistos the fire of heaven, which Zeus had withheld from mortals; and concealing it in a fennel-stalk, he brought it to man, thus incurring the wrath of the gods (Hesiod, *Op. et Dies*, 50). In punishment Zeus had chained him to a rock, but Herakles broke his shackles and set him free.

Prometheus was associated with the early Greek art of healing; and Aischylos (*Prometheus Vinctus*, 478 ff.) declares that he taught mankind not only divination, but

[240] Farnell, *op. cit.*, iv, 13.

[241] Adams, *op. cit.*, ii, 337.

[242] Gruppe, *op. cit.*, pp. 441-442, 1024-1026, 1402; Fox, *op. cit.*, pp. 12-14; Cook, *Zeus*, i, 325-330.

also the "mixing of gentle remedies" to replace the
drugs which hitherto had made sufferers pine away.
Mention is also made of a 'Promethian salve' (possibly
in origin a remedy for the venom of serpents),[243] with
which Iason was anointed by Medeia before ploughing
the magic field to gain the Golden Fleece (Apollonios
Rhodios, iii, 845; Valerius Flaccus, vii, 355).

At Athens he had an altar in common with Hephaistos
and Athena (Lysimachos, in *Frag. hist. Gr.*, iii, 341) and
he was honored by a festival called the Prometheia
(Xenophon, *Republica Atheniensium*, iii, 4).

RHEA

RHEA, the wife of Kronos and the mother of Zeus and
other Olympian deities, represented the same fundamental conception of the 'Great-Mother,' the 'Mother of
the Gods,' as the mighty earth-goddesses of fertility and
maternity of Oriental nations, so that she was identified
with the Phrygian Kybele, their names being used indis-
tinguishably in literature to denote the same divine personality and cult.[244] Modern investigations at Knossos
tend strongly to indicate that she was of Cretan origin.[245]
Her cult was emotional, with pronounced orgiastic and
mystic features which were represented by the noisy
band of 'Korybantes,' her servants, with whom the Kouretes and Daktyloi were associated.

There is little trace of definite healing in her cult,
except that she invented liniments for relieving the pains
of children, and had many remedies for them. It was supposed that the music and dancing of her followers, the
Korybantes, relieved mental terrors, vagaries, and other
nervous disorders.

[243] Gruppe, *op. cit.*, p. 573.
[244] Farnell, *op. cit.*, iii, 289 ff.
[245] *Ib.*, iii, 292 ff.

SABAZIOS

SABAZIOS was a deity of Thracian (or Phrygian) origin who gave life to all nature, and whose mystic and orgiastic cult was so similar to that of Dionysos that his name was regarded by many as merely an appellative of that divinity, whence the two were identified as Dionysos-Sabazios,[246] while Strabo (X, iii, 15 = p. 470 C) says that he may be considered a son of the great Mother-Goddess. His cult appeared in Athens about the fifth century B.C., attaching itself to that of Kybele and Attis, and in Asia being finally merged with that of Kybele. Persons initiated into the Mysteries of Sabazios wore his symbol, an ornamental golden snake on their robes over the breast; and Frazer[247] suggests that this may be a trace of the belief that women could be impregnated by serpents.[248] Notwithstanding sharp criticism and opposition because of its mysteries and their orgiastic features, the worship gained popularity; but its festivals, the Sabazia, were held at night, and eventually women took part in them with the Galloi in such a licentious manner that the cult was not considered respectable (Aristophanes, *Vespæ*, 9; Demosthenes, *de Corona*, 266). It prospered for a time, but disappeared about the beginning of the Christian era.

Sabazios was a healing deity, but was regarded as an impostor and a charlatan imitator of Asklepios. He is represented as healing by the laying-on of hands, and he aided child-birth in this manner.[249]

SARAPIS

SARAPIS was a foreign deity, allied with Isis, whose cult

[246] Farnell, *op. cit.*, iii, 297; v, 94 ff.; cf. also Gruppe, *op. cit.*, pp. 1532-1533; Kretschmer, *op. cit.*, pp. 195-198.

[247] *Adonis*, i, 90, note 4.

[248] Cf. *supra*, pp. 284-285.

[249] Weinreich, *op. cit.*, p. 18.

was brought to Greece during the latter half of the fourth century B.C. through the influence of Ptolemy I. He was a syncretistic creation of the Græco-Egyptian period, by some regarded as a fusion of Hades with the Egyptian Osor-Ḥap (Osiris-Apis), and by others held to be none other than the great Babylonian healing divinity, Ea of Eridu, *sar-apsi,* 'God of the Watery Deep.'[250] It has been said that Sarapis had "a Greek body haunted by an Egyptian soul."[250]

Sarapis was an iatromantic deity who gained favor by the use of divination, principally by the dream-oracle, or incubation.[251] Suppliants incubated for themselves or their friends; and priests, who might also incubate for their patients, interpreted the dreams and announced the results, with directions to be followed, as though possessed, or inspired, by the god. The cult made such rapid headway in Greece, largely because of its readiness to grant favors to its suppliants, that, at one time, its popularity and influence threatened the preëminence of the Asklepian cult; but its practices and mysteries caused scandals, brought it into disrepute, and aroused active opposition.

The healing methods of Sarapis and Isis, who were very like Asklepios and Hygieia, bore a strong resemblance to those of Asklepios, and their worships were not antagonistic.[252] There were indications of the use of hypnotism in cultic practice; incubation was a feature in both (Diodoros, i, 25); the general type and divinity of Asklepios and Sarapis were similar; the staff and the serpent were symbols of both; and as Aristeides (500, 19) saw

[250] Bouché-Leclercq, *Histoire de la divination,* iii, 378; also Gruppe, *op. cit.,* pp. 1576-1580; Cumont, *op. cit.,* pp. 74 ff.; J. G. Milne, "Græco-Egyptian Religion," in *ERE* vi, 376-378.

[251] Gruppe, *op. cit.,* p. 931; Hamilton, *op. cit.,* pp. 62, 98-107.

[252] Weinreich, *op. cit.,* pp. 117 ff.

them in a vision they were wonderfully like each other. Demetrios of Phaleron wrote pæans as votive offerings in honor of Sarapis in gratitude for the restoration of his sight (Diogenes Laertios, v, 76). The temples of Sarapis and Isis (the Sarapeia and Isideia) were very similar to the Asklepieia. Sarapis had a temple at Athens (Pausanias, I, xviii, 4) and Sparta (*ib.*, III, xiv, 5), as well as many others throughout Greece; while at Boiai both Asklepios and Sarapis had temples not far distant from each other (*ib.*, III, xxii, 13), and in the shrine of Apollo at Aigeira the statues of Sarapis and Isis were placed near that of Asklepios (*ib.*, VII, xxvi, 7).[253] A priest of Asklepios in Dacia dedicated a tablet to Sarapis (*CIL* III, i, 973), and the names of both gods have been found joined on the same coins.

TELESPHOROS

TELESPHOROS, a minor deity and a sort of famulus attached to the cult of Asklepios, and although mentioned about the time of Hadrian, was probably a very old figure for whose representation the Greeks adopted that of the Egyptian Harpokrates. It appears that the Greeks admired this divinity (Ḥar-pe-khrad, 'Horus the Child'), represented as a lame, undeveloped child, sitting on a lotos leaf with his fingers to his lips, and adopted the figure, but changed the fable, and set up statues to him under the name of Telesphoros, Euamerion, and Akesis, the attitude symbolizing the reserve customary concerning divine mysteries (Plutarch, *de Iside et Osiride*, 19, 68).[254] It is inferred that the priests attached him to Asklepios and Hygieia as having an in-

[253] Gruppe, *op. cit.*, p. 1579.

[254] Cf. Müller, *Mythology, Egyptian*, pp. 117, 243; also Milne, in *ERE* vi, 379-380; Gruppe, *op. cit.*, pp. 1562-1563; Schenck, *De Telesphoro Deo*, Göttingen, 1888.

fluence over healing and as suggesting the silence and secrecy which must be observed in respect to medical practice, whence he was called Sigalos ('Silent'), and physicians swore by him to hold inviolate the secrets of their profession.[255] He was worshipped at Pergamon and elsewhere along the coast of Asia Minor,[256] and was identified with Euamerion of Titane and Akesis of Epidauros (Pausanias, II, xi, 7); while at the latter site an inscription has been found in honor of "Asklepios [and] Hygieia Telesphoroi."[257] In a poem in his honor[258] he is called "bringer of life" (zoophoros); but later his name sank to mean 'ventriloquist' (e.g. *Etymol. mag., s.v.*).

Telesphoros is seldom referred to in literature, and the most of the information concerning him comes from monuments and coins, which indicate that his worship was prevalent throughout Asia Minor, spreading from Pergamon, where he was especially revered, and extending to Athens and Epidauros. His function is not clearly understood, but from the accepted meaning of his name, 'Accomplisher,' it has been assumed that he was the god of convalescence;[259] and possibly an incubation spirit;[260] and it is known that patients at the sanctuaries sacrificed to him during their recovery. At Pergamon he gave Aristeides a healing balsam which was applied in the bath

[255] Sprengel, *op. cit.*, i, 136.

[256] Gruppe, *op. cit.*, p. 1455; Usener, *op. cit.*, pp. 170-171.

[257] Baunack, in *SGAS*, 1886, i, 99 (cf. other inscriptions, merely mentioning the name of Telesphoros, *ib.*, pp. 91, 93, 98).

[258] Kaibel, ed. *Epigrammata Græca ex lapidis conlecta*, no. 1027, line 43.

[259] Prof. L. H. Gray suggests the meaning of the name as "he who brings the perfect end," and that he was an old 'departmental god' who put the finishing touches to a healing already practically complete.

[260] W. Wroth, "Telesphoros," in *JHS*, 1882, iii, 283 ff.; also J. Ziehen, "Studien zu den Asklepiosreliefs," in *MAIA*, 1892, xvii, 241.

while passing from the hot to the cold water;[261] and
Marinos (*Vita Prokli*, 7) relates that the boy, fair to see,
appeared to the philosopher Proklos in a vision, while he
was dangerously ill, and touched his forehead, whereupon he was straightway made whole. Telesphoros, in a
later period, is represented on monuments and coins as a
child wearing a hood and a long cloak which covers his
whole figure except the face; and he appears either alone,
with Asklepios, with Hygieia, or with both.[262] His worship
was recognized in Athens by a religious society named, in
his honor, the Ephebes of Telesphoros (*CIA* III, i, 1159).

Ianiscos, a hypothetical son of Asklepios (Scholion on
Aristophanes, *Plut.*, 701)[263] was another child-divinity
associated with the cult, one of whom little is known and
whose functional relation is obscure. On coins and in
marble he is represented as a small boy, nude or lightly
clad, standing by the side of the god, or alone, holding
some animal, most frequently a goose,[264] sometimes used
as a symbol of healing power.

THEMIS

THEMIS was the mother of the Horai and the Moirai
(Hesiod, *Theog.*, 901-906) and a birth-goddess,[265] receiving the epithet Themis Eileithyia (Nonnos, *Dionysiaca*,
xli, 162). At Troizen she was worshipped in the plural
as the Themides and the countless nymphs, the Themis-
tiades (Pausanias, II, xxxi, 5); and she received the
oracle at Delphoi from her mother, Earth, but was dis-
missed by Apollo, or she passed it to Phoibe, who pre-

---

[261] Bouché-Leclercq, *op. cit.*, iii, 302.
[262] Holländer, *op. cit.*, pp. 126 ff.
[263] Dindorf, *op. cit.*, iv, 228-230.
[264] Holländer, *op. cit.*, pp. 150 ff.
[265] A. Scheiffle, in Pauly-Wissowa, vi, 1788, ed. 1852.

sented it to Apollo as a birthday gift (Aischylos, *Eumen.*,
2-4; Strabo, IX, iii, 11 = p. 422 C).

TROPHONIOS

TROPHONIOS, a chthonic deity who presided over a celebrated oracle at Lebadeia in Boiotia, was, according to
Pausanias (IX, xxxvii, 4-5) and Strabo (IX, iii, 9 = p.
421 C), like his brother Agamedes, a builder who erected
a temple of Apollo at Delphoi and a treasury for Hyrieus.
He was reputed to have been a divinity of the Phlegyans,
and Cicero (*op. cit.*, iii, 22) gives him the same general
ancestry as Asklepios. Late authors have questioned the
propriety of considering him a god, but Celsus classed
him with other chthonic healing deities, such as Amphiaraos and Mopsos (Origenes, *contra* Celsum, vii, 35) while
Lucian (*Dialogi Mortuorum*, iii) spoke of him as compounded of man and god. Farnell calls him a 'faded
deity.'[266]

Trophonios had the same attributes as Asklepios, and
the ceremonies of his cult are said to have been a fair picture of the early ritual of Asklepios, who had a shrine at
Orchomenos in the same neighborhood; but his healing
functions appear never to have been developed beyond
the primitive stage and to have receded as those of Asklepios grew in importance. His oracle was near Lebadeia
in a grotto on the side of a hill above the Herkyna river,
where were images of the god and his daughter Herkyna
with serpents coiled around their scepters so that they
may have been taken for Asklepios and Hygieia. In the
grove was a temple with a statue of Trophonios by
Praxiteles that resembled Asklepios; and there were also
other shrines; one to Demeter Europa, and one to Apollo,
as well as images of Kronos, Hera, and Zeus (Pausanias,
IX, xxxix, 4-5).

[266] Farnell, in *ERE* vi, 405.

Those intending to consult the oracle, whether for healing or other reasons (*ib.*, IV, xxxii, 5), lodged for several
days in a building sacred to the Good Daimon and Good
Fortune, and observed rules of purity, avoiding hot
baths, bathing in the Herkyna river, and sacrificing to
the several gods, to Zeus Basileus, Hera the charioteer,
and others.[267] A soothsayer inspected the entrails of a
victim to learn if the suppliant would be graciously received by the deity, and on the evening before going to
the cave Agamedes was honored by the sacrifice of a ram,
whose entrails must tell the same tale to give the suppliant hope. Those who consulted the oracle paid a silver
coin into the treasury and offered ten cakes (*CIGGS*,
3055). Anointed by boys, he was then led by priests to
two springs where he drank first of the waters of Forget-
fulness and next of the waters of Memory (Frazer, *op.
cit.*, v, 198-204;[268] Pliny, *op. cit.*, xxxi, 5). Dressed in
white, bound with fillets, and wearing native boots, the
suppliant now approached the oracle, and, holding in his
hands barley cakes kneaded with honey as a sacrifice to
the serpents (Aristophanes, *Nubes*, 508), he descended
feet first into the cave. To some it was given to see, and
to others to hear, the oracle which was delivered by serpents.[269] After staying in the cave a varying length of
time, sometimes more than a day, the suppliant returned
as he entered, feet first, and was received by the priests,
who seated him in the chair of Memory, questioning him
as to all he had seen and heard. Later, still overpowered
by fear and quite unconscious, he was given into the
hands of his friends and returned to the House of the

[267] Farnell, *Cults*, i, 194.

[268] Frazer gives additional details and references.

[269] For the incubation of the Trophonios cult, see Hamilton, *op. cit.*,
pp. 88-93.

Good Daimon and Good Fortune, where he recovered his wits and finally his power of laughter.

ZEUS

ZEUS, the sovereign of the Greek pantheon and the chief of the Olympian circle of deities, was the god of the heavens, the potential ruler of the universe, the father of gods and men, and the undisputed master of lightning and thunder, who in his wrath used the thunderbolt as a weapon of punishment. He was the bringer of both good and evil, and could assume the functions of all other divinities, since his will was supreme.

The most ancient shrine of Zeus, and the most venerable oracle in Greece, was at Dodona in Epeiros (Herodotos, ii, 52 ff.), where there was a celebrated oak, sacred to him, which Sophokles called the "many-tongued oak" (*Trach.*, 1148) and which was commonly termed the whispering or talking oak, since the rustling of its leaves and the murmuring of the waters beneath it were believed to be the voice of the god. His priests, "the *selloi* of unwashen feet," interpreted these sounds as prophecies and instructions, and inscribed many of the divine decrees on tablets of lead. Recent excavations have unearthed a large number of these plates, inscribed with questions and prayers to Zeus Naïos and Dione and some replicas of these oracles, from a site supposed to be that of the old sanctuary.[270] These practices (*Il.*, xvi, 235) are assumed to be evidences of incubation in the primitive cult, and the inscriptions indicate that the oracle was consulted by persons from far and near both for personal and for state affairs,[271] as when Odysseus inquired of it to learn

[270] Carapanos, *Dodone et ses ruines*, i, 68-83; Plates 34-39.
[271] Gruppe, *op. cit.*, p. 355.

how he should return home (*Odys.*, xiv, 327; xix, 296).
At Dodona Zeus appears as in the earlier stage of his
development, half barbarian; whereas at Olympia he was
the center of the beauty, fancy, and greater activities of
the Greek life of the late centuries.[272] His statue there was
the highest expression of Greek art, was eagerly visited
by persons from every part of Greece, and was wonder-
ingly admired by all (Pausanias, V, xi, 1).

Zeus was regarded as the helper of weak and unfortunate humanity, and he was given many epithets, among
them being Paian at Rhodes (Hesychios, *s.v.* Παιαν Ζεύς)
and *apotropaios* ('averter of ill') at Erythrai, both expressive of the same idea of the deity,[273] but as a healer
he generally delegated his powers to others for application, although the sick consulted his oracle at Dodona.[274]
He was the divine physician at Rhodes; while votive
tablets, models of limbs, dedicated to him in gratitude for
healing, have been found at Athens in the Pnyx (*CIA* iii,
150-156) and also in Melos.[275] The allotment of a part of
the altar at the Amphiareion at Oropos establishes his
association with healing there (Pausanias, I, xxxiv, 3).
Pausanias (V, v, 5) intimates that Zeus Leukaios healed
leprosy at Lepreos, though this inference is disputed,[276]
and he was also known as a god who aided child-birth and
healed by the laying-on of hands, being assisted in this
phase of his character by Epaphos, being called Zeus
Epaphos, and receiving the epithet Hyperdexios.[277]

[272] Gardner, *op. cit.*, p. 407.
[273] Farnell, *op. cit.*, i, 67.
[274] *Ib.*, i, 40.
[275] Panofka, in *ABAW*, 1843, p. 258.
[276] Thrämer, in *ERE* vi, 545, note.
[277] Weinreich, *op. cit.*, p. 41; also Gruppe, *op. cit.*, p. 860.

DEMIGODS, HEROES, AND HEROINES ASSOCIATED
WITH HEALING

Achilles	Dexion	Mopsos
Agamede	The Dioskouroi	Mousaios
Amphilochos	Helena	Oione
Amynos (Alkon)	Heros-Iatros	Polyidos
Antikyreos	The Korybantes	Protesilaos
Apis	The Kouretes	Toxaris
Aristomachos	Medeia	[Glykon, the false
Bakis	Melampous	god or hero]
Cheiron	Molpadia Hemi-	
The Daktyloi	thea	

Supplementary List—Personalities not Discussed.[278]

Akesias	Epimenides	Ion	Paionaios
Akesidas	Eribotes	Iphykles	Panakeia
Alexanor	Eurostos	Kairos	Peleus
Alexida	Gorgasos	Kalchas	Perimedes
Alkeidas	Hektor	Linos	Phokos
Alkmene	Iapis	Medeios	Polydamas
Amphitrite	Iason	Medos	Prokris
Darron	Ias(i)os	Nikomachos	Sphyros
Dione	Ichnaia	Odysseus	Telamon
Epimedes	Idas	Orsilocheia	Teukros

ACHILLES

ACHILLES, a celebrated hero of the Trojan War and a
pupil of Cheiron, was not merely skilled in healing, but
also taught others the art (*Il.*, xi, 832). In Elis he was
worshipped as a hero possessing mantic powers (Pau-

[278] Note. The association of these heroes and heroines, and many
others, with healing was slight and occasional, except for the descendants of Asklepios, Panakeia, and the sons of Machaon, but their work
and that of later Asklepiads is sufficiently indicated in the text.

sanias, VI, xxiii, 3), and he had a dream shrine at Leuke (Arrianos, *Periplus*, xxiii), though this was concerned with sea-traffic rather than with healing.

The Sosias bowl represents him bandaging Patroklos;[279] appearing in a vision, he healed Leonymos, the boxer (Tertullian, *de Anima*, xlvi); and only the rust from his spear, which had inflicted the wound, could heal Telephos (cf. Pausanias, III, iii, 8). He is also mentioned in connection with the therapeutic heroines Medeia (Ibykos, *Frag.*, xxxvii; Simonides, *Frag.*, ccxiii; Lykophron, 174), Helena (Philostratos, *Heroica*, xix, 15-16), and Iphigeneia Orsilocheia (Eustathios, on *Il.*, iv, 306).

AGAMEDE

AGAMEDE, the daughter of Augeas, a prince of Elis, was a sorceress and one "who well understood as many drugs as the wide earth nourishes" (*Il.*, xi, 739).

AMPHILOCHOS

AMPHILOCHOS, the son of Amphiaraos and one of the heroes of the Theban War, inherited the mantic faculties of his father, with whom he was worshipped at the sanctuary of Oropos as a healing hero, his oracles, like those of his sire, being imparted by dreams (Tertullian, *op. cit.*, xlvi; Dion Kassios, lxxii, 7). He joined with Mopsos, one of his companions in the Theban War, to found the city of Mallos in Cilicia, where they set up a healing shrine (Strabo, XIV, v, 16 = p. 675 C); and Pausanias says (I, xxxiv, 3) that this oracle was considered the most infallible of that day.

AMYNOS (ALKON)

AMYNOS ('Averter') was a healing hero, or a demigod, who was worshipped at Athens before the arrival of

[279] Müller-Wieseler, *Denkmäler der alten Kunst;* Plate 45, no. 210.

Asklepios, and whose cult appears to have been associated (or confused) with that of a legendary therapeutic
hero, Alkon, of whom little is known except that he was
reared, together with Asklepios, by Cheiron (*Vita Sopho-
clis*, 11), and who is supposed to have occupied a *temenos*
at Athens.[280] The origin of Amynos and his cult is unknown, and it is said that he is not mentioned in Greek
literature, or by any of the Christian fathers except
Eusebios. He had been forgotten until excavations by
the German Archeological Institute in 1895 disclosed a
precinct on the western slope of the Akropolis, between
the Areiopagos and the Pnyx, with inscriptions to a healing divinity named Amynos. The precinct was an irregu-
lar quadrangle, about sixty-two feet long by forty-two
wide. It contained a well and the foundations of an old
chapel, the style of masonry suggesting that it was of
the date of Peisistratos (seventh century B.C.), and that
it was constructed on the site of a previous temple, dating
back possibly to 1000 B.C. Remains of the older, as well as
the later, style of pottery were discovered, with anatomical votive offerings in marble and bas-reliefs, the latter
being of the usual character, proving that the serpent was
the symbol of the hero, while one of them represents a
goddess, probably Hygieia, standing by a wreathed altar
receiving homage from a train of suppliants with a child.
These relics indicate that Amynos was held in high
esteem, but they do not give any intimation of his
methods of healing, or whether or not incubation was
used, except that one tablet shows a man and a woman
approaching the god with hands raised in the attitude of
supplication (Frazer, *op. cit.*, v, 499-500).[281]

Amynos had failed to avert an existing pestilence and
it was determined to bring Asklepios, who had gained an

[280] Walton, *op. cit.*, pp. 29-30.
[281] Körte, in *MAIA*, 1893, xviii, 231-256; 1896, xxi, 287-332.

enormous prestige in the Peloponnesos, to Athens, and it is believed that he was first made a guest at the *temenos* of Amynos, and that later he absorbed the cult.²⁸² Inscriptions of about the fourth century B.C., found in the *temenos*, indicate that Asklepios was also worshipped there, though as a secondary deity, and that there was also a third divinity, called Dexion (*q.v.*), who had a separate chapel. It is assumed that as the fame of Asklepios increased in Athens, Amynos faded until he was forgotten. The hero Alkon had a shrine at Sparta.²⁸²

ANTIKYREOS

ANTIKYREOS was a Greek healing hero who was reputed to have discovered hellebore in Phokis, and with it to have cured Herakles of madness.²⁸³

APIS

APIS, king of Argos, founder of the city of Apia in Argolis, and an iatromantis who had freed his state of monsters, was a son of Apollo who came from Naupaktos to Argolis, where he settled and cured its people, whence it was called the Apian land (Aischylos, *Supplices*, 250-260). He seems to have been, in reality, a hypostasis of Asklepios, his name being abbreviated from Apiodoros ('Giving Mild Gifts').²⁸⁴

ARISTOMACHOS

ARISTOMACHOS, a *heros-iatros* of ancient Greece and recognized as such at the Dionyseion at Marathon, had a healing shrine at that place and was worshipped at his grave.²⁸⁵

²⁸² Harrison, *Prologomena*, pp. 345-346.
²⁸³ Panofka, in *ABAW*, 1843, 257 ff.
²⁸⁴ Gruppe, *op. cit.*, pp. 172, 1441, 1452.
²⁸⁵ Thrämer, in *ERE* vi, 553.

BAKIS

BAKIS, one of the most distinguished seers of Greece, was a diviner and a purifier, while his reputation as a prophet almost equalled that of Melampous. He was said to be possessed by nymphs (Pausanias, X, xii, 11; Aristophanes, *Pax*, 1071), and his oracles, in hexameters like those of Delphoi and the Sibyl of Cumæ, were later collected (Pausanias, IV, xxvii, 4-5). Though a Boiotian seer, he was held in high esteem in Athens; and since both Athenians and Arkadians boasted of having a seer named Bakis (Suidas, *s.v.* Βάκις), it is entirely probable that the appellative became a collective for a family or was adopted by others.

The Boiotian Bakis is reputed to have cured a Lakedaimonian of a mental disorder by mysterious ceremonies and he was recommended by Apollo Pythios as one who could purify the Lakedaimonian women of the madness that possessed them (Suidas, *loc. cit.*).

CHEIRON

CHEIRON, one of the most celebrated heroes of ancient Greece, the most just and wise of the centaurs (*Il.*, xi, 830), and a great hunter, lived in a cave on Mount Pelion in Thessaly until driven out by the Lapithai, when he found refuge in the mountains of Lakonia (Apollodoros, ii, 5). Although generally ranked as a hero, he was a local divinity, possibly a very primitive, or pre-Hellenic, god whose cult was absorbed by Asklepios. The name, derived from a root meaning hand, may have referred to his skill in the arts, or the hand which he used with magic healing effect.[286] Cheiron was learned in all branches of human knowledge and was the reputed master of such sciences as botany, prophecy, healing, music (Plutarch, *de Mus.*,

[286] Weinreich, *op. cit.*, p. 16.

40), astronomy, and legislation; while many of the Greek heroes were his pupils, among them Achilles, Aktaion, Kastor, Polydeukes, Aristaios, Theseus, Amphiaraos, Iason, Nestor, Telamon, Teukros, Peleus, Odysseus, and Aineias. Accidentally wounded by a poisoned arrow from the bow of Herakles, Cheiron transferred his immortality to Prometheus (Apollodoros, *loc. cit.*) and was placed by Zeus among the stars as Sagittarius, thus being deified and sometimes classed as a god (Sophokles, *op. cit.*, 714-715).

Cheiron instructed Herakles and Asklepios in the art of healing. Pindar sings his praises (*op. cit.*, iii, 45-67) and sums up his instructions to Asklepios, whom he received as a babe, as healing by surgery, internal medication, and incantations. He knew the medicinal properties of all plants and roots, as well as their application (*Il.*, iv, 219; xi, 830-832), and was, accordingly, worshipped by the Magnesians, who sacrificed the first fruits of plants to him as a divine physician (Plutarch, *Quæstiones conviviales*, III, i, 3), and his teachings, as applied by his pupils during the Trojan War, and their descendants, were without magic (*Il.*, *ib.*). Hesiod wrote a poem concerning the "Precepts of Cheiron for the instruction of Achilles" (Pausanias, IX, xxxi, 5; cf. *Frag. hist. Gr.*, 182-185). Cheiron cured Phoinix of a blindness that was thought to be incurable (Apollodoros, iii, 13); in archaic times he was classed as a birth-god, possibly because of his 'pain-allaying hand' (*IG* XI, iii, 360); and he was regarded as the discoverer of the healing art (Hyginus, *op. cit.*, 274; Pliny, *op. cit.*, vii, 196). A tribe inhabiting the region of Mount Pelion claimed descent from him and maintained that their knowledge of herbs and healing was hereditary and sacred.

Cheiron was a specialist in herb-lore and represents the true forerunner of the rational school of therapeutics, in its transition from the occult to practical medicine, which Hippokrates sought to establish.

THE DAKTYLOI

THE DAKTYLOI were fabulous beings, who, living about Mount Ida in Phrygia or Crete, were superhuman in strength and were numbered from one to one hundred. The discovery of iron on Mount Ida was ascribed to them (Frazer, *op. cit.*, iii, 484), and they were skilled workers of metals by fire; but they were also the servants of Rhea-Kybele and were connected with her orgiastic Phrygian rites, whence they were related to, or identical with, the Kouretes, the Korybantes, and the Telchines (Pausanias, V, vii, 6; Strabo, X, iii, 7, 22 = pp. 466, 473 C). Like these groups the Idaian Daktyloi were famous magicians and practiced the art of healing by magic, possibly after the style of medicine-men.

DEXION

DEXION was a healing hero who was worshipped with Amynos and Asklepios at the Athenian Amyneion. Sophokles[287] had been a priest of Amynos, had been influential in bringing Asklepios to Athens, and, on arrival, had entertained him at his home (which may have been the *temenos* on the western slope of the Akropolis, at which, it may be assumed, Asklepios was a guest until the Asklepieion on the south slope had been prepared). After death the poet was heroized under the name of Dexion (*Etymol. mag., s.v.* Δεξίων) and gave distinction to the Amyneion-Asklepieion (Marinos, *op. cit.*, 29).

THE DIOSKOUROI

THE DIOSKOUROI, better known as Kastor and Polydeukes, were twin sons of Leda, Zeus being regarded as the

[287] Harrison, *op. cit.*, p. 345.

father of Polydeukes and Tyndareus of Kastor, though they are frequently referred to as the sons of either. They excelled in athletics and feats of arms, and were known for their bravery and dexterity; while at Sparta they were the exponents of heroic virtue and valor. In Lakonia and in Arkadia they were ranked as gods (Pausanias, III, xiii, 1; VIII, ii, 4). They were not only given the epithet *soteres* (e.g., Theokritos, xx, 6), but were also termed 'guardians' (*anakes;* e.g., Plutarch, *Theseus*, xxxiii);[288] and in this character were identified with the Kabeiroi as protecting seamen from dangers.[289] In Athens their sanctuary was known as the Anakeion (Frazer, *op. cit.*, iii, 164).

The Dioskouroi were healers, and their cult, widely diffused, was very popular in the late period, their cures being performed through incubation and the interpretation of dreams (*Frag. hist. Gr.*, iv, 149, 15). There is a possibility that they were sometimes regarded as helpers in child-birth.[290] In the late Roman period their principal temples were in Byzantium and Rome.

HELENA

HELENA, as her name implies, was a moon-goddess who was worshipped in the Peloponnesos (though possibly as a tree-spirit or a local daimon only),[291] and who, in Homeric mythology, was the daughter of Zeus and Leda, sister of Kastor and Polydeukes, and one of the most beautiful women of ancient Greece. Paris stole her from Menelaos, her husband, and carried her off to Ilion, thus causing the Trojan War.

[288] For this meaning, see Schulze, *op. cit.*, p. 505.

[289] Farnell, in *ERE* vii, 630.

[290] Gruppe, *op. cit.*, pp. 165, 860.

[291] Pearson, "Heroes and Hero-Gods (Greek and Roman)," in *ERE* vi, 654.

Helena was a healer who was skilled in the knowledge
of the medicinal qualities of plants and used nepenthe, a
soporific akin to opium and relieving sorrow and mourning, of which she learned from the Egyptian Polydama,
and which she gave to Telemachos (Herodotos, ii, 116;
Odys., iv, 219 ff.). She is said to have changed an ugly
child into a beautiful woman (Herodotos, vi, 61).

HEROS-IATROS

In the vicinity of the Theseion at Athens was a temple to
Heros-Iatros (Demosthenes, *Orat.,* xviii, 129; xix, 249),
who is referred to as the Hero of the city in an Eleusinian
inscription of the fifth century B.C. (*CIA* iv, 286 a, p.
145 f.). Whether this dedication was in honor of a definite
personality or of an abstract character is not known, but
the inscriptions show that the cult was not overshadowed
by that of Asklepios and that it was flourishing in the
third century B.C. (*CIA* ii, 403, 404). Silver offerings to
the divinity were melted down into sacred vessels from
time to time.[292]

THE KORYBANTES

The Korybantes were daimons or a mythical people of
uncertain origin who later were intimately connected
with the cult of Rhea-Kybele as her servants and priests,
especially as regarded her healing functions, probably
in the cathartic sense, as medicine-men driving away sickness and evil spirits.[293] They were associated, and perhaps identical, with the Kouretes, the Idaian Daktyloi,
and the Telchines (Strabo, X, iii, 7, 21, 22 = pp. 466,
473 C), and were prominent in the public festivals and
processions of Rhea-Kybele, appearing in women's gar-

[292] Usener, *op. cit.,* pp. 149-153.
[293] J. E. Harrison, "The Kouretes and Korybantes," *ERE* vii, 758-
760.

ments, with drums and cymbals, dancing through the streets, and conducting the orgiastic rites of the cult.

THE KOURETES

THE KOURETES were daimons or a mythical people of Oriental origin, said to have been brought to Greece by Deukalion and to have been the original inhabitants of Akarnania and Aitolia. They were identified with the Korybantes, the Telchines of Rhodes, and the Idaian Daktyloi, as servants of Rhea-Kybele, who entrusted the infant Zeus to the Cretan Kouretes for protection from Kronos (Pausanias, V, vii, 6). As followers of Rhea-Kybele they shaved their heads and, wearing women's garments, assisted at the festivals of the goddess in conducting the noisy, orgiastic Phrygian rites of her worship (Strabo, X, iii, 19, 22 = pp. 472, 473 C). They were the jugglers of Crete, but were active in advancing the arts of civilization and taught the healing art.[294]

MEDEIA

MEDEIA, whose name connects her with such healers as Agamede, Epimedes, Perimedes,[295] and her son Medos, was, according to the usual version of her legend, the daughter of Aietes, King of Kolchis, a priestess of Hekate, and a witch celebrated for her skill in magic and sorcery. She fell in love with Iason (also, in origin, a healing hero, as his name implies, and the son of Polymede), to whom she gave not only a magic salve which protected him from iron and fire, but also a magic potion with which to put the dragon to sleep, thus securing the Golden Fleece. She then fled with Iason, whose wife she became.

[294] Harrison, in *ERE* vii, 758-759.
[295] Usener, *op. cit.*, pp. 160-163.

Evidently a healing heroine of much importance in the earlier period, Medeia was reputed to be especially skilled in the knowledge of drugs (Pindar, *op. cit.*, iv, 233). She cured Herakles of his madness (Diodoros, iv, 55) and rejuvenated Iason's aged father.[296] She was apotheosized at Corinth (Scholion on Euripides, *Medea*, 10), and at Antioch a famous statue was erected in her honor (Malalas, p. 263). She is said to have discovered colchicum.

MELAMPOUS

MELAMPOUS, one of the most celebrated seers of ancient Hellas, was said to have been the first Greek endowed with prophetic powers. He lived before Asklepios, at a time variously estimated at from 150 to 500 years before the Trojan War, or, as more definitely stated, about 1400 B.C. He was an Argolian shepherd, whose ears, according to the legend, were cleansed by a serpent while he slept in the fields; and he thus gained remarkable perception, understanding the language of animals, interpreting the songs of birds, and acquiring the gift of prophecy. The name became a collective for his family and descendants, many of whom were prophets (*Odys.*, xv, 225) and healers, as Polyidos his nephew and Amphiaraos his grandson; while his lineage was divided into two branches, the Iamids and Klytids, the Elean seers (Iamids) being most famous.[297] It is claimed that Melampous was deified, but it appears more probable that he ranked as a hero or a demigod.

Melampous, who possessed the knowledge of all remedies, was the first Greek physician and was called 'divine.' He had a sanctuary at Aigosthena, where a yearly festi-

[296] Gruppe, *op. cit.*, p. 546.
[297] Halliday, *op. cit.*, p. 95.

val was held in his honor, but where no divination was practiced, either by dreams or in any other way (Pausanias, I, xliv, 5). He was famous for his cures of insanity, healing the women of Aigina of madness and being granted a large share of the kingdom in recompense (Herodotos, ix, 34). He gained his greatest fame, however, by curing the daughters of Proitos of their madness by the use of hellebore, which was named melampodion after him. Pliny says (*op. cit.*, xxv, 21) that they were healed by the milk of goats fed upon melampodion; and Ovid (*op. cit.*, xv, 326 ff.), that they were cured by herbs and incantations. It is claimed that this took place at Sikyon (Pausanias, II, vii, 8); at the Anigrian springs into which Melampous threw the things used for their purification, thus giving the water its bad odor (*ib.*, V, v, 10; Strabo, VIII, iii, 19 = p. 346 C); or, as more generally accepted, at the sanctuary of Artemis at Lousoi (Pausanias, VIII, xviii, 7), where the waters had been polluted in the same manner, so that persons drinking them lost their taste for wine and could not bear the smell of it (Frazer, *op. cit.*, iv, 259). As a reward Proitos gave Melampous one of his daughters, Iphianassa, in marriage, as well as a large part of his kingdom. Melampous is reputed to have visited Egypt and to have brought back the orgiastic and mystic rites of Dionysos (Herodotos, ii, 49).

MOLPADIA HEMITHEA

MOLPADIA HEMITHEA was the daughter of Staphylos of Thrace. While she and her sister, Parthenos, were guarding her father's wine-pots, they broke, and to avoid his wrath they threw themselves into the sea, Molpadia being later accorded divine honors and becoming celebrated for her dream-oracle. A temple was erected to her at Kastabos in the Thracian Cheronese, which became a popular resort for invalids, to whom the means of cure were indicated by incubation. She gained great repute for her assistance in child-birth and was appealed to especially by women who feared the difficulties and dangers of labor (Diodoros, v, 62).

MOPSOS

MOPSOS, the son of a Cretan seer named Rhakios, was one of the heroes of the Theban War and later joined Amphilochos in founding the city of Mallos in Cilicia, where they set up an oracle. Mopsos was worshipped as a healing hero both at Mallos and at Oropos, and was a prophet superior to Kalchas, who died of chagrin when he realized his defeat (Strabo, XIV, i, 27; XIV, v, 16 = pp. 642, 675 C).[298]

MOUSAIOS

MOUSAIOS, a mythical bard, seer, and priest of pre-Homeric times, was the son of Orpheus and Selene, or, as sometimes claimed, of Eumolpos; and he was usually considered as one of the Eumolpidai.

Aristophanes (*Ranæ*, 1033) makes Aischylos say that Mousaios taught oracles and the healing of disease.

OINONE

OINONE, a daughter of the river-god Kebren, and a rival of Helena for the love of Paris, had been given the art of prophecy and had received from Apollo the knowledge of healing herbs (Parthenios, *Erotica*, iv; Ovid, *Heroides*, v, 145-148). She alone could heal Paris when wounded by Philoktetes, but she refused to go to him. Repenting, she arrived too late and in her sorrow ended her own life (Parthenios, *loc. cit.*).

[298] See further, Gruppe, *op. cit.*, p. 553.

POLYIDOS

POLYIDOS, a descendant of Melampous and a celebrated seer of Corinth, Argos, or Megara, raised from the dead Glaukos, son of Minos, who had been strangled by falling into a vessel of honey. Shut in a room with the dead child, he killed a snake that had entered, and noticing that its companion had revived it by placing on it a certain herb or grass, he laid the same on the body of the child, thus restoring it to life (Apollodoros, III, iii, 1). This revivification is, however, often ascribed to Asklepios.[299]

PROTESILAOS

PROTESILAOS was a healing hero whose shrine was located at his grave on the shores of the Thracian Cheronese (Antiphilos, in *Anthol. Pal.*, vii, 171; Philostratos, *op. cit.*, ii, 15). He was slain by Hektor and descended to Hades, but returned to life for a short time.

TOXARIS

TOXARIS was a Scythian who came with Anacharsis to Athens, where he was heroized for his skill in the treatment of fevers. He was called a 'hero-physician,'[300] and in gratitude for stopping a disastrous plague the Athenians raised to him an altar at which they annually sacrificed a white goat.[301]

Supplement to Chapter VI.

GLYKON

[GLYKON was a false deity, a pretended reincarnation of Asklepios, who appeared about A.D. 150 when a certain

[299] See *supra*, page 251.

[300] W. W. Goodwin, "The Hero Physician," in *AJA*, 2d series, 1900, iv, 168.

[301] Thrämer, in Roscher, i, 2483 f.

Alexander of Abonouteichos, in Bithynia, on the shore
of the Black Sea, having learned magic and sorcery from
Apollonios of Tyana, set himself up as a physician after
the death of Apollonios; buying a tame snake in Macedonia, and conceiving the idea of establishing an oracle
in his native city. He accordingly buried some bronze
tablets in the temple of Apollo in Propontis, which, when
conveniently discovered, declared that Asklepios was to
return to earth and take up his abode in Abonouteichos.
A temple was later built there, and Asklepios duly appeared in the form of a snake on the finger of Alexander.
Notwithstanding the brazen imposition, he gained adherents and won popularity against violent opposition. A
certain Roman senator assisted the cult, and under the
name of Glykon it was introduced into Rome, where it
had a vogue for nearly a century before it was forgotten.[302] This pretended god of medicine, in the form of a
dragon with a human head, called Glykon, was proposed
for public veneration.][303]

[302] The chief source for this bit of charlatanism is Lucian's *Alexan-
dros*, or *Pseudomantis, passim*. It is also summarized by Sir Samuel
Dill, in *Roman Society from Nero to Marcus Aurelius*, pp. 473 *et sqq.*

[303] Besnier, *L'Ile tibérine*, p. 192; also E. Babelon, "Le faux
prophète, Alexandre d'Abonotichos," in *RN* (1900), 1.

CHAPTER SEVEN

ROMAN GODS

CHAPTER SEVEN

THE HEALING GODS OF ANCIENT ROME

PART I: GENERAL SURVEY

Foreign influences in Roman religion.

ALMOST from its earliest period, the religion of
Rome was constantly subjected to strong foreign
influences. During the centuries of her growth
and preëminent power, she adopted the gods of other
peoples who were brought under her domain, supporting
them at their home altars, inviting some within her own
walls, welcoming others, and permitting the deities of all
countries to find an abode at her capital. She neglected
and forgot her native divinities and finally yielded to the
moral supremacy of other races of more advanced civilization whose representatives came to her in large numbers as slaves, subjects, and visiting strangers. She held
the pantheon of the world, and during the Empire the
clashing of interests of many types of religions eventually made Rome the great religious battleground in
the final contest between paganism and Christianity. The
devotees of many foreign cults, often fanatical and barbaric, sought in many tongues to translate to the masses
a great diversity of religious beliefs and customs, and to
enlist their support. Thus Roman religion, as it passes
in review through the many centuries of the Kingdom,
the Republic, and the Empire, presents an ever changing,
kaleidoscopic aspect.

The resulting complexities.

Any study of the gods of Rome, mingled as they were in a great religious potpourri, encounters unusual complexities. The Hellenization of the old Roman cults obscured their original character; and the invasion of numerous Oriental cults, which finally exercised a dominating influence over Roman religion, added many perplexing facets for consideration. The Greek myths furnish the key to the character of the Hellenic cults that came to Rome, but the loss of the liturgies and much of the mythologies of the great nations of the East, which were swept away in the fall of paganism, has left a void that has been very imperfectly spanned by the recent discoveries of ancient records. Although the religions of Rome have been diligently studied, the healing function of their worship appears to have escaped the comprehensive examination which has been given to their other more general phases. With the exception of a very few cults, the healing of the sick was a minor or insignificant part of their religious activities; and, perhaps for the reason that it was a part of the mysteries of cultic practice, it received only cursory mention by contemporary writers. Even these comments still remain to be properly collated, critically studied, and adequately presented. They form the basis of the present study, which, however, resolves itself, in great part, into a survey of the religious healing rites of the Romans as practiced by the foreign worships in Rome, which may often be better understood by reference to their native religions.

The early Roman religion.

The Romans, originally a small group of agricultural and warlike people in close contact with other tribes, or clans, of similar peoples in a like stage of civil and religious development, grew in numbers and power by the absorption of neighboring communities. Their deities and cultic worship were much alike in conception; and, as the people came together, their religions were easily adjusted. Some gods of other tribes were accepted as an integral part of the common religion, and others were forgotten or blended; so that their names, when retained, were either those of independent deities or represented different phases of a more comprehensive divine personality.

The spiritual world.

The Roman religion developed from a pandæmonism, or multinuminism, to a polytheism, but always retained many of its earlier characteristics. The people believed that they were surrounded by a world of supernatural beings, spiritual powers, or *numina*, of undefined nature, known only by their activities. These beings were cold, colorless, abstract concepts with no personality, no human affections or relations except ritualistic; and their attitude toward man was ever doubtful. The early conception was simply that of a spirit and its function; only at a later stage did it develop into a god. Even when these powers, regarded as both the masters and the slaves of the people, were personified, they excited no emotions. They were never the companions of man, nor did he seek to know them; for the relation between man and his divinities was impersonal and merely contractual until the later period, when there came a tendency to consecrate oneself to the perpetual service of the deities.[1]

The deities as the supreme lords.

The Romans believed that "the gods are supreme lords

[1] Fowler, *The Religious Experience of the Roman People*, pp. 145-168; also Aust, *Die Religion der Römer*, p. 19; also Carter, *The Religion of Numa*, p. 116.

and governors of all things, and that all events are
directed by their influence, wisdom, and divine power"
(Cicero, *de Legibus,* ii, 7); so that all things came from
them, whether for good or for evil, according as their
disposition toward man was favorable or hostile. Misfortunes were a punishment for neglect or for some offense, and were the expressions of the wrath or displeasure of some divinity; and the people went in constant
terror and uncertainty concerning these unseen powers.

Functions of deity.

Some divinity presided over every human affair (Cicero, *de Natura Deorum,* iii, 18), and a spirit was assigned
to everything existing, to the man, to the state, to the
family storeroom, the counterpart of the natural phenomena in the spiritual domain.[2] The great divinities
represented the larger spheres embraced in the abstrac-
tion, and there were lesser gods and a swarm of *numina,*
named and unnamed, each with a definite circle of activity, a certain thing to do, whence the number of gods
became so great that Petronius remarked (*Satiræ,* 17)
that "Italy was so filled with *numina* that it was easier
to find a god than a man." The greater number of *numina*
remained as "vague and dimly-outlined forces, animate
yet scarcely personal,"[3] but others received thinly trans-
parent names significant of their function, the result, it
is said, of priestly elaboration, and are found in the pon-
tifical litanies.[4] The names given these subsidiary deities
and *numina* often appertained to a greater god, indicative of the capacities in which the divinity might function, and were recognized by the sacred law as belonging
to one god, but among the common people it frequently

[2] Mommsen, *The History of Rome,* i, 34.
[3] L. R. Farnell, "Greek Religion," in *ERE* vi, 394.
[4] Wissowa, *Die Religion und Kultus der Römer,* p. 23.

happened that they were looked upon as separate deities.[5] Such functional *numina* for each minute detail assisted Iuno Lucina and Diana in child-birth and in the supervision of childhood; Antevorta provided a position favorable to delivery; Opigena aided the birth; Potina taught the infant to drink; Edusa to eat; Sentina gave it understanding; Locutius taught it to speak correctly; and Ossipaga hardened the bones. Similarly there were no less than twelve subsidiary deities between the seeding and the harvest, the *numina agentis*. Tellus was the mother earth who received the seed and bore the fruit; Saturnus represented the seeding; Flora, the blossoming; Ceres, the growth; Pomona, the fruit; and Consus and Ops, the harvest.

The nature of the religion.

Religion consisted in sacrifice and in divination by birds, to which was added prediction by oracles (Cicero, *op. cit.*, iii, 2). For all practical purposes, it consisted in knowledge of the right power to be invoked and in knowing the manner, time, and place for propitiating the divinity by performing the ritual of worship. The spiritual powers concerned were often confused; and since they could not always be determined, all the gods were frequently invoked, lest if one be addressed, other interested deities might be neglected. The rites were both private and public in character, and were for purification and expiation of involuntary acts of omission or commission; while by their observance the people sought to appease the wrath of any divinities who were offended, to gain their favor and avert the evil which might emanate from a malevolent spirit, and to establish and maintain a *pax deorum*. Having performed these rituals, man had fulfilled his whole duty to the gods as understood by the

[5] Wissowa, *op. cit.*, p. 53.

contract; and the deities, having accepted the homage, were expected to fulfil the duties pertaining to their sphere of activity and to preserve man from all harm.[6] This religion was exceedingly practical, prosaic, grave, and unemotional, a religion of duty. In the early days there were—at least so far as the records go—no myths or poetic tales to stimulate an interest in the gods; these came later with Hellenic influences.

The great gods.

The center of the early religious life was the household. Vesta, the hearth, was the central divine figure; Ianus was the door; the Di Penates represented the storeroom, and the Di Parentum the ancestors; Lar guarded the fields and family property; and the *paterfamilias* was the priest. The oldest order of gods was Ianus, Iupiter, Mars, Quirinus, and Vesta; and this order was succeeded by the first triad: Iupiter, the sky-god who furnished the rain, as the chief of the pantheon; Mars, the god of war; and Quirinus, a phase of Mars in a civil capacity. Varro at a later time divided the pantheon into three categories; the celestial or sky-gods, the deities of the earth, and the divinities of the Underworld.

The early sanctuary.

For the first centuries of the city, until the sanctuary of the reconstructed triad was established on the Capitoline (*circa* 532 B.C.; Livy, i, 55, 56), the deities were not represented by pictures or statues; and there were no divine dwellings, except that of Vesta, which was roofed to protect the sacred fire.[7] Pits for receiving the sacrifices, sacred groves, altars, and fanes (*loca sacra*) were provided for worship from public consecrated ground.

[6] W. W. Fowler, "Roman Religion," in *ERE* x, 823.

[7] Wissowa, *op. cit.*, p. 28.

Di Manes, *Genius, and Iuno.*

In the early belief of the Romans two classes of beings intervened between man and his gods. The spirits of the dead, the *Di Manes* or 'kindly deities,' still had an influence over the living; and their powers were so dreaded, when they returned as ghosts and specters, that offerings were made to them to induce them to refrain from visiting man and doing him harm. Further, there was the personal divinity, or double,—the Genius of the male, and the Iuno of the female,—who came into being with each individual to initiate him into the mysteries of life, and who remained until death as counsellor and guide.[8]

Organization of religion.

Romulus had instituted divination, and Numa had established sacrifice, the observance of these rites causing the gods to be propitious and enabling Rome to reach the height of her grandeur (Cicero, *op. cit.,* iii, 2). The divine law (*ius sacrum*), being a part of the civil code (*ius civile*), concerned the safety of the State and was inseparable from it; religion organized by Numa, very early became a State institution; and the king, as the father of the State, was the chief priest. The catalogue of gods recognized by the State, the *di indigetes,* or 'indigenous gods,' was determined and closed forever, and their festivals were fixed on the calendar, all deities subsequently receiving official recognition being termed *di novensides,* or 'newly settled gods.' Each divinity worshipped must be publicly acknowledged or he was looked upon with suspicion, and his rites were deemed 'new and strange' (Cicero, *de Leg.,* ii, 8). All religious affairs were under the control of three *pontifices,* who were organized into

[8] Fowler, in *ERE* x, 845; also Preller, *Römische Mythologie,* i, 78 ff.; Wissowa, *op. cit.* (ed. 1902), pp. 154 ff.

a college with a *pontifex maximus,* the number being afterward increased to eight, to nine, and, still later, to fifteen. The *flamines* conducted the worship of the several gods and were subject to the *pontifices;* while the king was the *rex sacrorum* until the establishment of the Republic, when the chief priest of Ianus assumed that office; the religious authority, which was then separated from the civil, being given to the magistrates.

The rituals.

The *pontifices* arranged the rituals of worship and the ceremonies for festivals and other religious celebrations. The rituals were simple, without pomp or extravagance, but traditional in form; and it was essential that they should be performed with exactness and with attention to the minutest detail in word, voice, and gesture, lest the deity addressed be offended, for the slightest error vitiated the whole, so that it must be repeated with a piacular offering. Purification was obtained by the rites of lustration and expiation, and was the symbol for divine favor, and the sacrifices consisted of agricultural products, of animals, as of sheep, swine, cattle, and dogs; while for certain purposes the blood of the October horse was used. Public festivals were usually in honor of particular gods and were held on their natal days, which were kept sacred for the purpose, as the Vestalia to Vesta on June 9, and the Matralia to Mater Matuta on June 11. Additional sacrifices, supplications, festivals, and holidays (*feriæ*) were ordered by the Senate in time of public emergency, as for famine and pestilence, or to avert the calamities of war, and for thanksgivings; while on some occasions vows were made by the people (*vota publica*) to propitiate the divinities (Livy, xxxi, 9). Such extraordinary appeals to the deities were usually ordered on the advice of the augurs after they had consulted the *aus-*

picia, or the Sibylline books, and the ceremonies prescribed included special supplications and sacrifices for
purification and expiation, fasts, prostrations, humilia-
tions, processions with choruses, extra festivals, and
holidays with games, plays, and other spectacles.

Augury.

In the early religion, there were no oracles, but the
gods sent messages to man by the flight of birds, the
action of animals, the entrails of victims, celestial phenomena, and ill omens of nature (*prodigia*), thus indicating their disposition as propitious or otherwise. Presages
were supposed to be attached to all things, and it was of
the utmost importance for the safety of the State and of
the individual that they should be correctly interpreted.[9]
Three official diviners were appointed to consider every
omen and prodigy, to determine its meaning, and to
advise concerning measures necessary to appease the
gods, to avoid disaster, and to take advantage of their
favor. No serious business, public or private, was begun
without first consulting the auspices to learn the attitude
of the gods, and any action contrary to the omens was
sure to bring dire punishment or disaster (Cicero, *de
Divinatione,* i, 35). The signs of the heavens proceeded
from Iupiter as his divine will; augury was a part of his
cult; and the *augures* were his servants (*id., de Leg.,* ii,
8). A college of Augures was formed, and their number
was increased to nine with a *rex;* but they had no part in
the worship, though with the *pontifices* they formed the
consulting staff of the king and of the Senate. The highest
magistrates also had the right of *spectio,* or taking public
auspices, and they joined the *pontifices* in conciliating the
gods; but all doubtful and important matters were referred to the augurs. The religion of the State was thus

[9] G. Wissowa, "Divination (Roman)," in *ERE* iv, 820-826.

regulated by the two great *collegia* of Pontifices and Augures, the king, and the Senate, this organization remaining practically unchanged after the abolition of the Kingdom and throughout the Republic.

The Etruscan haruspices.

Following the accession of the Tarquins to the throne, the Etruscans on the north, of a different and more Oriental type of civilization, began to exercise an influence over religion; and Mars and Quirinus were displaced in favor of Iuno and Minerva, who, with Iupiter, now composed the great Capitoline triad. Thenceforth, until the third century of the Empire, they continued to be the supreme deities of Rome, whose temple, in the Etruscan style, was for many centuries the center of Roman religion and authority. The Etruscans were masters in the arts of divination and magic (Cicero, *de Div.*, i, 41), which, in their cult, strongly resembled those of Babylonia;[10] and their specialty was the interpretation of the signs of the heavens, of portents, and of prodigies by reading the livers and entrails of victims. Their methods were different from the Roman auspices, and on several occasions alarming prodigies were referred to their *haruspicia* for interpretation, but little reference is found to the use of Etruscan divination until the third century B.C., when the *Disciplina Etrusca* came into vogue, and Roman youths of patrician families were sent to Etruria for instruction in the art.[11]

The oracle of the Cumæan Sibyl.

From early times the Romans had recognized the Greeks as masters of divine lore, and the Sibyl of Cumæ, who had become renowned for her oracles, which had

[10] Jastrow, *Die Religion Babyloniens und Assyriens*, ii, 213 ff.
[11] Fowler, *Religious Experience*, pp. 292-311.

acquired such an authority that they were ascribed to the Delphic Apollo, possessed 'Books' that were believed to enshrine the precious results of Hellenic experience.[12] Tarquinius Superbus, who had consulted her when the native gods had not availed, ultimately obtained her 'prophetic books,' placing them in the custody of the Capitoline temple in charge of two augurs, the Duoviri Sacris Faciundis, who, not understanding their contents, which were expressed in enigmatical terms, sent for two Greek interpreters (Dion Kassios, i, 75). These volumes, reputed to contain revelations for the future, were used as "religious prescriptions" for ceremonies in times of public emergency; and Cicero says (op. cit., ii, 54) that an ordinance of their ancestors required that the 'books' should not even be read except by decree of the Senate, and that they were to be used for putting down rather than for taking up religious fancies. The oracle was Greek and naturally advised the introduction of Hellenic deities and ceremonies, so that the use of the 'books' was thus "destined to change the form and content of Roman religion." In this movement the worship of Apollo was naturally the leader. The rites of the foreign gods, as they came to Rome, differed from the Italic cults, and while the latter were under the control of the *pontifices*, the former were placed in the charge of the Duoviri. The number in charge of the 'books' was increased to nine, then to ten, the Decemviri (367 B.C.); and, in the last year of the Republic, to fifteen, the Quindecemviri.

Three types of divination.

In their excessive fear of the spiritual powers, the Romans had introduced the science of divination from

[12] J. S. Reid, "Worship (Roman)," in *ERE* xii, 809; also Fowler, in *ERE* x, 850-851; Marquardt, *Römische Staatsverwaltung*, iii, 352, note 7; Fowler, *Religious Experience*, p. 247.

Etruria, lest any form be neglected, and so had three kinds at their command: their own auspices; the Etruscan haruspices; and the oracles contained in the Sibylline books (Cicero, *ib.*, i, 2); while, in addition, they occasionally consulted the Pythian oracle at Delphoi (Livy, i, 56; v, 15; xxix, 10). The Romans had thus accepted two foreign teachers in religion: the Etruscans, who had a moderate early influence; and the virile, aggressive Greeks of Magna Græcia.

The religious invasion.

Before the Republic, prominent Italic deities, such as Minerva of Etruria, Diana of Aricia, and Hercules of Tibur (Livy, i, 45), had been received in Rome without disturbing the sobriety of the religious morale or the sense of duty of the citizens to their gods; and when, in the first years of the Republic, famine threatened (496 B.C.), the Senate, following the directions found in the 'books,' invited three Greek divinities, Dionysos, Demeter, and Kore, to Rome. They were given the names of similar old Roman deities, Liber, Ceres, and Libera; but their cults remained entirely Greek; and since the city was reserved for native gods, these foreigners were given a temple outside the *pomœrium* which marked the sacred limits (Livy, i, 44). In time, Ceres displaced the old earth-mother Tellus, and set an example for Hellenic deities to overshadow native divinities. For some years, other Greek gods came to Rome, but then a reaction followed, and the 'books' were silent for nearly two centuries. The immigration practically ceased, except that Apollo (as Apollo Medicus) was introduced very early, and Aphrodite arrived under the Italic name of Venus. The old official deities remained unchanged, but new fashions prevailed; and since the ancient divinities proved inefficient, they were neglected, the worship of new gods with strange ceremonies becoming such a public disgrace that, in 425 B.C., the ædiles were instructed to see that the citizens should worship no other than native deities (Livy, iv, 30).

Greek and Semitic deities.

Foreign influence had an early effect on religion as shown by the worship of both Greek and Roman deities and by the more emotional Greek rites (*ritus Græcus*) observed at the first *lectisternium* (399 B.C.), which was ordered by the Duoviri, "ex Sibyllinis libris," on account of a pestilence (Livy, v, 13). In 293 B.C., by the advice of the Decemviri, Asklepios was invited to Rome to stay a pestilence, and thenceforth the immigration of Greek gods was renewed with increased vigor, so that, by the end of the third century B.C., there was a host of Greek divinities outside the *pomœrium*. Meanwhile, Semitic deities were introduced from Syria (Atargatis and others) by slaves and merchants;[13] and the Romans, uncertain of the identity of these divinities, but wishing to protect the State from the malevolence of any of them, accepted *di novensides* freely. Many were enrolled by the magistrates as State gods, and legal obligations to them were assumed.

Magna Mater.

In 216 B.C., when the people were in despair because of many prodigies and through fear of Hannibal, devotion to alien cults gained the upper hand to such an extent that the authorities could no longer control the people, and the Senate ordered that all books of soothsayers must be given up so that no sacrifice could be made according to new and foreign rites (Livy, xxv, 1). When, in this emergency, the Decemviri finally had recourse to the Sibylline books, they reported that only the Idaian

[13] Cumont, *The Oriental Religions in Roman Paganism*, pp. 103 ff.

mother-goddess (Mater Deum Magna Idæa), Kybele (Rhea) of Pessinus, could free Rome and Italy from her enemies (*ib.*, xxix, 10, 11). Accordingly, brought to Rome in 204 B.C. as Magna Mater, she was received with acclaim and was accorded the highest honors, including a temple within the *pomœrium* on the Palatine. She brought relief and fulfilled all the promises made for her, but the orgiastic and barbaric character of her cult, and the conduct of her followers (the emasculated 'Galli') on the streets, scandalized the Romans; and she was the only Oriental deity invited to Rome. The people, and especially the youth of the city, were contaminated by the demoralizing influence of her cult; and shortly afterward, when the mysteries of Bacchus were surreptitiously introduced, very many yielded to their enticements. The debaucheries under cover of the frequent Bacchanalia were finally disclosed to the Senate (186 B.C.), the guilty were severely punished, and the cult was officially placed under heavy restrictions (*ib.*, xxxix, 8-19).

Oriental influences.

The sacred barrier of Rome had been invaded. Any foreign deity was now permitted to have an altar in the city, and it became difficult to find a contrast between Roman and Græco-Roman gods. Cults of Semitic divinities, Oriental Magi, Chaldæan *mathematici* or astrologers, Greek philosophers, physicians, craftsmen, and merchants from all parts flocked to Rome, exploiting their intellectual and religious wares and giving counsel. On the other hand, urgent protests against these alien influences, which were rapidly undermining the old faith of the Romans, the sobriety of religion, and the citizen's sense of duty to the State, were not lacking. In 173 B.C. the Epicureans were expelled; in 161, all philosophers were forced to leave; and in 139, the Chaldæi were

driven from the city and Italy by order of the Senate
(Valerius Maximus, I, iii, 3). In 155 B.C. philosophers
came to Rome on a peaceful mission, and Stoicism,
which though sceptic laid strong emphasis on ethics, appealed as the best among philosophies, with the result
that it became the national philosophy.[14] Nevertheless, it
came too late; the ancient virtues and conservative traits
of the Romans, which had caused them to keep a jealous
supervision over their native religion, were enfeebled;
and their ideals were becoming antiquated; while, under
the influence of Greek religions and philosophies, the people generally were lacking in duty to their gods. The
definite spiritual conquest of Rome had begun during
the third century B.C.; and during the second century, the
State religion had difficulty in holding its own against
these adverse influences. The Chaldæans and philosophers had never lacked defenders and patrons; and when
they returned to the city, their teachings attracted more
and more the attention of the serious-minded. Greek art
and literature filtered through many agencies; but after
the victory over Macedonia, the Hellenization of Rome
proceeded more rapidly and without effective resistance.

Decline of native religion. Greek influences.

The old Roman religion was disintegrating, and all the
influences of Hellas combined for a comparison between
her deities and the Roman gods, thus leading to a confusion of the two pantheons.[15] It was assumed that parallels
existed between the deities of the two States; and as
these were ascertained, their divinities were fused or
adjustments were made, so that a blending was effected.
Roman gods for whom no similarities were found and
for whom no compromises were possible were displaced

[14] Carter, *op. cit.*, pp. 123 ff.
[15] *Ib.*, pp. 112 ff.

and forgotten, both as to name and function, unless they were recorded on the old calendars. Temples to divinities under Roman titles were actually shrines of Greek deities, this process of syncretism being fostered by Hellenic art and mythology, and the substitution continued during the last two centuries of the Republic until all the Roman gods had been supplanted except Vesta (a symbol of the State's vitality), who appears throughout to have retained her original character and name. Little of the Roman religion remained except the old household cult. By the end of the first century B.C., the identification of the old Roman deities was all but impossible, and Varro was obliged to include in his list many *di incerti*,[16] or divinities for whom no function was known. The gods of Rome who had risen above the class of *numina* and *indigitamenta,* who always "remained in the amorphous twilight of religious perception,"[17] had now acquired a personality, and many had become anthropomorphic, so that Greek craftsmen represented them in art, though always after the Greek pattern. Similarly, Greek myths were adapted to Roman deities, and, as used by poets and other writers, formed the basis of Roman mythology, while Greece furnished Rome with her philosophers and physicians, and her teachers educated the Roman youth.

Emotional cults.

The many Oriental cults coming to Rome from Phrygia, Persia, Syria, and Egypt contributed very largely to the religious unrest. Semitic deities with their followers, priests, slaves, and merchants, and the closely related Chaldæans with their Oriental lore, had long been resident in Rome; while sailors and soldiers returning from the wars in the East brought with them other cults

[16] Wissowa, *Religion,* p. 72.
[17] Farnell, in *ERE* vi, 404.

of the Orient with which they had come in contact, notably those of Mithras of Persia and the goddess Komana
of Pontus, originally Mâ of Cappadocia, who was equated
with Atargatis and Kybele, and who was assimilated to
the ancient war-deity, Bellona, whom she supplanted and
whose name she assumed, though distinguished as Mâ-
Bellona.[18] About the same time, the partially Hellenized
Egyptian divinities, Isis and Serapis, came from Southern Italy. These Eastern religions had encouraged a taste
for the sensational, and the people came to care more for
Bellona and Isis than for all the gods of Numa.[19] The
devotees of the various Oriental cults were inclined to give
expression to their exuberant enthusiasm for these emotional religions; but as they became aggressive and gave
offense, sharp measures were taken to suppress them.
The altars of Isis were repeatedly destroyed by orders
of the Senate and as often restored by the zeal of her followers, until finally the Triumviri adopted a pliant attitude.[20] The doctrines brought in by these cults were
strange to the Occident and made a strong appeal to the
imagination, especially those of the Asianic cults. Underlying the orgiastic features, emphasized by fanatical followers, was a serious content that appealed to the conscience, gratified the cravings of the heart, and possessed
an irresistible personal charm for those who penetrated
their mysteries.[21]

Further decline of the Roman religion.

The emotional attractions and demoralizing influences
of these Oriental religions, as well as the scepticism of
Greek philosophies, had weakened the State religion,

[18] Carter, *op. cit.*, pp. 137 ff.
[19] *Ib.*, p. 141.
[20] *Ib.*, pp. 136 ff.
[21] Cumont, *op. cit.*, pp. 28, 30.

subjected as it was to politics and debauched conditions, and hastened its decline as an effective agency of government.[22] The people had grown indifferent toward it, and those who had supervision over it were themselves doubters, fast losing faith in its efficacy. The priesthoods, no longer avenues of advancement, fell into partial, and some into complete, neglect. The administration of the temples had grown lax; the priests shirked their duties; and many *flaminia* became vacant and were not refilled. Sacrilege and thefts of statues and other sacred objects occurred; many temples were neglected and in ruins; the cults losing their vitality, failed to uphold their obligations to State and people. Without standards for uprightness and incentives for accord, came a general lowering of personal morality. Corruption was cultivated as a science, wickedness in high places was unashamed, and a strong proletariat was drifting into turbulence.[23]

Religious tolerance.

Although scepticism was rife among the educated and influential classes of Roman citizens, the various peoples of the city, gathered at their several altars, worshipped their own gods in their own fashion, or as it has been expressed by a Christian controversialist (Minucius, *Octavius,* vi, 1): "Other cities worshipped their own gods, but the Romans worshipped everybody's."[24] Gibbon states,[25] in a well-known passage, that

The various modes of worship, which prevailed in the Roman world, were all considered by the people as equally true; by the

[22] Carter, *op. cit.,* pp. 124 ff.

[23] Fowler, in *ERE* x, 838-839; also Carter, *The Religious Life of Ancient Rome,* pp. 53-56.

[24] Moore, *The History of Religions,* p. 576.

[25] *The Decline and Fall of the Roman Empire,* i, 30-32; cf. Toutain, *Les Cultes païens dans l'empire romain,* i, 232.

philosopher, as equally false; and by the magistrate, as equally useful. Thus toleration produced not only mutual indulgence, but even religious concord.

The superstition of the people was not embittered by any mixture of theological rancor; nor was it confined by the chains of any speculative system. The devout polytheist, though fondly attached to his national rites, admitted with implicit faith the different religions of the earth. . . . The deities of a thousand groves and a thousand streams possessed, in peace, their local and respective influence; nor could the Roman who deprecated the wrath of the Tiber, deride the Egyptian who presented his offering to the beneficent genius of the Nile. The visible powers of nature, the planets, and the elements, were the same throughout the universe. The invisible governors of the moral world were inevitably cast in a similar mould of fiction and allegory. . . . Such was the mild spirit of antiquity, that the nations were less attentive to the difference, than to the resemblance, of their religious worship. The Greek, the Roman, and the Barbarian, as they met before their respective altars, easily persuaded themselves, that under various names, and with various ceremonies, they adored the same deities. The elegant mythology of Homer gave a beautiful, and almost regular form, to the polytheism of the ancient world.

Religious reforms.

The reforms in religion and politics which were urgently demanded (Horace, *Odæ*, iii, 6; *Epodæ*, xvi), were planned by Iulius Cæsar, but the task of guiding the disordered State fell upon Augustus. He at once endeavored to reëstablish the authority of the State religion; he solicited and received the aid of historians and poets (Horace, *Odæ*, iii, 6) ; he drew the attention of the people to their old familiar deities and sought to restore their sense of *religio* and *pietas*,[26] to renew the appreciation of

[26] Wissowa, *op. cit.*, p. 235; Fowler, *Religious Experience*, pp. 8-9, 174.

their duty of service to the gods and their obligations of loyalty to their ancestors and the State. It was too late to bring back the simplicity and content of the old faith, but he effected, so far as possible, the appearance of a return to the religion of the forefathers. He rebuilt the temples (Ovid, *Fasti*, ii, 59) and revived the ancient cults and forms of worship, as well as the venerable sacrificial priesthoods and sodalities, all under the direction of the recognized authority of the colleges of Pontifices, Augures, and Quindecemviri. Apollo had become the official god of prophecy, and Augustus had adopted him as his personal and family deity. He erected a temple to him on the Palatine and, exercising his prerogative as Pontifex Maximus, he directed the Sibylline books to be copied and the originals (the books as rewritten after the fire of 81 b.c.) to be removed from the custody of the temple of Iupiter to that of Apollo on the Palatine, thus making this shrine the headquarters of the new Græco-Roman religion. Heretofore the Greek divinities had been subordinated to the Roman deities, but now Apollo was brought into direct rivalry with, and made equal, if not superior, to Iupiter Optimus Maximus,[27] who, though the great national deity, had always been more of a political than a religious god. Augustus depended on *religio*, 'that which binds,' to revive the waning sense of morality and public duty, and to secure tranquillity and stability to the State. The old Roman religion had been rehabilitated in large measure; and after his death, his successors on the throne conscientiously endeavored to continue his policies and make them effective.

Growth of Oriental influences.

Rome was drifting under the influence of doubt and of the philosophic platitudes of Neo-Platonism, then current

[27] Carter, *Numa*, pp. 164-169.

among her citizens high in authority; while the middle and lower classes, wearied and careless of the cold, prosaic, and impersonal faith, were feeling the strong attractions of the sensational Oriental cults. Roman religion was beset by enemies; and the spirit of a new era, now under the nominal direction of imperialism, was evolving momentous religious activities that were beginning to excite the passions of the Occident and were destined to submerge the old order that Greece and Rome had zealously built up. The conservative Romans, little concerned by this undercurrent, remained officially faithful to their ancient gods. The temples were kept in repair, and the *flamines* continued to observe the old forms of worship in all their minutiæ for upwards of two centuries before they yielded to the subtile influence of the Orient. Antoninus Pius was honored for his care of the antique rites, but even then the vital spirit of Roman religion was gone.

Oriental religions.

During this imperial period, the Oriental faiths and customs (the *ritus peregrini*), were steadily making headway in Rome and the Latin provinces.[28] These religions were first confined to the foreign minority, principally slaves and freedmen; but by degrees converts were attracted from the better classes, beginning with soldiers and sailors, their officers, and minor government officials. The worship was individual, and the ceremonies were attended, usually in secret, by small but enthusiastic groups at private altars in cellars or small underground chapels (*spelæa*). They gave little outward evidence of activity; but as they grew stronger, some cults (notably

---

[28] Toutain, *op. cit.*, vol. ii; also Frazer, *Adonis, Attis, Osiris*, i, 298-312; A. C. Pearson, "Mother of the Gods (Greek and Roman)," in *ERE* viii, 850-851; Cumont, *op. cit.*, pp. 22 ff.

Mithraism) developed an organized propaganda, chiefly through army channels, and made rapid progress both in the city and in the provinces. Although the immoral practices of the rites of Isis had been repressed and severely punished, and although the worship of the goddess still aroused indignation among many, she was allowed a temple in the Campus Martius in A.D. 39 which had been voted eighty-two years before, and shortly thereafter she received favors from Emperors. The exotic cults from the East, at first despised, were permeating the more educated classes, and finally made their way into the highest circles, gaining the avowed support of the most authoritative citizens, and highest officials.[29]

Astrology.

Notwithstanding the liability of the Chaldæi (*mathematici* or *genethliaci*, Aulus Gellius, I, ix, 6; XIV, 1, 1) to expulsion and other severe penalties (Tacitus, *Annales*, ii, 32; xii, 52; *Historia*, ii, 62; Dion Kassios, LXVI, ix, 2), which did not materially diminish their activity (Juvenal, *Satiræ*, vi, 553 ff.), they set forth Babylonian astrology and magic with such persuasive skill that they won over the best minds of Rome and these arts were used by Emperors, astrology in particular being declared to be an exact science in predicting the future both in public and in personal affairs. The old *auspicia* and *haruspicia*, which could not compare with it in authority, were consulted less and less; even the Sibylline books were neglected (Cicero, *op. cit.*, i, 15; *de Nat. Deor.*, ii, 3); the oracles became silent and were abandoned; and the new science of the heavens supplanted the old forms of divination.[30]

[29] Cumont, *op. cit.*, p. 6.
[30] *Ib.*, pp. 162 ff.

Seductions of Oriental cults.

All the countries of Western Asia and Northern Africa were represented in Rome by their numerous deities, and the people were offered the choice of a great diversity of heterogeneous doctrines of various values, many of which gained authority as the vitality of the old religion declined. Gods from the provinces streamed into the city, and Ammianus Marcellinus (XVII, iv, 13) spoke of Rome as the sanctuary of the entire world ("templum mundi totius"). The traditional, fabulous wisdom of the East possessed a seductive charm for the Occidental mind, inured to practical affairs and an impersonal worship of duty; and the Semitic cults, when stripped of their orgiastic features, appealed both to the conscience and to the intelligence.[31] They aroused latent hopes, offered alluring prospects of attaining the most ardent aspirations of the soul, and satisfied the thirst for religious emotions. Side by side with Christianity, they promised those initiated in their mysteries purification, redemption from sin, salvation, and a blessed immortality as the reward of faithfulness. Of all these worships, those of Mithras, Isis, and Magna Mater attained the greatest prominence, leading in the struggle between paganism and Christianity; but Mithraism, which was fostered under cover of Chaldæan wisdom, presented the highest type of heathenism and penetrated to the better classes of Roman society. The Chaldæo-Persian religion foretold a sublime dwelling place for all purified souls in the heavens; from which they had come, shedding their celestial attributes on the way. After initiation and cleansing, they received the password for the guardian of the gateway, and divesting themselves of acquired passions and inclinations, at death, under the conduct of Psychopompos,

[31] Cumont, *op. cit.,* pp. 29-30.

they resumed their discarded celestial garments and returned to the heavens.[32] The seductive mysteries of these Oriental cults were enhanced by ceremonies, impressive in their solemnity, profoundly suggestive in their symbolism, and appealing to the eye and ear; while the fascinating pomp and magnificence of the processions, accompanied by languishing melodies and song, won the ardent, enthusiastic support of their worshippers. During cultic festivals, realistic dramas were performed based upon the myths of the lives of their respective deities, symbolizing their struggles in overcoming unrighteousness, as well as their sufferings, death, and resurrection, all being enacted in detail during the several days of the festival and arousing the deepest emotions among those who witnessed them, from profound grief and sorrow to ecstatic joy.[33]

Supremacy of Oriental religions.

The progress of this religious invasion had been slow, but by a "peaceful infiltration" the Oriental religions had finally won the support of the patricians and of the masses until, in the third century of the Empire, they attained their zenith and held undisputed sway. Under Caracalla, all restrictions which had excluded the worship of foreign deities within the limits of the sacred city were removed; and they entered Rome on an equality with the old State gods. Roman idolatry was dethroned. The ancient religion and the national ideals had been overwhelmed by those of the Orient. The Syrian sun, "leader of the planetary choir," became "king and leader of the whole world";[34] and the Aurelian State cult of Sol Invictus, Iupiter Cælus, displaced Iupiter Optimus Maximus

[32] Cumont, op. cit., pp. 126, 177-178.
[33] Ib., p. 29.
[34] Ib., p. 175.

as the supreme national deity. The *pontifices,* augurs, consuls, and Quindecemviri were now regarded as archaic; and the whole of the old religious organization lost every vestige of vitality.

Downfall of paganism.

With the gathering of popularity and power, strife was engendered between the pagan worships by the very similarity of their doctrines, and bitter antagonisms were developed as each struggled for supremacy; but the cults of Mithras, Isis, and Magna Mater, finding a common ground in their fierce opposition to Christianity, were foremost in the final fight for paganism. The new faith was definitely triumphant only in the closing years of the fourth century, when the defeat of Eugenius, the last open defender of heathenism, gave the authorities sufficient strength to enforce the edict of Theodosius (A.D. 391) and effectually to suppress the proscribed pagan religions throughout the Roman world.

Remains of the Roman faith.

The temporary supremacy of the Oriental religions in the Occident and the victory of Christianity could not at once and entirely destroy the tenacious faith of the Romans in their old and tried divinities. Their temples were preserved when Constantine visited Italy in the fourth century; and many votive inscriptions of that period give ample evidence that belief in the great triad and in other deities, such as Apollo, Diana, Mars, Hercules, and Fortuna, still survived.

No specific healing deities.

Although the Romans were convinced that every affair in nature and human life was directed by some specialized divinity, so that the pantheon was crowded with functional gods and *indigitamenta,* no specific deity of healing has been identified among the *di indigetes,* and the trend of belief suggests that none were required. It has been surmised, however, that the Romans always worshipped powers of healing, although their names under the old régime are not known, except possibly as they were connected with the Lymphæ (divinities of the healing power of water, who were supplanted by the Greek nymphs),[35] or with gods of springs and waters, as Faunus and Albunea of Tibur.[36] It appears that the early Romans were satisfied with the general apotropaic powers of their gods for the preservation of their health; and the people having performed their duty in observance of ritual and sacrifice, the deities were bound to preserve them from all harm, including physical ills. When disease and suffering came, and death threatened, they regarded it as a visitation of the wrath of some offended god or gods, or as the malevolent act of some evil spirit or deity. Gods, who were supposed to have sent disease, must be appeased, and in epidemics the State consulted the auspices to determine, if possible, the identity of the divinity concerned and the measures required to effect a reconciliation with the deity, or to drive away the malignant spirit.[37] Peace and harmony must be restored; this effected, health would return, the further course of the disease and the convalescence requiring no act of competence or direction by a special healing divinity. If the appeal was not followed by relief, the proper god had not been addressed, the ceremony had not been correctly performed, or possibly the old deities had failed and new ones must be sought.

[35] Wissowa, *op. cit.,* p. 182 (ed. 1902).

[36] Carter, *op. cit.,* p. 83.

[37] F. Kissel, "Die symbolische Medicin der Römer," in *Janus,* 1848, iii, 646 ff.

Early efforts for healing.

The relation of the individual to his gods in the matter of disease, and the relation of the State in respect to pestilence, were essentially the same; but simple as they appeared, they were full of perplexities and difficulties. During the reign of Tullus (640 B.C.), alarming prodigies occurred which were interpreted as divine warnings because of neglect of certain religious rites, and an expiatory festival was ordered. The prodigies recurred, however, and a festival of nine days was held, but later a pestilence came among the people. Tullus himself was seized with a lingering illness, and observed many religious scruples without avail; but receiving no help, the people became restless and wished to return to the old precepts of Numa (Livy, i, 12),[38] thinking that the only relief for their sickly bodies was by obtaining pardon and peace from the gods. The king turned to the commentaries of Numa, and learning of a secret and solemn sacrifice to Iupiter, he shut himself up and set about its performance. Though the rite was duly conducted, he received no favor from heaven; but, on the contrary, Iupiter, exasperated at the impropriety of the ceremony, struck him and his home with lightning, burning them to ashes (Livy, i, 31). Infernal deities from the realm of Dis and Proserpina released frightful maladies upon mankind, and death was their active agent.

Diseases as deities.

Since it was often impossible to determine the identity of the gods sending the disease, the Romans, when perplexed, spiritualized the malady itself and addressed it, raising it to the rank of a deity, building temples in its honor, and sacrificing to it, as to Febris, representing

[38] "Unam opem ægris corporibus relictam si pax veniaque ab diis impetrata esset."

fever, and to Mefitis and Cloacina, as apotheoses of noxious vapors causing disease and death. Thus it came
about that practically each form of illness was so worshipped and invoked for relief; but when a malady disappeared, the worship and temples fell into disuse, this
being illustrated by an altar unearthed in 1876, dedicated
to a previously unknown god, Verminus ('Wormy'), at
a time of plague among cattle (*CIL* vi, 3732).[39]

Pestilence and deity.

Pestilence of a virulent character, "killing without
illness," occasionally devastated Rome, driving her citizens to gloomy terrors and despair. Such scourges were
looked upon as mysterious natural phenomena and regarded as an especial calamity to the State, depriving it
of its most valued asset, its citizens. At such times the
Senate and public officials instituted inquiries to ascer-
tain the cause, the gods offended, and what must be done
to propitiate them and to avoid further disaster. Tarquin
had preferred Greek oracles to Roman seers, and following his example of lack of faith in native divinities, the
Senate, when their own deities failed, directed the augurs
to consult the Sibylline books for the remedy. In 462 B.C.,
the mortality at Rome by disease was not less than by
the sword of the enemy; the Consul and eminent men
died; the malady spread extensively; and the Senate,
destitute of human aid, directed the attention of the people to the gods and prayer, ordering them to go with
their wives and children and earnestly implore the protection of heaven. They filled all the shrines; and the
prostrate matrons, sweeping the temples with their hair,
begged remission of the divine displeasure and termina-
tion of the pestilence (Livy, iii, 7). During the plague of
433-432 B.C., Apollo Medicus was invoked, and a temple

[39] Wissowa, *op. cit.*, p. 55.

was vowed for the health of the people (*ib.*, iv, 21, 25). In 399 B.C., on the occasion of an intractable plague, the Duoviri, after consulting the 'books,' reported that a *lectisternium*, or 'banquet of the gods,' must be held, in which both Greek and Roman gods should be honored according to the Greek rites. Three couches were accordingly prepared with the greatest magnificence; images representing Apollo and Latona were placed on one, Hercules and Diana on another, and Neptunus and Mercurius on the third; and tables sumptuously supplied with food were set before them. For eight days the people implored the gods for relief, while solemn rites were performed in public and private, and general hospitality was observed. The doors of all houses were thrown open; strangers were invited to meals and lodgings; prisoners were released; all refrained from quarrelling; and everything was held in common (*ib.*, v, 13). During the plague of 364 B.C., which continued the next year, the third *lectisternium* was ordered by advice of the Decemviri; but the violence of the disease was alleviated neither by human measures nor by divine interference. Scenic plays were, for the first time, instituted in Rome, and actors were brought from Etruria to conduct them, with dancing to the measures of a musician in a graceful manner after the Tuscan fashion, native performances being added, with gestures, chants, and dialogues, which by practice were converted from a source of mirth to an art. These plays, as first introduced, were intended as a religious expiation, but they neither relieved the minds of anxiety nor the bodies from disease; and they were interrupted by an alarming inundation of the Tiber which overflowed the Circus and excited the people to terror, indicating that their efforts had not soothed the wrath of the gods. The officials were anxiously searching for other expiations when it was learned from the memory of the aged "that a pestilence had formerly been relieved by a nail driven by a dictator." The Senate therefore appointed a dictator to fix the nail according to the "ancient law written in antique letters and words," which declared that a nail should be driven on the Ides of September; and it was accordingly struck into the right side of the temple of Iupiter Optimus Maximus, in the part consecrated to Minerva, since it was surmised that it originally marked the lapse of years, and number was the invention of Minerva (*ib.*, vii, 1, 2, 3).[40] The nail was again driven in 330 b.c. to restore the sanity of the people, who were terrified by fatal poisonings at the hands of Roman matrons (*ib.*, viii, 18). Upon the advice of the Decemviri, after an inspection of the 'books,' the fourth *lectisternium* was held because of the pestilence of 347 b.c. (*ib.*, vii, 27); and the fifth in 325 b.c. in honor of the same gods (*ib.*, viii, 24). The *lectisternia* were observed later for other public emergencies; but the custom then declined until Marcus Aurelius celebrated one for seven days during the great epidemic which preceded the war with the Marcomanni.[41]

Æsculapius and later epidemics.

During the severe plague of 293 b.c., Asklepios of Epidauros, invited to Rome to stop it, was brought to the city under the name of Æsculapius and on the Insula Tiberina was erected a sanctuary which was dedicated to him in January, 291 b.c. (Livy, *Epitome*, xi). During the Punic wars, a plague occurred; and in 212 b.c., by the advice of Marcius, confirmed by the 'books,' Apollinarian games, according to the Greek customs, were held to check its spread, this being the usual belief, although

[40] Fowler, *Roman Festivals of the Period of the Republic*, pp. 234-235.

[41] Wissowa, *op. cit.*, p. 422.

Livy (xxv, 12) held that they were for victory in war, and not for the restoration of health. These games were first celebrated by the prætors each year for single occasions only, and on no certain day; and the sacrifices were made to Apollo and Latona. In the summer of 209 or 208 B.C., a grievous plague occurred, more protracted than fatal; a supplication was performed in every street in the city; and the people vowed that Apollinarian games should be held on a certain day forever, July 13 being thereafter kept sacred for that purpose (ib., xxvii, 23). This vow, which was made to Apollo and Æsculapius, was frequent in epidemics (CIL vi, 2074; i, 23 ff.).[42]

Holidays as expiations.

Again, in 183 B.C., pestilence carried off many distinguished men. The Decemviri consulted the 'books,' and as they advised, the Senate ordered, throughout Italy, a supplication for one day and a cessation of work for three days (*feriæ;* Livy, xl, 19). In this supplication, Salus was included with Apollo and Æsculapius; and in gratitude to these gods the officials erected a temple to Apollo Medicus (ib., xl, 51), while the Pontifex Maximus ordered gilded statues of each of the deities to be placed in it (ib., xl, 37). In 176 B.C. a pestilence left a serious disorder among those who recovered, turning into a quartan ague; and by direction of the Sibylline books a supplication of one day was ordered, the people assembling in the Forum and vowing that, "if the sickness and pestilence should be removed from Roman territory, they would solemnize a festival and thanksgiving of two days continuance" (ib., xli, 21). In times of less danger, the officials assumed the responsibility and directed ceremonies of prayers and processions to avert epidemics.

[42] Cf. Wissowa, *op. cit.,* p. 383.

Healing and magic.

The Romans received early instruction from others in primitive methods of healing as they had in matters of religion. The Sabines contributed their folklore medicine and the Marsians sent their seers and enchantresses to Rome with their remedial herbs. Etruria was a land of magic and magicians, and its people had taught the Romans, who had adopted their haruspices, to apply the arts of divination and magic, as well as the use of incantations, songs, and chants in the healing of disease, a knowledge of which, according to tradition, they had received from the Greeks of Arkadia and Phrygia.[43] As elsewhere, magic and religion were inseparably related, but the Romans endeavored to differentiate between them, regarding the gods who were officially recognized by the State, and their ceremonials, as orthodox, others being heterodox and their practices suspect, or magic. Faiths that had been superseded became magic. Magic had a bad name, it was mistrusted, and on several occasions it was made illicit and proscribed, but it could not be suppressed.[44] There are many evidences of its use in connection with the treatment of disease, but it would appear that, in the early days of Rome at least, it was not so much an integral part of the religion as it was an adoption from other peoples, and that the intimate relation of magic with religious healing in the later period was largely the result of foreign influences. Pliny asserts (*Historia Naturalis,* xxx, 1-6) that magic had its origin in medicine, as a higher and holier branch of it; yet he regards it as the most deceptive of all arts, frivolous, lying, and containing only the shadow of truth; and he does not connect it with religion.

[43] Kissel, in *Janus,* 1848, iii, 696; also Sprengel, *Histoire de la médecine,* i, 177-178.

[44] K. F. Smith, "Magic (Greek and Roman)," in *ERE* viii, 269-276.

Patrician healing customs.

The Romans had no theology to guide them, but appear to have placed quite as much reliance, if not more, upon their rituals of worship as upon their gods; and in the matter of disease of the individual, they did not trust entirely to either; but like other primitive peoples combined their religious ceremonials with resort to the simples of herb lore. The master of the Roman home, the *paterfamilias,* was the doctor for the members of the family, unless, as in many of the larger households, he appointed a slave or freedman, who showed an aptitude for medicine, to care for the family; and this often happened to be a Greek physician. Cato, the Elder, who was venerated for his pristine virtues and conservatism, left records (*de Agri Cultura,* 134, 139, 141) indicating the popular family practice of his day (third century B.C.), which had undoubtedly come to him from early traditions, of addressing certain deities, as Mars, Iupiter, and Ianus, and all the gods (*si deus, si dea es*), with supplications, ritual processions, and sacrifices, to protect his family, his cattle, and his crops, and to ward off the hostile spirits that sent maladies.[45] When disease came, appeals were made to the divinities, and various remedies were used with magic incantations. Of the many remedies used, the several kinds of cabbage (*brassica*) were most prominent, and their dietetic and therapeutic merits were extolled as panaceas for both ills and injuries (Pliny, *op. cit.,* xx, 78). It is surmised that a monograph of Chrysippos,[46] a Knidian physician, was the source of Cato's confidence in the cabbage (*op. cit.,* chs. 156-158), especially as he used similar prescriptions, consisting of cabbage with water for fistulas, with honey for sores (Pliny, *op.*

---

[45] Fowler, in *ERE* x, 829.
[46] M. Wellman, in Pauly-Wissowa, iii, 2510, no. 15.

cit., xx, 93). If a bone was dislocated, a cabbage poultice was applied; and if this failed magic was used during manipulations. A green rod, four or five feet long, cleft through the middle, was used as a conjuring rod; and while the patient was held by two men, the following incantation was recited and repeated: "mœtas væta daries dardaries asiadarides una petes," or "motas væta daries dardares astataries dissunapiter." If this failed, another incantation suggestive of more violent manipulations was spoken and repeated: "huat hauat huat ista pista sista dannabo dannaustra," or "huat haut haut istasis tarsis ardannabou dannaustra" (Cato, *op. cit.,* 160; cf. Pliny, *op. cit.,* xx, 33-36).[47] Other sources of information concerning the use of remedies with magic are found in the *de Medicamentis* of Marcellus, probably intended for home use; the later *Theriaca* and *Alexipharmica,* poems of Nikandros; the long passage on snakes in the poem of Lucan (ix, 607-937); and the detailed compilation by Pliny (*op. cit.,* xviii-xxxvi) of the many remedies of his day, the beliefs concerning them, the manner of preparation, and their use with magic and incantations. The efficacy of these remedies for cures, in many instances, depended on the purity of the person gathering and administering them, this duty often being deputed to a boy or girl, or to the Vestals (*ib.,* xxvi, 60).

Healing in general.

When a Roman was ill, the auspices and soothsayers (Pliny, *Epistolæ,* ii, 20, 2 ff.) were consulted. Diviners studied the signs of the heavens, the conjunction of planets, the constellations, the movements of the clouds, the breeze in the trees, the action of song-birds, the man-

[47] Heim, *Incantamenta Magica Græca Latina,* pp. 533-534; also *ib.,* in *JCP,* Supplement, 1893, xix, 463-565; F. Skutsch, "Addenda et Corrigenda," in *ib.,* 565-568.

ner in which fowls took their grain, and the conduct of
domestic animals and bees; or they examined the entrails
of sacrificial animals, especially the formation of the
liver. The least circumstance in nature might be an important guide to the proper manner of treating the sick.
Other forms of magic were used, as 'words of power,'
incantations, songs, chants, symbolism, substitution of a
victim, 'binding and loosing,' analogies, sympathy, talismans, and amulets. There were many popular beliefs,
e.g., that the foot of Cæsar had healing power, as when
Vespasian cured blindness and restored a cripple by
placing his foot upon the suppliants (Tacitus, *op. cit.*, iv,
81; Suetonius, *Vita Vespasiani*, 7). Kissing as a means of
cure is obscurely mentioned, and a blind woman is reputed to have been cured by kissing Hadrian's knee.[48]
Geodes, aëtites, or eagle-stones, were supposed to possess
magic powers and facilitate propagation and healing.
Attached to a woman or placed beneath the skin of an
animal, they prevented miscarriage; but it was necessary
to remove them at the time of parturition, else it could
not take place (Pliny, *Hist. Nat.*, xxxvi, 39). Dreams were
highly esteemed by the Romans, and persons seriously
ill were often brought to the atrium or peristyle of the
house, where they were given a sleeping potion in the
hope of exciting a dream that would convey indications of
a method of cure. Constellations were believed to have
the good and bad qualities of the mythical beings whom
they represented, and thus to influence human life, as
when the serpent in the northern heavens (the constellation Ophiuchus) was held to be the author of cures, because the reptile was sacred to Æsculapius.[49] Hydrotherapy was always considered of great value among the

---

[48] Weinreich, *Antike Heilungswunder*, p. 73.
[49] Cumont, *op. cit.*, p. 173; also cf. Hyginus, *Astronomica*, ii, 14,
for the identification of this constellation with the god.

Romans, who not only frequented hot and cold baths in the city, but sought the medicinal fountains of the provinces over which nymphs and deities presided, and near which sacred serpents often lived. The springs at Tibur were popular, and Augustus resorted to hot sulphur wells, the Aquæ Abulæ, where were, at a later time, temples to Isis, Hygia, and Apollo, as well as a stately bathhouse.

Æsculapius and charlatans.

Upon his arrival in Rome, Æsculapius had become the chief healing divinity of the State; and his worship initiated a new epoch in the medical history of the city as being the first to care for sporadic disease and offer healing to the individual. Apollo had been a healing deity in the broader sense of an averter of pestilence, but it is believed that his function of actual healing was not developed until long after Æsculapius was settled in Rome. The cults of other foreign deities who were known as healers, cults in which healing was incidental or a minor part of their activities, reached Rome from time to time; while claimants of divine rank, reputed healers, charlatans, and impostors, masquerading under their own or under Greek characters, often using the name of Æsculapius, and pretending to his methods, practiced healing in Rome and claimed the patronage of the people. The foreign cults that practiced healing had each its own rituals and ceremonies; and, at least until the second century A.D., when Roman citizens were no longer restrained from officiating in these rites, they were conducted by native priests, with whom secrecy was habitual in the use of divination, in the mysteries of their magic, and in their modes of healing. The details of cultic practice do not appear to have been disclosed and cannot be definitely stated, but allusions by satirists and other

writers, and inscriptions of late date, afford ample proof
that the methods followed at Rome were essentially those
of the Orient (Festus, p. 110). All information obtainable
indicates that the chief features of their healing practice
consisted in the use of divination, the dream-oracle (incubation) with official interpretation by *coniectores,* and
sacerdotal magic with material remedies.

Divination.

Cicero's study of divination and dreams shows that the
Romans held the same views concerning them as did the
Greeks; that they were nearly akin, divinely inspired, and
prophetic. Cicero (*de Div.,* i, 30) quotes Poseidonios as
imagining that men might dream in three ways under the
impulse given by the gods; (*a*) the mind intuitively perceives things by the relation which they bear to the
deities; (*b*) the perception arises from the fact that the
air is full of immortal spirits in whom all signs of truth
are stamped and visible; and (*c*) the divinities themselves converse with sleepers, especially before death,
since the soul, when disentangled from the cares of the
body, perceives forewarnings of the future. Divination by
dreams was similar to the presentiments which happen
to the diviner when awake, and consisted in the ability
to discern and express the signs given by the gods to man
as portents; while interpretation was the power of re-
vealing those things which the deities signify in dreams
(*ib.,* ii, 63). Evidence of the antiquity of the dream-oracle
in Rome is afforded by Vergil in relating the consultation
of King Latinus with his prophetic sire, Faunus, in his
sanctuary at Tibur. Servius (*ad Æneidem,* vii, 85-92), in
commenting on this passage, defines incubation,[50] and
Tertullian (*de Anima,* 94) called those who sleep in
temples for dreams "incubatores fanorum."

[50] "Incubare dicuntur hi qui dormiunt ad accipienda responsa."

Incubation.

Temple-sleep, or incubation, as practiced by the cults was preceded by ceremonial purification and by fasting from wine and food. Pallets for the sick were placed in the porticoes of the temples; and after the usual sacrifice the priest offered a prayer, and the patients slept.[51] In Greece, and probably in Rome, the patients were visited at some time during the night by a representative of the god and by attendants with the sacred animals; and possibly a few words were passed concerning the disease, or the disordered part of the body was touched or anointed, or licked by the serpents. Celsus states (Origenes *contra* Celsum, iii, 24) that both Greeks and Barbarians asserted that they had seen, and still saw the deity daily, in his own person, healing the sick, succoring men, and foretelling the future. In the morning the dreams and visions of the night were reported and were interpreted by the priests as divine monitions for effecting a cure. There were always suggestions of the marvellous powers of the divinity, supplemented by directions for the use of supposedly potent remedies, which were considered as 'the hands of the god,' to be used internally and externally, with baths, rubbings with ointments, diet, and other hygienic regimen. The cures were announced as illustrations of the superhuman powers of the deity and were spread abroad as miracles of healing, serving as pious tales to strengthen the faith of the clientele and to forward the propaganda of the cult. It would appear that in the Roman practice there was less of personal healing by the god and more use of symbolic magic and suggestion than in Greece. Those who were not cured at once remained under the charge of the priests for treatment or further temple-sleep. It has been claimed that many

[51] Hamilton, *Incubation*, pp. 5, 63-68.

of the priests practicing in the temple of Æsculapius, and especially in that of Serapis, were educated physicians.

Laying-on of hands.

Sacerdotal magic with suggestion was common to all Oriental cults and was doubtless freely used at Rome in connection with material remedies. The laying-on of hands was regarded as a most efficient means of transferring the divine power for healing, especially in the cults of Æsculapius and Sabazius. The patient was approached and the right hand was applied, the open right hand, or thumb and two fingers open and the other two closed, as often used in blessing and portrayed on vases, being potent, while the left hand had a maleficent influence. The position of the hands and legs was important among the Romans both in council and in religion. In council, at sacrifices, and during prayers, no one was permitted to sit with legs crossed or hands clasped, as such posture impeded what was going on (Pliny, *op. cit.*, xxviii, 17). The touching of sacred objects, the altar, or the image of the god frequently conveyed to the individual the power of healing himself. Flagellation was used in the cults of Faunus and Magna Mater for the februation of women, to drive away hostile spirits which prevented pregnancy.[52]

Sacred serpents and dogs.

Sacred serpents and dogs were kept at the healing temples of Rome (Festus, p. 110), and their ministrations were highly esteemed, the licking of ulcers and other external diseases by the tongue of either animal being regarded as particularly efficacious. Women resorted to the temples for the relief of sterility, and there were several legends of impregnation by the god in the form

[52] Fowler, *op. cit.*, p. 104.

of a serpent, as in the tradition that Atia, the mother of
Augustus Cæsar, asserted that he had been engendered
by intercourse which she thought she had had with
Apollo, in the form of a serpent, while she slept in his
temple (Dion Kassios, xlv, 2; cf. Suetonius, *Vita Augustæ*,
94; Aulus Gellius, VI, i, 3; Livy, xxvi, 19). Pliny states
(*op. cit.*, xxix, 22) that the sacred Æsculapian serpents
were first brought from Epidauros and were commonly
raised in the houses of Rome to such an extent, if they
had not been kept down by frequent conflagrations, it
would have been impossible to make headway against
their rapid increase. The original Epidaurian reptiles
were harmless, but Pliny says that these were water-
snakes and venomous, and that their livers were used to
remedy the ill effects of their bites. Other parts of the
serpents were also used as remedies. The serpent, as
dwelling in a hole in the ground, and often under the
house, came to be regarded as the guardian spirit of the
household, and hence as symbolizing Genius and Iuno.[53]

Votive offerings.

Those who had been healed at the temples not only
paid fees when able, but left *donaria* of various kinds as
an expression of their gratitude, these objects covering
a wide range from works of art and inscribed tablets to
relics and silver, bronze, or terra-cotta models of the
parts diseased.

Greek medicine in Rome.

While religious healing was gaining popularity among
the citizens of Rome, the germs of more scientific methods
of treatment of disease had been transplanted from Knidos, Kos, and Alexandria by many Greek physicians.

[53] J. A. MacCulloch, "Serpent-Worship (Introductory and Primitive)," in *ERE* xi, 405; also Wissowa, *op. cit.* (ed. 1902), p. 24.

Notwithstanding the violent hatred of the Elder Cato and other Romans toward the earlier Hellenic doctors, and despite the cold reception given them, they came in increasing numbers, many of them gaining respect, influence, and popularity. It appears that the great majority of the educated Romans eventually preferred their traditional medical treatment or the physicians, such as they were, to the religious healing of the temples, which they regarded with scepticism and scorn, often as being too plebeian for personal patronage, at least until long after the establishment of the Empire. These Greek doctors had their offices on the streets and in the Forum, and accepted patients at their homes. During the second and third centuries A.D., the cult of Æsculapius gained materially in the estimation of the better classes of Rome, and it became a common practice for the wealthier families to seek the aid of the Greek healing god elsewhere, particularly at his sanctuaries of Epidauros and Pergamon.

Scepticism toward cult-healing.

That there was a widespread scepticism toward all religious medicine among the more intelligent citizens of Rome, especially among the followers of the Stoic philosophy, is evidenced by the concluding remarks of Cicero on the subject of dreams and divination: "Now whence comes this distinction between true dreams and false? And if true dreams are sent by God, whence do the false ones rise?—What can be more ignorant than to excite the minds of mortals by false and deceitful visions?—What authority is there for making such a distinction as, 'God did this, and nature that?' " (op. cit., ii, 62). "How, then, can it be reasonable for invalids to seek healing from an interpreter of dreams rather than from a physician? Can Æsculapius or Serapis, by a dream, prescribe to us a cure for weak health? And cannot Neptune do the same for pilots? Or will Minerva give medicine without a doctor, and the Muses not give dreamers knowledge of writing, reading, and other arts? But if healing of feeble health were given, all these things which I have mentioned would be given. Since they are not given, neither is medicine; and if that be the case, all authority of dreams is at an end" (*ib.*, ii, 59). "Let this divination of dreams be rejected with the rest. For, to speak truly, that superstition, spreading through the world, has oppressed the intellectual energies of nearly all men, and has seized upon the weakness of humanity. This I have argued in my treatise 'On the Nature of the Gods,' and I especially labored to prove it in this discussion 'On Divination.' For I thought I should be doing a great benefit to myself and to my countrymen if I could eradicate that belief" (*ib.*, ii, 72). Cicero expresses himself definitely in respect to religious healing: "I believe that those who recover from illness are more indebted to the care of Hippocrates than to the power of Æsculapius" (*de Nat. Deor.*, iii, 38).

PART II: THE HEALING DEITIES

THE list here presented includes the names of the chief deities who were concerned with the healing art in ancient Rome, and whose cults and activities are considered in the following sections. The classification adopted is an arbitrary one which has appeared to be the most convenient for the discussion of their special functions in connection with the sick and the preservation of health.[54]

---

[54] In a Supplement to this chapter are listed a number of minor deities and *numina* representing the lesser phases of divine activity within the spheres of greater gods, and illustrating the subdivision of functions ascribed to subordinate divinities.

I. Roman Deities.

(A) *Deities of General Functions.*

Angerona (or	Fecunditas	Picus
Angeronia)	Feronia	Salus (or Hygia)
Angitia	Fessona	Saturnus
Anna Perenna	Fortuna	Silvanus
Bona Dea	Hercules	Soranus
Caia Cæcilia (or	Iupiter	Strenia
Tanaquil)	Liber	Tiberinus
Clitumnus	Mars	Vacuna
Fascinus	Meditrina	
Fauna (Fatua,	Minerva	
or Fatuella)	Neptunus	
Faunus (Fatuus,	Nortia	
Fatuellus, or	Picumnus and	
Inuus)	Pilumnus	

(B) *Child-birth Deities.*

Carmentis (or	Genita Mana	Natio (or
Carmenta)	Iuno (or Iuno	Nascio)
Comitia	Lucina)	Nixi dii
Diana	Iuturna	Ops
Egeria	Mater Matuta	Virbius

(C) *Underworld Deities.*

Carna   Dis (Dis Pater, or Orcus)   Lares   ʹProserpina

(D) *Deities of Disease.*

Angina   Cloacina   Febris   Mefitis   Scabies

(E) *Deities with minor functions related to healing,*
but not discussed.

Abonius	Honos	Pavor	Spes
Concordia	Orbona	Pax	Victoria
Felicitas	Pallor	Pudicitia	Virtus

II. Foreign Deities.

Adonis	Hygia	Mithras
Æsculapius	Isis	Sabazius
Apollo	Magna Mater	Serapis

Note.—The cults of many of these deities—not only Roman but Græco-Roman and Oriental—extended to the confines of the Latin provinces; but usually they continued true to the Roman types, though frequently syncretized with local gods. For details, see Toutain, *op. cit.*

I. Roman Deities.

(A) *Deities of General Functions.*

ANGERONA (OR ANGERONIA)

Angeron(i)a was an ancient Roman goddess whose functions had become so obscure that her real character was practically unknown. A statue in the temple of Volupia representing her with her mouth bound with a fillet (Pliny, *op. cit.*, iii, 9) probably implied ignorance of her true nature, but it led to the fancy that she symbolized fear and the silence inculcated by the early Romans concerning religious matters. Hence she was supposed to have been the guardian divinity of the city of Rome and to keep inviolate its secret and sacred name; while, through a popular etymology Angerona was regarded as another name for Angitia, and some believed she was called Angerona because Romans afflicted with the disease called *angina* (quinsy, or *angor*) were cured after making vows to her (Macrobius, *Saturnalia*, i, 10; Paulus, pp. 8, 17),[55] and she was invoked for relief from plagues (*a pellendis angoribus*).[56] As a matter of fact, since her festival was celebrated on December 21,[57] she was prob-

[55] Le Clerc, *Histoire de la médecine*, ed. 1702, p. 65.
[56] Wissowa, *op. cit.*, ed. 1912, p. 241.
[57] Fowler, *op. cit.*, pp. 274-275.

ably, in origin, the goddess of the winter solstice, and her name should be interpreted as 'The Up-Bringer (of the Sun).'

ANGITIA

ANGITIA, though a primitive Italian goddess (especially Marsian), was reputed to be of Greek origin, the sister of both Kirke and Medeia, and identical in character with the latter (Servius, *op. cit.*, vii, 750). She was a beneficent deity of healing, skilled in knowledge of medicinal properties of plants, and the discoverer of their poisons and their antidotes, besides being a snake-charmer and using her magic to cure the people of venomous bites. The chief seat of her cult was in the Lucus Angitiæ, on the shores of Lake Fucinus, which abounded with healing herbs (Vergil, *Æneid*, vii, 758-759); but after the conquest of the Marsians and the neighboring tribes (304 B.C.), her worship did not find favor in the Roman State pantheon, though she continued to be reverenced by individuals even in Imperial times.[58] Her name, which is probably connected etymologically with the Latin *indiges*,[59] appears in the plural in an inscription (*CIL* ix, 3074) from Sulmo, in the Pælignian region, in the *Dis Ancitibus* of an inscription (*CIL* ix, 3515) from Turfo, in the Vestinian district, and possibly in the Acetus of the Inguvine Tables (II *a*, 14); and the goddess was probably identical with the Oscan Anagtia Diiva, as well as the Pælignian Anceta.

ANNA PERENNA

ANNA PERENNA was an ancient Italian goddess of the year,[60] and thus came to be regarded as the giver of

---

[58] Le Clerc, *loc. cit.;* also Wissowa, *op. cit.*, pp. 49-50.

[59] Walde, *Etymologisches Wörterbuch der lateinischen Sprache*, p. 383.

[60] For hypotheses concerning her name, see Walde, *ib.*, pp. 44-45.

health and plenty, and as one of the earliest deities to watch over the life, health, and prosperity of the adult.[61] Nevertheless, her origin and identity were obscure, whence she was the subject of several speculative myths. To these Ovid refers (*op. cit.*, iii, 543-696), relating one story that she was Anna, the sister of Dido, who came to Latium and there met Æneas; another, that she was a nymph, a daughter of Atlas; a third, that equated her with the Greek Themis; and, lastly, that she was an old woman (*anus*) who befooled Mars. Her festival was held on March 15 (the beginning of the Roman civil year) in the Campus Martius near the Tiber with the license common to New Year celebrations, and was attended by the plebs, who paired off and passed the day in drinking, dancing, and carousing (*ib.*, iii, 523-540).[62]

BONA DEA

BONA DEA was a renowned but mysterious goddess whose name was not otherwise identified, although she was generally popular and greatly beloved. Originally she was probably an earth-spirit who gave health and blessings; and developing under a variety of names and aspects with the indefiniteness of Roman deities, she represented chiefly the earth and its bounties, absorbing the names and cults of other divinities.[63] It is also suggested that, in the beginning, she was an attribute of Fauna, with whom she became identified as Bona Dea Fauna; and evolving an individuality under this title, the surname finally supplanted that of Fauna, though it is sometimes urged that the development was in the reverse order.

[61] Hartung, *Die Religion der Römer*, ii, 229; also Kissel, in *Janus*, 1848, iii, 596.

[62] Fowler, *op. cit.*, pp. 50 ff.

[63] *Ib.*, p. 106.

Bona Dea was essentially a deity of women, symbolizing their fertility; and was very nearly akin to Iuno and
Genius. She was closely associated with Mater Matuta,
Ops, Terra, and Tellus, and was originally of a nature
similar to Silvanus, Pales, and Ceres, though later she
lost her rusticity in her organized city worship.[64] The
Greek Damia was identified with Bona Dea, and the rites
of her worship were so similar that the cult usurped the
name, thus assisting in eliminating that of Fauna, while
the priestess of Bona Dea was called 'Damiatrix' (Paulus,
p. 68).

Bona Dea, the symbol of health and life, was a prophetic deity with an oracle and practiced healing. Her
chief temple in Rome, on the slope of the Aventine beneath a large rock, was a sort of herbarium, stored with
medicinal herbs; and sacred serpents were kept there,
but neither myrtle nor wine was allowed in her shrines
owing to the legends concerning Fauna, except that wine
was sometimes taken there in honey vases under the name
of milk (Macrobius, op. cit., I, xii, 25 f.). The temples
were cared for by women; women conducted all cultic
ceremonies, and only women took part, but the cures were
not limited to the female sex, since inscriptions show that
ailments of men were also treated.[64] In her therapeutic
aspects, Bona Dea was identified with the Greek Panakeia, while as a healer of eyes she was called Oculata
Lucifera, and of the ears, Bona Dea Aurita (CIL v, 759;
vi, 68). The great festival of Bona Dea was held on May
1,[65] but she was also honored at the festivals of Faunus,
especially at the Faunalia Rustica on December 5, which
was celebrated on the Insula Tiberina.[66] Bona Dea likewise enjoyed a worship with sacrifice that did not appear

[64] Fowler, op. cit., pp. 103-104.
[65] Ib., p. 101; also Wissowa, op. cit., pp. 216-219.
[66] Fowler, op. cit., pp. 255-256.

THE HEALING GODS

on the calendar, this taking place early in December, on the third or fourth, in the house of a prætor or consul, not in a temple, and being attended by vestals and women only. This was probably a survival of an old custom when the wife of the chief of the community, her daughters, and other matrons made sacrifice of a young pig, or pigs, to the goddess of fertility.[67] It was originally a decorous rite and so continued until the sacrilege of Clodius, who invaded the ceremonies in female attire, wearing the mitre; but under the Empire it was accompanied by orgies to which Juvenal refers (*op. cit.*, ii, 86 ff.; vi, 313 ff.). Bona Dea may also be the same as *Cubrar matrer*, 'Good Mother,' of a short Umbrian inscription found at Fossato di Vico.[68]

CAIA CÆCILIA (OR TANAQUIL)

CAIA CÆCILIA, the wife of Tarquinius Priscus, was apotheosized after her death and became a healing goddess. A statue, reputed to be of her, stood in the temple of Semo Sancus Dius Fidius on the Quirinal as the ideal Roman matron, and in her girdle the people found healing herbs (Festus, p. 234).

CLITUMNUS

CLITUMNUS, an Umbrian river-god and an oracular deity who was highly revered, had a sanctuary near a spring in a forest at the head-waters of a stream of the same name (Pliny, *Epist.*, viii, 8). His cult flourished especially during the Empire, and many votive tablets have been found expressing the gratitude of those to whom he had revealed the future and given aid in illness.[69]

[67] Fowler, *op. cit.*, p. 254; also Wissowa, *op. cit.*, p. 60.

[68] Conway, *The Italic Dialects*, p. 610; also Bücheler, *Umbrica*, p. 173.

[69] Wissowa, *op. cit.*, p. 224; also Hopf, *Die Heilgötter und Heilstätten des Altertums*, p. 44.

FASCINUS

FASCINUS, a Roman divinity representing the phallus, was identified with Mutunus Tutunus and often regarded as merely another form of Lar.[70] His cult was similar to that of the Lares; and as they guarded the property of the State, he watched over the home. He was a symbol of the power most efficacious in averting evil influences, and was the protector against sorcery and malignant demons; while as a healing deity he protected the members of the family from illness and women until they had conceived. Children wore his image around their necks to avoid witchcraft and envy, and he was invoked just before the marriage ceremony, by young women, who sacrificed their maiden clothing to him.[71] The State set up a statue in his honor.

FAUNA (FATUA, OR FATUELLA)

FAUNA was an ancient Italian goddess, described as the wife, sister, or daughter of Faunus (Fauna Fauni), and a deity of women as Faunus was of men. According to legend, she was beaten to death by Faunus with myrtle branches because, as his wife, she drank to excess; or, as his sister or daughter and a virgin, she would not drink wine and submit to his incestuous love.[72] She was regarded as the symbol of the genii or *Manes* who give life; and, in another legend, was impregnated by Faunus in the form of a serpent.[73]

Fauna, personifying the earth and its fertility, was originally an agricultural and prophetic divinity who bestowed health and blessing through her oracle. She was closely related to Ops and Mater Matuta, and was iden-

---

[70] Kissel, in *Janus*, 1848, iii, 628-629.
[71] Wissowa, *op. cit.*, p. 243.
[72] Fowler, *op. cit.*, p. 103.
[73] Preller, *op. cit.*, p. 340.

tified not only with Tellus, Terra, and the Greek Damia, but especially with Bona Dea, so that it was supposed that, the name clinging to her and finally supplanting her own, she was regarded as the same, her cult becoming known as that of the 'Good Goddess.'[74] Fauna shared the honors of Faunus's festival, the Faunalia Rustica, on December 5,[75] and in so far as Fatuus was regarded as identical with Faunus, she was also known as Fatua and Fatuella.

FAUNUS (FATUUS, FATUELLUS, OR INUUS)

FAUNUS ('Kindly One,' 'speaker, or foreteller'), an ancient Italian deity of the woodland, pastures, and of shepherds, identified with the old god Tellumo ('earth') and with the Greek Pan, was one of the legendary founders of the Roman religion. He had a complex character, and neither his origin nor his development has been clearly followed or definitely interpreted. Faunus appears in various aspects and under several names, apparently of other independent divinities with whom he was syncretized or, more probably, whose characters were so nearly akin that he was identified with them and assumed their names.[76] He was regarded as dangerous to women and children; and if offended, he would call upon Silvanus and his woodland nymphs, or upon the Fauni, who caused fright and panic, mental disorders and cramps, and in this aspect he was known as Incubus, and Ficarius (Augustine, *de Civitate Dei*, xv, 23).[77] In his capacity as an earth-god, he was said, in one legend, to have assumed the form of a serpent when he impregnated Fauna.[78]

[74] Wissowa, *op. cit.*, pp. 216-219.
[75] Fowler, *op. cit.*, p. 256.
[76] *Ib.*, pp. 257 ff.
[77] Kissel, in *Janus*, 1848, iii, 609.
[78] Preller, *op. cit.*, p. 340.

Faunus was the second State deity of healing and a prophetic divinity, giving his divinations in verse; and being known, therefore, as Fatuus[79] (Servius, *op. cit.*, vi, 775) and Fatuellus,[80] he practiced healing with his oracle and by the use of the magic remedies of his father, Picus. His most celebrated sanctuary was in a sacred grove at Tibur, where was a sulphur spring over which the nymph Albunea (said to be of divine origin) presided. Those seeking his counsel lay down on a sheep-skin, and the fumes from the spring caused hallucinations which were interpreted as the revelations of the god (Vergil, *op. cit.*, vii, 81-91; Ovid, *op. cit.*, iv, 660 ff.). A similar healing-oracle shrine was located at the hot springs of Abona, southwest of Padua, where many inscriptions to the spring-god Abonius have been found (Lucan, vii, 193). Faunus also possessed a sacred grove on the Aventine, and on the Cælian a circular temple surrounded with columns. Introduced into Rome in 196 B.C., Faunus averted a pestilence and unfruitfulness, whence, in recognition of his services, a temple was vowed to him, erected on the Insula Tiberina, and dedicated in 194 B.C. (Livy, xxxiii, 42; xxxiv, 53). His festival, the Faunalia Rustica, was held there on December 5 (Horace, *op. cit.*, iii, 18).[81]

One of the oldest Roman feasts was the Lupercalia, celebrated on February 15 (Ovid, *op. cit.*, ii, 268).[82] Chiefly because of its name, it has been assumed by some that a god Lupercus was thus honored; but it is generally agreed that there was no such deity, and that the festival received its name from the priests of Faunus, who were known as Luperci (also called priests of Pan).[83] The ritual indi-

[79] Cf. Fowler, *op. cit.*, p. 259.
[80] Wissowa, *op. cit.*, p. 211.
[81] Fowler, *op. cit.*, p. 256.
[82] *Ib.*, pp. 310-321.
[83] Wissowa, *op. cit.*, pp. 208-216.

424 THE HEALING GODS

cates purification and expiation with the magic favoring
and attending impregnation. The characteristic features
of the ceremony were the Luperci (called *creppi*,[84] 'he-
goats,' Festus, p. 57), young men, wearing only a goat-
skin girdle, who ran around the Palatine hill in opposite
directions and struck, with thongs of goat-skin, all whom
they met, especially the matrons, who, when sterile, sub-
mitted their backs to the lash (Ovid, *op. cit.*, ii, 425-428,
445-448), or, placing themselves in the way, held out their
hands to the nimble Luperci (Juvenal, *op. cit.*, ii, 140-
142). This was the 'februation of women,' which was supposed to drive away hostile spirits that prevented fruit-
fulness and failure in their duty to the family and State
(Ovid, *op. cit.*, ii, 31-32, 427 ff.; v, 101).[85] Because of this
rite Faunus received the name of another god, Februus,
and appears as the god of impregnation whose priests
come into relation with Iuno Lanuvina as the goddess of
conception.[86] Faunus was likewise identified with another
early Italian divinity Inuus (Livy, i, 5), probably a deity
presiding first over the coition of animals, and then over
conjugal union of human beings.[87]

FECUNDITAS

FECUNDITAS was an abstract conception representing fertility and was appealed to as an independent divinity for
impregnation. Sacrifices were made to her after successful parturition, as in the case of Poppæa on her return to
Rome after the birth of her child by Nero;[88] and, in celebration of this event, the Senate built a temple to the
goddess in A.D. 63 (Tacitus, *Ann.*, xv, 23).

[84] Fowler, *op. cit.*, pp. 262, 318.
[85] *Ib.*, pp. 179, 302, 318-321. *Note.*—The Luperci were not abolished
until the time of Anastasius in the sixth century A.D.
[86] Wissowa, *op. cit.*, p. 185.
[87] H. Steuding, in Roscher, ii, 262-263.
[88] Wissowa, *op. cit.*, p. 336.

FERONIA

FERONIA was originally a deity of the Sabines and other central Italian, non-Latian tribes who presided over the harvest and markets,[89] while at Præneste, where her festival was celebrated on the same day as that of Fortuna, she represented fertility and plenty. She was beloved by the freed slaves (Servius, *op. cit.*, viii, 564); by some she was considered a goddess of liberty (Livy, xxii, 1); and inscriptions declare her to have been a nymph of springs in Central Italy.[90] Like Febris, she appeared as a mediator between man and the deities of light and darkness according as they purified for life and health or for death; and she brought healing by fire, though it differed from that of Febris in being external.[91]

Feronia was a goddess of Capena, in Etruria; and her principal sanctuary, in the Lucus Capenatis or Feroniæ, at the foot of Mount Soracte, where her priests, like those of Soranus, walked with bare feet over living coals unhurt (Vergil, *op. cit.*, vii, 800; Strabo, V, ii, 9 = p. 226 C; Pliny, *Hist. Nat.*, iii, 51), was attended by Sabines, Etruscans, and Latins, becoming so rich that it attracted the attention of Hannibal, who plundered it in 211 B.C. (Livy, xxvi, 11). She also had a celebrated temple at Terracina, as well as at Trebula Mutusca, in Sabine territory.[92] After the conquest of the Veii by Rome, she became a State deity and was given a temple in the Campus Martius; and in 217 B.C., during the Punic War, the women of Rome made a collection for her (Livy, xxii, 1). Her festival, Feroniæ *in campo*, was held on November 13.[92]

[89] Fowler, *op. cit.*, p. 199.
[90] Wissowa, *op. cit.*, pp. 285-286.
[91] Kissel, in *Janus*, 1848, iii, 616-617.
[92] Fowler, *op. cit.*, pp. 252-254.

FESSONA

FESSONA, a goddess who gave aid to the weary and restored their strength, was invoked for health and strength by those having chronic and exhausting diseases (Augustine, *op. cit.*, iv, 21).

FORTUNA

FORTUNA, an ancient Italian goddess of extra-Roman origin, who presided over an old and famous oracle, seems to have been originally a deity of women, her character as Fors Fortuna, the fickle goddess of Fortune, being a later development. This view is supported by the oldest known inscriptions to her at Præneste; one ('nationu cratia'=*nationis cratia, CIL* xiv, 2863) from a matron in gratitude for child-birth,[93] which mentions her as the first-born daughter of Iupiter;[94] and another in which she is represented as suckling two infants (Cicero, *de Div.*, ii, 41, 85)[95] (popularly, but probably erroneously, regarded as Iupiter and Iuno); and it may possibly be strengthened by the etymology of the name which is connected with the Latin *fero*, 'bear,' 'birth.'[96]

Servius Tullius, who considered himself a favorite of the goddess (Ovid, *op. cit.*, vi, 573 ff.), erected two temples to her in Rome, one on the banks of the Tiber and the other, to Fors Fortuna, in the Forum Boarium (*ib.*, vi, 775 ff.), the latter shrine containing a veiled wooden statue assumed to be Pudicitia (Festus, p. 242), the protectress of the purity of the marriage relation. Another temple to her as Fortuna Muliebris was located at the fourth mile-stone on the Via Latina, and none but women who were living in their first and only marriage (*uni-*

[93] Fowler, *op. cit.*, p. 168, note.
[94] *Ib.*, pp. 166, 223-225.
[95] Wissowa, *op. cit.*, p. 259.
[96] Fowler, *op. cit.*, p. 167; also Walde, *op. cit.*, pp. 284-285, 309, 311.

viræ) were permitted to enter this sanctuary and to touch the statue (Livy, x, 23). Her temple in the ox-market was near one dedicated to Mater Matuta, with whom Fortuna was closely related, and their festivals, the Matralia, were held at the same place on the same day, June 11 (Ovid, *op. cit.*, vi, 569).[97]

The chief seats of the earlier worship of Fortuna were at Antium and Præneste. As Fortuna Primigenia, she had a splendid temple at Præneste, where she presided over an oracle, foretelling the future by sortilege (*CIL* xiv, 2989; Cicero, *op. cit.*, ii, 41). Here she was the object of special devotion from mothers and from women expecting children and praying for an easy, safe delivery.[98] It is surmised that Primigenia was originally an independent deity presiding over the first parturition. This cult at Præneste was not acceptable to the Romans until after the second Punic War, when Fortuna Primigenia was brought to the city (*circa* 199 B.C.), a temple being erected in her honor on the Quirinal in 196 B.C. (Livy, xxix, 36; xxxiv, 53).

Fortuna had many aspects and titles. As Fortuna Virginalis the dresses of maidens were dedicated to her (Arnobius, *adversus Nationes*, ii, 67); as Fortuna Virginensis she was worshipped by newly married women; and as Fortuna Virilis she gave good luck to women in their relations with men (Ovid, *op. cit.*, iv, 149 ff.). She was called Fortuna Balneorum; as Fortuna Salutaris (*CIL* vi, 184, 201, 202) she was connected with health and healing, as is clearly shown by the votive inscription of Godesberg (*CIL* xiii, 2, 7994), 'Fortunis Salutaribus Æsculapio Hygiæ,' and as Fortuna Mala she had an altar on the Esquiline (Cicero, *de Nat. Deor.*, iii, xxv). Fortuna was equated with the Etruscan goddess Nortia, and

[97] Fowler, *op. cit.*, pp. 154-156.
[98] *Ib.*, p. 167.

under that name was adored at Volsinii. Her festival, which was popular with the plebs, freedmen, and slaves, was held on June 24.[99]

HERCULES

HERCULES, an old Italian divinity of Tibur, one of the *di novensides*, was believed by the Romans to be, in some fashion, a survival of the same religious conception that was represented by the ancient divinities Semo Sancus and Dius Fidius (Ovid, *op. cit.*, vi, 213), fidelity, the sanctity of the oath, and possibly the male principle expressed in the conception of Genius, very nearly akin to, or impersonations of, certain aspects of Iupiter.[100] In this conception of his character, as a deity of men, Hercules was placed in opposition to Iuno, the female principle, and all women were excluded from his worship. As the representative of the male, he was honored at births, a table (*mensa*) being prepared for him in the *atrium* (Servius, *Eclogæ*, iv, 62). Men made pledges and swore by their Genius, by Iupiter by the oath *medius fidius*, or by Hercules in the open air in the form *me hercule*, these being the synonymous, familiar forms of oath.[101]

In the Oscan Tabula Agnonensis (lines 13, 41),[102] a statue and an altar are mentioned as set up for 'Hereklúí Kerríúí' ('Cerealian Hercules') in a grove of Ceres; and since she was a goddess of the fruitful earth, and other divinities recorded in this inscription were likewise connected with fertility, Hercules also must be conceived in this capacity.

[99] Fowler, *op. cit.*, pp. 161 ff.; and for further details concerning the goddess, see Wissowa, *op. cit.*, pp. 257-262; also W. W. Fowler, "Fortune (Roman)," in *ERE* vi, 98-99.

[100] Fowler, *Festivals*, pp. 137-138.

[101] *Ib.*, pp. 138-144.

[102] Conway, *op. cit.*, pp. 191-192.

The earliest appearance of Hercules at Rome was at the first *lectisternium,* in 399 B.C., when he, with other deities, was invoked to stay pestilence. He was the presiding divinity at healing springs, and inscriptions and votive tablets dedicated to him for his cures have been found at some of these places.[103] Hercules Domesticus guarded the welfare of homes and kept away all ills (*CIL* vi, 294-297, etc.).

Hercules, also called 'Salutifer' and 'Salutaris' (*CIL* vi, 237, 338 f.), was assimilated to the Greek Herakles, and was related to Silvanus (*CIL* vi, 288, 293, 295-297, 309-310, etc.) ; while the goddesses Febris and Orbona are said to have belonged to his retinue. He had two temples in Rome. The principal one, built in 82 B.C. by Sulla, was near the Circus Flaminius, and the worship there was similar to that of the Greek Herakles *Alexikakos,* the dedication being held on June 4; the other, a round shrine to Hercules Invictus, stood between the river and the Circus Maximus, near the Porta Trigemina,[104] dedicated by a festival held August 13. Hercules also received homage in the honors paid to Dius Fidius on June 5.

IUPITER

IUPITER, or Iuppiter, was the chief deity of the Roman pantheon, to whom, as the divine guardian of the city and State, the fair name and fame of Rome were entrusted. He was assimilated to the Greek Zeus and was associated with Iuno in a ritual relation, though not as a husband until Greek influences prevailed, when she was identified with Hera. In origin a sky-god, whence the eagle was sacred to him, his particular domain was the upper atmosphere and the heavens with its lightning and thunder, a conception which was common to all Italian

103 Hopf, *op. cit.,* p. 38.
104 Fowler, *op. cit.,* pp. 135, 201.

peoples. He developed, in one aspect, into a divinity of
justice, fidelity, and solemn contracts, witnessing oaths
taken in making treatises of State; this phase of his
character being represented by Dius Fidius, and he was
invoked by the common Roman oath *medius fidius.*[105] As
guardian of mankind, he gave his psychic emanation in
the form of the *numen* Genius (symbolizing the developed
powers and capacities of man) to every man as the divine
spirit which accompanied and guided him throughout his
life, comparable to the Iunones of women.[106] His temples
were on the summits of hills, the earliest in Rome being
a small shrine on the Capitoline, consecrated to him as
Iupiter Feretrius (Livy, i, 10); but this was overshadowed by the later temple on a different part of the
hill, dedicated to the triad, Iupiter, Iuno, and Minerva,
which became the center of the religious life of the nation,
the seat of the power of Iupiter and of the authority of
Rome.

Iupiter had broad general powers and many aspects
which were indicated by his various names, surnames,
and forms of cults. His functions extended to healing,
both in a general and specific sense, so that the mother
of a child who had been ill and confined to bed for many
months appealed to him "O Iupiter! who sendest and
removest terrible sufferings" (Horace, *Satiræ*, II, iii,
288-292). He had a temple on the Insula Tiberina, erected
in 196 B.C. (Livy, xxxiv, 53), at which he appeared as a
healer.[107] He was given the epithet 'Salutaris' (*CIL* xiii,
240).

The Ides of every month were sacred to him as being

[105] Fowler, *op. cit.*, pp. 138, 141; also *id., Religious Experience*, p.
130; Wissowa, *op. cit.*, p. 118.
[106] Kissel, in *Janus*, 1848, iii, 590.
[107] Bruzon, *La Médecine et les religions*, p. 135.

the nights of the full moon, and he was also honored at
many seasonal festivals.

LIBER (BACCHUS)

LIBER, a member of the oldest cycle of Roman gods and
the name of an ill-defined spirit, may have been an
emanation from, or a cult-title of, Iupiter, developing
into an independent deity, whose nature was overgrown
with Greek ideas and rites, but the Liber cult later became attached to that of Iupiter.[108] Primarily he appears
to have been a god of impregnation both of plants and
animals,[109] and he was honored by a phallus carried about
the country in a wagon (Varro, in Augustine, *op. cit.*,
vii, 21).

When in 496 B.C., on account of a famine, Demeter,
Dionysos, and Kore were brought to Rome, they were
Latinized by the names Ceres, Liber, and Libera, and a
temple, the 'ædes Cereria,' erected to them at the foot of
the Aventine, near the Circus Maximus, was dedicated
in 493 B.C. (Livy, iii, 55; xli, 28). The consort of Liber was
Libera; and their festival, the Liberalia, was held on
March 17.[110]

It was only after this identification with Dionysos that
Liber was associated with the culture of the vine, and his
character then underwent a change, so that the cult took
on mystic and orgiastic features which became familiar
under the more common cult name of Bacchus. When the
people had acquired a taste for sensationalism in religion

---

[108] Fowler, *Festivals*, pp. 54, 55, 338. *Note.*—In a list of eleven gods
on a bronze found in a Prænestine tomb, Leiber is mentioned as a
distinct divinity along with Iouos, Apolo, Minuerua, etc. (*CIL* xiv,
4105); and an archaic inscription from Pisaurum (*CIL* i, 174) has a
dedication 'Lebro' (Conway, *op. cit.*, pp. 318, 434).

[109] Walde, *op. cit.*, p. 426.

[110] Fowler, *op. cit.*, p. 54.

after the arrival of Magna Mater in Rome, these aspects were developed in the cult and were surreptiously introduced in many gatherings of its worshippers, finally leading to wild debaucheries in the frequent Bacchanalia which were exposed to the Senate in 186 B.C., the result being imposition of severe restrictions upon the cult and its Orphic and mystic ceremonies (Livy, xxxix, 18-19). Augustus organized a new cult of Liber, half Oriental and orgiastic, and erected a temple to the god on the heights of the Velia, near that of Magna Mater, which is referred to by Martial (I, lxx, 9). During the second century A.D., this cult played an important part in the secret cults of Isis, Magna Mater, and Mithras, and especially of Hekate during the third century.[111]

Healing was practiced in the name of the cult, and impotence, madness, bladder and venereal diseases are among those mentioned as being treated. The priests of Bacchus conducted offices for the sale of drugs and prayers to the god, one of which was situated in the Forum.[112]

MARS

MARS ranked next to Iupiter in the old Roman triad, as one of the three highest deities of the State; and as the great god of war he was equated with the Greek Ares. Originally he appears as a vegetation divinity to whom husbandmen prayed for the prosperity of their crops, and twice yearly (in March and October) sacrificed to Mars Silvanus ('Mars of the Woods') for the welfare of their cattle.[113] Cato (de Re Rustica, 141) makes a broader appeal, not only for the safety of his cattle and to prevent

[111] Wissowa, op. cit., pp. 297-304, 378.
[112] Bruzon, op. cit., p. 136.
[113] Frazer, The Scapegoat, pp. 229 ff.; Fowler, op. cit., pp. 41, 45-48, 64, 249.

bad weather and failure of his crops, but for defense against disease and the preservation of the health of his family.

Mars was the first of the State deities associated with health and healing, as a protector rather than a healer, since it was one of his duties to protect the people from epidemics, especially summer pestilence. He also sent such diseases, and thus, in the *Carmen Arvale*, he is entreated, "Neither let plague (nor) ruin fall on more; be sated, O fierce Mars" (*CIL* i, 28). His priests, twelve in number, called 'Salii' ('Leapers'), were expellers of evil, whose rites of leaping, dancing, and smiting their shields with their staffs were intended, in part at least, to put to flight the host of demons that lurked in the houses, temples, and other edifices, for transference to scapegoats, and to counteract all maleficent activities which injured the prospects of the farmer.[113] It is asserted that in his civil capacity he was a seer or prophet who diagnosed disease and decided upon the manner of its treatment.

March, as the time for opening hostilities, was named for him, and his festival was held on the first of this month, the commencement of the old Roman religious year. Numerous temples were dedicated to him, the chief of which was outside the Porta Capena on the Appian Way, the next in importance being erected in the Forum of Augustus to Mars Ultor in 2 b.c.

MEDITRINA

MEDITRINA is mentioned by Festus (p. 123) as an ancient goddess of viticulture and healing; but modern writers deny any real evidence of such a deity[114] and hold that she had her beginnings in the speculations of grammarians.[115] She is sometimes described as though she were

---

[114] Fowler, *op. cit.*, p. 239.
[115] Wissowa, *op. cit.*, p. 115.

a sister of Salus and related to Mars; and she was reputed to restore health by the use of wine, herbs, and
magic formulas. The Meditrinalia, on October 11,[116] was
a festival at which the wine of the new vintage was tested,
and the ceremonies were conducted under the auspices
of the Flamen Martialis, who consecrated the wine as a
remedy by repeating the following words: "Novum vetus
vinum bibo; novo veteri vino morbo medeor" ("An old
man, I drink new wine; with new wine I cure old disease"). The name Meditrina is cognate with Latin
medeor, 'I heal.'[117]

MINERVA

MINERVA, an ancient Falerian goddess,[118] was one of the
di novensides and had a temple on the Capitoline before
the formation of the second State triad of which she was
a member. She was a divinity of handicrafts, of artificers,
and of artists' and workmen's guilds; and was the special
tutelary deity of physicians.[119] Although she was known
as Minerva Medica, it is not clear that her cult, with a
temple on the Esquiline, practiced healing in Rome;[120]
but it was common for leeches to appeal to her for
guidance and power to cure the sick, and Cicero (*de Div.,*
ii, 59) even remarks that "Minerva will give medicine
without a physician"; while inscriptions found at the
temple of Minerva Memor et Medica Cabardiacensis near
Placentia indicate that there she prescribed medicines,
healed diseases of the ear, and even restored the hair
(*CIL* xi, 1292-1310).[121]

[116] Fowler, *op. cit.,* p. 236.
[117] Lindsay, *The Latin Language,* p. 347.
[118] Wissowa, *op. cit.,* pp. 247 ff.
[119] Preller, *Regionen der Stadt Rom,* p. 133.
[120] Wissowa, *op. cit.,* p. 255, note 1.
[121] E. Thrämer, "Health and Gods of Healing (Greek and Roman),"
in *ERE* vi, 554.

Toward the close of the Republic, the cult of Minerva was blended with that of the Greek Athena, who was known as Minerva and Minerva Fatidica or Medica, and who practically supplanted the old Roman goddess during the Empire. Outside of Rome, however, the cult of the Italian Minerva continued in its purity,[122] and extended, even to Britain, where figures of the goddess, now preserved at Chester, have been found.[123] She was worshipped at the State temple of Iupiter on the Capitoline, the right cella of which was dedicated to her, and she also had temples on the Esquiline, the Cælian, and the Aventine. At least one of these was consecrated on March 19, her natal day,[124] and the festival of Quinquatrus (Festus, p. 257; Ovid, *op. cit.*, iii, 809), held from March 18 to 23, was in her honor,[125] while she was also associated in the ceremonies of Feriæ Iovi on June 13. During the epidemic of 363 B.C., a nail was driven in her temple on the Capitoline in the hope of checking the pestilence (Livy, vii, 3).

NEPTUNUS

NEPTUNUS, god of the seas, streams, springs, and fresh waters, had the same attributes as the Greek Poseidon, with whom the Romans identified him. With other divinities, he was honored as an averter of pestilence at the first *lectisternium* in 399 B.C. (Livy, v, 13), and inscriptions found at Como in Italy and at Plombières in France indicate that there he was regarded as a healing deity.[126] His festival, the Neptunalia, was held on July 23, and it has been conjectured that it was in fact utilized to propi-

[122] Wissowa, *op. cit.*, p. 254.
[123] H. Barnes, "On Roman Medicine and Roman Inscriptions found in Britain," in *PRSM*, 1913-1914, vii, 80.
[124] Fowler, *op. cit.*, p. 59.
[125] *Ib.*, p. 158.
[126] Hopf, *op. cit.*, p. 45.

tiate the divinity of waters and springs that the disastrous heat and droughts of summer might be averted.[127]

NORTIA

NORTIA, a Tuscan goddess who had healing functions, was a special deity of the Volsci (Tertullian, *Apologeticus,* 24) ; and it was customary to drive a nail in the walls of her temple at Volsinii each year "as indices of the number of years" (Livy, vii, 3).[128] This statement has recently been confirmed by the discovery of the remains of the temple at Pozzarello near Bolsena, and votive tablets found there bear witness that she was a healing divinity, allied to Fortuna. Votive poems (*CIL* vi, 537) and inscriptions were addressed to her (*CIL* xi, 2685 f.), but she was not admitted as a State goddess at Rome.[129]

PICUMNUS AND PILUMNUS

PICUMNUS and Pilumnus, two divinities said to be brothers and declared to be alike in character, acted as beneficent deities of matrimony. With Intercidona and Deverra they protected parturient women and their children from evil spirits and from attacks of Silvanus; and when a birth had taken place, a couch (*lectus*) being spread for them as *di coniugales,* they were worshipped as *di infantium,* who attended to the proper development of the child (Augustine, *op. cit.,* vi, 9; Servius, *ad Æn.,* ix, 4; x, 76; Nonnos, p. 528).[130]

PICUS

PICUS was an old Latin prophetic deity, supposed to be the son of Saturn (Vergil, *op. cit.,* vii, 48-49) and closely

[127] Fowler, *op. cit.,* pp. 186-187.
[128] *Ib.,* pp. 172, 234.
[129] Wissowa, *op. cit.,* p. 288.
[130] R. Peter, in Roscher, ii, 197, 199, 213-215.

associated with Faunus (Ovid, *Metamorphoses,* iii, 291
ff.; Plutarch, *Vita Numæ,* 15). He had an oracle at Tiora
and healed the sick.

SALUS

SALUS ('Welfare'), originally a Sabine goddess, first appears in the Roman pantheon as a divine impersonation
of the general welfare of city and State. Primarily she
was associated closely with Semo Sancus Dius Fidius,
for an elevation on the Quirinal near the shrine of the
latter deity was called Collis Salutaris, while the gate
leading to it was named Porta Salutaris; and she herself
was occasionally termed Salus Semonia (e.g., Macrobius,
op. cit., I, xvi, 8). In 302 B.C., a temple was dedicated on
the Quirinal to her as Salus Publica (Livy, ix, 43); its
walls were painted in 269 B.C.; it was struck by lightning
at least four times; and it was burned to the ground during the reign of Claudius.[131]

It was only after the Greek goddess Hygieia came
to Rome that Salus, through identification with her, became a divinity of health rather than of welfare. This
Hellenic deity was the only one of the divine associates
of Asklepios who appeared in Rome, and her name was
Latinized to Hygia. During the pestilence of 180 B.C.
Salus was invoked with Apollo and Æsculapius (Livy, xl,
19, 37), showing that she was being transformed to a
likeness of Hygieia; and she was afterward equated with
Hygieia as Salus Hygia, being represented in statues and
pictures with the characteristic drapery of the double
garment of the Greek goddess.[132] Inscriptions to this cult-
companion of Æsculapius were sometimes addressed to
Hygia and sometimes to Salus, and occasionally they

[131] Fowler, *op. cit.,* p. 191.
[132] Wissowa, *op. cit.,* p. 337.

438 THE HEALING GODS

were definitely distinguished as 'Salus eius' (*CIL* vi, 164) and 'Hygia' (*CIL* ix, 17-19, 20234). An altar to Æsculapius and Salus, for the health and safety of the Romans, was found at Chester, England, in 1779, and a votive tablet to these deities was unearthed at Binchester in 1879.[133] A temple at Lambesa by Marcus Aurelius was dedicated 'Æsculapio et Saluti' (*CIL* vii, 2579 f.; cf. also Terence, *Hecyra*, 338); but it would appear that the name and ultimate character of Salus were more properly represented by the Marsian deity Valetudo (*CIL* ix, 3812-3813; cf. Martianus Capella, i, 16), under which title Salus was addressed (*CIL* iii, 7279; cf. also iii, 5149; viii, 9610) besides being so represented on a denarius of M' Acilius Glabrio. It seems probable that Valentia, a deity of the Umbrian town Ocriculum, was a similar divinity of physical health (*CIL* xi, 4082; Tertullian, *op. cit.*, 24).

The later functions of Salus were those of a goddess of health, attending upon her chief and caring for the sacred serpents, but she never appears as a healing divinity. She is represented as holding a branch of laurel or with a cup and a serpent, standing or sitting by Æsculapius, and a statue of the goddess, as Salus Publica, stood in the temple of Concordia (Dion Kassios, liv, xxxv, 2).

SATURNUS

SATURNUS, an ancient Italian agricultural deity who presided over the seeding of the fields, was later assimilated to the Greek Kronos. Saturnus and his descendants were seers and healing divinities, averters of ills, and especially entrusted with the welfare of each citizen. His temple was on the Capitoline, but an altar and evidences of an older temple were located at the foot of the hill.[134] His festival, the Saturnalia, began on December 17, and

---

[133] Barnes, in *PRSM*, 1913-1914, vii, 78.
[134] Fowler, *op. cit.*, p. 269.

was not only popular but the occasion of such license that Seneca said (*Epistolæ*, xviii, 1; cf. Martial, xii, 62) all Rome went mad.[135]

SILVANUS

SILVANUS was an ancient deity of the wood and wild, an off-shoot of Mars, and in many respects similar to Diana (*CIL* iii, 7775, 13368), but was reclaimed and brought into useful and friendly relations with the farmer.[136] He was at times associated with Liber (*CIL* vi, 462) and was closely akin to Faunus and Fauna, or Bona Dea (*CIL* x, 5998 f.) ; while, like Faunus, he was dangerous to women and children, and in this aspect the term Incubus was applied to him, whence the divinities Intercidona, Deverra, and Pilumnus were believed to protect young mothers and their infants from attacks by him (Augustine, *op. cit.*, vi, 9; Servius, *op. cit.*, ix, 4; x, 76; Nonnos, p. 528).

In some of his aspects, Silvanus was regarded as a healing deity, and sacrifices were made to him in that capacity;[137] while he was occasionally associated with Hercules at healing springs and with Hercules Domesticus (*CIL* vi, 288, 293, 295-297, etc.). Cato (*op. cit.*, 83) addressed a prayer to him for the health of his cattle; and in later days he was admitted to the cult of Mithras as the protector of horses and agriculture.[138]

SORANUS

SORANUS, an ancient Roman god, apparently of Sabine origin, and possibly a chthonic deity, was a mediator between man and the higher divinities, bringing health and

[135] Fowler, *op. cit.*, pp. 268-273.

[136] *Ib.*, pp. 55, 201, 262.

[137] Sprengel, *op. cit.*, i, 184.

[138] Cumont, *Textes et monuments figurés relatifs aux mystères de Mithra*, i, 147; and *The Mysteries of Mithra*, pp. 66, 112, 137.

deliverance from disease by the purification of external
fire. He was usually identified with Apollo, and the chief
seat of his worship was on Mount Soracte, near Falerii,
where he was called Apollo Soranus (Vergil, *op. cit.*, xi,
785). His priests, the 'Hirpi Sorani' ('wolves of Soranus'), dressed and acting like wolves to avert pestilence,[139]
performed a yearly ritual of atonement by walking over
red-hot coals with bare feet, and worshippers passed
through the flames (Pliny, *op. cit.*, vii, 19), which custom
was continued in Imperial times. Soranus, whose festival
was held on November 13, was also called Soranus Pater
and, later, Dis Pater (Servius, *op. cit.*, xi, 785).

STRENIA

STRENIA was originally a Sabine goddess whose name,
connected with the Latin *strenuus*,[140] meant 'health'
(Ioannes Lydos, *de Mensibus*, iv, 4), although no details
are known of her cult.[141] A temple and grove at the head
of the Via Sacra were dedicated to her, and from 153 B.C.
onward, it became the custom to give presents and ex-
change congratulatory greetings on the first day of the
year, when the consuls took office, as good omens or
strenæ (Varro, *de Lingua Latina*, v, 47; Symmachus,
Epistolæ, x, 35; Augustine, *op. cit.*, IV, ii, 6).[142]

TIBERINUS

TIBERINUS, the river-god of the Tiber, identified with
Volturnus as Volturnus Tiberinus, and finally known as
Tiberinus Pater, is occasionally referred to as a healing
deity, since he was able, when propitiated, to heal the
diseases which his waters were supposed to bring (Aulus

---

[139] Fowler, *op. cit.*, p. 84.
[140] Walde, *op. cit.*, p. 743.
[141] Preller, *Römische Mythologie*, i, 234.
[142] Fowler, *op. cit.*, p. 278.

Gellius, X, xv, 30). It is believed by modern scholars,[143] that he was worshipped at the Sacra Argeorum, celebrated March 16 and 17, and May 14, when the Romans went in procession to the twenty-four Sacella Argeorum, and at the May festival, after the mourning Flaminica Dialis and Vestals had gathered at the Pons Sublicius, dummies of straw (held to represent old men bound hand and foot, and symbolic of former human sacrifice) were thrown into the Tiber by the Vestals. Tiberinus was also honored at the festival of the Volturnalia on August 27, and on December 8, the anniversary of the founding of his temple on the Insula Tiberina.[144]

VACUNA

VACUNA, an ancient Sabine goddess, was worshipped in numerous places throughout the Sabine territory, particularly in the valley of the upper Velinus, above Reate (Horace, *Epistolæ*, I, x, 49). Latin writers identified her variously with Bellona, Ceres, Diana, Minerva, and Venus, but especially with Victoria (cf. the Scholiasts on Horace, *ad loc.*); and they connect her name with *vaco*, "to be empty, free from." It is clear that her original nature was quite forgotten; but it is significant that vows were made to her for a safe journey and for recovery from illness (*CIL* ix, 4636, 4751-4752);[145] and it may be inferred that her functions were negative rather than positive, so that, for example, she caused freedom from disease rather than good health itself.

---

[143] Fowler, *op. cit.*, pp. 112-120. Ancient writers differed as to the deity honored, naming both Saturnus and Dis Pater. See further, R. Wünsch, "Human Sacrifice (Roman)," in *ERE* vi, 860-861; and G. A. F. Knight, "Bridge," in *ERE* ii, 848-849.

[144] Wissowa, *op. cit.*, p. 225.

[145] Conway, *op. cit.*, p. 358.

I. (B) *Child-birth Deities.*

THE principal deities of child-birth in the later Roman pantheon were Iuno Lucina and Diana, both divinities of women in the broadest sense, presiding over the functions and relations peculiar to their sex. Although the honors were divided, Iuno Lucina was always the more prominent; and she, rather than Diana, extended her protection and supervision over children from birth to maturity. These two chief goddesses had many assistants and deities of lower rank associated with the processes of gestation and birth, some of whom had originally been independent divinities and had retained their names, although their cults had lost their individuality and become more or less blended with those of Iuno Lucina and Diana; while others had surrendered their cults and remained mere surnames or as variants and phases of the more exalted pair.[146] Thus the ancient goddesses Carmentis and Mater Matuta could no longer maintain their independence,[147] and Natio had lost her cult; while Parca, originally a deity of child-birth,[148] was later identified with the Greek divinities of Fate, the Moirai, and like them, developed into three personalities. Both Iuno Lucina and Diana were equated with the Greek Eileithyia, under whose name they were frequently referred to.

The functions connected with conception, gestation, birth, and the growth of offspring to maturity and marriage were infinitely subdivided and distributed among a large class of *indigitamenta*, subsidiary physiological divinities, conceived as supervising each detail, being evolved from—or amalgamated with—the activities of the chief goddesses, as Lucina Ossipaga and Diana Ale-

---

[146] L. Deubner, "Birth (Greek and Roman)," in *ERE* ii, 649.
[147] Wissowa, *op. cit.*, p. 63.
[148] Walde, *op. cit.*, p. 561.

mona.[149] In the matter of conception, if the potency of the male was in question, the men invoked Liber, Libera, Subigus, Dea Perfica, Dea Prema, or Dea Pertunda (Augustine, *op. cit.*, vi, 9); and if women feared sterility they appealed to the gods Pilumnus, Mutunus Tutunus, and Fascinus (Arnobius, *op. cit.*, iv, 131), or to the goddesses Rumina, Deverra, Mena, or Cunina (Augustine, *op. cit.*, ii, 11, 21; vi, 9; vii, 2; Tertullian, *ad Nationes*, ii, 11; Arnobius, *op. cit.*, iv, 7).[150]

Little mention is made of the details of the theurgic methods used in child-birth, but in general they appear to have consisted of magic formulas, songs, incantations, and the laying-on of hands, so that "gentle Lucina applies her hands and utters words which promote delivery" (Ovid, *op. cit.*, x, 511). Only the right hand favored delivery, as shown on vases and by models of the hand left as votive offerings. It was usual for newly delivered mothers to bring flowers to the temples of the birth-goddesses.

Roman families were accustomed to honor various deities on the occasion of a birth, the male Genius and the female Iuno being reverenced by spreading a table for Hercules and placing a couch for Lucina in the atrium (Servius, *Eclogæ*, iv, 62), or possibly the table only would be prepared, and this to an impersonal divinity.[151] At other times a couch was set for Pilumnus and Picumnus, protectors of mother and child, and they were supposed to partake of a meal after the birth. Varro (*apud* Augustine, *op. cit.*, vi, 9) relates that after a birth, if the babe was acknowledged by the father (*sublatus*), three men came at night to the threshold of the house and struck it repeatedly with a hatchet, a mortar, and a besom, that

[149] See Supplement to this chapter.
[150] Hopf, *op. cit.*, p. 40.
[151] Wissowa, *op. cit.*, p. 422.

"by these signs of agriculture Silvanus might be prevented from entering," this rite being supposed to symbolize Intercidona, Deverra, and Pilumnus, who guarded mother and child from the spirit of the wild. The eighth day after birth for girls, and the ninth for boys, was the *dies lustricus,* the day of purification, when they were accepted into the family.

After the successful delivery of the Empress Poppæa, wife of Nero, the Arval brothers included Spes, as Augusta Spes, in the list of divinities to whom it was customary to sacrifice on such occasions (*CIL* vi, 758-760); and Fecunditas likewise received honors.[152]

The birth of an hermaphrodite was of foul and ill omen. On one occasion it was destroyed by being thrown into the sea, while the Decemviri decreed that a litany should be sung by a chorus of thrice nine virgins, sacrifices should be offered by the matrons of the city, and processions with sacrifices should be made at the temple of Iuno Regina (Livy, xxvii, 37; xxxi, 12).

CARMENTIS (OR CARMENTA)

CARMENTIS, an ancient Italic goddess and a prophetic deity of great repute,[153] though overshadowed by the Cumæan Sibyl (Vergil, *op. cit.,* viii, 337-341), appears originally to have been a nymph of springs and a healing divinity (sometimes identified with Albunea of Tibur), and later to have interpreted divine symbols and announced decrees of Fate. Aside from prophecy, her most prominent characteristic was her influence over childbirth, though her functions here were subordinate to Iuno Lucina and Diana.[154] She coöperated with Lucina, assisting in delivery by reciting her magic formulas; and

---

[152] Wissowa, *op. cit.,* pp. 330, 336.
[153] Kissel, in *Janus,* 1848, iii, 652.
[154] Wissowa, *op. cit.,* pp. 219-221.

hence, being a prophetess for the infant into whose future she looked and from whom she warded off impending evils, she became a mantic deity in general.[155] Her priests, the Carmentarii, lit the sacrificial fires and were the official interpreters of her oracles.

Carmentis had a temple at the foot of the Capitoline, a sacred grove and temple in the Vicus Patricius open only to women, and an altar near the Porta Carmentalis; and her festivals, the Carmentalia, attended only by women, were held January 11 and 15.[155] At these celebrations the Flamen Carmentalis called upon her, as Carmentis Prorsa, Porrima, or Antevorta, to aid those who invoked her by giving the child a position favorable for easy delivery, thus bringing about a fission of the deity into a plurality of Carmentes.

COMITIA

COMITIA was assimilated to, if she was not identical with, Carmentis as a deity of child-birth and a healing goddess. She dwelt with the Sabines at Lake Cutilia, near Reate, the waters of which were cold and used for their medicinal properties, where was a floating island on which grew trees and many healing herbs (Varro, *de Ling. Lat.*, p. 1063, 48).

DIANA

DIANA ('the Divine')[156] was originally an Italian goddess of the wild, a spirit of the forest and vegetation, and very nearly related to Silvanus; but in her general aspect she was identified with the Greek Artemis, by whom she was eventually supplanted, and in whose name she was afterwards worshipped in anniversary games (Catullus, *Car-*

---

155 Fowler, *op. cit.*, p. 167.
156 Walde, *op. cit.*, p. 231.

mina, xxxiv). As Diana Lucifera she was a moon-deity and was often called Diana Lucina (Cicero, *de Nat. Deor.,* ii, 27); while as a divinity of magic she was equated with Hekate, whence she was sometimes regarded as of triple aspect (e.g., Vergil, *op. cit.,* iv, 511). She was a divine protectress of women in all the needs peculiar to their sex, and a child-birth deity who was often ranked as the equal of Iuno Lucina; ''Goddess of triple form, who, thrice invoked, dost hear and save from death young mothers in their labor pangs'' (Horace, *Odæ,* III, xxii, 2-4). She had a large retinue of deities and *numina* who presided over many subordinate functions incidental to her activities, and whose appellatives were often given her as surnames. She was sometimes called Diana Sospita, and at Nemi she was worshipped as Diana Opifera and Diana Lucina (to whom the girdle of the first birth was consecrated),[157] being invoked especially for diseases of women, for successful deliveries, and for happiness in married life; while as Diana Nemorensis she was assisted in her obstetric functions by the local associated divinities, Egeria and Virbius.[158] Her sanctuary at Nemi was a celebrated resort for hydrotherapy, and healing springs were dedicated to Diana Thermia, who presided over such fountains in the Campagna, at Arethusa in Sicily, and at Aix-les-Bains in Savoy.[159]

Diana was worshipped very generally throughout Italy but her most renowned shrine was at Nemi on the north shore of Lake Nemus in the Alban mountains. Her temple was small, being only fifty by eighty feet, but the grove in which it stood, not far from Aricia, was one of the largest known in antiquity, having an area of 44,000

[157] Hecker, *Geschichte der Heilkunde,* i, 358-361.
[158] Frazer, *The Magic Art,* i, 41.
[159] Hopf, *op. cit.,* pp. 37-38.

square meters.[160] Commonly known as Nemus Aricinum,
it was reputed to be the religious center of Italy; and in
Aricia Diana, as the tutelary goddess of the city and the
protecting deity of the 'League of Latium,' had her altar,
over which her chief priest, the 'Rex Nemorensis,' presided (Suetonius, *Caligula*, 35), winning his position at
Nemi by slaying his predecessor (Strabo, V, iii, 12 = p.
239 C).[161]

This League of Latin cities was overthrown in 338 B.C.;
and it is inferred that when its seat was moved to Rome,
the cult of Diana followed, especially as she is said to
have been among the first of the *di novensides* to enter
Rome. Her temple on the Aventine was a League sanctuary and the center of her worship until she was superseded by Artemis; but her shrines in Rome and her
sacred grove in the Vicus Patricius (Livy, i, 45) were
open only to women (Plutarch, *Quæstiones Romanæ*, 3).
Her festival, with the dedication of her temples at Rome,
was held on August 13, and at Aricia probably on the
same day, processions at Rome and from all Latium
going to her sanctuaries in her honor. Women made pilgrimages to Nemi with torches and wreaths to implore
the goddess to grant them children and easy delivery;
and in her temples were hung many votive tablets and
ex-votos representing all parts of the body, though chiefly
the genital organs of both sexes, mothers with nursing
babes, and other *donaria*.[160] Diana had many other
shrines in Italy, but the wealthiest, and the one favored
by Sulla, was that at Mount Tifata near Capua, known
as the Mons Dianæ Tifatinæ (*CIL* x, 3933, 4564). Her cult
was so popular that foreign goddesses were worshipped

[160] Contessa Gautier, "An excursion to the Lake of Nemi and Civita
Lavinia," in *JBASR*, 1890-1898, ii, 448 ff.; also R. Lanciani, "The
Mysterious Wreck of Nemi," in *ib.*, pp. 300 ff.

[161] Frazer, *op. cit.*, i, 10-11.

in her name, or her name was connected with theirs, as with the Carthagenian Tanit, known as Dea Cælestis.[162] Diana was commonly depicted in the dress of a huntress, but in her obstetric function the torch was her permanent attribute.

EGERIA

EGERIA, originally a water-nymph,[163] was associated with Diana as a deity of child-birth and healing at the sacred grove of Nemi, near Aricia. According to legend, she was the friend, mistress, or wife of Numa, whom she met at night and counselled concerning legislation, especially hygienic laws, in a cave on the Palatine, or at a grotto-spring with healing properties outside the Porta Capena on the Via Appia (Juvenal, op. cit., iii, 11-12). After the death of Numa, she retired to the grove at Nemi, where her inconsolable grief disturbed the worship of Diana (Ovid, Fasti, iii, 262 ff.; Metam., xv, 480 ff.). At the roots of an oak in the sacred grove was the 'Spring of Egeria,' which had received her tears and was resorted to for healing, its waters, as those of other springs, being credited with power to facilitate conception and delivery.[164] In her obstetric function she was associated with Virbius, another divinity connected with the sacred precincts at Nemi. When the cult of Diana was removed to Rome, Egeria followed and she was worshipped in the sacred grove of the Camenæ, below the Aventine.[165]

GENITA MANA

GENITA MANA, as her name ('Birth-Death')[166] implies,

[162] Wissowa, op. cit., pp. 248-252.
[163] Frazer, op. cit,, i, 17-19.
[164] Ib., ii, 171 ff.
[165] Wissowa, op. cit., pp. 160, 219, 247.
[166] Cf. Walde, op. cit., pp. 338, 341, 460-461.

was an ancient Italian goddess who had power over life and death,[167] so that when sacrifices were made to her the suppliants prayed that no one of the household should become 'manus' (*i.e.*, one of the *Manes*). Her cult was obscure, but she had a great influence over child-birth; and it is said that she was a rival of Iuno Lucina. She was honored at the festival Compitalia, and nursing bitches were sacrificed to her (Plutarch, *op. cit.*, 53). As Geneta she had a statue and an altar in the grove of Ceres at Agnone in Samnium.[168]

IUNO (OR IUNO LUCINA)

IUNO ('Youthful'?),[169] one of the chief goddesses of the Roman pantheon, formed the great State triad with Iupiter and Minerva; but though, by a false analogy with the Greek Hera, she was often referred to as the wife of Iupiter, there is no well-authenticated myth of this until the anthropomorphic period following the acceptance of Greek ideas.[170] She was the divinity of the lower atmosphere in distinction to the domain of Iupiter in the heavens, and was originally the elemental spirit of womanhood, representing the female principle in human life as Hercules did the male. Each woman had her Iuno, a spirit who guarded her throughout life, corresponding to Genius for men, and by whom she swore; whence Iuno became the great tutelary deity of woman in all her functions and activities.

In several of her aspects, especially as Iuno Lucina, Iuno was the chief goddess of child-birth and presided over every process and activity of the offspring until the period of manhood and womanhood. Lucina was her most

[167] Wissowa, *op. cit.*, p. 240.
[168] Conway, *op. cit.*, pp. 191-192.
[169] Walde, *op. cit.*, pp. 398-399.
[170] Fowler, *op. cit.*, p. 134.

frequent epithet (Ovid, *Fasti*, ii, 449-451), and one by
which poets addressed her (Horace, *Epodæ*, v, 5-6); and
the name, meaning 'light,' was derived from Luna
('Moon'; Cicero, *op. cit.*, ii, 27), being supposed to have
been given her because she brought children into the
light. She also received many other epithets expressive
of the various phases of her character, as Conservatrix,
Opigena (Festus, p. 200), and very commonly Sospita or
Sispes, by which she was known at Lanuvium (*CIL* xiv,
2088 ff.); and a temple in the herb-market at Rome was
dedicated to her in 197 B.C. (Livy, xxxiv, 53).[171] She was
often assimilated with, and called, Diana and Ilithyia, or
she sometimes preferred the name of Genitalis (Horace,
Carmen Seculare, 13-16). Iuno Lucina apparently supplanted the old birth-goddess Natio; Lucina and the Nixi
dii were associated in the obstetric function; and old
Roman goddesses were subsidiary to her. Lucina was not
only invoked for her aid but also to save women in confinement (Terence, *Andria*, 473; *Adelphæ*, 487); and she
was similarly implored to be propitious to infants, as to
the boy who was to usher in the Golden Age (Vergil,
Eclogæ, iv, 8-10).

Iuno frequently appears in very minor functional capacities under the surname of one or another of the many
numina of her retinue, as Lucina Ossipaga, or Fluonia
(Arnobius, *op. cit.*, iii, 30, 118); as the divine match-
maker, she was Iuno Iuga (Paulus, p. 104); as the divine
bridesmaid, Iuno Pronuba (Vergil, *Æn.*, iv, 166); and as
Iuno Populona she protected against devastation and
was responsible for the increase of the population.[172]
According to an old legend of the sacred grove near the
Suburra, which surrounded her temple on the Esquiline,

[171] Fowler, *op. cit.*, p. 302.
[172] Wissowa, *op. cit.*, p. 189.

the Sabine women carried off by the Romans proved
sterile, so that couples made pilgrimages there and heard
a voice from the trees which indicated the remedy (Ovid,
op. cit., ii, 431-450).

Iuno shared honors at the Capitoline temple with Iupiter and Minerva, but her most renowned sanctuary in
Rome was on the Esquiline, where a gift was brought to
the goddess after every birth, where flowers were offered
her (*ib.*, iii, 253-254), and which no one wearing something knotted was allowed to approach, a knot being supposed to hinder birth (Servius, *op. cit.*, iv, 518).

Iuno was universally regarded as the goddess of matrons and chastity, and the wives of Romans joined in,the
festival of the Matronalia which celebrated the dedication of her temple on March 1, when pigs were sacrificed
as substitutes for lambs.[173] She also had a sacred grove at
Lanuvium, one of the great sanctuaries of Latium; and
her oracles, which were announced from the mouths of
serpents, enjoyed great renown in Rome. The goat was
sacred to her and at Lanuvium she was represented as
wearing a goat's skin. The thongs ('amicula Iunonis,'
Arnobius, *op. cit.*, ii, 23) used by the priests of Faunus,
for the purification of sterile women,[174] were taken from
the skin of the goat, and from this custom Iuno received
the name Februa and was brought into relation to
Faunus as the goddess of conception (Paulus, p. 85; Martianus Capella, ii, 149; Arnobius, *op. cit.*, iii, 30). The
festival of Iuno Regina was celebrated on the Aventine
by processions of women, the sacrifice of cows, and other
ceremonies (Livy, v, 31; xxi, 62; xxii, 1; xxvii, 37; xxxi,
12); and another festival was held at Falerii (Ovid, *op.
cit.*, ii, 427).

The oldest strictly women's celebration in Rome was

---

[173] Fowler, *op. cit.*, pp. 38, 105.
[174] *Ib.*, pp. 179, 318-321.

the Nonæ Caprotinæ,[175] held on July 7, when sacrifices
and feasts were held under the wild fig-tree (*CIL* iv,
1555), and at which sham battles took place between
servant maids who exchanged scurrilous epithets and
speeches. The origin and significance of this festival have
been lost, but it is supposed to have had something to do
with sex-life, perhaps the bearing of children, since Iuno
bore the name Caprotina and was evidently associated
with it.[176] The term is connected with Latin *caper*
('goat').[177]

IUTURNA

IUTURNA, associated with Carmentis in child-birth, was a
water-nymph, representing the healing powers of water
and presiding over a spring named for her at Lanuvium
(Servius, *op. cit.*, xii, 139; Varro, *op. cit.*, v, 71).[178] After
the first Punic War, her cult was transferred to Rome,
and a temple was built for her on the Campus Martius;
while an old *lacus* of Iuturna was situated in the Forum
near the shrine of Castor and Pollux (Ovid, *op. cit.*, i,
706-708). Recent excavations have disclosed this shrine of
Iuturna,[179] the construction of which suggests that it was
used for incubation. Her festival, the Iuturnalia, was celebrated on January 11 simultaneously with the Carmentalia, and was attended especially by those whose occupa-
tions associated them with spring water, such as fullers
(Servius, *loc. cit.*).

[175] Wissowa, *op. cit.*, p. 184; also Fowler, *Religious Experience*,
p. 143; *id., Festivals*, pp. 175, 178-179.

[176] Wissowa, *op. cit.*, p. 184.

[177] Walde, *op. cit.*, p. 128.

[178] *Note.*—Fons (or Fontus) was the god of springs and had a temple at Rome and a festival in his honor, the Fontinalia, on October 13
(Varro, *op. cit.*, vi, 22).

[179] H. L. Bishop, "The Fountain of Juturna in the Roman Forum,"
in *RP*, 1903, ii, 174-180.

MATER MATUTA

MATER MATUTA was an ancient Italian goddess who presided over the early morning hour;[180] and as the birth of day from darkness was symbolized by Ianus, so she is said to have unlocked the womb and brought the child into the light.[181] At the close of the Republic she was identified with the Greek Leukothea (Cicero, *op. cit.*, iii, 19; Paulus, p. 125); but she was overshadowed in her obstetric functions by Iuno Lucina, for whom Matuta was occasionally used as a surname. She was always a deity of matrons and children, like Carmentis, Fortuna, and Bona Dea, and it is suggested that she was a form of the latter.[182]

The temple of Mater Matuta, in the Forum Boarium, dated from 396 B.C., and was dedicated on June 11, thus giving rise to the Matralia. Only women officiated at this rite, which was attended solely by matrons who were living with their first husbands; while a female slave, ritually brought into her temple, was cuffed and driven out (Ovid, *op. cit.*, vi, 475 ff.; Plutarch, *Vita Camilli*, 5). Women prayed there for their nephews and nieces before their own children (Plutarch, *Quæst. Rom.*, 16, 17), a mark of the extreme antiquity of the worship of this divinity.

The cult of Mater Matuta was widespread throughout Central Italy, and even extended to Africa, while inscriptions to her have been found in Umbria, at Præneste, and among the Volsci. The temple in the harbor of Pyrgi, the port of Cære in Etruria, dedicated to Ilithyia, is believed to have been hers,[183] and she also had shrines at Satricum and Cora.

[180] Cf. Walde, *op. cit.*, pp. 470-471.
[181] Wissowa, *op. cit.*, p. 110.
[182] Fowler, *op. cit.*, p. 156.
[183] *Ib.*, p. 155, note 4.

NATIO (OR NASCIO)

NATIO (or Nascio) was an ancient Roman goddess of child-birth who had been supplanted by Iuno Lucina, and who, according to Cicero (*op. cit.*, iii, 18), had formerly been honored by sacrifice and processions in the district of Ardea.

NIXI DII

NIXI DII were obscure divinities of whom little is known except that they assisted in child-birth. They were reputed (though probably in error) to have been brought from Syria by the Consul M' Acilius Glabrio after his defeat of Antiochus in 191 B.C., and Festus (p. 174) mentions them as three guardians of women in labor, whose statues, in a kneeling position (whence their name, 'they who bow down, kneel'),[184] stood before the chapel of Minerva on the Capitoline. Both Lucina and the Nixi dii were invoked in one cry by Alcmene at the birth of Hercules (Ovid, *Metam.*, ix, 294).

OPS

OPS was an ancient harvest goddess who assisted in child-birth. As an agricultural deity she was closely associated with Consus in protecting the crops during the harvest, and hence she was called Consiva (Varro, *op. cit.*, vi, 21), though she never developed a personality but always remained a *numen*.[185] It was sometimes assumed in antiquity that she was the spouse of Consus (Festus, p. 186; Macrobius, *op. cit.*, iii, ix, 4), but of this there is no well-attested myth, and more frequently she was referred to as the wife of Saturn (e.g., Plautus, *Cistellaria*, 514-515),

---

[184] Sommer, *Handbuch der lateinischen Laut- und Formenlehre*, p. 646.

[185] Fowler, *op. cit.*, p. 338.

though even this is doubtful, despite their functional relation.[186] Ops in her aspect as the earth was identical with Terra,[187] and it is believed that Fauna and Bona Dea were at times called Ops.

It was as Opifera that she was the helpful mother to new-born children, and those who invoked her touched the ground. Shortly after birth, every infant was placed on the ground in honor of Ops, the great mother, and under the supervision of Levana, the father raised it up (sublatus), by this act acknowledging his paternity, whence Ops and Levana were witnesses to the legitimacy of children (Augustine, op. cit., iv, 11).[188]

Ops shared the temple of Saturn, and the Opalia, in her honor, was celebrated on December 19, during the Saturnalia.[189] She divided another shrine, situated in the Vicus Iugarius, with Ceres; and her own festival, the Opiconsivia, at which none were admitted to the sacrifice but the Pontifex Maximus and the Vestals, was held on August 25.[190] Both the Opiconsivia and the Opalia fell, it should be noted, four days after the Consualia, thus further establishing the relation between Ops and Consus.

VIRBIUS

VIRBIUS was a minor deity associated with child-birth in the cults of Diana and Egeria at Aricia (Vergil, op. cit., vii, 761-782), and was reputed to be Hippolytos, who had been done to death by the curses of Theseus, but raised from the dead by Asklepios. He had then fled to Italy, where he consecrated a precinct to Diana (Artemis) at Aricia (Pausanias, II, xxvii, 4), and was called her chief

---

[186] Fowler, op. cit., p. 212; id., Religious Experience, pp. 156, 482.
[187] Fowler, op. cit., p. 156.
[188] Ib., p. 83.
[189] Id., Festivals, pp. 273-274.
[190] Ib., pp. 212-214.

priest (Ovid, *op. cit.*, xv, 543 ff.). He has also been regarded as the consort of Diana, having the same relation
as Adonis to Aphrodite, and Attis to Kybele,[191] and possibly he was a local form of Iupiter.[192] Virbius was represented as an old man not unlike Æsculapius,[193] and at
Naples had a Flamen Virbialis (*CIL* x, 1493).

I. (C) *Underworld Deities.*

Dis, or Dis Pater, and Proserpina ruled over underworld
regions inhabited by a vast horde of spirits, of all kinds
and degrees of rank, and possessing a certain, though
indefinite, existence. The original conception of these
superhuman beings, as well as their character, powers,
and classification, were largely forgotten during the Republic, and Latin writers on the subject are vague and
confused; but it appears clear that the early Romans
never imagined any such organized Underworld as was
evolved by the Greeks and adopted by Vergil in the
Æneid. Nevertheless, the dead had some sort of continued existence in this subterranean realm; and although
no definite lines were drawn, in general, those who had
been duly buried according to the customary ceremonies
became the respected ancestors, the *Di Parentum,* often
called *Di Manes;* while those who had died away from
home or who had not received proper rites, as well as
spirits of evil men, became specters, the *Larvæ* or
Lemures, who returned to their old abodes and troubled
the living. From among these myriad spirits a few had
been personified, as the Lares and their mythical mother,
Mania.

The evil spirits and deities who were hostile to man

---

[191] Frazer, *op. cit.*, i, 41.
[192] *Ib.*, ii, 379.
[193] Wissowa, *op. cit.*, p. 248.

appeared on earth as ghosts and apparitions of the night, tormenting and terrifying the living, and causing sickness and misfortune. They were the willing slaves of disease, bringing pestilence and death into the state and afflicting individuals with many ills, especially such neuroses and psychic disturbances as epilepsy, hysteria, hydrophobia, and mania.

These were the general conceptions underlying the several festivals designed to pay respect and honor to the good ancestors, and to propitiate, appease, and drive away those deities and spirits who were hostile. The rites were essentially those of purification, atonement, sacrifice, and the bestowal of gifts; and these religious obligations gave rise to many cults and ceremonies which vanished at an early period, being represented in historic times by the *dies parentales,* or nine days which ended February 21 in the State festival of the Feralia with a general atoning sacrifice (Ovid, *Fasti,* ii, 533 ff.); and the Lemuria of May 9, 11, and 13, sacred to the *Lemures* and *Larvæ.*[194] It was considered an essential duty of every family to fulfil their religious obligations to the *Di Manes* at the Parentalia on February 13 and to make atonement for all involuntary offenses of commission and omission, whereas those which were voluntary could not be expiated in this way. During the Parentalia and Lemuria, all temples were closed; and since marriages performed on those days would be unfortunate, none were contracted (Ovid, *op. cit.,* v, 485-488). The Lemuria is supposed to have been originally both a State and a private function; but in historic times the share of the State was uncertain, if, indeed, it was still retained. The private rites were performed by the *paterfamilias,* who rose at midnight and walked barefoot through the house,

[194] Wissowa, *op. cit.,* pp. 174, 235-236, 239.

signing "with his fingers joined with the middle of his thumb."[195] He then washed his hands thrice, and taking black beans in his mouth, spat them out with averted face, repeating nine times the words, "These I offer; with these beans I ransom myself and mine." Again he touched water, struck a brazen vessel, and after crying nine times, "Go forth, ancestral Manes," could once more look behind him (Ovid, *op. cit.*, v, 431-444).

CARNA

CARNA was an ancient Italian goddess of the Underworld who presided over the vital portions of the body,[196] particularly the heart and digestive organs, and incidentally over nutrition, her own diet being simple like that of the olden time, without dainties or luxuries (Ovid, *op. cit.*, vi, 169-172). Her festival, the Carnaria, was held on June 1. "Prayers are offered to the goddess, for the good preservation of liver, heart, and the other internal organs of our bodies," and "her sacrifices are bean-meal and lard, because this is the best food for the nourishment of the body" (Macrobius, *op. cit.*, I, xii, 32). Those who sacrificed to her and ate bean-gruel and pig's fat on that day secured a good digestion for the year.[197] She practiced beneficent magic and healing, for Ianus had given her a branch of white thorn (? arbutus) which was reputed to avert evils and to ward off the attacks of the *striges* who sought to suck the blood of children and cause death, as when she saved the life of Phocas by touching the doorposts three times with her twig of arbutus, sprinkling the threshold with water containing drugs, holding the entrails of a sow two months old, and saying: "Heart for

[195] The well-known apotropaic sign of the *fico*.
[196] Her name is connected etymologically with Latin *caro*, 'flesh' (Lindsay, *op. cit.*, p. 317).
[197] Wissowa, *op. cit.*, p. 236.

heart, take vitals for vitals! this life we give you instead
of one better'' (Ovid, *op. cit.*, vi, 129-168).[198] She was
confused with the totally different deity, Cardea, the goddess of the door-hinge (*ib.*, vi, 101-102, 127).

DIS (DIS PATER, OR ORCUS)

Dis, Dis Pater, and Orcus were names given by Roman
writers to the god of the dead and Underworld. Dis was
the Latinized form of the Greek Plouton, with whom he
was equated, referring to the wealth under his control
(Varro, *op. cit.*, V, x, 20; Cicero, *op. cit.*, ii, 26), and
Orcus (Death, ? Viduus) was used to designate the god
who separated the soul from the body and took it to himself (Festus, p. 202).[199] His consort was Proserpina,
identical with Persephone, who had been brought to
Rome with Demeter and Dionysos in 496 B.C. and named
Libera.

Dis and Proserpina sent disease and death among mankind, Dis to men and Proserpina to women and children;
but they also had the power of averting sickness and
death, and of healing disease.[200] Accordingly, honors and
sacrifices were offered them to release their victims from
maladies and to restore health, and waters heated upon
their altars had curative powers (Valerius Maximus, II,
iv, 5). The cult of Dis and Proserpina was first brought
to Rome about 249 B.C. from Tarentum and was established at an underground altar in the Campus Martius
near the Tiber, where the strange rites of the Ludi Taren-
tini, with a nocturnal ritual and sacrifice of black animals,
were performed (Festus, p. 154; Macrobius, *op. cit.*, I,

[198] For similar incantations and offerings of substitute victims among
the Babylonians, see *supra*, p. 112.

[199] Preller (*op. cit.*, p. 453) interprets Orcus as the cause of death,
probably meaning 'the Restrainer,' see Walde, *op. cit.*, p. 546.

[200] Kissel, in *Janus*, 1848, iii, 623-624.

xvi, 17).²⁰¹ During three days, August 24, October 5, and November 8, the 'mundus' on the Palatine, claimed by these deities, remained uncovered.²⁰² These divinities also had an altar on the Capitoline.

LARES

THE Lares were deities of the Underworld, but were often identified with the *Di Manes* and were regarded primarily as the shades of those who had founded the family or State, good men who, after death, loved to hover about their old homes and to preserve the welfare of ,their families and possessions,²⁰³ but who must be appeased by special gifts (Ovid, *op. cit.*, ii, 535, 633; vi, 791). The State Lares guarded the State as a whole, helped its citizens in distress, and guarded against pestilence; while the household Lares (*Lares domestici*) were generally good spirits who protected the family against illness, though, if they were offended, they had the power of causing disease, especially neuroses and psychic disorders (Festus, p. 119; Nonius, p. 44). The family recognized their beneficent influence by hanging wreaths in their home to the Lares on happy occasions, as when a member recovered from disease. There were also Lares of the roads and cross-roads, where they watched over the farms and other property of the family. The festival of the Laralia, or Compitales, usually held about January 3-5, was celebrated in their honor (Varro, *op. cit.*, vi, 25).²⁰⁴

PROSERPINA

PROSERPINA was the chief goddess of the Underworld and the consort of Dis. (For her functions see under DIS.)

²⁰¹ Fowler, *Religious Experience*, pp. 440-441.
²⁰² *Id., Festivals*, pp. 211-212.
²⁰³ Wissowa, *op. cit.*, p. 235.
²⁰⁴ Fowler, *op. cit.*, p. 279; *id., Religious Experience*, p. 78.

I. (D) *Deities of Disease.*

DISEASE, both sporadic and epidemic, was regarded as the expression of divine disfavor, primarily as punishment for sin or some offense toward the gods, and restoration of good relations depended upon conciliation obtained by sacrifice and by purification, which was regarded as the symbol of divine grace.[205] Romans revered their sin as a divinity who might become friendly and inclined to them, hence they also venerated disease, but they seldom went so far as to group symptoms as of a single disease, and conceived the various symptoms as divinities who should be revered and invoked for cure (Varro, *apud* Nonius, p. 46).

ANGINA

ANGINA, the name under which a *numen* or goddess was venerated as the impersonation of sore throat, supposed to have been quinsy, was invoked for its cure, although Romans afflicted with this malady believed they were cured after having invoked Angerona (Macrobius, *op. cit.*, I, 10; Paulus, pp. 8, 17, 28).

CLOACINA

CLOACINA, a goddess who presided over the drains of Rome, especially the Cloaca Maxima, was a *numen* who personified the stench arising from them. She was invoked for protection from diseases due to the drains and was euphemistically addressed as 'sweet Cloacina.'

It is related by Pliny (*op. cit.*, xv, 119) that the Romans and Sabines, when about to engage in battle on account of the rape of the Sabine virgins, lay down their arms and made atonement with branches of myrtle on the spot where later the statue of Venus Cloacina stood. The deri-

[205] Kissel, in *Janus*, 1848, iii, 408-409.

vation of the name Cloacina (*cluere*) denoted the same as the later word to cleanse (*purgare*) (Festus, p. 55), and Venus was the goddess of myrtle and marriage. Hence Venus Cloacina was invoked for purification from forbidden sexual indulgence and its results, and, in her cult, marriage was an atonement for such transgressions and the consequences (Servius, *op. cit.*, i, 720; Augustine, *op. cit.*, vi, 10; iv, 23). It was in the temple of Cloacina that Virginia met death at the hands of her father in protection of her honor (Livy, iii, 48).

FEBRIS

FEBRIS, an ancient *numen* personifying fevers, especially the malarias of the Roman marshes, was supposed to cause such fevers as were sent in punishment and also to heal the fever-stricken by a purifying fire within the body which delivered them from the divine displeasure.[206] Later the goddess, usually addressed as Dea Febris, was specialized as Dea Tertiana and Dea Quartana, and inscriptions (*CIL* vii, 999; xii, 3129) show that these deities were venerated as the disease itself and were directly appealed to as being able to heal by destroying the malady.[207] Febris was regarded as a mediator between mankind and the gods, even such divinities as Iupiter and Iuno when the disease led to light and health, and those of the lower world, as Dis Pater or Orcus, when purification led to death (Macrobius, *op. cit.*, I, 13). She was a popular deity and had at least three temples in Rome, one each on the Palatine, the Esquiline, and the Quirinal (Valerius Maximus, II, v, 6).[208] She was believed to be well-disposed toward mankind and, having magic cures for both kinds of fever, to prosper the many reme-

[206] Kissel, in *Janus*, 1848, iii, 616.
[207] Wissowa, *op. cit.*, p. 245.
[208] Thrämer, in *ERE* vi, 554.

dies which were consecrated and stored in her fanes (Valerius Maximus, *loc. cit.;* Pliny, *op. cit.,* xxviii, 46). Patients were carried to her temples, but their recovery was supposed to be due to the severe regimen which they were obliged to undergo rather than the remedies given (Valerius Maximus, II, v, 55).

MEFITIS

MEFITIS, an ancient Italian goddess personifying stench (Servius, *op. cit.,* vii, 82; *CIL* ix, 1421), more particularly miasms arising from the earth, was invoked not only to protect her worshippers from malarial fevers, vapors from marshes, and poisonous gases from springs and clefts in the earth, but also to cure those who were ill after exposure to them.[209] She had temples on the Mons Cispius (Varro, *de Ling. Lat.,* v, 49; Festus, pp. 217, 261, 351), outside the gates of Cremona (Tacitus, *Hist.,* iii, 33), and in the famous Amsanctus valley,[210] in the land of the Hirpini, about four miles from Frigento, where the gusts of sulphuretted hydrogen coming from the earth were believed to be the breath of Pluto himself, while near by was a bubbling pool giving off carbonic acid gas in such quantities as to be deadly when raised above the ground by the wind (Pliny, *op. cit.,* ii, 108). Mefitis appears to have originated in Central Italy, but the extension of her cult, of which little is known, may be traced from Lucania across the Po into Gaul.[211]

SCABIES

SCABIES was a *numen* or deity who is supposed to have personified diseases of the skin characterized by itching,

[209] Kissel, in *Janus,* 1848, iii, 612-613.
[210] Frazer, *Adonis,* i, 204.
[211] Wissowa, *op. cit.,* p. 246.

and as such was invoked for relief (Prudentius, *Hamartigenia*, 220); although it is sometimes claimed that she was not an incarnation and should not have been considered a divinity.[212]

II. FOREIGN DEITIES.

ADONIS

ADONIS, a deity developed in Syria and Phœnicia, was originally a corn-spirit, born in the myrtle tree which was his emblem, and made the subject of idyllic poetry.[213] A late importation into Greece, he was brought to Rome in partially Hellenized form, identified with Attis and connected with the cults of Magna Mater and the Dea Syria (Macrobius, *op. cit.*, I, xxi, 1). A divinity to whom women appealed especially in their love affairs, and called the 'indiscreet god,' he was reputed to cause the menses to return when arrested, to prevent maidens from suffering in losing their virginity, and to give young wives sexual passions.[214]

ÆSCULAPIUS

ÆSCULAPIUS was the Greek god of healing, Asklepios, who had been brought to Rome under this Latinized name. During the severe pestilence of 293 B.C., which had afflicted the city and country with prodigious mortality, the Sibylline Books had been construed as directing that Asklepios must be brought from Epidauros, but the Consuls, being then fully occupied with a war, postponed the matter, ordering instead a supplication for one day and prayers to Asklepios (Livy, x, 47), so that it was not until

212 Kissel, in *Janus*, 1848, iii, 613-614.
213 Farnell, *The Cults of the Greek States,* ii, 644, 648.
214 Bruzon, *op. cit.,* pp. 136-137.

ÆSCULAPIUS

IT IS BELIEVED THAT THE EMPEROR AUGUSTUS REMOVED THE HEAD
OF ASKLEPIOS FROM THIS STATUE AND REPLACED IT BY THAT
OF HIS FAVORITE PHYSICIAN, ANTONIUS MUSA.

*The original is in the Vatican Museum, Rome. Reproduced
from a photograph supplied by the courtesy of The
New York Academy of Medicine Library.*

the following year that an embassy, headed by Q. Ogulnius, was sent to invite the deity to Rome. Ovid (*Metam.*,
xv, 622 ff.) relates that the embassy, on consulting the
oracle at Delphoi, were informed that Apollo was not
needed to diminish the grief of the city, but that they
should go to Epidauros and with a good omen invite his
son. This was done, but the priests hesitating to comply
with the request, the divinity himself appeared to the
commission during the night and promised to go in the
form of the snake which encircled his staff. On the following day, to the surprise of the priests, the god appeared in the temple in all his serpent majesty, and descending to the beach, leaped on board the trireme,
weighting it down with his great bulk and appropriating
the comfortable quarters of Ogulnius. All went well until
they approached the shores of Italy, when a storm arose,
and the ship put into the harbor of Antium, where stood
a sanctuary of Apollo. The serpent without warning left
the galley to pay a visit of respect to his father, coiling
himself in the top of a palm tree within the sacred precincts; and the embassy were in despair until, after three
days, he came down of his own accord and again boarded
the vessel, allowing it to proceed to Rome. Passing up the
Tiber, the people on the banks welcomed the god and
burned incense in his honor; but upon approaching the
city, the serpent is said to have risen up and, resting his
head against the mast, to have inspected the shores, after
which, suddenly leaving the ship, he disappeared in the
reeds of the Insula Tiberina (Livy, *Epitome,* xi; Valerius
Maximus, I, viii, 2; Aurelius Victor, *de Viris Illustribus,*
22). The embassy brought back the visible presence of
the god, or his incarnation, "anguem in quo ipsum numen
esse constabit," the form in which it was customary to
transfer the divinity in establishing a new sanctuary.

There was a legend that this Insula Tiberina had been

formed by corn sown by Tarquin in the Campus Martius, but which had been cut and thrown into the river by the people and had lodged on the shallows, mounds being added later and the banks raised so that the surface was capable of sustaining buildings (Livy, ii, 5). The god having indicated his choice, the island, sometimes called the 'Island of the Epidaurian serpent' (Apollinaris Sidonius, *Epistolæ*, I, vii, 12) or the 'Island of Æsculapius' (Suetonius, *Vita Claudii*, 25), was selected as the site of his temple, which was dedicated on January 1, 291 B.C., and which contained statues of Hygieia and Telesphoros.[215] In commemoration of the event, the festival of Æsculapius was fixed for that day, and subsequently, in 196 B.C., temples were built on the island, in compliance with vows, in honor of Iupiter (or Veiovis) and Faunus (Livy, xxxiv, 53). In 171 B.C., Lucretius decorated the Æsculapium with pictures taken in Greece as spoils of war (Livy, xliii, 4), and toward the end of the Republic the island, which was about one thousand feet long by three hundred wide and reached by two bridges, the Pons Cestius from the Ianiculum, and the Pons Fabricius from the Campus Martius, was made into the shape of a boat to celebrate the trireme which had brought the god to Rome, travertine blocks being placed for the prow and stern, while in Imperial times an obelisk in the shape of a mast stood in the center of the island. Plutarch, who called it the 'Sacred Island,' said that it contained "temples of the gods and porticoes" (*Vita Poblicolæ*, 8) ; and it is believed that practically all of it was devoted to the sick. Æsculapius had another temple in Rome believed to have been in connection with the baths of Diocletian (*CIL* i, 329).[216]

The old *di indigetes* who had been displaced by Apollo

215 Besnier, *L'Ile tibérine dans l'antiquité*, p. 197.
216 Wissowa, *op. cit.*, p. 306.

were pushed still further into the background by the coming of Æsculapius, and even Apollo took second rank as an averter of disease. Nevertheless, writers of the later years of the Republic have little to say concerning Æsculapius and his cult, and it is believed that it played a modest part in the religion of this period. Those who appealed to the god were, for the most part, the humbler class of citizens who did not care to pay much (or could not) and the slaves. Many masters sought to escape the burden of slaves who had protracted illnesses by sending them to Æsculapius and then neglecting them; and this became such an abuse that a law was passed which freed all slaves who recovered after being sent to the sanctuary (Suetonius, *op. cit.*, 25; Dion Kassios, lx, 29).

During the last centuries of the Republic, several foreign deities with healing cults came to Rome, where they assumed the name and attributes of Æsculapius; but his worship was the first to be derived from Greece and was the only genuine Greek foundation in the capital enjoying the authority of the Sibylline Books.[217] From the moment of his arrival the god had been the divine protector of the city against pestilence and had applied his therapeutic powers to the individual, whence the Epidaurian Æsculapius had precedence and official recognition, and, continuing to be distinguished above all others claiming his name, he retained throughout his supremacy as a healer.

Asklepiads, or physician-priests, from Epidauros accompanied the deity to Rome, where their habit of cultic secrecy, combined with the rule which forbade Romans to become priests of foreign worships, was conducive to the continuance of their rites unchanged. They brought the sacred serpents (Pliny, *op. cit.*, xxix, 22) and dogs with them (Festus, p. 110), so that the cultic practices

[217] Fowler, *Festivals*, p. 340.

were the same as in Greece (Festus, p. 237; Valerius Maximus, I, viii, 2), consisting of ritual purification and fasting, prayers, sacrifice, incubation, magic formulas, and the use of rational remedial measures with a general hygienic regimen. There remains no direct evidence of the use of incubation during the earlier centuries of the cult in Rome, but there can be no doubt that it was practiced there as in Greece, especially since prophetic oracles and divinely inspired dreams were known in the worship of the old native gods and could not fail to have been used at the Æsculapium, though positive evidence comes only with the Flavian period (*CIL* vi, 8).[218]

The Romans, susceptible to the marvellous, craved miracles, and cures suggestive of such wondrous powers of the divinity were freely noised abroad. In the eyes of the people Æsculapius possessed not only the mystic powers of a healer, but also of a preserver, saving in battle, protecting from murder and shipwreck, and finding lost articles. There was a general belief in the healing power of the hand and the sacredness of the altar, and the laying-on of hands was a common practice, as when the hand of a divinity wiped the pest away from the children of Valerius (Valerius Maximus, II, iv, 5). The 'Maffeian Inscriptions' (*CIG*, 5980) of the Insula Tiberina relate cures effected by applying the directions or oracles given in dreams—they were theurgic in character, and symbolic magic was associated with the chthonic ritual. The dreams and the visions of the nocturnal visitations of the god were interpreted by official *coniectores* as divine directions for means of cure by internal and external remedies, diet, regimen, and other methods common to the period; but although surgery was practiced by the lay practitioners of the city, as proved by surgical

[218] Thrämer, in *ERE* vi, 555; Preller, *op. cit.*, pp. 607, 609. Deubner, *De Incubatione*, p. 44.

instruments and appliances of iron and bronze, some
beautifully inlaid with silver, now deposited in museums,
there is little evidence of its use at the Æsculapium.[219]

Such inscriptions as the following, from the work of
Hieronymus Mercurialis,[220] illustrate cultic methods:

In these days the god [Æsculapius], admonished by the oracle,
answered one Gaius, who was blind, that he should go to the
right side of the altar and worship; afterwards, from the right he
should go to the left, and place his five fingers upon the altar,
and lift up his hands, and lay them upon his own eyes; and he
recovered his sight directly, the people standing by and rejoic-
ing together with him that such great miracles were performed
under our Emperor Antoninus.

The god [Æsculapius] answered by the oracle to Lucius, who
had a pleurisy and was despaired of by every man, that he should
come and take from the altar some ashes, and mix them together
with wine, and put them on his side; and he was cured; and he
publicly returned thanks to the god, and the people congratulated him.

The god [Æsculapius], by means of the oracle, admonished
Iulianus, who vomited blood and was despaired of by every man,
to come and take pine berries from the altar, and eat them with
honey for three days; and he was cured; and coming forth, he
publicly returned thanks before the people (CIG, 5980).[221]

The god [Æsculapius] admonished, by means of the oracle,
Valerius Aper, a blind soldier, to come and take the blood of
a white cock, to beat it up with honey and collyrium, and for
three days to put it on his eyes; and he came forth and gave
thanks in a public manner to the god.[222]

[219] Milne, *Surgical Instruments in Greek and Roman Times*, pp. 10-
23; also W. H. Buckler and R. Caton, "Medical and Surgical Instruments found at Kolophon," in *PRSM*, 1913-1914, vii, 235 ff.

[220] *De Arte Gymnastica*, Venetiis, 1573, based on the Farnese collection.

[221] W. Wroth, "Hygieia," in *JHS*, 1884, v, 93 ff.

[222] Cf. Besnier, *op. cit.*, p. 213.

A small marble stand, the base of a silver offering, probably of the time of Augustus, was found on the Insula Tiberina with the following inscription:

To Asklepios, the great god, the savior and benefactor, saved by thy hands from a tumor of the spleen, of which this is a silver model, as a mark of gratitude to the god, Neochares Iulianus, a freedman of the Imperial household.[223]

A dedication, found in front of the Porta Appia, from M. Ulpius Honoratus to Æsculapius and Hygia "pro salute sua suorumque et L. Iuli Helicis medici, qui curam mei diligenter egit secundum deos," shows the coöperation of the physician with the god.[224]

Other inscriptions, in their original form, are as follows:[225]

Æsculapio. et. Hygiæ. L. Sept. Nigrinus. Patro. Coll. Fabr. Col. Apul. pro. Salute. sua. et. suorum. posuit.

Æsculapio. et. Hygiæ. ceterisq. huius. loci. salutarib. C. Iul. Frontonianus. vet. ex. B.F. Cos. Leg. U.M.P. redditis. sibi. luminibus. grat. ag. ex. viso. pro. se. et. Carteia. Maxima. coniug. et. Iul. Frontina. Filia. V.S.L.M.

Prov. salute. Iuliæ. Veneriæ. Filiæ. dulcissimæ. deliciæ. suæ. tabellam. hanc. marm. cum. signo. Æsculapii. in somno. admonitus. L. Valerius. Capito. Æd. Ann. . . . D.S.P.L.M.D.D.D.

Numini. Æsculapi. et. Hygiæ. pro. salute. dominor. N.N. Aug. Antrocius. Verna. ipsor. ex. disp. pos.

Asclepio. et. Saluti. Commilitonum. Sex. Titius. Alexander. Medicus. Coh. V. pr. donum. dedit. Aug. VIII. F. Flavio. Sabino. Cos.

Asclepio. et. Saluti. Commilitonum. Coh. VI. pr. voto. suscepto. Sex. Titius. Medic. Coh. VI. pr. D.D.

[223] Hamilton, *op. cit.*, p. 67; cf. Besnier, *op. cit.*, p. 212.
[224] Thrämer, in *ERE* vi, 555.
[225] Kissel, in *Janus*, 1848, iii, 665-666.

Patients leaving the Æsculapium were required to pay when able, and many left *donaria* in gratitude for services, these being hung on the walls of the sanctuary. Along the approaches to the island were shops for the sale of votive offerings which have been disclosed by modern excavations on the embankment of the river at this point and found to contain large numbers of tokens— images, tablets, portraits, and anatomical models in bronze or terra-cotta. Some are of heroic size, others show a correct anatomy, and still others illustrate diseased conditions, these specimens being of almost every part of the human body, occasionally presenting sections of the trunk and internal organs, while a group of father, mother, and child suggests a thank offering for relief of sterility.[226]

Beginning with the Christian era, the cult of Æsculapius appears to have attracted a greater amount of attention, and from the better classes of Rome, so that after the first century A.D. it steadily gained influence until the time of Antoninus Pius, when there was a definite revival of interest in it. This Emperor caused a coin to be struck and inscribed to Æsculapius, commemorating the legend of his arrival in Rome and showing the serpent-god springing to the island with the river-deity Tiberinus half-rising from the water to receive him.[227] From an inscription, it is learned that during the reign of Antoninus there was a college of Æsculapius and Health, composed of individuals who assembled on a certain day of the year, made sacrifices, received small gifts, and partook of a meal.[228] The members were limited to sixty and sons succeeded to their fathers. The Æsculapium on the

[226] L. Sambon, "Donaria of Medical Interest," in *BMJ*, 1895, ii, 146, 216.

[227] Besnier, *op. cit.*, p. 176.

[228] Spon, *Recherches curieuses d'antiquités*, p. 326.

Insula Tiberina was probably more like a general public hospital than a sanctuary that would attract the better classes, and many of the wealthier people who desired the aid of the divinity besought him at other shrines.[229] Herodian, the historian, relates that the Emperor Caracalla visited the shrine of Asklepios at Pergamon to obtain a cure by means of incubation, and the Emperor Iulian asserted that Æsculapius, by indicating remedies, had repeatedly cured him of his maladies (Kyrillos, in *Iulianum,* vii, 235). Epidauros became popular with the Romans and Antoninus improved the place, erecting a temple to the Epidotai, the 'benevolent gods,' and building, just outside the sacred precinct, a refuge for lying-in women and the dying.[230] Thus Æsculapius eventually gained the confidence and veneration of the Roman people, who regarded him as the most beneficent of all gods, and he retained his preëminence as a divine healer until the pagan worships were suppressed, proving one of the most stubborn obstacles to Christianity (Eusebios, *Vita Constantini,* iii, 56). The Emperor Iulian endeavored to continue the cult (Kyrillos, *loc. cit.*), and Libanios praised Æsculapius (*Epistolæ,* 607); while at Rome he was 'Lord,' 'Savior,' 'King,' and 'Friend of Man,' and efforts were made to have his manifestations, marvels, and oracles prevail against the Christians.[231]

The Æsculapium on the Insula Tiberina was always the center from which the propaganda of the cult spread until Æsculapius was recognized throughout the Roman world as a divine physician, devoted only to the physical welfare of suffering humanity. In this expansion throughout the Latin provinces the divinity was worshipped separately, frequently as the Greek Asklepios, once as

[229] Pater, *Marius the Epicurean,* i, 27-42.
[230] See *supra,* pp. 264-265, 267-268, 282.
[231] Preller, *op. cit.,* p. 609.

'Deus Salutifer' (*CIL* viii, 20961), and also with other
deities; with Apollo (*CIL* iii, 2004; xiii, 6621), and sometimes with Hygia, usually called Salus, Dea Salus (*CIL*
vii, 164; viii, 2579ᵃ), or Valetudo, and also 'Bonæ Valetudo sacrum' (*CIL* viii, 9610, Mauretania) and 'Bonæ
Deæ Hygiæ' (*CIL* viii, 20747). From Northern Africa to
Caledonia, from the coast of Lusitania to the Black Sea
and Syria, Æsculapius and Hygia were invoked to con-
serve and reëstablish health, and were usually represented in the familiar forms of Græco-Roman art. In the
larger part of the provinces their worship was in or near
camps and their cult partook of a military character, while
in Syria, Spain, and Britain votive inscriptions have been
found in which he appears as a Roman officer.[232] At Carthage, the temple that crowned Byrsa hill was ascribed
to Æsculapius during the Empire, but doubtless it was
dedicated to the Punic Eshmun, with whom the divinity
was frequently confused.[233]

Æsculapius was also connected with many medicinal
springs in the provinces, and inscriptions show that he
was syncretized with local deities and associated with
many Nymphæ, who, presiding over springs having medicinal properties, were given appropriate epithets, 'Medi-
cæ' (*CIL* iii, 10595), 'Salutares' (*CIL* iii, 10891, 10893),
and 'Salutiferæ' (*CIL* iii, 1397), and votive tablets with
inscriptions have been found in Gaul, Britain, Spain, and
the Danube provinces, showing that they were venerated
and held in high esteem.[234]

Roman altars and other remains of the cult of Æsculapius and Hygia have been uncovered in many provinces.
In England the following relics have been unearthed: an
elaborately carved altar to Æsculapius and Salus at

[232] Toutain, *op. cit.*, i, 330-338.
[233] Cumont, *Oriental Religions*, p. 21; also Toutain, *op. cit.*, i, 336.
[234] Toutain, *op. cit.*, i, 380-381.

Chester; a hooded figure of Telesphoros at Birdoswald in Cumberland; two hooded figures of Telesphoros from the Castle Yard at Carlisle; sculptured figures of Æsculapius and Salus at Binchester; an altar dedicated to Asklepios and Hygieia at Tunstall; and minor evidences at Lancaster.[235]

From its first occupancy by Æsculapius until the present day, upwards of twenty-two centuries, the Insula Tiberina has been an Insula Sacra for the sick at Rome. In A.D. 1000 Emperor Otho erected a hospital on the foundations of the ancient temple, and from that time the island and hospital have borne the name San Bartolomeo. What is said to be the old Æsculapian well is a prominent feature of the altar-steps of the present church, first erected in the twelfth century and rebuilt in the seventeenth. About 120 feet deep, it has a circular curb of white marble carved with images of saints, and the Romans still use its waters for their medicinal properties. Excavations on the island in 1867 exposed layers of travertine rock which formed the prow of the island boat and disclosed the remains of a human bust and the symbols of the god, his staff and serpent, carved on the rock;[236] but these characteristic old relics were later covered by the mud and shifting sands of the river.

APOLLO

Apollo, primarily adopted into the Roman pantheon as an averter of pestilence and later becoming a divine healer, was the first of the Greek deities to be naturalized by Rome, even his name being retained unchanged in its Hellenic form.

The cult of this chief god of prophecy and presiding

[235] Barnes, in *PRSM*, 1913-1914, vii, 71 ff.
[236] Holländer, *Plastik und Medizin*, p. 91, fig. 96.

genius of the Delphic oracle had been brought to Magna
Græcia at so early a date that he was almost an indigenous Italian divinity. Tradition associated him with the
Sibyl of Cumæ, whose oracles he was believed to have
inspired, so that they were regarded as his own commands; and when the Sibylline Books were taken over by
Rome, he became the leader of the Greek movement. Tarquin had been acquainted with him as the Etruscan deity
Aplu, who possessed a sanctuary at the home of the Tarquin family at Cære.[237] According to tradition, the King
having lived at Corinth and preferring Greek oracles to
Roman seers, sent an embassy to Delphoi for instructions
when in difficulty (Livy, i, 56), while Dionysios says (iv,
69) he was the first to invoke the god for Rome on the
occasion of an epidemic which had attacked children and
pregnant women.

Apollo came to Rome from one of the Greek colonies of
Southern Italy, probably in advance of the Sibylline
Books; and the tradition that his earliest Italian home
was Cumæ is strengthened by the fact that the Senate
ordered sacrifice to be made to him at that place.[238] He
was at first worshipped privately under the name Apello,
and at the end of the kingdom he was received in Rome
as a divine healer;[239] but though it has been stated that
he was invoked during the plague of 464-463 B.C., the first
definite record is of the appeal to him to stay the pestilence of 433 B.C. In recognition of his divine assistance
at this time, a temple was vowed to him, this being placed
outside the *pomœrium* in the Flaminian Field, before the
Porta Carmentalis, and being dedicated in 431 B.C. to
Apollo Medicus "pro valetudine Populi Romani" (Livy,

237 Fowler, *op. cit.*, p. 181.
238 Wissowa, *op. cit.*, p. 293.
239 Carter, *op. cit.*, p. 83.

iv, 25, 29). At some later period Apollo developed a cult as a healing divinity.[240]

Apollo with others was invoked at the first *lectisternium* during the intractable pestilence of 399 B.C. (Livy, v, 13). During the plague of 212 B.C. aid was sought from him and Latona, while the Apollinarian games were instituted and celebrated yearly by order of the Prætors until, in 208 B.C., because of a protracted epidemic, they were vowed to be held forever on the thirteenth of July (*ib.*, xxvi, 23).[241] He was invoked during the pestilence of 181 B.C. with Æsculapius and Salus, and in gratitude for their services M. Fulvius dedicated a temple to him as Apollo Medicus in 180 B.C. (*ib.*, xl, 51), gilded statues of the three deities being placed within the shrine (*ib.*, xl, 37). This fane stood outside the Porta Carmentalis on the site of a former Apollinar (*ib.*, iii, 63); and in view of the positive statement of Asconius[242] that it was the only one to the god in Rome until the Palatine temple of Augustus, it was, in all probability, a restoration.

Apollo had usurped a large share of the functions of the old Roman deities as averters of disease, and in his turn he was overshadowed by the arrival of Æsculapius. His cult had never exercised any important religious or political influence in Rome, and apparently his worship gradually declined until after the battle of Actium, when Augustus, ascribing his success to the assistance given by the god, and in recognition of his favor, restored the temple of the divinity on the promontory of Actium, embellished it with a portion of the spoils, and made the worship of the deity a family cult. In 28 B.C., Augustus erected a temple of unusual splendor to the god on his private property on the Palatine, and in it he placed the

---

[240] Thrämer, in *ERE* vi, 554; also Wissowa, *op. cit.*, p. 294.

[241] Fowler, *op. cit.*, pp. 179-180.

[242] Ed. Kiessling and Schöll, Berlin, 1875, p. 81.

triad of Apollo, Latona, and Diana, with the new Greek ritual (Dionysius Halicarnasensis, XII, ix, 2).

Apollo became identified with Soranus in Etruria and the celebrated shrine on the summit of Mount Soracte was sacred to him as Apollo Soranus, the worshippers at this fane sacrificing to him annually by passing through the flames and pressing with undaunted foot the burning coals (Vergil, *op. cit.*, xi, 785-788), whence his priests, the 'Hirpi,' were exempted from military service (Pliny, *op. cit.*, vii, 2).

After Apollo became prominent in general Roman religion, he was made to say: "The healing art is my discovery, and throughout the world I am honored as the bearer of help; and the properties of simples are subject to us" (Ovid, *op. cit.*, i, 521-522); while Horace (*op. cit.*, 60) addresses him:

> Thou who restorest with thy healing art,
> The weakened limbs of the body.

In Imperial times, Apollo was believed to be the cause of disease as well as a healer; and his cures seem to have been wrought by his general divine powers and by symbolic magic, although the usual ritual of religious healing, of supplications, and of expiatory rites with sacrifices, regimen, and remedies were observed.[243] It is claimed that incubation was practiced in his cult; but, although this is entirely probable, positive evidence is lacking. Those who sought his aid addressed him as 'Apollo Salutaris et Medicinalis,' as appears on a Roman dedication (*CIL* vi, 39); and the details were entrusted to Vestals who invoked the god, crying aloud, "Apollo Medice, Apollo Pæan" (Macrobius, *op. cit.*, I, xvii, 15), and giving medicines in a state of nakedness, since nudity

---

[243] Kissel, in *Janus*, 1848, iii, 659.

was believed to be a magic preventive.[244] The patient must have fasted, and while touching him with the back of her hand, the Vestal must say: "Apollo forbids a disease to increase which a naked virgin restrains"[245] (Pliny, *op. cit.*, xxvi, 60), this being repeated thrice after she withdraws her hand, and both of them spitting on the ground each time.

The cult of Apollo, essentially in the phase of healing, extended to the Latin provinces, where the god was worshipped with Diana, but more frequently separately. He was often associated with Æsculapius (*CIL* iii, 2004; xiii, 6621); physicians invoked him (*CIL* xiii, 5079); and he had a cult at thermal springs, as at Aquæ Calidæ in Gaul (*CIL* ii, 4487, 4490). He was adored in Gaul as a healer ("Apollinem morbos depellere," Cæsar, *de Bello Gallico*, vi, 17), and his worship spread in the Rhine and Danube valleys, and to Britain. Apollo was identified with the Celtic gods Belenus, Borvo, Grannos, and others (*CIL* vi, 36; iii, 5586).[246]

HYGIA

SEE under the heading SALUS.

ISIS

THE worship of Isis, the most beloved and most popular goddess of the Egyptian pantheon, was united to that of Serapis in a cult which spread to the majority of the countries bordering on the Mediterranean, and to the Latin provinces. Possessing many religious features which had popularized the adoration of Demeter and Dionysos, and famed for healing, it had been well re-

[244] E. Riess, in Pauly-Wissowa, i, 35.

[245] "Negat Apollo pestem posse crescere, cui nude virgo restinguat," Heim, *op. cit.*, p. 506.

[246] Wissowa, *op. cit.*, p. 297; also Toutain, *op. cit.*, i, 314-318.

ceived in Greece, where it had been partially Hellenized and whence it had been brought to Magna Græcia, established at Puteoli and Pompeii,[247] and invaded Rome, but its temples there had been destroyed in 217 B.C. by order of the Senate (Valerius Maximus, i, 3).[248] During the time of Sulla (Apuleius, *Metamorphoses*, xi, 30), it was introduced into Rome at first as a private worship, Anubis and Harpokrates being associated with the cult in minor capacities, and the memory of Osiris being particularly honored. The rituals were symbolic and mysterious, but they appealed to the imagination of the people brought in contact with them; and, for the first time in Rome, a cult gave its faithful initiates assurance of purification, forgiveness of sins, communion with deity, regeneration of the soul, and blessed immortality.[249] Organized by its Egyptian priests, the worship attracted enthusiastic adherents, who rapidly grew in numbers. Its altars invaded the Capitoline (Ovid, *op. cit.*, xv, 826-828; Vergil, *op. cit.*, viii, 696-700; Propertius, IV, x, 39-46); its practices created official distrust; and because the augurs interpreted certain prodigies as evidence of the jealousy of the gods on account of the invasion, the Senate, in 58 B.C., ordered the destruction of all the altars of the cult, fifty-three in number. The altars were rebuilt and again officially destroyed in 54, 50, and 48 B.C.; but these repressive measures did little to restrain the ardor of its worshippers, whose influence became so great that, in 43 B.C., the triumvirs withdrew active opposition and decreed a temple, which, however, was not built until much later (Dion Kassios, xl, 47; xlvii, 15). Augustus forbade its chapels within the *pomœrium* (Suetonius, *Vit. Aug.*, 93), but as this order was disregarded, Agrippa, in 21 B.C., denied

---

[247] Wissowa, *op. cit.*, pp. 351-359.
[248] Teubner edition, Halm, ed. 1865, p. 17.
[249] Cumont, *op. cit.*, p. 100.

the cult any privileges within seven and a half stades of the city limits (Dion Kassios, liii, 2). In A.D. 19, owing to the debauching of a noble lady in one of the temples, Tiberius threw the image of Isis into the Tiber, destroyed the shrines, and crucified or banished the priests (Josephus, *Antiquitates,* xviii, 65 ff.; cf. Tacitus, *Ann.,* ii, 85). Under Caligula, however, the cult appears to have been recognized by the State, and although it received no public funds a temple to Isis Campensis was erected outside the *pomœrium* on the Campus Martius in A.D. 39 (Apuleius, *op. cit.,* xi, 26). In A.D. 71, Vespasian and Titus passed the night before their triumph at this shrine, and the procession started from it (Josephus, *de Bello Iudaico,* vii, 123); Domitian escaped from the populace in the garb of a priest of Isis; and after the destruction of the temple by the fire of A.D. 80 he and Alexander Severus and Diocletian replaced it by the most splendid structure in Rome (Suetonius, *Vita Domitiani,* 1; Eutropius, VII, xxiii, 5).[250] These favors to Isis were the first examples of an essentially popular religious movement triumphing over the continued resistance of the public authorities and official clergy,[251] and signalized the progress of Oriental religions in the Occident. No repression was now exercised against the cult outside the city, and its popularity spread from the Sahara to Britain and the mouths of the Danube. After the restrictions excluding foreign worships from within the *pomœrium* were removed in the third century A.D., Caracalla built a great temple to Isis and Serapis on the Quirinal (*CIL* vi, 570, 573), and perhaps the Iseum et Serapeum on the Cælian Hill (Scriptores Historiæ Augustæ, *Triginta Tyranni,* xxv, 4).

[250] Platner, *The Topography and Monuments of Ancient Rome,* pp. 62, 358.
[251] Cumont, *op. cit.,* p. 81.

During its earlier years in Rome, the worship drew its supporters mostly from the poorer classes, and many of the devotees were the dissolute men and women of the city who used the cult as a cloak for their orgies (e.g., Juvenal, *op. cit.*, vi, 486 ff.); but later it attracted many of the best patrician families, and Emperors were among its adherents.[252] From the time of the Antonines, when the cult reached its fullest development, it was the most bitter and effective opponent of Christianity until paganism was proscribed; while during the three months of the uprising of Eugenius in A.D. 394, and until his final overthrow, it was revived with great enthusiasm, a magnificent festival being held in honor of the goddess.

Of all the foreign cults in Rome, that of Isis and Serapis is said to have been the most civilized; and to this fact are due its success and continued worship in the Latin world during five centuries. It had some of the very qualities which existed in Christianity in a fuller and perhaps less artificial form, so that "the transition to Christianity was quite as much a process of blending as a violent displacement."[253]

Isis, a divinity of universal character embracing the virtues of all other goddesses, was the tutelary deity of women, the goddess of love, fertility, and healing, to whom all could appeal with assurance of sympathy and aid, and she was loved with a passionate devotion by large numbers of enthusiastic worshippers.

The priesthood of the cult was organized after the Egyptian model. Both the priests and priestesses were carefully chosen, trained in cultic usages, and punctilious in their daily duties.[254] The heads and faces of the priests

[252] Carter, *Religious Life*, pp. 84 ff.

[253] G. Showerman, "Isis," in *ERE* vii, 435-437; also Preller, *op. cit.*, ii, 373-385; Marquardt, *op. cit.*, iii, 77-81.

[254] Wissowa, *op. cit.*, p. 357.

were shaven, and they wore white linen. Worshippers were assured that if they would purify the body, Isis would cleanse the soul, wherefore they appointed 'nights sacred to Isis,' which they passed in her temples. The cultic ceremonies were attractive, fascinating, and impressive in dignity and solemnity. Two services were held each day. In the early morning, the temple was opened by priests who 'waked the deity,' unveiled and refreshed the images, lighted the fires, and with prayers, sacrifice, and libations greeted the dawn with loud acclamations (Apulieus, *op. cit.*, xi, 20). In the afternoon, a vase of consecrated water from the Nile was held before the people as the first principle of all things (Martial, X, xlviii, 1), ancient hymns of divine efficacy were intoned with the playing of the flute, the images were veiled, the worshippers bade farewell to the day, and the temple was closed.

The festivals of Isis were held from October 28 to November 3, the chief *motif* of the festival being a 'passion play' commemorating by a mystic drama the principal events in the life of Osiris, his struggles, his death, the search for and the discovery of his body, and his resurrection, all enacted with the aid of a large chorus. These events were celebrated with appropriate ceremonies on different days, and the mourning over the death of the god was followed by exultations over the 'finding of Osiris,' commemorated by the Hilaria, on October 31; the triumph of life over death; and these rejoicings were continued for three days.

The healing functions of Isis (Diodoros, i, 25) were in all essential respects those of Serapis, except that she was the especial favorite of women. Isis was usually represented as wearing one or another of her attributes on the head, the lotus (resurrection),[255] the uræus, or

---

[255] Lafaye, *Histoire du culte des divinités d'Alexandrie, Serapis, Isis, Harpocrate et Anubis, hors de l'Égypte*, pp. 167-170.

some cereal plant, such as wheat, as the goddess of fertility and vegetation (Apuleius, *op. cit.*, xi, 3).

MAGNA MATER

MAGNA MATER (an abbreviated form for Mater Deum Magna Idæa), the great Asiatic Mother-Goddess and the 'Mother of the Gods,' was brought to Rome as a Hellenic divinity during the second Punic War when the Roman State was threatened, and when the people were in danger of demoralization through belief that they had incurred the hatred of some deity. All religious expedients had been tried in vain when the Decemviri discovered in the 'Books' that Italy could be freed only by bringing from Pessinus, in Galatia, the sacred stone representing the goddess. Accordingly, the divinity, in the form of a black meteorite, was formally received at Rome in 204 B.C. by the most worthy Romans, and with great pomp and solemnity was escorted to the temple of Victory on the Palatine (Livy, xxix, 10, 14; Ovid, *Fasti*, iv, 255 ff.). The crops at once improved; Hannibal was forced out of Italy; and the goddess, having accomplished all that had been expected of her, was honored by being admitted to State worship, while a temple, Ædes Matris Deum Magnæ Idææ, was erected on the Palatine and dedicated to her April 10, 191 B.C. Like other Greek worships it was placed under the charge of the Decemviri. Her festival, the Megalesia, was held on April 4, the anniversary of her entry into Rome, and was celebrated by the matrons of the city, being accompanied by scenic plays, the Ludi Megalenses (Livy, xxxvi, 36), which continued from April 4 to 10 (*CIL* i, 314). Her temple was burned in A.D. 3 (Valerius Maximus, I, viii, 11), but was restored by Augustus (*Monumentum Ancyranum*, iv, 8).

Magna Mater represented the broad, universal conception of a 'Mother-Goddess' embracing the ideas underlying the many Oriental goddesses. They were held to be identical with her, and their personalities, when brought to Rome under their local names, were either blended with hers, so they lost their identity, as Rhea, Kybele, and Mâ; or they became variants with a closely related worship, as Isis, Atargatis (Dea Syria), Tanit (Dea Cælestis), and Mâ-Bellona.[256] Magna Mater was also assimilated to the Roman earth-goddess Ops, whose worship was always distinct, and to Mater Matuta in her obstetric function.

In coming to Rome, Magna Mater was accompanied by her Phrygian Korybantes, the eunuch priests called 'Galli,' who appeared in woman's dress. Their worship was enthusiastic and wild, and was accompanied by orgiastic, barbaric Oriental rites; while their public processions were characterized by dancing and by noisy clashing of cymbals. Rome was scandalized, but the cult so fascinated and excited the ardor of the lower classes that it was not only placed under the supervision of the Decemviri, but, anticipating trouble, the Senate adopted restrictive police regulations, confining the pageants to certain days of the year and limiting the strange ceremonies to the precincts of the Palatine temple (Dionysius Halicarnasensis, *Antiquitates Romanæ,* II, xix, 4 f.; Ovid, *Fasti,* iv, 377). Roman citizens were forbidden to become priests of the rite or to attend its ceremonies, and these measures were continued until the Empire, only to be relaxed in the second century A.D., when the worship was reorganized, and the Archigalli and all priests and priestesses were Romans, confirmed by the Quindecemviri.

The more extravagant developments were evolved during the Empire. Attis and Adonis had been brought to

[256] Wissowa, *op. cit.,* pp. 359 ff.

Rome with their respective female cults, and Attis finally became the more prominent religious figure, even over-shadowing Magna Mater in her own realm; while festivals were organized to celebrate the myths of these vegetation-deities, and to commemorate their deaths and revivification, symbolic of the disappearance of vegetation in the fall and its revival in the spring (Plutarch, *de Iside et Osiride*, 69). These feasts and their pageants were conducted in the name of Magna Mater and were first introduced by Claudius for March 27; but later were extended to seven days. The *Canna intrat* was celebrated on March 15; the *Arbor intrat,* on the twenty-second; the *Sanguen,* when devotees madly performed self-mutilation, on the twenty-fourth; the *Hilaria,* when the festival reached its zenith in the wild rejoicings of the worshippers on the reawakening of Attis, on the twenty-fifth; followed by a day of rest, the *Requietio,* on the twenty-sixth. The only part of the ceremony in which the State and citizens had a share was the *Lavatio,*[257] directed by the Quindecemviri, when, on March 27, the symbol of the goddess (the meteoric stone) was drawn in a wagon by cows to the Porta Capena and bathed in the Almo, a tributary of the Tiber (Lucan, i, 599 f.). At a later date self-mutilation on the day of blood was symbolized by an incision in the arm of the chief priest and sprinkling the blood (Tertullian, *Apol.,* 25). The *taurobolium,* the baptism in the blood of the bull, also a prominent feature of Mithraism, was celebrated in this cult on March 28 as a symbol of purification and as a dedication to the priesthood,[258] and after undergoing both the *taurobolium* and *criobolium* (baptism in the blood of a ram) worshippers were born again for eternal life ("renatus ad æternum,"

[257] Frazer, *op. cit.,* ii, 266-274; also Pearson, in *ERE* viii, 850.

[258] G. Showerman, "Taurobolium," in *ERE* xii, 214-215; also Frazer, *op. cit.,* i, 274-275.

CIL vi, 510).²⁵⁹ In the later Imperial period, a sanctuary of Magna Mater stood on the right bank of the Tiber on the site of the present Vatican grounds, and excavations, especially those for the foundations of the Basilica of St. Peter, have disclosed so many taurobolium altars that this was apparently the chief center of the ceremony (*CIL* vi, 497-504; *IG* xiv, 1019, 1020).

The cult of Magna Mater became influential in Rome during the Empire and was among the most prominent in its opposition to Christianity until the pagan worships were suppressed; but it is claimed that its influence was always harmful, and that it caused more demoralization among the people than all the other eastern rites.

Healing was a prominent feature of the cultic functions. Sterile women appealed to the goddess for fertility and were lashed over the loins by the 'Galli,' both at the temples and during the processions on the streets; while 'metragyrtes' (minor officials of the cult) went through city and country attending the sick and selling images of the goddess, amulets which were assumed to cure all ills, and especially talismans of the phallus carved from a pomegranate root.²⁶⁰

MITHRAS

MITHRAS was an ancient Indo-Iranian divinity of heavenly light, of righteousness, and of the plighted word; and his was the last of the Oriental religions that reached Rome, being brought there about 67 B.C. by pirates of Asia Minor captured by Pompey (Plutarch, *Vita Pompei,* 24). The cult found favor among the sailors and soldiers who worshipped Mithras as the protecting genius of arms and

²⁵⁹ J. S. Reid, "Asceticism," in *ERE* ii, 107; also G. Showerman, "Criobolium," in *ERE* iv, 314.

²⁶⁰ Bruzon, *op. cit.,* pp. 135-136; also Wissowa, *op. cit.,* pp. 63-64, 317-326.

the tutelary deity of armies;[261] and thanks to the ardent support of the troops, the worship spread rapidly throughout the Roman provinces, especially Gaul, Britain, Germania, and the valley of the Danube, where many centers of Mithraism were established, while slaves and freedmen of private households of Rome, and many who were government officials, were enthusiastic devotees and active in propagating the new religion among the people. The cult attracted little attention till toward the end of the first century A.D.;[262] but it had slowly penetrated among the masses, and now was steadily permeating the better classes until it finally won the support of the cream of Roman society and of the highest officials of the State,[263] so that during the third and fourth centuries, the worship of Mithras became by far the most influential of all the Oriental rites, before which others faded into comparative insignificance.[264] The cult was the chief exponent of the scientific methods of divination by astrology, and penetrated under cover of the sidereal theology taught by the 'Magi' and 'Chaldæi'; but although its doctrines were accepted, it never received the authority of a State religion. Representing a pantheistic sun-worship, Emperors adopted it and regarded Mithras as the protecting divinity of their imperial power, as the "master and god by right of birth," this being illustrated by the dedication of an altar to Mithras, "fautori imperii sui," by Diocletian at Carnuntum on the Danube in A.D. 307.[265] The sun-god Elagabal[266] of Emessa, set up early in

[261] Cumont, *op. cit.*, p. 144.

[262] H. S. Jones, "Mithraism," in *ERE* viii, 755-759.

[263] It is believed that Commodus was one of the initiates (*CIL* vi, 2271), his successors were lenient toward the cult, and Alexander Severus showed Mithraism the same respect paid to Christianity.

[264] Carter, *op. cit.*, pp. 87-88.

[265] Cumont, *op. cit.*, p. 150.

[266] Probably the form for the Hebrew word meaning 'Mountain-God.'

the third century A.D., was superseded by the Aurelian State cult of Sol Invictus, a name under which Mithras was absorbed into the solar pantheon as 'invictus Mithras' and 'deus Sol invictus Mithras'; and, until the conquest of Constantine overwhelmed paganism, Mithraism bade fair to become a world-wide religion.

Mithras was beneficent, the friend of mankind who had furnished the moisture essential to life, and was represented as sacrificing the bull, the source of all generation, by whose death he overcame unrighteousness, and spreading its blood, which impregnated all things, brought about fertility and regeneration. Mithras personified moral light, truth and justice,[267] the two essentials developed in the Mithraic theology as necessary for purity, moral and mystic, and the conception of the destiny of the soul after death. Life was an ordeal, a struggle against evil. Purity, in thought, word, and action, was indispensable to victory. After death came the judgment, the soul being condemned to torture in the abyss with Ahriman; or, protected and assisted by Mithras, shaking off all earthly taint, was accorded the privilege of returning through the seven planetary spheres to the eighth heaven and there enjoying the sublime essence, the light in which the gods sojourned in an eternal beatitude. The romantic story of Mithras' struggles for humanity, as the minister of Ahura Mazda, together with the profoundly religious content of his doctrines of redemption, salvation, and the attainment of ideal hopes of immortality, of which the *taurobolium*,[268] or baptism of blood, was the pledge, made the strongest possible appeal to the deepest emotions; while initiation in the seven grades of the Mithraic Mysteries, from Corax (the Raven) to Pater (Father) (*CIL* vi, 749-753; Jerome, *Epistolæ*, cvii, *ad Lætam;* Tertullian,

[267] Reinach, *Cults, Myths, and Religions,* pp. 180 ff.
[268] Frazer, *op. cit.,* i, 274; also Showerman, in *ERE* xii, 214-215.

op. cit., 8) gave full assurance of forgiveness of sins by
expiation and personal consecration to the god. Mithraism, a religion of revelation which brought light and
purity to the minds of men, banished all evil, and inculcated the brotherhood of man, became the most formi-
dable antagonist of Christianity and at one time threatened to prevail over it.[269]

Little is known of the rites of the cult, which appear to
have consisted in the usual lustrations, libations, and
sacrifice, and, in addition, initiation in the Mysteries with
their revelations. The seven degrees of Mithraism corresponded to the seven zones through which the soul of the
deceased must pass for its several transformations before reaching that of eternal peace. The initiation, which
gave the worship its originality and strength, was designed as an earthly rehearsal to prepare the soul for the
vicissitudes it was assumed it would meet on its journey
after death, and the requirements for passage through
the gates of each of these zones to its home of eternal
rest.[270] These ceremonies, conducted in costume and character appropriate to the several grades, are asserted to
have been ordeals by fire, cold, hunger, thirst, etc., with
the requirement of showing steadfastness in the face of
threats of death (Tertullian, *de Corona*, 15). The communities of the cult acquired an internal solidarity. The
members were called brothers (*fratres*), and all others
were excluded from its temples.[271] The ceremonies of the
cult were conducted in small underground chapels
(*spelæa* or *Mithræa, CIL* iii, 4420), holding not more than
one hundred each, on the walls of which were depicted the
slaying of the bull by the god. The largest Mithræum
known was discovered in 1912 in the Thermæ Caracallæ

[269] Carter, *op. cit.*, pp. 120 ff., 138 ff.

[270] Jones, in *ERE* viii, 756; also Elderkin, *Kantharos*, p. 32.

[271] Toutain, *op. cit.*, ii, 121-177.

in Rome, with an inscription to Zeus-Helios-Serapis-Mithras. Mithraism was essentially a man's religion; and since its votaries wished their wives to have similar religious advantages, a union was made with certain female cults which supplied to them what Mithraism could not offer, a notable example being the alliance with the worship of Magna Mater.[272]

The priests of Mithras were past masters in the arts of magic and the pseudo-science of astrology, and the cult concerned itself with politics, science, etiquette, and personal affairs. Healing was a prominent part of the cult functions; and the priests cured the sick by divination, astrology, magic, and the use of medicinal herbs which had sprung from the blood of the bull.[273]

The festival of December 25, sacred to Sol Invictus (*Natalis invicti Solis*), was in practice a festival of the nativity of Mithras, the Unconquered Sun (*Soli invicto Mithræ*),[274] although the rites were addressed to the Sun as the State deity.[275] In the fourth century A.D., the day was adopted by the Western and Eastern branches of the Christian Church (at Antioch about A.D. 375) as the true date of the Nativity of Christ.[276]

SABAZIUS

SABAZIUS, originally a Thracian or Phrygian deity of a nature similar to that of Dionysos, was the presiding divinity of a mystic and orgiastic cult which invaded Rome from Greece. The Romans associated him with Iupiter as Iupiter-Sabazius; but though it is said that he was known in Rome during the Republic, there appears to be

---

[272] Cumont, *Mysteries*, p. 179; also Jones, *op. cit.*, in *ERE* viii, 759.
[273] Bruzon, *op. cit.*, pp. 136, 138.
[274] Cumont, *Textes*, ii, 99 ff.
[275] Wissowa, *op. cit.*, pp. 90-91.
[276] Frazer, *op. cit.*, i, 302-305.

no positive proof that the cult and its mysteries, the
Sacra Savadia, gained a foothold in the city and in Italy
before A.D. 2.[277] The worship was attached to that of
Magna Mater and was finally absorbed by it. In the late
period, holy marriages, or sex communion with the god
or goddess, was a part of its mysteries as conveying a
sense of deity, and this was assailed as obscene by the
early Christian Fathers, though it was claimed that the
ritual was only symbolic and was at most only very indirectly detrimental to morals.

Sabazius was a healing deity, acclaimed a second Æsculapius. His hand had both prophylactic and therapeutic
powers, and healing by the laying-on of hands was common in his cult. The right hand of the god placed on
the abdomen warded off evil, assisted child-birth, and
effected delivery; while, with at least three fingers out-
stretched, it was used in healing and as a symbol of protection and blessing. It was customary for women who
had been assisted in confinement to dedicate votive hands
to Sabazius in gratitude, and many such offerings have
been found with fingers open, and often with figures of
animals, or of the eagle and the eagle-stone, carved upon
them, supposed to represent the 'healing hand of Sabazius.'[278] The serpent was the emblem of the divinity, and
his initiates wore a golden snake attached to the breast
of their garments (Clemens Alexandrinus, *Protrepticus,*
ii, 16, p. 14, ed. Potter).

SERAPIS

SERAPIS was a prominent divinity of the later Egyptian
pantheon who, through the influence of Ptolemy I, supplanted Osiris and Apis, acquired their functions and

[277] Wissowa, *op. cit.,* p. 376.
[278] Weinreich, *op. cit.,* pp. 16, 18, 28.

attributes, and was joined with Isis in worship. The cult had gained fame for cures at Alexandria and had reached Rome with its prestige enhanced by the success it had won in Greece.[279]

Serapis, celebrated as a healer, was easily the leader of all the foreign healing deities who came to Rome in rivalry with Æsculapius, whether claiming his name or arrogating an equality in therapeutic powers; and his methods were singularly like those in vogue in the cult of the Greek Asklepios at Pergamon and elsewhere, which had been adopted at Alexandria.[280] Its essential features were incubation, either by the patients themselves, by friends, or by priests, with hieratic interpretation, divination, magic formulas and incantations, medicines, diet, and general hygienic measures. Suppliants, after undergoing a ceremonial purification, made sacrifices before passing the night in the temple; and while they slept, the god and his attendants visited them, often touched the diseased part, and applied some remedy. Dreams and visions were interpreted; and if the cure had not been effected by a miracle, the divine directions for healing were followed (Iamblichos, de Mysteriis, iii, 3; Artemidoros, iv, 22). Many of the priests of Isis and Serapis are said to have been educated physicians who prescribed for the patients according to their technical knowledge and pursued a systematic treatment.[281]

Isis, who was invoked by women, especially for the troubles peculiar to their sex, conferred fertility and gave nursing mothers full breasts; while nursing women applied at the temple for employment, and after swearing that they were free from all disease, underwent a complete and searching physical examination by the priests.

---

[279] J. G. Milne, "Græco-Egyptian Religion," in ERE vi, 376-378.
[280] Wissowa, op. cit., pp. 351-359; also Bruzon, op. cit., p. 137.
[281] Bruzon, loc. cit.

If approved, the priests consecrated the first milk pressed from the breasts, and the women remained as wet-nurses, for hire if free women, or for sale if slaves.[281]

The walls of the temples of Isis and Serapis were adorned by numerous votive tablets, inscriptions, and anatomical models, many of which were of the male and female genital organs.[282] One of the inscriptions was the gift of a man named Saurana in recognition of the cure of his son;[283] and another text declares that Serapis directed two sick men to go to Vespasian and allow him to touch the one with his spittle and the other with his foot, thus healing blindness and a crippled hand (Suetonius, *Vita Vesp.*, 7; Tacitus, *Hist.*, iv, 81). A votive medallion to Serapis has been found showing the mystic tripod and the attributes of Æsculapius. The tripod is supported upon a vase standing on the heads of three rams and encircled by a serpent whose head is raised above the vase as if to partake of its contents; and at the base are three cocks eating sacred barley.[284]

The following inscriptions, expressing thanks to these deities for a return of health, have been found:[285]

Isi. sacr. L. Magius. Phileas. Vi. Vir. Aquil. ob. salut. Grattiani. Filii. et. Grattiæ.

Isidi. et. Serap. sacrum. ex. voto. pro. filioli. salute. suscepto. Saurana. fecit.

I.S.I.P.D.M. Isidi. salutari. pro. sal. Q. Vergilii. Modesti. Cassia. Mat. V.S.D.

Serapis was usually represented with the emblems of Æsculapius, the serpent and staff; and on an ancient

[282] F. Buret, "La Médecine chez les Romains avant l'ère chrétienne," in *Janus*, 1896, i, 522.

[283] Kissel, in *Janus*, 1848, iii, 670; also Sprengel, *op. cit.*, i, 184.

[284] Sprengel, *op. cit.*, i, 183, 185.

[285] Kissel, *loc. cit.*

monument the god is shown with the serpent coiled around his body and an aureole upon the head.[284]

(For the history of the cult in Rome and for its general character, see under the heading Isis.)

Supplement to Chapter VII.

THE following are a few examples of minor Roman functional deities and *numina* who supervised some of the less prominent spheres of divine activity, with prescribed subdivision of duties, as illustrated by auxiliary divinities in the cults of Iuno Lucina and Diana, especially in relation to protection, physiological processes, and human development; of (A) conception, gestation, and birth, and (B) the care and growth of children from infancy to the maturity of adult life.

(A) *Minor Deities and* Numina *Associated with Child-Bearing.*

ANTEVORTA, Porrima, Prorsa, and Prosa were practically identical and were invoked for head presentations and easy delivery (Macrobius, *Saturnalia,* I, vii, 20; Ovid, *Fasti,* i, 633-636; Varro, *apud* Aulus Gellius, XVI, xvi, 4 ff.).

AVERRUNCUS was a deity who guarded women during parturition and afterwards from the assaults of Silvanus (Varro, *de Ling. Lat.,* VII, v, 100; Aulus Gellius, V, xii).

CANDELIFERA lighted and carried the candles during confinement (Tertullian, *ad Nationes,* ii, 11).

CINXIA loosened the bride's girdle after marriage (Festus, p. 92).

CURITIS protected married women and gave them promise of strong children (*ib.,* p. 147).

DECIMA, one of the Fates, guarded women during the tenth lunar month of pregnancy, determined the date of delivery, and presided over the accouchements (Aulus Gellius, III, xvi, 10-11).

DEVERRA, with Intercidona and Pilumnus, guarded the young mother from attacks of Silvanus, one striking the threshold with an axe and the other with a pestle, while Deverra swept it with a broom to prevent him from entering the house (Augustine, de Civitate Dei, vi, 9).

FEBRUA was a goddess of purification who presided over the delivery of the after-birth and over purgation (Festus, p. 85).

FEBRUUS (and Februlis) purified women to favor fecundity and coöperated with the Luperci at the Lupercalia to drive away the hostile spirits that prevented impregnation. What Februlis did for women Februus did for men (ib.).

FLUONIA (or Fluona) stopped the menses after conception and prevented hemorrhages during pregnancy (Paulus, p. 92).

INTERCIDONA guarded the navel and coöperated with Pilumnus and Deverra in protecting the lying-in woman against Silvanus (Augustine, loc. cit.).

MENA presided over menstruation, inducing it during adolescence, and remaining idle during pregnancy (Augustine, op. cit., iv, 11; vii, 2-3).

NONA, one of the Fates, coöperated with Decima in determining the proper date of birth (Varro, apud Aulus Gellius, III, xvi, 10; Tertullian, de Anima, 37).

NUMERIA, the goddess of counting, was also the divinity of speedy, successful births (Varro, apud Nonius, p. 352).

OPIGENA, a divine midwife, aided in child-birth, particularly in the cult of Iuno Lucina (Festus, p. 200).

PARTULA presided over the delivery and placed the binder (Tertullian, *loc. cit.*).

PERFICA was a completing goddess who presided over coition (Arnobius, *adversus Nationes*, iv, 131).

PERTUNDA presided over the first coition (Arnobius, *loc. cit.;* Augustine, *op. cit.*, vi, 9).

POPULONA, a phase of Iuno, protected against devastation and promoted an increase in population (Augustine, *op. cit.*, vi, 10).

PORRIMA, see Antevorta.

POSTVORTA presided over breech presentations (Varro, *apud* Aulus Gellius, XVI, xvi, 4 ff.).

PREMA presided over the coition of newly married couples (Augustine, *op. cit.*, vi, 9, note 3).

PRORSA (or Prosa), see Antevorta.

SENTINUS and Sentina gave the embryo sensation (Tertullian, *ad Nationes*, ii, 11; Augustine, *op. cit.*, vii, 2-3).

SUBIGUS was the tutelary god of the wedding night (Augustine, *op. cit.*, vi, 9).

VAGITANUS opened the mouth for the first cry and promoted breathing and squalling (Varro, *apud* Aulus Gellius, XVI, xvii, 2).

VITUMNUS bestowed upon the child the faculty of life (Tertullian, *loc. cit.;* Augustine, *op. cit.*, vii, 2-3).

(B) *Minor Deities and* Numina *Associated with the Care and Growth of Children from Infancy to Maturity.*

ABEONA watched over the goings of the child (Augustine, *op. cit.*, iv, 21; vii, 3).

ADEONA watched over the comings of the child (Augustine, *loc. cit.*).

AGENORIA bestowed the power of reaction to stimulation (Augustine, *op. cit.*, iv, 11).

ALEMONA presided over the nutrition of the embryo and child (Tertullian, *de Anima*, 37).

CATIUS, a protector of boys, awakened and molded the child's intellect (Augustine, *op. cit.*, iv, 21).

CUBA presided over the passing of the child from the mother to the cradle and blessed its sleep (Varro, *apud* Donatus, in *Terentii Phormionem*, I, i, 15; Augustine, *op. cit.*, iv, 11; vii, 11).

CUNINA protected the infant in the cradle (Varro, *apud* Nonius, p. 167).

DOMIDUCUS presided over conducting the bride to her husband and new home (Augustine, *op. cit.*, vi, 9); while Domiduca led children home (Tertullian, *ad Nationes*, ii, 11).

EDUSA taught the infant to take food and was invoked to bless its first nourishment (Varro, *apud* Nonius, p. 108; *id.*, *apud* Donatus, *loc. cit.*; Tertullian, *loc. cit.*; Augustine, *op. cit.*, iv, 11; xxxiv, 6, 9).

FABULINUS awakened the understanding and taught the child the articulation of words (Varro, *apud* Nonius, p. 532).

FATA SCRIBUNDA recorded the destiny of the child as determined by Fatum, but during the first week of its life, before it was inscribed, the Romans prayed that it might be favorable (Tertullian, *de Anima*, 39; Aulus Gellius, II, xvi, 9-11).

FORTUNA BARBATA provided for the growth of the beard (Augustine, *op. cit.*, iv, 11).

ITERDUCA guarded the child in its journeyings to and from school (Augustine, *op. cit.*, vi, 9; vii, 3).

Iuga, or Iugalis, originated the marriage bond and carried the courting to engagement (Festus, p. 63).

Iugatinus was the god of marriage (Augustine, *op. cit.*, iv, 11; vi, 9).

Iuventas, the goddess of youth, beautified and guided youthful development (Augustine, *op. cit.*, iv, 11; Tertullian, *ad Nationes*, ii, 11).

Latius awakened and molded the intellect (see Fabulinus) (Nonius, p. 532).

Levana supervised the raising of the infant from the ground by the father (see Ops) and bore witness to its legitimacy (Tertullian and Augustine, *locc. citt.*).

Locutius taught the child to speak correctly (Tertullian, *loc. cit.*; Nonius, *loc. cit.*; Augustine, *op. cit.*, iv, 21; vii, 3).

Mens was the goddess who conferred high intellectual powers (Nonius, *loc. cit.*; Augustine, *op. cit.*, iv, 21).

Nundina supervised the purification and naming of children, which took place on the eighth day for girls and on the ninth day for boys, the *dies lustricus,* when they were adopted by the family and received their names and the *bulla,* or amulet, which they wore as a protection against all evil, especially sorcery (Macrobius, *op. cit.*, I, xvi, 36).

Ossipaga presided over the growth and hardening of the bones of the embryo and child (Arnobius, *op. cit.*, IV, vii, 8).

Parca was one of the Fates who determined the destiny of the child about one week after birth (Arnobius, *op. cit.*, iv, 85; Aulus Gellius, III, xvi, 9-11).

Paventia guarded the infant from all causes of sudden terror and fright (Tertullian, *loc. cit.*; Augustine, *op. cit.*, iv, 11).

POTINA presided over the child's drinking, and sacrifices were made to bless the first liquid which the infant took (Tertullian and Augustine, *locc. citt.*; Varro, *apud* Nonius, p. 108; *id., apud* Donatus, in *Terentii Phormionem*, I, i, 15).

RUMINA (or Rumilia) caused the breasts to swell and presided over the suckling of the infant (Tertullian and Augustine, *locc. citt.*).

SENTIA gave the child discernment and wisdom (Augustine, *op. cit.*, iv, 11).

STATULINUS, Statanus and Statina were divinities who taught the child to stand and walk (Varro, *apud* Nonius, p. 532; Tertullian, *de Anima*, 39).

STIMULA made the child sensitive to impressions that result in action (Augustine, *loc. cit.*).

VATICANUS was the maker and developer of the human voice, the first cry of the infant corresponding to the first syllable of its future name (Varro, *apud* Aulus Gellius, XVI, xxxvii; Augustine, *op. cit.*, vii, 2).

VENILIA promised future success for the child (Augustine, *op. cit.*, vii, 22).

VIRGINENSIS presided over the loss of maidenhood and made the girl a married woman (Augustine, *op. cit.*, iv, 11; vi, 9).

VOLUMNUS and Volumna gave the child the will to do right (Augustine, *op. cit.*, iv, 21; vii, 3).

VOLUPIA granted the capacity for pleasure and present enjoyment (Tertullian, *ad Nationes*, ii, 11; Augustine, *op. cit.*, iv, 8, 11).

CHAPTER EIGHT
CELTIC GODS

CHAPTER EIGHT

THE HEALING GODS OF THE ANCIENT CELTS

PART I: GENERAL SURVEY

The ancient Celts and their records.

THE earliest home of the Celts in Europe seems to have been in the basin of the upper Danube, in the basin of the Main, to the east of the Rhine, and in the areas corresponding to modern Baden, Württemberg, and Bavaria, spreading thence to Gaul, the British Isles, Spain, and northern Italy, while to the east they migrated to Pannonia, Illyria, and Dacia, and even to Asia Minor.[1] Their ancient beliefs and practices regarding matters of health and of disease and its treatment, seem to have corresponded very closely to those of other peoples in the early stages of development toward civilization; when misfortune and disease came upon them they looked to the gods for relief and appealed to them through the medium of their priests. The scanty and fragmentary data concerning their religious faith and cultic usages are scattered over western Europe, for the Celts left no records except brief inscriptions (found mainly in the region of ancient Gaul and the Rhenish provinces, and in lesser number in Britain) and traditions, mythical tales, and folklore (especially in Ireland and Wales). Nevertheless, this material presents a general uniformity which is indicative of a tenacious retention of the essentials of

[1] Dottin, *Les anciens peuples de l'Europe,* pp. 201-211; Schrader, *Atlas de géographie historique,* Map 11.

their native faith, but it is so lacking in detail that, although generously supplemented by the comments of contemporaneous classical writers,[2] it is barely sufficient to reconstruct even an approximately satisfactory outline of their religion and religious customs. To add to the difficulties, this system was undermined in Gaul and Britain by the advent of the Romans, and its purity was invaded by the cults of foreign gods from Rome and the East. Augustus forbade Roman citizens to attend Druid ceremonies (Suetonius, *Vita Claudii*, 25); Roman ritual was introduced, shrines and temples were erected on Roman models, and the Celtic deities were assimilated with Roman divinities and received Roman names. Thereafter the native Celtic religion bore the strong impress of Roman influences and domination, while in Ireland the victory of Christianity obscured the figures of the ancient gods.[3]

The Celtic religion.

Celtic religion centered about the great activities of nature, especially around the deities of fertility and growth; and over all nature's activities presided superhuman beings differing in character, rank, power, and functions. With the development of religious conceptions, the vague primitive *numina* of the more important aspects of nature tended to become definite as gods and goddesses, and received names. The spirits of vegetation, notably those of corn and general agriculture, were apparently evolved very early and were regarded as female until the men, the hunters and warriors, joined the women in tilling the soil. Natural objects, such as trees and forests, wells and springs, streams and rivers, moun-

[2] H. d'Arbois de Jubainville, *Principaux auteurs à consulter sur l'histoire des Celtes*, Paris, 1902.

[3] MacCulloch, *Celtic Mythology*, pp. 17-20, 206-213.

tains and sky, sun and moon, had indwelling deities who presided over them; and there were civilization-divinities of the arts and crafts, of music, of commerce, and of war. There were also spirits of the earth and of the 'other-world,' and these, occurring singly or in groups, were beneficent, maleficent, or of mixed character like human beings.[4] They were believed to have magic skill and to live in forests or in caves and other recesses of the earth, whence they emerged to manifest themselves, preferably at night. There were many of these groups, such as the benignant Lugoves, the malignant Dusii (Augustine, *de Civitate Dei*, xv, 29), the Castæci and Castæcæ, the Icotii or Icotiæ, the Di Silvani and Deæ Silvanæ, the Di Casses, and the Nervini or Nervinæ. From the divinities of fertility and growth the greater seasonal gods of agriculture were evolved; and from the cults of vegetation-deities the women developed the worship of the nature-god-desses of fertile 'Mother-Earth,' of the Matres and the Matronæ, the Proximæ and the Iunones, 'Mothers' or 'Kinswomen,' who were the protecting divinities of various localities.

Celtic gods.

Most of the Celtic deities were local in name, although like many others in character and function. Each tribe, group, and town had its own tutelary divinity, whose rôle, while local, was similar to those of other groups or places having different or kindred names. Wells and springs were divine and gave their gifts of fertility and healing to the people, each well having its presiding genius, a spirit or nymph who protected it or who was associated with the deity of the fountain. These divinities of thermal or mineral springs with medicinal qualities were always healing deities, this aspect appearing as a local survival

---

[4] E. Anwyl, "Demons and Spirits (Celtic)," in *ERE* iv, 573-574.

of a general ancient belief; and in later times the principal therapeutic gods shared their functions with Apollo,
Æsculapius, and the nymphs of the forests and waters.

The pantheon.

The Celtic pantheon appears to have been very large,
and the names of about two hundred and eighty deities
have survived in inscriptions, although many of these are
duplications of the same divinity under different names
in various places.[5] Some of these occur but once, and
nothing more is known concerning them; while doubtless
many names have entirely disappeared. Cæsar (de Bello
Gallico, vi, 17-18), recognizing among the Celtic gods
certain deities with functions and characters similar to
those of Roman divinities, named six of them: Mercury,
Apollo, Mars, Iupiter, Minerva, and Dis Pater; while the
deities Grannos, Belenus, and others were not only assimilated to Roman gods, but their names were compounded in inscriptions,[6] such identifications and surnames indicating their character and functions, as
Apollo-Grannos and Apollo-Belenus, who, like Apollo,
dispensed light, warmth, and healing. Cæsar (ib., vi, 17)
termed the Celtic 'Apollo' the divinity of healing
("Apollinem morbos depellere"), and this may explain
the great frequency of his name in these equations of
therapeutic deities.

Religiosity.

Classical writers describe the Celts as a religious people who never forgot or transgressed the laws of their
gods, but who were diligent in the observance of all religious rites and ceremonies and who referred all matters
pertaining to religion to their priests.

[5] Renel, Les Religions de la Gaule avant le christianisme, pp. 391-406.
[6] Dottin, Manuel pour servir à l'étude de l'antiquité celtique, 2d ed.,
pp. 304-309.

Druidism.

Although it has been asserted[7] that Druidism was "the common religion of the aboriginal inhabitants from the Baltic to Gibraltar," it would seem that there is little ground for the belief that the Druids were pre-Celtic and were adopted by the Celts, but rather that they were "a native priesthood common to both branches of the Celtic people, and that they had grown up side by side with the growth of the native religion," so that "the Celtic religion, in effect, was Druidism."[8] The Druids, a guild with an elective chief, were the priests and instructors of the people, and those who disobeyed them were forbidden the privilege of the sacrifice. They are declared to have "tamed the people as wild animals are tamed" (Diodoros Sikelos, V, xxxi, 5); and with a firm and jealous grasp they held within their own class all matters pertaining to religion, regulating all its ceremonies and determining the myths concerning the gods. Acting as arbiters and judges in other matters than religion, they acquired enormous political power, so that Cæsar (op. cit., vi, 13-14) called them nobles, a learned, priestly class, and the chief expounders and guardians of the law; while Pliny (Historia Naturalis, xxx, 4) refers to them as wizards and physicians ("Druidas et hoc genus vatum medicorumque"), although the latter are supposed to have formed a special subdivision.[9] They were also bards, magicians, and soothsayers who practiced all kinds of divination and made prophecies.[10]

---

[7] Rhŷs, Celtic Britain, 2d ed., p. 72.

[8] J. A. MacCulloch, "Druids," in ERE v, 83, 84; cf. id., The Religion of the Ancient Celts, p. 301.

[9] MacCulloch, in ERE v, 85; and id., Religion, p. 300.

[10] G. Dottin, "Divination (Celtic)," in ERE iv, 787-788.

Religious ceremonies.

Of the ceremonies and practices of the native religion very little is known except that they were liberally mingled with magic; many appear to have been secret or to have had a mystic significance attributed to them; and the religious rites were held in the open, in a forest or 'sacred grove,' or in a *nemeton,* an enclosure or 'consecrated place,' as when Diodoros (ii, 47) speaks of a circular temple on the Island of the Hyperboreans (*i.e.,* Celts).[11] The gods were invoked by prayers, sacrifices, incantations, and magic, with the chanting of mystic verses; and in the exercise of these rites priestesses, later called Druidesses, were employed, especially in divination and in prophecy. The Druids sacrificed animals and even human beings, in Gaul more particularly; and classical writers, shocked by the cruelties practiced in the name of religion, describe the horrors of the Druidic rites in the forests (Strabo, IV, iv, 5 = p. 198 C; Lucan, *Pharsalia,* iii, 399-425; Dion Kassios, lxi, 7). Because of their 'magic arts,' Tiberius (Pliny, *loc. cit.*) and Claudius (Suetonius, *loc. cit.*), making an exception to the otherwise universal toleration of the Romans, issued edicts intended to abolish the Druidic religion with its human sacrifices and cruelties. These prohibitions in the interest of humanity were ostensibly based on the political ground that the Druids had resisted the majesty of Rome, and were not aimed directly at their religion; but it would seem that they did little more than abolish human sacrifice, which thereafter was celebrated symbolically by letting of harmless blood (Pomponius Mela, iii, 18), while the Druids retired farther into the forests to perform their rites (Lucan, *op. cit.,* i, 450-454), where they lingered on until paganism finally disappeared.

[11] Cf. Dottin, *Manuel,* pp. 22-23.

Disease and healing.

The Celts regarded disease with terror; and since it was believed to be a visitation from the gods or the work of some maleficent being of the 'other-world,' it came within the purview of religion, so that the people appealed to their divinities for relief through the priests as mediators and as representatives of the deities, the treatment consisting of prayers with sacrifices, incantations, magic, and the administration of various herbs. It has been asserted[12] that temple-sleep for healing was known and practiced in Gaul, but there is no evidence that it was used in the cults of the native deities, and since the practices of Æsculapius[13] and Serapis[14] were well known in Gaul, it is entirely probable that incubation was used in the rituals there as it was in Rome. The adoration of Mithras, popular among the Roman soldiers, found its way to the Danube and Upper Rhone valleys,[15] and this cult also exercised healing functions. Remains of these worships have occasionally been found in the regions of ancient Gaul and Britain.

Mythic healing tales.

Numerous mythic tales and traditions of the ancient Celtic deities have been handed down with the folklore, especially in Britain. Many herbs were used with the theurgic medicine of the Celts, and whatever grew on trees was regarded as coming from heaven. Among the herbs the mistletoe held the first rank, whence the Druids had great veneration for it and for the oak on which it grew. It was a gift direct from the Celtic Zeus; it was the 'sacred bough' of the Druids, being known as the 'all

[12] Hopf, *Die Heilgötter und Heilstätten des Altertums*, pp. 52, 54.
[13] Toutain, *Les Cultes païen dans l'empire romain*, i, 380-381.
[14] Renel, *op. cit.*, pp. 333-334.
[15] Cumont, *The Mysteries of Mithra*, pp. 69-70, 79.

healer,' and in Wales as 'the tree of pure gold' (Pliny, *op. cit.*, xvi, 95); and at the New Year's festival, with mystic ceremonies and the sacrifice of white oxen, it was gathered by a priest clad in white, using a golden sickle and collecting it in a white cloth. With its life-giving powers, it was believed to be a cure for sterility in man and beast, a protection against poison, and a cure for epilepsy. Pliny (*ib.*, xxiv, 62) mentions another plant, the *selago*, identified with the savin-tree, a species of juniper which was burned and used for eye-troubles; while the *samolus* was gathered, to the accompaniment of magic ceremonies, to cure diseases of cattle and swine (*ib.*, xxiv, 63).

The 'cauldron of renovation.'

The myth of the 'cauldron of renovation' is prominently associated with the Irish god of healing, Díancecht, and figures in some of the Welsh Mabinogion tales. The cauldron had been brought out of the lake in Ireland and given to Bren, son of Llyr, while in the Welsh tale it was represented as a talisman of healing in the story of Branwen, daughter of Llyr. "The Irish kindled a fire under the cauldron of renovation, and they cast the dead bodies into the cauldron until it was full, and the next day they came forth fighting-men as good as before, except that they were not able to speak."[16] It was the equivalent of the cauldron of Dagda of Irish legend, and one of the treasures of the Tuatha Dé Danann; and it also represented the cauldron of sciences from which Gwion received three drops.[17] Its fires were fed by nine maidens, and it was called 'undry,' because it was never empty.

[16] *Mabinogion*, ed. A. Nutt, p. 39.

[17] T. Barns, "Disease and Medicine (Celtic)," in *ERE* iv, 748; see also MacCulloch, *op. cit.*, pp. 381-383; and *id., Mythology*, pp. 95-96, 120, 192, 203.

PART II: THE HEALING DEITIES

Belenus	Díancecht	Miach or Midach
Borvo or Bormo	Goibniu	Mogounos or
Brigit, Brigantia,	Grannos	Mogon
or Brigindo	Lug	Sirona
Damona	Mabon or Ma-	Sul
	ponos	

Supplementary List: Deities named in various inscriptions as being connected with healing of whom little or nothing more is known.

Abnoba	Ivaos or	Ollototæ
Addus	Ivavus	Segeta
Arduinna	Laha	Sequana
Griselicæ	Lelhunnus	Sinquatis
Nymphæ	Lenus	Virotutis
Ilixo	Luxovius	

BELENUS

THIS deity, whose name probably means 'the shining one,'[18] seems primarily to have been a solar divinity, whence he was frequently equated with Apollo. His cult centered mainly in Aquileia (*CIL* v, 732-755, 8212, 8250) and the neighboring regions (*ib.,* 1829, 1866, 2143-2146; iii, 4774), but no traces of it are found in Gaul except for two somewhat dubious allusions by Ansonius (*Professores,* v, 7; xi, 24), though it is possible that the god was identical with the Welsh Beli.[19] He apparently had a feminine counterpart in Belisama, 'the most shining one,'[20] who was identified with Minerva,[21] and after whom

[18] Stokes, *Urkeltischer Sprachschatz,* p. 164.

[19] MacCulloch, *Religion,* pp. 112-113.

[20] Pedersen, *Vergleichende Grammatik der keltischen Sprachen,* ii, 122.

[21] H. Steuding, in Roscher, i, 757. See in general on these two deities, H. d'Arbois de Jubainville, "Le Dieu gaulois Belenus, la déese gauloise Belisama," in *RA,* 1873, xxv, 197-206.

the Mersey was called (Ptolemaios, II, iii, 2). He was especially honored at the springs of Aquileia and was often addressed as Fons Belenus (*CIL* v, 754, 755, 8250); the springs at Bordeaux and Nimes were dedicated to him; and he had rich temples near the warm springs of Toulouse and Antun over which he presided.[22] The plant *bilinountia* or *bellinuntia,* 'henbane' (Dioskorides, iv, 69; pseudo-Apuleius, *de Herbis,* 4), probably received its name from him.[23]

BORVO OR BORMO

THE divinity called Borvo or Bormo in Central France, Bormanus in Provence, and Bormanicus in Portugal, was a therapeutic deity who presided over healing springs and health resorts. At Bourbonne-les-Bains (Haute-Marne) an inscription was found dedicated "Deo Apollini Borvoni et Damonæ," and he (or his feminine counterpart Bormonia) was associated with this same goddess also at Bourbon-Lancy (Saône-et-Loire); while at Aix-en-Diois (Drôme) he appears together with Bormana, who is again mentioned at Lagnieu (Ain). He had shrines at Borma on the Rhine and at the baths of Bormio in the extreme north of Italy; two inscriptions in honor of Bormanicus have been discovered at the healing springs near Oporto; and Bormanus is mentioned at Aix-en Provence. Other places recalling one or the other of these divinities are Bormanni in Gallia Narbonensis, Bourbon-l'Archambault (Allier), Bourboule (Puy-de-Dôme), Bourbriac (Côtes-du-Nord), and Bormida (Montferrat).[24] The names of these deities are connected with Irish *verbaim,* 'I boil,' Welsh *berw,* 'boiling,' Latin

[22] Hopf, *op. cit.,* pp. 51-52.

[23] Dottin, *La Langue gauloise,* pp. 232-244.

[24] Renel, *op. cit.,* pp. 178-179, 309; Steuding, in Roscher, i, 814, 815.

ferveo, 'I boil, ferment,'[25] and hence were peculiarly appropriate to their functions.

BRIGIT, BRIGANTIA, OR BRIGINDO

ACCORDING to Irish myth, one of the Brigit triad was a goddess of healing, the other two being respectively a poetess and seeress and the patroness of smiths. She had a female priesthood and men are said to have been excluded from her cult. In the hymn *Brigit be bithmaith* she is addressed as 'golden, sparkling flame,' and is invoked to "break before us the battles of every plague.'"[26] She may have been the goddess identified by Cæsar (*op. cit.*, vi, 17) with Minerva as "giving the beginnings of crafts and arts" and she appears in Gaul as Brigindo (*CIL* xiii, 2638) and as Brigantia in Britain, where she was the eponymous deity of the Brigantes.[27] Originally she seems to have been a divinity of fire and of fertility, and her name means 'the high one.'[28]

DAMONA

THIS goddess is associated with the therapeutic deity Borvo in inscriptions found at Bourbonne-les-Bains (Haute-Marne) and Bourbon-Lancy (Saône-et-Loire);[29] but she was, in reality, an animal-divinity, her name being connected with Irish *dam,* 'ox,' Welsh *dafad,* 'sheep,' etc.[30]

---

[25] Dottin, *op. cit.,* p. 235; Walde, *Etymologisches Wörterbuch der lateinischen Sprache,* p. 286.

[26] Stokes and Strachan, *Thesaurus Palæohibernicus,* ii, 325.

[27] Steuding, in Roscher, i, 819; MacCulloch, *op. cit.,* pp. 68-70.

[28] Pedersen, *op. cit.,* i, 100.

[29] Steuding, in Roscher, i, 946.

[30] MacCulloch, *op. cit.,* pp. 43, 215.

DÍANCECHT

DÍANCECHT (? 'Swift-Power'), the Irish god of healing *par excellence,* was of the number of the Tuatha Dé Danann and was the son of Dagda, the father of another therapeutic deity, Miach, and grandfather of Lug, who also possessed similar powers. His surgical prowess is particularly prominent in the Middle Irish account of the second battle of Moytura (*Cath Maige Turedh*).[31] In this combat, the hand of Nuada being stricken off, Díancecht, with the aid of the smith, Credne, replaced it with a hand of silver which was capable of every motion possessed by a hand of flesh; but Miach, after thrice three days and nights, restored to Nuada his natural hand, whence Díancecht slew his son and confused the healing herbs which grew from the corpse. Díancecht is the leech of the Tuatha Dé Danann; and in the conflict says: "Every man who shall be wounded there, unless his head be cut off, or the membrane of his brain or his spinal (?) marrow be severed, I will make quite whole in the battle on the morrow." In fact, the slain and mortally wounded were cast into a healing well over which Díancecht, his sons Miach and Octriuil, and his daughter Airmed sang incantations; and all were restored to full vigor. In a St. Gall manuscript of the eighth or ninth century we read: "I put my trust in the salve which Díancecht left with his family that whole may be that whereon it goes."[32]

GOIBNIU

GOIBNIU was an Irish divinity of smiths (cf. Irish *gobas,* 'smith') whose ale preserved the gods from old age, disease, and death.[33]

---

[31] §§ 11, 33-35, 64, 98-99, 123; ed. and tr. W. Stokes, "The Second Battle of Moytura," in *RC,* 1891, xii, 56-111.

[32] Stokes and Strachan, *op. cit.,* ii, 249.

[33] MacCulloch, *Mythology,* pp. 51-54.

GRANNOS

GRANNOS was a healing deity of great renown whose cult seems to have been especially important among the Celts along the upper Danube, where he was equated with Apollo (*CIL* iii, 5870, 5871, 5874, 5876, 5881) and was associated with Hygieia, with the Nymphs, and with Sirona (*ib.*, 5861, 5873, 5888). He again appears together with Sirona in an inscription from Rome (*ib.*, vi, 36), and epigraphs to him have been found at Musselburgh in Scotland (*ib.*, vii, 1082) and even in Vestmanland in Sweden;[34] while it is possible that certain inscriptions mentioning Sirona and Apollo, as that from Graux in the Vosges, may really refer to her and Grannos.[35] He was likewise associated with the local goddess Avantia and Vesunna, who have given their names to Avenches (Switzerland) and Vesona; while he had a statue in the temple of the Seine-goddess, Sequana.[36] Aix-la-Chapelle was known as Aquæ Granni, and the stream receiving the waters from Plombières in the Vosges is called Eaux Graunnes.

The name of Grannos is usually connected with Irish *grian*, 'sun,' *gor*, 'warmth';[37] and he and Sirona possibly represent the ever-young sun-god and the old goddess, who may be likened to Apollo and his mother, Leto, of Greek mythology.[38] Apollo Grannos was associated with Æsculapius and Serapis by Caracalla, who appealed to them in a second illness when other gods had failed him (Dion Kassios, lxxvii, 15).[39]

[34] I. Undset, "Inscrizioni latine ritrovate nella Scandinavia," in *BIA*, 1883, p. 237; also M. Ihm, in Pauly-Wissowa, vii, 1826; Steuding and W. Drexler, in Roscher, i, 1739.

[35] Renel, *op. cit.*, p. 310.

[36] MacCulloch, *Religion*, p. 43.

[37] Stokes, *Sprachschatz*, p. 114.

[38] Barns, in *ERE* iv, 747.

[39] Ihm, in Pauly-Wissowa, vii, 1825.

The memory of Grannos is still preserved in the Auvergne at the festival of the Brands when, on the first Sunday in Lent, fires are lighted in every village, and the ceremony of Grannasmias takes place after a dance. A torch of straw, called Granno-mio, is lighted and carried around the orchards; and in the character of a sun-god the deity is invoked in song as "Granno . . . my friend . . . my father . . . my mother," these processions being followed by feasting. The torches are carried in the fields and gardens wherever there are fruit trees, and the ceremonial is intended to ensure fertility and the sun's heat for the ripening of the fruit.[40]

LUG

Lug, an ancient and important member of the Tuatha Dé Danann, seems to have been in origin a civilization-hero[41] concerning whom many tales are told in Middle Irish literature. In the story of the second battle of Moytura,[42] he is described as the grandson of Díancecht and comes to the Tuatha Dé as they feast at Tara, offering his services in many capacities, including that of physician, only to be told, in this connection, that "we have for a leech Díancecht." He finally wins entrance, however, as being *samildánach* ("skilled in many arts together"), an epithet which suggests his identification with the Gaulish god described, under the name of Mercury, as, *inter alia*, "the inventor of all arts" (Cæsar, *op. cit.*, vi, 17). Although no Gallic inscription to him has yet been found, and though it is by no means clear that the Lugoves mentioned in an inscription from Avenches in Switzerland and in another from Osma in Spain are to be considered as plural forms of Lug (it is not even certain whether

---

[40] Barns, *loc. cit.*
[41] MacCulloch, "Celts," in *ERE* iii, 285-286.
[42] §§ 55 ff.

these are masculine or feminine),[43] the widespread character of his cult is shown by the place-names Lugudunum ('fortress of Lug': Lyons, St. Bertrand-de-Comminges [Gers], Leyden), Luguvallum ('rampart of Lug': Carlisle), and Louth (*i.e.*, Lug-magh: 'plain of Lug'). The meaning of the name is uncertain, but it may be connected with Gallic *lugos*, 'crow,'[44] or, more probably, with Irish *lug*, 'lynx,'[45] or it may signify 'the bright one.'[46]

MABON OR MAPONOS

THE Welsh deity Mabon ('Youth'), one with the Gaulish Maponos, appears among the figures of the Arthurian cycle[47] and is mentioned under his Gallic name in inscriptions from Hexham, Ribchester, and Armthwaite in England.[48] Assimilated to Apollo, he was perhaps a divinity of healing springs,[49] and, from his name, was probably the same as the 'bonus puer' associated with Apollo in Dacian inscriptions (*CIL* iii, 1133, 1138).[50]

MIACH OR MIDACH

ACCORDING to the story of the second battle of Moytura,[51] Miach was a son of Díancecht and one of the four who sang charms over the healing well which brought back to life those who had fallen in the fray. After thrice seventy-two hours, he restored the hand of Nuada, which had been

[43] Ihm and Drexler, in Roscher, ii, 2153-2154.
[44] Renel, *op. cit.*, p. 206; cf. Pedersen, *op. cit.*, i, 186.
[45] Dottin, *op. cit.*, p. 268.
[46] Pedersen, *op. cit.*, i, 98 (for a much less plausible etymology see Stokes, *op. cit.*, p. 257).
[47] MacCulloch, *Mythology*, pp. 188-189.
[48] R. Peter, in Roscher, ii, 2332.
[49] MacCulloch, *Religion*, p. 123.
[50] Barns, *loc. cit.*
[51] §§ 33-35, 123.

severed in combat and for which Díancecht had substi-
tuted a silver hand; but, in anger, his father struck him
on the head with a sword. The first three blows Miach
healed, since they reached, respectively, only to the flesh,
the bone, and the membrane of the brain; but the fourth
stroke, cutting the brain, proved mortal. After his burial,
"herbs three hundred and sixty-five, according to the
number of his joints and sinews, grew through the
grave," and these were gathered by his sister, Airmed,
only to be so hopelessly confused by Díancecht that "no
one knows their proper cures unless the [Holy] Spirit
should teach them afterwards." The late character of the
deity is shown by his name, which is borrowed from
Latin *medicus*, 'physician.'[52]

MOGOUNOS OR MOGONS

Mogounos is once mentioned as an epithet of Apollo
Grannos in an inscription from Horburg (Haut-Rhin;
CIR, 1915). He is doubtless connected with the British
deity Mogon (*CIL* vii, 958, 996) and with the Gaulish
goddess Mogontia, who gave her name to Mogontiacum,
the modern Metz.[53] The name probably means 'the in-
creaser,' and may have denoted originally a solar
divinity.[54]

SIRONA

Sirona, whose name is also written Đirona, Dirona, probably connected with the Welsh *seren*, 'star,'[55] is sometimes associated, on Gaulish inscriptions, with Apollo
Grannos (e.g. *CIL* iii, 5588; xiii, 4129), or simply with
Apollo (*ib.*, xiii, 4661, 5424, 6272, 6458), and seems to

[52] Pedersen, *op. cit.*, i, 239.
[53] Ihm, in Roscher, ii, 3083, 3084.
[54] Stokes, *op. cit.*, p. 197; MacCulloch, *op. cit.*, p. 27.
[55] Pedersen, *op. cit.*, i, 78, 532.

have been a healing deity, though there is no certain evidence to support this hypothesis.[56]

SUL

THIS goddess presided over the healing springs of Aquæ Sulis, the modern Bath, and Solinus (xxii, 10) states that a perpetual fire burned in her temple. She was identified with Minerva (*CIL* vii, 42, 43), and inscriptions were dedicated to her "pro salute et incolumitate" (*ib.*, 40, 41).[57] Her name seems to be cognate with Irish *súil*, 'eye,' and Welsh *heol*, 'sun';[58] and she perhaps had Gaulish counterparts in the Suleviæ, beneficent and protecting 'mothers' or 'matrons.'[59]

The Supplementary List.

ABNOBA. This divinity of the Black Forest, who was identified with Diana, is mentioned as a goddess of child-birth (*CIL* xiii, 5334, 6283).

ADDUS. This seems to have been the name of a god, presumably Gaulish, to whom an inscription from Altripp was dedicated by a man "for the health of himself and his" (Steuding, in Roscher, i, 67).

ARDUINNA. Identified with Diana, she was the deity of the Ardennes Forest and is mentioned as a goddess of child-birth (*CIL* vi, 46).

GRISELICÆ NYMPHÆ. These were goddesses of the thermal springs of Gréoulx (Basses-Alpes) and were probably regarded as therapeutic divinities (Drexler, in Roscher, i, 1741).

ILIXO. This god is mentioned in three short inscriptions

[56] Ihm, in Roscher, iv, 952-957.
[57] Ihm, in Roscher, iv, 1591-1592.
[58] Dottin, *op. cit.*, p. 289.
[59] Ihm, in Roscher, iv, 1592-1600.

found at Bagnères-de-Luchon (Hautes-Pyrénées) and was probably the deity of the thermal springs at that place (Ihm, in Roscher, ii, 119). The word may possibly be cognate with Welsh *ilio*, 'to ferment.'

IVAOS OR IVAVUS. This divinity is named on a bronze key discovered at Evaux (Creuse) and was apparently the deity of the local springs (Ihm, in Roscher, ii, 766). The appellation seems to be cognate with Irish *eo*, 'good.'

LAHA. Some inscriptions in honor of this goddess have been found near Martres-Tolosanes (Haute-Garonne), and since one of them was dedicated "pro salutæ [*sic*] dominorum," she may possibly—though by no means certainly—have been a deity of health (Ihm, in Roscher, ii, 1799-1800).

LELHUNNUS. On inscriptions from Aire-sur-l'Adour (Landes) Mars receives this epithet in dedications "for the health of himself and his," etc. (Ihm, in Roscher, ii, 1937).

LENUS. Inscriptions found at Trèves and in Luxembourg give this epithet to Mars, and, on the basis of a bilingual text from the lower Moselle, the term evidently indicated a therapeutic divinity (Ihm, in Roscher, ii, 1942-1943).

LUXOVIUS. He was the deity of the thermal springs of Luxeuil-les-Bains (Haute-Saône) (Ihm, in Roscher, ii, 2163).

OLLOTOTÆ. This epithet is given to the 'Mothers' in an inscription from Binchester in England, dedicated "pro salute sua et suorum" (Ihm, in Roscher, iii, 833-834). The name means "pertaining to all the people."

SEGETA. This goddess presided over healing springs at Aquæ Segetæ, near Feurs (Loire) (Ihm, in Roscher, iv, 599).

SEQUANA. The Seine-goddess exercised healing functions at the river's source, where numerous ex-votos in her honor have been discovered, while one inscription (*CIL* xiii, 2862) is expressly recorded as given "pro-[sal]ute . . . ex voto" (Ihm, in Roscher, iv, 711).

SINQUATIS. This deity, whose name is given to Silvanus as an epithet, received a votive statue, found at Géromont, near Gérouville (Belgium), "pro salute" (*CIL* xiii, 3968) (Ihm, in Roscher, iv, 949).

VIROTUTIS. An altar dedicated "Apollini Virotuti" has been found near Annecy (Haute-Savoie) (*CIL* xii, 2525), and the name is explained (Dottin, *La Langue*, p. 95) as 'healer of men.'

BIBLIOGRAPHY

EGYPTIAN

AKMAR, E., *Le Papyrus magique Harris*. Upsala, 1916.

BAILLET, J., *Idées morales dans l'Égypte antique*. Blois, 1912.

BLACKMAN, A. M., "Some Remarks on an Emblem upon the Head of an Ancient Egyptian Birth-Goddess," in *Journal of Egyptian Archeology*, 1916, iii, 199-206.

"The Pharaoh's Placenta and the Moon-God Khons," in *ibid.*, pp. 235-249.

BOYLAN, P., *Thoth, The Hermes of Egypt*. Oxford, 1922.

BREASTED, J. H., *Ancient Records of Egypt*. 5 vols. Chicago, 1906-1907.

Development of Religion and Thought in Ancient Egypt. New York, 1912.

A History of the Ancient Egyptians. New York, 1912.

"The Edwin Smith Papyrus," in *New York Historical Society, Quarterly Bulletin*, April, 1922.

"The Edwin Smith Papyrus. Some Preliminary Observations," in *Recueil d'Études égyptologiques dédiées à la mémoire de Jean-François Champollion*, Paris, 1922, pp. 385-429.

BRUGSCH, H. K., *Ueber die medicinische Kenntniss der alten Ägypter*. Brunswick, 1853.

Hieroglyphisch-demotisches Wörterbuch. Leipzig, 1867-1882.

"Eine geographische Studie," in *Zeitschrift für ägyptische Sprache und Altertumskunde*, 1879, xvii, 1-29.

Die Aegyptologie. Leipzig, 1889-1890.

Religion und Mythologie der alten Ägypter. 2 vols., 2d ed. Leipzig, 1891.

BUDGE, E. A. W., *The Book of the Dead*. 3 vols. London, 1898.

Egyptian Magic. London, 1901.

The Gods of the Egyptians. 2 vols. London, 1904.

Egyptian Religion. London, 1908.

Facsimiles of Egyptian Hieratic Papyri, in the British Museum. London, 1910.

The Syriac Book of Medicines. 2 vols. London, 1913.

The Literature of the Egyptians. London, 1914.

CHABAS, F. J., *Le Papyrus magique Harris*. Châlon-sur-Saône, 1860.

524   THE HEALING GODS

"La Médecine des anciens Égyptiens," in *Mélanges égyptologiques*, 1 sér. Paris, 1862.

DARESSY, G., "Thouéris et Meskhenet," in *Recueil de travaux relatifs à la Philologie et à l'Archéologie égyptienne et assyrienne*, 1912, xxxiv, 189-193.

DAVIS, C. H. S., *The Egyptian Book of the Dead*. New York and London, 1894.

EBERS, G. M., *Papyrus Ebers: Die Maasse und das Kapitel über die Augenkrankheiten*. 2 vols. Leipzig, 1889. (*Königlich sächsische Gesellschaft der Wissenschaften. Abhandlungen der philologisch-historischen Classe*, Bd. 11, no. 2-3.)

ERMAN, A., *Die Märchen des Papyrus Westcar*. Berlin, 1890.

"Der Zauberpapyrus des Vatikan," in *Zeitschrift für ägyptische Sprache und Altertumskunde*, 1893, xxxi, 119-124.

Life in Ancient Egypt. London, 1894.

"Zaubersprüche für Mutter und Kind," in *Abhandlungen der königlich preussischen Akademie der Wissenschaften*, 1901, no. 1.

Hieratische Papyrus aus dem königlichen Museum zu Berlin. 5 vols. Leipzig, 1901-1911.

Die ägyptische Religion. 2d ed. Berlin, 1909. (English tr. A. S. Griffith, *Handbook of Egyptian Religion*. London, 1907.)

*FINLAYSON, J., "Ancient Egyptian Medicine," in *British Medical Journal*, 1893, i, 748-752; 1014-1016; 1061-1064.

FOUCART, G., "Imhotep," in *Revue de l'histoire des religions*, 1903, xlviii, 362-371.

"La Religion et l'Art dans l'Égypte ancienne. La Statuaire," in *Revue des idées*, 1908, v, 385-419.

GARDINER, A. H., "Imhotep and the Scribe's Libation," in *Zeitschrift für ägyptische Sprache und Altertumskunde*, 1902-1903, xl, 146.

GARRISON, F. H., "The Bone called Luz," in *The New York Medical Journal*, 1910, xcii, 149-151.

GRIFFITH, F. Ll., *The Petrie Papyri: Hieratic Papyri from Kahun and Gurob*. London, 1898.

Stories of the High Priests of Memphis. Oxford, 1900.

and THOMPSON, H., *The Demotic Magical Papyrus of London and Leiden*. London, 1904.

HAGEMANN, E., "Zur Hygiene der alten Aegypter," in *Janus*, 1904, ix, 214-229.

HIRSCHBERG, J., *Aegypten. Geschichtliche Studien eines Augenarztes*. Leipzig, 1890.

HOLMES, B., and KITTERMAN, P. G., "Medicine in Ancient Egypt," in *Cincinnati Lancet-Clinic*, 1913, cix, 566-570, 590-603, 624-629.

HOPFNER, T., *Der Tierkult der alten Ägypter.* Vienna, 1913.

JÉQUIER, G., "Nature et origine du dieu Bes," in *Recueil de travaux relatifs à la Philologie et à l'Archéologie égyptienne et assyrienne,* 1915, xxxvii, 114-118.

"Thouéris," in *ibid.,* pp. 118-120.

JOACHIM, H., *Papyrus Ebers. Das älteste Buch über Heilkunde.* Berlin, 1890.

KLEIN, C. H. VON, "The Medical Features of the Ebers Papyrus," in *Journal of the American Medical Association,* 1905, xlv, 1928-1935.

LACAU, P., "Suppressions et modifications de signes dans les textes funéraires," in *Zeitschrift für ägyptische Sprache und Altertumskunde,* 1914, li, 1-64.

Textes religieux égyptiens. Paris, 1910.

LETRONNE, J. A., "Notices et textes des papyrus grecs du Musée du Louvre et de la Bibliothèque impériale," in *Notices et extraits des manuscrits de la Bibliothèque impériale et autres bibliothèques,* L'Institut impérial de France, vol. 18, pt. 2.

MALLET, D., *Le Culte de Neit à Saïs.* Paris, 1888.

Kasr-el-Agouz. Cairo, 1909.

MANETHO, ed. C. Müller, *Fragmenta historicorum Græcorum.* Paris, 1848, ii, 511-616.

MARIETTE, A. E., *Les Mastabas de l'ancien empire.* Paris, 1889.

Les Papyrus égyptiens du Musée de Boulaq. 3 vols. Paris, 1871-1876.

MASPERO, G., *Mémoire sur quelques papyrus du Louvre.* Paris, 1875.

Études égyptiennes, 2 vols. Paris, 1889.

Études de mythologie et d'archéologie égyptiennes. 8 vols. Paris, 1893-1916.

Popular Stories of Ancient Egypt. New York and London, 1912.

MORET, A., *Le Rituel du culte divin journalier en Égypte.* Paris, 1902.

Le Magie dans l'Égypte ancienne. Paris, 1907.

Kings and Gods of Egypt. New York and London, 1912.

Mystères égyptiens. Paris, 1913.

MÜLLER, W. M., "Surgery in Egypt," in *Egyptological Researches.* Washington, 1906-1910.

Mythology, Egyptian, in *The Mythology of All Races,* vol. xii, Part I. Boston, 1918.

NAVILLE, E., *Études dédiées à Leemans.* Leyden, 1885.

La Religion des anciens Égyptiens. Paris, 1906. (English tr., *The Old Egyptian Faith.* London, 1909.)

OFFORD, J., "A New Egyptian Medical Papyrus," in *Proceedings of the Royal Society of Medicine,* 1912-1913, vi, *Section of the History of Medicine,* 97-102.

PEIRRET, P., *Le Pantheon égyptien.* Paris, 1879.

PETRIE, W. M. F., ed. *Egyptian Tales from the Papyri.* 2 vols. London, 1895.

The Religion of Ancient Egypt. London, 1906.

PLEYTE, W., *Étude sur un rouleau magique du Musée de Leyde.* Leyden, 1866.

and ROSSI, P., *Papyrus de Turin.* 2 vols. Leyden, 1869-1876.

REISNER, G., *The Hearst Medical Papyrus.* Leipzig, 1905.

RENOUF, P. LE PAGE, "Note on the Medical Papyrus of Berlin," in *Zeitschrift für ägyptische Sprache und Altertumskunde,* 1873, xi, 123-125.

The Religion of Ancient Egypt. London, 1880.

RÉVILLOUT, E., "Un page de l'histoire de la Nubie," in *Revue égyptologique,* 1888, v, 72-77.

["Letter upon Nubian oracles,"] in *Proceedings of the Society of Biblical Archeology,* 1888, x, 55-59.

SANDWITH, F. M., "The Earliest Known Physician," in *British Medical Journal,* 1902, ii, 1419-1420.

"Notes on Medical History in Egypt," in *Practitioner,* 1904, lxxii, 430-438.

SCHAEFER, H., "Eine altägyptische Schreibersitte," in *Zeitschrift für ägyptische Sprache und Altertumskunde,* 1898, xxxvi, 147-148.

Die Mysterien des Osiris in Abydos unter König Sosostris. Leipzig, 1904.

SCHNEIDER, H., *Kultur und Denken der alten Aegypter.* Leipzig, 1907.

SETHE, K., "Imhotep, der Asklepios der Aegypter," in *Untersuchungen zur Geschichte und Altertumskunde Aegyptens,* 1902, ii, 93-118.

"Zur altägyptischen Sage vom Sonnenauge, das in der Fremde war," *ibid.,* 1912, v, 117-156.

Die altägyptischen Pyramidentexte. 2 vols. Leipzig, 1908-1910.

SMITH, G. E., *The Ancient Egyptians.* London, 1911.

SPIEGELBERG, W., *Aegyptologische Randglossen zum alten Testament.* Strassburg, 1904.

"Ἑρμῆς ὁ θηβατος," in *Zeitschrift für ägyptische Sprache und Altertumskunde,* 1908-1909, xlv, 89-90.

"Specialistentum in der ägyptischen medizin," in *ibid.,* 1917, liii, 111.

STERN, L., *Papyrus Ebers.* 2 vols. Leipzig, 1875.

VIREY, PH., *La Religion de l'ancienne Égypte.* Paris, 1910.

WALSH, J. J., "The First Pictures of Surgical Operations Extant," in *Journal of the American Medical Association,* 1907, xlix, 1593-1595.

WIEDEMANN, A., *Die Religion der alten Ägypter*. Munster, 1890.
(English tr. London, 1897.)
 Magie und Zauberei im alten Ägypten. Leipzig, 1905.
 Altägyptische Sagen und Märchen. Leipzig, 1906.
 Die Amulette der alten Ägypter. Leipzig, 1910.
 Der Tierkult der alten Ägypter. Leipzig, 1912.
 Das alte Ägypten. Heidelberg, 1921.
WILKINSON, J. G., *Manners and Customs of the Ancient Egyptians*.
3 vols. London, 1837.
WRESZINSKI, W., *Der grosse medizinische Papyrus des Berliner
Museums*. Leipzig, 1909.
 Der Londoner medizinische Papyrus und der Papyrus Hearst.
Leipzig, 1912.
 Der Papyrus Ebers. Heft 1. Leipzig, 1913.

ASSYRO-BABYLONIAN

ANONYMOUS, "The Laws of Hammurabi, King of Babylon," in
Records of the Past, 1903, ii, 84-85.
JASTROW, M., JR., *Die Religion Babyloniens und Assyriens*. 3 vols.
Giessen, 1905-1912. (The second edition of *The Religion of Baby-
lonia and Assyria*. Boston, 1898.)
 *The Aspects of Religious Belief and Practice in Babylonia and
Assyria*. New York, 1911.
 The Civilization of Babylonia and Assyria. Philadelphia, 1915.
 "The Medicine of the Babylonians and Assyrians," in *Proceed-
ings of the Royal Society of Medicine*, 1913-1914, vii, *Section
of the History of Medicine*, 109-176; also in *Lancet*, 1913, ii,
1136-1142.
 "Babylonian and Assyrian Medicine," in *Annals of Medical
History*, 1917, i, 231-257.
 "Sumerian and Akkadian Views of the Beginnings," in *Journal
of the American Oriental Society*, 1916, xxxvi, 274-299.
KING, L. W., *Babylonian Magic and Sorcery*. London, 1896.
 Babylonian Religion and Mythology. London, 1899.
KÜCHLER, F., *Beiträge zur Kenntniss der assyrisch-babylonischen
Medizin*. Leipzig, 1904.
LÖW, I., *Aramische Pflanzennamen*. Leipzig, 1881.
LUTZ, H. F., "A Contribution to the Knowledge of Assyro-Babylonian
Medicine," in *American Journal of Semitic Languages and Litera-
tures*, 1919, xxxvi, 67-83.
 "An Omen Text Referring to the Action of a Dreamer," in *ibid.*,
1919, xxxv, 145-157.
OEFELE, F. VON, *Keilschriftmedizin in Parelleln*. Leipzig, 1902.
PREUSS, J., *Biblisch-talmudische Medizin*. 2d ed. Berlin, 1921.

SAYCE, A. H., *The Religion of the Ancient Babylonians*. London, 1888.

The Babylonians and Assyrians. New York, 1909.

THOMPSON, R. C., *Devils and Evil Spirits of Babylonia*. 2 vols. London, 1904.

Semitic Magic. London, 1908.

"Assyrian Prescriptions for Diseases of the Head," in *American Journal of Semitic Languages and Literatures*, 1907-1908, xxiv, 1-6, 323-353.

WARD, WM. H., *The Seal Cylinders of Western Asia*. Washington, D. C., 1890.

WEBER, O., *Dämonen-Beschwörung bei den Babyloniern und Assyriern*. Leipzig, 1906.

Die Literatur der Babylonier und Assyrer. Ein Überblick. Leipzig, 1907.

WINCKLER, H., *Die Völker Vorderasiens*. Leipzig, 1903.

ZIMMERN, H., *Beiträge zur Kenntniss der babylonischen Religion*. Leipzig, 1901.

PAGAN SEMITES OF THE WEST

ANONYMOUS, "The Figure of Æsculapius in Ancient Art," in *Lancet*, 1904, ii, 1362-1363.

BAETHGEN, F., *Beiträge zur semitischen Religionsgeschichte*. Berlin, 1888.

BAUDISSIN, W. W., GRAF VON, "Der phönizische Gott Esmun," in *Zeitschrift der deutschen morgenländischen Gesellschaft*, 1905, lix, 459-522.

"Zu 'Esmun' ZDMG 59, S. 471 f.," in *ibid.*, 1911, lxv, 567-569.

Adonis und Esmun. Leipzig, 1911.

BERGER, P., "Tanit Pene-Baal," in *Journal asiatique*, 1877, ix, 147-160.

COOKE, G. A., *A Text-Book of North Semitic Inscriptions*. Oxford, 1903.

EISELEN, F. C., *Sidon. A Study in Oriental History*. New York, 1907.

LANDAU, W. VON, "Vorläufige Nachrichten über die im Eshmuntempel bei Sidon gefundenen phönizischen Alterthümer," im *Mittheilungen der vorderasiatischen Gesellschaft*, 1904, ix, 279-350; 1905, x, 1-16.

LIDZBARSKI, M., "Der Name des Gottes Esmun," in *Ephemeris für semitische Epigraphik*, 1915, iii, 260-265.

MAURY, A., "Sur une statuette du dieu Aschmoun ou Esmoun trouvée à Cherchell," in *Revue archéologique*, 1846, iii, 763-793.

RAWLINSON, G., *Phœnicia*. New York, 1904.

TEXIER, C., "Extrait d'un aperçu statistique du monuments de l'Algérie," in *Revue archéologique*, 1846, iii, 724-735.

TORREY, C. C., "A Phœnician Royal Inscription," in *Journal of the American Oriental Society*, 1902, xxiii, 156-173.

WINCKLER, H., "Bruchstücke von Keilschrifttexten," in *Altorientalische Forschungen*, 1898, ii, 1-96; "Nachträge und Verbesserungen," p. 192.

INDIAN

BERGAIGNE, A., *La Religion védique.* 3 vols. Paris, 1878-1883.

BLOOMFIELD, M., "Jalāṣah, Jalāṣabheṣajaḥ, Jalāṣam and Jālāṣam," in *American Journal of Philology*, 1891, xii, 425-429.

"The Story of Indra and Namuci," in *Journal of the American Oriental Society*, [1891]-1893, xv, 143-163.

"The Atharvaveda," in *Grundriss der indo-arischen Philologie und Altertumskunde*, III, B. Strasbourg, 1899; also in *The Sacred Books of the East*, vol. xlii.

The Religion of the Veda. New York and London, 1908.

CALAND, W., *Altindische Zauberei.* Amsterdam, 1908.

CROOKE, W. B. A., *The Popular Religion and Folklore of Northern India.* 2d ed., 2 vols. Westminster, 1896.

FAUSBØLL, V., *Indian Mythology according to the Mahābhārata.* London, 1905.

GETTY, A., *The Gods of Northern Buddhism.* London, 1914.

GRAY, L. H., "The Indian God Dhanvantari," in *Journal of the American Oriental Society*, 1922, xlii, 323-337.

HENRY, V., *La Magie dans l'Inde antique.* Paris, 1904.

HILLEBRANDT, A., *Varuṇa und Mitra.* Breslau, 1877.

Vedische Mythologie. 3 vols. Breslau, 1891-1902.

HOPKINS, E. W., "Henotheism in the Rig-Veda," in *Classical Studies in Honour of Henry Drisler.* New York, 1894.

The Religions of India. Boston, 1895.

India, Old and New. New York, 1902.

Epic Mythology. Strasbourg, 1915.

JOLLY, J., "Zur Quellenkunde der indischen Medicin," in *Zeitschrift der deutschen morgenländischen Gesellschaft*, 1900, liv, S. 260-274.

"(Indische) Medicin," in *Grundriss der indo-arischen Philologie und Altertumskunde.* Strasbourg, 1901.

KAVIRATRIA, A. C., tr., *Charaka-Saṁhitā.* Calcutta, 1897.

KEITH, A. B., *Indian Mythology,* in *The Mythology of All Races,* vol. vi, Part I. Boston, 1917.

KERN, H., tr., *Saddharmapuṇḍarīka.* Oxford, 1884; also in *The Sacred Books of the East*, vol. xxi.

530   THE HEALING GODS

MACDONELL, A. A., "Vedic Mythology," in *Grundriss der indo-arischen Philologie und Altertumskunde.* Strasbourg, 1897.
The History of Sanskrit Literature. London, 1900.
and KEITH, A. B., *Vedic Index of Names and Subjects.* 2 vols. London, 1912.
MONIER-WILLIAMS, M., *Religious Thought and Life in India.* London, 1883.
MOOR, ED., *The Hindu Pantheon.* London, 1810.
MUIR, J., *Original Sanskrit Texts.* 5 vols. London, 1868-1874.
MUKHOPĀDHYĀYA, G., *History of Indian Medicine.* University of Calcutta, 1923.
MYRIANTHEUS, L., *Die Aśvins oder arischen Dioskuren.* Munich, 1876.
OLDENBERG, H., *Die Religion des Veda.* Berlin, 1894.
QUACKENBOS, G. P., *The Sanskrit Poems of Mayūra.* New York, 1917.
TEMPLE, R. C., *The Legends of the Punjab.* 2 vols. Bombay, n.d.
WILKIN, W. J., *Hindu Mythology—Vedic and Puranic.* Calcutta, 1882.
WILSON, H. H., *Viṣṇu Purāṇa.* London, 1864.
WISE, T. A., *Review of the History of Medicine in Asia.* 2 vols. London, 1867.
ZIMMER, H., *Altindisches Leben.* Berlin, 1879.

IRANIAN

BARTHOLOMAE, C., "Arica I," in *Indogermanische Forschungen,* 1892, i, 180-182.
CARNOY, A. J., *Iranian Mythology,* in *The Mythology of All Races,* vol. vi, Part II. Boston, 1917.
"The Iranian Gods of Healing," in *Journal of the American Oriental Society,* 1918, xxxviii, 294-307.
CASERTELLI, L. C., "Traité de médecine mazdéene," in *Le Muséon,* 1886, v, 296-316, 531-558. (An independent English translation of *The Dinkard,* ed. and tr. Peshotun Dustoor Behramjee Sunjana, and others. Bombay, 1874.)
DARMESTETER, J., *Le Zend-Avesta.* 3 vols. Paris, 1892-1893.
DHALLA, M. N., *Zoroastrian Theology.* New York, 1914.
Zoroastrian Civilization. New York, 1922.
DITTENBERGER, W., *Orientis græci inscriptiones selectæ.* No. 383. Leipzig, 1903-1905.
FIRDAUSI, A., *Shāh-Nāmah,* tr. A. G. and E. Warner. London, 1905.
GIEGER, W., *Ostiranische Kultur im Altertum.* Erlangen, 1882.
GELZER, H., "Zur armenischen Götterlehre," in *Berichte über die*

BIBLIOGRAPHY 531

Verhandlungen der königlichen sächsischen Gesellschaft der Wissenschaften. Philosophisch-historische Classe, 1896, xlvi, 99-148.

HAUG, M., *Essays on . . . the Parsis.* 3d ed. London, 1884.

HENRY, V., *Le Parsisme.* Paris, 1905.

JACKSON, A. V. W., "Die iranische Religion," in *Grundriss der iranischen Philologie.* Strasbourg, 1904, ii, 612-708.

KANGA, K. E., "King Farīdūn and a few of his Amulets and Charms," in *The K. R. Cama Memorial Volume,* Bombay, 1900, pp. 144-145.

MEILLET, A., "Le Dieu indo-iranian Mitra," in *Journal asiatique,* X, 1907, x, 143-159.

MIRKOND, M., *The History of the Early Kings of Persia.* Tr. D. Shea. Paris, 1832.

MODI, J. J., "Charms and Amulets for some Diseases of the Eye," in his *Anthropological Papers,* Bombay, 1911, 43-50.

MOULTON, J. H., *Early Zoroastrianism.* London, 1913.
The Treasure of the Magi. Oxford, 1917.

PETTAZZONI, R., *La Religione di Zarathusthra.* Bologna, 1920.

SCHROEDER, L. VON, *Arische Religion.* 2 vols. Leipzig, 1914.

STEIN, M. A., "Zoroastrian Deities on Indo-Scythian Coins," in *Babylonian and Oriental Record,* 1887, i, 155-166.

WOLFF, F., *Avesta; die heiligen Bücher der Parsen übersetzt.* Strasbourg, 1910.

GREEK

ADAMS, F., *The Genuine Works of Hippocrates.* 2 vols. New York, 1886.

ANONYMOUS, "Healing Shrines in Old Greece," in *Practitioner,* 1898, lx, 384-389.

BABELON, E. C. F., "Le faux prophète, Alexandre d'Abonotichos," in *Revue numismatique,* 4 sér., 1900, iv, 1-30.

BAUNACK, J., *Arische Studien.* Leipzig, 1886.
"Inschriften aus dem Asklepieion zu Epidauros," in *Studien auf dem Gebiete der griechischen und der arischen Sprachen,* Leipzig, 1886, i, 79-162.
"Epigraphische Kleinigkeiten aus Griechenland," in *Philologus,* 1889, xlviii, 385-427, 576, 768.

BAUNACK, TH., "Inschriften aus dem kretischen Asklepieion," in *ibid.,* 1890, xlix, 577-606.
"Bruchstück einer Grabinschrift aus Kreta," in *ibid.,* 1891, l, 577-582.
"Neue Bruchstücke gortynische Gesetze," in *ibid.,* 1896, lv, 474-490.

BERGK, TH., ed., *Poetæ lyrici Græci; tertius curis recensuit.* 3 vols. Leipzig, 1866-1867.

532   THE HEALING GODS

BLACKIE, J. S., *Horæ Hellenicæ*. London, 1874.

BLINKENBERG, C., "Epidaurische Weigeschenke," in *Mittheilungen des kaiserlich deutschen archäologischen Instituts in Athen*, 1898, xxiii, 1-23; 1899, xxiv, 294-309, 379-397.

BOHN, R., "Zur Basis der Athena Hygieia," in *ibid.*, 1880, v, 331-334.

BOISACQ, E., *Dictionnaire étymologique de la langue grecque*. Paris, 1913.

BOUCHÉ-LECLERCQ, A., *L'Astrologie grecque*. Paris, 1899.

BRUCKMAN, C. F. H., *Epitheta deorum quæ apud poetas Græcos leguntur*. Leipzig, 1893.

CATON, R., "The Ancient Temples of Asklepios," in *British Medical Journal*, 1898, i, 1509-1513, 1572-1575.

   The Temples and Ritual of Asklepios at Epidauros and Athens. London, 1902.

   "Hippocrates and the Newly Discovered Temples of Kos," in *British Medical Journal*, 1906, i, 571-574.

   "Health Temples of Ancient Greece," etc., in *Proceedings of the Royal Society of Medicine*, 1913-1914, vii, *Section of the History of Medicine*, 57-70.

CARAPANOS, C., *Dodone et ses ruines*. 2 vols. Paris, 1878.

COOK, A. B., *Zeus, the Indo-European Sky-God*. Cambridge, 1914.

CORYLLOS, P., "Les Sanctuaires médicaux de la Grèce et le culte d'Æsculape," in *Æsculape*, 1912, i, 97-103.

CURTIN, R. G., "Æsculapian Temples of Health compared with our Modern Resorts," in *Transactions of the American Climatological Association*, 1906, xxii, 204-214.

DANA, C. L., "The Cult of Æsculapius, his Statues and Temples," in *Proceedings of the Charaka Club*, 1902, i, 59-73.

DAREMBERG, C., *La Médecine dans Homère*. Paris, 1865.

   État de la médecine entre Homère et Hippocrate. Paris, 1869.

DAUFRESNE, C., *Épidaure, ses prêtres, ses guérisons*. Paris, 1909.

DEFRASSE, A., et LECHAT, H., *Épidaure*. Paris, 1895.

DIEHL, C., *Excursions in Greece*. London, 1893.

DILL, S., *Roman Society from Nero to Marcus Aurelius*. London, 1905.

DINDORF, G., ed., *Aristophanis Comœdiæ*. 4 vols. Oxford, 1838.

DITTENBERGER, W., *Sylloge Inscriptionum Græcarum*. 2 vols. Leipzig, 1898-1901.

DYER, L., *Studies of the Gods of Greece*. London, 1894.

ELDERKIN, G. W., *Kantharos*. Princeton University Press, 1924.

FARNELL, L. R., *The Evolution of Religion*. London, 1895.

   The Cults of the Greek States. 5 vols. London, 1896-1909.

   The Higher Aspects of the Greek Religion. London, 1912.

FENTON, J. DE, "A Greek Hospital 600 B.C.," in *Transvaal Medical Journal*, 1908-1909, iv, 285-289.

FLOQUET, A., *Homère médecine*. Paris, 1912.

FOWLER, H. M., "The Statue of Asklepios," in *American Journal of Archeology*, 1887, iii, 32-37.

FRAENDER, H., *Asklepios*. Copenhagen, 1893.

GARDNER, P., *New Chapters in Greek History*. London, 1892.

GARRISON, F. H., "The Greek Cult of the Dead and the Chthonian Deities in Ancient Medicine," in *Annals of Medical History*, 1917, i, 35-53.

"The Gods of the Underworld in Ancient Medicine," in *Proceedings of the Charaka Club*, 1919, v, 35-51.

GIRARD, P., *L'Asclépieion d'Athènes d'après de récentes découvertes*. Paris, 1881; also in *Bibliothèque de l'écoles françaises d'Athènes et de Rome*, X, *fasciculus* xxiii.

GOODWIN, W. W., "The Hero Physician," in *American Journal of Archeology*, 1900, iv, 168-169.

GRUPPE, O., *Griechische Mythologie und Religionsgeschichte*. Munich, 1906.

HALLIDAY, W. R., *Greek Divination*. London, 1913.

HARRIS, J. R., *The Origin of the Cult of Aphrodite*. London, 1900.

HARRISON, J. E., *The Mythology and Monuments of Ancient Athens*. London, 1890.

Primitive Athens as Described by Thucydides. Cambridge, 1906.

Prologomena to the Study of Greek Religion. Cambridge, 1908.

HAUVETTE-BESNAULT, A., "Fouilles de Delos," in *Bulletin de Correspondance hellénique*, 1882, vi, 295-352; 1891, xvi, 671.

HERRLICH, S., *Epidauros, eine antike Heilstätte*. Berlin, 1898.

HIPPOCRATES, *Opera Omnia*, Foesius, A., ed. Geneva, 1662.

HOUDART, M. S., *Histoire de la médecine grecque depuis Esculape jusqu'à Hippocrate exclusivement*. Paris, 1856.

JONES, W. H. S., *The Doctor's Oath*. Cambridge, 1924.

KAIBEL, G., ed., *Epigrammata Græca ex lapidibus conlecta*, no. 1027. Berlin, 1878.

KAVVADIAS, P., *Fouilles d'Épidaure*. Athens, 1893.

KEIL, K., "Attische Kulte aus Inschriften," in *Philologus*, 1866, xxiii, 592-622.

KOEPP, F., "Die attische Hygieia," in *Mittheilungen des kaiserlich deutschen archäologischen Instituts in Athen*, 1885, x, 255-271.

KÖHLER, U., "Der Südabhang der Akropolis zu Athen nach den Ausgrabungen der archäologischen Gesellschaft," in *ibid.*, 1877, ii, 229-260.

KÖRTE, A., "Bezirk eines Heilgottes," in *ibid.*, 1893, xviii, 231-256; 1896, xxi, 287-332.

"Die attische Heilgötter und ihre Kultstätten," in *Verhandlun-*

gen der Gesellschaft der Naturforscher und Ärzte, 1899, lxx, 446-447.

KRETSCHMER, P., *Einleitung in die Geschichte der griechischen Sprache.* Göttingen, 1896.

KUBITSCHEK, W., and REICHEL, W., "Bericht über eine im Sommer 1893 ausgeführte Reise in Karien," in *Anzeiger der kaiserlichen Akademie der Wissenschaften. Philosophisch-historische Classe*, 1893, xxx, 104.

KÜHN, C. G., ed., *Medicorum Græcorum Opera.* Leipzig, 1821-1833.

KÜSTER, E., "Die Schlange in der griechischen Kunst und Religion," in *Religionsgeschichtliche Versuche und Vorarbeiten*, 1913, xiii, 1-172.

LANG, A., *The Homeric Age.* London, 1906.

LAWSON, J. C., *Modern Greek Folklore and Ancient Greek Religion.* Cambridge, 1910.

LE BLANT, E., "750 inscriptions de pierres gravées inédites ou peu connues," in *Mémoires de l'Institut national de France. Académie des Inscriptions et Belles-Lettres*, partie 1898, xxxvi, 1-210.

LEGGE, F., "The Greek Worship of Isis and Serapis," in *Proceedings of the Society of Biblical Archeology*, 1914, xxxvi, 79-99.

LIÉTARD, G. A., "Le médecin Charaka. Le serment des hippocratistes et le serment des médecins hindous," in *Bulletin de l'Académie de Médecine*, 3 sér., 1897, xxxvii, 565-575.

LITTRÉ, M. P. É., *Œuvres complètes d'Hippocrate.* 10 vols. Paris, 1836-1859.

MALGAIGNE, J. F., *Lettres sur l'histoire de la chirurgie.* Paris, 1842.

MAURY, L. P. A., *Histoire des religions de la Grèce antique.* Paris, 1857-1859.

MERRIAM, A. C., "The Treatment of Patients in the Temples of Æsculapius," in *Boston Medical and Surgical Journal*, 1885, cxii, 304-305.

"The Dogs of Æsculapius," in *American Antiquarian and Oriental Record*, 1885, vii, 285-289.

"Æsculapia as Revealed by Inscriptions," in *Transactions of the New York Academy of Medicine*, 1886, v, 187-217.

MICHAELIS, A., "Die Statue und der Altar der Athena Hygieia," in *Mittheilungen des kaiserlich deutschen archäologischen Instituts in Athen*, 1876, i, 284-294.

MILNE, J. C., "Greek Inscriptions from Egypt," in *Journal of Hellenic Studies*, 1901, xxi, 275-292.

MOLLET, M., *La Médecine chez les Grecs avant Hippocrate.* Paris, 1906.

MÜLLER, C., ed., *Fragmenta historicorum Græcorum.* Paris, 1868-1883.

MÜLLER, K. O., *Denkmäler der alten Kunst,* ed. Wieseler. Göttingen, 1854.

NILSSON, M. P., *Griechische Feste von religiöser Bedeutung.* Leipzig, 1906.

OSTHOFF, H., "Griechische und lateinische Wortdeutungen," in *Indogermanische Forschungen,* 1895, v, 275-324.

PANOFKA, T., "Die Heilgötter der Griechen," in *Abhandlungen der königlichen Akademie der Wissenschaften zu Berlin. Philosophischhistorische Classe,* 1843, 257-274.
"Asklepios und die Asklepiaden," in *ibid.,* 1845, 271-359.

PATER, W., *Greek Studies.* London, 1910.
Plato and Platonism. London, 1910.

PATON, W. R., and HICKS, E. L., *The Inscriptions of Kos.* Oxford, 1891.

PAUSANIAS, *Description of Greece,* tr. Frazer, J. G., 6 vols. London, 1898.

PRELLER, R., *Griechische Mythologie.* 4th ed., 2 vols., ed. Robert, C. Berlin, 1887-1894.

PROTT, I. VON, and ZIEHEN, L., *Leges Græcorum sacræ e titulis collectæ.* Leipzig, 1896.

REINACH, S., "Les Chiens dans le culte d'Esculape," in *Revue archéologique,* 3 sér., 1884, iv, 76-83.
"La seconde stèle des guérisons miraculeuses, découverte à Épidaure," in *ibid.,* 3 sér., 1885, v, 265-270.
"Les fouilles de Cos," in *ibid.,* 4 sér., 1904, iii, 127-131.

ROHDE, E., *Psyche,* 3d ed. Tübingen, 1904.

ROTH, R., "Indische Medicin. Caraka," in *Zeitschrift der deutschen morgenländischen Gesellschaft,* 1872, xxvi, 441-452.

SCHENCK, L., *De Telesphoro Deo.* Göttingen, 1888.

SCHMIDT, C. A., *De Aristidis incubatione.* Jena, 1818.

SCHULZE, W., *Quæstiones epicæ.* Gütersloh, 1892.

SINGER, C., *Greek Biology and Greek Medicine.* Oxford, 1922.

THORLACIUS, B., *De Somniis Serapicis præcipue Aristidis orationibus sacris delineatis.* Copenhagen, 1813.

THRÄMER, E., *Pergamos.* Leipzig, 1888.

UFFELMANN, J., *Die Entwicklung der altgriechischen Heilkunde.* Berlin, 1885.

VERCOUTRE, A., "La Médecine sacerdotale dans l'antiquité grecque," in *Revue archéologique,* 1885, vi, 273-292; 1886, vii, 22-26, 107-123.

WALTON, A., *The Cult of Asklepios.* Boston, 1894.

WELCKER, F. C., *Alte Denkmäler.* Göttingen, 1849-1864.
Zu den Alterthümern der Heilkunde bei den Griechen (Band III, *Kleine Schriften*). Bonn, 1850.
Griechische Götterlehre. 3 vols. Leipzig, 1857-1862.

WILIAMOWITZ-MÖLLENDORF, U. von, *Isyllos von Epidauros.* Berlin, 1886.

WOLTERS, P., "Zur Athena Hygieia des Pyrrhos," in *Mittheilungen des kaiserlich deutchen archäologischen Instituts in Athen,* 1891, xvi, 153-165.

WROTH, W., "Telesphoros," in *Journal of Hellenic Studies,* 1882, iii, 283-300.

"Hygieia," in *ibid.,* 1884, v, 82-101.

ZAREMBA, V. V., "Der Cult des Asklepios," in *Janus,* 1904, ix, 603-611; 1905, x, 12-21.

ZIEHEN, J., "Studien zu den Asklepiosreliefs," in *Mittheilungen des kaiserlich deutschen archäologischen Instituts in Athen,* 1892, xvii, 229-251.

ZINGERLE, J., "Heilinschrift von Lebena," in *ibid.,* 1896, xxi, 67-92.

ROMAN

ALLBUTT, T. C., "Greek Medicine in Rome," in *British Medical Journal,* 1909, ii, 1449-1455, 1515-1522, 1598-1606; 1910, ii, 1393-1401.

ANDERSON, J., "The Temples of Æsculapius," *ibid.,* 1887, ii, 904-905.

ANONYMOUS, "Medicine and Medical Practitioners in Ancient Rome," in *Practitioner,* 1895, liv, 59-63, 148-152.

AUST, E., *Die Religion der Römer.* Münster, 1899.

BARNES, H., "On Roman Medicine and Roman inscriptions found in Britain," in *Proceedings of the Royal Society of Medicine,* 1913-1914, vii, *Section of the History of Medicine,* 71-87.

BESNIER, M., *L'Ile tibérine dans l'antiquité.* Paris, 1871.

BISHOP, H. L., "The Fountain of Juturna in the Roman Forum," in *Records of the Past,* 1903, ii, 174-180.

BOUCHÉ-LECLERCQ, A., *Les Pontifices de l'ancienne Rome.* Paris, 1871.

BÜCHELER, F., *Umbrica.* Bonn, 1883.

BUCKLER, W. H., and CATON, R., "Account of a Group of Medical and Surgical Instruments found at Kolophon," in *Proceedings of the Royal Society of Medicine,* 1913-1914, vii, *Section of the History of Medicine,* 235-242.

BURET, F., "La Médecine chez les Romains avant l'ère chrétienne," in *Janus,* 1896, i, 517-526.

CARTER, J. B., *The Religion of Numa.* London, 1906.

The Religious Life of Ancient Rome. Boston, 1911.

CONWAY, R. S., *The Italic Dialects.* 2 vols. Cambridge, 1897.

CORDELL, E. F., "The Medicine and Doctors of Horace," in *Bulletin of the Johns Hopkins Hospital,* 1901, xii, 233-240.

"The Medicine and Doctors of Juvenal," *ibid.*, 1903, xiv, 283-287.

CRAWFURD, R., "Martial and Medicine," in *Proceedings of the Royal Society of Medicine*, 1913-1914, vii, *Section of the History of Medicine*, 15-29.

CUMONT, F., "Le Taurobole et le culte de Bellone," in *Revue d'Histoire et de Littérature religieuses*, 1901, vi, 97-110.

DANA, C. L., "The Medicine of Horace," in *Proceedings of the Charaka Club*, 1906, ii, 72-101.

DUPOUY, E., *Médecine et Mœurs de l'ancienne Rome, d'après les poètes latin.* Paris, 1892.

FOWLER, W. W., *Roman Festivals of the Period of the Republic.* London, 1899.

The Religious Experience of the Roman People. London, 1911.

GAUTIER, CONTESSA, "An Excursion to the Lake of Nemi and Civita Lavinia," in *The Journal of the British-American Archeological Society of Rome.* 1890-1898, ii, 448-454.

GIBBON, E., *The Decline and Fall of the Roman Empire.* 6 vols. London, 1846.

GLOVER, T. R., *The Conflict of Religions in the Early Roman Empire.* London, 1909.

HARTUNG, J. A., *Die Religion der Römer.* 2 vols. Erlangen, 1836.

HELME, F., "Les médecins practiciens à Rome," in *Presse Médicale*, 1910, xviii, 417-422.

KISSEL, F., "Die symbolische Medicin der Römer," in *Janus*, 1848, iii, 385-418, 577-674.

LAFAYE, G., *Histoire du culte des divinités de l'Alexandrie, Serapis, Isis, Harpocrate et Anubis, hors de l'Égypte.* Paris, 1884.

L'Initiation mithriaque. Paris, 1906 (in *Annales: Bibliothèque de Vulgarization Musée Guimet.* Vol. 18, 89-114).

LANCIANI, R., "On the Hygienic Laws and Sanitary Conditions of Ancient Rome," in *Boston Medical and Surgical Journal*, 1886, cxv, 537-541, 565-567.

"The Mysterious Wreck of Nemi," in *The Journal of the British-American Archeological Society of Rome*, 1890-1898, ii, 300-309.

LINDSAY, W., *The Latin Language.* Oxford, 1894.

MARQUARDT, J., *Römische Staatsverwaltung*, vol. iii, ed. Wissowa. Leipzig, 1885.

McKENZIE, D., "Some Healing Wells and Waters, with a Suggestion as to the Origin of the Votive Offering," in *Proceedings of the Royal Society of Medicine*, 1913-1914, vii, *Section of the History of Medicine*, 177-192.

MERCURIALIS, H., *De Arte Gymnastica.* Venice, 1573.

MOMMSEN, T., *The History of Rome*. 5 vols. New York, 1903.

PLATNER, S. B., *The Topography and Monuments of Ancient Rome*. Boston, 1911.

PRELLER, L., *Regionen der Stadt Rom*. Jena, 1846.

   Römische Mythologie. Berlin, 1858.

SAMBON, L., "Donaria of Medical Interest," in *British Medical Journal*, 1895, ii, 146-150, 216-219.

   "Medical Science amongst the Ancient Romans," in *The Journal of the British-American Archeological Society of Rome*. 1890-1898, ii, 166-174.

SOMMER, F., *Handbuch der lateinischen Laut- und Formenlehre*. Heidelberg, 1902.

SPON, J., *Recherches curieuses d'antiquités contenues en plusieurs dissertations sur les médailles, bas-reliefs, statues, mosaïques et inscriptions antiques*. Lyon, 1683.

TOUTAIN, J. F., *Les Cultes païens dans l'empire romain*. 2 vols. Paris, 1907-1911.

WALDE, A., *Etymologisches Wörterbuch der lateinischen Sprache*. 2d ed. Heidelberg, 1910.

WISSOWA, G., *Die Religion und Kultus der Römer*. Munich, 1902; 2d ed., 1912.

CELTIC

ANWYL, E., *The Celtic Religion*. London, 1906.

D'ARBOIS DE JUBAINVILLE, H., *Principaux auteurs à consulter sur l'histoire des Celtes*. Paris, 1902.

   "Le Dieu gaulois Belenus, la déesse gauloise Belisama," in *Revue archéologique*, 1873, xxv, 197-206.

DOTTIN, G., *Manuel pour servir à l'étude de l'antiquité celtique*. 2d ed. Paris, 1915.

   Les anciens peuple de l'Europe. Paris, 1916.

   La Langue gauloise. Paris, 1920.

JULLIAN, C., *Recherches sur la religion gauloise*. Bordeaux, 1903.

MacCULLOCH, J. A., *The Religion of the Ancient Celts*. Edinburgh, 1911.

   Celtic Mythology, in *The Mythology of All Races*, vol. iii, Part I. Boston, 1918.

NUTT, A. H., ed., *Mabinogion*. London, 1902.

PEDERSEN, H., *Vergleichende Grammatik der keltischen Sprachen*. 2 vols. Göttingen, 1909-1913.

RENEL, C., *Les Religions de la Gaule avant le christianisme*. Paris, 1906.

RHŶS, J., *Celtic Britain*. 2d ed. London, 1884.

SCHRADER, F., *Atlas de géographie historique*. Paris, 1896.

STOKES, W., ed. and tr., "The Second Battle of Moytura," in *Revue celtique*, 1891, xii, 56-111.

Urkeltischer Sprachschatz. Göttingen, 1894.

and Strachan, J., *Thesaurus Palæohibernicus.* 2 vols. Cambridge, 1901-1903.

UNDSET, I., "Inscrizioni latine ritrovate nella Scandinavia," in *Bulletino dell' instituto di correspondenza archeologica*, 1883, no. 12, pp. 234-238.

GENERAL

BAAS, H., *The History of Medicine*, tr. H. E. Handerson. New York, 1885.

BERNHEIM, H., *De la Suggestion.* 2d ed. Paris, 1887.

BERTRAND, A., *Traité du Somnambulisme.* Paris, 1823.

BLACK, W. G., *Folk-Medicine.* London, 1883.

BORDEU, TH. DE, *Recherches sur l'histoire de la médecine.* Paris, 1882.

BOUCHÉ-LECLERCQ, A., *Histoire de la divination dans l'antiquité.* 4 vols. Paris, 1879-1881.

BOUCHUT, E., *Histoire de la médecine.* Paris, 1873.

BRAID, J., *Neurypnology.* London, 1843.

BRAMWELL, J. M., *Hypnotism, its History, Practice, and Theory.* London, 1903.

BREYSIG, K., *Die Entstehung des Gottesgedankens und der Heilbringer.* Berlin, 1905.

BRUZON, P., *La Médecine et les religions.* Paris, 1904.

BUCK, A., *The Growth of Medicine from the Earliest Times to about 1800.* New Haven, 1917.

CATON, R., "The Gods of Healing of the Egyptians and Greeks," in *Nature* (London), 1907, lxxv, 499-500.

COMRIE, J. D., "Medicine among the Assyrians and Egyptians in about 1500 B.C.," in *Edinburgh Medical Journal*, 1909, ii, 101-129.

COX, G. W., *The Mythology of the Aryan Nations.* London, 1903.

CUMONT, F., *Textes et monuments figurés relatifs aux mystères de Mithra.* 2 vols. Brussels, 1896-1899.

The Mysteries of Mithra. Chicago, 1903.

The Oriental Religions in Roman Paganism. Chicago, 1911.

Astrology and Religion among the Greeks and Romans. New York, 1912.

CUTTEN, G. B., *Three Thousand Years of Mental Healing.* New York, 1911.

DAREMBERG, CH., *La Médecine, histoire et doctrines.* 2 vols. Paris, 1865.

Histoire des sciences médicales. 2 vols. Paris, 1870.

and SAGLIO, E., *Dictionnaire des antiquités grecques et romaines.* Paris, 1873-1911.

DEUBNER, L., *De Incubatione.* Leipzig, 1900.

ELLIOTT, J. S., *Outlines of Greek and Roman Medicine.* New York, 1914.

ELOY, N., *Dictionnaire historique de la médecine ancienne et moderne.* 4 vols. Mons, 1778.

FARNELL, L. R., *The Evolution of Religion.* London, 1905. *Greece and Babylon.* Edinburgh, 1911.

FASBENDER, H., *Geschichte der Geburtshülfe.* Jena, 1906.

FOX, W. S., *Mythology, Greek and Roman,* in *The Mythology of All Races,* vol. i. Boston, 1916.

FRAZER, J. G., *The Golden Bough.* 3d ed., 12 vols. London and New York, 1907-1915.

FRIDAULT, F., *Histoire de la médecine.* 2 vols. Paris, 1870.

GARRISON, F. H., *An Introduction to the History of Medicine.* 3d ed. Philadelphia, 1921.

GASTE, L. F., *Abrégé de l'histoire de la médecine.* Paris, 1835.

GAUTHIER, L. P. A., *Recherches historiques sur l'exercice de la médecine dans les temples, chez les peuples de l'antiquité.* Paris, 1844.

HAESER, H., *Lehrbuch der Geschichte der Medicin.* 3 vols. Jena, 1875-1882.

HAMILTON, M., *Incubation, or the Cure of Disease in Pagan Temples and Christian Churches.* London, 1906.

HARRIS, J. R., *The Cult of the Heavenly Twins.* Cambridge, 1906.

HASTINGS, J., ed., *Encyclopædia of Religion and Ethics.* 12 vols. Edinburgh, 1910-1922.

HECKER, J. F. K., *Geschichte der Heilkunde.* 2 vols. Berlin, 1822-1829.

HEIM, R., *Incantamenta Magica Græca Latina.* Leipzig, 1892; also in *Jahrbücher für classische Philologie,* 1893, xix, 463-565.

HERRLICH, S., *Antike Wunderkuren.* Berlin, 1911.

HIRSCHELL, B., *Compendium der Geschichte der Medicin.* Vienna, 1862.

HOLLÄNDER, E., *Plastik und Medizin.* Stuttgart, 1912.

HOPF, L., *Die Heilgötter und Heilstätten des Altertums.* Tübingen, 1904.

ISENSEE, E., *Die Geschichte der Medizin und Hülfswissenschaften.* 6 vols. Berlin, 1846.

JAMES, E. O., *Primitive Ritual and Belief.* London, 1917.

LAWRENCE, E., *Primitive Psycho-Therapy and Quackery.* Boston, 1910.

LECLERC, D., *Histoire de la médecine.* 2d ed. Amsterdam, 1702.

LEGGE, F., *Forerunners and Rivals of Christianity.* 2 vols. Cambridge, 1915.

MASPERO, G., *The History of Egypt, Chaldea, Syria, Babylon and Assyria*. 8 vols. London, 1906.

Life in Ancient Egypt and Assyria. London, 1892.

McKAY, W. J. S., *Ancient Gynecology*. New York, 1901.

MEIBOMIUS, J. H., *Disputatio de Incubatione in fanis deorum medicinæ causa olim facta*. Helmstadt, 1659.

MENZIES, A., *The History of Religions*. London, 1895.

MEUNIER, L., *Histoire de la médecine*. Paris, 1911.

MILNE, J. S., *Surgical Instruments in Greek and Roman Times*. Oxford, 1907.

MOLL, A., *Hypnotism*. 5th ed. London, 1901.

MOORE, G. F., *The History of Religions*. New York, 1913.

MÜLLER, F. MAX, ed., *The Sacred Books of the East*. 50 vols. Oxford, 1879-1897.

NEUBERGER, M., *The History of Medicine*. London, 1910.

and PAGEL, J., *Handbuch der Geschichte der Medicin*. 3 vols. Jena, 1903.

OSLER, SIR WM., *The Evolution of Modern Medicine*. New Haven, 1921.

PATER, W., *Marius the Epicurean*. 2 vols. London, 1911.

PAULY-WISSOWA, *Real-Encyklopädie der classischen Altertumswissenschaft*. 11 vols. Stuttgart, 1894-1922.

PUSCHMANN, T., *The History of Medical Education*. London, 1891.

RAWLINSON, G., *The Religions of the Ancient World*. New York, 1883.

REINACH, S., *Cultes, mythes, et religions*. 4 vols. Paris, 1905-1912. English ed. London, 1912.

RENOUARD, P. V., *The History of Medicine*, tr. C. G. Comegys. Philadelphia, 1867.

RITTERSHAIN, G. VON, *Der medizinische Wunderglaube und die Inkubation im Altertum*. Berlin, 1878.

RIVERS, W. H. R., *Medicine, Magic and Religion*. New York, 1924.

ROSCHER, W. H., ed., *Ausführliches Lexikon der griechischen und römischen Mythologie*. Leipzig, 1884-1922.

SAYCE, A. H., *The Religion of Ancient Egypt and Babylonia*. Edinburgh, 1902.

SCHRADER, O., *Reallexikon der indo-germanischen Altertumskunde*. Strasbourg, 1901.

SMITH, W. R., *The Religion of the Semites*, 2d ed. London, 1894.

SOZINSKY, T. S., *Medical Symbolism*. Philadelphia, 1891.

SPIEGEL, F., *Die arische Periode und ihre Zustände*. Leipzig, 1887.

SPRENGEL, K., *Histoire de la médecine*. 9 vols. Paris, 1815.

THORNDIKE, L., *A History of Magic and Experimental Science during the First Thirteen Centuries of Our Era*. 2 vols. New York, 1923.

TOURTELLE, E., *Histoire philosophique de la médecine*. Paris, 1804.

TUCKEY, C. L., *Treatment by Hypnotism and Suggestion*. 6th ed. London, 1913.

USENER, H., *Götternamen*. Bonn, 1896.

WEINREICH, O., *Antique Heilungswunder*. Giessen, 1909.

WELLCOME, H. S., *Historical Medical Museum*. London, 1913.

WITHINGTON, E. T., *The History of Medicine from Earliest Times*. London, 1894.

WITKOWSKI, G. J., *Accouchement chez tous les peuples*. Paris, n.d.

WORCESTER, E., and McCOMB, S., *Religion and Medicine*. New York, 1908.

INDEX

558 INDEX

Lochia, 322.
Locutius, 377, 498.
London Medical Papyrus, the, *37,* 47.
Louvre Papyrus, the, 37.
Lucina, 73; see also Diana Lucina, and Iuno Lucina.
Lug, *516-517.*
Lupercalia, the, 423.
Luperci, the, 423-424.
Luxovius, 520.

M

Mâ, of Cappadocia, 389, 484.
Ma'at, 14-15, 65, 75, 80, 83.
Mabon, *517.*
Machaon, 226, 242, 246, 247, 248, *249-250,* 285, 344.
'Maffeian Inscriptions,' the, 468.
Magi, the Oriental, 386, 487.
Magic, Egyptian, 24-27; the 'Magic Library,' at Heliopolis, 33-34; magico-religious rites, 42-48; Thoth, god of, 80; Babylonian and Assyrian, 96; Vedic, 154-159; in the cult of Mithra, 193; Greek, 226-228; healing and Roman, 404-406.
Magna Græcia, 475, 479.
Magna Mater, *385-386,* 395, *483-486.*
Makhir, a Babylonian dream goddess, 102.
Maklû series, the texts of the, 105.
Maleates, 243, *338.*
Ma-Ma, 121.
Mamú, see Makhir.
Mamu-da-ge, 102.
Mandara, Mount, 175.
Manes, the, 421, 449.
Manetho, 31, 34.

mantras, or *manthras,* 157, 186, 188.
Maponos, see Mabon.
Marathon, 318.
Marduk, 93, 94, 103, 108-110, 112, 116-117, 120, *123-125,* 126.
'Market god,' Hermes, the, 332.
Mars, 405, *432-433,* 520.
Maruts, the, 160, *171-172.*
Mater Matuta, 442, *453,* 484.
Materia medica, Egyptian, 50; of the Atharvaveda, 156-158.
Matralia, the, 453.
Matronalia, the, 451.
Mayūra, the Indian poet, 176.
Medeia, 345, *364-365,* 417.
Medeios, 355.
Medicine, in Egypt, 3-4; invention of, ascribed to Thoth, 32; of the medical papyri, 35-37; profane Egyptian, 50-51; origin of, ascribed to Apis, 54; Dhanvantari, the Indian god of, *166-169;* Indian genealogy of, 169 note; knowledge of, revealed to Indra, 171; cradle of Greek, 226, 269; origin of rational, in temple practice, 235-236; religious and practical, 236-237; descent of Greek, 238-239, 299-300; allusion to specialization in, 249; scientific and rational tendencies, 299; the Kabeiroi, inventors of, 337; Greek, in Rome, 412-413; Celtic, 509.
Meditrina, *433-434.*
Meditrinalia, the, 433.
Medos, 355.
Mefitis, 400, *463.*
Megala Asklepieia, the, 295-298.
Megalesia, the, 483.